ENCYCLOPEDIA OF
WORLD MYTHOLOGY

This edition published by Parragon in 2009

Parragon
Queen Street House
4 Queen Street
Bath, BA1 1HE, UK

ISBN: 978-1-4075-8145-3

Produced for Parragon by Foundry Design & Production

Thanks to: Claire Dashwood, Jennifer Kenna,
Sonya Newland, and Ian Powling.

Printed in Indonesia.

ENCYCLOPEDIA OF
WORLD MYTHOLOGY

Loren Auerbach, Professor Anne M. Birrell, Rev. Dr. Martin Boord, Miranda Bruce-Mitford, Peter A. Clayton, Dr. Ray Dunning, Dr. James H. Grayson, Dr. Niel Gunson, Stephen Hodge, Dr. Gwendolyn Leick, Dr. Helen Morales, Mark Nuttall, Richard Prime, Professor James Riordan, Dr. Nicholas J. Saunders, Professor Harold Scheub, Bruce Wannell, and Professor James Weiner.

GENERAL EDITOR
Arthur Cotterell

Parragon
Bath · New York · Singapore · Hong Kong · Cologne · Delhi · Melbourne

CONTENTS

Introduction 6

Ancient Near East 12
Egypt 44
Greece 54
Rome 68
The Celts 76
Central and Eastern Europe 102
Northern Europe 114
Siberia and the Arctic 132
India 144
Sri Lanka 160
Tibet 164
Mongolia 172
China 178
Japan 190
Korea 200
Southeast Asia 206
Oceania 216
Australia 234
Africa 248
The Caribbean 258
North America 266
Central and South America 282

Glossary 306
Author Biographies 309
Bibliography 310
Picture Credits 312
Index of Names 313
Subject Index 317

INTRODUCTION

WE OWE the word "myth," like many others in common use today, to the ancient Greeks. No modern language has a substitute, and so there can be no better way of understanding what mythology is about than by taking a look at the original meaning of the word.

Descended from the idea of speech itself, myth had, by the fifth century B.C.E., come to mean a story, a narrative of events. The historian Herodotus, who wrote an account of the wars between the Greeks and the Persians, was anxious to record everything he could about this great struggle, even if some of the tales might be regarded as myths or legends. He admitted that he was unsure of their factual accuracy, but such was their interest they simply could not be ignored. It was for his readers to decide what could or could not be believed. This suggestion of a myth being a tall story, something fictitious rather than a statement of fact, was pushed even farther by the philosopher Plato, who was concerned to distinguish between those things we can accept as being true and those we cannot.

But the rise of reasoning in Ancient Greece did not immediately undermine the importance of mythology, for it was realized how myths were traditional stories which embodied the heritage of the Greek speaking world. They contain, a mythologer would say today, the basic thought patterns by which the ancient Greeks knew themselves as a separate people. He might add that the strength of Greek mythology, like other notable traditions, lay in its collective nature. Unlike a story composed by a single author, a myth always stands on its own, with a plot and a set of characters easily recognized by those who listen to the storyteller, poet, or dramatist making use of it. When, for instance, the Athenians watched plays performed every year at their religious festivals, they were already aware of the events a playwright like Aeschylus or Sophocles would often choose to tell. The aftermath of the Trojan War never ceased to fascinate them, nor did the tragedy of Oedipus ever fail to hold their attention. That, after becoming aware of his terrible deeds of patricide and incest, Oedipus should have chosen to die in the grove of Colonus near Athens, made his tragedy a subject of intense local interest. Sophocles' play *Oedipus at Colonus* can indeed be said to draw together the deepest

feelings of the Greeks about crime, punishment, and fate in the final release of the blind Theban ex-king.

In the fourth century B.C.E., Euhemerus, a philosopher resident at the Macedonian court, went as far as to argue that all myths and legends related to historical events, and that the gods were originally men who had achieved great success and who, after their death, received divine honors from a grateful people. Such a rational point of view might not seem far off the mark for the Trojan War: in the nineteenth century the ruins of a major city were located in Asia Minor, where Troy was once supposed to have flourished. Agamemnon, Ajax, Menelaus, Helen, Paris, Achilles, Hector, Nestor, Odysseus, Priam—the great names of Homer's two epic poems, the *Iliad* and the *Odyssey*—could have been part of an historic conflict which had occurred there. The problem is that this is too obvious an explanation. Study of Indian epics has revealed unexpected parallels with Homer, especially between the *Iliad*, the account of Troy's downfall, and the *Ramayana*, Rama's expedition to Sri Lanka in order to recover his abducted wife Sita. Both Greek and Indian storytellers must have drawn upon a shared Indo-European heritage, albeit later changed to suit the different historical experiences involved in migration and settlement of Greece and India. Even though he may have really been a Mycenaean king, the account of Agamemnon's leadership of the Greek expeditionary force has been absorbed into a story of divine rivalry, of gods and goddesses settling their personal disputes by backing either the Trojans or the Greeks. Yet a close reading of the text shows that in Helen herself (who was the cause of the conflict), we are dealing with a goddess rather than a wayward queen. Hatched from an egg, this daughter of Zeus was undoubtedly a pre-Greek tree goddess, whose cult involved both abduction and recovery. Her husband Menelaus, the Spartan ruler, is also known to have had a shrine of his own in historical times. In all likelihood he was made King Agamemnon's brother in the course of the innumerable retellings of the story which Homer finally recast as the *Iliad*.

What this more complex view of Homer should remind us of is the variety of forms in which myth actually survives. It can be handed down almost unchanged, as sacred narrative associated with theology and ritual, or in an altered form, as historical narrative that has lost contact with purely sacred events and instead deals with extraordinary secular happenings. Epics, sagas, puranas—these are perhaps the grandest expressions of mythology: but a great deal of our own knowledge comes from the writings of past mythologers. Much of Germanic mythology would have been lost without the efforts of the Icelandic scholar and statesman Snorri Sturluson. He wrote, in the early thirteenth century, a handbook for poets on the world of the pre-Christian gods, providing detailed explanations of their myths. He was recalling the sagas of the Viking period, approximately C.E. 750–1050, when a vigorous tradition formed around the wisdom and deeds of one-eyed Odin and giant-slayer Thor.

Myths bring divinity into focus and their subject matter inevitably touches upon the nature of existence, the world over which the gods rule. In ancient Sumer, present-day southern Iraq, the oldest surviving myths tell us that kingship "came down from heaven," the ruler being chosen and invested by the assembly of the gods. During the third millennium B.C.E. the local deity was imagined to be the actual owner of each Sumerian city, and his or her temple possessed and worked most of the irrigated land, with the result that the king was rather like a steward managing the god's estates. The temple, placed on a high brick-built platform, served as the house in which the deity was fed and clothed, and received worshipers. In the city of Eridu, the temple was called Apsu, after the freshwater ocean thought to lie under the earth. Because the climate of Sumer was semi-arid, with insufficient rainfall for sustaining a crop of cereals, or an orchard or a garden, agriculture was only possible through irrigation. Small schemes of canalization gradually grew into a large interdependent system needing constant supervision, dredging, and repair of breaches in the dykes to keep it functioning. Hardly surprising, therefore, is the circumstance that the

divine owner of the Apsu temple was named Enki, or "Productive Manager of the Soil." Characteristic of Enki was his craftiness, for in conflicts with other, usually more powerful deities, such as the wind god Enlil or Ninhursaga, goddess of fertility, he won by means of his wits, never by the use of force.

Crafty Enki outdid Ninhursaga in a myth about the creation of mankind. It was said that originally

the gods had to work themselves, performing the hard tasks of irrigation agriculture. They complained, and Enki and his mother Nammu produced people to relieve them of the toil. At a party to celebrate this event, the gods drank deeply and Ninhursaga boasted how she could make mankind's form good or ill at will. Enki accepted the challenge, saying whatever she might do, he would balance it so that every creature could earn a living. So he compensated for the various freaks she created. Then Enki turned the tables on Ninhursaga and asked her to cope with the creation he would make. It was a decrepit old man, so utterly broken down with years as to be useless: Ninhursaga gave up the competition in despair.

In the subsequent Babylonian and Assyrian periods, following the decline of Sumer after 2004 B.C.E., the gods in the region became more like national gods and were identified with the political aspirations of their nations, so that their relation to Nature came to seem more accidental, and their share of managing the world dwindled. Thus Marduk of Babylon and Ashur of Assyria assumed in turn a dominating position over the entire pantheon. The exploits of the older gods continued to be retold, however. In a parallel of the biblical story of the Flood, Enlil is credited with a series of assaults upon mankind. The population of the cities had grown so large that the din kept Enlil awake at night. Thoroughly annoyed, he persuaded the assembly of the gods that a plague should be sent down to thin out the people and reduce the noise. But a wise man named Atrahasis (sometimes Utnapishtim or Ziusudra) consulted Enki (or Ea) and learned of this terrible threat.

Mankind was told to be quiet, and so many offerings were made to Namtar, the plague god, that he did not dare to appear. When the crisis had passed and once again Enlil noticed the rising level of noise, he sent a drought which brought mankind to the verge of starvation. Only shoals of fish sent along the rivers and canals by Enki saved the situation. But he realized that this was only a temporary reprieve, since Enlil would next employ the combined power of heaven against mankind. So he warned Atrahasis to build a ship in order to escape a flood which lasted for seven days and seven nights. When the storm passed, the only survivors were Atrahasis, his family, and the animals he had taken on board. Other than Enlil, the gods were horrified by the extent of the destruction, until the devout Atrahasis landed on dry land and sacrificed to them. Then, smelling the goodness of the offering, they gathered "like flies around the priest and his sacrifice."

These two myths from the Ancient Near East could be termed cosmological, because they deal with such major happenings as the creation of mankind and its destruction, with the exception of a single family. Most traditions of mythology have stories dealing with events of similar importance, but the majority of myths tend to be more mundane. They usually deal with human conflicts and uncertainties, behind which divine activity is nonetheless apparent. Among other things treated by myths are misfortune, success, cruelty, love, death, family relations, betrayal, old versus new, youth versus age, magic, power, fate, war, chance, accident, madness, quests, and voyages. The richness of incident and description in mythology suggests a very deep origin in the human mind. Even though experts are by no means agreed on an explanation, the view put forward by Carl Jung in the early twentieth century seems the most likely. According to this German psychologist, everyone possesses both a personal and a collective unconscious. The personal one is filled with material peculiar to the experience of the individual, while the collective one holds the mental experience of all mankind. The common legacy of the latter, Jung maintained, gives rise to primordial images "which bring into our consciousness an unknown psychic life belonging to a remote past. The psychic life is the mind of our ancient ancestors, the way in which they conceived of life and the world, of gods and human beings."

Such a rich source of stories is bound to fascinate every generation, and especially our own which is so fortunate in enjoying access to the traditions of the whole world. This book invites you to explore the links and contrasts between these traditions with a fully global approach that provides the best possible introduction to the still unfathomed depths of mythology in all its diversity.

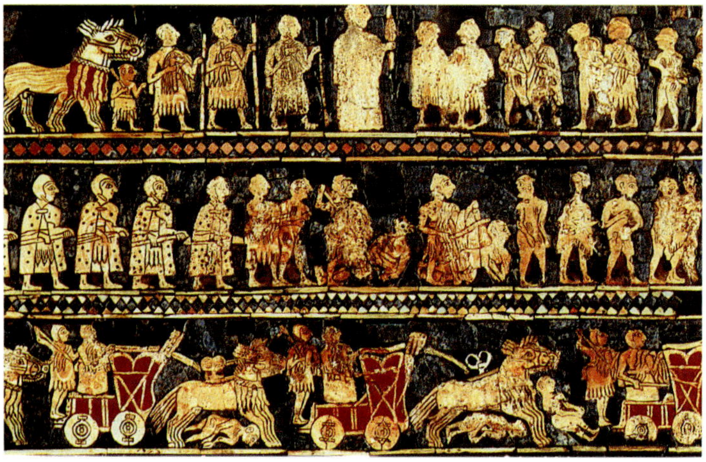

ARTHUR COTTERELL

HOW TO USE THIS BOOK

The mythologies in this encyclopedia are organized into broadly geographical chapters; those that cover a particularly large area, or regions that have a great diversity of mythological tradition, have been subdivided within the chapter for ease of reference.

- The Introduction and map at the beginning of each chapter or section offer a brief background to the history of the mythological tradition for each region.

- The key at the bottom of each spread explains the type of information given:

RETOLD MYTHS
accounts of some of the best known myths and tales.

CHARACTERS
offers more detailed information on the heroes, protagonists, and creatures that appear in the myths.

GODS
gives information about specific gods or spirits from the pantheon of each region.

REFLECTIONS
details the ways in which the myths and beliefs were depicted through different forms of art.

THEMES
highlights the most significant or recurring themes and subjects in the myths.

- A Glossary explaining unusual terms can be found on pages 306–308.

- The names of all gods, characters, and historical figures are listed in the Index of Names on pages 313–316.

- The themes, places, and all other elements of the mythologies are listed in the Subject Index on pages 317–320.

Ancient Near East

INTRODUCTION

THE ANCIENT NEAR EAST is a term that has both geographical and historical meaning. The area comprizes what is now known as the Middle East: western Asia from the eastern shores of the Mediterranean to the Iranian plateau. The northern border of the region is formed by the Black Sea and the Caucas mountain range, to the south by the Arabian desert and the Persian Gulf. Egypt is sometimes regarded as forming part of the Ancient Near East but is treated separately in this volume. The historical framework "Ancient" refers to all the Bronze and Iron Age cultures that flourished within the area insofar as they are accessible through written documents. The first literary sources date from around 2600 B.C.E., written in the cuneiform system in Sumerian and soon afterward also in several Semitic languages. Although the urban civilizations of Mesopotamia exerted a tremendous influence over the whole of western Asia, it was never culturally homogeneous but comprised nonsedentary tribal groups, semi-settled pastoralists and rural agricultural peoples of many different ethnic and linguistic affiliations. In the second and first millenna B.C.E some of these peoples either developed independent political units (chiefdoms or states) and acquired access to literacy, while others came under the direct control of powerful states and formed minority enclaves. The introduction of the horse (in the mid-second millennium) and the camel made it much easier to overcome distance and brought the various populations of the Near East into more intimate contact with each other and the more remote regions of the ancient world, including Egypt and Ethiopia, the Transcaucasus, and eastern Iran. The emergence of large, multi-ethnic, imperial states who competed with each other over colonial territories was characteristic for the period from *c.* 1500 B.C.E. to the middle of the first millennium. The collapse of the indigenous states—first of Assyria and then of Babylonia—paved the way for the Persian conquest under the Achaemenid kings who, for a short while, ruled the whole of the Near East as well as Egypt. Alexander the Great set out to challenge Persian control and, although his success was cut short by his untimely death, his conquests initiated foreign control over the whole region that was to last for centuries, first under Macedonian rule and then under Rome and Byzantium. The death of Alexander in C.E. 331, therefore, marks the "official" end of the Ancient Near East.

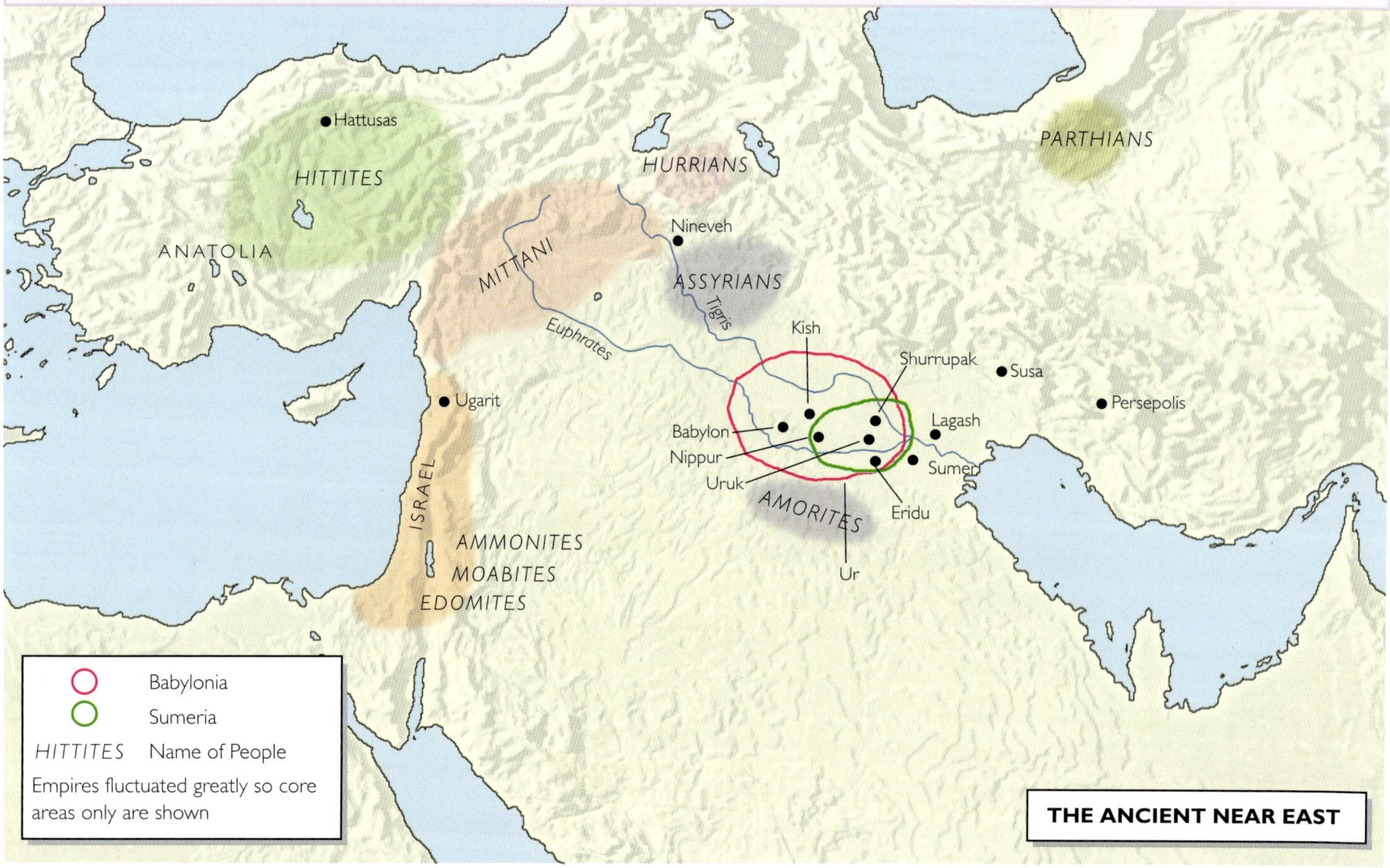

THE ANCIENT NEAR EAST

Sumerian Mythology

INTRODUCTION

THE SUMERIANS INHABITED the southern part of the alluvial basin formed by the Tigris and the Euphrates (in present-day Iraq). Their language was written on clay tablets in wedge-shaped (cuneiform) characters in a complicated system comprising signs for words, syllables and vowels. On linguistic grounds it cannot be linked to any other known language.

The beginnings of Sumerian civilization go back to the fourth millennium when the first cities with monumental mud-brick architecture appeared. The economic basis was agricultural, mainly producing grain on irrigated land as well as livestock. The surplus was exchanged for materials lacking in the region, most notably metal, timber, and precious stones, which stimulated long-distance trade. The characteristic political unit was the city with its surrounding arable land. In the second half of the third millennium, attempts were made to unify the country and impose a centralized political and administrative control. The most successful Sumerian state was that ruled by the Third Dynasty of Ur (*c.* 2113–2004 B.C.E.). In the eighteenth century, Semitic-speaking groups (known as the Amorites) formed a new state, Babylonia, and Sumerian ceased to be a spoken language, though written Sumerian continued to be used for religious purposes for more than a thousand years.

SUMERIAN MYTHS

MOST SUMERIAN myths are known from cuneiform tablets dating to the beginning of the second millennium B.C.E., although some compositions can be traced back some 700 years earlier. The tablets were discovered among the remains of temple archives, and most of the myths feature the deities worshiped in these temples. Their purpose also remains unclear; there are elements of popular narratives, some passages seem to refer to cult rituals, while others contain dialogue that may have been recited at festivals. The general background of the texts is a centralized urban bureaucratic state (the Sumerian empire of the Third Dynasty of Ur) which imposed control over smaller city statelike political units.

The reconstruction and translation of Sumerian myths is fraught with difficulties. Tablets are often fragmentary, with crucial passages missing. Furthermore, linguistic knowledge of the language is still developing and there is as yet no general consensus on the workings of Sumerian grammar. Hence all translations are at best provisional, and many older published versions are unreliable and out of date. Similarly, interpretations as to the meaning, function, and even context of individual compositions are often subjective and quickly superseded.

ENKI AND NINMAH

WHEN THE WORLD WAS FIRST created and generations of gods were born, each deity had a task in themaintenance of the land, especially its irrigation, with some gods being basket carriers and some acting as supervisors. The hard labor led to complaints and demands that Enki in his wisdom find a better solution. One day his mother Nammu wakes him from his sleep in the watery depths known as the Apsu and tells him to create man. He delegates the work to Nammu, instructing her to take some of the Apsu's fertile clay and shape it accordingly. She is helped by another goddess, Ninmah, who imposes the fate of hard work upon mankind. When the gods are celebrating in praise of Enki's wisdom, he and Ninmah drink too much beer and begin a contest in which one god creates beings and the other has to find a suitable fate or social role for them. Ninmah forms six creatures who have some physical defect. Three of them suffer from malfunctioning genitals, but Enki appoints them to be priests or other officials. When it is Enki's turn to make creatures the text becomes almost unintelligible, but the second being is completely unviable, unable to sit, walk, stand, or feed himself. Ninmah curses Enki in anger, condemning him to rest in the Apsu forever. The hapless creature (perhaps to be understood as an infant human being) is to be held on her lap.

◀ *Cylinder seal from the mid-third millennium B.C.E.*

ENKI

HE IS THE SON of the sky god An and his mother is Nammu, a goddess of water and creation. He lives in the Apsu, the watery depths below the earth, the source of all fertility and organic life. Since water in Mesopotamia also had an important magical role, Enki was invoked in magic spells and rituals and hence was regarded as the wise one among the gods, called upon to find solutions for difficult problems. On the other hand his sexual appetite and his weakness for drink account for the less-than-perfect conditions of life on earth. He is not a warlike god and his major adversaries are various goddesses, most notably Inanna, who tricks him into giving away divine prerogatives and powers.

INANNA

A SUMERIAN GODDESS with a complex mythological persona, perhaps the result of a syncretism between a local Sumerian deity associated with Uruk and the west Semitic Venus-star deity Ishtar, introduced by the Akkadian ruling dynasty in the mid-second millennium B.C.E. The former was regarded as the daughter of the supreme sky god An, the latter as the daughter of the moon god Nannar. The dual nature of the planet Venus was conceptualized as an androgynous deity, and this accounts for Inanna's association with warfare, aggression, and lust for power as well as childbirth and erotic attraction. The myths stress Inanna's irascible nature or the fatal consequences of her anger or her sexuality.

ENKI ON DILMUN (OR ENKI AND NINHURSAG)

DILMUN IS INTRODUCED as a place which has potential but does not as yet function fully in the absence of fresh water. The mother goddess complains about this state of affairs to the god of water, Enki, who produces rivers, canals, and cisterns. The fields are now ready to produce grain and the waterways allow profitable trade to be established. Then Enki copulates with a goddess in the marshland beyond the city. She conceives straight away and, after a pregnancy of nine days, gives birth to another goddess, who is eventually inseminated by Enki in turn. This happens several times until Ninhursaga intervenes and advises the nubile girl Uttu to avoid the advances of Enki by demanding fruits and vegetables which he produces by extending the water into the dry zones around the city. When Enki arrives laden with cucumbers and apples, Uttu lets him into her house and they embrace. Ninhursaga removes his seed from Uttu's womb to create eight plants. Enki desires these plants and eats them as soon as they have grown, which infuriates Ninhursaga so much that she curses Enki to become afflicted in eight parts of the body. Near death, he is only saved by the intervention of a fox who persuades the goddess to restore Enki to health. She takes him on her lap and gives birth to eight divine beings, one for each ailing part.

▼ *Modern picture of an Assyrian king.*

MYTHS OF NINURTA

The Return of Ninurta to Nippur

THIS TALE BEGINS with praises of Ninurta's victories on the battlefield. However, when he returns to Nippur, laden with spoils and accompanied by a huge retinue, his triumphal progress threatens the stability of the country. He is persuaded by Enlil's vizier Nusku to slow down his progress and though he relents somewhat, the assembled gods are overwhelmed by his trophies.

Ninurta and the Tablets of Destiny

THE TABLETS OF DESTINY were stolen from heaven by the stormbird Anzu. The young eaglet complains to Ninurta, who is responsible for them, that he dropped them into the watery abyss (the Apsu) because Ninurta had attacked him. When they go to the Apsu to persuade the god Enki to hand over the Tablets of Destiny, Enki refuses. In his frustration Ninurta turns on Enki's vizier. In retaliation Enki fashions a giant turtle which attacks the young god, biting his toes. Ninurta defends himself, but Enki digs a pit, into which he and his tormentor fall. Only the pleas of Ninurta's mother, Ninlil, persuade Enki to set him free.

THEMES

THE SUMERIAN theological works (hymns, prayers, incantations) and the extant myths reflect the emergence of a coherent cosmic order, represented by various deities, each fulfilling an essential role in the realization of divine harmony in heaven and on earth. This parallels the emergence of the Third Dynasty of Ur, when previously independent Sumerian cities were subsumed in one political body ruled by kings who assumed quasi-divine status. The creation and maintenance of such order (Enmesh and Enten, Lahar and Ashnan), and its protection against forces of chaos or rival claims, are a characteristic theme in Sumerian mythology (Inanna's Descent to the Underworld, Ninurta myths). Various myths of origin propose

◀ *A mosaic standard from "royal" graves of Ur.*

etiological accounts for Sumerian institutions, practices, and rituals (Enki and Ninmah, Enlil and Ninlil). However, successful myths function on several levels at once; they may reflect the socio-political background of a bureaucratic and hierarchical society and project the image of a well-managed universe, while at the same time addressing general human concerns and the ambiguities of life and death within a particular historical setting. Similarly the style and poetic artifice of Sumerian myths range from liturgical solemnity and litany-like repetition to raunchy dialogue and lyrical sentiment, often within one and the same text (Enki and Dilmun).

▲ *Terracotta relief of a winged goddess.*

INANNA'S DESCENT TO THE UNDERWORLD

INANNA, "QUEEN OF HEAVEN AND earth," decides to go down to the underworld. Realizing the danger that such an undertaking involves, even for a goddess of her power, she makes contingency plans. She not only dresses in all her regalia and magic amulets but instructs her vizier, Ninshubur, in emergency procedures.

At the gate of the underworld, Inanna demands to be admitted in order to attend the funeral of her brother-in-law. When the gatekeeper informs his mistress Ereshkigal, Inanna's sister and queen of the underworld, of this request, she is furious and instructs him to lock all the seven gates. At each of these gates Inanna has to divest herself of an item of her regalia. Naked and defenseless she finally appears before Ereshkigal, and her desperate attempts to seize the throne are swiftly thwarted. The summoned judges of the underworld condemn her to die, and her corpse is hung upon a peg on the wall.

When, after the appointed time, Inanna fails to appear, Ninshubur follows her instructions to the letter. She dons mourning and makes an appeal to other gods to help her secure Inanna's release. Both Enlil and Nannar refuse, saying that Inanna's unbridled ambition has got her where she is. Only Enki is prepared to assist. From the dirt under his fingernails he fashions two beings (their names reflect those of cult actors or transvestites associated with Inanna's rituals). They gain admission to Ereshkigal by pretending to be sympathetic to her suffering.

Flattered by such attention, she offers a reward and, instructed by Enki, they demand the corpse of Inanna which they sprinkle with the Water of Life provided by Enki. However, the judges of the underworld demand that she must provide a substitute for herself. A host of demons accompany her on the way back, as she pauses at each gate to clothe herself once more in her apparel. Emerging from the underworld she finds Ninshubur. When the demons try to seize her, Inanna refuses, nor does she allow them to take other gods of Uruk who have all been mourning her. Only when she sees her husband Dumuzi in splendid robes on a splendid throne does she indicate in anger that he is the one who will have to die for her, in punishment for his faithlessness. In the end Dumuzi's sister Geshtinanna shares in his fate, so that they each spend half the year in the underworld and half the year on earth.

◀ *Sumerian harp from Ur, decorated with a bull's head.*

▲ *Deity holding a vessel from which water flowed.*

DUMUZI

A SUMERIAN GOD associated with the steppe land outside the cultivated area; he is also known as the Shepherd. He is the lover and husband of Inanna, whom she prefers over the "Farmer" when both compete for her hand. While some poetic texts celebrate their marriage, others focus on his early death and his unsuccessful attempts to evade his fate. The love of his sister Geshtinanna secures his temporary relief from the underworld. In "Inanna's Descent to the Underworld" he has to take her place among the dead; in other myths no direct cause of his death is revealed, it is simply his fate as a "dying god" (one who moves cyclically between the earth and the underworld).

ENMESH AND ENTEN (SUMMER AND WINTER)

This is a fragmentary myth in the form of a dialogue.

WHEN THE GOD Enlil conceives the idea of making the earth fertile with plants and animals, he creates two brothers, Enmesh and Enten, to bring his work to completion. Enten is in charge of the animals: "causing the ewe to give birth to the lamb, the goat to the kid, cow, and calf to multiply." He populates the land with wild donkeys, sheep, and goats, fills the sky with birds and the rivers with fish. He plants palm groves and fruit trees and lays out gardens. Enmesh takes over from there by founding cities with houses and "temples as high as mountains." Having accomplished these tasks the brothers come to Enlil and present him with gifts that symbolize their achievements. Enmesh brings wild and domestic animals and plants, Enten offers precious metals and stones, trees and fish. They start to quarrel as to who has more merit and ask Enlil to decide. The great god declares that Enten, who is in charge of irrigation, the basis of Sumerian agriculture, can justly call himself "farmer of the gods." The brothers acknowledge this judgment. Enmesh bends his knee to Enten, they exchange gifts and pour libations to Enlil.

SUMERIAN GODS

ATTEMPTS TO ENUMERATE the many local gods and list them according to rank were made early in the third millennium B.C.E. These god lists are invariably headed by the sky god An. The most important deities were those of major shrines, such as Enlil of Nippur, Enki of Eridu and Inanna of Uruk. Astral deities were Uttu (Sun), Nannar (Moon), and Inanna (Venus). Female deities, often tutelary goddesses of cities, such as Baba of Lagash, Nammu of Eridu, and Ninhursaga of Kesh, were mother goddesses, while others had specific functions: Nisaba was patroness of scribes, Nanshe goddess of fish and magic, Ninisina the goddess of healing. Gods were envisaged as residing within their temple estates, represented by their image or statue. The divine household consisted of the god and his wife, their children and numerous servants. Included in the pantheon were demons and evil spirits, offspring of An and to some extent susceptible to magic spells and rituals of banishment.

ENLIL AND NINURTA

SON OF the supreme god An, Enlil is the leader of gods and he bestows kingship. He has the characteristics of a weather god whose rains ensure good harvests, but who also has an unpredictable temperament which causes him to punish a troublesome earth with plagues and floods.

Originally an agricultural and rain deity, Ninurta became a "young god," associated with violent storms and martial prowess. In one mythological text, known as the "Splendid Storm King," Ninurta defeated a demon and then made a giant stone dike to stop the waters of the Tigris from flowing eastward on top of the remains of his slain enemy.

▼ *Assyrian stone relief of the hero Gilgamesh with captured lion, from Khorsabad.*

MYTHS OF GILGAMESH

Gilgamesh and the Land of the Living

ACCOMPANIED BY his servant Enkidu, Gilgamesh ventures to the Land of the Living, sacred to the deity Enlil and protected by a powerful demon called Huwawa. When they reach their destination they begin to cut down trees, despite the terrible rays of divine splendor that Huwawa emits. They manage to capture the demon and, although Gilgamesh is prepared initially to spare his life, he cuts off his head, which they present to Enlil in his shrine at Nippur. The enraged Enlil turns the seven rays of splendor into agents of revenge to persecute Gilgamesh and his companion. The text breaks off there.

▲ *Modern depiction of Gilgamesh mourning the death of his friend and servant, Enkidu.*

Gilgamesh, Enkidu and the Netherworld

THE TALE BEGINS with Inanna growing a huluppu tree on the banks of the Euphrates. When the south wind keeps tearing at its branches, she has it transplanted to her shrine at Uruk, where she tends it well in order to fashion a bed and chair from its wood. When the tree has matured sufficiently, she discovers that she is unable to cut it down because it is inhabited by three demonic creatures: a serpent among the roots, a raptor bird in the crown, and a female demon in the trunk. Gilgamesh volunteers to help her and with his mighty battle-ax fells the tree and kills the snake, whereupon the demon and bird fly away. Apart from the furniture, Inanna makes two objects from the timber, which she presents to Gilgamesh as a reward, but for some reason they fall into the underworld. His servant Enkidu volunteers to retrieve them. Gilgamesh gives him careful instructions how to behave in this place, where all the normal rules of behavior are inverted. Enkidu goes down to the underworld but promptly forgets all his warnings and breaks every single taboo. Through the mediation of the deity Enki, Gilgamesh summons the spirit of Enkidu through a hole in the ground; he tells him of the conditions in the Land of the Dead, where one with three sons has water to drink, one with seven sons is close to the gods, but those whose bodies were never buried are destined to roam forever without rest.

ENLIL AND NINLIL

SET IN THE CITY of Nippur, the myth describes the courtship of Enlil and Ninlil and the birth of three underworld gods. Ninlil is a young girl who is seduced by Enlil when she goes to bathe in the canal, despite the warnings of her mother to beware of Enlil, who will desert her. When Enlil is banned from Nippur for his unlawful impregnation, Ninlil follows him. Although the god assumes disguise, she is not deceived and sleeps with him again, conceiving another child each time. The final passage praises Mother Ninlil and Father Enlil.

LAHAR AND ASHNAN (CATTLE AND GRAIN)

IN THE BEGINNING An created the Annunanki gods. However, because the world was not yet fully organized, they had to eat grass with their mouth like sheep and drink water from a ditch. Then Lahar, the cattle goddess, and Ashnan, the grain goddess, were created. They produced more food, especially milk, and things became better for the gods, but the Annunanki were still not satisfied. At this point, Enlil, advised by Enki, decides to send the goddesses to earth. They set up sheepfolds for Lahar and present a plow and a yoke to Ashnan. In this way agriculture and animal husbandry are brought to the "earth. Mankind, "destined for the service of the gods," is now able to supply the gods with abundant and suitable sustenance. However, the two goddesses begin to quarrel, each denigrating the contribution of the other and praising her own advantages. Enki and Enlil intervene and Ashnan is declared the winner.

Babylonian Mythology

INTRODUCTION

AT THE BEGINNING of the second millennium B.C.E. Semitic-speaking Amorite tribes established themselves in southern Syria and the middle Euphrates region and formed a state under the leadership of Hammurabi, who made the city of Babylon his capital (eighteenth century B.C.E). Like the preceding Sumerian civilization it continued to be urban and bureaucratic, based on irrigation, agriculture, and commerce. Most of the earlier institutions, especially temples, were maintained. Babylonian, written in the cuneiform system, became the medium of international communication in the mid-second millennium B.C.E. and Babylonian scribes were employed in all the major urban centers of the Ancient Near East, from Egypt to Anatolia. This disseminated Mesopotamian literary culture across a large area. Babylonia became one of the great powers in the first millennium B.C.E., especially during the reign of Nebuchadnezzar II, following the defeat of the Assyrian empire.

▲ *Modern representation of Marduk defeating Tiamat, goddess of the Deep, personification of evil.*

ENUMA ELISH (THE BABYLONIAN CREATION)

This long text, which exists in several edition from the twelfth to the seventh century B.C.E., was recited on the occasion of the Babylonian Near Festival. (In Assyria, a similar version, featuring their national god Assur rather than Marduk, was in use.) The bulk of the text is taken up with the recitation of Marduk's names, his glorification, and a praise of Babylon. The cosmogonic myth, reworking older creation accounts concerning other deities, such as Enlil and Ninurta, introduces the litanies.

IN THE BEGINNING, before Heaven and Earth were named, the primeval waters were mingled together. From this creative source three generations of gods emerge, leading to Anu and Ea (the Sumerian Enki). The young gods are restless and disturb the peace of Apsu, their ancestor, who decides to destroy them. His plan is thwarted by Ea, who puts a spell on Apsu to make him fall into a deep sleep while Ea takes over the watery depths as his own domain and lives there with his wife Damkina. She gives birth to Marduk, whose vigor disturbs Apsu's consort Tiamat. Urged on by the other old gods, she prepares to do battle against Marduk and assembles a host of monsters and serpents headed by her son Kingu. When Ea's magic fails to prevail against her host, he calls on Marduk to take on the fight. Marduk accepts, on condition that should he win he shall have supreme command among the gods. This is accepted and he is armed with irresistible weapons, including the seven winds. He raises a storm and charges against Tiamat, whom he catches in his net and immobilizes with the winds. He then rounds up the fleeing army and seizes Kingu, from whom he takes the Tablets of Destiny.

He splits open the prostrate body of Tiamat, whose upper part he fixes above to form the sky, complete with stars and planets. The lower part becomes the earth, and the Tigris and Euphrates flow from her eye sockets. Her knotted tail serves as a plug to keep the waters of Apsu from flooding the land. Solid pillars separate heaven and earth. The Tablets of Destiny he hands over to Anu for safekeeping, and then he is officially installed by the assembled gods. Kingu, blamed for causing the revolt, is executed and from his blood and clay Ea creates Man, imposing the services of the gods upon him which, frees the Annunanki gods from labor. In gratitude they build a sanctuary for Marduk, which he names Babylon. Then all the gods sit down to celebrate. The text goes on to continue the exaltation of Marduk.

◀ *Ancient Babylonian ceramic art depicting a lion, symbol of Ishtar.*

MARDUK

THE NATIONAL BABYLONIAN god rose to importance during the First Dynasty of Babylon. He was the son of Ea and, like him, had associations with magic. He also shared aspects of the solar deity, Shamash, especially in terms of justice, impartiality, and compassion. His mythological personification is that of a young warrior and dragon slayer (akin to Ninurta in Sumerian mythology), combined with executive functions (the order of the universe and the division of offices among the gods). His symbol was the horned and winged dragon, also known as Mushhushu.

THEMES OF BABYLONIAN MYTHOLOGY

WHILE THE BABYLONIANS inherited the culture and religious institutions of Sumer and translated a number of Sumerian myths, their religious sensibilities owe much to their pastoralist origin. The important Sumerian deities were simply renamed with a Semitic appellative (An: Anu; Enki: Ea; Enlil: Ellil; Inanna: Ishtar; Utu: Shamash; Nannar: Sin), but new deities were also introduced.

Important themes were justice, morality, and personal piety, as well as concerns with death and the underworld (Nergal, Ereshkigal, Adapa, Gilgamesh, Atra-hasis). Although a number of Sumerian myths were translated into Babylonian, their emphasis was changed to reflect a more pessimistic outlook, in keeping with the social and political instability of the second and early first millennium B.C.E. They are set in a more unpredictable world in which capricious gods at once uphold and threaten universal order. There is also a new consciousness of national identity and ideology, as exemplified by the rise of the god Marduk (see Epic of Creation, Erra).

ADAPA

ADAPA IS ONE of the Seven Sages, created by Ea (the Sumerian Enki) as an exemplary man with superhuman wisdom. He serves the god as a priest in Eridu. One day he is out fishing when the south wind overturns his boat. In anger he curses the wind to "break his wings," with the result that no south wind blows for a long time. The great god Anu hears of the matter and has Adapa summoned to heaven so that he can be made responsible. Ea, anxious for his protégé, instructs him how to prepare for his journey. He must don mourning and express his sympathies to two gods stationed before the gate, Dumuzi and Ningishzida, in order to win their support. The plan works, as Anu is mollified by the gods' intercession. When he hears that Adapa had acquired his wisdom (and magic) from Ea, he offers him the Water and Bread of Life, which would make him like the gods. However, forewarned by Ea not to accept the proffered Water and Bread of Death, Adapa rejects the offer. Anu breaks into laughter at his folly and sends him back to earth.

(This myth reinforces the Mesopotamian view that eternal life is for the gods; even when offered the chance of immortality, Adapa is unable to take advantage.)

◀ *Babylonian map of the world.*

ATRA-HASIS (OLD BABYLONIAN FLOOD MYTH)

The Babylonian flood myth has Sumerian antecedents which are only known from fragmentary texts that concern the flood-hero, called Ziusudra, who escapes the great deluge sent by the gods on the secret instructions of Enki.

THE BABYLONIAN VERSION begins at that time when the minor gods have to work hard for the great gods, which eventually causes a revolt. Enki offers to find a solution and asks the mother goddess to create man to "bear the yoke." Enlil orders one god to be killed and his flesh to be mixed with clay. From this she makes seven human couples and decrees rules to regulate procreation. Henceforth it is mankind's destiny to reproduce themselves and labor for the gods. However, after some time, humanity fills heaven and earth with noise and clamor, disturbing the peace of the gods. Enlil seeks to put a stop to this by sending first a plague, then famine, in order to decimate the people. His plans are foiled by Enki, who instructs Atra-hasis ("the exceedingly wise") to counteract the threat with appropriate measures, such as to bring offerings to the gods of healing and grain. Enlil is furious at the failure of his methods and decides to send a devastating flood to eradicate mankind once and for all. He makes the gods swear an oath of allegiance, but again Enki betrays his plan to Atra-hasis, appearing to him in a dream where he speaks to the reed-wall. He tells Atra-hasis to build a boat and load it with his family and various species of animals. When the flood is released, they are safe in the boat while everyone else is drowned.

The gods are in great distress, especially the mother goddess, who mourns the fate of her creatures. When the flood has subsided and Atra-hasis makes his first sacrifice, Enlil is furious that he has been tricked again. However, Enki points out that the gods rely on mankind's support and that Enlil had gone too far. He tells him that he should limit his anger and punish those who deserve it, while he himself will take measures to limit the population. Enki then decrees the existence of barren women, special categories of childless priestesses, as well as infant mortality personified by a child-snatching demon. Atra-hasis, like the Sumerian flood hero Ziusudra, is given eternal life.

▲ *Assyrian relief thought to depict Gilgamesh.*

THE FLOOD STORY FROM NINEVEH (ELEVENTH TABLET OF THE GILGAMESH EDITION)

The story is told to Gilgamesh by the flood hero Utnapishtim. The parallels with the biblical story of the flood are striking.

UTNAPISHTIM IS A CITIZEN of the Babylonian town of Shurrupak, when he receives a message from the god Ea (through the brick wall) that the gods are about to bring a deluge. Ea instructs him to build a boat, gives him the exact measurements, and warns him to tell his inquisitive fellow citizens that he is preparing to live with Ea in his watery abode below the earth. When the vessel is finished, he loads it with his family, silver and gold, and all species of living creatures. At the appointed time the dams burst, the groundwaters swell, and the rains come down. The storm is so fierce that even the gods "cower like dogs."

On the seventh day the flood subsides, and when Utnapishtim opens a vent to look out, he realizes that the ship has run aground. He lets out a dove which, finding no resting place, returns to the vessel. The swallow fares no better, and eventually he lets fly a raven, which eats and flies about and does not return to the boat. Utnapishtim then disembarks with his family and makes a sacrifice, pouring out libations and burning incense. "The gods smelling the sweet savor gather like flies about the priest and his offering." The mother goddess arrives, grieving over the destruction of her creatures and vowing never to forget what has happened. She blames Enlil for the almost total annihilation of mankind. Although Enlil is furious that one human family has escaped, Ea soothes his anger and confesses that it was he who engineered Utnapishtim's escape. Enlil, assuaged, blesses the flood hero and his wife and grants them eternal life.

◀ *Utnapishtim, the flood-hero, and his boat.*

ISHTAR

AN ANCIENT SEMITIC goddess, probably originally associated with the planet Venus. In the Akkadian period she was identified with the Sumerian Inanna but retained her warlike character. In the second millennium she was promoted to the role of queen of heaven as the consort of An(u), equal in rank with the other astral deities. Her martial prowess and violence (personified by her aspect of "bearded Ishtar") were offset by her mother goddess characteristics and by her particular concern: erotic attraction. She presided over all manifestations of sexuality, and her cult personnel included transvestites, eunuchs, and prostitutes of both sexes.

NERGAL AND ERRA

NERGAL IS AN ANCIENT Semitic god, known since the Akkadian period in the second half of the third millennium. He is primarily an underworld deity (see Nergal and Ereshkigal). Later he was also identified with the planet Mars, dividing his time between the underworld and heaven.

Erra is an old Semitic god who was particularly associated with the fertility of land, especially the steppe region. He was worshiped at Cutha as an underworld god. A myth recorded in the eighth century portrays Erra as a force of chaos who unleashes a breakdown of all social norms during the temporary absence of Marduk.

ERRA

ERRA, THE GOD of pestilence and rebellion, is sleeping in his underground abode when he is woken by the dangerous, demonic "Seven." They remind him of the glories of war and taunt him that his weapons have rusted from inertia. Unless he takes up his former ways, he will become the butt of jokes and, furthermore mankind has become too noisy. Erra decides to comply with their suggetion and goes to find the god Marduk. He criticizes the lackluster state of the god's regalia, and Marduk tells him that he cannot leave his palace untended while he goes to procure the necessary precious stones and metals since the last time he absented himself, terrible calamities befell the earth. Erra persuades Marduk to let him be his temporary representative and at the same time makes efforts to delay Marduk's quest. Erra vents his anger upon the earth, causing civil war, terrible violence, and anarchy. Ishum, his vizier, feels compassion for the suffering of the people and by flattery manages to direct Erra's destructive energy toward the enemies of Babylonia until his fury is spent and he is ready for a period of rest. Before his retirement he utters a blessing over the devastated lands to make them populous and fertile once again.

▶ *Neo-Hittite relief depicting a female deity standing on a lion.*

▲ *Sumerian cylinder seal depicting Zu being judged by Ea.*

NERGAL AND ERESHKIGAL

THE HEAVENLY GODS have a banquet and Ereshkigal, queen of the underworld, sends her envoy Namtar to receive her share of the feast. The only god who does not greet Namtar with due respect but remains seated is Nergal. Ereshkigal plans to avenge this insult by killing Nergal and so she summons him to the underworld. Ea equips Nergal with powerful magic and when he confronts Ereshkigal he roughly pulls her off the throne by her hair and prepares to cut her head off. Overcome, she pleads to be saved and offers to marry him and share the rulership over the underworld, to which he concedes.

Another version of this story again has Nergal failing to behave respectfully toward Namtar. Before his journey to the underworld Ea advises him how to behave: he must not sit down, drink beer, or eat bread or meat. He warns him particularly not to give in to sexual urges when he sees Ereshkigal. Nergal resists the food and drink but when Ereshkigal appears in a transparent gown after her bath he gives in "to his heart's desire" and they spend the next six days and nights in bed together. Nergal tricks Namtar into letting him leave the underworld and goes back to heaven. Ereshkigal is distraught when she discovers her lover's absence and sends her envoy to plead for his return, mentioning her loneliness since childhood and the fact that she is now unclean and cannot perform her divine functions. Ea's attempts to disguise Nergal's appearance fail and Nergal descends to the underworld again. He goes up to Ereshkigal, laughs, and pulls her off the throne, only to embrace her again passionately. From this time on he remains in the realm of the dead and becomes king of the underworld as the husband of Ereshkigal.

GILGAMESH

THE STORY OF GILGAMESH has survived in several different versions from different periods, beginning with the Sumerian tales (see Gilgamesh, Enkidu, and the Netherworld; Gilgamesh and the Land of the Living). It was known throughout the Ancient Near East and combines the theme of Mesopotamian *hubris*—the cutting of valuable timber in foreign territory—with a dragon-slaying motif (the trees are protected by a demonic creature). Added on to this core were other popular narratives, such as the flood story, the rebuttal of the love goddess's advances, and speculation about the underworld. The framework of the most coherent version, the so-called Twelve Tablet edition, probably dating to the late second millennium but best known from the recension discovered in the library at Nineveh from the seventh century B.C.E., revolves around male friendship and the question of man's mortality. The following résumé is based on this version.

THE STORY OF GILGAMESH

GILGAMESH, two-thirds god and one-third man, is the young king of Uruk. His continual feasting and debauchery anger his subjects, who complain to the gods. In response Anu instructs the mother goddess to create a being that would be his match and she fashions Enkidu, a wild man who lives in the steppeland and roams with the beasts. He is observed by a huntsman who comes to investigate why his snares remain empty. He brings the news of this strange and completely hairy creature to the king of Uruk. He also advises him to send one of the city's prostitutes to tame the wild man. Having had sex with the "voluptuous one," Enkidu becomes estranged from the animals and accompanies the woman to Uruk. There he will meet Gilgamesh who meanwhile has been dreaming about objects falling from the sky; his mother tells him that they represent a man who will become his best friend. After Enkidu's arrival the two men decide to win glory and leave the city for adventures. Their first journey is to the Cedar Mountain where, with the help of the sun god Shamash, they overcome the demon Humbaba.

When they return victorious to Uruk, the goddess Ishtar appears to Gilgamesh, offering herself as his bride; when he rejects her offer with blasphemous insults, she sends down the Bull of Heaven. Gilgamesh and Enkidu kill the creature, but as a punishment Enkidu falls ill and dies. In despair over his friend's death and confronted with his own mortality, Gilgamesh leaves the city and sets out to seek the floohero, Utnapishtim, who has been granted eternal life. Having overcome many dangers he reaches a garden full of precious stones where the ale wife Siduri lives. He relates his story to her and she warns him that only the sun god may cross the waters of death. Gilgamesh, however, is able to persuade the ferry man Urshanabi to take him across the waters to where Utnapishtim lives with his wife. Asked why he, a mere human, was exempt from death, Utnapishtim tells him the story of the flood (see The Flood Story from Nineveh, eleventh tablet of the Gilgamesh edition) and that his continuous existence reminds the gods of their promise not to destroy mankind again. Why, he asks, should they assemble for Gilgamesh's sake? However, moved by the latter's despair, he tells him to abstain from sleep for seven days and seven nights. When Gilgamesh fails this test, Utnapishtim gives him new clothes that will not wear out. As a last favor he tells him of a magic plant that makes the old grow young again, but on Gilgamesh's way home a serpent steals the plant, shedding its skin. Finally Gilgamesh returns to Uruk, where he climbs the walls to survey the brickwork and the city.

The Ninevite edition adds the Babylonian version of the old Sumerian narrative about Gilgamesh, Enkidu, and the Netherworld.

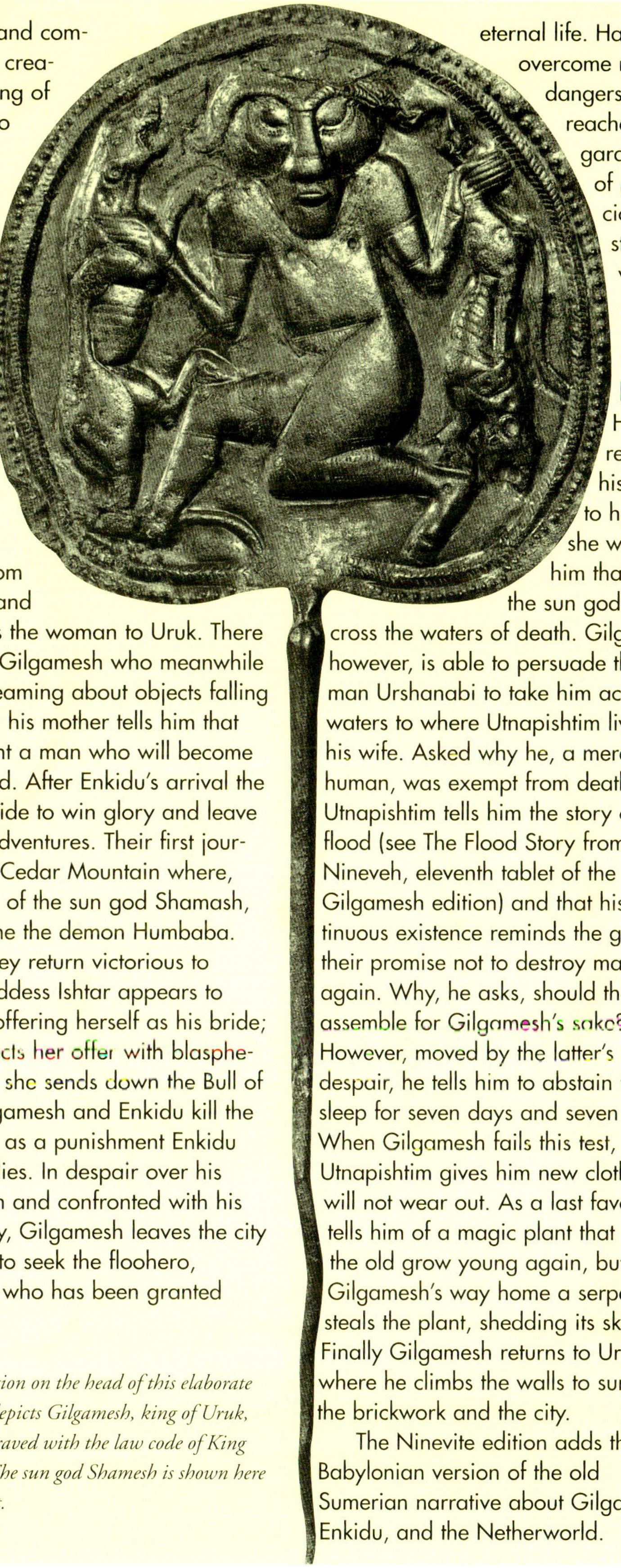

▲ *The decoration on the head of this elaborate bronze needle depicts Gilgamesh, king of Uruk,*

◀ *A pillar engraved with the law code of King Hammurabi. The sun god Shamesh is shown here seated, top right.*

◀ *The remains of a wall-painting from the Palace of Zimri-Lim in Mari showing Zimri-Lim in front of the goddess Ishtar.*

ISHTAR'S DESCENT

THE SURVIVING VERSION from the library at Nineveh is a condensed variation of the Sumerian myth "Inanna's Descent to the Underworld." The goddess decides to go to "the Land of No Return," ruled by Ereshkigal, a dark and gloomy place. She demands entry by threatening to smash the gates down and let out the dead, who would eat the living. As in the Sumerian tale she is stripped of her accoutrements. Ereshkigal fatally curses Ishtar, whose death has drastic consequences on earth: all copulation among beasts and man comes to an end. Ea (the Sumerian Enki) creates a handsome eunuch to visit Ereshkigal, win Ishtar's corpse through flattery, and revive it with the Water of Life. The ending is badly damaged but alludes to Tammuz (the Sumerian Dumuzi) who takes up Ishtar's place in the underworld.

ETANA

THIS MYTH IS only partially known; there are large gaps in the texts and the ending is missing. A prologue describes that, while the city of Kish has been created, it lacks a king. The next preserved episode concerns a tree inhabited by a snake and an eagle. They decide to overcome their mutual distrust, swear an oath of friendship before the sun god Shamash, and become partners sharing their food. All goes well until one day the eagle breaks their oath and eats up the young of the serpent, who cries out to Shamash for revenge.

The god kills a bull and tells the serpent to hide inside the cadaver. When the greedy eagle alights on the carcass to feed on his favorite intestines, the serpent strikes him, plucks out his feathers, and throws him in a pit. Meanwhile, in Kish, King Etana is still without an heir. He prays to Shamash, imploring him to show him the Plant of Birth, and the god tells him of an imprisoned eagle that will help him. Etana sets out and finds the bird languishing in the pit. For seven months he feeds the creature until its feathers have regrown. When the eagle offers a reward, Etana mentions the Plant of Birth. Since it cannot be found anywhere on earth, they fly to heaven together to consult Ishtar, the goddess of procreation. During the first attempt Etana falls off the eagle's back but after an auspicious dream they try once more and probably succeed (the text breaks off here).

ASSYRIAN MYTHOLOGY

WRITTEN VERSIONS of Assyrian myths are few in number and closely follow Babylonian prototypes due to the great influence of Babylonian culture and literature over the Assyrian elite. The main national deity was Assur, a type of weather god who was closely associated with the Assyrian king. In the Assyrian version of the Creation myth, Assur takes on the role of Marduk. Other important deities were Ishtar, who had a major temple of great antiquity at Nineveh, the storm god Adad, Ea, the master magician of the gods, and Nabu, son of the Babylonian god Marduk and patron of scribes.

▶ *Portion of a cuneiform tablet inscribed with the Babylonian myth of creation.*

THE THEOGONY OF DUNNU

DUNNU WAS A CITY in central Babylonia. The myth is partially preserved on tablets dated to the beginning of the second millennium B.C.E. It concerns the foundation of Dunnu and the genealogy of its gods and was probably related to seasonal festivals through the agricultural year.

Plough and Earth are the first divine couple. They cultivate the land, establish Dunnu and beget Shakan, the cattle god. Earth desires her son and marries him, having killed Plough. Shakan takes over from his father, whom he buries at Dunnu. He then marries Tiamat, his sister, who in turn kills Earth, her mother. The next generation kills both parents. Their children, a herding god and goddess, increase the fertility of the pastures. The herding god disposes of his parents and takes over the dominion of the land. Their son marries his sister and they kill their parents. On New Year's Day their son also marries his sister, but instead of killing his father and mother he merely imprisons them.

The rest of the composition is fragmentary, but it appears, since it mentions some well-known Mesopotamian gods such as Enlil and Ninurta, that relationships between parents and their offspring become increasingly normal and regulated.

▶ *Carved stone pillars such as this have withstood the tests of time, enabling us to piece together ancient mythologies from the script and the pictures.*

Hittite Mythology

INTRODUCTION

THE HITTITES WERE Indo-Europeans who settled in Anatolia (now Turkey) in the eighteenth century B.C.E. and developed an independent kingdom around their capital, Hattusa. The name Hittite derives from that of the indigenous population, known as the Hatti, who built a flourishing civilization in the Bronze Age (mid-third millennium B.C.E). In the fifteenth century B.C.E the Hittite empire controlled all of Anatolia, Upper Mesopotamia, and successfully challenged Egyptian supremacy in Syria and Palestine. Though the Hittite empire was destroyed in the thirteenth century B.C.E., Hittite principalities continued to exist well into the first millennium B.C.E. They wrote their language in the cuneiform system and later in a hieroglyphic form.

Knowledge about Hittite mythology derives from cuneiform tablets discovered in the archives of the capital Hattusa. The national and supreme deities were the weather god (he bore different names, according to local manifestations) and the sun goddess Arinna. The Hittite official pantheon comprised the "thousand gods of Hatti," a reference to the Hittite tendency to absorb local and foreign deities, especially Mesopotamian and Hurrian ones. Their mythology also borrows from neighboring countries, and Hurrian myths in particular were copied and translated into Hittite.

THE QUEEN OF NESHA

ONE YEAR the queen of Nesha gives birth to 30 sons. Worried about this extraordinary number of children, she decides to hide the matter. She puts the babies in reed baskets caulked with excrement and puts them in the river. Miraculously preserved, the children reach the seashore, and there the gods take pity on them and raise them. After some time the queen experiences another multiple birth, producing 30 daughters, though this time she keeps them. When the boys are grown up they decide to seek out the place of their birth. Their mother does not recognize them and gives her daughters in marriage to her sons. The youngest brothers warn the others against committing incest, but the siblings marry. The end of the tale is missing.

ILLUYANKA

The story of Illuyanka was recited on the occasion of the New Year celebrations at Nerik, the main shrine of the weather god. The tale probably comes from an old Hattian myth. The text survives in two versions.

ILLUYANKA IS A GIANT, dragon-like monster (rather like the Hurrian Hedammu) who defeats the weather god in a crucial fight. The mother goddess Inara decides to help. She prepares a banquet, filling various vessels with large quantities of alcoholic drink. However, she needs to enlist the assistance of a human being and asks a man called Hupashiya. He agrees to help but only on condition that she first has sex with him. She agrees to this and takes the man to the banquet to which she had invited Illuyanka and all his children. The dragon family get so drunk that they cannot leave. Hupashiya ties them up securely and keeps them ready for the weather god, who kills them forthwith. Inara now takes the man to a far-off place to live with her. However, she forbids him to look out of the window. After 20 days he can resist no longer and, looking out, he sees his wife and children. Filled with longing, he asks the goddess to let him return. The ending is lost, but it seems likely that she kills Hupashiya for his disobedience.

The second version of Illuyanka and the weather god also involves a human being. Again Illuyanka has managed to take away the power of the weather god, this time by depriving him of his heart and eyes. The vulnerable god marries the daughter of a "poor man" and she bears him a son, who in turn woos the daughter of Illuyanka. As a bride-price he demands the stolen organs of his father. When the weather god is restored to health, he renews his fight. He not only kills his old enemy but also his son, who is now part of his wife's clan and asks not to be spared.

▶ *Hittite basalt relief depicting the head of the goddess Kubaba.*

TELEPINU

The myth of Telepinu is preserved as part of a ritual intended to appease the anger of the gods in time of national emergency, and survives in fragmentary form in several versions.

THE BEGINNING is lost, but it is clear that Telepinu (a grain deity) has disappeared, which has dire consequences for the country. Fires go out in the hearths; gods and men feel exhausted; ewes and cows neglect their young; grain fails to ripen; neither animals nor men copulate. The sun god sends envoys to the eagle and also to the weather god asking that they search for Telepinu, but their efforts are in vain. Finally Hannahanna, the mother goddess, sends out a bee. The bee finds the god asleep and wakes him with a sting. Telepinu is furious and in his anger he causes more mayhem and destruction, which frightens even the gods. The divine magician Kamrushepa is called upon to calm the wrathful god. With magic spells and special rites she purifies him of his bad temper and restores his good qualities and goodwill toward mankind. Telepinu returns home and revives the fertility of the country.

Hurrian Mythology

INTRODUCTION

THE HURRIANS, WHO SPOKE an agglutinative, probably Indo-European language, first settled in northern Mesopotamia in the third millennium B.C.E. They made significant contributions to the culture of the Ancient Near East for the next 2,000 years and formed the majority of the population of the Mitanni empire in the fourteenth century B.CE. As long as their capital city remains undiscovered, an assessment of Hurrian civilization must remain provisional.

Their main gods were the weather god Teshub, the goddess Shaushga (identified with the Babylonian Ishtar), and Kumarbi. They also worshiped a sun god (Shimegi) and a moon god, Kusuh, and incorporated the major Mesopotamian deities within their pantheon. Hurrians also settled in southern Anatolia, and many of their gods and goddeses, myths and rituals were transmitted to the Hittites. Owing to the lack of Hurrian archives dealing with religious subject matter, almost all extant sources about their mythology come from either Mesopotamian or Hittite text versions. It seems that some of their myths reached the Greeks, perhaps via the Hittites.

KINGSHIP IN HEAVEN (KUMARBI)

KUMARBI (identified by the Hurrians with the Babylonian Ellil (Enlil) and by the Canaanites with El) was an agricultural deity.

"Kingship in Heaven," which survives in a Hittite version, describes the power struggle among the primeval gods.

Alalu is deposed by Anu, who in turn is attacked by his son Kumarbi. When Anu tries to escape, Kumarbi bites off his genitals. Anu tells him that this will make him pregnant with the weather god, the Tigris, and another deity. Kumarbi tries to spit out the semen, some of which falls to the ground and impregnates the earth, which gives birth to two children. The text is fragmentary from then on; it appears that Kumarbi does become pregnant and has considerable problems delivering the weather god, who in turn wrests the kingship from his progenitor.

▼ *Composite figures, part animal, part human, are a common theme in Ancient Near Eastern art.*

▶ *Stone relief of a warrior from the Hittite capital Hattusa.*

ULLIKUMMI

KUMARBI PLOTS to overthrow the weather god. To this purpose he impregnates a great rock, which bears a stone monster called Ullikummi. Kumarbi installs him on the right shoulder of the giant Upelluri, who lives in a distant place. The sun god spots the rapidly growing monster and informs the weather god, who goes to inspect Ullikummi, accompanied by several gods. Ishtar tries to seduce him with her charms but this fails since the stony creature can neither see nor hear. Kumarbi now assembles all the gods, in an effort to annihilate the monster, but he has grown so big that they cannot harm him. Ea goes to find Upelluri, who is unaware of Ullikummi and only complains of a slight pain in his shoulder. Ea asks the primeval gods to lend him a cutting tool that was originally used to sever the earth from the sky. With this he manages to cut Ullikummi off the giant's shoulder, which immediately reduces his power. The gods now renew their attack and presumably succeed, though the ending is not preserved.

KUMARBI

KUMARBI MARRIES the daughter of the sea god and she gives birth to Hedammu, a dragonlike creature who emerges daily from the sea to devour vast quantities of domestic animals and people. The goddess Ishtar discovers the monster and informs the weather god, who for some reason (the text is badly preserved here) can do nothing about it. Ishtar decides to deal with the situation herself, bathes and anoints herself and goes down to the water's edge. Hedammu is untamed and tries to eat her too. Next time she approaches the shore, she comes with magic and turns the seawater into a sleeping potion. Hedammu succumbs and, enticed by her charms, leaves the water. The ending is unclear owing to the fragmentary state of the text, but it seems that the weather god eventually subdues Hedammu.

Biblical Mythology

INTRODUCTION

THE SACRED TRADITIONS of the Hebrew people, collected in the *Torah* and the prophetic books, contain various references to gods and cult practices of Israel's neighbors, such as the Canaanites, Edomites, Ammonites, and Moabites, as well as Babylonia and Assyria. There are also elements of mythological themes which either borrow themes from other Ancient Near Eastern cultures or elaborate on current patterns. As a result of the emphasis on a single god of Israel as sole creator, mediator, and savior of the nation and mankind, the mythological drama so characteristic in polytheistic religions is largely absent. Furthermore, none of the extant written sources of the *Old Testament* are older than the Hellenistic age (the earliest scrolls of the Qumran caves date to the first century B.C.E.). By that time the various texts had undergone several series of editions to produce a theological coherence that minimized mythological elements. The first chapters of the *Book of Genesis* have a mythological structure and content, as paradigmatic narratives that account for the form and nature of the world and humankind. The flood-story is clearly based on the Babylonian version although the myth was retold with a radically different theological intention for the Hebrew audience.

THE GARDEN OF EDEN AND MAN'S DISOBEDIENCE (GENESIS II: 4–III: 24)

IN THE BEGINNING, when God created heaven and earth, the earth had no vegetation since God had not caused rain to fall and there was no man to till the fields, only fog moistened the earth. Because of this, God makes a man from the soil and breathes the breath of life into his nostrils. He plants a garden, called Eden, and he puts the man in this garden that he plants with different trees, all tempting to look at and good to eat. Among them are the Tree of Life and the Tree of Knowledge of Good and Evil. From the garden flow four streams, including the Tigris and the Euphrates.

God instructs the man to look after the garden and tells him that he may eat from all of the trees except the Tree of the Knowledge of Good and Evil. Should he do so he will die. God realizes that the man is lonely and decides to make a companion for him. He calls together all the animals and asks the man to name them. Then he lets the man fall into a deep sleep and from his rib he makes a woman. He shows her to the man and tells him that she is of his flesh and that for her sake he will leave father and mother to become one flesh with her. Both of them are naked but feel no shame.

Now the serpent, more cunning than all the other animals, addresses the woman, asking her why God has forbidden them to eat fruit from the trees of the garden. The woman explains that they are allowed to taste them all except for the one in the middle of the garden, on pain of death. The serpent insinuates that this injunction was only made to stop them becoming like God, able to differentiate between good and evil. The woman looks at the fruit of this tree and sees that it would be good to eat. She takes one to eat and also gives it to the man. No sooner have they eaten than they become aware of their nakedness and make themselves aprons of leaves.

▲ *Modern portrayal of God and his angels enthroned on high in the Heavens.*

◀ *The serpent tempts Eve to eat the apple from the forbidden Tree of Knowledge growing in the Garden of Eden.*

CREATION OF THE WORLD (GENESIS I–II: 4)

THE BIBLICAL CREATION account is set within a temporal sequence of seven days. The act of creation is through the uttered command of God. It begins with heaven and earth, with the earth being empty and in darkness. Then God causes light to appear, which divides night from day. He separates the waters of above from the waters of the deep by a solid barrier. The upper part becomes the sky and the lower solid part becomes the earth. The following day he assembles the waters below the sky to form seas which leave dry land, to be called earth. He next decrees that the earth sprout vegetation and instigates the self-propagation of plants through seeds. On the fourth day he fixes the lights on the heavenly body: stars and planets to regulate time. Then he fills the sea and the sky with watery creatures and birds, followed by the animals that live on land, wild beasts and domestic animals, clean and unclean. He creates human beings, male and female, and gives them dominion over all the creatures of heaven, earth, and sea, and he makes them in his image. On the seventh day God surveys his work and, satisfied, rests from his labors.

MAN'S PUNISHMENT

GOD CALLS to them, asking why they are hiding, and when they answer that they are ashamed of their nakedness he accuses them of having tasted from the forbidden tree. Questioned why it happened, the woman blames the serpent and God curses it among all animals, to creep on its belly for evermore and to become the eternal enemy of the woman and all her descendants. He tells the woman that she will have trouble in her pregnancy and that she should long for the man who will be her master.

He turns to the man and decrees that because of his disobedience the earth of the field shall be cursed and filled with weeds and thistles. Man will have to earn his bread in the sweat of his brow and, being made from dust, he will return to dust. The man then names the woman Eve and she becomes the mother of all human beings. Then god makes them garments of fur and declares that now man is able to tell good from evil he must not stretch out his hand to eat from the Tree of Life. He sends the man and the woman away from the garden of Eden and sets divine creatures with flaming swords to guard the way to the Tree of Life.

SONS OF GOD AND DAUGHTERS OF MAN

MEN MULTIPLY on earth and daughters are born to them. The sons of God see that the daughters of men are beautiful and they marry them. God decides that his spirit should not live within man and limits their lifespan to 120 years. The offspring of the union between the daughters of man and the sons of God are the giants, famous heroes of the old time.

CAIN AND ABEL (GENESIS IV: 1–22)

ADAM AND HIS WIFE EVE have two sons, first Cain and then Abel. Abel becomes a farmer and Cain a shepherd. Cain makes a sacrifice, offering from the fruits of his fields, and so does Abel, who offers the firstborn of his herds. God looks favorably on Abel's offer but disregards that of Cain, who is upset by this slight. God notices his anger and warns him to control his impulse, but Cain invites his brother to come to his fields where he kills him. Asked by God where Abel is, he replies that he is not his keeper. God curses him, saying that because of this bloodshed the earth will not yield to him any longer and that he will be a fugitive. Cain leaves and goes east of Eden and his wife bears him a son, Enoch, whose descendants are people who "live in tents and keep herds," lute and flute players, as well as metalsmiths.

(For a similar rivalry between farmers and pastoralists, but favoring the latter, see the Sumerian myths Enmesh and Enten, Lahar and Ashnan.)

◀ *Adam and Eve are sent away from the Garden of Eden in disgrace, having disobeyed God and eaten the fruit from the Forbidden Tree.*

▲ *Noah and his family sit and wait aboard the ark for the floods to subside.*

THE FLOOD

GOD SEES THAT MANKIND has only evil in mind and he regrets having created them. He decides to annihilate them from the face of the earth, together with all the animals. Only Noah finds grace in his eyes because he is without fault. God speaks to Noah, warning him that he is going to destroy all flesh. He instructs him to built an ark, a boxlike craft of pinewood, to make it watertight with bitumen, and to put in several decks since he will send a devastating flood, which will destroy everything on earth. Noah should take his wife, his sons, a pair each of all the animals, and enough food for them all.

Noah does exactly as bidden. Then all the wells of the deep open, rain falls for 40 days and 40 nights and the waters cover the earth and lift the craft of Noah. Everything on earth dies in the flood. After some time God remembers Noah and all the animals within the ark. He plugs up the wells of the deep and the windows of heaven, and the rain stops so that the waters gradually diminish.

After 40 days Noah lets out a dove but she can find no place to rest and returns to the ark. Seven days later he sends her out again and this time she returns with the twig of an olive tree in her beak. He waits for another week, and when he lets the bird out again she does not come back. Noah sees that the earth is dry again and God tells him to leave the ark, with his wife and sons and all the animals. Noah makes an altar and, taking some of all clean animals and birds, he sacrifices to God, who smells the sweet fragrance and decides in his heart not to curse the earth again for the sake of man, since evil is in man's heart. He blesses Noah and his sons and decrees that the animals should live in fear of human beings henceforth, and as a sign of his covenant he sets the rainbow in the sky.

THE TOWER OF BABEL

THERE WAS ONLY one language on earth. But in the journey east, men came to Mesopotamia and decided to build a city of burnt brick.

They begin to build a tower that will reach the sky so that they can make a name for themselves and not be dispersed all over the earth. God comes down to look at the city and the tower and sees that, with one language, nothing will stop mankind from achieving anything they want. He therefore decides to confound their language so that no one can understand the other's tongue. He disperses them into all the lands and they have to desist from building the city. This is why the city and tower is called Babel.

▼ *The magnificent Tower of Babel, built to reach the sky.*

Ugaritic Mythology

INTRODUCTION

UGARIT IS THE NAME of an ancient city on the Syrian coast (modern Ras Shamra near Lattakia). In the mid-second millennium B.C.E. it became the center of a small but influential and wealthy state, based on agricultural exploitation of the fertile soil and benefiting from the international trade between Egypt, Mesopotamia, and the Hittite empire to the north. The inhabitants, like the other Canaanite peoples in Syro-Palestine, spoke a west Semitic dialect. They used Babylonian cuneiform for official record keeping and correspondence but invented an alphabetic system, also written on clay, for their ritual and mythological compositions. Ugarit was destroyed in the thirteenth century B.C.E. Most of the gods of Ugaritic mythology were weather gods and associated with rainfall, crucial for the agriculture of the Fertile Crescent that depends on natural precipitation.

Most of the myths of Ugarit are known from the tablets discovered in the ruins of a priests' house in the city. The texts written in the Ugaritic alphabetic system still pose considerable problems in terms of vocabulary, syntax, and grammar. Even the sequence of the tablets is disputed, and new translations and editions keep appearing to replace existing versions.

The main deities featured in the myths of Ugarit were the creator god El, his son, the storm god Baal, who was thought to reside on Mount Zaphon, the peak that towers above the city, and the goddesses Astart and Anat, an Ishtar-like deity of war and sexual love.

THE BAAL MYTHS

THE NAME BAAL simply means "lord" or "master." It was a common appellative of west Semitic deities. There are local manifestations of this weather god, usually named after a mountain peak, which his habitual domain. The Baal featured in the Ugaritic texts is Baal-Zaphon (present-day Jebel el-Aqra). He is identified with the ancient Syrian deity Hadad (see the Mesopotamian Adad). He is called "Rider of the Cloud," manifest in the storms that herald the fall season with thunder and lightning. In the myths he battles against the unruly waters of the sea (personified as the god Yam, "Sea")—Ugarit depended on maritime traffic for its prosperity and against the scorching heat of the summer. Baal is regularly overcome by his foes but destined to rise again in a cyclical waning and waxing of power. As he represents fertility and the renewal of life, he is often associated with the bull, an ancient symbol of vitality and sexual vigor.

BAAL MYTHS (I)

THE TEXTS FORM an interrelated cycle of narratives, all of which illustrate the nature and activities of Baal. The tablets are not well preserved and especially the beginnings and endings are often missing, which makes it difficult to establish the exact sequence of events. The following synopsis is based on Johannes de Moor's 1987 *Anthology of Religious Texts from Ugarit.*

THE GODDESS ANAT bathes and anoints herself before she goes down to the seashore, where she causes a bloodbath among the people. Hung with the severed heads and hands of her victims, she wants still more violence and turns her household furniture into an army until she wades knee-deep in blood and gore. Then she returns to normality and washes herself with dew and rain. Meanwhile Baal has sent a messenger from Mount Zaphon, asking her to join him there. He complains that he alone of all the gods has no house or court. Anat promises to take up his case and goes to visit her father El, who seems to prevaricate. Somebody suggests he send for Kothar-and-Hasis, the clever craftsman, who leaves Egypt to take up the commission. Because of a plot against Baal, El is swayed to offer the palace to Yam.

Baal has a premonition that he is soon to be "bound between the stones of the stream." Yam sends word to El to deliver Baal up to him, and although Baal defends himself he is overcome. Yam tries to take up residence in the unfinished palace originally built for Baal. However, he is too big for it, and Kothar-and-Hasis is told to make another, larger palace for him. The craftsman god goes to find Baal, who "cowers under the chair of Prince Yam," and tells him that the time has now come to challenge Yam and claim his kingdom. He gives him two magical weapons, which Baal uses to defeat Yam, who is taken captive.

Baal departs with Anat to visit Astart, the Lady Asherah of the Sea, El's estranged wife, in order to persuade El to allow the building of Baal's palace to proceed. Astart, pleased by the rich presents they have brought, agrees to plead with El, who is so pleasantly surprised by her visit that he finally consents to the building of the palace. Kothar-and-Hasis is called and Baal tells him not to put any windows in.

EL

THE ETYMOLOGICAL origin of the word El is still unclear. It was the common designation for "god" in all Semitic languages, from the Akkadian Ilum to the Arabic Allah. In the Ugaritic myths El, like the Sumerian An, represents divine authority and cosmic order. He is the father of all gods (except of Baal, who is the son of Dagan) and, like Enlil in Mesopotamia, the source of royal power. He is also the "Father of Mankind" and has connections with human fertility and childbirth (see Aqat and Keret). His relationship with Baal is ambiguous, especially as the Baal myths show that there is tension between them.

BAAL MYTHS (II)

WHEN ALL IS FINISHED El prepares a banquet to celebrate. Baal returns, having sacked 90 cities, and revokes his earlier decision not to have windows. He raises his voice until the earth shakes and is enthroned in the palace. But at the height of his power he knows that his destiny is to "descend into the gullet of Mot" (death). He sees the dust storms (envoys of Mot) and sends an invitation to Mot to come to his palace. Mot refuses the request and threatens to swallow Baal in two gulps. Baal has to obey his summons to go down to the underworld and receives instructions on how to get there. On the way he sees a heifer and copulates with her, which results in the birth of an ox, called his "twin brother." Messengers arrive at El's palace and announce the death of Baal. They lament him and Anat goes in search of his body to bury him with all honors on Mount Zaphon. El calls for Astar, one of the sons of Astart's, who is eager to promote her own offspring, to mount the throne of Baal. He proves too small to occupy Baal's enormous seat.

Anat now decides to go to the underworld to look for Baal. When Mot admits that he has indeed eaten the young god, she is filled with fury and seizes Mot, splits, sieves, burns, grinds, and mills him. El meanwhile is asked to perform a dream oracle which will reveal whether Baal is still alive. Should he dream that the heavens rain oil and the valleys run with honey then Baal is not fully dead. El does indeed dream in this manner and sends Anat, accompanied by the sun goddess Shapash, to look for Baal. El describes the sun-parched fields that await the harrowing (wetting) by Baal. Shapash instructs Anat to pour "sparkling wine into the wine skins" and to bring wreaths; presumably Baal returns since after seven years Mot, now also revived, sends another challenge.

He orders one of Baal's brothers to be killed in order to atone for the wrongs done to him by Anat. Baal pretends to comply, but he intends to outwit Mot by offering him "brothers of Mot" (perhaps wild boars, the usual sacrifice to chthonic gods in Ugarit). When Mot discovers that he has eaten his own kin he comes to Zaphon and attacks Baal. They fight bitterly, but neither can defeat the other. Shapash intervenes and warns Mot that El will take away his kingship over the underworld if he continues to fight Baal. Mot retreats. The final passages contain a hymnlike conclusion, celebrating Baal's "eternal kingship." The gods sit down to a banquet and the sun-goddess is asked to rule over the spirits of the dead with Kothar-and-Hasis' assistance.

▶ *Stele or funeral stone, depicting the god Baal, hurling a bolt of lightning.*

ANAT

ANAT, WHOSE NAME may be related to the Akkadian word *ettu* ("active will",) was a goddess popular throughout the western areas of the Near East, including Egypt. In the Ugaritic myths her epithets are "Virgin Anat" and "Destroyer." Like the Babylonian Ishtar, she is a beautiful woman as well as a ferocious and bloodthirsty warrior. She is the lover of Baal and ever ready to fight for him. Their love is consummated in the guise of bovines when Baal the Bull mounts Anat the Heifer. As the "Widow of the Nation" she mourns for him in his periods of absence; there may have been a ritual connection between Anat and funerary rites.

AQAT

This story is partially preserved on tablets written by Elimelek, priest of Baal at Ugarit.

KING DANEL HAS NO SON and heir. He asks Baal for help, and Baal intercedes with the great god El, who grants his wish. A son, named Aqat, is born. Sometime later, the craftsman of the gods, Kothar-and-Hasis, arrives and is received with all honors. In return for the hospitality he presents Danel with a beautifully fashioned bow. This bow passes into the possession of Aqat; one day he meets the goddess Anat, who tells Aqat that the bow was originally meant for her and that he should hand it over. When he is reluctant to do so she offers him gold and silver, finally even immortality. Aqat retorts that he would rather share the fate of common men and casts doubts on her ability to bestow immortal life. He goes on to taunt the goddess that such a bow is not fit for mere women and then departs.

Anat threatens retribution and goes to her father El, whom she bullies to comply with her plans. Anat finds Yatpan who, in the shape of a vulture, flies out to find Aqat and kills him. He snatches up the bow, only to lose it when he drops it into the sea. Anat begins a lament over the dead body of Aqat and the failure of the crops, an atonement for his spilled blood. When Danel hears the news of his son's demize, he calls out to Baal to break the wings of the vultures circling overhead and duly finds the remains of Aqat in the mother bird. Danel curses three cities near the scene of the crime and returns to his palace to mourn his son for seven years. Pugat, his daughter, sets off to avenge her brother, and, disguised as Anat, rouged and with a sword over her dress, she finds Yatpan among the nomads. Yatpan in his drunkenness boasts about the murder of Aqat. From here on the text becomes very fragmentary. It appears that Pugat kills Yatpan. Danel asks Baal for help as he cannot forget his son, and Baal seems to propose a ritual that summons the souls of the dead.

▼ *Detailed carving of the god Baal, an enduring figure in Ancient Near Eastern mythology.*

MOT

THE WORD MOT MEANS "death" and he personifies death in all its aspects; to "be eaten by Mot" is to die. In the Ugaritic myths he is the main adversary of Baal, whom he can never completely vanquish. It has been proposed that their antagonism dramatizes the agricultural year, with Baal ensuring the rainfall that allows seeds to germinate and grow, and Mot representing the dryness of summer and the ripening of the corn. It is not clear to what extent Mot was a deity with a cult or a fictional character in a poetic and perhaps ritual context.

YAM

YAM, WHOSE name means "sea," was an important deity in Ugarit and probably along the Syrian littoral generally, where the economy depended on seaborne trade. His mythological character seems to reflect two temperaments, perhaps reflecting the calm summer when maritime expeditions are feasible and the stormy winter. In the Baal myths he fights against Baal and is defeated with magic weapons. Unlike Mot he was part of the official cult at Ugarit and received regular offerings.

KERET

This myth too belongs to the fragmentary tablets written by Elimelek.

KERET, THE KING of Khubur, is deeply unhappy. Not only has he lost all his male relatives, but none of the seven wives whom he married in succession lived long enough to bear him children. The god El appears to him in dream and tells him what to do. He is to sacrifice a bull on a tower to him first, and then he must depart on a military campaign against the neighboring kingdom. When the besieged king sues for peace, offering tribute and treasure, he is to reject it all and demand his daughter Hariya in marriage instead. Keret does exactly as bidden.

Having raised a formidable army that includes even the newly married men, he sets off. On the way he stops at a shrine of the goddess Astart. He promises to give her threefold the weight of his wife in gold if his mission should be successful. All goes according to plan. He weds the beautiful Hariya and all the gods come to the wedding feast. El pronounces that Hariya will bear eight sons and eight daughters. After some time, when all the 16 children have been born, the goddess Astart remembers the promise Keret made, which has never been honored. She announces that she will make him ill and advises that he should make arrangements for his funeral; he instructs his wife to prepare sacrificial banquets.

The people begin to lament his impending death, but he sends them all away and asks for his youngest daughter, "whose passion is strongest," to weep for him. While the king is ill, all vegetation withers. The gods call for an assembly to debate the case and finally El declares that he will create a female being able to cast out the disease. He makes a winged woman called Shatiqtu. He gives her a flower and puts "a charm on her lips." She flies into town and cures Keret, washing him clean of his sweat and restoring his appetite. Keret straight away calls to his wife to prepare a fat lamb. After two days he is well enough to ascend his throne again. His son Yassub enters the hall and challenges his father to abdicate in his favor. The king has only scorn for his son and calls on the god Horon to smash his skull in. The text becomes very fragmentary but it appears that Keret loses all his children but the youngest daughter.

▲ *Bronze statue of the Ugaritic god Baal.*

▶ *This decorative pendant shows the Syrian goddess of fertility, Astart.*

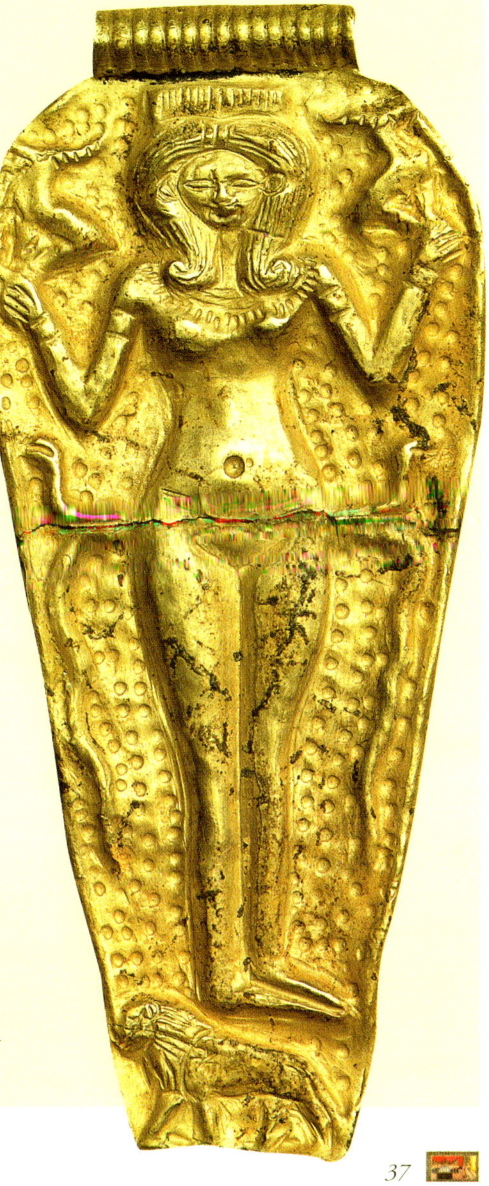

Persian Mythology

INTRODUCTION

THE PERSIANS are a branch of the Aryan family of peoples as defined by language; more specifically they belong to the Indo-Iranian branch. Originally horse- and cattle-tending nomads on the steppes of Central Asia, they migrated to the Iranian plateau around 1000 B.C.E. Other Iranian tribes—Medes, Parthians, Scythians—were migrating at the same time. Some Persian tribes settled, others remained nomadic. Those that settled took over many customs of the older urban cultures of West Asia, especially when Cyrus (559–530 B.C.E.) began to conquer Elam, Assyria, and Babylon. The erstwhile nomads became rulers of a multi-ethnic cosmopolitan empire stretching from the Mediterranean to the Oxus and the Indus.

At some period before Cyrus (scholars do not agree when), the traditional religion of the Iranians was reformed, probably in the northeast of Greater Iran, by a priest (*zaotar*), the prophet Zarat-hushtra (variously translated as "gold" or "old camel"), known to the Greeks as Zoroaster. Zoroaster approached monotheism: Ahura Mazda, constantly invoked in the inscriptions of Darius the Achaemenid (521–486 B.C.E.) and subsequent rulers of the Achaemenid dynasty (550–330 B.C.E.) descended from the clan ancestor Hakhamenesh (Achaemenes in Greek), is the supreme Wise Lord of Zoroastrianism, even though the faith emphasized the utter separation and conflict of the Holy Thought and the Evil Thought.

▲ *Second-century fresco of a Zoroastrian priest.*

ENVIRONMENT, MIGRATIONS, EMPIRE

BY 640 B.C.E. the senior clan of the senior tribe of the Persians, the Achaemenids of the Pasargadae, were ruling the old Elamite province of Anshan in the southwest of the Iranian plateau (Persis or Fars). The Medes settled further north, the Parthians, Soghdians, and Bactrians remained in the northeast and the Scythians in the steppes of eastern Europe.

Cyrus took the Elamite city Susa as his winter capital and the Median city Ecbatana as his summer capital. He founded a ceremonial capital at his family fief, Pasargadae, where the New Year ceremonies of spring were celebrated, in imitation of those performed at Babylon. These were later moved to nearby Persepolis by Darius.

In 330 B.C.E. the invasion of Alexander of Macedon imposed a supremacy of Greek ideals which lasted two centuries. Ardeshir the Sasanian consciously attempted to restore Achaemenid norms and legitimacy, but their successors could escape neither the Hellenistic heritage nor the pressure to imitate the rival empire, Byzantium.

The Arab victory at the battle of Qadisiya in C.E. 636 and their occupation of the capital Ctesiphon put an end not only to the Sasanian state but also to the Zoroastrian state church. Destruction of temples and libraries, massacres and forced conversions reduced the intellectual vitality of the Iranian national religion, which went into hibernation or exile.

◀ *A relief depicting a Persian guard from Xerxes' Palace.*

▶ *This door relief is all that remains to indicate Cyrus' palace's former splendor.*

GUARDIAN SPIRIT AT PASARGADAE

CYRUS (c. 559–530 B.C.E.) built the palace and tomb at Pasargadae near Anshan, his family's fief in Pars. His extant inscriptions merely state: "I am Cyrus, the King, the Achaemenid." There is no indication of his religious beliefs. The figure on the remaining doorjamb of the ruined palace has been interpreted as a protective spirit, comparable to the four-winged figure in the Assyrian palace at Khorsabad; here it wears an Egyptian-style triple crown resting on rams' horns. This is characteristic of the eclectic court style of the early Achaemenids, where elements from Media, Elam, Babylon, Assyria, Egypt, and Asia Minor were borrowed and blended.

THE GOOD CREATION, THE IRRUPTION OF EVIL, THE FINAL BATTLE

The *Bundahishn*, the Creation, is a late cosmological and chronological compilation collated from earlier sources during the early tenth century C.E.

THE HISTORY of the universe lasts 12,000 years. At first Ohrmazd's world of light coexists with Ahriman's world of darkness, potential in the spirit (*menog*). Ahriman (earlier known as Angra Mainyu) sees the light, and hears Ohrmazd's proposed 9,000-year war between light and dark, and falls back into the abyss. After another 3,000 years, Ohrmazd (earlier known as Ahura Mazda) creates the physical world (*getig*), the primal bull Gosh and the first living mortal Gayomard.

Ahriman determines to destroy the good creation. He smashes his way through the crystal vault of the sky, speeds through the waters which turn bitter and salt, turns the earth into desert and mountains, and sullies everything, killing the plants, the primal bull, and the living mortal. Gayomard's sperm is taken to the sun and Gosh's to the moon. From the moon-preserved seed come new plants and life, renewed by the rains of Tir, and from the sun-preserved seed grows—after 40 years underground—an androgynous rhubarb (*rivas*) out of which step the first human couple, Mashyagh and his mate Mashyanagh.

So the next 3,000-year period begins, called the period of the mixing of good and evil (*gumizeshn*), when Ahriman makes man greedy, lethargic, vicious, and diseased. At the end of this period, the birth of the prophet Zoroaster brings In the last period of 3,000 years. In this final period, after every thousand years a savior, Soshans, is born from the sperm of Zoroaster preserved in Lake Hamun in Seistan, where it miraculously fertilizes virgins who go swimming there. At the birth of the third savior, the last battle begins, and all the heroes and monsters of myth are revived to take part in the fight. Evil is defeated in a final fire ordeal of molten metal that covers the earth, Ahriman is banished to outer darkness forever, and the earth once more becomes flat. This is the great renewal (Frashokereti, or Frashgerd), the end of history.

RELIGIOUS CULTS, INFLUENCES, TEXTS

FOR CENTURIES, the liturgies of the Avesta were transmitted orally, as the Vedas were in India. Writing was alien to traditional Persian culture, being a Semitic import described in legend as "taught by the demons." The Semitic Aramaic language and script came to be used for trade and administration throughout the Achaemenid empire. The cuneiform script of Babylon was adapted for royal inscriptions in Old Persian but had little use beyond this. Zoroastrian religious hierarchies were suspicious of writing at least until the mid-Sasanian period—late fifth to early sixth centuries—when the Avestan script was devised with 46 letters, improving on the clumsy, Aramaic-derived Pahlavi alphabet used for secular and non-liturgical texts.

The prophet Zoroaster's 17 visionary hymns, the Gatha, survive after centuries of oral transmission, embedded in much later compositions in a different dialect. Scholars do not agree about the precise translations of these hymns, and the fragmentary literary record often does not agree with the patchy and much-plundered archeological record. What survives of the Avesta is what is used in the ritual and practices of the Zoroastrian clergy, which often date from after the Arab conquest.

▼ *A lion-griffin from the palace of Darius I, king of Persia.*

HUNT OF BAHRAM V WITH THE HARPIST AZADEH

BAHRAM "GUR" (c. C.E. 420–38) was entrusted in childhood to Mundhir, vassal king of Hira, and in adolescence became a keen horseman and hunter. His guardian bought him a Byzantine captive, Azadeh, among 40 slave girls; she accompanies Bahram on his swift hunting camel with her harp. She challenges her lover to perform a dazzling feat of archery: grazing a young antelope's ear with a pellet and immediately, as it raised its hoof to scratch its ear, transfixing hoof and ear with the same arrow. Bahram achieves this, but Azadeh snubs him and accuses him of being Ahriman, the evil god. The prince knocks her off the camel and tramples her to death.

TALES FROM THE SHAHNAMA

Ferdowsi's reworking of the Sasanian Book of Kings, the Shahnama which he wrote for Sultan Mahmud of Ghazni (998–1030 C.E.), remains one of the major and most accessible sources of Persian myths and historical legends.

JAMSHID, Yima Khshaeta (Yama in the Vedas), is the fourth of the primal founder heroes of Iranshahr, who teaches crafts and organizes society. After a long and peaceful reign, he boasts that he should be called "Jehan-Afarin," the creator of the world. At this, the royal glory abandons him, flying off like a bird, and his courtiers flock to the rising Arab leader Zuhhak. Jamshid is chased out and eventually sawn in two.

Ahriman gives Zuhhak a parting poisoned kiss that leaves him with two snakes growing out of his shoulders (recalling his original form as the dragon demon Azhi Dahaka). Zuhhak becomes a tyrant and exacts a daily sacrifice of young Persians to feed their brains to his snakes.

After a thousand years of tyranny, a revolt is sparked off by the fearless blacksmith Kaveh, whose sons have been sacrificed to feed Zuhhak's snakes. He rouses the crowd around his leather apron flag and marches off to find Fereydun (Thraetaona in the Avesta), descended from the legitimate royal line, whose father had also died under the Arab tyranny. The growing army, camped out in tents like guerrillas, is led by Fereydun wielding his bull-headed mace. Zuhhak is defeated and bound in chains and imprisoned in a cave on Mount Damavand. The earthquakes of the region are the monstrous Zuhhak rattling his chains under the mountains.

TOMB OF DARIUS I AT NAQSH RUSTAM

IN 522 B.C.E., DARIUS overthrew a Magian posing as Cyrus' grandson. He prepared his own tomb cut into the rockface at Naqsh Rustam, where he is shown on a dais supported by the subject peoples of the empire, standing with hand upraised in salutation of the regnal fire burning on the stepped fire altar before him. With his other hand he holds a bow, a motif that reappears on his gold coins. Above hovers the solar winged disk, which has been taken as representing Ahura Mazda, the supreme god, or the Khwarna, royal glory of divine rule. The winged disk originated in Egypt, but the Assyrians added the small human figure floating in the middle.

CULT OF FIRE AND EPHEDRA

THE CULT OF FIRE and the use of the intoxicating haoma plant go back to the earliest phase of Aryan nomad religion. Atar (Adhur) was categorized into five types by the Sasanian clergy: Atash Bahram, the fire in temple and hearth; Vohufryana, the fire life-principle in men; Urvazista, the fire life-principle in plants; Vazista, the fire or lightning in clouds; Spanishta, the pure fire that burns in paradise before Ohrmazd, with the royal glory, Khwarna.

The major fire temples were Adhar Farn-Bag at Karyan in Fars, Adhar Gushn-Asp at Shiz in Adharbaijan, and Adhar Burzin-Mehr on Mount Revand in Khorasan; they were associated respectively with the three classes of society: priests, warrior nobility, and farmers.

Haoma, the ephedra which grows on the mountains of Iran (Vedic soma), is pounded in a mortar at the dawn prayer, strained, and drunk with milk as part of the Yasna ritual. It is addressed as "Haoma, golden flowered, growing on the heights, drink that restores us and drives death afar!"

In the late Zoroastrian apocalypse, Arda Viraz Namag, the pious Arda Viraz agrees to drink the potentially lethal "mey o mang" wine and henbane in order to pass to the underworld to see the rewards of the just and the punishments of sinners. After seven days and nights of coma he wakes in the fire temple, as if from a happy sleep and dream, and tells the priests of his vision.

▲ *North entrance to the Hall of 100 Columns, showing Darius supported by flanks of soldiers.*

▶ *A human-headed capital from the fifth-century B.C.E. Apadana.*

MITHRA

THE INDO-IRANIAN tribes of the Hittites moved into Asia Minor, and in one of their treaties, dated to 1350 B.C.E., they invoke, among other gods, Mithra, Varuna, and Indra. In the commentary on the earliest religious composition of the Indo-Iranians in India, the Rig Veda, the name Mithra is translated as "friend"; in Iran, he is associated with agreements, like his Babylonian counterpart, Shamash the all-seeing sun who guards legal contracts. In the Mihr Yasht, Mithra is described watching over the land of the Iranians from the Alborz mountains, and marching out to support their fight against cattle raiders.

Mithra's popularity is attested by the wealth of personal names derived from his name, e.g. Mithra-dates (the later form is Mihr-dad). The feast of Mithra in the month of Mithra—the Mihrgan at the beginning of fall—was a great feast with wine-drinking and royal gifts.

The initiation mysteries of Mithraism spread throughout the Roman empire. The central symbol of Mithraism is the rejuvenating sacrifice by the young god of the bull, which parallels the killing of the primal bull Gosh by Ahriman in the Zoroastrian tradition. Associated with the unconquerable power of the sun, the Roman Mithraic feast of Sol Invictus gave the traditional birth date of Christ, December 25.

ZAL, THE SIMORGH, RUSTAM, ISFANDYAR, SOHRAB

Rustam is the most famous of the heroes of the Persian epic, yet his story stems from the cycle of Saka legends from Seistan, not Pars. His father Zal, born abnormal, with white hair, was left exposed on a mountainside. He was saved and fostered by a giant bird, the Simurgh (linked to the Sasanian Senmurv), which later comes, with its magically potent feathers, to help Rustam overcome the hero Isfandyar.

RUSTAM has a remarkable horse, Rakhsh, which once, when he is dozing after hunting and feasting on roast onager, wanders off and is taken to Samangan. There, Rustam follows it and is entertained by the local ruler, whose daughter Tahmina comes at night to the warrior's room. From their union, Sohrab is born and grows up not knowing his father, yet eager to equal his exploits. Rustam is the foremost warrior of the shah of Iran, and Sohrab becomes the warrior of Afrasyab of Turan (originally Fransiyan of Turya, later identified with the Turks who had by the late Sasanian period taken over the area of Samarqand and Transoxus—again the transformation of mythical figures reflects the historical antagonisms of the Persians, against the Arabs and against the Turks).

Father and son are pitted against each other in battle, each not guessing who the other is, until the son receives a mortal wound from his father and they discover each other's identity. Appeals sent to the shah of Iran to send the "nush-daru" medicine that could save Sohrab remain unanswered. Sohrab dies and Rustam goes, mourning, to Zabulestan.

AHURA MAZDA AND THE AMESHA SPENTAS

AHURA MAZDA, the Wise Lord, is thought originally to be the Iranian equivalent of the Vedic Asura Varuna, both guardians of the true law, Asha or Arta.

Zoroaster had a vision of the Amesha Spenta Vohu Manu as he was emerging from the river where he had gone to fetch water for the dawn pressing of haoma at the spring festival; he was led into the presence of Ahura Mazda, the only god, the all-good, all-wise creator. There is a radical separation of good, Spenta Mainyu (Holy Thought), an emanation of Ahura Mazda, and evil, Angra Mainyu (Evil Thought), whose struggle will last until the end of the world. Everything in the spiritual (*menog*) and physical (*getig*) creation partakes of this struggle. The followers of the Good Religion do all in their power to hasten the victory of light.

Ahura Mazda was supported by abstractions called the Holy Immortals, Amesha Spenta: Vohu Manah (Bah-man, Good Thought) who protects cattle; Asha Vahishta (Urdi-bihisht, Best Truth) who protects fire; Spenta Armaiti (Isfand-armud, Holy Devotion) who protects

◄ *Stone carving showing Sasanian warriors on horseback.*

earth; Khshathra Vairya (Shahri-var, Dominion Chosen) who protects minerals; Haurvartat (Khurdad, Wholeness) who protects water; and A-mertat (A-murdad, Immortality) who protects plants.

WARRIORS AND WISE MEN

THE WARRIOR who fights for his king and his religion against monsters, demons, and foreigners recurs throughout Persian mythology: Fereydun, who defeats the tyrant Zuhhak and finally chains him in a cave under Mount Damavand; Isfandyar, who is only defeated when the magic bird aids Rustam with one of its feathers; and Garshasp, who will come at the end of the world to help in the final defeat of evil. Later heroes of epic, Ali and Hamza, are depicted in the style of the great pre-Islamic heroes.

The figure of the wise man, the sage, is also central, like Bozorgmehr who guesses the rules of the Indian game of chess and counters it with his own invention, backgammon.

GOOD AND EVIL

ZOROASTRIANISM, like the monotheistic religions, is not rich in mythical narratives. It has basically just one myth, the fight of good against evil, re-enacted constantly on every level until the end of the world; evil is seen in filth, vermin, diseases, and death as well as in moral impurity, such as lying. Man and the natural creation, being basically good, must be kept pure or returned to a state of purity and order. Observance of the purity laws in life and death, avoiding pollution of Fire, Water, or Earth, prayer in the presence of the bright flaming fire that recalls divine energy and life force: these have been features of Zoroastrianism since earliest days.

AHRIMAN, DRUGH, JADU, PAIRIKA

ANGRA MAINYU (Ahriman), the destructive evil spirit, is the total opposite of Ahura Mazda, the all-wise creator; into the good creation Angra Mainyu brings disease, drought, famine, darkness, and death. He dwells in northern darkness, in the House of Lies; with him come Drugh the Lie and force of disorder, evil thought Aka Manah, Nasu the fly that crawls over rotting corpses, Azhi Dahaka (Zuhhak the Arab tyrant, Ezhdeha the dragon), Yatu (Jadu) the magician, Pairika (Pari) the evil fairies, and Mush the mouse that eats the grain harvest. These are some of the demons that surrounded primitive Persian man with fear. It was to counter this pervasive fear that the Vi-dev-dad was collected, the Law against Demons, the priestly ritual against demonic forces.

Aeshma Daeva, the gory-clubbed demon of wrath, appears in the Bible (or rather, the Apocrypha) in the Book of Tobit, as Ashmedai (Asmodeus), who kills the husbands of Tobias' bride on the first night of each wedding until she is exorcized by the burning of a fish's liver and heart.

Az, the demon of greed and concupiscence, was seen—perhaps under Buddhist influence—to be the root of unhappiness in the world, for which the cure, according to the communist heresy of the Sasanian Mazdak, was to pool all goods and chattels, including gold, land, and especially women.

▲ *Vase depicting a battle between mythological creatures, possibly the combat of Enkidu.*
▶ *Frieze of an archer of the Persian king's guard.*

Egypt

INTRODUCTION

EGYPT, AS THE GREEK HISTORIAN Herodotus wrote on visiting the country in *c.* 450 B.C.E., was "the gift of the Nile." This was by virtue of the annual inundation, the rising of the waters of the Nile in July that then spread the fertile mud across the landscape and gave Egypt life. Without the Nile and its flood Egypt could not have existed. It was this regularity, despite times of low Nile—famine—and of high Nile—disaster, the gods being beneficent or angry—that gave a stability to ancient Egyptian ideas about life and death. The concept of Ma'at, the goddess who embodied stability and law, therefore governed all aspects of Egyptian life and religion.

The Egyptians envisaged a hereafter, Kherneter, or the Fields of Iahru (the Elysian Fields in Greek mythology), located not in the heavens above but in the west, the land of the setting sun. One of the titles of Osiris, the god of the dead, was "First Lord of the Westerners." In order to achieve entry into that afterworld it was first necessary to preserve the body—which gave rise to the process of mummification—and to have been judged a righteous person, *ma'at heru* (True of Voice), by the 42 gods in the Hall of Judgment, each of whom asked the deceased a direct question to which the truthful answer had to be "No." This was known as the Negative Confession. A green hard stone heart scarab within the bandages of the mummy was inscribed with Chapter 30A or B of the Book of the Dead, "Whereby my heart shall not speak falsehood against me in the Hall of Judgment." Other gods and goddesses appear in some of the myths but have no individual mythical background.

Since the Classical times of Greece and Rome the religion of ancient Egypt has been a source of wonderment and incredulity, even down to the modern day. Although the Classical world had a large pantheon of gods with Zeus (Jupiter in the Roman world) at its head, as did ancient Egypt (with Amun-Re as chief of the gods), it was the theriomorphic (animal) forms of the Egyptian gods that caused concern. Herodotus also wrote that in Egypt the animals "are without exception held to be sacred," and he declined to discuss the religious principles involved.

Egyptian mythology is, in fact, quite tightly focused; there are not as many myths by comparison with the Ancient Near East and the later Mediterranean civilizations. Essentially, the Egyptian myths are concerned with the Creation, the Destruction of Mankind, the story of Isis and Osiris, the Contendings of Horus and Seth, and the sun god Re's journey across the daytime sky and then through the 12 terrible dark hours of the night to be safely reborn at dawn in the east.

THE CREATION

WHILE CHRISTIAN THEOLOGY has a single creation story there were four accounts in ancient Egypt, each connected with a major city—Heliopolis, Memphis, Hermopolis and Esna—as well as with a major god—Atum (later assimilated with Re), Ptah, Thoth, and Khnum, respectively.

HELIOPOLIS (THE CREATION)

AT HELIOPOLIS, "City of the Sun," Atum was alone on a muddy bank that had emerged from the primeval Waters of Nun covering the world (like the inundation of the Nile). Realizing that he needed other gods to assist in the creation, he masturbated and from his semen emerged two other gods: Shu, god of the sky, and Tefnut, his sister, goddess of moisture. Their children were Geb, god of the earth, and Nut, goddess of the sky (such relationships, consanguineous marriages, usually abhorred as incest in the modern world, were not uncommon in ancient mythology). In the papyri Nut appears arched over Geb and they are being separated to their respective

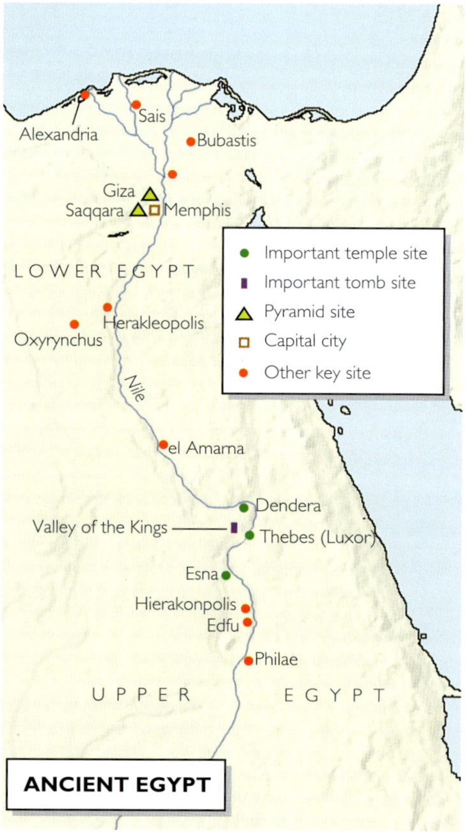

spheres by Shu. Geb and Nut had five children: Osiris, Isis, Horus the Elder, Set, and Nephthys—born on five consecutive days, outside the normal calendar of 360 days. This was (and it has reflections in Classical mythology) because of a prophecy that Nut's children would surpass the power of Atum-Re (as the children of Kronos by Rhea would surpass their father). Being born on noncalendar days overcame the problem of the curse that Nut could not give birth on any day of the year.

THE BENU BIRD

ALSO ASSOCIATED with the sun cult at Heliopolis was the benu bird, represented in Egyptian art as a heron but referred to as a phoenix, and in that capacity a symbol of the resurrection (in other mythologies it rises alive from the ashes of its own funeral pyre). At Heliopolis the benu bird is shown alighting on the top of a stunted, pyramidal shaped stone, the *ben-ben*. This was the origin of the huge obelisks that stood in pairs before the high protective pylon entrances to the temples. Dedicated to the sun god, their pyramidal apexes were often embellished with gold, silver, or electrum (a natural alloy of gold and silver) so that they caught and reflected the first rays of the sun, the god Re-Harakhte "rising in his horizon." Many of these obelisks were removed from Egypt from late antiquity onward and now adorn many modern capitals, invariably being misnamed "Cleopatra's Needles," being much earlier and nothing to do with that last Egyptian queen who committed suicide in August of the year 30 B.C.E.

▲ *Wall painting in the tomb of Sennedjem in Thebes depicting the Fields of Iahru, the Egyptian equivalent to the Afterworld.*

► *Gold and lapis lazuli trinity of Osorkon II, Osiris flanked by Isis and Horus.*

MEMPHIS AND HERMOPOLIS (THE CREATION)

Memphis

AT MEMPHIS, the secular capital of Egypt from the First Dynasty, *c.* 3100 B.C.E, the major deity was the creator god Ptah. According to the legend, Ptah took precedence over Atum because he had created the heart and tongue of Atum. Ptah was particularly revered as the god of craftsmen and workers, and among his many titles was that of "father and mother of all gods."

Hermopolis

A THIRD CREATION legend was identified at Hermopolis, a revered cult center of the god Thoth. He was often represented with the head of an ibis, and the baboon was an animal particularly regarded as sacred and associated with him. He was the god of wisdom and learning who had invented hieroglyphs, literally "the sacred writings." He was especially the patron god of scribes and was also associated with the moon. The variation on the creation legend here said that it was at Hermopolis and not Heliopolis that the primeval mound had emerged from the Waters of Nun. From an egg lying on the mound emerged the sun god or, in an alternative version, a lotus flower grew from the mound and its leaves opened to reveal the young god of creation, Nefertum.

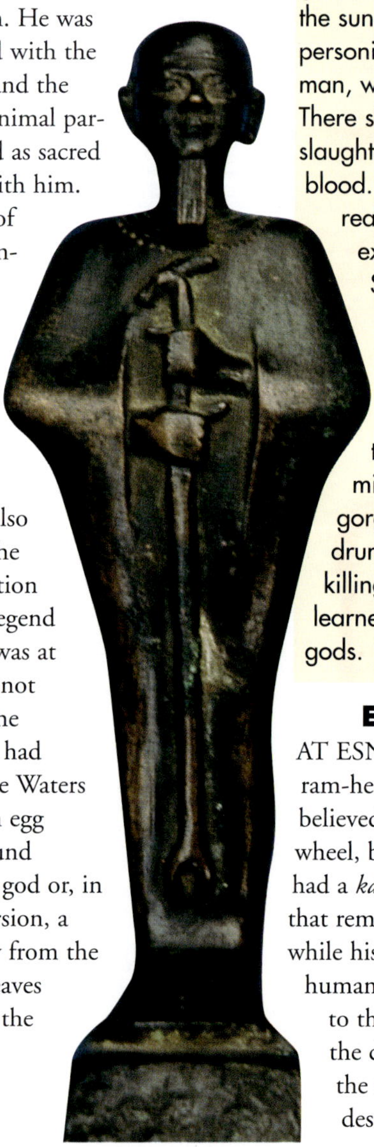

THE DESTRUCTION

THE WORLD AND MAN having been created, the gods then proliferated, most being closely related to each other (as with the 12 gods of Mount Olympus in Greek mythology). However, as in the Christian tradition, there is a story of destruction. Man had become too full of himself and was ignoring the gods and not making the proper offerings to them. Re, as chief of the gods, took council with the rest to see how best to punish man and make him continue the proper religious observances. It was agreed that Sekhmet, a lion-headed goddess who represented the power of the sun at midday and hence was the personification of evil, being able to kill man, would be sent down to earth. There she began an indiscriminate slaughter, delighting in the taste of blood. The gods were appalled as they realized the eventual outcome, the extinction of mankind, but Sekhmet had a bloodlust and would not stop. She was eventually brought to heel by a trick of the gods, who flooded a field with a red drink (khakadi) that looked like blood but was mixed with strong beer. Sekhmet gorged herself on it and fell into a drunken stupor. When she awoke the killing had stopped and man had learned his lesson not to disregard the gods.

▲ *Granite seated statue of the lion-headed goddess Sekhmet in the temple of Mut, Karnak.*

◀ *Bronze statuette of the god of Creation and craftsmen, Ptah.*

ESNA (THE CREATION)

AT ESNA the temple was dedicated to the ram-headed god Khnum. He, it was believed, fashioned man on his potter's wheel, but in duplicate because everyone had a *ka,* or double. This was the spirit that remained near the dead man's tomb while his *ba,* his soul, in the shape of a human-headed bird, flew away at death to the next world. The fullest version of the creation is carved on the walls of the temple at Esna, and tells of a goddess called Neith, associated with the city of Sais in the Delta, who came into being even before the primeval mound, emerging from the Waters of Nun to create the world.

While to the modern religious mind four basic versions of the story of creation would cause concern and questions, to the ancient Egyptian this posed no problems. Each creation legend took precedence at its appropriate place, although overall it was the Heliopolitan version that held prime position because of its association with the sun and the chief of the gods, Re, who was later assimilated with Amun of Thebes to become the great god Amun-Re.

ISIS

ISIS WAS THE MOST important deity of the Egyptian pantheon for the average Egyptian. She was the embodiment of all that human life stood for and was governed by. She was the "Great Mother," the ever-loving wife, the "Queen of Heaven" (a title she shared with the Virgin Mary in Christianity) and fierce protector of the family and family values. She is most commonly represented as a seated mother suckling her small son Horus on her lap. The iconography is very similar to that of Mary and the Christ Child, and caused many violent religious arguments among the early Christian Church fathers. Her principal temple was on the island of Philae, near Aswan. Her worship lived on after the fall of Egyptian civilization and temples to her are known into Roman times and in far-flung parts of the empire, even Roman London.

▲ *Bronze statuette of the Goddess Isis nursing her infant son Horus.*

OSIRIS AND ISIS

THE MOST IMPORTANT MYTH of which Egyptians took note and to which they had the greatest affinity was that of Osiris and his wife and sister Isis. As is so often the case, it is a story of jealousy, the opposition of evil against good, the adversities suffered by good, and the eventual triumph of good over evil, invariably leading to some kind of benefice, everlasting life, etc. The scenario is a potent aspect of so many myths of the ancient world (and, indeed, of the modern world) that it is difficult to positively identify its origins, although some suggest that Osiris was a god who came into Egypt from the area of the Fertile Crescent in the Ancient Near East.

Osiris, the good king, had a jealous brother, Set, who, by a trick, contrived to have him killed. To celebrate his brother Osiris' return from a foreign visit, Set arranged a huge party in the palace. In the course of it a magnificently decorated chest was brought in by Set's retainers. Set suggested that all the guests lie down in it and, if one of them fitted the chest exactly, then he would win the magnificent object. All tried and all failed, being too tall, short, fat, or thin (this has parallels with the later Greek myth of Theseus and the giant Prokrustes who "adjusted" passersby who slept on his bed by lopping off extremities or extending them to fit). At last Set persuaded his brother Osiris to join in the game and try the chest for size. Naturally, it fitted Osiris exactly since Set had made it to his measurements. At the signal, Set's adherents rushed into the hall, drove off the supporters of Osiris, sealed down the lid of the chest, which now became Osiris' coffin, and cast it into the Nile.

The chest enclosing Osiris' body floated out to sea and was washed up on the shore at the city of Byblos in the Lebanon. Landing close to a freshwater spring running down to the sea, the chest was caught up in the roots of a large tree that grew and enclosed the chest/coffin within its trunk. The king of Byblos saw the magnificent tree and had it felled to become the central pillar of his new palace.

▼ *The temple at Esna, dedicated to the creator god Khnum.*

ISIS AT BYBLOS

THE GRIEVING WIDOW, Isis, searched throughout Egypt for the chest and eventually, through her magic, located the body at Byblos. Knowing that the chest and body were now part of the palace, she had to find a way of access to them. She disguised herself as an old woman, seating herself by the freshwater stream that came down to the seashore where the maids of the queen of Byblos came to do their washing. They found her and took pity on the "old lady," bringing her food and treating her kindly. In return she taught them to braid their hair, but the scent of the goddess was upon her fingers and the queen noticed the new hairstyles and perfume and inquired about this change. The maids told her of the lonely old lady they had befriended by the seashore who sat there day after day, apparently grieving, although she would not tell them the cause of her sorrow.

The queen had recently given birth to a son and heir and was looking for a suitable nurse: the old lady sounded ideal and she was brought to the palace. Isis (in her disguise) accepted the post of nurse on condition that she was left alone with the child throughout the night hours. Although it seemed an odd request to the queen, she agreed. At night the goddess shut herself in the great hall, alone with the baby. The maids reported hearing a strange sound after dark, rather like the twittering of a bird, and they told the queen. One night she hid herself behind some drapery and, when she heard the twittering sound, emerged to find her baby lying in the red-hot coals of the fire and a swallow (Isis having transformed herself) flying around the pillar twittering. In terror the queen snatched up her child, whereupon the goddess revealed herself and admonished the queen as a foolish woman because she, the goddess, was burning away the child's mortality. The king was called, and both monarchs worshiped the goddess and asked what they could give her. She requested the tree trunk pillar that concealed the chest holding the corpse of her husband. Her request was naturally granted, the roof of the great hall fell, and Isis took the body of Osiris back to Egypt, hiding it in the marshes of the Delta and guarding it with her sister Nephthys.

OSIRIS

OSIRIS, BROTHER of the goddesses Isis and Nephthys, and husband of Isis, became the god of the dead. As such hewas one of the most revered gods of ancient Egypt. It was only by passing through the Hall of Judgment and being presented to him as a just person (*ma'at heru*—"true of voice") that the deceased could ever hope for a life in the afterworld. The Egyptian "heaven" was located in the far west toward the setting sun: one of the major titles of Osiris was "First Lord of the Westerners." In later periods the ushabti figures, provided to work in place of the dead person in the next world, associated the deceased with the god and the inscription on them identifies him as "The Osiris N." Abydos, the center of the cult of Osiris, was the most sacred site in ancient Egypt, and there Seti I (1291–1278 B.C.E.) built the finest of all the Egyptian temples.

◀ *Pectoral depicting the god of the afterworld, Osiris, from Tutankhamun's tomb.*

ISIS RETURNS TO EGYPT WITH HER HUSBAND'S BODY

HOVERING OVER the body of Osiris in the form of a hawk, which is depicted on the walls of the Osiris shrine in the temple at Abydos, Isis became pregnant and in due course gave birth to their son Horus. However, the evil usurper of the throne of Osiris, Set, while out hunting one day, discovered the body in the marshes. Both goddesses were absent so he tore the body into 14 pieces and had them scattered far and wide throughout Egypt. Once more the mourning widow Isis set off to retrieve her husband's body, now in fragments. Legend has it that she traveled on a papyrus skiff and, knowing the reason for her forlorn journey, the crocodiles did not attack it (neither do they today, in modern folklore, as they remember the goddess and her quest).

One version of the myth says that Isis buried each portion of her husband's corpse where she found it and there founded a temple. Another says that she brought all the pieces together, save for one, his phallus, that could not be retrieved because the oxyrhynchus fish had swallowed it. Thereafter the fish was abhorred, except in the city of Oxyrhynchus in the Fayum, where it was held to be sacred. The body (or only the head, according to another version) was buried at Abydos, which became the most sacred site of ancient Egypt and where one of the most beautifully decorated temples was built under the pharaoh Seti I (1291–1278 B.C.E.). Unusually for an Egyptian temple it has seven sanctuaries, dedicated respectively to the king himself, Ptah, Re-Harakhte, Amun-Re, Osiris, Isis, and Horus.

The jackal-headed god Anubis came to Isis' assistance when she had assembled the 13 fragments, and it was he who embalmed the body of Osiris. He acted not only as the embalmer god but as the guide for souls as they made their way to the west, the location of the Egyptian "heaven."

HORUS AND SET

SET HAD DECLARED himself to be king and Isis, now with her small son Horus, went into hiding. When Horus reached young manhood he challenged his evil uncle Set for his father's throne. Their various battles, known as the Contendings of Horus and Set, are inscribed and illustrated in long texts and reliefs on the walls of the temple of Horus at Edfu—one of the two finest preserved and complete temples from ancient Egypt. In the carvings of the two gods as they battle against each other Set is often shown as a rather diminutive male hippopotamus being speared with Horus' long lance. (While the male hippopotamus was the embodiment of evil in ancient Egypt the female, by contrast, was associated with the goddess Taurt and was particularly worshiped by women as their protector in childbirth.)

At one point Set, finding Horus asleep in the desert (which is Set's domain), gouged out his eyes, which in the mythology represent the sun and the moon. However, the goddess Hathor (often conflated with Isis in later Egyptian mythology) restored the sight of Horus, bathing his damaged eyes in gazelle's milk. The eye of Horus (the *udjat*) became one of the most powerful protective amulets of Egypt, worn by children around their necks or on a bracelet and incorporated into fine jewelry, such as the bracelet with a large *udjat* eye found on the mummy of the boy pharaoh Tutankhamun.

Eventually the gods tired of the continual conflict, and Horus and Set were brought before the Council of Gods to state their case and for the gods, under the presidency of Re, to make a decision in favor of one or the other. The court case dragged on for several years. There were various reverses of decision when first Set and then some of the other gods threatened dreadful things, not least Osiris, who said that if no decision was swiftly reached in favor of his son Horus he would let loose his vicious dog-headed messengers who feared no gods. The gods eventually decided in favor of Horus as the rightful king. His father Osiris, whose shattered body had been embalmed by the jackal-headed god Anubis, was confirmed as the god of the dead. Set was banished to the desert, a place of evil, and was also made the god of storms. Thereafter the ruling pharaoh was recognized as the god Horus on earth and became a god among the gods at his death.

▲ *A bronze statue of the Oxyrhynchus fish, sacred in the city of that name, from the fertile area of the Fayum.*

▶ *The outer ambulatory of the Temple of Horus at Edfu, inscribed with the story of his fight with Set.*

▲ *This eye of Horus amulet, the* udjat, *made from glazed pottery, would have been worn to protect the health and fortune of the bearer.*

HORUS

HORUS, THE SON of Osiris and Isis, was identified as the dutiful son who avenged his murdered father. The pharaoh on earth was identified with the god: the third of the pharaoh's five titles was his "Golden Horus Name," and he was referred to as "the living Horus." As a falcon god Horus was Lord of the Sky and took bird form, yet he could also be seen as a small child being nursed on the lap of his mother Isis. His principal temple was at Edfu, south of Luxor, and it is one of the two best preserved temples from ancient Egypt, although the present structure is of the Ptolemaic (Greek) period in Egypt.

ISIS LEARNS THE SECRET NAME OF RE THE SUN GOD

AFTER THE SUN GOD RE, Isis was the most powerful of the Egyptian deities because she discovered the secret name of Re. To know a name was to have power, and Isis wanted that power, so she schemed to obtain knowledge of Re's secret name from him. As Re got elderly he dozed a lot and spittle dribbled onto his chin. Isis carefully gathered some and used it to moisten some mud, which she fashioned into a poisonous mud snake. Gods could only be harmed by something of their own making, so Isis gave the snake life and left it in the path of Re as he walked by. Naturally, the snake bit him and injected its poison as he passed. Re was in agony from the bite because, unbeknown to him, the snake was partly composed of Re's magical essence, his spittle. Re shook with fever and found it difficult to speak. Isis asked him what ailed him, knowing full well the cause. He described his terrible symptoms and she offered to cure him, but only if he told her his secret name. He held back, then gave her a string of descriptive names, but she knew that none of them was the secret name. So she caused the poison to bite deeper and asked Re again for his name. In the end he could stand the pain no longer and agreed to tell her, but only in private and away from the other gods. She had to promise that she would not divulge it to anyone. Having gained the knowledge she wanted, she cured Re and extracted the poison. She now knew his secret name which, should she ever need to use it, would give her power over him. There was no cause for her ever to make use of her knowledge, but she was satisfied in simply knowing that she had the power, if need be.

THE JOURNEY THROUGH THE UNDERWORLD

WHEN THE SUN SET—that is died—in the west each day it was imperative that it should be reborn the next dawn. To do this, the god Re had to travel underground through the dark hours of the night, each hour's doorway being guarded by frightening and obnoxious demons which the god had to succeed in passing. Many parts of this journey are represented on the wall paintings in the royal tombs in the Valley of the Kings. There were three major compositions that acted as safeguards to make the journey possible: the *Book of Am-Duat* (also known as the *Book of That Which is in the Underworld*), the *Book of Gates*, and the *Book of Caverns.*

THE *BOOK OF AM-DUAT*

THE FULLEST VERSION of this book, which concerns the sun god Re's journey from his "death" at sunset to his "rebirth" at sunrise, is drawn on the walls of the burial chamber of the pharaoh Tuthmosis III (d. *c.* 1450 B.C.E.) and in the tomb of his son Amenophis II (d. *c.* 1419 B.C.E.), in the Valley of the Kings at Thebes (modern Luxor). The god travels in a boat with lookouts and steersmen, and he is accompanied by various other deities. Although at first this magic book was confined to royalty, gradually it was appropriated by senior officials and used in their tombs also, so the deceased often appears as the steersman of the bark of Re.

Each hour is associated with various gods or animals. For example, in the First Hour baboons sing and open the doors for Re, and a dozen serpent goddesses provide light. Grain gods feature in the Second and Third Hours, in the latter of which Re revives Osiris. Snakes are prominent in the Fourth Hour and have great potency because it was believed that, in being able to slough their skins, they were the embodiment of the resurrection. (This belief was widely held throughout the ancient world and very prominent in the worship in the healing shrines of the Greek world dedicated to Asklepios at Epidaurus and on the island of Kos.) In the Sixth Hour, Re takes on the aspect of the sacred beetle, Khepri, believed to roll the sun's disk across the sky in the daytime, and thus passes by the two lions of the Horizon (Aker). And so the journey goes on with its various difficulties—cats wielding large knives and beheading evil serpents (Apophis), goddesses spitting fire at Re's enemies or decapitating them—until the final Twelfth Hour is reached. Here the snake imagery reappears as Re enters the tail of a serpent's body to emerge from its mouth in his manifestation as Khepri, the sacred beetle. He rests momentarily before then being born as a disk through the thighs of the goddess of the night and sky, Nut—a scene represented in several royal tombs where the goddess arches over the ceiling of the burial chamber protecting the king's sarcophagus below her.

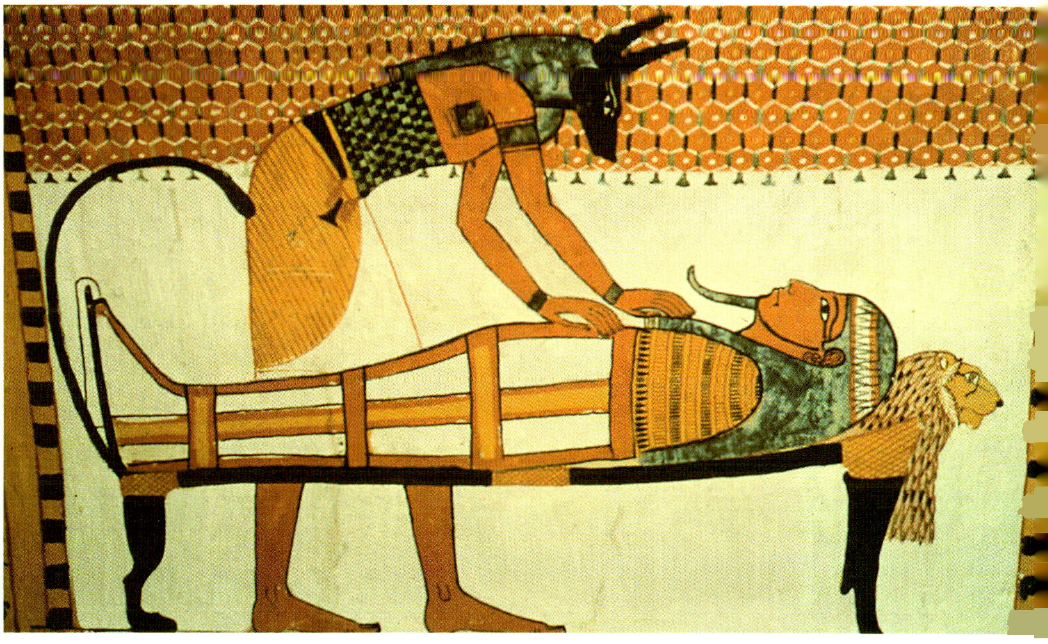

▶ *The jackel-headed god of embalming, Anubis, bends over the mummy of Sennedjen in his tomb at Deir el Medineh, Thebes.*

THE *BOOK OF GATES*

THIS TEXT IS CARVED and brightly painted on the walls of the tomb of Rameses VI (*c.* 1133 B.C.E.), and occurs in its finest form carved in exquisite small hieroglyphs on the alabaster sarcophagus of Seti I (d. *c.* 1278 B.C.E.) now on display in Sir John Soane's Museum, London. Once again 12 gates must be passed, and a lot of imagery of serpents spitting fire is involved, but Re knows the names of his adversaries, and passes through safely. The power inherent in knowing another person's name is, again, found widely in the mythologies of the ancient world. The evil serpent Apophis, seen being slain by a cat in the *Book of Am-Duat*, is at several of the gates barring the way. But the god prevails, and his imminent birth and resurrection at dawn is proclaimed by a team of baboons sacred to the god of learning, Thoth. Baboons are to be found carved at the pedestal base of obelisks, itself a symbol of the sun god, raising their paws in greeting and adoration to him. As they were the first living creatures to greet the sun at its rising with their chattering, they were thought to be especially pious.

THE *BOOK OF CAVERNS*

THE FULLEST VERSION of this also occurs in the tomb of Rameses VI (*c.* 1133 B.C.E.). However, instead of the emphasis being on the Twelve Hours of the Night, it concentrates only on six divisions, or caverns. The focus here is on the division between good and evil. Re, as the all-powerful god, has the knowledge of names and can therefore easily sweep aside the wrong-doer. So he passes safely to his rebirth, taking once again the aspect of the sacred beetle Khepri, ready to begin trundling the sun's disk across the heavens at dawn.

THE *BOOK OF THE DEAD*

ANOTHER WELL-KNOWN Egyptian composition was the *Book of the Dead*, which consisted of a series of some 200 chapters, "spells" or "utterances." designed to help the deceased on his journey from this life to the next. Parts of some of the myths are also incorporated in several of the chapters, but the most important for the dead person were Chapter 125 (often illustrated in the papyri), relating to the Weighing of the Heart in the Hall of Judgment; Chapter 30B, whereby the deceased's heart would not speak evil against him at the Judgment; and Chapter 6, the "Ushabti chapter." Chapter 6 is most frequently found as a text painted, carved or moulded on the mummiform ushabti figures provided in a burial. Each is represented carrying a pick and hoe and with a seed bag on its back over its left shoulder; sometimes it also has water pots represented on its back. These figures, which can vary enormously in size from almost a meter in height (granite examples provided for Amenophis III) to a matter of a few inches, were thought to be a necessary part of a burial from the Middle Kingdom onwards (the twentieth century B.C.E). Some of the finest and fullest texts are found on Later Period ushabtis of the Twenty-sixth Dynasty (664–525 B.C.E.), which often have finely molded faces. They were intended to answer any summons and answer "Here am I" if called upon and stand in place of the deceased to carry out any tasks in his/her place in the afterworld. The major task—hence the provision of picks and hoes—was to keep the irrigation canals clean and sweet, the dreaded corvée. In a complete burial, 365 ushabtis were provided, one for each day of the year. To keep this gang of workers in order, an overseer (reis) ushabti was necessary. The latter are not mummiform like the workers but dressed in civil dress wearing a kilt and carrying a whip. One reis was provided for every 10 workers, and the inscription on them often identifies them by the owner's name as "Chief of 10."

ANUBIS

ANUBIS, THE jackal-headed god, was a god of the dead and especially of embalming. He performed this service on the dead god Osiris. His Egyptian name was Inpu and also Wepwawet, which means "Opener of the Ways" as he was believed to lead the souls of the dead into the west to the Hall of Judgment. At the ceremony of the Opening of the Mouth performed on the upright mummy before it was placed in the tomb, a priest would wear a jackal-headed mask to simulate the god (such a terracotta mask has survived in the Pelizaeus Museum, Hildesheim). Although a major god in the cult of the dead, Anubis had no large temple dedicated to him, unlike many of the other gods and goddesses.

◀◀ *Wooden panel from a coffin, showing Osiris holding a crook and flail.*

◀ *Vignette of Chapter 25 of the* Book of the Dead, *showing Ani watching his heart being weighed in the Hall of Judgment.*

▶ *This wooden coffin is from the tomb of an unknown woman. The coffins were intricately decorated with scenes of the underworld.*

Greece

INTRODUCTION

GREEK MYTHOLOGY has exercised a profound and unparalleled influence upon Western culture. Dramatists, artists, and philosophers from Roman times, through the great revival of interest in antiquity in the Renaissance, up to the present day, have been inspired by the thrilling legacy of ancient Greece. The origins of these myths are impossible to determine and there is no one true version of any myth. Instead, every city in the ancient Greek world, spanning from southern Italy across the Aegean and Adriatic islands to the coast of Asia Minor, created its own myths. This can result in confusion, as many different, and often contradictory, versions of the myths exist.

Originally passed on, adapted and developed by an oral tradition of storytelling, the basic canon of gods and heroes was well established by the time the myths came to be written down, from about 750 B.C.E. The literature from this period, in particular Homer's epic poems the *Iliad* and the *Odyssey* and the works of the writer Hesiod, are one of our major sources for Greek myths. The *Iliad* dramatizes a few days at the end of the myth of the Trojan War, and the *Odyssey* tells of the adventures of the hero Odysseus as he returns home after fighting at Troy. Hesiod's *Theogony* is a poem concerned with the origins of the world and the gods who rule it. The creation myths in the *Theogony* show strong affinities with Near Eastern creation myths. Greek mythology has many similarities with Indo-European mythology and was either influenced by it or shared common sources.

OUR WORD "MYTH" comes from the Greek word *mythos* ("speech"). The meaning of *mythos* changed over the centuries. At the beginning of Greek literature (mid-eighth century B.C.E.) *mythos* did not necessarily denote a fictional tale. By the fifth century B.C.E. *mythos* was predominantly used in contrast with the word *logos*, which also means "speech." *Logos* has connotations of rational speech and writing and *mythos* came to mean "fiction" or "story."

The poetry recital, where poems were sung by professional reciters called rhapsodes, was one of the two major institutions for the performance of myth in Classical Athens. The other was the theater, one of the greatest achievements of Athenian culture. Some 16,000 people thronged to see the lavish spectacles, including the riotous comedies of Aristophanes and the great tragedies of Aeschylus, Sophocles, and Euripides, whose plays drew almost exclusively upon the Greek myths. The plays were performed in the theater of Dionysus on the southern slope of the Acropolis and formed part of the festivals of the Great Dionysia and the Lenaia, which were held in honor of the god. These were state occasions that combined religious worship and thrilling entertainment with debating mythology and the role of the gods and heroes in fifth-century B.C.E. civic life. The Greeks never simply believed in or took for granted the traditional narratives handed down to them. Their mythology was dynamic and was constantly interpreted and reinterpreted.

Philosophy played a crucial role in this. Pre-Socratic thinkers challenged literal belief in, and the morality of, mythology. Empedocles, writing in the mid-fifth century B.C.E., approaches mythology as a type of physical allegory. For him, the gods represent the four main elements of the world: Zeus is fire, Hera is air, Hades is earth, and the little known Nestis ("starvation") is water. The great philosopher Plato (428–348 B.C.E.) had an ambivalent attitude toward mythology. In Plato's *Republic* he debunks most myths and argues that they should have no place in an ideal society; Homer and Hesiod are particularly at fault for presenting the gods and heroes as weak and vengeful. Plato would not ban all myths but would only keep those that supported, rather than undermined, proper values.

The Olympian gods were fickle and it was not expected that they would watch over humans all the time. It was up to the human worshiper to make contact with a deity, and one of the most important means of communication was through sacrifice. At official rites like the Panathenaia and City Dionysia, priests would perform a blood sacrifice *(thysia)*. This could involve mass slaughter. Imagine the sight, sound, and smell of the City Dionysia in the year 333 B.C.E. when 240 bulls were sacrificed to Dionysus! Like the dedication of votive offerings and libations (ritual offerings of food and drink), sacrifice was a way of seeking the gods' approval and protection.

THE ROLE OF MYTH

THE TIME OF CLASSICAL ATHENS was a time of enormous creativity—politically, culturally, and artistically. Mythology permeated every area of life, public and private. It was an essential part of education, as children would be required to learn and recite the stories recounted in the works of Homer and Hesiod. Myths played an important role in the philosophy and

▲ *The remains of the Parthenon in Athens.*

science of the period and were portrayed in art, from images of vase paintings and jewelry to the great sculptures and statues seen adorning temples. The *Iliad* and *Odyssey* were recited in full at the Great Panathenaia, the most important religious festival at Athens when worshipers came from all over Greece to honor Athens' patron goddess, Athene. The Greek myths commonly involved extreme circumstances in which human beings transgressed established norms (one example of this is Oedipus killing his father and marrying his mother). In doing so, they repeatedly debated, challenged, and reaffirmed the traditional values of the societies that produced them.

ATHENE AND THE NAMING OF ATHENS

THE GODDESS ATHENE sprang into the world fully armed and ready to do battle. She was conceived by Zeus, the king of the gods, and Metis, "Cunning Wisdom," but Zeus heard a prophecy that any child born of Metis would be greater than its father and to prevent this he swallowed up Metis whole. Soon after he suffered a terrible headache, his head split open and the fully grown Athene appeared. Athene inherited her mother's wisdom and was patron goddess of skilled crafts such as shipbuilding and weaving. The owl, the wisest of birds, was one of her special symbols.

Myth had it that Athene and Poseidon quarreled over who should be patron of Athens, and it was decided that whoever provided the best gift for the city would win. Poseidon made salt water spring from the Acropolis (the hill above Athens), thus giving Athens access to the sea. Athene created the olive tree, whose oil is important for lighting, cooking, and trade. This was judged the better invention and the people named their city after Athene. They built a shrine to her on the Acropolis, called the Parthenon, from one of Athene's epithets, *parthenos*, which means "*virgin*."

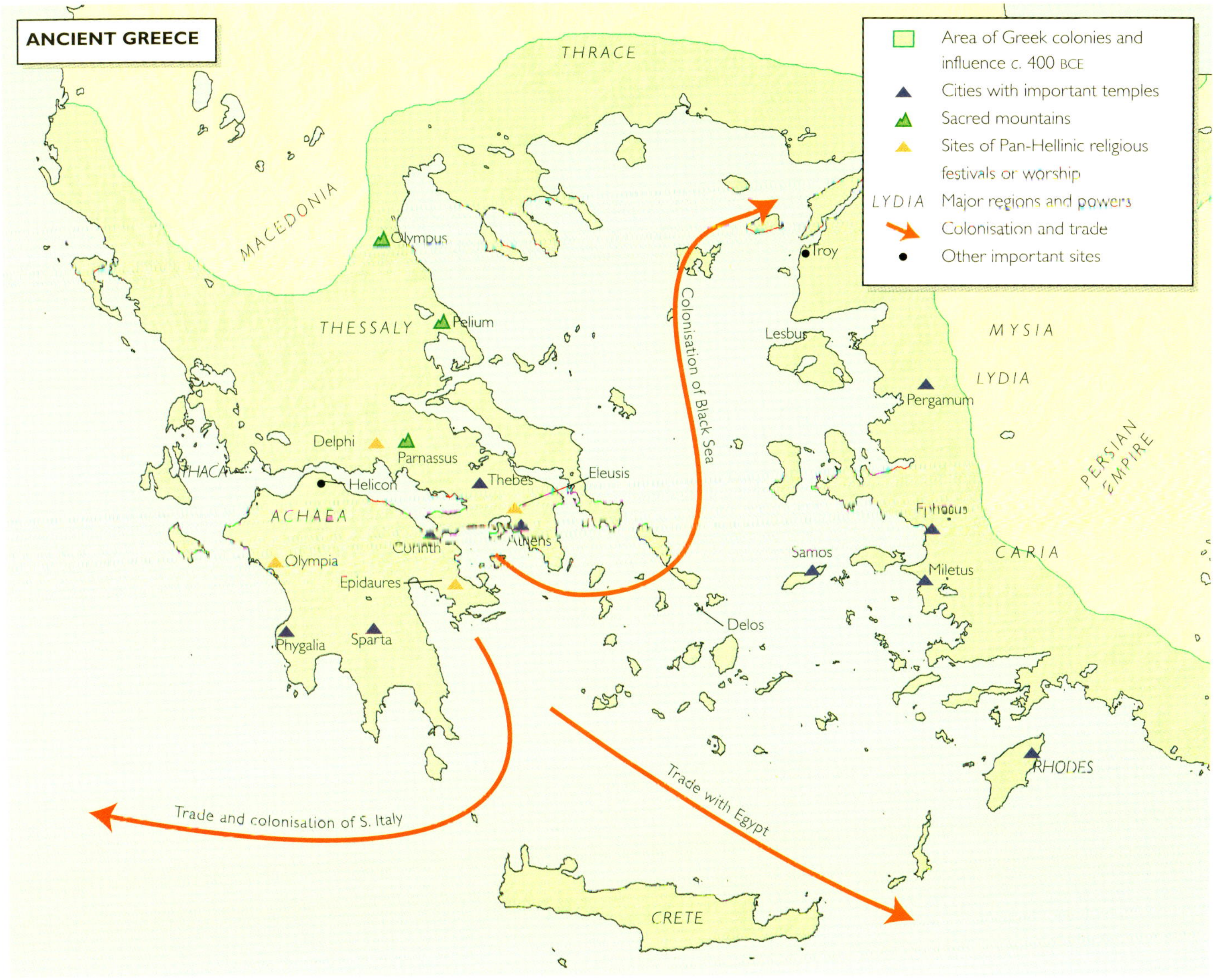

THE OLYMPIC PANTHEON

THE PRINCIPAL DEITIES were thought to live on Mount Olympus, which was the highest mountain in Greece, in the north of the country. They were represented as anthropomorphic and often quarrelsome. Supreme among the gods was Zeus, whose dominion was the sky. One of his brothers, Poseidon, ruled over the sea and the other, Hades, was sovereign of the underworld, the realm of the dead. His sister Hestia was goddess of the hearth and home and Demeter, whose name means "grain mother," was goddess of agriculture. Zeus' sister Hera also became his wife. They gave birth to Ares, the god of war; Hephaestus, the god of fire and metalworking; Hebe, goddess of youth; and Eileithyia, goddess of childbirth.

With Metis Zeus fathered Athene and with Demeter he fathered Persephone, who became goddess of the underworld. The virgin huntress goddess, Artemis, and her brother, Apollo, god of music and poetry, resulted from an affair between Zeus and the Titan Leto. With the divine Maia, Zeus had Hermes, the messenger of the gods, and with a mortal woman, Semele, he fathered Dionysus, god of wine and religious ecstasy. Zeus' daughter Aphrodite, goddess of desire, sprang from the foaming sea.

POSEIDON, LORD OF THE SEA

POSEIDON IS AS FEARSOME as his brother Zeus. He holds sway over the sea and forces of nature, particularly tempests. One of his cult titles is Enosichthon, which means "earth shaker." His symbols include the trident, with which he could split open the earth, the bull (possibly representing his aggressiveness), and the horse, since he was supposed to have created the first horse. Poseidon was often warring with Athene. He is ancestor of some of the most awesome monsters in Greek myth: the Echidna, Cerberus, the Hydra, and the Sphinx.

►Trompe l'oeil *from the Sala dei Giganti, showing the gods of Olympus.*

BIRTH FROM THE SOIL

OF THE MANY DIFFERENT accounts of the birth of humanity, perhaps the most important is the idea of birth from the earth itself, autochthony. Zeus, enraged with mankind, sent a flood to destroy them. Prometheus managed to warn his son Deucalion and Deucalion's wife Pyrrha, who survived by building an ark. When the waters subsided, they made sacrifices to Zeus who sent the Titan Themis to help them. She advised them to walk along, throwing stones over their shoulders. The stones thrown by Deucalion turned into men and those thrown by Pyrrha into women. The human race was thus re-created from the earth.

Myths of autochthony were particularly important to the Athenians, who emphasized their ancestry from the earth to show their superiority over other Greeks and barbarians, they claimed, did not have such a special relationshipthe land. In Euripides' play, Erechtheus the, wife of the king of Athens talks about her people: "Our people did not immigrate from some other place; we are born of the earth. Other cities, founded on the whim of the dice, are imported from other cities. Whoever inhabits a city derived from another, like a joint fitted poorly in wood, is a citizen in name, not in fact" (fragment 50).

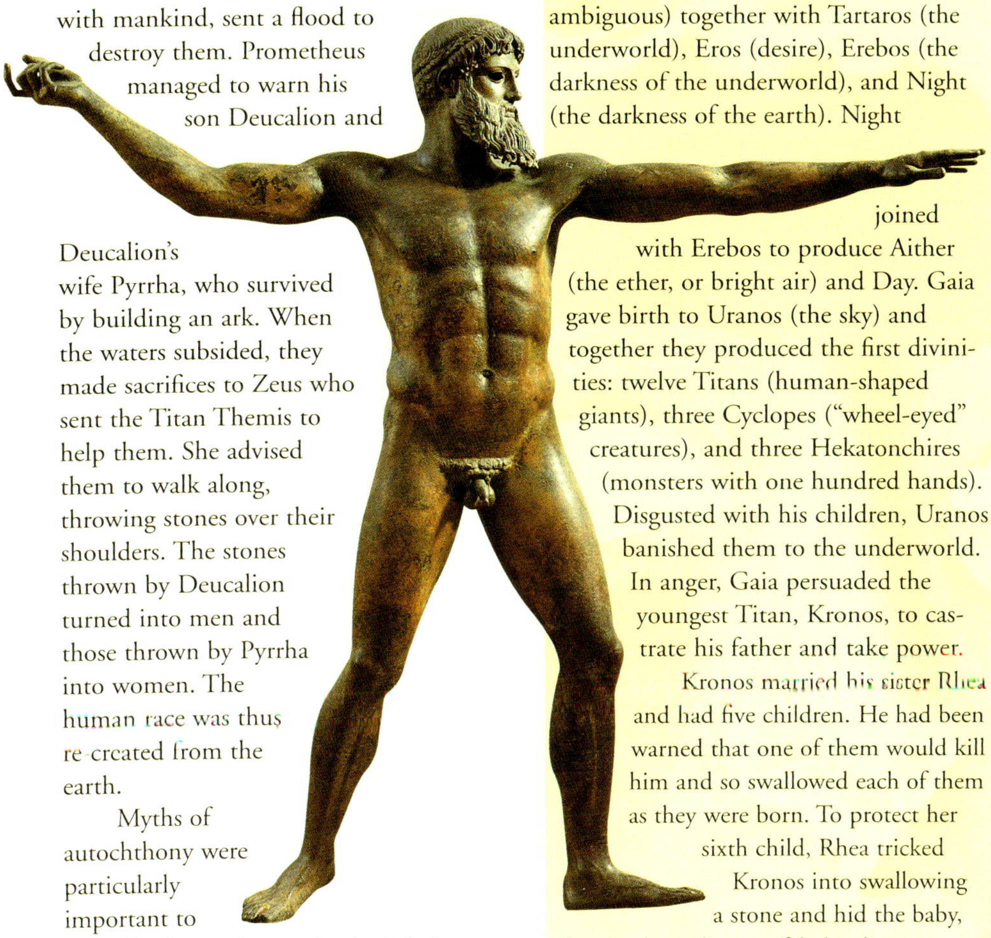

▲▶ *The mighty Zeus, king of the gods, hurling his thunderbolt.*

FROM CHAOS TO CREATION

FIRST THERE ONLY EXISTED Chaos, "the void," from which Gaia (earth) was formed (exactly how remains ambiguous) together with Tartaros (the underworld), Eros (desire), Erebos (the darkness of the underworld), and Night (the darkness of the earth). Night joined with Erebos to produce Aither (the ether, or bright air) and Day. Gaia gave birth to Uranos (the sky) and together they produced the first divinities: twelve Titans (human-shaped giants), three Cyclopes ("wheel-eyed" creatures), and three Hekatonchires (monsters with one hundred hands). Disgusted with his children, Uranos banished them to the underworld. In anger, Gaia persuaded the youngest Titan, Kronos, to castrate his father and take power.

Kronos married his sister Rhea and had five children. He had been warned that one of them would kill him and so swallowed each of them as they were born. To protect her sixth child, Rhea tricked Kronos into swallowing a stone and hid the baby, who was brought up safely by the nymphs. This child was Zeus, who returned as an adult and fought a mighty battle against the Titans, the Titanomachy. With the help of the freed Cyclopes and Hekatonchires, Zeus was victorious. He made Kronos vomit up his sisters and brothers and became king of the gods.

THE HARDSHIPS OF HUMANITY

THE HARDSHIPS SUFFERED by humanity were explained in the myths of Prometheus and Pandora. Prometheus (whose name means "forethought") was a Titan who befriended mankind but incurred the wrath of Zeus. He tricked the king of the gods out of the best part of the sacrifice, the meat, giving him the bones instead. (From that time, the people offered Zeus the bones of a sacrificed animal but ate the meat themselves.) As punishment, Zeus refused to let humans have the gift of fire, but Prometheus outwitted him again by stealing a flame and bringing it to earth. Enraged, Zeus ordered Violence and Strength to bind Prometheus to a stake on Mount Caucasus, where an eagle pecked out his liver. As an immortal, Prometheus could not die, and his liver was renewed every night for the torture to begin again every morning.

Zeus also punished mankind for accepting the gift of fire. He commissioned Hephaistus to create a woman from clay and sent her to Prometheus' brother Epimetheus with a jar ("Pandora's box"). Despite Prometheus' warnings, Epimetheus, whose name means "afterthought," accepted Pandora. She opened the jar, releasing evil and sickness into the world. Only hope remained, a sign that mankind should not despair.

HEROES AND HERO CULTS

HEROES WERE USUALLY born of a god and a mortal woman. The hero Perseus was the result of Zeus' love affair with the mortal Danae and the mighty Herakles was born to Zeus and the mortal Alkmene. They were not divine, but their spirits were thought to be eternal and they often intervened to help mortals in need. Heroes were not worshiped in Homer's time, but by the fifth century B.C.E., the hero cult had become a widespread form of religious worship. Heroes were worshiped at shrines built on the supposed sites of their burial or death. Because heroes were thought to possess exemplary courage and honor, to be associated with them was thought to bring good fortune. Similarly, to neglect a hero risked provoking his anger. Many Greek states claimed a hero as their founder or protector, creating myths to support their lineage, and noble families often claimed to be descended from a hero. There were many local heroes, and heroes often became associated with particular places, for example Oedipus at Colonus, Ajax at Salamis and Theseus at Athens. Heroes' power brought both good and evil. For example, the hero Oedipus saved his city but committed terrible crimes.

▶ *The city of Troy is destroyed by flames during the Trojan War.*

▲ *Ajax and Cassandra in a scene from the Battle of Troy.*

THE TROJAN WAR

ARCHAEOLOGICAL EVIDENCE tells us that the city of Troy (called Ilion or Ilium in antiquity) in northwest Asia Minor was destroyed in a war in about 1250 B.C.E. Perhaps this was the war between the Greeks and Trojans that was the subject of Homer's *Iliad*—we just do not know whether or not the myth of the Trojan War had any basis in reality.

The trouble starts when the king and queen of Troy, Priam and Hecuba, expose their baby son Paris to the elements, leaving him to die, because they are frightened by an omen suggesting that he will destroy the city. Paris survives and is eventually welcomed back into the family.

Zeus sets Paris the task of judging whom of the three goddesses Hera, Athene, and Aphrodite is "the fairest." Paris chooses Aphrodite, who has promised him the most beautiful woman in the world—Helen—as his wife. Paris elopes with Helen, much to the displeasure of her husband, Menelaus. Supporting Menelaus, the Greeks sail to Troy and wage war to recapture Helen.

During the siege, Agamemnon wins Chryseis, daughter of Chryses, the Trojan priest of Apollo, as war booty. Apollo sends a devastating plague upon the Greeks and Agamemnon is forced to return Chryseis. Piqued, Agamemnon steals Achilles' war prize, Briseis. Achilles is furious and sulks in his tent, refusing to fight. This allows the Trojans to slaughter many Greeks. Hector, Priam, and Hecuba's eldest son, kill Patroclus, who has gone into the fray wearing Achilles' armor to try to intimidate the Trojans. Achilles is stricken with grief and guilt and lunges into battle, bent on revenge. He pursues Hector three times around the walls of Troy, kills him in single combat and drags his corpse around the city behind his chariot. Priam begs to be allowed to give his son a proper burial and the angry gods intervene and force Achilles to return the corpse. Achilles dies when Paris' arrow hits him in his only vulnerable spot, his heel.

The Greeks win the war with a trick devised by Odysseus. They build a giant hollow wooden horse, in which the best warriors hide while the fleet sails away as if in defeat. Believing the horse to be an offering to the gods, the Trojans drag it inside the city gates. At night, the Greeks slip out of its belly, burn the city, and enslave the women. Thus Hecuba's omen that Paris would bring destruction to Troy proves true.

PROPAGANDA MYTHS IN ART

GREEK ART OFTEN featured mythology which reinforced the Greeks' superiority over non-Greek others. Athenians, in particular, used mythological scenes as propaganda. This frieze shows the Athenians fighting and vanquishing the Amazons, a mythical race of warrior women who were unlike Athenians in every way. The frieze is taken from that monument to Athenian supremacy, the Parthenon. Other "foreign" enemies whom art shows Athenians fighting include the Persians (Athens' nonmythical foe) and the fabulous race of the centaurs: half men, half horses. By including the Persians among these mythical oddities, the Athenians emphasized their enemies' difference and inferiority.

THESEUS, THE ALL-ATHENIAN HERO

THESEUS WAS the official hero of Athens. He was not born in Athens and his most famous exploit took place in Crete, where he slew the Minotaur, the man-bull hybrid who lived in a labyrinth and terrorized Athenian youth. However, in the sixth century B.C.E., the tyrant Pisistratus appropriated Theseus as a pan-Athenian hero. Athenian citizens were encouraged to emulate Theseus, and any songs that presented the hero in an unfavorable light were censored. Around 510 B.C.E. an epic celebrating his exploits was composed, called the *Theseis*. It is lost to us now but might have told how Theseus slew Sinis, the "pine bender," who would bend two pine trees together, strap his victim between them, and then let the trees go, ripping the man in two. Or perhaps it recounted Theseus' defeat of Prokrustes, who victimized travelers by giving them hospitality but making them "fit" the bed. Those whose legs were too short, he would stretch on the rack until they fitted, and those whose legs were too long, he chopped down to size. It is unlikely that the real Theseus existed, but Athenians honored him for unifying Attica (the region of which Athens was the supreme city) into one single state.

HERAKLES, THE HYPER-HERO

HERAKLES, WHO was called Hercules by the Romans, was the greatest Greek hero. He was one of the earliest mythological figures to be featured in Greek art (as early as the eighth century B.C.E.) and he was the only hero to be revered throughout Greece. He exemplified the problem that heroes presented to Classical Greeks: he was an outstanding individual whose extremity was both a source of admiration and yet also resulted in destruction and dishonor.

Among his spectacular achievements are his 12 labors, overseen by King Eurystheus as punishment for killing his family in a fit of madness visited on him by Hera, jealous of Zeus' liaison with Herakles' mother, Alkmene. Less glorious was his reputation for uncontrollable lust (myth has it that he slept with the 50 daughters of King Thespios in a single night), drinking, and gluttony. It was lust that led to Herakles' death. Distressed by Herakles' affection for Iole, his wife Deianeira tried to win back his love with a potion that turned out to be poison. The dying Herakles was placed on a funeral pyre but, as the flames licked around, his father Zeus snatched him up to heaven, where he was the only hero to be given immortality.

▼ *Herakles and Apollo engage in battle.*

THE 12 LABORS OF HERAKLES

1. The Nemean Lion
The lion that terrorized Nemea had a hide so tough that no weapon was able to pierce it. Herakles stunned it with his club before strangling it. He wore its skin for protection.

2. The Lernaean Hydra
In the swamps of Lerna lurked the Hydra, a water snake with nine heads. Whenever Herakles slashed off one serpent head, two more grew in its place. After cutting off a head, Herakles cauterized the stump with a burning torch, thus preventing any heads from growing back.

3. The Cerynean Hind
Herakles had to capture the hind unharmed. It had bronze hooves and gold horns, lived on Mount Cerynea and was sacred to the goddess Artemis. After stalking the hind for a year, Herakles trapped it in a net.

4. The Eurymathian Boar
Herakles managed to chain this boar, who was so fearsome that when Eurystheus saw him he was terrified and hid inside a bronze urn.

5. The Augean Stables
The stables of King Augeus had never been cleaned and were piled high with dung. Herakles had to clean them out in one day, a task he only accomplished by diverting two nearby rivers through the stables to wash the filth away.

6. The Stymphalion Birds
These man-eating birds had beaks, claws, and wings of iron. Herakles frightened them off Lake Stymphalos by clashing cymbals and then shot them with his arrows.

7. The Cretan Bull
This monstrous bull ran amok on Crete. Only Herakles was able to overpower it and capture it alive.

8. The Mares of Diomedes
Diomedes fed his wild mares on human flesh. Herakles killed Diomedes and fed his body to the mares, who became calm and were easily tamed.

9. Hippolyte's belt
Herakles defeated the warrior women Amazons in order to steal the belt of t

10. The Cattle of Geryon
Geryon was a three-bodied monster who guarded his cattle with the help of Orthus, a two-headed dog. Herakles killed them both and drove the cattle home, establishing the Straits of Gibraltar on the way.

11. The Apples of the Hesperides
The apples were tended by the Hesperides nymphs and guarded by a dragon that Herakles had to slay before stealing them.

12. Cerberus
Herakles' final task was to show Eurystheus Cerberus, the three-headed dog who guarded the gates of the underworld. He wrestled with the beast and took him to Eurystheus, but returned him to Hades.

◀ *Greek amphora showing Herakles capturing Cerberus.*

THE ETERNAL SUFFERER

EVERY CULTURE has its myths of those that are punished by the gods and sentenced to eternal damnation. Tantalus suffered a particularly nasty fate. He had dishonored the gods by serving them human flesh (his own son!) instead of meat, and Zeus banished him to the underworld. He was made to stand in a pool of fresh water which had fruit trees growing overhead. Whenever he tried to eat or drink, the branches and water moved away, condemning him to perpetual hunger and thirst. This myth gives us the word "tantalize."

TEMPLES

AWESOME IN THEIR SIZE, scale, and beauty, temples were privileged public sites for the expression of Greek culture. Temple friezes and pediments often displayed mythological battles, celebrating the victories of the civilized (the Olympians and the city-state) over the uncivilized (giants, monsters, and hybrids). The battle between the Lapiths (a tribe in Thessaly) and the Centaurs (half men, half horses) was featured on the Parthenon, in the frieze at the temple of Apollo at Bassae, and in the sculptures from the west pediment of the temple of Zeus at Olympia. The Parthenon also portrays the Panathenaic procession, whose participants are not mythical, but anonymous Athenians. Here myth and everyday life merge; both serve to reassert Athenian superiority.

GODS OF HEARTH AND HOME

EVERY HOUSE had a hearth and it was protected by the goddess Hestia. Hestia features in few mythological tales, but she had immense importance as a figure of stability and prosperity for the household. A few days after the birth of a baby, a ceremony was held to name the child and place it under the protection of Hestia. This involved running with the baby around the hearth and so was called the Amphidromia ("running around").

Outside the house, at the doorway, a statue of the god Hermes stood guard. Hermes was thought to bring good luck and, like his Roman counterpart Mercury, was the god of communication. Flashing his winged sandals and cap and brandishing his magic staff, Hermes was messenger to the gods. His verbal dexterity also made him a slippery customer, and he presided over thieves and deceivers. In one notorious myth Hermes stole Apollo's cattle, driving them backwards so that their footprints would not lead Apollo to them. When Zeus tried to punish him, he wriggled out of it by lying about his age and then playing the lyre so beautifully that Apollo forgave him.

THE VOYEUR: ACTAEON

ACTAEON WAS A POTENT reminder of the perils of looking upon forbidden sights. While out in the woods one day this legendary hunter unwittingly came across Artemis bathing naked. Livid at the intrusion, the goddess turned Actaeon in a stag, whereupon he was torn to pieces by his own hounds. Several myths follow a similar pattern. The prophet Teiresias was punished with blindness after he saw Athene bathing. In a less well known myth, Erymanthus, son of Apollo, saw Aphrodite bathing after she had made love to Adonis and he, too, was blinded for his infringement.

ARTEMIS AND RITES OF PASSAGE

ARTEMIS IS THE TWIN sister of the god Apollo and is best known as the goddess of the hunt. She is often depicted in hunting dress, with a bow and arrows. She was a virgin goddess and exacted a terrible revenge upon anyone who threatened her chastity. When the great hunter Orion tried to rape her, she made a scorpion spring up from the earth which stung to death both Orion and his dog. Orion was placed in the sky as a constellation of stars and his dog became Sirius, the Dog Star. In what might seem like a contradiction, Artemis also presided over childbirth.

Many of Artemis' cults were associated with female rites of passage such as birth, puberty, and death. It appears—although our evidence is far from conclusive—that there were various myths about Artemis (and other gods) that grew up from association with rituals. Before marriage, Athenian girls went to Brauron, a few miles away from Athens, to serve Artemis in a ritual that involved them acting as bears (the *arkteia*). Myth has it that originally a real bear was killed and girls were made to perform the *arkteia* to appease the angry goddess.

◀ *The majestic remains of the Parthenon, Athens.*
▲ *Greek statue of the mighty Zeus.*

METAMORPHOSIS

MANY GREEK MYTHS involved metamorphosis, the fantastic transformation of shape. Sometimes metamorphosis was imposed as a punishment. Tereus, king of Thrace, married Procne and had a child with her named Itys. When Procne's sister Philomela visited them, Tereus raped her and cut out her tongue so that she could not tell anyone. But Philomela wove a tapestry depicting the outrage and showed it to her sister. Procne and Philomela took revenge by killing Itys and serving him as a meal to Tereus. All three were turned into birds: Tereus a hoopoe, Procne a swallow, and Philomela a nightingale. The Romans were also very fond of myths of metamorphosis.

THE ABDUCTION OF PERSEPHONE

DEMETER, THE SISTER of Zeus, Poseidon, and Hades and the goddess of grain and agriculture, had a daughter called Persephone. One day, when Persephone was out with friends picking flowers, Hades kidnapped her and took her back to the underworld. Demeter was grief stricken at the loss and wandered the earth looking for Persephone. She traveled for nine days without pausing to eat or sleep. On the tenth day she met Helios, the sun god, who told her that Hades had abducted her daughter but that he had done so with permission from Zeus. Devastated, Demeter left Olympus and continued her wanderings among mortals, disgused as an old woman called Doso.

She arrived at a place called Eleusis, where the daughters of the king, Celeus, persuaded their father to take the old woman in. As Doso, Demeter was employed as an attendant of Queen Metaneira, but when the queen saw her, she recognized her godlike nobility and bade her be seated and eat and drink. Demeter, still in mourning for Persephone, refused and stood in silence until a slave woman, called Iambe, lifted up her skirts and made Demeter laugh. (Iambe gives her name to iambic poetry, which is often comic and satirical.) Demeter/Doso stayed at the palace as a nurse to the baby prince Demophoon. She planned to make the child immortal by feeding him ambrosia, the food of the gods, and by placing him in the fire every night. She did this in secret, but one night was disturbed by Metaneira as she was laying Demophoon in the fire. Metaneira screamed in horror and the goddess took the child away from the flames, angrily declaring that he would now never be immortal. Revealing her identity, Demeter left the palace after establishing rites to be held in her honor: the Eleusinian Mysteries.

▲ *This silver decadrachma bears the head of the goddess Persephone.*

In her renewed grief, Demeter refused to allow grain to be cultivated or any crops to grow. Humanity began to starve, so Zeus intervened and said he would allow Persephone to be returned to her mother if she had not eaten anything during her time in the underworld. Hades, however, had persuaded the maiden to eat some pomegranate seeds, a symbol of marriage. Despite this, Zeus allowed a compromise: Persephone was to spend two-thirds of the year with her mother, but for the other third she must return to Hades. Every year, during Persephone's absence, Demeter mourns anew and the crops perish. We call this time winter.

▲ *This bas-relief shows a priest and priestess carrying out a ritual ceremony.*

DEMETER AND THE MYSTERIES

A MYSTERY RELIGION is one that requires its followers to undergo a secret initiation ceremony. There were various mystery cults, and one of the most popular was dedicated to the worship of the goddess Demeter and her daughter Persephone. This was known as the Eleusinian Mysteries. *The Homeric Hymn to Demeter,* a poem believed to have been based on the rituals involved in the Eleusinian Mysteries, states "To the kings of Eleusis Demeter showed the conduct of her rites and taught them her mysteries, awful mysteries which no one can transgress or utter." The death penalty was imposed on anyone who leaked the secrets of the rituals.

Consequently, our knowledge of the mysteries is scant, but we do know that they were concerned with the afterlife and agriculture, two central themes in the myth of Demeter and Persephone. Each year in September and October an international festival was held, with a procession from

▲ *Bronze portrayal of the god Apollo.*

Athens to Eleusis followed by a two-day initiation ceremony. It is possible that this involved a reenactment of Hades' abduction of Persephone. Initiates were promised life after death. The mysteries were celebrated at Eleusis for over a thousand years and were (rightly) perceived as a threat by early Christians.

APOLLO AND DELPHI

APOLLO, THE SON OF ZEUS and Leto and twin brother of the goddess Artemis, had many associations. He was often referred to as Phoebus ("Brilliant", his grandmother was the Titan Phoebe) and he was god of the sun and light. Apollo was patron of the arts and music and is often depicted playing a lyre. One myth tells how the satyr Marsyas challenged Apollo to a music competition and lost. Apollo punished Marsyas's impertinence by having him flayed alive. He was also the god of healing and fathered Asklepios, the mythical founder of medicine. Paradoxically, however, Apollo sometimes visited plagues upon people with his arrows.

Apollo was worshiped at Delos, where he was born, and at Delphi, where he had a sanctuary and oracle. Delphi was thought to be the center of the world. Apollo slew a dragon there called Pytho, which was celebrated by the Pythian Games held every four years and which gave the name Pythia to Apollo's priestess. She sat on a tripod and delivered answers to questions in an inspired trance. The oracle was consulted by many individuals and cities, and its predictions were believed always to come true, despite often having been first misunderstood.

ASKLEPIOS, GOD OF HEALING

FROM THE FOURTH century B.C.E. people visited the sanctuary at Epidauros—in much the same way as the sick make pilgrimages to Lourdes today—in the hope of being cured of their ailments by the god Asklepios. According to one tradition, Asklepios was a mortal who was taught the healing arts by the centaur Chiron, but another suggests that Apollo (whose powers included healing) was his father. The Asklepios cult flourished and was introduced to Rome after a plague in 293 B.C.E. Asklepios is said to have been killed by a thunderbolt from Zeus after he transgressed by trying to raise the dead.

THE TRAGEDY OF OEDIPUS

The most celebrated version of the Oedipus myth is that dramatized in Sophocles' play *Oedipus the King*. It presents a man on a remarkable journey of self-discovery.

THE DELPHIC ORACLE

prophesied that the child of King Laius and Queen Jocasta of Thebes would grow up to kill his father and sleep with his mother, so when the royal couple had a son, they left him to die on the mountainside. In doing so they pierced his feet and bound them together. A shepherd found the baby and took him to Corinth, where he became adopted by the king and queen, Polybus and Merope. They called the boy Oedipus, which means "swollen foot."

When he was a young man, Oedipus was taunted by a stranger who said that he was not the son of Polybus. Disconcerted, Oedipus consulted the Delphic oracle, who told him that he would kill his father and marry his mother. Assuming that the prophecy referred to Polybus and Merope, Oedipus left Corinth immediately. On the road to Thebes, he fell into an argument with a stranger who insulted him. In his anger, Oedipus killed the man, thus fulfilling the first part of the prophecy: the man was Laius.

At this time Thebes was terrorized by the Sphinx, a monster with the head of a woman and body of a lion who came from Egypt. She would ask the riddle: "What is it that walks on four legs in the morning, on two at noon, and on three in the evening?" She strangled and devoured anyone who was unable to answer, and Thebes was littered with her victims. Oedipus answered correctly that it was Man, who first crawls on all fours, then walks on two and in old age uses a stick as a third leg. In fury, the Sphinx hurled herself from a rock and was dashed to pieces. Thebes rejoiced and made Oedipus their king. He married the recently widowed queen Jocasta, thus fulfilling the second part of the prophecy.

After a while the city was struck by plague, drought, and famine. The Delphic oracle advised that only when Laius' murderer was expelled would the crisis end. Oedipus made a thorough inquiry and soon learned the terrible truth from the blind prophet Teiresias and the shepherd who had saved him as a child. Jocasta hanged herself and Oedipus, having gained this terrible insight, gouged out his eyes and left Thebes.

▲ *The illustrations painted on this Greek vessel show a sacrificial procession in honor of the Delphic oracle.*

TRANSGRESSION

MANY MYTHS, like that of Oedipus, warn against mortals transgressing, both overstepping the bounds of decent behavior and showing arrogance (hubris) toward the gods. Ixion transgressed when he tried to rape Hera, queen of the gods. Zeus' punishment was severe: Ixion was strapped to a burning wheel, where he was condemned to rotate forever in Hades. Atreus was a notorious transgressor. When his brother Thyestes seduced Atreus' wife, Atreus slaughtered Thyestes' children and served them to him as a meal. This myth was also enjoyed by the Romans and was the subject of the playwright Seneca's drama *Thyestes.*

MURDEROUS WIVES

FROM AX-MURDERESSES to poisoners, Greek mythology is filled with stories of wives murdering their husbands. One of these tells how Danaus, a descendent of Zeus, had 50 daughters—known as the Danaids—and his brother Aegyptus had 50 sons. Aegyptus wanted the daughters and sons to marry, but the women were unwilling and Danaus refused. When Aegyptus persisted, Danaus relented but told his daughters to kill their husbands on their wedding night. They all obeyed except Hypermnestra, who had fallen in love with her husband, Lynceus. The 49 murderesses were punished in the underworld by having to fill jars through sieves: a never-ending task.

Medea and Clytemnestra are the most famous husband slayers. Clytemnestra hated her husband Agamemnon after he sacrificed their eldest daughter, Iphigeneia, at the goddess Artemis' command, to enable the Greeks to sail to Troy to fight the Trojan War. When Agamemnon returned from Troy, he brought with him a new lover, Apollo's priestess, Cassandra. Further enraged, Clytemnestra, with the help of her new lover Aegisthus, lured Agamemnon into the house. While he was taking a bath, she trapped him in a net and stabbed him to death. These myths perhaps testify to men's fear that women might destroy them.

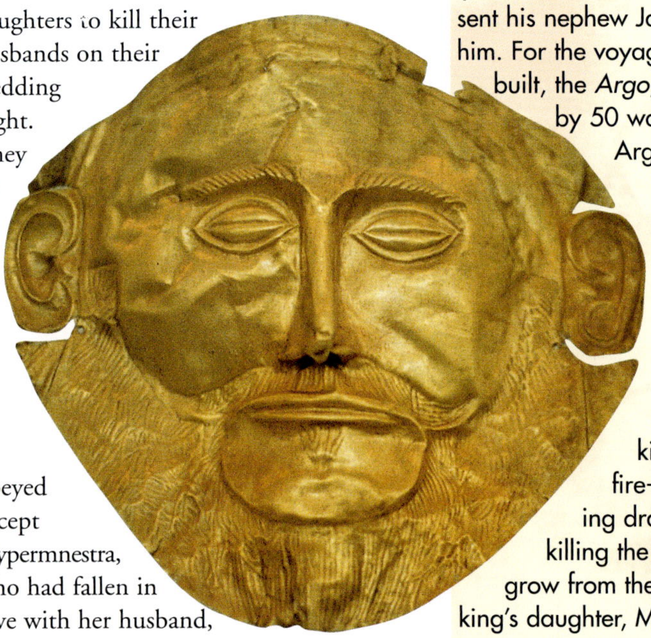

▲ *The golden funerary mask of Agamemnon.*

JASON AND MEDEA

Medea is one of the most notorious murderers in Greek mythology. She was the wife of Jason, the hero famous for his quest for the golden fleece.

AT COLCHIS THERE HUNG a golden ram's fleece which belonged to King Aeetes and was closely guarded by a dragon which never slept. Peleus, the tyrant at Iolcus, coveted the fleece and sent his nephew Jason to obtain it for him. For the voyage, Jason had a ship built, the *Argo*, which was manned by 50 warriors known as the Argonauts. After numerous adventures, the crew landed at Colchis where King Aeetes promised to give Jason the fleece if he accomplished various tasks: yoking the king's bronze-hooved, fire-breathing bulls, sowing dragon's teeth and killing the giants who would grow from the planted teeth. The king's daughter, Medea, fell in love with

▲ *With Medea's help, the hero Jason retrieves the golden fleece.*

Jason. She was a sorceress and used potions and spells to help him fulfil these tasks. She then drugged the dragon and Jason stole the fleece. Aeetes pursued them, but Medea slowed his ship down by murdering her own brother, Apsyrtus, and throwing chunks of his body into the sea. Aeetes stopped to gather them and the *Argo* escaped.

When Jason and Medea arrived back in Iolcus, they plotted to avenge the death of Jason's father, who had been killed by Peleus. Medea devised a particularly cruel plan. She persuaded Pelias' daughters that she would rejuvenate their elderly father with a secret spell but, in preparation for this, they had to chop Pelias up and boil him. Foolishly the daughters agreed: they killed Pelias and cooked his body and only then did Medea reveal that she had tricked them. The people were so outraged that they hounded Jason and Medea out of Iolcus, from where they fled to Corinth. They settled there and had children.

Years later, King Creon of Corinth offered Jason a politically advantageous marriage to his daughter, Glauce, which

Jason was keen to agree to. He proposed that he divorce Medea and that she go into exile. According to the version of the myth told in Euripides' *Medea*, Medea was enraged and embittered by this betrayal. Her revenge was terrifying. First, she sent poisoned robes to Creon and Glauce which burned them to death. Then—in order to cause Jason maximum pain—she cut the throats of her own children. She escaped in a chariot pulled by dragons, mocking her broken husband.

THE WOMAN SCORNED

STHENEBOIA LUSTED after the young and handsome Bellerophon. When he rejected her advances, she told her husband, the king of Argos, the lie that he had tried to rape her. The king plotted (unsuccessfully) to have Bellerophon killed. Hippolytus was less fortunate. He was the object of desire of his stepmother Phaedra, an affection he found repulsive. Scorned and humiliated, Phaedra committed suicide, leaving a note to her husband Theseus in which she accused Hippolytus of attempted rape. Theseus called on Poseidon to destroy his son and Hippolytus was thrown from his chariot and died. These myths are akin to the biblical tale of Joseph and Potiphar's wife.

AMAZONS: WARRIOR WOMEN

MYTHS OF AMAZONS represented the nightmarish, topsy-turvy world that might exist were women ever to take up arms and seize control. Amazons lived in women-only societies, hunted on horseback, wore men's clothing and fought battles. They represented the reverse of civilized norms: they lived in the east and dressed as Persians (they were, therefore, "barbarians") and they did not grow crops or live in cities, as the civilized Greeks did. They were only allowed to fight in battles after they had killed at least one man. They were said to keep men as slaves or to have sex with men periodically, but only in order to get pregnant. Male children were exposed to die; only girls were raised to adulthood.

Some sources suggest that the Amazons used to slice off their right breasts so as to make shooting with a bow and arrow easier—*a-mazos* means "without a breast"—but in art Amazons are always depicted with two. The great Athenian heroes fought against the Amazons. Herakles' ninth labor involved seizing the belt of the Amazon queen Hippolyte, whom Theseus later abducted. Amazons always lost these battles, thus ultimately reinforcing Greek male superiority.

MEDUSA'S DEADLY GAZE

MEDUSA WAS ONE of the three Gorgons, monstrous females with writhing serpents for hair. Anyone who looked directly at her was turned into stone. Medusa was eventually killed by the hero Perseus, the son of Zeus, and a mortal woman, Danae. Perseus was ordered to bring back a Gorgon's head by the wicked king Polydectes, but Hermes and Athena helped him achieve this mission. They gave him a sickle, a bag, a helmet of invisibility, winged sandals so that he could fly, and a shield. Perseus was able to decapitate Medusa by looking not at her but at her reflection in the shield, and he put the head in the bag lest he accidentally catch sight of it. As he was flying home, Perseus saw a beautiful maiden chained to a rock by the sea. She was Andromeda, who was about to be sacrificed to a sea monster to appease the wrath of Poseidon, after her mother boasted that she was more beautiful than the sea nymphs. Revealing Medusa's head, Perseus turned the sea monster into stone, rescued Andromeda, and married her. Having returned and killed Polydectes in the same way, Perseus gave Medusa's head to Athena, who wears it on her breastplate as a petrifying warning to her enemies.

▲ *A clay tablet in the form of a Gorgon's head from the temple of Apollo.*

◀ *Sculpture of the great god of the sea, Poseidon.*

▲ *The enraged Cyclops, Polyphemus, hurls rocks at Odysseus and his remaining crew as they escape.*
▶ *Relief showing the reclining figure of Dionysus being served wine by a satyr.*

MYTHICAL MONSTERS

MANY FABULOUS, frightening, and grotesque creatures lurk in Greek mythology. Like Amazons, monsters existed to be confronted by the Greek gods and heroes and to be conquered by them. When the world was first created, Zeus defeated Typhon, described by the poet Hesiod as having a hundred snake's heads, fire-flashing eyes and with voices that could imitate the speech of any god or animal. Typhon spawned the Echidna, a repulsive creature with the upper body of a nymph and the lower body of a viper. Many monsters were hybrids of women and animals. The Harpies ("Snatchers") were birds with women's faces. They tormented the blind prophet Phineus by swooping down on his food and seizing it or defecating upon it. He was rescued by the hero Jason. The Sirens were winged creatures with women's heads and voices so enchantingly beautiful that every sailor who passed by and heard them felt compelled to draw closer and listen. The sailor's boat would crash on the rocks and the Sirens lured many men to their deaths in this way. Odysseus plugged his crew's ears with wax and had himself strapped to the mast so that he could hear the Sirens but escape their bewitching trap.

ODYSSEUS AND THE CYCLOPS

THE HERO ODYSSEUS had many strange adventures on his long journey returning home to Ithaca after the Trojan War. In one of them, Odysseus and his crew landed on an island inhabited by Cyclopes, one-eyed giants who lived in caves. The men explored the island in search for provisions and entered the cave of the Cyclops Polyphemus. Polyphemus returned with his flock of sheep and blocked the entrance to the cave with a huge boulder. When he discovered the Greeks, he ate two of them raw for supper and two more for breakfast. The Greeks were in a desperate situation because none of them was strong enough to move the boulder. However Odysseus, who was famed for his cunning, devised a plan. He got Polyphemus drunk and, when asked his name, replied "Nobody." He then blinded the giant's eye with a burning stake. When the Cyclopes heard screaming and called to Polyphemus, he replied, "Nobody is hurting me," and so they did not come to help. Odysseus and his men escaped by tying themselves under the bellies of the sheep, which were let out the next morning. From the safety of his ship Odysseus taunted Polyphemus, who cursed him. Polyphemus' father, Poseidon, made Odysseus wander the ocean for ten years.

LOVE AND WAR

ARES WAS THE FEARSOME and often brutal god of war. He was the son of Zeus and Hera, and in the *Iliad* he supported the Trojan warriors on the battlefield. Ares does not feature in many myths and is perhaps best known as the lover of Aphrodite. Homer's *Odyssey* recounts the story of Aphrodite's adulterous affair with Ares. Aphrodite was married to the god of fire and metalwork, Hephaistos, but took Ares as her lover. Helios, the Sun, spotted the two together and told Hephaistos. He spun a fine, strong net and cast it over the lovers as they lay in bed, trapping them in their shame. Hephaistos called the other Olympians to witness their humiliation, but they only laughed, some even suggesting that it was worth the embarrassment just to sleep with Aphrodite.

Aphrodite was associated with all aspects of love and physical attraction. Her name means "born of foam" and she was said to have sprung up from the sea around Cyprus. She had many lovers, one of whom, the gorgeous hunter Adonis, was killed by a wild boar. Aphrodite was said to be devastated, and ritual songs were sung in honor of her beloved every year at the Athenian festival of the Thesmophoria.

DIONYSUS, GOD OF WILDNESS AND WINE

DIONYSUS WAS, in Euripides' words, "most gentle and most terrible." He was the god of illusion and disguise and drama festivals were held in his honor. He was also the god of wine, which was a sacred drink whose consumption was ritualized. His followers went into states of religious ecstasy and roamed wild. Dionysus symbolized passion and a dangerous lack of restraint. He was also worshiped in secret mysteries which persisted well into Roman times. His associations with fertility (the phallus—Greek *phallos*—was a common symbol of Dionysus) led to his identification with other male fertility gods of the Ancient Near East, including the Egyptian Osiris and the Mesopotamian and Syrian Tammuz or Dumuzi.

SATYRS AND MAENADS

SATYRS AND MAENADS were followers of Dionysus, god of the theater, but also of wine, religious ecstasy, and the irrational.

▲ *This detail of a wall painting shows the Dance of a Bacchantine, the initiation of Bacchantes in to the Dionysus cult.*

Satyrs were part man, part goat (with cloven feet and pointed ears) and had horses' tails. They were mischievous, wine-loving creatures, who were usually depicted in a permanent state of sexual arousal, chasing nymphs or maenads. Their licentiousness was extreme, and one of the functions of representations of satyrs was to define the limits of normative male behavior. Unlike satyrs, myth suggests, the typical man should have a sense of moderation about his pleasure seeking (as one Greek maxim puts it, "Nothing in excess"). Satyrs were frequently depicted in art and were the subjects of the Athenian satyr play, riotous comedies that were usually performed after a tragic trilogy in the dramatic festivals.

Maenads (also known as Bacchantes) were women incited into religious frenzy by Dionysus, as dramatized by Euripides in his play *The Bacchae*. They left their homes and roamed wild around the countryside. Each carried a special staff known as a thyrsus. Maenads were so liberated from normal human conventions that they ripped apart live animals with their bare hands and ate the raw flesh.

DRINK AND DECORATION

MYTHICAL SCENES were used to decorate many household objects, especially the drinking vessels used for the symposium, an important social event for Greek men. *Symposion* means "drinking together" and the men would indeed drink (with the pouring of ritual libations) and socialize. Women were present only as entertainers, for dance, music, and sex. A regular entertainment was the recitation of poems with mythological themes. As befitted their use at an occasion involving drink and sex, drinking cups often depicted Dionysiac themes: satyrs, maenads, or other scenes of revelry.

THE UNDERWORLD

THE GREEKS DID NOT have a heaven and hell like many religions, but they did believe in various sorts of afterlife. The most frequently encountered was the underworld, known as Hades ("the unseeing" or "the unseen place"), which was also the name of its joyless ruler. The god Hades was the brother of Zeus and Poseidon but was rarely included in the Olympian pantheon because his gloomy realm was opposed to that of celestial Olympus. There were regions of the underworld—Erebos and Tartaros—reserved for those whose crimes sentenced them to an afterlife of eternal punishment, like Tantalus and the Danaids. There were also the lands of the divine dead, called the Elysian Fields or Islands of the Blessed, which were the resting places for brave warriors and others of the chosen few.

It was important that the dead be buried with proper ceremony to ensure a smooth passage down to the underworld. Hermes Psychopompos would lead the dead down into Hades. Charon, the ferryman of the underworld, then took the dead across the infernal rivers: the River Styx (river of hate), Acheron (river of woe), Lethe (river of forgetfulness), Cocytus (river of wailing), and Phlegethon (river of fire).

▲ *The scene depicted on this vessel retells one of the myths surrounding Apollo and Artemis.*

Rome

INTRODUCTION

MANY OF THE GREEK myths were adopted and modified by the Romans, whose empire was the dominant power over and beyond most of the area that we now know as modern Europe for the first four centuries C.E The speed and extent of Rome's expansion was quite extraordinary. When Rome became a republic (governed by elected magistrates) in 509 B.C.E., it controlled relatively little, but by 241 B.C.E. it had control of most of Italy and by 31 B.C.E., when Rome became an empire under the leadership of Augustus, it was well on the way to ruling virtually the entire Mediterranean world. Rome's subjects numbered over 50 million people, with one million populating the city itself.

The Greek pantheon was absorbed into the Roman one, primarily via the Etruscans, an important civilization on the Italian peninsula between 900 and 500 B.C.E. Thus, for example, the Roman equivalent of Zeus was Jupiter; of Hera, Juno; of Athene, Minerva; of Artemis, Diana; and of Aphrodite, Venus. There were no native myths in which these gods played a part, nor did the Romans have any creation myth. The Roman derivatives proved colorless counterparts to the Greek divinities. The Greek gods were anthropomorphic in more than shape; like humans they fought, swindled, loved, and avenged. The Roman deities did not possess human psychology. Instead, they were mostly personifications of various abstract qualities and their personalities were much less important than their functions.

HOWEVER, THE ROMANS did more than take over and water down the Greek pantheon. They refocused the myths to serve Roman concerns. Wisdom and enlightenment were of less concern to the Romans than agriculture and feeding the growing population. This is reflected in the diminution in importance of Minerva (Roman goddess of wisdom) and Apollo (god of self-knowledge, like his Greek counterpart of the same name), in stark contrast to the dominance of Athena and Apollo in Classical Greece.

◀ *God of love, Eros, is punished in front of Aphrodite.*

▲ *Gold coin bearing the portrait of Emperor Augustus Caesar.*

Correspondingly, the importance of Ceres, the goddess of agriculture and Roman equivalent to Demeter, is substantially increased. Likewise, whereas the Greeks did not lay much emphasis on their war god Ares, the Romans proudly embraced Mars as their ancestor and the embodiment of the martial spirit necessary to fulfil Rome's imperial ambitions. Roman myths were also more historicized than Greek myths and it is impossible to demarcate any clear line between Roman myth and its early history. On the whole, Roman mythology is less fantastic and more realistically grounded in time and place than Greek mythology. The Greek writer Plutarch (C.E *c.* 46–126) treated Romulus and Remus, the mythical founders of Rome, as historical figures. When points of fact and legend become so intermingled, the distinction between myth and history becomes redundant.

Rome was first populated through an act of violence. After it had been founded and named, there was no one to live in the city. Part of this problem was solved when Romulus allowed criminals from all over Italy to settle in Rome as citizens. But it became clear that they needed wives with whom they could have children and increase in number. Romulus approached various local communities, but no one was willing to let his daughter marry a Roman bandit. Romulus resorted to subterfuge. He invited neighboring Sabine tribes to celebrate a religious festival, and when they had gathered he gave his men the signal to abduct the marriageable women.

The Sabine king, Titus Tatius, marshaled an army to retaliate and the Sabines invaded Rome. The battle raged fiercely until the Sabine women, who now had loyalties to their new husbands, intervened and peace was made.

Titus Tatius ruled Rome jointly with Romulus until his death, when Romulus took over as Rome's first offical king. When Romulus died he became a god and was worshiped as the Roman spirit Quirinus.

THE BIRTH OF ROMAN MYTHOLOGY

THE EXTENT of Rome's dominion is the key to understanding its mythology. The Roman state was simply too large and mutable for only one set of mythological and religious traditions to suffice. As Rome expanded its territories, it incorporated the myths of the conquered peoples into its own. The result is eclectic: Roman mythology is a strange hotchpotch of Greek, Egyptian, Celtic, and many other myths. All of these, once assimilated, became Roman myths. For example, at the end of the second century B.C.E., the Egyptian goddess Isis was introduced into Italy. A mother goddess, associated with fertility, Isis soon became popular and she was sometimes linked with the Roman Fortuna, spirit of fertility, agriculture, and love, becoming Isis-Fortuna. Another Egyptian deity, the ram-horned god Amon, became Ammon in Greek mythology and in Rome was incorporated into the imperial cult. He was a protector of the Roman armies and his image appears on breastplates and medallions.

JANUS

JANUS WAS a Roman god with no Greek equivalent. He is often depicted on coins as facing in two directions. This is because he was the spirit of doors and archways—at entrances and exits it is sensible to look ahead and behind.

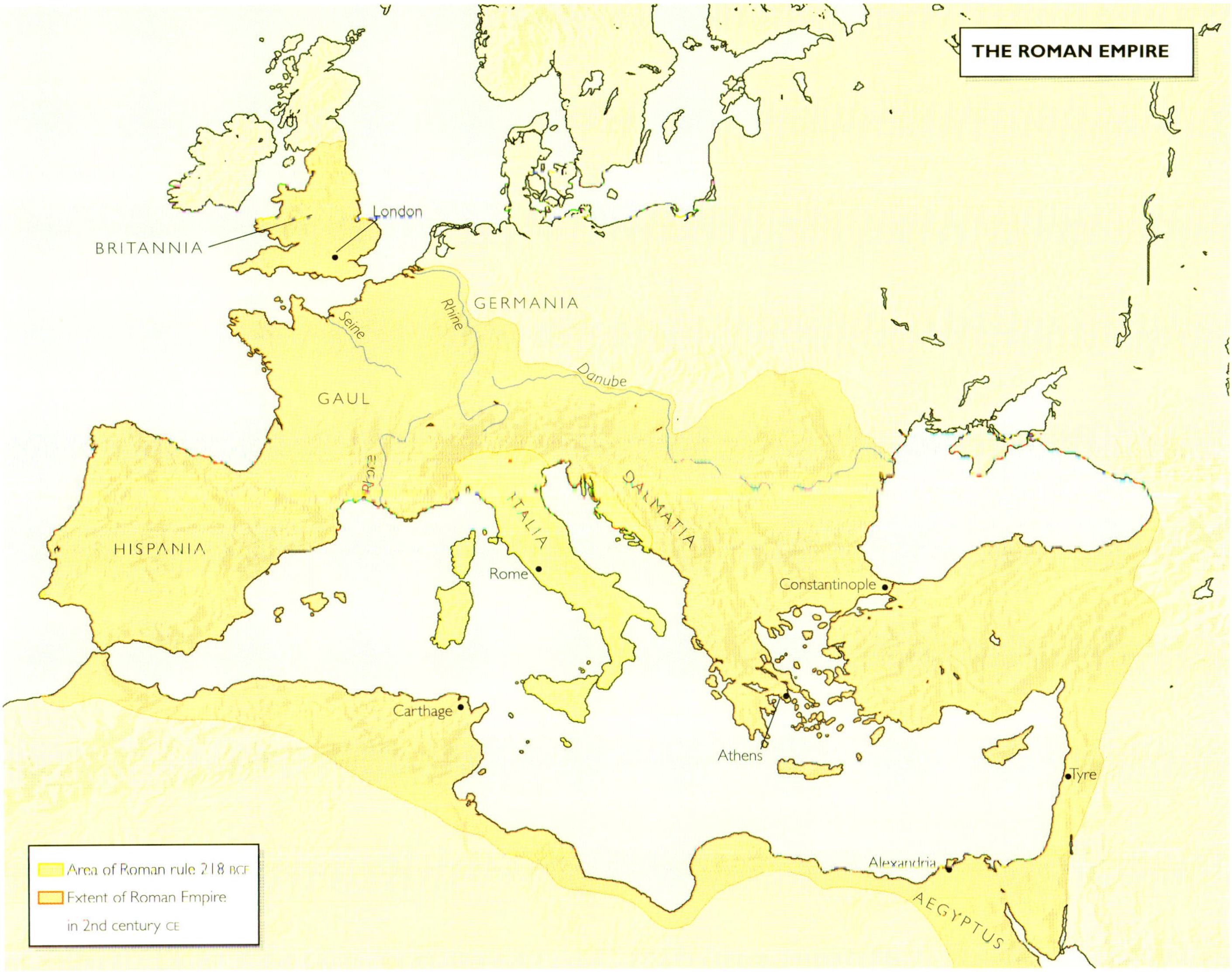

INSPIRED WOMEN

WHEN AENEAS DESCENDS to the underworld in the sixth book of the *Aeneid*, his guide is the Sybil at Cumae. Myth has it that she was so old because of a punishment inflicted on her by Apollo. The god offered her as many years of life as she could scoop up grains of sand. The Sibyl accepted, but when she rejected Apollo he kept his word but made her shrivel up like a grasshopper. It is often women who are mouthpieces for prophecy. The oracle at Delphi was spoken through the Pythia, and in the Bible the Witch of Endor foretells the future to King Saul.

EXPOSED CHILDREN

ROMULUS AND REMUS were exposed by the banks of the River Tiber where they were expected to die. A she-wolf rescued them, and the image of her suckling the twin babies was used by Rome as a symbol of her growing power. Babies being abandoned in the wild, then being saved by an animal or country worker and returning to take their rightful place in society, is a common theme in myth. In Greek mythology, Oedipus was exposed on the mountainside. In fairy tales it is common for babies or older children like Snow White and Hansel and Gretel to be abandoned in the woods.

THE GREAT MOTHER

ONE OF THE MOST extraordinary deities introduced to Rome was that of the "Great Mother" or "Magna Mater", the Roman name for the Phrygian fertility goddess Cybele. Her cult was brought into Rome in 204 B.C.E. on the advice of an oracle. In one version of the myth, by the Christian writer Arnobius (fourth century C.E.), Cybele was born from a great rock in Phrygia (the one from which Deucalion and Pyrrha took the stones that became human beings). Zeus attacked Cybele and spilled some semen on the rock, which became pregnant. The rock bore a son, Agdestis, a violent and uncontrollable creature. Dionysus drugged him with wine and made vines grow from his genitals. Agdestis tripped over the vines and ripped his genitals. From the blood sprang a pomegranate tree whose fruit made a maiden pregnant. Her child, Attis, became Cybele's favorite and Agdestis protected him. When the king of the capital of Phrygia arranged for Attis to marry his daughter, Agdestis in anger drove the wedding guests mad and one castrated himself. The distraught Attis castrated himself likewise. This is all very bizarre, and the disturbing elements of self-castration and ecstatic ravings were mirrored in the cult practices of the followers of the Magna Mater.

▲ *Dionysus reclines amongst his entourage.*
▼ *A she-wolf suckles the abandoned Romulus and Remus.*

ROMULUS AND REMUS

ACCORDING TO THIS famous myth, Rome was founded on fratricide. Romulus and Remus were twin brothers born to Rhea Silvia, a woman from the royal family in Alba Longa who was raped by the war god Mars. When her uncle, the king Amulius, noticed her pregnancy, he imprisoned Rhea Silvia and, once the babies were born, he exposed them to die by the banks of the River Tiber. The twins were discovered by a she-wolf, who suckled them until a shepherd named Faustulus found and adopted them. When they were young men, Romulus and Remus tried to rob some of Amulius' shepherds and Remus was caught and taken before the king. Meanwhile, Faustulus decided to explain to Romulus the circumstances of his birth. When he learned the facts, Romulus rescued Remus, murdered Amulius, and made his grandfather, Numitor, king of Alba Longa. Romulus and Remus resolved to found their own city on the site where the she-wolf had nurtured them. However, they argued about the exact location of the site and the dispute ended with Romulus murdering his brother and becoming the sole king of Rome. He gave his name to the city (*Roma* in Latin).

THE ORIGINS OF ROME

AENEAS, WHO WAS A minor Trojan hero in the Greek epics of Homer, was a significant figure in Roman mythology. Aeneas was revered as the mythical founder of Rome from as early as the third century B.C.E., but it is in Virgil's monumental epic poem, the *Aeneid*, that this tale of national origin receives its most celebrated treatment. Written in the first century B.C.E., the *Aeneid* narrates Aeneas' escape from Troy, his voyage around the Mediterranean to Italy, and his fight with Turnus for the hand in marriage of the princess of the Italian kingdom of Latium. In a visit to the underworld, Aeneas is shown the city he will later found, the future greatness of Rome and the souls of famous Romans of the future who are yet to be born. The poem ends with the defeat of Turnus, but another version of the myth told how Aeneas' son founded Alba Longa. This version made the myth compatible with the myth of Rome's foundation by Romulus, who was descended from the royalty of Alba Longa. Through his *pietas* (devotion to duty) Aeneas was a paradigm of Roman moral values and the emperor Augustus claimed to be descended from him.

AENEAS AND DIDO

BEFORE AENEAS arrives in Italy, he lands at Carthage on the coast of North Africa. The queen of Carthage, called Dido, has fled from her home city of Tyre in Phoenicia after her husband Sychaeus was brutally murdered. Dido has sworn a vow of perpetual fidelity to Sychaeus' ghost, but Aeneas' mother, the goddess Venus, sends Cupid to inspire Dido with passion. Dido falls in love with Aeneas and her thoughts turn to marriage. One day while she and Aeneas are out hunting, they huddle together in a cave while sheltering from a storm and make love there. Their affair blossoms until Mercury, the messenger of the gods, is sent by Jupiter to remind Aeneas that his destiny is to found the Roman race. Aeneas makes secret plans to leave Carthage, but Dido discovers his intentions and confronts him angrily. Aeneas is resolute, and after he departs Dido commits suicide. When Aeneas visits the underworld later in the epic, he sees Dido's ghost reunited with the ghost of her husband. This part of the myth is more than a poignant romance. With her infidelity, seductive passion, and self-destruction, Dido symbolizes Carthage, Rome's greatest enemy, which, under Hannibal (247–183 B.C.E.), almost destroyed Rome.

▼ *Aeneas relates the tales of Troy to Queen Dido.*

VENUS AND CUPID

VENUS, GODDESS of sexual desire, plays a major role in the Roman epic poem, the *Aeneid*. As the mother of Aeneas, on several occasions she intervenes to help her son. Aeneas' father, Anchises, was a mortal man.

Venus is accompanied by Cupid, who is depicted in art as a beautiful winged boy with bows and arrows (much like the modern St Valentine's Day image). Venus is the Roman equivalent of the Greek Aphrodite and also shares similarities with the Sumerian fertility goddess Inanna and the Akkadian fertility goddess Ishtar.

THE ROMAN HERO

THE ROMAN HERO contrasts strongly with the heroes of Greek mythology. The Greek hero was often driven by a quest for personal glory and the desire for individual fame. This led him to behave antisocially, like Achilles sulking in his tent while his fellow Greeks died on the battlefield at Troy. The Roman hero, however, exemplified the ideal Roman citizen, wholly focused on championing the great city and its ideals. In contrast to Achilles and Herakles, Aeneas was a paradigm of *gravitas* (devotion to duty, especially toward the state), *frugalitas* (a rejection of excess and indulgence), and *pietas* (devotion to duty and Roman religion): the three most important Roman values.

TARPEIA'S TREACHERY

DURING THE BATTLE between the Romans and the Sabines following the abduction of the Sabine women, the Romans were betrayed by a young woman, Tarpeia. Tarpeia was the daughter of the Roman commander in charge of the Capitol. One tradition holds that she fell in love with the Sabine king, Titus Tatius, and agreed to let the Sabine army into the Capitoline Hill only if the king promised to marry her. Another version suggests that she was motivated by greed. She let the army gain entry and demanded in return "what the Sabines wear on their left arms," meaning their thick gold bracelets. Once inside, Titus Tatius was not prepared to reward an infidel. They did indeed give Tarpeia "what the Sabines wear on their left arms"—not their bracelets, but their heavy shields, which they threw on top of her and so crushed her to death. The cliff on the Capitoline Hill, the place where Tarpeia was supposed to have allowed the Sabine army into the fortifications, was named after her. The "Tarpeian Rock" became a place of execution from which murderers and traitors were thrown to their deaths.

VIOLENCE

ROMAN MYTH was strikingly patriarchal. The majority of myths feature themes of rape or threatened rape and are concerned with female chastity and virginity. Greek mythology is also largely patriarchal, but myths like that of Demeter and Persephone present a female perspective on male violence and also celebrate women's close relations and power. In Greek myth, when the Centaurs attempt to rape the Lapith women, their behavior is seen as abhorrent and uncivilized and they are driven off by the Greeks. In contrast, when the early Romans rape the Sabine women, they benefit by getting wives and land. The gods and even the women themselves, in time, approve of the violence.

LUCRETIA AND THE NEW REPUBLIC

THE MYTH OF LUCRETIA explains how this virtuous woman brought down the monarchy. She was the wife of

◀ *The arrival of Aeneas at Pallanteum.*

Collatinus and was renowned for her goodness. When the Roman men returned unexpectedly from military service they found most of the women drinking and behaving in an unruly fashion, but Lucretia was spinning wool with her women servants. Sextus Tarquin, son of the last king of Rome, called Tarquin the Proud, desired Lucretia. He went to her house while her husband was away and she received him politely. He then drew his sword and insisted that he make love to her. She absolutely refused, so Sextus had to resort to blackmail. He threatened not only to kill her, but to kill a slave and lie their bodies together to make it look as if they had been caught in adultery. Lucretia had no choice but to give in. Afterwards, she summoned her husband and father and told them what had happened. Despite their exhortations that she was guiltless, she threw herself on her dagger and died. In revenge, Lucretia's family overthrew the Tarquins and from that time on there was no monarchy. A new order was established, the *res publica,* a "public affair." Collatinus was one of its first magistrates.

▼ *The virtuous Lucretia, who threw herself upon a dagger following the attack of Sextus Tarqin.*

HERO AND LEANDER

UNLIKE LUCRETIA, the maiden Hero willingly disobeyed her parents. She was the loveliest maiden in Sestos and, at her parents' insistence, she served the goddess Venus as a priestess who, rather contrarily, was obliged to remain a virgin. One day a festival in honor of the goddess was held at Sestos and among the many worshipers was Leander, a young man whose attractiveness in his hometown of Abydos rivaled that of Heros in Sestos. He fell in love with Hero at first sight and she reciprocated his desire. Their parents would not consent to them marrying, so Hero and Leander were driven to meet in secret. Abydos and Sestos were separated by the River Hellespont, so each night Leander swam across the river, guided by a lamp lit by Hero in her tower, and spent the night with his lover, only to swim back before dawn broke. One night there was a terrible storm and the wind extinguished the candle in Hero's lamp. With no light to guide him and tossed by vicious waves, Leander drowned. When first light came the distraught Hero scanned the shore for Leander and saw his body washed up nearby. Overcome by anguish, she hurled herself from the window and the two lovers were once again joined—in death.

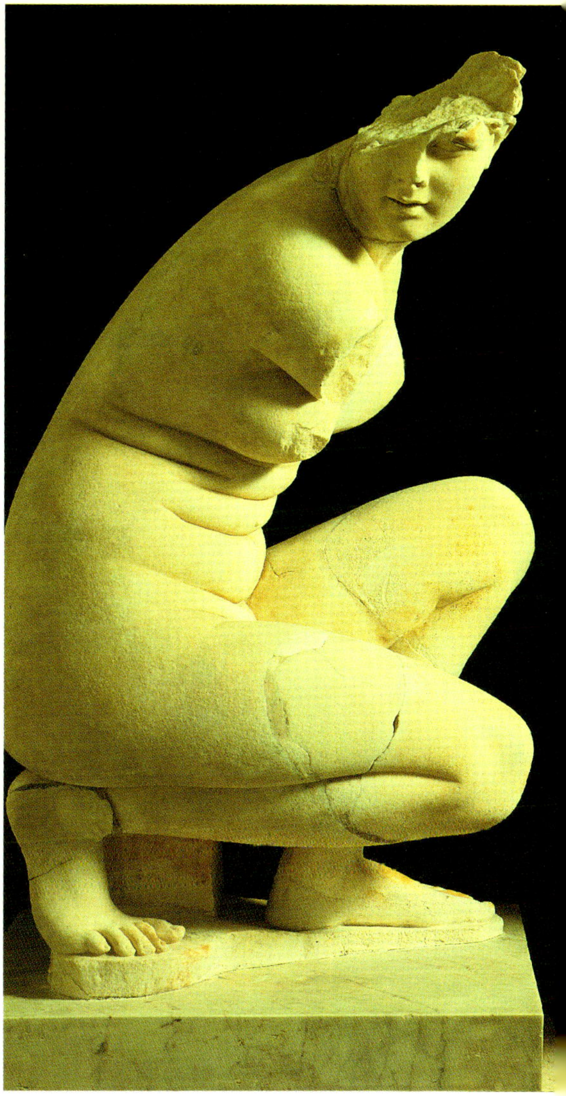

▲ *The voluptuous goddess of desire, Venus.*

METAMORPHOSES

THE *METAMORPHOSES,* vivid tales of "bodies transformed" by the poet Ovid (43 B.C.E.–C.E. 17), refashioned many Greek myths into Latin poetry. It is one of our most important sources of information about Greco-Roman mythology and has been immensely influential on Western literature, most recently having been adapted by one of Britain's late poet laureates, Ted Hughes. Many of the tales in the *Metamorphoses* concern the pursuit of nymphs or women by the gods. For example, the god Apollo blazed with desire for the nymph Daphne, who rejected men and marriage. Apollo pursued her until Daphne's father, a river god, took pity on her and turned her into a laurel tree. Like many such stories, this is an etiological story, designed to explain why the laurel was Apollo's sacred tree ("Daphne" means "laurel"). However, there may be a more politicized point to Ovid's rendering of the myth. The god Apollo was given prominence in Rome by the emperor Augustus, who liked to be associated with him. By making Apollo look ridiculous, grasping a tree trunk rather than a nymph, Ovid may have been poking fun at the emperor. The poem ends with "The Deification of Caesar," but the tone of this tribute to Rome is also hard to read.

ECHO AND NARCISSUS

ONE OF THE TRAGIC TALES of transformation related in Ovid's *Metamorphoses* is that of Echo and Narcissus. Echo was a nymph whose endless chatter distracted the goddess Hera from catching Zeus in the act of adultery. As a punishment, Hera deprived Echo of normal speech, allowing her only to imitate faintly the words of others. Echo fell in love with Narcissus, the son of Cephisus, the river god, and the nymph Leirope. Narcissus was famous for his handsome looks, but he was also conceited and hard-hearted. He did not return Echo's love, and the poor nymph followed him around, endlessly repeating the ends of his phrases, until she had completely pined away in sorrow, leaving only her echoing voice. Some say that Echo cursed Narcissus, others that he spurned many other lovers and so the goddess Artemis decided to punish him. One day he came across a pool of water and caught sight of his reflection on the shimmering surface. Entranced, he fell in love with his own image and, when it failed to return his love, Narcissus pined away and died. As he lay dying, he was transformed into the narcissus flower.

MOSAICS AND WALL PAINTINGS

MANY WONDERFUL images from mythology survive in Roman wall paintings, which were used to decorate the interiors of Roman villas. We have particularly rich evidence from the houses at Pompeii and Herculaneum, cities that were destroyed in C.E. 79 by the eruption of Mount Vesuvius. However, paintings and mosaics can be found in the Roman remains almost everywhere their empire extended. The mosaic below, depicting the serpent-headed Medusa, comes from the floor of a thermal spring at Dar Smala in Tunisia.

▲ *Roman statue known as the "Lizard Killer."*

PRIAPUS, GOD OF THE PHALLUS

PRIAPUS WAS A FERTILITY god whose cult spread through Greece and Italy from the third century B.C.E. His paternity was attributed to various gods, including Zeus and Dionysus. Statues of Priapus were placed in gardens and orchards to ward off thieves. He is often represented as an ugly old man with a red-painted face and huge, erect phallus. The donkey was his special animal, an apt choice, because donkeys were thought to symbolize lust. Priapus features in many comic and obscene poems, and in wall paintings he is depicted weighing his oversized member on a pair of scales.

ORPHEUS AND EURYDICE

ORPHEUS WAS THE SON of Calliope, the muse of poetry and song, and he was famous for being the greatest of all singers. When his wife Eurydice died from a poisonous snakebite,

▼ *This detail of a Roman floor mosaic shows the head of the Gorgon, Medusa. Mosaics such as this have enabled us to gain an insight into ancient Roman mythology.*

▲ *A painting showing Orpheus, mourning on the beach accompanied by his harp.*

Orpheus was heartbroken and went to the underworld in search of her. His enchanting music lulled Cerberus, the three-headed guard dog of Hades, into letting him pass and so captivated Hades and Persephone that they agreed to let him take Eurydice back to the realm of the living under one condition: Orpheus must not look round as he led her into the light. However, as he reached the exit of the underworld, Orpheus was so overwhelmed with desire and fear that he did look back to see Eurydice. Now she was lost to him forever. So grief-stricken was Orpheus that he renounced the company of women completely. This rejection incensed a group of Thracian women who ripped Orpheus apart and scattered his severed limbs over the earth. Even when dismembered and cast into the sea, Orpheus' head remained alive and singing. The gods punished his murderers by turning them into oak trees. Orpheus' lyre metamorphosed into the constellation Lyra and his soul was granted immortality in Elysium.

THE HOUSEHOLD GODS

IN THEIR HOMES, the Romans worshiped three kinds of gods: the Lares, the Penates and the goddess Vesta. The Lares were spirits who protected the household. They were often depicted carrying drinking horns and bowls and were worshiped at small shrines placed at the crossroads between farm boundaries. The Penates were spirits who guarded the household's storehouse (*penus* means "cupboard"), food, and possessions.

The goddess Vesta corresponds to the Greek goddess Hestia. Like her, Vesta watched over the hearth and home. The Romans treated the family as a miniature version of the state. Vesta was worshiped in the city where she was served by six maidens known as Vestal Virgins. They were chosen from noble families at the age of seven and were devoted to the goddess for 30 years, after which, should they wish, they were allowed to marry. If a Vestal was caught having sex, the punishment was severe: she was buried alive. The Vestal Virgins performed public tasks that paralleled the work done by unmarried girls in the home. They cleaned the round temple of Vesta which stood in the Roman Forum and insured that the sacred fire, which was said to have been brought back from Troy by Aeneas, burned eternally.

CUPID AND PSYCHE

PSYCHE WAS a young woman so superhumanly beautiful that her parents boasted she was as lovely as Venus herself. To punish them for their arrogance, Venus sent her son, Cupid, with orders that he should prick Psyche with one of his arrows and make her fall in love with a monster. Cupid, however, pricked himself by mistake and fell deeply in love with Psyche. He married her and gave her a beautiful palace to live in, but she was never allowed to see the god; she promised Cupid that he would always remain invisible to her. Psyche's sisters visited her palace and were so jealous that they goaded her into doubting that it was Cupid who was her husband. To find out, she shone a lamp on Cupid as he slept. He awoke and, in a rage, left Psyche. She wandered in search of her beloved, suffering, until Venus let her prove herself worthy of Cupid. Among Venus' tests was to fetch a jar from Proserpina (the Roman Persephone). Once again, curiosity got the better of Psyche and she opened the jar, releasing the sleep of death on to her. Eventually Cupid appealed to Jupiter and was reunited with Psyche, who became immortal.

The Celts

INTRODUCTION

THE CELTS WERE among the great founding peoples of Europe. Centuries before the time of the Roman empire, Celtic kingdoms occupied much of Europe north of the Alps. In the period of maximum expansion, between the fifth and third centuries B.C.E., their world stretched from Ireland and parts of Spain in the west to central Turkey in the east.

It used to be thought that the Celts invaded Western Europe some time in the second millennium B.C.E. The less dramatic but more likely view is that the peoples who had inhabited the area for thousands of years gradually adopted the characteristics we call Celtic.

The Celts were not a united group with a self-conscious ethnic identity. They did not form an empire. Their world was a mosaic of richly diverse chiefdoms and extended families linked by little more than a common language and culture. Nevertheless, these apparently disorganized peoples dominated Europe for 500 years before they were conquered by the Romans and later driven to the edges of the known world, to Ireland, Wales, Scotland, Cornwall, and Brittany.

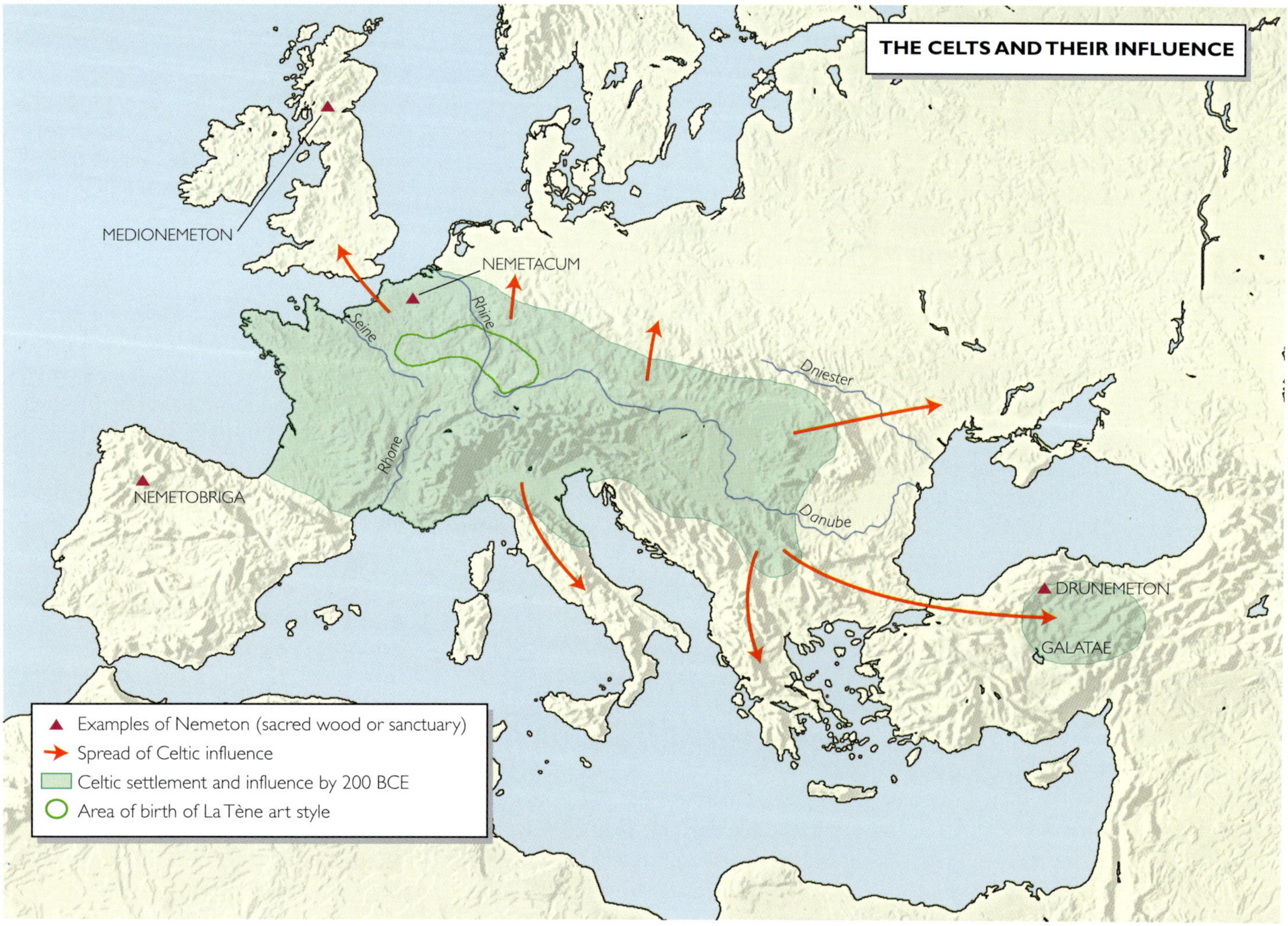

◀ *Heads held spiritual protective power for the Celts.*

▶ *Ornate gold openwork on a Schwazenbrach Celtic decorative bowl.*

THE CELTS IN HISTORY

CELTIC ROOTS LIE in the Hallstatt Culture which extended across Central Europe between the thirteenth and fifth centuries B.C.E. It is named after Hallstatt in Austria, where important discoveries were made of artifacts dating from this period. In the fifth century B.C.E., the Hallstatt princedoms were succeeded by wealthy, Celtic-speaking warrior societies from the north which developed the material culture called "La Tène," the pinnacle of Celtic achievement.

Around 400 B.C.E. Celts began pouring over the Alps to settle in northern Italy. Others swept east along the Danube from where, a century later, they invaded Greece and Asia Minor. The tide turned toward the end of the third century B.C.E., however, when the resistance of the Romans in the south, the Germans in the north, and the Dacians in the east strengthened. Over the next two centuries the Romans conquered Celtic strongholds until, by the first century C.E, only Ireland and parts of Britain remained truly Celtic.

Christianity was adopted by the Celts in Roman times, including those on the Celtic fringe. After Rome fell in the fifth century C.E, the old Celtic lands came under Germanic rule. In Ireland and outlying parts of Britain, however, there was a resurgence of Celtic culture between the sixth and eighth centuries.

SOURCES

THE PAGAN CELTS left no written records. They passed down their laws, traditions, and religious beliefs by word of mouth. Consequently our knowledge of their culture is based on the testimonies of Classical Greek and Roman observers, archaeological remains, and later Irish and Welsh texts.

At first the ancients did not understand the customs of the Celts and later they needed excuses to conquer and "civilize" them. So their portrayal of these people as fearsome, undisciplined barbarians who gloried in war and indulged in disgusting rituals is not reliable. Some of their observations, however, have been confirmed by archaeology.

From artifacts and Romano-Celtic inscriptions, archaeology has also discovered much about Celtic life which is not mentioned by Classical writers. Such discoveries show the Celts to have been an intelligent, complex, and wealthy people whose art and technical brilliance was unsurpassed in prehistoric Europe.

The Irish and Welsh texts were written down much later by monks in a post-Roman, Christian setting and they relate entirely to geographical areas which were peripheral to pre-Roman, Celtic Europe. As such, their use is limited in helping us to form a true picture of the mythology of the pagan Celts. Nonetheless, these texts are of enormous interest in themselves and they provide invaluable insights, particularly into those mythological traditions that were to inspire the great Arthurian romances of medieval Europe.

RELIGIOUS FESTIVALS

THE MAIN CELTIC religious festivals, which feature prominently in the mythology, were held on four days in the year.

The eve of February 1was called Imbolc. It was sacred to the fertility goddess, Brigit, and it marked the coming into milk of the ewes. It was subsequently taken over by the Christians as the feast of St. Brigid.

At Beltaine, which was held on the eve of May 1, people lit bonfires and honored the god Bel. He was a god of life and death, and the festival was seen as a purification or a fresh start. Under Christianity it became the feast of St. John the Baptist.

The third festival was Lughnasa, which the Christians renamed Lammas. It was introduced by the sun god, Lugh, to commemorate his foster mother, Tailtu, and it took place in August.

Samain was celebrated on the evening of October 31 and marked the end of one pastoral year and the beginning of the next. It was the one period when spirits from the Otherworld became visible to men. With the coming of Christianity this celebration became Harvest Festival. It has also come down to us as All Hallows Eve, or Halloween.

FIRE

THE GREAT CELTIC bonfire festivals were an acknowledgment of fire as the earthly counterpart of the sun. Like the sun, fire sustains and destroys life. It also purifies, and growth springs anew from the ashes. After a bonfire the Celts spread the ashes on their fields as fertilizer.

The main fire ceremonies were Samain and Beltaine, which divided the year into summer and winter. They were meant to encourage the sun in its annual cycle and to persuade it to return from its seasonal death. Not surprisingly, therefore, veneration of fire was a particular feature of the cold, northern parts of Europe with their long, dark winters.

In Celtic mythology significant events frequently occur at festival times consistent with the themes of transformation, renewal, death, and rebirth. In the *Book of Invasions* (an Irish text compiled in the twelfth century C.E—see p. 79), the great Battle of Mag Tuiread, between the Tuatha Dé Danann and the Fomorians, happened at Samain. Also at Samain Cúchulainn met his death and Gawain left Arthur's court to seek the Green Knight. Stories associated with Beltaine are nearly always about overcoming the enchantment of the Otherworld. An example is the return of Rhiannon's baby, Pryderi, which had been stolen by a clawed demon.

ANIMAL IMAGERY

ANIMALS WERE revered by the Celts for their strength, speed, fertility, and so on, and both wild and domesticated animals feature symbolically in Celtic mythology. The bull, as seen in the *Táin* (see The Ulster Cycle), is a symbol of power and wealth, while the boar is closely associated with war.

The pagan Celts adorned their metalwork and coins with depictions of animals, often highly stylized and hidden amid complex patterns. In the Romano-Celtic period, images of animals appear alone, as small bronze or clay figurines, or in company with deities. Epona, for example, is nearly always depicted with horses and Nealennia with dolphins.

EPONA

EPONA WAS an important goddess of the Continental Celts, commemorated in more surviving sculpture and inscriptions than any other early goddess. Her name means "Great Mare" and she is usually portrayed on horseback sitting sidesaddle and accompanied by a bird, a dog, and a foal.

Epona was imported to Britain by the Romans and was the only Celtic deity to be cited in the Roman pantheon. She was popular with the Roman cavalry: she was associated with husbandry and fertility, and shrines were made in stables for her worship and favor. In Britain her cult merged with those of Macha and Rhiannon.

▼ *A monolith with Celtic inscriptions.*

GODS OF THE PAGAN CELTS

FROM THE ROMANS we get a simplistic interpretation of Celtic religion which reduces the abundance and variety of Celtic deities to a convenient system modeled on their own. Hence the Celtic god Lugh is equated with Mercury, Brigit with Minerva, and so on.

Fortunately for archaeology the Celts were influenced by the Romans when they were absorbed into the empire. This led to a large scale representation of their gods in durable materials and to the production of religious inscriptions. Many Celtic gods discovered in the form of figurines, reliefs, and sculpture turned out to be quite alien to the Classical system and the inscriptions have provided us with names for a number of them.

The Celts had many gods associated with the most important aspects of life: warfare, hunting, fertility, healing, good harvests, and so on. A few, like Lugh, were worshiped by Celts across Europe. In much greater numbers there were local, tribal, or family deities. Certain gods were associated with particular places such as sacred groves, remote mountains, and lakes. In Gaul, for example, Borvo and Grannos were associated with wells, and in Britain the goddess Sulis gave her name to the healing springs at Aquae Sulis, present-day Bath.

CERNUNNOS

CERNUNNOS WAS A PRINCIPAL god among the pagan Celts. His name means the "Horned One" and he was a lord of nature, animals, agriculture, prosperity, and the underworld. He is portrayed with a man's body and the antlers of a stag; he adopts a characteristic "Buddha" posture, and he wears or holds the sacred torc in one hand and a ram-headed serpent in the other.

Cernunnos is possibly the closest the Celts got to a universal father god. There are traces of him in the literary traditions of Ireland and Wales and he is the model in later Christian iconography for the Devil.

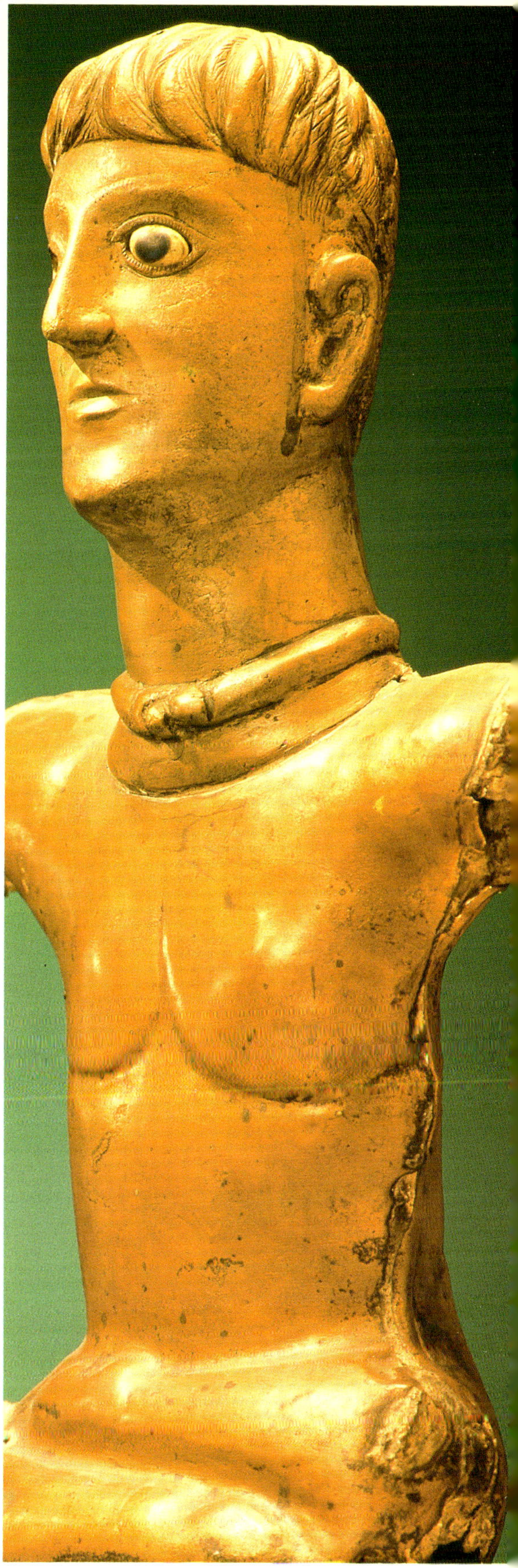

HEROES

THE HEROES Cúchulainn (pronounced "Koo Hoolin") and Finn mac Cool dominate Irish literature. In Britain only the Arthurian legends achieved such popularity. Among the lesser heroes women were as prominent as men, particularly, as the story of Deirdre shows, in the theater of love and war.

There is a pattern to the lives of Celtic heroes which can be seen in the kinds of tale told about them. These include stories of their unusual conception and birth, their afflictions or *geasa*, how they got their names, how they proved themselves, their loves, ordeals, battles, quests, and death. Cúchulainn, for example, had three fathers. His *geis* forbade him to eat dog meat and he earned his name, the "Hound of Culann," by killing a ferocious canine. Lugh had to prove himself by winning at chess before he was admitted to Tara, and Gawain's ordeal was to take part in the beheading game with the Green Knight. In many love stories, such as those of Deirdre and Grainne, the heroine places the hero under a *geis* to elope with her.

This pattern or sequence provided a lengthy cycle of tales connected with a particular hero, or group of heroes, which would keep the storyteller going indefinitely.

THE MYTHOLOGICAL CYCLE

AMONG THE IRISH TEXTS is a collection of prose stories which includes the *Book of Invasions* and the *History of Places*. Both texts were compiled in the twelfth century C.E., but the more interesting *Book of Invasions* has its origins in earlier attempts by monastic scholars of the sixth and seventh centuries to construct a history of Ireland. In effect it is an Irish creation myth which follows a succession of legendary invasions of the country from the Flood to the coming of the Gaels, or Celts.

The most important invasion is that of the Tuatha Dé Danann, the "People of the Goddess Danu," the divine race of Ireland. To establish themselves, they had to expel the Fir Bolg and overcome the demonic Fomorians. Their father god was the Dagda, the "Good God." Other deities included a triad of craft gods called Goibniu, Luchta, and Credne, and King Nuadu who handed over power to Lugh after he lost an arm in battle. Myths involving Lugh are not confined to the *Book of Invasions*. He turns up elsewhere as the father of the hero Cúchulainn.

The Tuatha Dé Danann are said to have retreated underground when the Gaels conquered Ireland.

▲ *Cernunnos, "The Horned One."*

▶ *Sheet bronze Celtic divinity with torque.*

THE COMING OF LUGH

NUADA, THE ONE-HANDED leader of the Tuatha Dé Danann, was holding a great feast at Tara when a young man appeared at the gate. Challenged, the youth identified himself as Lugh, son of Cian of the Tuatha Dé Danann and grandson of their enemy Balor. He had come, he said, to help their incapacitated leader in the imminent battle between the Tuatha Dé Danann and the Fomorians.

No one was allowed into Tara without a skill and Lugh was asked what arts he could offer. He said he was a carpenter, but the gatekeeper was unimpressed. There was already a carpenter in the citadel, he scoffed, by the name of Luchtar. Lugh tried again. This time he said he was a smith. There was already a smith at Tara, came the reply, by the name of Colum Cuaillemech; he was very talented and he had already invented three new techniques.

In successive attempts Lugh told the gatekeeper that he was a champion, a harpist, a warrior, a poet, a historian, a magician, and a metalworker. He said he was even prepared to serve as a cupbearer. But nothing he offered was needed. The Tuatha Dé Danann, he was told, had people who possessed all of these skills.

Eventually Lugh bade the gatekeeper to ask Nuada if there was any one man in his company who possessed all of the skills that he professed. If there was, said Lugh, he would withdraw. So the gatekeeper went to the king and told him that there was a man at the door whose name was Lugh, but it should have been Ildanach, the Master of All Arts, because all of the things that different people could do in the Tuatha Dé Danann, he could do himself.

Intrigued, Nuada suggested a test to see just how good Lugh was. He sent the gatekeeper back with a chessboard and told him to pit the young man against their best player. After winning convincingly, Lugh was brought to the king, who set him a further test. Ogma, the king's principal champion, hurled a heavy flagstone out of the citadel and Lugh was challenged to return it. Effortlessly, Lugh hurled it back inside, where it fell into its original position.

The king was so impressed that he handed over his crown to Lugh, who successfully led the Tuatha Dé Danann in their fight against the Fomorians.

▲ *Cúchulainn is shown here with the Swan Maidens who have come to seek his help.*

▼ *Lugh the sun god passes his first test by beating Nuada's best chess player.*

LIGHT AND ENLIGHTENMENT

THE CELTS BELIEVED that there were divine forces at work in all aspects of nature and they perceived the sun as the most important natural phenomenon. Not only did they see it as the source of life and a promoter of fertility but also as a healing force and a comfort for the dead.

The Irish god Lugh is associated with the sun and the sky. His name means "the shining one" and he is one of the most important of the Celtic gods. He was a master of all the arts and crafts, the "Gaulish Mercury" as Caesar called him, and he brought light in the form of enlightenment with him from the Otherworld.

The coming of Lugh occasioned two very important developments in early Irish mythology. First, he introduced the idea of a single god with many skills and, second, he created a new order of deities who drove out the degenerate primal beings and brought knowledge and order to the land. He became king of the Tuatha Dé Danann, the people of light; he drove out the artless Fomorians and he went on to father the great Ulster hero, Cúchulainn.

Lugh's Welsh equivalent is Lleu, the "Bright One of the Skilful Hand."

FEASTING

RECURRING THEMES in Celtic mythology are the Otherworld feast and the feast where dramatic events occur. Tales regarding Briccriu and Mac Da Thó revolve around disputes over the champion's portion at feasts; Grainne seduces Diarmaid at a feast; Deirdre is born at one; and the beautiful butterfly, Etain, is born again as a human after landing in a glass of mead at a feast. In the story of Branwen, marriage arrangements and a peace treaty are settled over a feast; Fergus is tragically distracted while feasting; and Bres is satirized by the poet Cairbre for failing to provide lavish hospitality.

▲ *This bronze and wood bucket may have been used at banquets for diluting and serving the wine.*

THE WOOING OF ETAIN

ETAIN, THE MOST BEAUTIFUL woman in Ireland, married Midhir, a god of the Otherworld, who lived in the barrow of Bri Leith. Midhir's first wife, Fuamnach, was jealous and she used magic to turn Etain into a pool of water, then into a worm, and then into an exquisite butterfly whose music and perfume suffused the air.

Midhir was happy with Etain's new form, so Fuamnach again resorted to magic. This time she created a wind which blew Etain to a rocky shore where she lay helpless for seven years. At last Midhir's foster son, Oengus, found her. He was able to change her back to her human form at nights and they lived happily together until Fuamnach found out. She conjured up another wind and this time Etain was blown into a cup of mead. The woman holding the cup did not notice the butterfly struggling in her drink and she swallowed Etain.

Etain swam down into the woman's womb and was born again as a human girl one thousand and twelve years after her first incarnation. This time she was Etain, daughter of King Etar of Ulster.

When she was old enough Eochaid Airem, the king of Ireland, married her. Midhir discovered that Etain had been born again and he went to Eochaid to reclaim her. However, Etain would not leave her new husband without his consent, so Midhir challenged Eochaid to a chess tournament. He won, but when he went to claim his prize he found all the doors of Eochaid's palace were barred against him. This did not deter Midhir, who materialized suddenly in the hall and seized Etain. The two then escaped through the smoke hole in the roof as a pair of swans.

Eochaid marched to Bri Leith and laid siege to the barrow for nine years. Eventually Midhir came out and promised to return Etain. Then 50 women appeared, all looking like her. Eochaid examined them all carefully before making his choice and returning home to Tara.

Some years later Midhir revealed to the king that the woman he had selected was not Etain. Etain had been pregnant with Eochaid's child when she and Midhir had fled from him as swans. The woman Eochaid had mistaken for his wife was his own daughter.

By this time Eochaid had fathered a son who became the hero Conaire Mor, so some good came of the wooing of Etain.

THE DAGDA

KNOWN AS THE "GOOD GOD," the "Great Father" and the "Most Learned," the Dagda was the leader of the Tuatha Dé Danann. His attributes include a magic cauldron and a mighty club towed on wheels. The cauldron satisfied all who fed from it, while the club not only killed enemies but also resurrected dead friends. The Dagda is credited with the ability to determine the weather and to control the harvest. He combines elements of a sky father, a storm god, a war god, a fertility deity, and the sun itself, yet he is often portrayed as oafish and even comical.

THE ULSTER CYCLE

THIS IS THE NAME given to a collection of Irish epic prose stories of which the most important is a group called the *Táin* (pronounced "toyn") or the *Cattle Raid of Cooley*. The oldest manuscript, which was compiled in the twelfth century CE, is called the *Book of the Dun Cow*. The story is much older in origin, however, and can be traced to the eighth century and possibly earlier.

The *Táin* is not a tale of mundane cattle rustling; it is about supernatural beasts around whom a battle myth is woven. The fighting over the Brown Bull, the Donn, and the White Bull, Finnbennach, symbolizes the prolonged and fruitless struggle between Ulster and Connacht, the two most northerly of the five ancient provinces of Ireland. Traditional rivalry between the provinces is suggested by the fact that the bulls have already pursued their ferocious conflicts in various guises.

Compiled in a Christian setting, the story must have undergone some reinterpretation. Nevertheless, a considerable mythological content remains: the superhuman warrior Cúchulainn champions the Ulster cause; Connacht is ruled by the queen-goddess Medb (pronounced "Maeve"); and the destiny of the two kingdoms is in the hands of the death and destruction goddess, the Morrigan.

THE MORRIGAN

THE MORRIGAN was the supreme Celtic goddess of war. She stalked battlefields filling warriors with fury and picking over the corpses of the fallen. She had the power of prophecy and she was a shape-shifter, assuming the form of a crow or a raven.

The Morrigan was a three-fold deity and she features in the Irish legends either as herself or in the guise of one of her subsidiaries: Badb, Macha and Nemain. She combines death and destruction with an intense sexual potency and she is thought to have been the model for Morgan Le Fay in the Arthurian legends.

◀ *Cúchulainn is led by the shining wheel toward the Shadow Land.*

▼ *Queen Medb of Connacht on her throne.*

THE BROWN BULL OF ULSTER

QUEEN MEDB of Connacht and her consort, Ailill, lay chatting in bed one night, boasting of their possessions. They were evenly matched except for Finnbennach, the great, white-horned bull owned by Ailill.

Medb searched her lands in vain for a comparable beast until she heard of the Donn, the magnificent Brown Bull of Ulster which was owned by Daire mac Fiachniu. Daire might have been willing to lend Medb the Donn for a year if he had been made a generous offer, but he overheard the queen's drunken envoys bragging that they would take the animal with or without his consent. So he refused to cooperate and sent the bull into hiding.

On hearing the news, Medb was livid and she bullied Ailill into invading Ulster to steal the Brown Bull. They amassed a huge force including a well disciplined contingent from Leinster. Jealous of their performance, the evil Medb contemplated sending them home, or even killing them. However, wise counsel prevailed, and she was talked into dispersing them throughout the rest of her army to spread their good influence.

A bitter struggle ensued between the forces of Connacht and King Conchobar of Ulster, often pitting relations and old friends against each other. For much of the time the great warrior Cúchulainn fought the Connacht army single-handed because he was the only Ulster hero unaffected by a curse of weakness which descended periodically on the men of the land. Medb failed to defeat him with bribes and tricks, and he killed large numbers of her men, many sent against him in single combat and others attacking as a hundred at a time. Eventually the men of Ulster regained their strength and, rallying in support of Cúchulainn, they routed Medb's army.

In the meantime, Medb's scouts had found the Donn and they had driven it back to Connacht along with 50 heifers which followed it from Daire's herd. When the Brown Bull came into contact with Ailill's white-horned animal, there was instant hatred between them. The great beasts lowered their horns and fought a tremendous battle, rampaging over the whole of Ireland. At last the Brown Bull was seen galloping back victorious to Ulster, scattering Finnbennach's entrails across the plain. But the Donn was exhausted and mortally wounded, and it died soon after.

Thus, in the space of a month, thousands died over a greedy whim and neither side won the great bull.

▲ *Queen Medb seeks the advice of a druid regarding the hero, Cúchulainn.*

DECAPITATION

THE CELTS BELIEVED that the soul resides in the head. They decapitated their war victims as an act of triumph and kept the heads as trophies or offered them up to the gods in temples.

Decapitation is a prominent feature in Celtic myths, where it is common for heads to remain alive separated from their bodies. In the *Mabinogion* the head of Brân the Blessed is cut off and brings good fortune to his companions. In the Irish story of Finn mac Cool's fool, Lomna, his head is removed and impaled on a stake, still able to speak. The head of the Ulster hero Conall Cernach is enormous and, used as a vessel for drinking milk, could revive the debilitated men of Ulster.

Another common aspect of the cult of the head in myth is the "beheading game" found in the Ulster Cycle in Briccriu's Feast and in the story of Gawain and the Green Knight. The emphasis in these tales is on the courage or cowardice shown by the characters involved, and the issue of honor. In putting their heads on the block, Cúchulainn and Gawain are prepared to risk everything to prove their valor and integrity.

▼*Cúchulainn sets out on his journey to Emain Macha.*

BRICCRIU'S FEAST

BRICCRIU OF THE POISONED Tongue built a wonderful hall at Emain Macha to impress his guests, and he invited all the men of Ulster and Connacht, traditional rivals, to a great feast at the hall. No one wanted to go. They knew Briccriu of old and his love of mischief. But he threatened such retribution if they refused him that they had no choice.

Now it was the privilege of the most noble warrior present to take the choicest joint of meat at a feast. Briccriu was quick to use this heroic etiquette as an opportunity to cause trouble. He went in turn to the three main contenders, Loegaire Buadach, Conall Cernach, and Cúchulainn, and persuaded each of them to claim the "champion's portion." To be sure of a fight he also set their wives against each other.

As Briccriu had planned, there was a brawl which was stopped only by the wisdom of Sencha mac Ailella, who suggested that the three heroes should take the issue to Connacht, to Queen Medb, to decide. After a fearsome ordeal, Medb gave the honor to Cúchulainn but, on their return to Emain Macha, Loegaire and Conall claimed that the queen had been bribed and they refused to accept the verdict.

So the three went to Munster to seek the judgment of the great warrior king, Cú Roí mac Dairi. Following further trials of valor, he also chose Cúchulainn, but again there was a refusal on the part of the other two to accept defeat.

The matter was unresolved until, one night when all the men of Ulster were assembled at Emain, an oafish giant entered the hall. In turn he challenged Loegaire, Conall and Cúchulainn to cut off his head on the understanding that he would return the following night to remove theirs. All

three agreed and Loegaire took the first turn, decapitating the churl, who left carrying his head under his arm. Next evening the giant, with his head restored, returned for his revenge, but the cowardly Loeghaire reneged and refused to submit.

The same thing happened in Conall's case. Only Cúchulainn, when it was his turn, was prepared to pay the price. He knelt and waited for the blow. But it did not come. The giant turned out to be Cú Roí mac Dairi himself, come to confirm his previous judgment. He spared Cúchulainn the ordeal and the hero was declared undisputed champion of all Ireland.

GIANTS

GIANTS OCCUR in Celtic mythology in several forms. Heroes such as the Irish Finn mac Cool or the Welsh Brân are so great that they are pictured as giants. Some giants are instrumental in the deeds of heroes, such as Wrnach, whose sword was one of the items Culhwch had to steal for the hand of Olwen. Others issue challenges, like Cú Roí mac Dairi at Briccriu's Feast. The remainder are either foolish and gentle, or they exist for weaker men to vanquish.

Giantesses also feature in Celtic mythology: Bébinn in the Fenian Cycle, for example, and Cymidei Cymeinfoll in the story of Branwen.

THE FENIAN CYCLE

THE EARLIEST MANUSCRIPT fragments of the Irish Fenian Cycle date from the eighth century C.E., although the tales are thought to derive stylistically from the third century C.E. The first complete synthesis of its eight major parts did not appear until the twelfth century CE, however. The cycle comprises a very large body of verse and prose romances from which, it has been argued, the themes of the Arthurian sagas are derived.

The supernatural hero of this cycle is the poet and seer Finn mac Cool, a late development of the earlier god, Lugh. He is the leader of an elite and highly disciplined band of Irish warriors, the Fianna, who are pledged to defend the king and who are chosen for their strength and courage.

Finn's divine status is confirmed by many features of his life. He is brought up by a druidess and he marries an enchanted woman transformed into a deer. He acquires wisdom from contact with the Salmon of Knowledge, he has the gift of prophecy, he uses magic, and he is a superhuman warrior.

These stories are sometimes referred to as the Ossianic Cycle after Finn's principal son, the great poet and warrior Oisin (pronounced "Usheen"), who features prominently in the later tales.

◀ *Surviving stone carvings give an insight into the characters and protagonists of Celtic mythology.*

▼ *A fifteenth-century manuscript showing the crowning of King Arthur.*

THE SALMON OF KNOWLEDGE

FINNECES THE BARD had been fishing at Linn Feic, on the River Boyne, for seven years in the hope of catching Fintan, the fabled Salmon of Knowledge. It had been prophesied that whoever tasted the salmon would be blessed with boundless knowledge and that person would be called Finn. Finneces was not worried, therefore when one day a lad called Demna asked to become his pupil.

Shortly, to Finneces' great joy, they caught Fintan. It was the most beautiful fish he had ever seen and he gave it to Demna to cook. He told the boy that on no account was he to eat any of it; after all this time, he did not want to be beaten to the post.

What Finneces did not know was that Demna was the nickname of the young Finn mac Cool. As Finn was cooking the salmon he burned his thumb on its skin and sucked it to relieve the pain. He tasted the salmon, therefore, and its knowledge rightfully became his.

When all this was revealed to Finneces he said grumpily that Finn might as well eat the whole fish. He did, and thereafter he was able to see into the future.

DEIRDRE OF THE SORROWS

BEFORE DEIRDRE WAS BORN it was prophesied by the druid Cathbad that she would be very beautiful and she would be the cause of much suffering in Ulster. As a result, at her birth there were some who wanted to kill her, but King Conchobar thought he could change Deirdre's fate by bringing her up himself and marrying her when she came of age.

Deirdre was raised in a secluded hunting lodge by Leborcham, Conchobar's nurse, until she became the beautiful young woman that Cathbad had predicted and she was nearly ready to marry the king. One day, however, she saw a raven drinking blood spilled in the snow after a calf had been slaughtered and she asked Leborcham if all husbands were wrinkled and gray like Conchobar or if there were any with lips as red as blood, skin as white as snow and raven-black hair. Forgetful of the prophecy, Leborcham let slip that Naoise, son of Uisnech, had these qualities and Deirdre immediately resolved to meet him.

She contrived a meeting and the two fell in love at once. Naoise knew that Deirdre was betrothed to the king, however, and he was reluctant to take it any farther. But Deirdre threatened to compromise him and so, to preserve his honor, he enlisted the help of his brothers, Ardan and Ainnle, and the lovers eloped to Scotland.

Conchobar was furious and pursued them with an army. There was bitter fighting, but after a while Conchobar was persuaded to call a truce. He sent three warriors, Fergus mac Roich, Dubthach Doeltenga, and Cormac, to invite the fugitives to come home and to guarantee their safety. But as soon as they had returned to Ulster, Conchobar broke his word and got Eogan mac Durthacht to murder all three sons of Uisnech.

Fergus and his men were enraged at this treachery. They attacked Conchobar and killed 300 of his men before deserting to Connacht, Ulster's traditional enemy.

So Cathbad's prophecy was fulfilled and Deirdre was inconsolable. She was married to Conchobar, but they were not happy. After a year, Conchobar asked her what were the two things she disliked most. Deirdre said she hated him most of all and, after him, Eogan mac Durthacht. So the king decided that, having spent a year with him, she should spend the next with Eogan. On her way to Eogan's court, Deirdre flung herself from the carriage and died.

◀ *Deirdre holds the severed head of her lover, Naoise, killed by the jealous king Conchobar.*

DIVINE LOVERS

LOVE IS A CENTRAL THEME in many Celtic myths. It may be between two supernatural characters or a god and a human being. Often it involves three people: a handsome youth, a beautiful girl or woman, and an unsuccessful suitor or a husband who may be much older. The Irish stories of Diarmaid and Grainne, and Deirdre and Naoise, are typical of such love triangles and they show that the result is often tragic. The Welsh story of Pwll and Rhiannon is comparable to the Irish tales. In this story, trickery against Gwawl,

▲ *Finn Mac Cool as a young man, shown here with the Princess Tasha.*

Rhiannon's rejected suitor, causes the enchantment of Dyfed, in which everyone except the subjects of the story disappears.

Irish mythology also contains the notion of sacral kingship and sovereignty where the union of the king and the goddess of love and fertility insures prosperity in the land. Often the goddess appears as a hag but, when the king has performed his duty, she becomes young and beautiful.

The image of divine love and marriage is often found in the archaeological evidence for pagan Celtic religion. Divine couples were venerated in inscriptions and in sculpture where they were seen as symbolic of harmony, health, wealth, protection, or abundance.

THE PURSUIT OF DIARMAID AND GRAINNE

FINN MAC COOL, leader of the Fianna, was growing old, but he decided to get married again. After careful deliberation he chose Grainne, the daughter of Cormac mac Airt, the high king at Tara. Grainne could not love an old man and at the wedding feast she took an interest in a handsome warrior called Diarmaid. She sent for a sleeping potion and, when all of the wedding guests except Diarmaid were asleep, Grainne begged him to take her away.

Diarmaid was loyal to Finn and he refused at first. But Grainne called his manhood into question and he weakened. They took some horses and a chariot from the stable and left while everyone was still sleeping.

When Finn woke and realized what had happened he was very angry. He had lost his new bride to one of his most trusted lieutenants. He ordered the Fianna to hunt them down ruthlessly with hounds and not give them a moment's rest until they were captured.

Diarmaid and Grainne fled in terror, their pursuers hot on their heels. So unrelenting was the chase, they hardly had time to eat or sleep. The only way they managed any rest was through the magic of Angus, Diarmaid's foster father, who lent them his cloak of invisibility. For 16 years they traveled all over Ireland, sleeping rough, eating what they could hunt or gather, and having many adventures with a host of natural and supernatural forces.

Eventually Angus and Grainne's father got together and begged forgiveness for the couple. Finn agreed to stop the hunt if Diarmaid promised not to flaunt Grainne. A feast of reconciliation was held at Tara and the high king returned Diarmaid's lands to him.

For some years Diarmaid and Grainne were happy. But Finn never stopped hating Diarmaid, and one day he contrived to involve him in a hunt for the Boar of Boann Ghulban. It was prophesied that Diarmaid would meet his death in confrontation with this beast which was, in fact, his enchanted half brother.

As predicted, Diarmaid was mortally wounded and his only chance of survival lay in Finn's magic powers. Finn could revive dying warriors with water carried in his cupped hands. He went through the motions for Diarmaid, but twice on his way back from the spring he managed to spill the water. The third time he succeeded, but it was too late—Diarmaid was dead.

▼ *The raven of ill-omen comes to Cúchulainn.*

ANIMALS

VARIOUS CREATURES, both wild and domestic, appear in Celtic mythology. Oisin and Lanval are transported to the Otherworld on magnificent white horses; Ulster and Connacht are represented as battling bulls; Culhwch is associated with pigs; Etain becomes a beautiful butterfly; Finn receives knowledge from a salmon; Deirdre's sorrows begin with the sight of a raven drinking the blood of a slaughtered calf; St. Patrick assumes the shape of a deer; and Pwll strays into the Otherworld while hunting stag.

Animals played a very important part in the life of the Celts and this is reflected in their storytelling. Horses, for example, were prestigious animals, revered for their beauty, speed, bravery, and sexual vigor. As such they became a symbol of the aristocratic warrior elite. What better animal to carry a hero to the Otherworld? Cattle provided the Celts with most of their everyday needs: meat, dairy products, leather, bone, and horn for implements. Oxen were essential draft animals, while bulls reflected the owner's power and wealth.

Hunting was a sporting and also a prestige activity, and there was a spiritual bond between the hunter and the hunted. Similarly animals such as the boar, the meat of feasts, were treated with respect. The sacrifice of animal life stirred the Otherworld.

▼ *St. Patrick, who converted Oisin to Christianity.*

OISIN IN THE LAND OF FOREVER YOUNG

OISIN, THE SON of Finn mac Cool, was out hunting one day with his father and their elite band of warriors, the Fianna. They were joined by a beautiful, fairylike woman on a white horse. Her name was Naim of the Golden Hair and she had come, she said, to take Oisin home with her to Tir na nOg, the Land of Forever Young.

Naim told them that she had loved Oisin since she and her father had ridden through Ireland some years before. She had watched him then, running like a young deer through the meadows, looking every inch a huntsman and a warrior. For seven years and seven days she had returned, invisible, to watch him grow up and, at last, her father had given her permission to declare her love.

She cast a spell over Oisin so that he loved her too, and they rode away on Naim's white steed across lakes, rivers, and the misty sea to Tir na nOg. There they married and lived happily for 300 years, a period that seemed like only three weeks to Oisin.

Eventually Oisin became homesick. He longed to see his father and his friends again. Naim did all she could to dissuade him from returning to Ireland. She could not change his mind, however, so she gave him her white horse to make the journey and she warned him not to dismount or he would never return.

When Oisin got back to Ireland he found that everything was different. The countryside had changed, his father and the Fianna were long dead and a new faith was being practiced. Deeply saddened, Oisin turned and began his journey back to his fairy wife. He had not gone far, however, when a group of peasants struggling to lift a heavy stone into a wagon asked him for help. He agreed

willingly but, as he stooped, his reins broke and Oisin fell to the ground. Immediately, the horse vanished and Oisin was transformed dramatically into a very old man, blind and near to death.

He was carried to St. Patrick, who was walking the land and preaching of the new god. The saint received him into the new faith. He also managed to take down some of Oisin's stories of the old days when the Fianna ruled the land. But soon the warrior poet, and the world he had known, passed away forever.

EARLY WELSH MYTHS

THE MASTERWORK of medieval Welsh literature is the *Mabinogion,* made up of the Four Branches, or tales, of the Mabinogi and various other stories, numbering 12 in all.

The earliest surviving manuscripts of the *Mabinogion* are the *White Book of Rhydderch* and the *Red Book of Hergest* which date from the fourteenth century. The stories must be much older than this, however, because they contain so many ancient Celtic elements, such as godike heroes, enchanted animals, the love of feasting, and the Otherworld. By the time they came to be written down they were overlaid with elements of chivalry, knights on quests and ladies in distress, which are all products of later, Continental influence.

The Four Branches, three of which concern the hero Pryderi, are the stories of Pwll, Branwen, Manawydan, and Math. The remaining stories fall into two groups: "Four Independent Native Tales" and "Three Romances." The story of Taliesin is included in later compilations.

Among the "Native Tales," the collection boasts the earliest surviving Arthurian tale in Welsh, *Culhwch and Olwen,* which shows forms of eleventh-century style, vocabulary, and custom. In this story, Arthur appears as something between a crude, Celtic chieftain and a courtly king.

THE FAMILY

CELTIC TRIBES, or *tuath*, were ruled by kings through general assemblies of the people. Celtic communities were rigidly hierarchical and divided into four main groups: nobles, warriors, farmers, and the intelligentsia. The latter might be holy men (druids), poets (bards), or skilled craftsmen such as metalworkers. Kinship was important and Celts lived, worked, and fought in extended families which could embrace hundreds if not thousands of "relatives." It is understandable, therefore, that heroes such as Culhwch or Peredur might not recognize an "aunt" or a "cousin" on their travels.

The Welsh tales in the Four Branches of the Mabinogi revolve around two great, divine families: the houses of Don and Llyr. Don, a mother goddess cognate with the Gaelic Ana, is married to Beli Mawr, "Bile" to the Irish. Their descendants are the children of light, or the sky, comparable to the Tuatha Dé Danann in Irish mythology.

By contrast, the descendants of the sea god, Llyr (the Gaelic Lir), are more like the Fomorians and they are seen as a remnant of an earlier, less enlightened age. Brân the Blessed and Branwen are children of Llyr.

The two families are often portrayed in conflict but, as with their Irish equivalents, they are allied by intermarriage.

◀ *The Gundestrup Cauldron, one of the most famous and most beautiful of the survivng cauldrons.*

BRANWEN, DAUGHTER OF LLYR

Branwen was the sister of Brân the Blessed of Wales. To insure peace between Wales and Ireland she was betrothed to the Irish king Matholwch. Her other brother Efnisien objected to the match, however, and he insulted Matholwch when he traveled to Harlech for the wedding by mutilating his horses so badly that they had to be destroyed.

Brân appeased his guests with apologies and gifts, the most precious being a magic cauldron of Irish origin which could restore dead warriors to life, lacking only the power of speech.

Branwen was taken to Ireland as Matholwch's queen and they lived happily together for awhile. But the king's resentment smoldered, fueled by his counselors, and he began to take it out on his wife. He relegated her to the kitchens, where she was subject to daily bullying by the servants, and he took measures to insure that Brân would not find out. However, Branwen trained a starling to carry a message to her brother, who responded by invading Ireland.

Brân was a giant and he waded across the Irish Sea, leading his fleet and carrying his harpists and lute players on his back. The Irish retreated beyond the river Shannon and destroyed the crossing. But Brân was so huge that he was able to form a bridge for his army to cross over.

To pacify Brân, Matholwch told him that he was giving up the crown in favor of the son Branwen had given him. But, at the investiture, Efnisien felt slighted and threw the boy into the fire. Fighting resumed and, using the magic cauldron, the Irish were gaining the upper hand. However, Efnisien destroyed the cauldron and himself in the process, and the Welsh won with only seven men left.

Brân himself was mortally wounded by a magic dart and he decreed that his head should be cut off and borne to the White Mount in London, where it was to be buried facing east to deter invaders. On the way the party rested at Harlech for seven years. They visited the Otherworld of Gwales and they spent eight years in Pembroke. All the while the head remained alive and did not decay; indeed, it was a most congenial companion.

Eventually the head was buried in accordance with Brân's instructions. As for Branwen, she died of a broken heart in Wales lamenting that, because of her, two great countries were in ruins.

▼ *Detail from the magnificent Gundestrup Cauldron.*

FABULOUS CAULDRONS

MAGIC CAULDRONS feature repeatedly in both Irish and Welsh mythology. Some, like the Dagda's, never empty, except for cowards; some, like Brân's, revive the dead; while others contain *greals* or brews of wisdom. Ultimately the miraculous cauldron becomes the Holy Grail, which promises immortality to those who have earned it.

Surviving cauldrons from the pagan Celtic period are made of bronze, copper, or silver and they are richly decorated. The best example is the Gundestrop Cauldron from the first century B.C.E. displaying what is thought to be the embossed figure of the god Cernunnos holding a torc and a serpent.

THE OTHERWORLD

BEFORE THEY BECAME Christian, the Celts had no conception of heaven or hell as a reward or punishment for their earthly lives. They thought that rebirth into the afterlife was automatic. So firm was their belief in the afterlife that they would put off paying debts until they met there! This accounts for the heroic way they threw themselves into battle, with no apparent fear of death.

The Otherworld of Celtic myth is an invisible realm of gods, spirits, fairies, and giants, and it takes many forms. Sometimes it is a heaven which entices dreamers such as Oisin, and sometimes it is purgatory. When they were driven underground, the Tuatha Dé Danann lived in comfortable "*sidhe*" which were, in reality, prehistoric burial chambers. The Fomorians before them, however, were doomed to dwell damply beneath lakes and seas.

The divide between the visible and invisible worlds is not clearly defined in Celtic myth. Seers inhabit both realms while heroes, such as Cúchulainn and Finn mac Cool, are frequent Otherworld visitors. Pwll wandered into the Otherworld while hunting and offended Arawn, a winter deity. He had to pay for this mistake by swapping places with him for a year and fighting the annual battle with Hafgan, the spirit of summer.

▲ *The Broighter ship, possibly a votive offering to the king of the Ocean Manannan mac Lir.*

LORD OF THE OTHERWORLD

WHILE HUNTING one day, Pwll, the prince of Dyfed, insulted Arawn, king of the Otherworld, by driving his hounds from a stag they had caught. To make amends he agreed to a proposition.

There was a neighboring king called Hafgan who was always threatening Arawn's kingdom. Pwll was asked to take on Arawn's appearance and spend a year in the Otherworld in his place. At the end of this time he was to kill Hafgan.

Pwyll was willing, but he was concerned about what would happen to his own lands in his absence. Arawn had thought of that; he would assume Pwll's appearance and take his place in Dyfed. This satisfied Pwll and the two exchanged shapes. Before they parted, however, Arawn warned Pwll that if Hafgan was struck a second time after receiving a mortal blow, he would revive.

Pwll behaved honorably and, although Arawn's wife believed him to be her husband, he did not lie with her once. At the end of a year he killed Hafgan with a single blow and returned home to find his kingdom had been in good hands. When he told his people what had happened they gave him the title Lord of the Otherworld.

OTHERWORLD VOYAGES

THE "*IMRAM*," or voyage, is a class of Old and Middle Irish narrative in which travelers explore an Otherworld, usually an archipelago of wondrous islands in the western ocean. Typical is the seventh- or eighth-century *Imram Brain*, the *Voyage of Bran, Son of Febal.* Brân's Otherworld goal is the Land of Women where there is no grieving, winter, or want. After many adventures he returns home to find that a considerable time has passed in his absence. His family and friends are long dead, and his voyage is remembered as an ancient story. Other notable voyages were made by Maíle Dúin and St. Brendan.

◀ *Religious illustration depicting St. Patrick.*

Many myths surrounding the saints involve a Celtic sympathy with animals and even the suggestion of shape-shifting. St. Patrick, again, was said to be able to take the form of a deer to avoid his enemies. St. Ciaran of Clonmacnoise trained a fox to carry his copy of the psalms, St. Kevin of Glendalough had his psalter returned by an otter when he dropped it in a lake, and St. Columba of Iona subdued the Loch Ness monster.

THE CRY OF THE DEER

ST. PATRICK AND HIS NOVICE, Benen, were traveling to Tara to try to convert Loegaire mac Neill, the high king of Ireland, and his followers to the new faith. It was Easter and, as they drew near to the citadel, Patrick stopped to light a bonfire in celebration.

That same night Loegaire was also preparing a bonfire. To him the festival was Beltaine when, for hundreds of years, his people had lit fires to celebrate the rebirth of spring. No sooner had his fire started to blaze, however, than he saw Patrick's glowing on the horizon. He was angry at this competition and he called his druids for their advice. They prophesied that Patrick's flame would burn forever,

SAGES AND SEERS

THE MOST FAMOUS SAGE in Celtic mythology is Merlin, Arthur's mentor. There were many others, however, including Amairgin, Cathbad, Mug Ruith, and Taliesin. They were in contact with the Otherworld and they commanded tremendous respect.

Many were druids, a name derived from the Celtic word for the oak, a sacred tree. It was forbidden for their secrets to be written down. Their knowledge was passed from one generation to the next in verse which had to be memorized. Consequently, laws, histories, traditions, and magic formulae, which could take a novice up to 20 years to learn, died with them.

CELTIC SAINTS

CHRISTIANITY may have preserved Celtic mythology, albeit in a sanitized form, but it also incorporated mythological themes into its own traditions. In particular it adapted stories of Celtic warriors and heroes as wondrous events in the lives of the saints. Saints could not excel in battle, of course, but they could perform miracles to help preach the word.

The greatest number of miracles are attributed to St. Patrick. Many of these arise from his struggle against the the druids, who had most to lose by the spread of a new faith. At the court of King Loegaire at Tara, Patrick had to destroy two druids, Lochru and Lucetmail, by miraculous means in order to convince the king and his entire court to convert to Christianity.

▼*A fifteenth-century illustration of King Arthur and his knights.*

▲ *Knights surrounding the Round Table, in the center of which sits the Holy Grail.*

and it would overwhelm his own. This angered Loegaire even more and he vowed to prevent this happening.

The king took this as a challenge and he led an army forward from Tara to confront the saint. As he approached he saw Patrick raise his arms in prayer; he then watched as a mist descended and obscured the view. When the air cleared, there was no sign of Patrick or his companion. However, as Loegaire turned to leave, a deer and a fawn were seen walking in the direction of Tara.

CELTIC ILLUMINATION

CHRISTIANITY HELPED to preserve Celtic mythology by adapting the legends as miraculous events in the lives of Celtic saints. Some of the exploits of St. Patrick, for example, echo those of Cúchulainn. Symbolic imagery, involving animals and plants, was also adapted, as in the character of St. Columba, whose name means "dove." This imagery, expressed in the traditional, highly decorative style developed by the pagan Celts, resulted in the magnificent illuminated manuscripts produced for Christian missionary work in the seventh and eighth centuries C.E. The most famous are the *Book of Durrow*, the *Lindisfarne Gospels* and the *Book of Kells*.

ARTHUR

ARTHUR RECURS in Welsh, Irish, and other Celtic mythologies. He was probably a warrior living in Britain in the late fifth century, famed for resisting the Saxons. By the Middle Ages, however, he and his knights were firmly embedded in myth, sharing many of the attributes of Finn mac Cool and the Fianna.

Early references to Arthur appear in a Welsh poem by Aneirin (sixth century C.E.), the writings of the British monk Gildas (sixth century C.E.), and in those of the Celtic historian Nennius (eighth century C.E.). A tenth-century Latin history of Wales lists his victories and his defeat at the battle of Camlan.

ARTHURIAN ROMANCES

THE ORIGINS of these are obscure. *Culhwch and Olwen* is the earliest, fully-fledged Arthurian tale in a Celtic language and the tenth century Welsh poem, 'The Spoils of Annwn," is a prototype for the Grail quest. Arthurian tales became popular in Irish literature because of the similarities with Finn mac Cool and the Fianna, but the Irish Arthur is a rapacious invader.

It was Geoffrey of Monmouth who began the popular myth of King Arthur. His twelfth-century *History of the Kings of Britain* inspired the Norman poet Wace, whose version provided a more courtly setting and introduced the Round Table. Later in the twelfth century the story was expanded by the French poet, Chrétien de Troyes, who introduced novel elements from Continental sources. He added the idea of courtly love and provided the earliest version of the Grail legend.

There followed an English version by Layamon, mixing in some Celtic folk traditions, and in the thirteenth century there was a German contribution. The fourteenth century saw the writing of the greatest single Arthurian legend in Middle English, *Sir Gawain and the Green Knight,* and in the fifteenth century Sir Thomas Malory gave the saga its final shape in *Le Morte d'Arthur*.

SHAPE-SHIFTERS

THE ABILITY TO CHANGE shape, or to transform into another object or creature, is common in Celtic mythology. The Morrigan, the terrifying Irish goddess of war, appears as a crow feeding off the bodies of fallen warriors. Arawn, king of the Welsh Otherworld, exchanges forms with Pwll, and Sadb, the enchanted mother of Oisin, takes on the form of a doe.

Merlin, of course, can also change his shape as well as that of others. He facilitates the union between Arthur's father, Uther, and Igraine, the wife of Gorlois, the Duke of Cornwall, by casting a spell to make Uther appear temporarily as Gorlois.

▲ *Bronze figure of a boar, possibly used as a votive offering. The boar is very widely depicted in Celtic art.*

WATER

THE CELTS PERCEIVED water as both a creator and a destroyer of life and these contrasting images are reflected in the differing tales told of Merlin's demise.

In *Le Morte d'Arthur,* by Sir Thomas Malory, Merlin is seduced by the scheming temptress Nimue. She is the daughter of a British sea deity, Dylan, and she is sometimes identified with the Lady of the Lake. Nimue tricks Merlin into revealing the secrets of his magic and, when she has learned all she can from him, she uses her knowledge to trap him forever in a cave. This is an example of the Celtic distrust of fairies and the dangers of associating too closely with them.

In the Breton version, Vivien's association with water is witnessed by the presence of a fountain where she and Merlin meet in the forest of Broceliande. They fall in love and the magician is wistfully complicit in his withdrawal from the world. It ends positively, with the lovers dwelling happily ever after in their Joyous Garden.

Nimue and Vivien are, of course, the same character and their contrasting natures reflect the different faces of water as represented by different storytelling traditions. The later, Breton version fits the more romantic mood of its time.

CULHWCH AND OLWEN

CULHWCH RECEIVED HIS NAME from the pig run in which he was born. As a young man he angered his stepmother, who swore that he would never know the touch of a woman until he won the hand of Olwen, the beautiful daughter of the giant Ysbaddaden.

Culhwch went to the court of Arthur, his cousin, to ask for help. There, a group of extraordinary characters was

◀ *This fourteenth-century poem, written in French, describes King Arthur's flight from the Emperor Lucius.*

assembled to accompany him in his search for Ysbaddaden's castle. In their travels they encountered the giant's herdsman whose wife turned out to be Culhwch's aunt. When she heard of his quest, she was reluctant to help, having lost 23 of her 24 sons to the giant. Nevertheless, she arranged a meeting between Culhwch and Olwen.

Olwen was more beautiful than Culhwch could have imagined and he swore his undying love for her. Olwen was equally smitten, but she would not leave her father without his consent because it was destined that he would die on her wedding day. Culhwch would have to go to Ysbaddaden, she said, and ask him what he would accept in exchange for her hand.

Culhwch and his companions fought their way into the castle where Ysbaddaden kept them waiting for three days for his reply. Eventually he relented and gave Culhwch a daunting list of tasks to perform. There were 39 in all, many of which revolved around the hunting of Twrch Trwyth, the son of Prince Taredd, who had been magically transformed into a wild boar. Ysbaddaden was particularly keen to acquire a comb and shears from between the ears of the boar: none of his own were strong enough to give him a decent shave.

Arthur himself led the expedition which finally tracked down Twrch Trwyth and his seven young pigs to Tsgeir Oervel in Ireland. After a long and bitter battle, Arthur and his men chased them across the sea to Wales. There they continued to create havoc before the boar was driven into the River Severn. As he struggled against the current, two of Arthur's men snatched the comb and shears from between his ears.

Culhwch returned to Ysbaddaden's castle with these and all the other objects he had been challenged to collect. He claimed Olwen as his bride, and the giant was shaved of his beard. Then Goreu, the last remaining son of the herdsman, cut off Ysbaddaden's head and displayed it on a stake.

THE GIANT'S DAUGHTER

THE STORY of Culhwch and Olwen, told in the *Mabinogion,* is one of the most important for students of Arthurian legend because of its Celtic authenticity. It was probably first written down in the eleventh century, but its kinship to earlier Irish

▼ *Jason and Medea retrieve the golden fleece.*

texts shows that it comes from a much older tradition.

Probably of more interest to scholars than the story itself is the list of Arthurian characters it introduces. Culhwch alone mentions 200 names, including an inventory of Arthur's court. Equally important is the text's early, unadorned treatment of themes that recur in later narratives with medieval, Continental embellishments.

The tale has a number of supernatural elements. For example, there is a suggestion of shape-shifting in the hero, whose name means "pig run" and whose birth-link with pigs is developed in his final struggle with Twrch Trwyth, a prince transformed into a boar. Also, Culhwch is portrayed as a god like hero, radiant from head to foot.

There are some typical elements, too. The story is a quest tale comparable to the Labors of Hercules in Classical tradition, and the main plot, comparable to that of the Classical Jason and Medea, falls into a category of folklore known as "The Giant's Daughter."

BRETON TALES

ALTHOUGH GERALD of Wales wrote of "tale-telling Bretons," no Breton literature survives from before 1450 other than the so-called "Breton Lais," and there is nothing to compare with the earlier Irish and Welsh manuscripts.

The twelfth-century writer, Marie de France, popularized the "Breton Lai," a short narrative poem in French which dealt with Celtic and Arthurian themes. Breton folk tales, as such, were not collected until the nineteenth century, when stories from people living in remote villages were gathered under the title *Songs of Brittany*.

Nevertheless, some scholars believe there were Arthurian traditions in Brittany surviving from the influx of Irish, Welsh, and Cornish refugees in the fifth century C.E., and that it was these, and not the Welsh sources, that inspired Chrétien de Troyes' twelfth-century romances. Extended passages of the Arthurian story are set in Brittany; Geoffrey of Monmouth claimed that his seminal work was based on a "Breton book"; and Marie de France held that her tales were drawn from old Breton sources since lost.

The story of Lanval is taken from a Breton Lai and it shows one characteristic of Marie's view of love: that is, an almost inevitable association between joy and suffering.

LANVAL

LANVAL WAS ENVIED for his bravery and good looks, and he was not popular. One day he was feeling disconsolate when he was invited to the pavilion of the most beautiful woman. She said she had come from afar to see if Lanval was as fair and courteous as she had heard. They made love and afterwards the woman told Lanval never to speak of her to anyone. If he kept this bargain, she said, she would always appear when he needed her and he would be rich.

◀ *French art showing Arthur and his knights seated at the Round Table.*

◀ *A maiden bears the Holy Grail to show one of Arthur's Knights.*

Lanval agreed and returned to court, where he proved extremely generous with his new wealth. His reputation grew and one day Queen Guinevere made a pass at him. He rejected her, saying that he was faithful to a much fairer lady. Guinevere told Arthur that Lanval had insulted her and must be punished.

Lanval was brought to trial and challenged to produce the lady who was more beautiful than Guinevere. He refused and things were looking bad until his lady appeared, radiant on a white horse. Everyone agreed that Lanval had spoken the truth and he was released. They rode off together to Avalon and neither was seen again.

HEROIC QUESTS

THE MOST FAMOUS QUEST of all is the pursuit of the elusive Holy Grail by the Knights of the Round Table. There are many others, particularly among the Arthurian sagas. To win Olwen, Culhwch sets off to find 39 objects for her father, the giant Ysbaddaden. Owain, inspired by Cynon, son of Clydno, goes in search of the Castle of the Fountain, and Peredur enters upon a long series of adventures to avenge Cei's insult to a dwarf. Whatever the goal of the quest, whether divine or trivial, it is the journey itself that is the object of the story.

THE GRAIL

IN ARTHURIAN myth, the Holy Grail is a mystical vessel sought by the Knights of the Round Table.

The earliest story of the Grail is told by Chrétien de Troyes. It involves Sir Percival, who fails to find the Grail because he does not ask the right questions. Further stories have a succession of knights, including Lancelot, also failing. The only one deemed pure enough to succeed in the quest, and to be taken up to heaven with the Grail, is Galahad, Lancelot's son. Later versions allow more knights to achieve it, including Percival and Bors.

Forerunners of the Grail quest may be found in older Celtic myth. In "The Spoils of Annwn," an early Welsh poem, Arthur leads a disastrous expedition to Ireland to obtain a cauldron, one of the Thirteen Treasures of Britain. A variant of this appears in the tale of Culhwch and Olwen in which a cauldron numbers among the objects the hero must find with Arthur's help. The story of Peredur in the *Mabinogion* has been described as a Grail legend without the Grail. Peredur is the Welsh form of Percival, while Gwalchmai, who also appears in the story, is the Welsh form of Gawain.

◀ *Oisin and Naim arrive at the Land of Forever Young.*

PEREDUR, SON OF EFRAWG

FOLLOWING THE DEATH of his father and six brothers in battle, young Peredur was taken by his mother to live quietly in a place where he would not be tempted to take up arms. One day, however, he was impressed by three knights passing on horseback and he left his mother to follow them to Arthur's court.

On his arrival his appearance and naivety caused amusement, but he soon proved himself by defeating and killing a knight who had insulted Queen Guinevere. But he refused to become one of Arthur's knights until he had avenged another insult. He had witnessed Cei, Arthur's irritable companion, hitting and kicking two dwarfs and he would not accept the honor of joining the company until Cei accepted his challenge.

In the meantime Peredur went off on his travels and whenever he encountered an enemy of Arthur he defeated him and sent him, as the price for his life, to beg Arthur's forgiveness and to tell him that it was Peredur's doing. As a result, Arthur became very keen to embrace the brave warrior and he set out to find Peredur.

Peredur's wanderings took him to two uncles, one after the other. The first, a lame fisherman, told him never to ask about things he did not understand. At the court of the second he saw a mysterious severed head on a salver and he was careful not to ask about it. After this he fell in love with a rosy cheeked maiden, and he stayed for a time with the warrior witches of Caerloyw who instructed him in weaponry.

Arthur eventually caught up with Peredur, who was on a hilltop day dreaming about his love's black hair, white skin and red lips. Arthur sent several knights to arrange a meeting, including Cei, but they intruded rudely on Peredur's reverie and he sent them back battered and bleeding. Gwalchmai, being more polite, succeeded where the others had failed and when Peredur learned that Cei had been among the warriors he had beaten, he joined Arthur's knights at last.

At court Peredur had many adventures until one day he learned that the severed head he had seen at his uncle's house had been that of a cousin who had been murdered by the witches of Caerloyw. So Peredur made his way belatedly to the Castle of Wonders, where he and Arthur's war band wreaked terrible vengeance on the witches.

MAGIC AND ENCHANTMENT

CELTIC MYTHS are full of magic, which fulfils a number of functions in the narrative. It is commonly used as a means of escape. Etain and Midir make their getaway from Eochaid's palace as swans, while Diarmaid and Grainne evade Finn's huntsmen by using Oengus' magic cloak of invisibility. It is also used to deceive, as in the cases of Cú Roí and Sir Bartilek, who are magically transformed into unrecognizable giants for the beheading game. Heroes and ogres often have magical powers to confirm their greatness and power. Finn has the ability to see into the future, while Balor has a magic eye and his gaze is lethal.

Enchantment comes in many forms, but it is most often used in the service of love. Oisin is enchanted by Naim's beauty; a love potion is the undoing of Tristan and Iseult; Diarmaid is enchanted by Grainne; and Naoise is enchanted by Deirdre. Places such as groves, springs, and pools are said to be enchanted and they serve as entrances to the Otherworld. It is in the Forest of Broceliande that Merlin falls under the spell of Vivien, and it is from a lake that Arthur receives his enchanted sword.

TRINITIES

THE NUMBER THREE was sacred to the Celts. Knowledge was preserved in triadic verses, while in art a common form is the triple face.

In mythology, mother goddesses are commonly represented in threes, and the Morrigan is often represented by her terrifying sisters.

Sometimes a trio represents different aspects of the same character; Naoise, the lover of Deirdre, has two brothers, but they are distinguished only by the tones of their voices.

Many Celtic romances, like that of Lancelot and Guinevere, involve love triangles. Sometimes one of the rivals is young and handsome, like Tristan, while the other is an oppressive husband or guardian.

◀ *Thirteenth-century illustration of Tristan and Iseult.*

TRISTAN AND ISEULT

TRISTAN WAS LIVING with his uncle, King Mark of Cornwall, when Mark stopped paying tribute money to Ireland. An Irish champion was sent to collect it and Tristan killed him. He was injured in the fight, however, and his wound became poisoned. A cure was found in Ireland, where Tristan was sent under an assumed name. There he was restored to health by Iseult, daughter of the Irish king.

To restore peace a marriage was arranged between Mark and Iseult, and Tristan was sent to fetch her. Coming back, they accidentally drank a love potion that Iseult's mother had given her, and they fell helplessly in love.

On her wedding night Iseult had to disguise the fact that she was not pure. So under cover of darkness her maid took her place in Mark's bed. Thereafter, Tristan and Iseult continued to deceive Mark and they met secretively at every opportunity.

Inevitably, rumors reached Mark. Traps were laid, and the lovers came close to being caught. Ultimately Iseult agreed to swear on her life that she was not an adulteress. Tristan attended the ritual disguised as a beggar. Pretending to trip into his arms, Iseult was able to say, quite truthfully, that she had never been held by anyone other than her husband and this beggar.

Recognizing their love was doomed, Tristan left for Brittany where he married the daughter of King Hoel. He missed Iseult so much, however, that he was unable to consummate the marriage and his wife became very jealous.

One day Tristan received another wound which became poisoned and he believed that only his beloved Iseult could make him better. So he sent a ship to bring her to him. Tristan was not sure that Iseult would agree to come and, to be forewarned, he ordered the captain to hoist white sails on the return journey if she was on board, and black ones if she was not.

Tristan sent his wife to look out for the returning ship. When she spotted it, she lied to him and told Tristan that the sails were black. On hearing this he gave up the ghost and died, broken-hearted. Arriving to find Tristan dead, Iseult was so grief-stricken that she also died.

King Mark buried them side by side in Cornwall. From Tristan's grave there grew a vine and from Iseult's a rose. As they grew, the two plants became inseparably entwined.

▲*This double head is believed to be a symbol of defeated enemies.*

THE SACRED HEAD

CELTIC MYTHOLOGY is full of stories in which giants and enemies are beheaded or heroes are challenged to decapitation contests. We know, too, that the Celts were headhunters; they kept them as trophies or sacrificial offerings, believing them to contain the essence of the person to whom they belonged and to be a source of wisdom. While human figures are rare in Celtic art, the head or face alone is not, although in two dimensional art forms the face may be difficult to make out among the decorative details. The wearing of jewelry decorated with faces may have followed from the belief that it possessed protective powers.

GAWAIN AND THE GREEN KNIGHT

AT ARTHUR'S COURT one New Year's Eve, the merriment was interrupted when a green knight with an ax entered and challenged anyone present to cut off his head. The catch was that they would have to submit to the same treatment on the following New Year's Eve.

Arthur's nephew Gawain accepted the challenge and removed the stranger's head with a single blow. Believing the game to be at an end, everyone was amazed to see the green body pick up the head and leave the hall. On the way, the head called to Gawain and told him to be at the Green Chapel in 12 months' time.

Gawain set out 10 months later to find the Green Chapel. He came upon a castle on Christmas Eve, within a short distance of his goal, and he was invited by the lord, Sir Bertilak, to stay for Christmas. Bertilak proposed that Gawain should rest before his ordeal and be entertained by his wife. He intended to spend the time hunting, and he decreed that every evening he and Gawain would exchange what they had gained during the day.

Each day for three days Bertilak disappeared with his hounds while his wife visited Gawain's bedroom. Gawain took no more than kisses from her and these he exchanged with his host each night for the trophies of the hunt. Gawain did take something more from the lady on the third day, however, a green girdle which he concealed from the lord.

When the time came, a guide was provided to lead Gawain to the Green Chapel. The man tried to deter him with fearsome warnings about the occupant, but Gawain pressed on bravely. At the chapel the Green Knight was waiting with his axe ready. Gawain removed his helmet and knelt before him while the knight dealt him three feinted blows to the neck. The third made light contact and drew blood.

Gawain was puzzled, until his tormentor explained that he was none other than Bertilak, transformed by the sorceress Morgan, to test the bravery of Arthur's knights. The first two blows he had dealt with the axe were for the two occasions on which Gawain faithfully gave him his day's gains. The third, which drew blood, was a mild reproof for Gawain's failure to hand over the gift of the green girdle.

Thereafter Gawain always wore the green girdle to remind him of his lapse.

◀ *In another Celtic myth, the Green Knight meets Beaumains at the ford and is beaten in combat.*

Central and Eastern Europe

INTRODUCTION

WITH THE NOTABLE exception of the Romanians, Hungarians, and Albanians, the peoples of Central and Eastern Europe are predominantly of the Slav family, which established an ethnic identity some 1,500 years ago. About that time, in the fifth century C.E,, the Slavs began to migrate through Eastern Europe: up to the Baltic Sea in the north; down to the Adriatic in the south; from Bohemia in the center eastwards, traveling halfway around the world to the Pacific Ocean.

Those who settled in the north—the Poles, Belorussians, and Russians—found themselves mainly in a flat and marshy terrain, interspersed with broad rivers and covered in snow for up to six months in the year.

Those who inhabited the central parts—the Czechs, Slovaks, and Ukrainians—encountered a largely treeless steppe of feather grass.

THE TRIBES that trekked south through the Balkans—the Yugoslavs (meaning "southern Slavs": Serbs, Croats, Slovenes, and Macedonians) and the Bulgarians—found a milder climate beside the warm Adriatic, Aegean, and Black Seas, surrounded by snow-topped mountains.

The hardy tribes that went due east—the Rus or Russians—cleared a way by ax and fire through dense forest watered by bog and lake and nourishing large numbers of wild animals. According to the historian Vasily Kluchevsky (1841–1911), we must learn about the forest, river, and steppe in order to understand Slav culture:

The forest provided the Slav with oak and pine to build his house, it warmed him with aspen and birch, it lit his hut with birchwood splinters, it shod him in bast sandals, it gave him plates and dishes, clothed him in hides and furs and fed him honey. It was the best shelter from his foes.

But life in the forest was tough and dangerous: wolves and bears stalked man and beast. It was an awe inspiring world of weird sounds and menacing shadows. The forest taught caution and kindled fantasy.

The steppe put quite a different imprint on the Slav soul. Its endless expanse gave the feeling of vast horizons and distant dreams. Yet it was even more menacing than the forest, for it offered no hiding place from the marauding nomads

◀ *The* kibitka *or tent that the early Russian migrants would have lived in.*
▶ *Fundamental to Central and Eastern mythology is the fish-faced creator god.*

and the dreaded Mongol-Tartars. The forest and steppe, therefore, evoked conflicting feelings as both friend and foe. Not so the river, as Kluchevsky explains:

He loved his river. There is no other feature of the land so fondly sung of in folklore. And for good reason. In his meanderings, she showed him the way; in his settlements, she was his constant companion; he placed his home upon her banks. For most of the year she fed him. For the trader she was the perfect summer and winter road. She taught the Slav order and sociability; she made men brothers, made them feel part of society, taught them to respect the customs of others, to trade goods and experience, to invent and adapt.

The rivers and lakes, too, had their mysteries. In a world inhabited by demons it is easy to understand how primitive Slavs thought the spirit of the river murmured when pleased or roared when angry. The continual motion of the water very naturally suggested that it was alive; so each river and lake had its male sprite and female water nymph. Here, then, are the main offspring of Mother Nature that formed Slav culture and lent Slav myth its special character.

RELIGIOUS CUSTOMS, CULTS, AND INFLUENCES

THE UNIQUE ARTISTRY of Slav myths must be largely attributed to the storytellers, who cultivated their bardic art and passed on stories by word of mouth from generation to generation. These minstrels, jesters, blind pedlars were welcome in the strung out, isolated settlements, especially of a long winter evening. Before modern life spread into the remotest corners of the countryside, the recounting of myths was a favorite entertainment in the quietness and monotony of the long evenings.

It is interesting that myths were not simply for the common people; they were for the entertainment of gentlefolk too. A good storyteller was a much prized possession in many well-to-do homes, including that of the emperor himself. The first Russian tsar, Ivan the Terrible, was said to be a great admirer of Slav myths and had at court three blind men who would take turns at his bedside, telling stories to lull him to sleep. Myths told by serf nurses to young aristocratic gentlefolk provided themes for innumerable Slav masterpieces (*Sadko*, *The Snowmaiden*, and *The Golden Cockerel* of Rimsky-Korsakov; *The Firebird* and *The Rite of Spring* of Stravinsky; *Rusalka* of Dvorak).

But storytellers had not always been so welcome. Tsar Alexei Mikhailovich, father of Peter the Great, had all the storytellers rounded up and their tongues cut out. In the famous royal edict of 1649 it was proclaimed: *"Many persons stupidly believe in dreams, the evil eye and birdsong, and they propound riddles and myths; by idle talk and merry-making and blasphemy, they destroy their souls."*

THE *VODYANOI*

RIVERS, LAKES, AND SEAS were very important to the ancient Slavs, and the motion of water naturally suggested that it was alive. Each stretch of water therefore had its spirit, the *vodyanoi*. The *vodyanoi* was old, ugly, slime covered, and green bearded. He controlled the "life" of the water: when drunk he made the waters overflow; when pleased, he guided the fish into nets; when cross, he raised storms, sank ships, and drowned sailors.

Palekh papier-mache *plaque showing the Snowmaiden watching the villagers dancing.*

SNOWMAIDEN

SNOWMAIDEN (SNEGUROCHKA) was the daughter of Fair Spring and old Red-Nose Frost. Until she was 16, she grew up in her father's icy realm—lest Yarilo the sun god see her and melt her away.

Late one winter, when her parents met, they argued about Snowmaiden's fate. While her mother wanted her to be free, her father was afraid of the sun. Finally, they decided to put her into the care of an old couple. So one morning, as the old man and woman were walking in the snowy forest, the man set to making a "snowgirl" (the Slav equivalent of a "snowman.") To his surprise, the snowgirl's lips grew red, her eyes opened and she stepped out of the snow—a real, live girl.

Snowmaiden grew up not by the day but by the hour. Soon spring sunshine warmed the land and patches of green grass appeared. Yet the young girl hid from the sun, sought the chill shadow and stretched out her pale arms to the rain.

One day, as summer is approaching, some village girls invite Snowmaiden out to play. Reluctantly, she joins them, picking flowers, singing songs, and dancing with the village lads. She hangs back until Lel, a shepherd boy, plays his flute for her, then takes her by the hand and whirls her round in a dance. From that day on, Lel the shepherd calls on Snowmaiden. But though he loves her dearly, he feels no response in her cold heart. Finally, he leaves her for another village girl. In her grief, Snowmaiden runs to a lake in the middle of the forest and begs her mother Lo to give her a human heart: to love even for a brief moment is more precious than to live forever with a frozen heart.

Her mother takes pity on her, places a crown of lilies on her head and warns her to guard her love from Yarilo's fiery gaze.

Rushing through the trees, Snowmaiden finds Lel and declares her love for him. As she speaks, the radiant sun rises higher in the cloudless sky, dispelling the mists of dawn and melting the remaining snow. A ray of sunshine falls on her and, with a cry of pain, she begs Lel to play her one last tune. As he plays, her body sinks into the ground; all that remains is a crown of lilies.

Yet as one life passes, another is born. Sunshine awakens the frozen earth with a kiss and gives birth to plants and flowers. As for Lel, he waits for the winter snows to bring him back his beloved Snowmaiden.

RECORDING THE MYTHS

UNLIKE THE SUMERIANS, Egyptians, Aztecs, and ancient Greeks, the Slavs left no written record of their myths. Only after their christianization in the late tenth century did literacy and literature appear.

The first significant and unsurpassed collection of Slav myths and legends was made by Alexander Afanasiev (1826–1871), whose vast enterprise appeared in eight volumes between 1855 and 1867 and contained as many as 640 myths, legends, and folktales—by far the largest collection by one man anywhere in the world. Afanasiev took down the stories second-hand, from the records of other people, yet this modest lawyer from Russia's Voronezh region became one of the most influential figures in Russian national culture.

Afanasiev's interest in the intrinsic beauty of peasant language—at a time when aristocratic Slav society was aping foreign fashions and conversing in French—brought him to admire myths for their musical quality, their poetic artistry, sincerity, purity, and childlike simplicity. But his work stirred up opposition in some quarters.

The second edition of his myths was confiscated and later burned, and Afanasiev was brought before a special investigating committee in St. Petersburg. He was disgraced, dismissed from his employment, and deprived of his Moscow house. Nevertheless, despite illness and poverty,

Afanasiev spent every free moment on a new work: *The Poetic Interpretations of Nature by the Slavs.*

THE HOUSEHOLD SPIRITS

EVERYWHERE THE ANCIENT Slavs turned, they found spirits good, bad, and temperamental. Each had to be treated with care: because they were usually related to the spirits of ancestors, the prosperity of the household depended on their well-being. The Slavs kept the memory of dead ancestors alive through elaborate rituals, such as leaving food beside the grave at various times of the year and talking to the grave when important decisions had to be taken. Such ancestor worship is illustrated in tales of the youngest son, often "The Fool," who is slovenly and slow witted. Yet because he honors his dead father he invariably receives a just reward (sometimes becoming handsome and smart, and marrying a beautiful princess).

PALEKH FOLK ART

THE ANCIENT RUSSIAN folk art, palekh, was born in the village of Palekh, some 300 miles to the northeast of Moscow. Palekh-lacquered miniatures are paintings, mainly on papier-mâché jewelry boxes and brooches. They most frequently depict folk themes (such as the Firebird, Sadko, Bába Yagá) or religious images. An impressive collection of icons can be seen in Palekh's beautiful Krestodvizhensky Cathedral.

For the paint, finely ground pigments are rubbed into an emulsion made of egg yolk; the separated yolk is returned to the shell, water and vinegar are added, and the emulsion is stirred with a special nine-hole whisk.

◀ *The magnificent Krestodvizhensky Cathedral, depicted here by the palekh artists, itself contains many other such artworks.*

AFANASIEV'S THEORIES OF THE SYMBOLS OF FOLK MYTHOLOGY

ALEXANDER AFANASIEV sought to understand how the myths had arisen and what was the hidden meaning behind them, to understand the world of the primitive storyteller, whose feeling in regard to his surroundings was of some mysterious and fantastic power that controlled all the elements of nature.

In the story of Márya Morévna, he believed that the three bird-bridegrooms who arrive at Prince Ivan's palace to the accompaniment of thunder, whirlwinds, and lightning are really the rain, thunder, and wind. The three princesses they marry are the sun, moon, and stars. Seeing how the light went out of the sky during a storm, the early Slavs created an explanation of the abducted maidens in the poetic language of myth.

Márya Morévna (Marya "Daughter of the Sea") herself is really the sun which, at dawn and dusk, "bathes" in the sea. The ogre Koshchay Bessmertny ("Old Bones the Immortal"), fettered by iron chains, is the storm cloud chained by the winter frosts. He gains strength when he drinks his fill of water as spring melts the snows; then he tears himself free and carries off Márya Morévna, thus clouding over the sun.

Prince Ivan is really Perun, the pagan Slav god of thunder and lightning, who smashes the storm cloud with a mighty blow of his sword and saves the sun, leading her out of darkness from behind the mountains.

▲ *An illustration from Bilibine's stories about Márya Morévna.*

VAMPIRES

THE BEST KNOWN malevolent mythical creature of the Slavs and Central Europeans is the vampire—from the southern Slav word *vampir*. With the advent of Christianity, the Church directed vampire myths against heretics and pagans, and those it wished to brand in order to frighten society into conformity: witches, sorcerers, the godless, thieves, prostitutes, and other undesirables. All such "unclean" people were said never to rest on death but to turn into vampires. Such "undead" visited homes at midnight to suck blood or have sex with the sleeping victims who then wasted away and died, or turned into vampires themselves.

◀ *Vampires were used to frighten heretics and pagans and to threaten those who did not conform with the conventions of the society.*

MÁRYA MORÉVNA

WHILE OUT RIDING one day, Prince Ivan comes upon the slain army of Old Bones the Immortal; it has been defeated single-handedly by the warrior queen Márya Morévna. Ivan rides on, finds the queen, falls in love with her and they marry. Before she goes off to war again, she warns him not to enter a sealed room in her palace.

As soon as she is gone Ivan opens the forbidden chamber and finds an old man chained inside an iron pot over a blazing fire. Taking pity on him, Prince Ivan gives him a drink of water. At once Old Bones' strength returns, he bursts his bonds and carries off Ivan to his own realm.

When Márya Morévna finds out, she rides off to rescue her husband but is caught and cut to pieces. At this point, Ivan's brothers-in-law—a falcon, raven, and eagle—come to the rescue and sprinkle the water of life over the pieces of the corpse. The body grows whole and Marya comes back to life.

This time, to rescue Ivan, Márya Morévna sets off to obtain the only horse that can outpace Old Bones' steed. It belongs to Bába Yagá the witch, who lives beyond the Land of One Score and Nine, in the realm of One Score and Ten; and to get there Márya Morévna must cross a burning river.

With a magic scarf taken from Old Bones, Márya Morévna crosses the Burning River (with three waves of the magic scarf) and arrives at Bába Yagá's hut, telling the witch that she has come to earn one of her steeds. The witch gives her three days to keep the horses safe in their pasture; then she may have one of her finest steeds as reward. Should she fail, however, her head would be stuck on the last pole of the skull fence.

Eventually Márya Morévna succeeds in herding the horses and is told by a queen bee to go to the stables and saddle a mangy colt wallowing in the mire. That is the horse that can ride round the world in a single day.

▲ *Illustration of Bilibine's tale showing Prince Ivan fleeing with his beautiful wife, Queen Márya Morévna.*

She does so and returns over the Burning River with the aid of the magic scarf; meanwhile Bába Yagá falls into the fire and is burned to death. Márya Morévna rescues Prince Ivan and together they ride the fiery steed (for such the mangy colt has become), pursued by Old Bones. But the ogre's horse stumbles and throws its rider to the ground, smashing his head against a stone. Marya finishes him off with his own sword, burns the body, and scatters the ashes to the winds. Then she and Prince Ivan return to her realm to hold a feast to which the whole world is invited.

KOSHCHAY THE IMMORTAL

A PURELY SLAV villain or ogre is Koshchay Bessmertny—Old Bones the Immortal. This wizened, evil old man specializes in carrying off fair maidens. Chained and imprisoned, usually by a bold warrior maiden (like Márya Morévna), he features in a forbidden chamber incident common to the Bluebeard cycle of West European tales. His name, Koshchay, appears to derive from either the Old Slavonic (meaning "bones") or the Turkic *koshchi* (meaning "prisoner.") The constant struggle between Slavs and nomadic Turkic tribes, including the Polovtsians and Tartars, has bequeathed many names and figures to Slav tales.

DRAGON AND WITCH STORIES

TO AFANASIEV, myths were the primitive Slav's story of nature; the heroes are the gods of sun, sky, light, thunder, and water, while their foes are the gods of darkness, winter, cold, storms, mountains, and caves.

In the story of Fair Vassilisa and Bába Yagá, the witch (Bába Yagá) symbolizes the dark storm cloud that wants to destroy the sunlight (the young girl Vassilisa). At the end of the tale, Vassilisa escapes and causes the death of her two wicked stepsisters and stepmother at home. To Afanasiev, it is the sun freeing itself from the power of the storm and other dark clouds.

In the dragon stories, once again it is the sun (the hero or, more often, the heroine) oppressed by storm clouds that bring snow and hail. But there is invariably a happy ending, with the sun destroying and dispersing the clouds with lightning (his or her sword), and the dragon is slain.

In a typical Slav divergence from West European myths and folktales, it is the prince who is awakened by a maiden's kiss after she has overcome unimaginable obstacles. To Afanasiev, the story behind the myth is of nature being woken by spring, the earth being kissed by the sun and brought back to life.

Because of this mythological approach, Afanasiev attached no value to information concerning the storytellers from whom the tales had been taken. He did not think style of delivery important since myth, like language, was a product of collective work down the ages.

FAIR VASSILISA AND BÁBA YAGÁ

THERE ONCE LIVED an old man and woman with their daughter Vassilisa. One day, the old woman fell sick and, before she died, gave her daughter a little doll, telling her that whenever she needed help, she was to give the doll a bite to eat and ask her advice.

After his wife's death, the old man married a widow with two daughters of her own; all three were jealous of Vassilisa. One day, when the old man had gone to market and it was growing dark, the stepmother sent Vassilisa to Bába Yagá's house for a birch splinter to light the hut.

Now Bába Yagá was a witch who lived in the depths of a dark wood. Vassilisa put the doll in her pocket and set off. Finally, she came to a wooden hut on hens' feet surrounded by a fence of human bones crowned with skulls. The gateposts were dead men's legs, the bolts were dead men's arms and the lock was made of dead men's teeth. Just then, Bába Yagá came flying out of the forest in her mortar, driving herself along with a pestle and sweeping her traces away with a broom.

When Vassilisa had explained her mission, the witch said she must work for her to earn a reward. Then began evidently impossible tasks—picking husks from grain and black-eyed peas from poppy seed. Yet in the space of two nights, and with the doll's help, the tasks were completed.

By now, Vassilisa knew that the witch had no intention of letting her go. So while she was asleep Vassilisa ran away, taking from the fence a skull with burning eyes. On her flight through the forest she was passed by three horsemen: one white, representing the light of day; one red, representing the rising sun; one black, representing dark night. They guided her on her way.

▲ *Bába Yagá the witch—an illustration from the tale of the beautiful Vassilisa.*

◀ *A beautiful princess is held captive by the dragon that lies sleeping, its head cradled in her lap.*

When she came home, the stepmother and stepsisters snatched the skull from her hands; yet the skull's glowing eyes fixed themselves upon them and burned them to cinders. Only Vassilisa remained unharmed. Next morning she buried the skull deep beneath the soil, and in time a bush of dark red roses grew upon the spot. From then on, Vassilisa lived with her father in peace and comfort, always keeping the little doll safely in her pocket—just in case she needed her again.

REFLECTIONS IN ART

WHILE WE KNOW some of the names of the old Slav pagan gods, little of their appearance or cults survives, even in decorative representation. As in music, literature, and art, the Orthodox Church succeeded in suppressing much of the folk heritage and pagan myth.

In the wooden cottages, wood carving continued down the ages to depict the old deities, such as the Slav fertility goddess Makosh and the goddess of life and death Bába Yagá. But particularly popular—and "safer" —were anthropomorphic and totemistic figures, such as the bear (Mikhail Potapich), the goat (Kozma), the vixen (Lisa Patrikeyevna—the midwife, herbalist, gossip, and sage), and the cockerel (Petya).

BÁBA YAGÁ

THE SLAV WITCH is an old hag who typically sits on a wooden bench or stone stove, one leg curled beneath her, the other dangling, her crooked nose reaching to the ceiling. She lives in a revolving hut on hens' feet, sometimes with, sometimes without, windows and doors.

Bába Yagá rides through the air in an iron mortar, propelling herself with a pestle, stirring up terrible storms and leaving a trail of disease and death in her wake. She is a cannibal, specializing in devouring young children. It is noteworthy that, in several stories, the witch is helpful, thereby reverting to her earlier functions in the Mother Ale of mythology, when she represented the priestess in whom all love and wisdom were embodied.

MATRIARCHAL INFLUENCE ON SLAV MYTHS

TRADITIONAL SLAV myths are full of fantasy and stock descriptions: the heroes and heroines are bold young men and innocent maidens (or vice versa) assisted by helpful beasts and magic implements, the villains are dragons, witches, sorcerers, and evil kings. And the lucky number is three, thus presenting a triad of witches, tasks, sons, princesses, nights, and dragons' heads.

The strong matriarchal influence on Slav myth is apparent in that the main role is frequently played by a woman—who may be a warrior and all-conquering queen, as in the case of Márya Morévna, or a wise young girl, like Fair Vassilisa, or an enchanted wife like the Dove Maiden in The Archer or The Frog Princess (once again, a gender reversal from the West European version of the tale).

With social changes that made men the center of the social group, especially as a result of Christian influence, the power and knowledge of women were broken down and the priestess became the wicked witch; her superior wisdom dabbling in witchcraft—was reason enough to have her burned at the stake or, in most Slav lands, set loose across the plain tied to a horse's tail. The lateness of such social change over the Slav region has left many myths unaffected by the new "political correctness."

WEREWOLVES

ANYONE BORN with a particularly prominent birthmark, an afterbirth caul on the head, or tufts of hair on any part of the body was thought to have the potential for becoming a werewolf. To some tribes it was a sign of good luck: such a child would possess second sight as well as the power to change shape into an animal or a fish. Malevolent characters, though, preferred to turn into a bloodthirsty wolf. So prevalent was this belief in medieval Russia that the Church in the sixteenth century condemned "beliefs in birthmarks, cauls, and hair tufts, and their werewolf associations."

◀ *A gentleman demonstrates to his wife his ability to turn himself into a werewolf, surprising both her and his dogs!*

▼ *The spectacular St. Andrews Church in Kiev. The introduction of Christianity had a great effect on the traditions of the Eastern Europeans, shifting the balance of power from the women to the men.*

THE TWELVE MONTHS

IN A LITTLE VILLAGE in Bohemia there once lived an old woman with her daughter and stepdaughter. The woman doted on her own child, yet her stepdaughter could do nothing to please her.

One evening, in the depths of winter, the cruel stepmother unlatched the cottage door and told her stepdaughter to go into the forest and pick snowdrops for her sister's birthday on the morrow. Of course, she well knew that snowdrops only appeared in March, and it was now January.

The little girl went out into the driving snow and after a time was surprised to see a light flickering through the trees. Then she smelled warm smoke and heard the crackle of burning logs. Before she realized it she found herself in a clearing; round a bonfire sat twelve men quietly talking. Three were old, three of middle years, three youths, and three just boys still. These were the Twelve Months!

After she had explained why she had come, the months talked among themselves. They knew her well enough; she was a maid for all seasons, washing clothes at the ice hole, collecting sticks in the forest. And they decided to help her pick snowdrops.

Brother March asked old January and February to let him take their place for an hour, and it was agreed. All at once a carpet of brown earth stretched beneath her feet and buds began sprouting from branches. The ground was simply thick with snowdrops. The girl picked a whole basketful then hurried back to the glade. But it was empty.

She ran home with her basket of flowers. When she had told her story, however, the stepsister rushed into the snowy forest to seek a much richer reward from the Twelve Months. When she reached them, seated round the bonfire, they did not recognize her and, in response to her demands, they angrily blew up a snowstorm which soon swallowed her up. When her mother came in search of her, she too stumbled into a snowdrift and died.

The young girl lived on contentedly in her cottage. And round about, so folk say, there appeared the most delightful garden; in it roses bloomed, berries ripened, and apples and pears grew in abundance the whole year round. After all, she had all Twelve Months visiting her every day of the year.

THE LESCHI

BEYOND THE HOUSEHOLD lay the dense, dark forest which, naturally, was peopled by all manner of spirits, mostly malevolent. Most common was the leschi, an evil one eyed spirit or woodsprite who amused himself by leading people astray so that they perished in the depths of the forest. He took the form of a small, treelike creature, although often he was invisible and it would be his singing or whistling that guided travelers to their doom.

THE SOUL AND MAGIC CHARMS

A FEATURE OF SLAV primitive belief is that the soul dwells outside the body. Not only can the soul depart from the body upon death, but sometimes even when a person is asleep. Among the Serbs, such souls may gather on hilltops at night and fight one another; victory brings good fortune to the sleeping owner of the soul, but if the soul is defeated, its owner may never awake. In the eastern Slav lands (Russia, Belarus, and the Ukraine), the soul can take the form of a *kikimora*, a tiny, ugly old woman with long flowing hair who normally lives in the home but, like the Irish banshee, can presage a death by her wailing.

◀ *This gold dress ornament shows a seated goddess. Such jewels and ornaments have survived as records of ancient mythology.*

In some myths, trees and plants are tenanted by the souls of the dead, thus becoming personified and endowed with human qualities. This superstition led to certain trees being regarded as sacred, to legends of speaking or bleeding plants and to the planting of trees as life tokens. If the hero dies, the tree withers and falls because the hero's soul resides in it.

Such primitive beliefs are loosely associated with the contemporary notion of breaking a mirror and, in Slav lands, a person whistling indoors (summoning the Devil)—both said to presage death or bad luck. On the other hand, today's lucky charms may be compared with the magic swords, self-laying tablecloths and magic sacks in the myths.

THE OTHERWORLD

THE "OTHERWORLD" is sometimes portrayed as an island, Booyán, far out to sea (where the sun goes down and rises), a place of eternal sunshine and happiness. This is where the souls of the dead and those not yet born dwell—as well as the seeds, plants, and birds that appear in springtime.

To reach this mystic isle, the hero has to travel beyond the realm of Three Times Ten, often on foot, wearing out three pairs of iron shoes and three stone staffs, eating through three stone loaves and climbing a mountain of iron or glass. The person making the journey is often a simple peasant girl, thus emphasizing matriarchal power in Slav mythology.

▶ *Serbian painting depicting a beautiful princess removing her golden dress.*

THE FIREBIRD

ACROSS THE MISTY MOUNTAINS, over deep rolling seas, there lived a king who had an orchard that was the apple of his eye. For in the orchard grew a golden apple tree. One night a thief came and stole some apples. The king was most upset and had his stable lad Ivan stand guard all night long.

Half the night passed and then, all of a sudden, Ivan saw a firebird swoop down and start pecking at the apples. He grabbed the Firebird's tail, but it tore free and flew away, leaving a feather in Ivan's hand.

The king sent Ivan in search of the magical firebird. He had not gone far when a big gray wolf suddenly appeared and promised to help him find the thief. He advised Ivan to mix some beer with bread and cheese and scatter it on the ground. When the firebirds ate the bread and cheese, they were soon reeling about; and Ivan was able to seize one and thrust it into his sack. Then, leaping upon the wolf's back, he raced back to the king.

Now, the king had heard of a princess, Yelena the Fair, who lived beyond the seas. And he sent Ivan on another errand, to fetch the lovely maid. Once again, the big gray wolf came to his aid, and they sped off to a fairytale castle beyond the seas.

The princess was seized, and both she and Ivan sat astride the wolf for the journey back to the old king. On the way, however, Ivan fell in love with Yelena the Fair and she with him. When they told the wolf of their dilemma, he told them to leave everything to him.

Once in the king's palace, the gray wolf turned himself into the living likeness of the fair princess, and Ivan led the "wolf-princess" to the king. The king was overjoyed, and summoned all his nobles to witness the crowning of his new queen. But just as he went to kiss the bride his lips met the cold muzzle of the big gray wolf. The shock was too severe, and the old king died upon the spot.

So Ivan married Yelena the Fair and became king himself. As for the firebird, it was set free to fly away. But never again did it nibble at apples or bread and cheese.

◀ *The Slavic divinity Vodianoï was believed to favor stretches of water near mills.*

THE COMING OF CHRISTIANITY

WHEN SLAV PRINCES adopted Christianity in the tenth century (the western Slavs—Poles, Czechs, and Slovaks—took their religion from Rome; the eastern and southern Slavs from Greek Byzantium), the Church outlawed the pagan gods and did its best to stamp out the myths surrounding them. But the old cults continued: either they were adopted by the Church as its own rites or they became magic. Thus Perun (god of thunder and lightning) became Ilya the prophet; Volos (guardian of herds and flocks) became St. Vlasia; Kupalnitsa (goddess of rivers and lakes) became St. Agrippina; Kupala (god of sun and light) became John the Baptist.

The rites of spring now coincided with Easter (the main Orthodox Church celebration), the winter Calendae was replaced by Christmas, and the festival of Yarilo (also pagan god of the sun and all earthly life) became St. John's Day.

THE *RUSALKA*

IN THE DEPTHS of the waters lived the *rusalka*, or water nymph—a lovely naked girl with skin the color of moonlight, who so charmed passersby with her laughter and song that some would drown themselves for her sake. The *rusalka* was the dead soul of an infant, or a drowned or unhappy young woman. Although the *rusalka* later became associated with the dead, the original association, before the coming of Christianity, was probably with fertility.

THE *VILA*

THE LANE EQUIVALENT of the *rusalka*, or water nymph, was the *vila*, an eternally youthful and lovely woman with long fair tresses. She was commonly a girl who had died unbaptized (a Christian belief) or been jilted by her fiancé, or who was simply "flighty" and whose soul flitted somewhere between heaven and earth. She usually appeared at night to sing and dance, causing any human who saw her to dance themselves to death.

SPIRITS OF THE FARMSTEAD

ALL PARTS of the farmstead had their own spirits. The farmyard spirit was the *dvorovoi*—responsible for the area surrounding the house. Newborn or purchased animals had to be introduced to him, and it was important to keep only animals of the color he was thought to favor. He was mostly invisible, but those who caught a glimpse of him say he was a gray-bearded old man covered all over in hair. The *dvorovoi's* realm was confined to the open air. Once inside the farmyard buildings, he handed over guardian duties to the appropriate spirits.

The threshing shed had its *ovinnik*, who was an irascible, even dangerous character. You had to be on your guard or he would trip you up or maim you with the threshing tools. A much more merry fellow was the *bannik*, the spirit of the bathhouse, although he was not averse to playing unpleasant tricks on visitors, especially when they went to the bathhouse for the purposes of divination. Young women, for example, sometimes used it to divine their future spouses. If they left a comb, it might later contain the hair of their future husband (though the *bannik* was not unknown to place a horse hair there!).

▼ *A Vila causes mischief by thwarting the builders' attempts to construct a castle until they have accomplished the feats she sets for them.*

▲ *The farmyard spirit,* dvorovoi, *protected the people and the animals on the farm.*

Many of the modern names for supernatural beings have their derivation in these primitive ideas. Thus, the English "bogeyman" is related to the Slav name for god, *bog*—an illustration of how the word "devil" was originally the same as a god, being a corruption of *deva*, the Sanskrit name for god. Hence *div* and *divitsa* (the ancient Slav pagan deities), the Latin Zeus, the French dieu and the English word "deuce" (meaning "a little devil") can be traced to the same root.

SADKO THE MINSTREL

SADKO LIVED in Novgorod and played his maplewood lute at banquets for rich merchants. But times grew hard and no one wished to pay for his music. One day, as he was walking along the riverbank, he sat down and played his lute. Hardly had he finished than the waters started to foam and the mighty head of the sea god rose from the deep. So much did he enjoy Sadko's music that he commanded him to play in his underwater palace, promising him a handsome reward.

No sooner had Sadko agreed than he found himself upon the ocean bed in a palace of white stone; there was the sea god in a great hall, sitting on a coral throne. As soon as Sadko struck up a tune, the sea god began to dance. Overhead the waters frothed and foamed, and waves as big as hills rolled across the swell, dragging ships down into the depths.

After a while, Sadko grew tired; he could barely play another note. All at once he felt a hand upon his shoulder and, glancing round, he saw a white bearded man. The sage advised him to break the strings of his lute in order to stop the dance. Thereupon the sea god would offer him a bride as his reward. But he was not to be hasty in his choice, letting the first three hundred maidens, and the second and the third, pass by – choosing the very last one as his wife. But the sage gave Sadko a warning: he must not touch his bride or he would remain forever beneath the sea.

Sadko snapped the strings of his lute and the dancing ceased. Although the sea god grumbled, he insisted that Sadko claim his reward: he had to pick a bride from among his daughters. A procession of maidens appeared, each more lovely than the one before. Sadko let the first three hundred pass, then the second and the third. Last of all came Chernava, the fairest of them all. And Sadko claimed his bride.

Later that night, when Sadko was left alone with his new wife, he recalled the old man's warning; so he lay down without touching his bride. In the middle of the night, however, he turned over in the bed and touched her with his foot. So cold was she that he woke up with a start.

He found himself lying on the steep bank of the Chernava River, his left foot dangling in the icy waters. For the rest of his life he was to remain lame in that foot. But by his side was a sackful of gold which made him very wealthy. There are those who say that when a storm rages upon sea or lake, it is really Sadko the minstrel playing his lute and the sea god dancing a jig upon the ocean bed.

Northern Europe

INTRODUCTION

NORTHERN MYTHS tell of conflict between gods and giants, between chaos and order. The evidence for the myths is fragmentary, but this mythology's influence on the English speaking world is far-reaching and its position as an important heritage of English speaking people undeniable. Indeed, in English some days of the week are still named after northern gods: Tuesday—Tyr's day; Wednesday—Woden/Odin's day; Thursday—Thor's day; Friday—Frigg's day.

When the Roman empire declined, Germanic tribes pushed forward from east of the Rhine over lands formerly defended by the Romans. The Germanic peoples were those who spoke Germanic languages, as opposed to Celtic, Slav or Latin based tongues. From the fourth to the sixth century C.E. Europe was the scene of continual movement. Some Germanic dialects disappeared and the rest developed eventually into what are now German, Dutch, Flemish, English, Danish, Swedish, Norwegian and Icelandic. To these regions the Germanic people brought not only their language but also their myths, religion, and beliefs. In mainland Europe and England relatively early conversion to Christianity means that little evidence for these beliefs remains, so we have to turn to Sweden, Denmark, Norway, and particularly Iceland, where Christianity was embraced much later (only finally taking over in the eleventh century), to construct a picture of Germanic myth.

THE ONLY CONTEMPORARY written evidence we have is from such outside observers as the Roman historian Tacitus, as the Germanic people did not write. Their runic alphabet, which had mystical significance, was designed for carving inscriptions on wood or stone—not for lengthy treatises. The most important written sources for mythology date from around the thirteenth century, when the authors were already Christian, and come from Iceland, where interest in the old gods lasted the longest. In around 1220, Snorri Sturluson, a brilliant Icelandic scholar who was also a major landowner, an important political figure, and a Christian, wrote a book about the heathen gods and myths so that they would not be lost forever to poets of the future. It is from Snorri's book, the *Edda,* that we have our fullest picture of northern mythology. Also written down in thirteenth-century Iceland, though presumably dating from earlier, was another major source: a collection

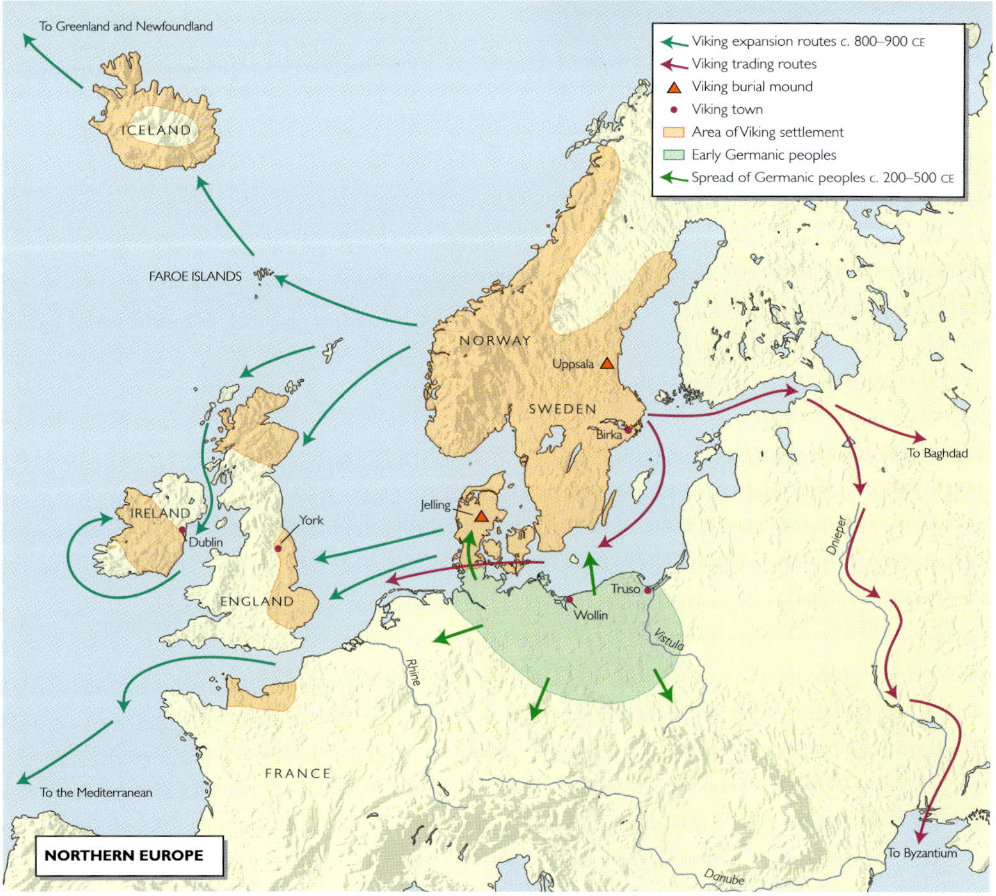

◀ *Church carvings such as this, were a means of insuring that tales stayed part of a culture's heritage through time.*

▶ *The illustrations and texts of ancient manuscripts record myths and legends for prosperity.*

of mythological poems known as the *Poetic Edda*. Additionally we have fragmentary evidence from Icelandic sagas and evidence from archaeology, such as the finds from the magnificent ship burials excavated at Oseberg and Sutton Hoo.

THE ENVIRONMENT

LIFE WAS THOUGHT by the northern people to have begun with the fusion of ice and fire, and they thought that at Ragnarok, the end of the world, flames would reach the sky and the earth would sink into the sea. Destruction by fire and water must have been a familiar image to poets writing down the myths in volcanic Iceland, and their vision of steam and flames rising to the skies could well have been inspired by volcanic eruptions. Descriptions of major eruptions through the ages bear a great resemblance to the sequence of events of Ragnarok: mountains shaken by earthquakes, the sun going dark from the clouds of smoke, and ash, followed by flames, smoke, and steam filling the sky and melting ice causing serious flooding alongside rivers of burning lava. The great winter and the darkening of the sun, lasting for three years with no summer, was also something the people of the north, with their long, dark winters, had reason to dread. Iceland, in particular, saw summers with no darkness and winters with no light. This apocalyptic vision, however, also has much in common with conceptions of the end of the world in other cultures.

RELIGIOUS CUSTOMS

WORSHIP OF NORTHERN gods was conducted in many different ways. Huge statues of Thor, Odin, and Freyr resided in the magnificent temple at Uppsala in Sweden, where sacrifices apparently included humans. At other, less splendid temples priests would sacrifice animals, particularly to Thor or Freyr. People also worshiped less dramatically: sacrifices were brought to groves, rocks, and stones in which patron gods were thought to reside. This type of sacrifice was more likely to be foodstuffs. Simple altars of piled stones were also set up in the open air for such sacrifices.

Specially built temples could be very simple, or natural sacred places might be chosen, such as Helgafell (Holy Mountain) in western Iceland. Thorolf Mostur-Beard, a devoted follower of Thor, held this mountain to be so sacred that no one could look at it unwashed and no living creature could be harmed there.

The same Thorolf also followed widespread custom by throwing the wooden pillars of his high seat overboard, as his ship approached Iceland, to allow Thor to guide them to where he should make his home. Thorolf held the site thus chosen by Thor as so holy that no one might desecrate it with bloodshed or excrement.

CREATION

IN THE BEGINNING there was Ginnungagap—a gaping void. Fiery Muspell lay to the south of this and freezing Niflheim to the north. Eleven rivers flowed from the heart of Niflheim, whose poisonous flow hardened into ice. Vapor rising from the poison froze into rime, and layer upon layer the rime increased until it spread right across Ginnungagap.

The part of Ginnungagap facing Niflheim was filled with ice and rime, but the southern part was warmed by hot wind coming from Muspell. When the ice met the heat this fusion brought about the first signs of life.

The melting drops of ice formed into a huge giant, Ymir. Three gods—Odin, Vili and Ve—killed Ymir and created the world from his body. They carried him into the middle of Ginnungagap and formed the earth from his flesh and rocks from his bones. His blood they made into lakes and the sea. They formed the sky from Ymir's skull and set it up over the earth, placing one of four dwarfs—Nordri, Sudri, Austri, and Vestri—at each corner. Ymir's hair the gods used to create plants and trees, and they scattered his brains into the sky to form clouds.

THE CREATION OF LIFE

FROM YMIR, the primeval giant who came into being at the beginning of time, descended the race of giants. As Ymir slept, he sweated, and a male and female grew under his armpit, while one of his legs begot a monstrous son on the other.

The great Ymir was sustained by a cow, Audhumla, also engendered spontaneously at the beginning of creation. She licked the salty rime stones for nourishment. As she licked, a man's hair began to emerge, on the second day a head, and by the end of the third day there was a complete man, Buri, who was tall, strong, and handsome. He had a son, Bor, who married Bestla, a giant's daughter. They produced three sons: the gods Odin, Vili, and Ve.

These three gods killed Ymir and created the world from his body, and they also created humankind by forming a man and woman from two tree trunks they found on the seashore. Odin gave the new beings breath and life, Vili gave consciousness and movement, and Ve gave them faces, speech, hearing, and sight. They called the man Ask (ash tree) and the woman Embla (of unknown meaning). From these two beings the human race descended.

▲ *Odin, skilled magician and god of war.*
◀ *Tapestry detail showing one-eyed Odin carrying an ax, Thor carrying his symbolic hammer, and the fertility god, Frey.*

FAMILY LIFE

LIFE FOR THE PEOPLE of Northern Europe was difficult. The unforgiving climate and terrain had to yield enough food to last through the long, cold, dark winters. In Iceland, where the myths survived longest, the weather could be pitiless and travel often impossible. Under these conditions family relationships were crucial. Families had to be self-reliant, and family ties gave a guarantee of support in times of difficulty. This is reflected in the myths of the gods, who had many risky adventures, but who were a close-knit group that helped and supported each other, with very clear loyalties to their own kind.

▶ *The motif on the chest of this figure, that forms part of a bucket handle, is a symbol of the god, Thor.*

CREATION OF THE DIFFERENT CLASSES

CREATION OF DIFFERENT social classes was attributed to the enigmatic god Heimdall. One day, in disguise, Heimdall was received at a farm by Ai and Edda (great-grandfather and great-grandmother) who fed him coarse bread and broth. Heimdall stayed with them for three nights, sleeping between the couple. Nine months later Edda gave birth to a son, a swarthy, ugly child who was named Thrall. Thrall spent his life in manual labor, and slaves descended from him.

Next Heimdall came to a dwelling where a well dressed couple, Afi and Amma (grandfather and grandmother), gave him hospitality and a trencher of meat. He slept three nights between them. Nine months later Amma bore a bright-eyed son, with a rosy complexion, who was called Karl (freeman) and grew up to farm and build. All freemen descended from Karl.

Heimdall then came to a luxurious home, where Fadir and Modir (father and mother) entertained him with a sumptuous meal of bread, meat, poultry, and wine. Heimdall stayed three nights, sleeping between them, and in nine months a boy was born with glittering eyes and fair skin and hair, named Jarl (earl). Jarl grew up highly accomplished, and the nobility descended from him.

COSMOLOGY

THE WORLD was thought to consist of three levels, one above the other like a series of plates. The group of gods known as the Aesir lived in Asgard, on the top level. Also on this level was Vanaheim, dwelling place of the Vanir (another group of gods), and Alfheim, domain of the elves. On the level below was Midgard, where men lived; Jotunheim, land of the giants; Svartalfheim, the abode of the black elves; and Nidavellir, home of the dwarfs. Asgard and Midgard were connected by a flaming bridge called Bifrost, otherwise known as the rainbow. On the level below was cold Niflheim.

The central column of the World Tree, the great ash Yggdrasill, passed through each level. Yggdrasill's branches extended over the whole earth and its three roots burrowed into the three levels of the universe. The well of Urd (fate), where the gods held council each day, lay under the root that reached into Asgard. Beneath the second root, which delved into Jotunheim, was the well of Mimir, where Odin pledged one of his eyes in return for a wisdom-giving drink. Under the root which extended into Niflheim was the spring of Hvergelmir, the source of the 11 rivers of the creation.

THOR

ARMED WITH HIS HAMMER, Thor, god of thunder, protected the world. His most famous attribute was his mighty strength, excelling that of all others. He was enormous, with red hair, a red beard, red eyebrows, and fierce red flashing eyes. Thor's main occupation was destroying the giants who constantly threatened the worlds of gods and men. Thor actively sought these beings out, with the express intention of their annihilation, and seldom hesitated to raise his hammer aloft when he encountered one. Should any of the other gods be threatened he could also be called upon and would instantly appear.

GIANTS

GIANTS, HUGE AND usually hostile, played a major part in Norse myths. In general they represented forces of chaos and negativity, against whose influence the gods were forced to contend to maintain the order of their universe. However, this was not always the case—the relationship was not always straightforward. While the gods' daily business consisted mostly of protecting themselves from giants, giants were not invariably the enemy. Occasionally they presented a helpful aspect, and furthermore many gods had affairs with giantesses or even married them. (For example: Freyr married Gerd, a giant's daughter; Njord married Skadi, also a giantess.) Odin himself was descended from a giant and had several affairs with giantesses. Nevertheless, more often than not, the mode of handling giants involved the crashing down of Thor's hammer.

Famous giants include Hrungnir, who challenged Thor to a duel, and Thjazi, who stole the golden apples of youth. Utgarda-Loki, a lord of the giants, used magical art to outwit Thor and his company. Helpful giants tend to be of the female variety and include the giantess Grid, who lent Thor a staff and belt of strength when he was without. Thor also had two sons with a giantess, Jarnsaxa.

THOR LOSES HIS HAMMER

THE MYTH OF THE THEFT of Thor's hammer, Mjollnir, shows how important the protection of the hammer was to the gods, and the lengths they would go to get it back. It also demonstrates the hammer's range of functions.

Thor awoke one morning to find his hammer missing. He woke Loki and told him the hammer had been stolen. Loki decided they should go to see Freyja.

"Will you lend us your falcon shape to look for my hammer?," asked Thor. "Gladly," replied Freyja, "I would give it even if it were made of gold or silver if it would help to find Mjollnir."

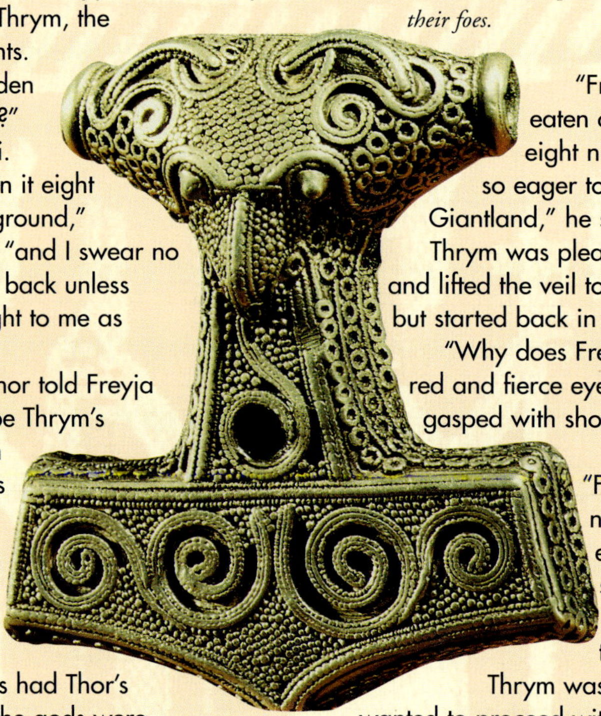

▼ *Thor's hammer, used to protect the gods from their foes.*

Loki flew off in Freyja's falcon shape until he found Thrym, the lord of the giants. "Have you hidden Thor's hammer?" demanded Loki.

"I've hidden it eight leagues underground," replied Thrym, "and I swear no one shall get it back unless Freyja is brought to me as my bride."

Loki and Thor told Freyja to prepare to be Thrym's bride, at which she was furious and flatly refused. Alarmed, the gods met to decide what to do. If the giants had Thor's hammer, then the gods were defenseless against attack and Asgard would soon be overrun—but if Freyja would not marry Thrym how could they get the hammer back? Heimdall came up with an idea.

"Let us dress Thor as a bride and send him to Thrym in Freyja's place."

Thor was aghast at this suggestion, protesting that he could not possibly be dressed up in women's clothing, but Loki reminded him of the fate that lay in store for Asgard if he did not get Mjollnir back. So Thor was dressed in bridal clothes with jewels on his breast and a veil over his head. The necklace of the Brisings was put around his neck. Loki accompanied the disguised Thor, dressed as his handmaiden.

Thrym was exceedingly pleased to see Freyja arrive, and his servants laid out a great feast before them. Thor set to and ate a whole ox, eight salmon, and all the dainties reserved for the women, washed down with three horns of mead. Thrym watched this with some alarm, saying he had never seen a maiden eat and drink so much. Loki had to think quickly to avoid discovery.

"Freyja has not eaten or drunk for eight nights, she was so eager to come to Giantland," he said.

Thrym was pleased at that and lifted the veil to kiss Freyja but started back in horror.

"Why does Freyja have such red and fierce eyes?" he gasped with shock.

Loki said, "Freyja has had no sleep for eight nights, she was so eager to come to Giantland."

Thrym was satisfied and wanted to proceed with the wedding. He ordered Mjollnir to be brought to hallow the couple. The hammer was laid on the bride's lap. As soon as Thor had the hammer things were very different. He jumped up, tearing off the veil, and crushed all the giants in the hall, starting with Thrym.

THOR'S HAMMER AS PROTECTOR

AMULETS IN THE SHAPE of Thor's hammer, made of silver or other metals, have been found in Scandinavian graves, demonstrating the faith placed in Thor's protection. Most date from the later tenth century and were found in Denmark, southern Norway, and south-eastern Sweden. Some are very tiny, perhaps two centimeters long, and many have loops attached, showing they could be worn. As a protective symbol, they were perhaps the pagan version of the miniature cross worn by Christians. Molds have been found in which hammers and crosses could be manufactured side by side to suit the requirements of customers with different beliefs.

ELVES AND DWARFS

ELVES APPEAR in most Northern European mythology associated with the land. However, they could also be considered dangerous. The Anglo-Saxons, Norwegians, and Icelanders believed they could cause illness and nightmares. Light elves, more beautiful than the sun, with matching characters, lived in Alfheim, while dark elves, blacker than pitch and evil natured, lived underground.

Another race of beings living underground were the dwarfs. Although not particularly small, they were usually thought of as ugly. Dwarfs originally generated from the soil, forming as maggots in the flesh of Ymir, the primeval giant, whereupon the gods gave them consciousness and intelligence.

Dwarfs were master craftsmen and amazingly skilful smiths who fashioned objects with extraordinary properties, particularly from gold. They created many treasures belonging to the gods, including Thor's hammer Mjollnir, Odin's ring Draupnir and Freyja's famous necklace. Gleipnir, the only fetter that could restrain the wolf Fenrir, was also the work of their hands.

Dwarfs would sometimes place curses upon treasures, particularly when they were forced to forge them or to give them up. For example, two dwarfs were compelled to forge a magic sword and laid the curse upon it that it could never be drawn without causing death.

◄ *This pendant represents the goddess Freya. She is wearing the Brisingamen necklace, made for her by the dwarf craftsmen.*

▼ *Illustration of an elf procession. The bright colors suggest that these are likely to be kind, light elves.*

LAW AND ORDER

THE THEME OF ORDER pervades northern mythology, where the gods constantly strive to maintain or restore order in the face of dark and unpredictable forces, mainly in the shape of giants. Thor's strength and his hammer are the main weapons in this fight, and Thor's overriding concerns are justice, law, and order. Therefore, among men, Thor was closely associated with the law, and the populace relied on and placed their trust in him. The annual Icelandic assembly, at which the laws were recited, disputes were settled, and legal cases heard, always opened on a Thursday, the day sacred to Thor.

THE WORLD TREE

THE ASH TREE Yggdrasill, the World Tree, was the axis of the universe. Nothing is recorded of Yggdrasill's origins. It was populated by specific creatures: an all-knowing eagle sat high in it, with a hawk, Vedrfolnir, between its eyes. A vile serpent, Nidhogg, lay in Niflheim, gnawing at Yggdrasill's roots. Ratatosk, a squirrel, ran up and down the tree carrying insults between Nidhogg and the eagle. Four stags also lived in the branches: Dain, Dvalin, Duneyr, and Durathror.

The tree was a source of life and succor to the creatures that lived in and under it, but it suffered anguish and hardship, caused by the very creatures it sustained. Nidhogg and his entourage of serpents gnawed its roots, and the stags ate its leaves and shoots. The squirrel bit it, and its sides constantly rotted away. Thus the central support and sustenance of the world also bore its trials and tribulations.

To counteract this suffering, Norns that lived by the well of Urd took water together with mud that lay around the well and poured it over the branches every day. This mixture was so holy that everything it touched turned white, and it protected the tree from decaying.

FATE AND DESTINY

THE INFLUENCE OF FATE is felt throughout northern mythology: destiny is preordained and cannot be avoided. Ragnarok—the end of the world—is inevitable. The destiny of individuals was allotted by Norns, female spirits who were thought to visit each child at birth and brought either good or bad fortune. Discrepancy in individual lives was because good Norns allotted good lives, but malevolent Norns allotted misfortune. Individual destiny was faced with stoicism and humor. A hero's death was much honored, adversity was cheerfully accepted, and to face death with a final humorous remark was the most honorable act of all.

▲ *This picture of Yggdrasill, the World Tree, clearly shows the all-knowing eagle at the top, with the vile serpent Nidhogg entwined in the roots.*

▼ *Thor and his hammer Mjölner, and his spear Gungner.*

LIFE AFTER DEATH

THERE WERE SEVERAL possibilities for the afterlife.

Warriors who died in battle, particularly by the spear which was sacred to Odin, might go to Odin's great hall, Valhalla. A warrior's death was considered most noble, and this fate was to be aspired to. A nobleman dying at home who wished to go to Valhalla instead of Hel, where those went who died in their beds, could have himself cut with a spear and "marked for Odin," ensuring reception into Valhalla.

Freyja also received slain warriors. She rode out to battles in her cat-drawn chariot and took half the slain, while the other half went to Odin. The warriors she received went to her hall, Sessrumnir (place of many seats). Dead women went to Freyja too. In Egils' saga a woman bent on suicide claimed she would not eat or drink until she supped with Freyja. The goddess Gefjun also received dead women, being responsible for all the girls and women who died unmarried.

Those dying of illness, accident or old age went to the underworld realm of Hel (not to be confused with the Christian hell), overseen by Loki's daughter, also called Hel. The drowned were taken into Aegir and Ran's underwater palace.

▲ *Odin rides his horse, Sleipner, who is also used to carry dead warriors in Valhalla.*

BALDER'S DEATH

BALDER DREAMED of mortal danger to his life, which was of great concern to the Aesir. His mother Frigg hit on a plan to safeguard him. She extracted oaths from everything not to harm Balder: from fire, water, animals, birds, snakes, plants, stones, trees, earth, metals, diseases, and poison.

The Aesir then found it greatly amusing for Balder to stand up and the other gods to throw things at him, for nothing would harm him. When Loki saw this, he changed himself into a woman and went to visit Frigg. He told Frigg the Aesir were all shooting at Balder, but he was not being hurt. Frigg said. "Neither weapons nor wood will harm Balder, I have received oaths from them all."

"Has every single thing sworn an oath not to hurt Balder?" Loki asked. Frigg replied that one plant, mistletoe, had seemed too young to swear an oath.

Loki went and found the mistletoe and pulled it up. He approached the blind god Hod, who was standing alone, and asked why he was not shooting at Balder.

"Because I cannot see where he is," replied Hod, "and besides, I have no weapon."

"I will help you to honor Balder," said Loki. "I will show you where he is and you can shoot at him with this stick."

Hod took the mistletoe and shot as Loki directed. The stick pierced Balder through and he fell down dead. When they saw Balder fall, all the Aesir were speechless with shock. All they could do was weep. Frigg eventually spoke. She asked who amongst the gods would ride down to Hel, the underworld, to find Balder, and offer a ransom to Hel's guardian, also called Hel, to let Balder come back to Asgard. Hermod, Balder's brother, volunteered. Odin's horse Sleipnir was fetched, and Hermod galloped away.

Hermod rode until he came to the gates of Hel, where he saw Balder in the seat of honor. Hermod begged Hel to let Balder come home to Asgard, describing the great weeping among the Aesir. Hel said the strength of feeling for Balder must be tested before she would release him. "If all things in the world will weep for Balder, then I will let him go, but if any object refuses to weep then I will keep him."

The Aesir sent messengers all over the world to ask that Balder be wept out of Hel. Everyone and everything did this—people and animals, the earth, stones, trees and every metal.

On their way back, the messengers came across a giantess called Thokk. They asked her to weep Balder out of Hel, but she refused, saying, "Thokk will weep dry tears for Balder. Let Hel keep what she has." So Balder was not released. It was widely thought that Thokk was Loki in disguise.

THE AESIR

CHIEF OF THE GROUP of gods known as the Aesir was Odin, a skilled magician and the god of war, death, kings, poetry, and magic. Odin was a frightening character, not always to be trusted, who was more concerned with magical power than with his subjects. His queen was the beautiful and gracious Frigg, who shared with him the ability to foresee the future.

Thor, protector of Asgard, was Odin's son and the god of thunder. He was always called upon if the gods were in trouble with giants and would instantly appear, wielding his invincible hammer, to save the day. This role as protector also extended to men: Thor could be relied upon and the population put their trust in him.

Balder, another son of Odin, is the best known of the other Aesir, mainly on account of the myth of his death. Balder was the wisest, kindest, most beautiful, and most beloved among the gods—but was tragically killed through Loki's treachery. Tyr, also a god of war, was the bravest of the gods. Bragi, god of poetry, and Ull, god of archery and hunting, were also of the Aesir.

▲ *Detail of a carved funerary stone. The soldiers in the top panel carry their swords pointing down, signifying death.*

▼ *Tyr, god of the sky, with a chained animal, probably Fenrir, whom Tyr fettered at the cost of his hand.*

VALHALLA

NOBLES AND HEROES who died in battle were believed to go to Odin's magnificent hall, Valhalla (hall of the slain), where they became part of the Einherjar, Odin's personal army. They dwelled there gloriously, feasting and sporting, until the end of the world, when they would be called upon to fight for Odin in the last great battle.

Valhalla was an enormous building with many doors. Its rafters were fashioned from spear shafts and its tiles from shields. Every day the Einherjar would put on war gear and fight one another for their entertainment. At the end of the fighting all those who had fallen miraculously rose, and in the evening they all sat together again: eating, drinking, and carousing.

The warriors ate the meat of a boar named Saehrimnir, which was cooked each day in the pot Eldhrimnir by the cook Andhrimnir. Saehrimnir's flesh would always be sufficient to feed the Einherjar, regardless of their number, and each morning it was whole again, ready to be cooked for the next day. The Einherjar's drink was an endless supply of mead produced by a goat named Heidrun which, each day, filled a vat big enough for all to drink their fill.

VALKYRIES

THOSE WHO were to die in battle were chosen on Odin's behalf by Valkyries. The name Valkyrie means literally "chooser of the slain" and these female spirits went to the battlefields to grant victory according to Odin's will and lead the slain back to Valhalla. They also waited on the dead warriors in Valhalla, serving their food and drink. In poetic sources Valkyries are described wearing armor and on horseback, and the popular conception arises from this, but it appears that possibly much more mysterious and bloodthirsty supernatural female figures were associated with battles and the slain from early Germanic times.

THOR FISHES FOR THE WORLD SERPENT

THOR'S PARTICULAR ADVERSARY was the monstrous Jormangand, the World Serpent, who lay coiled around the world at the bottom of the sea. On one occasion, Thor assumed the appearance of a young boy and lodged for a night with a giant called Hymir. When Hymir prepared to go fishing the next day, Thor asked to accompany him. Hymir sneered that he would be useless as he was so young and small. Infuriated, Thor retorted that he was not sure who would be the first to beg to row back and was just about to crash his hammer down on Hymir's head when he remembered his secret plan to test his strength elsewhere. Instead he asked Hymir what they would use for bait. "Get your own bait," said Hymir, whereupon Thor tore the head off the biggest ox in Hymir's herd.

Thor took the oars first, and it struck Hymir that Thor rowed particularly hard. When they reached the usual fishing ground, Thor said he wanted to row farther out. A little later, Hymir warned they were now so far out it would be dangerous to proceed on account of the World Serpent. Thor said he would row on, and did so, which made Hymir very anxious.

When Thor finally laid down the oars he fastened the ox head onto the end of a line and threw it overboard. Deep under the sea the serpent closed its mouth around the bait. Inside was a huge hook which stuck into the roof of its mouth, and the serpent jerked violently. Holding the other end of the line, Thor summoned all his strength against the serpent. He pushed down so hard that both his feet went through the bottom of the boat, bracing him against the seabed. He pulled up the serpent, but Hymir panicked and went very pale, and just at the moment Thor lifted his hammer to strike the serpent its deathblow Hymir cut Thor's line. The serpent sank back into the sea and Thor threw his hammer after it. Thor was furious at Hymir's ruining of his plan and punched him so hard that he fell overboard. That was the end of Hymir, and Thor waded ashore.

THE VANIR

FERTILITY DEITIES known as the Vanir lived alongside the Aesir. Njord, god of the sea and its bounty, was invoked for riches, success in fishing, and sea travel. He lived at Noatun (ship enclosure/harbor) and was the father of the twins Freyr and Freyja.

The principal fertility god, Freyr, was a radiant and bountiful god of sunshine and increase. He ruled harvests by controlling the sun and the rain. Marriages were also occasions to invoke Freyr, as he was responsible for human increase too. Freyr was called upon for prosperity and thought to be a bringer of peace. Weapons were banned in his temples and the shedding of blood in his sacred places was taboo.

Freyja, principal goddess of the Vanir, was more than just a fertility goddess: she was also the goddess of love, an expert in magic, and a receiver of the slain.

▲ *Thor with his symbolic hammer, catches Jormangand, the World Serpent.*

BOARS

BOARS WERE SACRED to the fertility deities. Freyr and Freyja owned and rode boars, and were possibly sometimes envisaged in boar form. Boars were also sacrificed to Freyr to insure a good harvest. Boar images are found on ceremonial objects: an heirloom of the Swedish kings was the Sviagriss, a ring bearing the figure of a pig, and early Swedish kings treasured helmets carrying images of boars. Like Freyja's boar, one of these magnificent helmets was known as Hildisvin. Such a helmet is also mentioned in the Anglo-Saxon poem *Beowulf*, where the boar crest protected the life of the wearer.

LOKI—FRIEND AND FOE OF THE GODS

ONE OF THE MOST extraordinary characters in northern mythology is Loki. Not strictly a god (he was descended from giants), he lived among the Aesir, joining in their escapades and often helping them out. However, while he was the gods' friend and companion, and blood brother of Odin, Loki was also their adversary and at Ragnarok—the end of the world—he would fight against the gods on the side of the giants.

Loki was handsome and witty but malicious and sly. He was also extremely cunning and always full of tricks and schemes. A shape-shifter, he was able to take on the shapes of animals or birds when wreaking his mischief. Snorri refers to Loki as the slanderer of the gods and the origin of all lies and falsehood.

There is no evidence that Loki was worshiped, but he was integral to the mythological canon. His presence causes many of the events in the mythology. Loki's mysterious nature is revealed by the fact that although he constantly caused trouble for the gods, it was often his quick thinking and cunning that got them out of trouble again, and his influence could be beneficial to them as well as malign.

▲ *Detail of a forge stone incised with the face of Loki with his lips sewn together.*

◀ *Bronze statue of Freyr, the god of fertility.*

LOKI AND IDUNN

THE GODDESS Idunn guarded the golden apples of eternal youth which the gods had to eat to keep from growing old. Mischievous Loki caused both Idunn and her apples to be stolen away by a giant, yet it was also Loki's cunning that reversed this calamity and brought Idunn back again.

Loki was captured by a giant called Thjazi, who refused to free him unless he promised to bring Idunn out of Asgard with her apples. Loki at once vowed to do this and the giant let him go. Loki went to Idunn and told her he had seen some apples in the forest that she might think were very precious. He suggested that she come to see and bring her apples with her to compare. As soon as the two were outside the walls of Asgard, Thjazi arrived in the shape of an eagle and snatched up Idunn with the apples, taking her back to his home.

The disappearance of Idunn and the apples affected the gods greatly and

◀ *Both Loki and Thjazi transform themselves into birds in this myth in order to overcome their adversary.*

they began to grow old and gray. They met to discuss the last sighting of Idunn and realized the last time she had been seen she was going out of Asgard with Loki. Loki was seized and threatened with torture and death. Terrified, he promised to go and look for Idunn if Freyja would lend him her falcon shape.

Transformed into a falcon, Loki flew to Giantland and came to Thjazi's castle. Thjazi was away and Loki found Idunn alone. He quickly turned Idunn into a nut and flew home to Asgard with her in his claws.

When Thjazi returned and discovered that Idunn had been taken, he transformed himself once more into an eagle and gave chase. The Aesir saw the falcon flying with the nut and the eagle following and built a fire in Asgard. The falcon, Loki, flew in over the wall and dropped straight down, but the eagle could not stop and flew over the fire and caught alight. So the Aesir killed Thjazi, and Loki had both caused the disappearance of Idunn and her apples and brought them back.

LOKI'S CHILDREN

LOKI PRODUCED three monstrous offspring with a giantess called Angrboda: Jormangand, a gigantic serpent; a daughter, Hel, who was half alive and half corpse; and the huge wolf Fenrir. These creatures were all significant in the mythology. Indeed Jormangand and Fenrir would destroy Thor and Odin respectively at Ragnarok. Odin rounded Loki's offspring up, but the gods could not simply annihilate them. They had to find other ways to deal with them.

The gods were all extremely worried when it was discovered that Loki had produced these three children. They had heard prophecies that great harm would come to them from the siblings. Odin sent gods to find the children and bring them to Asgard. When they were brought, Odin first threw Jormangand, the serpent, into the sea that lay around the world. There it grew until it encircled the whole world, biting on its tail. Then Odin placed Hel, Loki's hideous daughter, down in Niflheim, the land of the dead, and charged her with providing food and lodging to all the dead who went there. Fenrir, the vicious wolf, the Aesir kept and brought up in Asgard, although only Tyr was brave enough to look after it.

LOKI'S PUNISHMENT

AFTER LOKI HAD caused the death of Balder through his malice, he realized the gods' anger would not be appeased and he ran away. He built a house on a mountain as his hiding place, with four doors so he could keep watch on all sides. By day he transformed himself into a salmon and hid in a nearby river. Sitting in his house one night, he wondered what sort of device the Aesir might use to catch him, and thus he invented the first fishing net.

Then Loki realized the Aesir had discovered him and they were not far away. He threw the net into the fire and ran to the river. The Aesir noticed the shape of the net in the ashes where it had burned and realized this must be a device to catch fish. Quickly making one themselves, the Aesir took it to the river. They dragged the net through the water, but Loki squeezed himself between two stones on the riverbed and the net dragged over him. They dragged the river again, this time weighting the net down so that nothing could pass underneath. Loki kept ahead of it, but he realized he would soon be in the open sea. He leaped up over the net and swam back upstream.

The Aesir dragged the river a third time, and now Thor waded ahead of the net. Loki faced either the mortal danger of entering the sea or the equal threat of Thor. He decided to try to leap over the net as fast as possible, but Thor caught the transformed Loki by his tail—which is why a salmon tapers toward the tail.

Now the Aesir were not about to show Loki any mercy. They took him to a cave, where they set up three stone slabs, making a hole in each. They fetched Loki's sons Vali and Narfi and turned Vali into a wolf, whereupon he tore his brother Narfi to pieces. The gods pulled out Narfi's intestines and used them to bind Loki across the three stones. The bonds immediately turned to iron. Skadi fixed a poisonous snake securely over Loki's head so that poison dripped onto his face. Loki is destined to lie there until he breaks free at Ragnarok. Sigyn, his wife, stands beside him catching the poison in a bowl, but when it is full she has to pour the poison away and the drops reach Loki's face. Then he wrenches away so hard that the whole earth shakes, which is called an earthquake.

◀ *Odin, the god of war.*

Fenrir will advance with mouth gaping. Beside him will be Jormangand, spitting poison. They will advance to Vigrid, the plain where the last battle will take place, as will the gods with the Einherjar, led by Odin who will make for Fenrir. Thor will vanquish the serpent but will succumb to its poison. Fenrir will swallow Odin. Flames, smoke, and steam will shoot up to the firmament. The sky will turn black and the stars will disappear. The earth will sink into the engulfing sea.

However, Ragnarok will not be the end of everything. Eventually the world will reemerge, green and fertile, and a new age will be ushered in. Crops will grow unsown. The children of the old gods will sit on the grass where Asgard had previously been and discuss former times.

The human world will be repopulated by two people, Lif and Lifthrasir, who will have hidden in the ash tree Yggdrasill. Thus the end will contain a new beginning, and the cycle will recommence.

ODIN

ODIN, KING of the gods, was powerful and terrifying—certainly not a benevolent father figure. He was the special god of kings, nobles, and poets and a god of war, magic, and wisdom. Odin's mastery of magic was legendary. He could change his shape at will, and his magical abilities made him a formidable opponent. He had only one eye, having pledged the other at the well of Mimir in return for a knowledge giving drink. Odin was invoked for victory in battle, but the promotion of strife was in his interests and he was often accused of awarding triumph unjustly.

RAGNAROK

DESTINY COULD NOT be avoided. This concept culminated in Ragnarok (destiny of the gods), the inevitable destruction of the world. Ragnarok will be presaged by three years of fierce battles, followed by three years of terrible winter with no summer. Then a huge earthquake will break all bonds. The wolf Fenrir will become free, and so will Loki. Jormangand, the World Serpent, will come to shore, making the ocean surge onto the land. The ship *Naglfar,* made from dead men's nails, will be carried along on the flood, filled with giants, with Loki at the helm.

TYR AND FENRIR

THE AESIR KEPT the wolf Fenrir, child of Loki, in Asgard to keep an eye on him, but only Tyr was courageous enough to look after him. When they saw how enormous Fenrir was growing the gods decided to restrain him. They brought a huge iron fetter to the wolf and suggested he try his strength against it as a game. Fenrir thought little of the fetter, so he let them do as they pleased. When the fetter was secured the wolf freed himself with one kick.

The gods quickly forged another fetter, twice as strong, and exhorted Fenrir to try again, saying he would be renowned for his might if he broke free from this one. Fenrir was keen to achieve that kind of fame, so he allowed himself to be bound. Although he had to struggle slightly more than before, again he quickly escaped.

The Aesir became worried that they would never restrain Fenrir. They sent to the dwarfs, who made a fetter called Gleipnir. Gleipnir was silky like a ribbon but was made of six magical ingredients: a cat's footfall; a woman's beard; the breath of a fish; the roots of a mountain; the sinews of a bear; and a bird's spittle. The Aesir took Gleipnir to Fenrir, who looked at it carefully.

"I do not think I will get much credit for breaking a thin ribbon," he said, "but if this is forged by magic then, however thin it is, it is not going around me."

The Aesir said he would surely break such a delicate band, seeing as he had broken huge iron fetters, "but if you cannot break this, we will free you, for you will seem no threat to us."

Fenrir replied, "If I cannot free myself I'll wait a very long time before you free me, so I do not care for this game. But rather than have you think me cowardly, I'll take part if one of you puts his hand in my mouth as a pledge of good faith."

The Aesir looked at each other then and did not know what to do, until Tyr volunteered to place his hand in the wolf's mouth. At that Fenrir allowed himself to be bound, but the harder he kicked the stronger the fetter became and he could not free himself. The Aesir all laughed then—except Tyr: he lost his hand.

GODDESSES

THE NORTHERN pantheon included powerful female deities. The most prominent were Odin's gracious wife, Frigg, and Freyja, goddess of fecundity and sensuality. These two have sometimes been suggested to be aspects of one goddess—Frigg representing wife and mother, and Freyja mistress and lover. They also shared some functions: they were both invoked in childbirth to protect and assist women in labor and were also involved in the naming of newborn children.

Other goddesses were mostly related to fertility. Some of these are possibly merely aspects of Freyja and Frigg: Saga, Hlin, Vor, Syn, and Snotra seem to be aspects of Frigg, while Sjofn, Lofn, and Gefion appear to be aspects of Freyja. Fulla and Gna were Frigg's handmaidens. They attended Frigg, carried her casket, looked after her shoes, and shared her secrets. Some other goddesses were in fact giantesses, given the status of goddess by virtue of marriage into the community of gods. Skadi, wife of Njord, was the daughter of the giant Thjazi but was accepted into the Aesir and appears to have been worshiped in her own right. Freyr's wife, Gerd, also came from the race of giants and attained the status of goddess on her marriage.

▲ *The Andreas Stone with a relief depicting Odin being eaten by the Fenrir, from the story of the Doomsday of the Gods.*

◀ *Brooch in the form of the World Serpent, who will come to shore at the final destruction of the world.*

THE NECKLACE OF THE BRISINGS

THE STORY of how the goddess Freyja obtained her famous and magnificent gold necklace, the necklace of the Brisings, demonstrates the passionate and lustful side of her nature.

One day Freyja came upon four dwarfs. They were fashioning an object from gold, as was often their occupation, for dwarfs were renowned for their skill in working the precious metal. What they were making was an exquisite necklace, more beautiful than Freyja had ever seen before. Freyja coveted the marvelous necklace greatly. Surely no neck other than hers should sport such a gorgeous adornment. She told the dwarfs she wanted it and offered to buy it from them, but they refused to sell. Freyja offered a large amount of gold and silver, but still they would not part with the necklace.

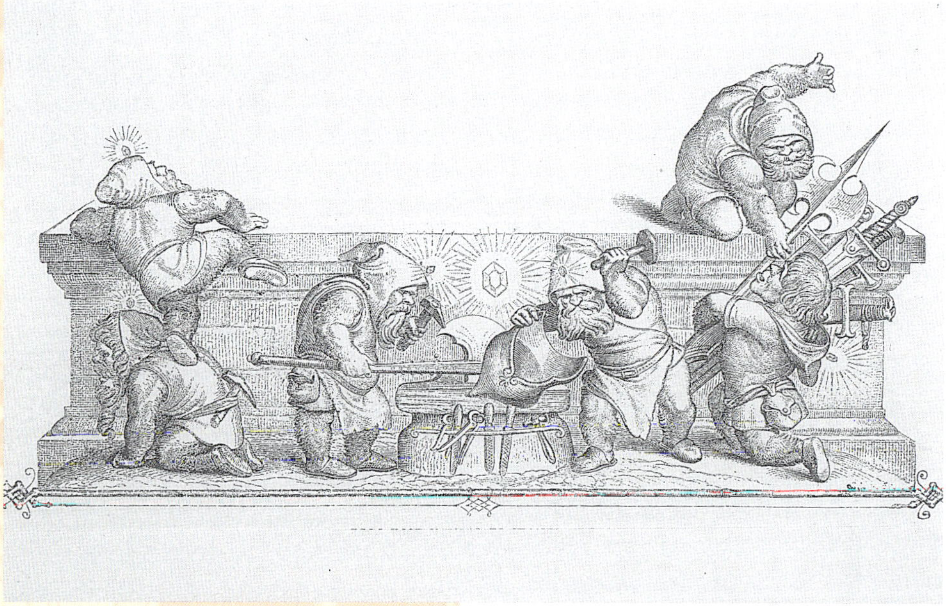

▲ *Dwarfs were excellent metalworkers and crafted a necklace for the beautiful goddess Freyja.*

◀ *Freyja, goddess of love, marriage, and the dead, sits here spinning the clouds.*

Freyja was consumed with a desire to own it. She offered more and more things of value, but the dwarfs were not interested—until eventually they named their price.

"All that we want, we already have. The only thing that we desire, Freyja, is you. If you would spend one whole night with each of us, then we would each give you our share of the necklace."

Freyja was shocked. She looked at the four ugly, misshapen dwarfs, who leered back at her, and was not pleased, but her desire for the necklace was a burning fire. Four nights did not seem too high a price to pay to own the necklace forever and, besides, no one would know. She agreed to the dwarfs' terms.

Freyja stayed with the dwarfs for four nights, and each in turn had his way with her. After she had kept her side of the bargain they kept theirs and gave her the necklace. Freyja went home with it, pretending nothing had happened, and the necklace became one of her most prized possessions.

FREYJA

POWERFUL, PASSIONATE, and beautiful, Freyja was the principal goddess of the Vanir. As well as being a major fertility deity she was goddess of erotic and sensual love, expert in the practice of magic and a receiver of the dead. Freyja participates in many myths and is depicted as both desirable and desirous. She was the target of the giants' lust—when attacking Asgard they often sought possession of her—but was also accused of "running about at night after men like a goat in heat" and of taking as lovers all the gods and elves, including her own brother.

DEITIES OF THE SEA

THE SEA was greatly important to the people of Northern Europe, both as a source of food and as a means of acquiring fame and glory through travel, trade, or raiding. The best known deity of the sea was Njord (one of the Vanir), but Aegir, who appears to have personified the mighty ocean itself, also ruled there. Aegir dwelled far from land, and Viking poetry talks of the jaws of Aegir swallowing ships at sea.

Aegir and his wife Ran received the drowned into their palace on the ocean floor. The sagas tell that if drowned seafarers appeared at their own funerals, Ran had given them a good welcome. It was considered lucky to have some gold on one's person at sea, so as not to arrive empty handed at Ran's dwelling.

The hospitality of Aegir and Ran was not entirely malevolent, however. Aegir was famous for the bounty of feasts held at his hall. Thor journeyed to visit the giant Hymir especially to obtain a cauldron large enough for the mead at Aegir's feasts and, in a poem of mourning for a drowned son, the father wishes to avenge himself on Aegir but at the same time refers to him as the "Ale-brewer."

NJORD AND SKADI

SKADI WAS THE DAUGHTER OF the giant Thjazi, killed by the Aesir after he stole their golden apples of youth. She eventually married the sea god Njord, and the myth of this marriage tells of the linking of a fertility deity with a representative of winter and darkness.

When the news of the death of Thjazi reached his daughter Skadi, she armed herself, donning helmet and mailcoat, and went to Asgard to seek vengeance for her father. The Aesir offered to compensate her for Thjazi's killing, and part of the settlement was that she could choose a husband for herself from among the Aesir. However, she was to see only the feet of the potential suitors and must choose by these alone.

A parade of all the unmarried gods was set up where only their feet were visible. Skadi inspected all the feet. One pair was by far the cleanest and whitest of them all. She felt sure that this must be Balder, the most beautiful and whitest of the gods, so she quickly claimed her husband.

When the owner of the feet was revealed, it turned out to be Njord, god of the sea. His feet were so beautifully clean because the sea washed over them all the time. Skadi was a little taken aback, but nevertheless the two were married.

The marriage was a difficult one. Skadi was the daughter of a mountain giant and longed to live in her mountain home, but Njord only felt comfortable near the sea. They tried to make it work: they agreed to live alternately for nine nights in Thrymheim, Skadi's mountain castle, and nine nights at Noatun, Njord's home at the seashore. Unfortunately this arrangement did not last long. Each was desperately unhappy in the other's home: Njord could not bear being up in the mountains, listening to the howling of the wolves, and Skadi could not stand the open sea and detested the screaming of the seagulls. Eventually they agreed to live separately, and Njord remained by the ocean while Skadi lived up in the mountains, where she was often seen traveling about on skis or snowshoes.

▼ *This illustration shows Aegir, the god who personified the great ocean, causing a mighty storm.*

◀ *A pair of harness mounts decorated with the form of the eagle commonly associated with Odin. The exaggerated beaks and talons emphasize their ferocity.*

ODIN'S ANIMALS

ODIN NEEDED no food. He lived purely on wine, giving his food to two wolves, Geri and Freki, who sat at his feet. He also had two ravens, Huginn and Muninn (thought and memory), who flew over the world every day to bring him news. In the evening they returned to sit on Odin's shoulders and tell him what they had seen. These creatures are often depicted with Odin in artistic representations and are associated with his role as god of war: wolves and ravens are traditionally linked with battle and death, both in poetry and in actuality (they were commonly found in the aftermath of battles, feeding on corpses).

Odin's other animal was his extraordinary horse Sleipnir, progeny of Loki. Sleipnir had eight legs and was the fastest of horses, able to carry Odin through the air and over the sea. Sleipnir was held to be one of Odin's great treasures.

TREASURES OF THE GODS

THE GODS OWNED special treasures made by dwarfs, the most skilled craftsmen in the mythical world. Odin had a spear, Gungnir, whose thrust could never be stopped, and a gold ring, Draupnir, from which eight rings of equal weight and value dropped every ninth night. Freyr owned a ship, Skidbladnir, which always got a fair wind when its sail was raised but could be folded up and kept in a pocket when not in use, and a golden boar which ran across sky and sea faster than any horse and illuminated the night with light from its bristles.

The most important treasure belonged to Thor. This was his hammer, Mjollnir, which would never fail to strike, could never miss when thrown, and always returned to his hand. The gods relied on the hammer greatly and felt it was the best treasure of all as it afforded them such protection against giants. Mjollnir's properties were so special that it was not only used for physical protection, but was raised over objects to bless them, such as Balder's funeral ship; and raising it over the bones of Thor's two goats brought them back to life after they had been killed and eaten.

THE NUMBER NINE

IT IS NOT KNOWN WHY, but the number nine is significant in Norse mythology. Odin hung for nine nights to learn nine spells. Heimdall had nine mothers, Aegir nine daughters. Hermod traveled nine nights to find Balder, Freyr waited nine nights for his bride Gerd. Njord and Skadi lived nine nights in each other's homes. Every ninth night eight more rings dropped from Odin's ring, Draupnir. Thor will retreat nine paces from Jormangand before dying. A great festival was also held for nine days every nine years at Uppsala in Sweden, where nine of every living creature (including humans) were sacrificed.

RUNES

THE EARLY Northern European runic alphabet was designed for cutting on wood, stone, or metal and consisted of straight lines, easier to carve than curves. Runes were not used for long documents. They have been found extensively on memorial stones, on wooden tallies used in trade, and on weapons. Runes were also thought to have magical significance, and spells could be cast by carving them or protection afforded by wearing them. Odin, powerful god of magic, was thought to have introduced the runes to the world by performing an excruciating self-sacrifice: hanging for nine nights on the World Tree.

ODIN AND THE MEAD OF POETRY

ODIN WAS the god of poetry, which perhaps explains the prominence the poetic sources accord him. Odin himself spoke only in poetry, and poetic ability and inspiration was his to bestow: upon one of his favorites, for example, he conferred the ability to compose poetry as fast as he could speak.

Odin procured the precious mead of poetic inspiration for the gods and for men. The mead was originally made by dwarfs from the blood of a being called Kvasir, created by the gods as a symbol of peace after a war between the Aesir and the Vanir. Kvasir was so wise that there was no question he could not answer. He traveled far and wide imparting his knowledge but eventually was murdered by two dwarfs who mixed his blood with honey and created a rich mead. Drinking the mead imparted the ability to compose poetry or spout words of wisdom.

The mead was later taken from the dwarfs by a giant called Suttung, as they had made the mistake of murdering Suttung's parents. Odin, through his wily ways, regained the priceless mead for the gods and men. He seduced the giant's daughter, Gunnlod, who had been put in charge of the mead, and when she consented to let him have three sips he drained it all and, in the form of an eagle, flew back to Asgard where he regurgitated it. A few drops of mead fell outside Asgard, and that was the portion available to men.

◀ *Carved dragon-head post from the burial ship discovered at Oseberg.*

▲ *A Rune stone, once believed to have held magical or protective power.*

SHIP BURIALS

THE ANGLO-SAXON EPIC poem *Beowulf* describes a spectacular ship funeral given for the Danish king, where the dead king was laid in a ship with much valuable cargo and a gold standard above him. The ship was launched and bore him away. In Norse mythology the god Balder also has an elaborate ship funeral. The ship is sent blazing into the ocean.

These mythological funerals reflected real burials: a magnificent burial in a ship of a ninth century woman, surrounded by much treasure, was discovered at Oseberg in Norway, and ship burials have been found in other parts of Northern Europe.

Siberia and the Arctic

INTRODUCTION

THE ARCTIC REGIONS of Siberia, Alaska, Canada, Greenland, and northern Scandinavia are homelands for diverse groups of indigenous peoples. In Siberia these peoples include the Chukchi, Even, Evenk, Nenets, Nivkhi, Itelmen, Chuvan, Yukagir and Khant; in Alaska they are known as Inupiaq and Yup'ik Eskimos, Alutiiq, and Athabaskans; in Canada and Greenland they are the Inuit; while in Scandinavia the indigenous population is the Saami. The Saami also inhabit the Kola Peninsula in northwest Russia, while Yup'ik Eskimos also live along the far eastern coasts of Siberia. The circumpolar peoples are hunters, fishers, and reindeer herders. They have similar origins in Central Asia: the Inuit, for example, are nomadic migrants who arrived in Alaska from Siberia during the last Ice Age and moved gradually across the vast tundra plains of northern Canada, eventually reaching the mountainous and ice-filled coasts of Greenland some 4,500 years ago.

Whatever the differences in lifestyle, language, and social and economic organization, the indigenous peoples of the Arctic have one thing in common—they have a unique and special relationship with the Arctic environment which is essential for social identity and cultural survival. Whether they depend on reindeer herding or hunt seals, whales, and caribou, the peoples of the Arctic are not only sustained by the environment in an economic sense, but the Arctic nourishes them spiritually and provides a fundamental basis for their distinctive cultures and ways of life.

THIS RELATIONSHIP of Arctic peoples with their environment is reflected in the richness of their mythology and underscored by an elaborate system of beliefs and moral codes. Spiritual forces are inherent in humans, animals and all natural phenomena. Because of this, the Arctic is perceived as an environment of risk, fraught with danger and uncertainty. Part of this danger is due to the fact that hunting peoples such as the Inuit rely on hunting animals, which have souls that must be propitiated by the hunter after being killed. Similarly, reindeer herders such as the Evenk must make sure that reindeer are slaughtered correctly and their meat, bones, and hide utilized in ways that will not offend the animals' guardian spirit.

Sometimes the rites practiced both before and after the killing of animals took the form of complex animal ceremonialism, such as the bear festival in Siberia, the Bladder Festival in northern Alaska, and other festivals associated with the hunting of sea mammals. The purpose of these festivals was to honor the animal, to ask forgiveness for slaying it, and to insure the safe return of its soul to the spirit world. Offenses by an individual against animals and spirits in the natural world can

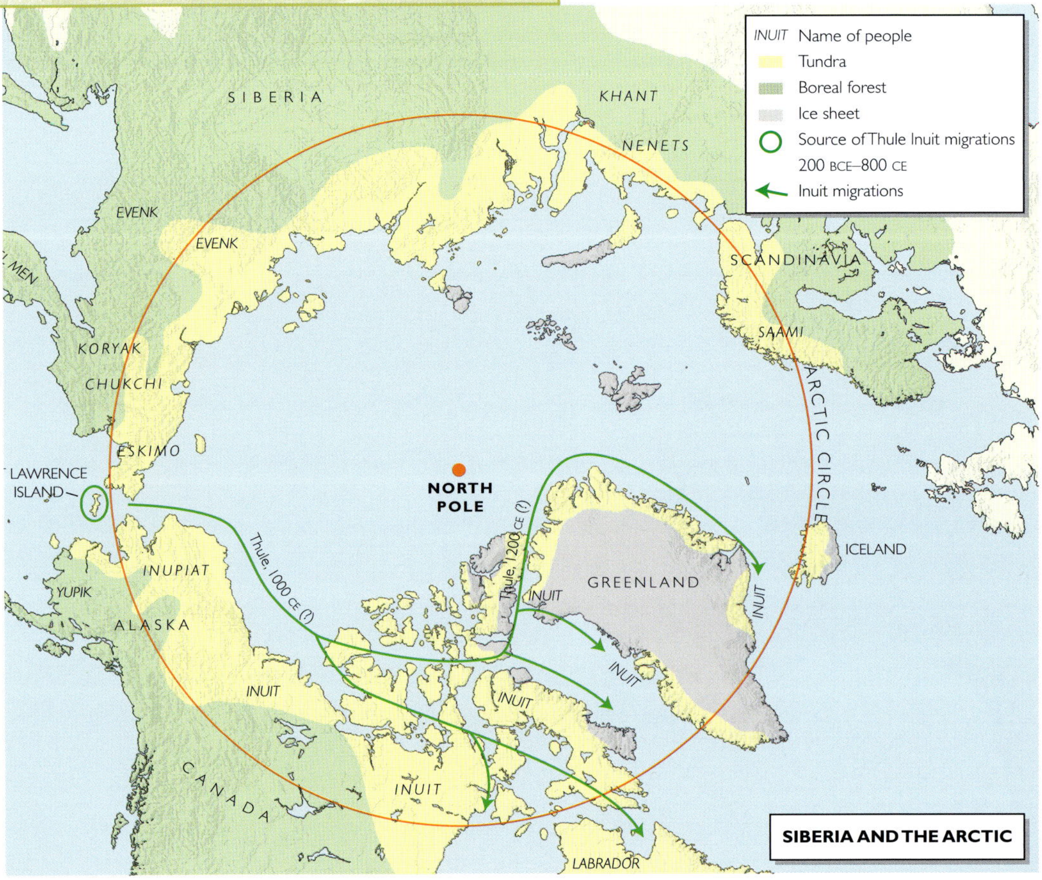

cause pain to the souls of recently killed animals and entice vindictive and malevolent spirits, putting an entire community at risk. Myths relate how poor hunting, illness, misfortune, famine, and bad weather come about because of a violation of the relations between people and the natural world. This finely tuned balance between humans and the environment can be restored through the intervention of the shaman, who visits the spirit world and acts as a curer of illness, affliction, and misfortune.

The compelling similarities between the mythology, religious beliefs, and ceremonial life of the peoples of the Arctic can be accounted for, in part, by the fact that these peoples can not only trace similar origins and share elements of material culture and subsistence technology but had extensive contact with and knowledge of each other prior to the arrival of Europeans. The archaeological and ethnohistorical record shows that the peoples of northeastern Siberia and western Alaska participated in long distance trade, trade fairs and even warfare. At the same time, they participated in ritual exchanges, festivals, and religious ceremonies. This activity linked them to other peoples in wider ranging economic, social, and ritual networks. For Alaskan and Siberian peoples, these networks extended right across Siberia and south to Korea, Japan, and China; while Alaskan Eskimos and Athabaskans also had links with peoples to the east in Canada and farther south with the various Indian groups on the Pacific Northwest Coast.

Undoubtedly, such contacts provided the opportunity for mutual influence in terms of material culture and mythology. Raven myths, for example, provide strong evidence of contact between the Chukchi and Koryak in Siberia and the peoples of western Alaska, while there are similarities in origin myths and myths about spiritual transformation and reincarnation. Across the Arctic, similar figures and themes occur in different myths. Whether the myth comes from the Chukchi, Koryak, Yukagir, or Inuit, or many other Arctic peoples, the narratives and motifs are recognizable. There are encounters between humans and nonhumans (animals, giants, sea monsters); the transformation of humans into animals and vice versa; accounts of the origin and descent of humans; stories about the power and magic of women and the journeys of the shaman's soul; and narratives about the deeds of deities and heroic characters.

▲ *Indigenous peoples have learned to survive the Arctic conditions of semi-permanent ice and darkness.*

▼ *The Evenk people ensure that they respect the guardian spirit of the reindeer by using the meat, hide, and bones without causing offence.*

RESPECT FOR THE SOULS OF ANIMALS

THE MYTHS AND ORAL histories of the Arctic peoples mainly emphasize the spiritual relationship between humans and animals. Animals are the principal supply of food, and elaborate rituals are associated with the hunting of animals and their subsequent treatment. Among the Nenets, Chukchi, and Evenk of Siberia, reindeer, bears, wolves, and foxes are dominant animal characters in myths and stories, whereas Inuit myths revolve around seals, whales, walrus, and fish such as Arctic char. For Arctic peoples, animals are spiritual beings endowed with souls. As such, they are potentially dangerous to humans if mistreated. The everyday and ambivalent preoccupations of Arctic hunting peoples are their hopes for good hunting and for an abundance of game, but also their fears of starvation and bad luck. Specific measures must be taken to insure a successful hunt, and myths describe how the animal must be propitiated and respected in order to ward off vengeance of its soul. A fundamental belief across the Arctic is that animals have a guardian, or master, who releases the animals in their care only if people treat them with courtesy and respect. The Inuit myth of the Sea Woman (Sedna or Nuliayuk) reflects a belief in the unity of all life but also symbolizes the tensions between the human and animal worlds, of which Sedna is mediator.

▲ *The arctic fox is hunted for its pelt, yet they also command respect from the Arctic peoples as they are believed to have souls.*

▼ *This polar bear, made from marine ivory, originates from the Inuit culture.*

THE SEDNA MYTH

SEDNA WAS A GIRL who refused to get married. As punishment, her father married her to a dog and they went to live on a nearby island. One day, when her dog-husband was away from home, a stranger appeared in a boat and called to her to join him. Sedna seized this opportunity to leave the island and stepped into the stranger's boat.

After a long journey, they reached his village and Sedna took him as her new husband. Sedna soon discovered that her husband was not a man after all, but a petrel who could assume the appearance of a human. Sedna was now afraid and wished she could escape from her new husband. Sedna's father, in the meantime, had been searching for his daughter, and when he found her he hid behind some rocks and waited for the petrel to go fishing. When the petrel was gone, Sedna and her father left the village. The petrel returned in time to see the boat disappearing. Chasing after it, he caused a

heavy storm, which rocked the boat. To save himself, Sedna's father threw her overboard into the sea.

Clinging onto the side of the boat, Sedna pleaded with her father to save her. The storm grew wilder and, one by one, Sedna's father cut off the joints of her fingers. As they hit the water, Sedna's fingers were transformed into seals, whales, and narwhals. Before Sedna slipped beneath the waves, her father poked out one of her eyes. Sedna descended to the lower world at the bottom of the sea, where she became mistress and keeper of the sea mammals which had once been her fingers. Sedna's father reached his village. He was lying in his tent, when the tide rose and swept him away. He now lives in Sedna's house and her dog guards the entrance.

Sedna is usually generous to humans and releases the sea mammals in her care. But there are also times when she retains them because hunters have caused pain to the animals' soul. When the animals are scarce, a shaman must journey to Sedna's abode and plead with her to release them. Sometimes the sea mammals are tangled in Sedna's hair, which has been made dirty by humans violating taboos. When this happens, the shaman must visit Sedna and comb her hair, and so release the seals, whales, and other animals.

INUIT SOAPSTONE AND IVORY CARVINGS

IN CANADIAN INUIT mythology, the entire universe was dormant until creative human acts brought it into existence. This notion of humans as revealers is reflected in the carvings of animals such as seal, whale, walrus, caribou, and polar bear. Images of animals are said to lie hidden in soapstone and ivory, waiting to be released by the carver's knife. Inuit carvers say that they do not create the animal but merely help it to emerge. The carving of animal figures is done for ornamental, religious, or ritual reasons, and, as the image is believed to contain the essence of the animal itself, the hunter can influence the spirit of what he is about to hunt.

THE MASTER OF THE ANIMALS

ARCTIC PEOPLES believed that a great spirit protected the animals, embodied their essence, and supervised their correct ritual treatment by humans. This master, guardian or owner of the animals also prevented or facilitated the hunting of animals. In Siberian reindeer herding societies, such as the Chukchi and Nenets, the master is protector of the herds. The Naskapi of Labrador visualized the caribou guardian as a white-bearded man who could also take the form of a bear. For the Inuit, the Sea Woman is owner of the sea mammals. A widespread myth throughout the North Pacific coasts of Siberia and Alaska relates how the master of the water is a killer whale.

THE SUPREME BEING

FOR SIBERIAN PEOPLES, the supreme being is distant and often detached from human affairs and seldom intercedes when human life is threatened by disease or evil spirits. In the mythological past, the relations between the supreme being and people were close, and shamans would regularly ascend skywards to communicate with the supreme being. A common motif in Siberian mythology is that a human transgression offended the supreme being, who then withdrew far into the heavens. The human world became subject to the influence and actions of the spirits of the ancestors, animals, and natural phenomena. In some myths, the supreme being sent the first shaman to protect people from famine, disease, and malevolent spirits.

▼ *Reindeer, which can provide transport as well as food and clothing.*

MYTHS ABOUT THE SUPREME BEING

FOR THE PEOPLES of the Arctic everything in the world has a life force and shares the same spiritual nature. Some groups, such as the Chukchi, believe in a supreme being which they call the Creator, or Life-giving Being. But the nature of the supreme being is uncertain and difficult to conceptualize. For the Chukchi the supreme being is indistinguishable from the master of the reindeer herds and is also known as Reindeer Being. The Evenk believe the supreme being consists of two aspects: Amaka, which looks after the fortunes of people; and Ekseri, which rules over all animal guardians and the great Siberian forests. Amaka is also the Evenki word for bear, which is visualized as the form of both the supreme being and the master of the animals.

The supreme being personifies the life force which flows through and animates both the human and animal worlds. The Inuit call this vital principle *inua*. But they also talk of *sila*, the ruler of the elements and the universe. *Sila* is all of the individual powers and forces of nature, the fundamental principle which pervades the natural world. *Sila* is also manifest in each and every individual person and is the vital force that connects and integrates a person fully with their immediate environment.

▲ *An Inuit woman drinks from one of many melt-water streams.*

▼ *This shaman in ritual clothing invites the spirit of the fire to give a blessing.*

THE SHAMAN

THE SHAMAN is a universal figure across the Arctic, acting as intermediary in the transactions between humans, the souls of animals, and the master of the animals. Myths relate how the shaman must first undergo a long, solitary, and arduous initiation, wrestling with spirits and aquiring his powers, before returning home. As the shaman goes into a trance, his soul leaves his body and journeys to the spirit world. Once there, the shaman bargains with the master or guardian of animals for the animals to be sent to the hunter to be converted into food, and for the return of human souls that may have been captured by malevolent spirits.

ORIGIN MYTHS

A RICH AND WIDE variety of myths tell of how the world came into being. A common theme is that, before the beginning of time, there existed only darkness until a trickster figure created the world. The Inupiaq Eskimos have oral histories which describe how Raven Man was first created by the figure of a primal shaman. Raven Man harpoons a whale whose body becomes land, then Raven reveals the daylight and creates the first people. Raven

▲ *In some parts of the N. American Arctic, Inuit winter villages would have consisted of snow houses.*

Man appears in several variants of a myth which tells how, set adrift on an ice floe, Raven comes across a village of people and takes a wife from among them. Raven and his wife have children who, traveling to their father's land, become ravens themselves, retaining the power to change back into human form. Eventually, their descendants forget how to change into people and remain ravens. Other myths describe the origin of the elements, the sun and the moon, and other celestial bodies, which are related to myths about the balance between daylight and darkness, time and space, and the year's hunting activities.

THE ORIGIN OF THE SUN AND THE MOON

LONG AGO, before the world had taken its present form, a man lived in a coastal village. He had no wife, but he did have a younger sister with whom he was in love. At night, when she put out the seal oil lamp in her igloo, she found that a man would come in and make love to her. In the darkness, she could not see who the man was, but she was determined to find out. One night, before she put out the light, she dipped her fingers in the soot at the bottom of the lamp. When the man came in and made love to her that evening, she smeared his forehead with the soot.

The following day, she went looking for the man and found her brother sitting in the men's house with lamp soot on his forehead. The girl was both ashamed and angry. In a fit of rage she cut off one of her breasts and placed it on a dish, which she then offered to her brother, saying, "Since you desire me so much, eat it!." Her brother refused and chased her as she ran off, still carrying the dish. As she was running, the girl picked a clump of moss and lit it. Her brother did the same. The girl ran faster and faster until she ascended skywards and became the sun. Her brother followed her, but the flame on his moss went out, leaving only the burning embers, and he became the moon. To this day, the sun is still chased by the moon. Occasionally they embrace, causing an eclipse. The sun loses height in the middle of winter but gains in strength and beauty throughout the spring and summer, which only increases the moon's desire for her. The moon is without food and gradually wanes from hunger until it is lost from sight, but then the sun reaches out and feeds it from the breast which the girl had placed on the dish. Once the moon is nourished it continues to chase the sun, which allows it to starve again before allowing it to feed once more.

THE MOON

IN INUIT MYTH it was once possible for any person to journey to the moon. This would happen when the moon visited earth and took a man or woman of his choosing back with him on the dog sledge he used to travel around the sky. Some Inuit groups believed that the moon influenced the fertility and movement of animals. If the moon was angered by a human breach of a taboo, it was possible that he would punish the Inuit by sending the animals elsewhere or by preventing female animals from conceiving. Shamans would make frequent visits to the moon to appease his anger.

RAVEN AS PRIMEVAL FIGURE

FOR THE CHUKCHI, Itelmen, Koryak and Yup'ik of northeastern Siberia, and for the various Inuit groups in Alaska, Canada and Greenland, Raven is a central mythological figure. Raven is the primeval ancestor who brought daylight for the people. In some Chukchi, Koryak, and Itelmen myths, Raven created the earth and taught people how to make clothes from animal furs, how to make boats and canoes, and how to weave nets for fishing. In other variants of Siberian myths, the first people originated from an incestuous union between Raven's son and daughter, while for the Koryak, Raven is a trickster figure.

THE SACRED LANDSCAPE

RESPECT FOR NATURE and animals is a fundamental theme in the traditional worldview of Arctic peoples and is reflected in both mythology and practice. Many features in the landscape are sacred places, where animals reveal themselves to hunters in dreams, or where people encounter animal spirits while traveling. In Siberia, reindeer antlers are placed at sacred sites and adorned with gifts; in Greenland, pieces of the vertebrae or hide of a hunted polar bear are left to flutter in the wind to insure the release of its spirit; while in northern Scandinavia, the Saami place sacred stones (*seiteh*) on mountaintops and near lakes and rivers.

HUMANS AND ANIMALS IN A DUAL EXISTENCE

MANY MYTHS SERVE to remind people that, in the distant past, humans and animals were not as clearly distinguished as they are today. Koryak, Chukchi, and Yup'ik Eskimo myths from Siberia; Inupiaq Eskimo myths from Alaska; and Inuit myths from Greenland and Canada relate how all animate beings have a dual existence, so that an animal can become a human at will, or vice versa. All human persons have the power and ability to change their form, while the guardian spirit of an animal can not only assume the shape of the animal it protects but take the form of any other animal as well as becoming a person. Because of this, the hunter can never be entirely sure of the true nature of any animal he encounters, and great care must be taken when approaching it. As well as being a guardian spirit, an animal could be the free soul of a sleeping person, the soul of a powerful shaman, or the soul of someone who has recently died and has assumed animal form while waiting to be reborn. The Koryak of Siberia believed that a black bear was a human wearing a bearskin. The following story, which illustrates these themes, was told to the author in northern Greenland.

▼ *Walrus being hunted by Greenlanders.*

THE WALRUS AND THE HARPOON HEAD

THERE WAS ONCE a man who made a beautiful harpoon head. The first time he went out hunting with it he spotted a walrus on an ice floe. He paddled his kayak very carefully until he was close enough to the walrus to throw his harpoon. He took aim and threw it, but the walrus dived into the water. Pulling in his harpoon, he noticed the harpoon head had disappeared, but the shaft and the bladder float were still there. He looked around but could not see the walrus. He waited in silence for some time, trying to think where the walrus would surface. Then he paddled around the ice floes in his kayak but still could not see the walrus.

Feeling depressed at the disappearance of the walrus and the loss of the harpoon head, he returned home. Later, during the evening, he went to visit his friend who was a great hunter. Still in low spirits, he told his friend of the day's events and of the loss of the beautiful harpoon head. However, his friend laughed and, reaching into his pocket, he said: "Today I was out in my kayak and you thought I was a walrus! Here is your harpoon head!"

▼ *The Inuit believe that the souls of the deceased either go to the underworld, a happy, hunger-free place where kin are reunited, or to an afterlife of cold and starvation, an environment even more hostile than that in which they lived.*

▲ *The Chukchi respect polar bears as nonhuman persons. They live in communities, are believed to have intelligence and therefore deserve human respect.*

ANIMALS AS NONHUMAN PERSONS

ACROSS THE ARCTIC, animals are conceptualized as nonhuman persons and are endowed with consciousness and intelligence. Some species of animal are said to live in communities that are similar in social organization to that of human communities. For the Chukchi there are polar bear people, wolf people, mouse people, and spider people, while the Yup'ik say that seals live according to the same kinds of rules that humans are subject to. Yup'ik stories describe how young seals learn appropriate rules from their elders, such as knowing the dangers of approaching a hunter who appears to be a careless and disrespectful person.

MYTHS CONCERNING REINCARNATION OF THE HUMAN SOUL

MYTHS AND STORIES surrounding personal names and human reincarnation are universal themes throughout the Arctic. The person consists of three souls: the personal soul, the breath or free soul, and the name soul. In Greenland, the Inuit believed that after death the personal soul traveled to either the underworld, a place with an abundance of game animals and where the souls of dead kin and friends would be reunited, or to an upper world of eternal starvation and cold. The breath or free soul can leave the body at will, often when the person is asleep. If it strays too far, it may have to be retrieved by a shaman. Throughout Siberia, Alaska, Canada, and Greenland, people believe that a person's name is also a soul. At death the name soul leaves a person's body and is said to remain "homeless" until it is recalled to reside in the body of a newborn child. Names have power, and some of the good personal qualities of the deceased are inherited by the receiver of the name. Myths and stories commonly tell of the soul's wanderings after death and relate how, through the name soul, the deceased become the guardian spirits of their descendants.

◀ *Shamans still play an important role in modern communities.*

THE SOUL'S JOURNEY TO THE LAND OF SHADOWS

UPON DEATH a person's three souls separate. One stays with the body, remaining in the land of the living as a spirit or ghost, one journeys to the heavens and eventually finds its way to Pon, the supreme being, while the third goes to the land of shadows, where it becomes a shadow itself. Sometimes, a person's soul journeys to the land of shadows when a person is asleep or ill. The shaman must follow, retrieve the soul, and return it to the person's body. The journey to the land of shadows is long and arduous. The soul enters a passage underneath the funeral pyre, travels along a road and first meets an old woman with a dog, who guards the boundary between the edge of the world and what lies beyond. The soul then reaches a river which it must cross in a boat. When the river has been crossed, the soul has reached the land of shadows. Once the soul has become a shadow, it continues to lead the same life it has known in the land of the living. The shadow soul joins the shadow souls of the relatives and friends it had on earth. In the land of shadows, each family has its own house or tent. The shadow souls of people hunt the shadow souls of animals and fish for the shadow souls of fish.

The souls of the dead eventually leave the land of shadows and return to earth to be reborn. If the living do not respect the souls of the dead, then they refuse to leave the land of shadows and women are unable to conceive. When this happens, the shaman's soul, with the assistance of his helping spirits, must journey to the land of shadows and bargain with the dead to release their souls so that women can conceive once more. The shaman cannot always persuade the souls of the dead to return to earth themselves, or to release some of their relatives, and sometimes has to steal a shadow soul to place in the womb of a woman. The shaman steals the soul by breathing deeply in order to swallow it. The shaman then returns swiftly to the land of the living. Because the stolen soul has been forced, rather than chosen, to be reborn, the child does not live long and the soul returns to the land of shadows as soon as it can.

THE QIVITTOQ

ALL OVER GREENLAND, stories are told about the *qivittoq,* a mysterious, supernatural wanderer, originally a person who has left their community to live alone in the mountains. After some time living in the wilderness, the senses of the *qivittoq* sharpen; his eyes, ears, and nostrils grow larger to enable him to see, hear, and smell animals, and his teeth and fingernails grow long and sharp. His body becomes covered in a thick coating of fur and his head hair becomes long and matted. The *qivittoq* takes on raw animal characteristics and depends on himself for survival. During the long, dark Arctic winter, the *qivittoq* returns to his home community to peer through windows and to pilfer meat and fish.

THE NORTHERN LIGHTS IN MYTH

WHILE THE DECEASED are waiting to be reborn, their souls form the *Aurora borealis,* the northern lights. A Labrador Inuit myth tells how at the end of the world there is a great abyss, with a dangerous pathway leading through a hole in the sky and on to the land of the dead. The souls of those who have crossed over light torches to guide the new souls. A recurring theme in Inuit myth is that the land of the dead is a land of plenty. The souls of those who go there can be seen feasting and playing ball with the skull of a walrus, and this appears as the *Aurora borealis.* Variants from Greenland and the central Canadian Arctic relate how, as the souls run across the frost hardened snow of the heavens, they make a crackling sound. The souls of the dead do not wish to remain apart from the living and try to communicate with them by whistling. If a person hears this whistling, they must answer with a soft whisper or whistle, and the lights will come closer out of curiosity. The Chuvan of Siberia believe the northern lights bring relief to a woman in childbirth, while the

Saami of Finland have a story which relates how the northern lights are ever present, even in daylight, and offer protection from sorcery and evil.

▲ Aurora borealis, *believed to be the souls of those awaiting rebirth.*

▼ *A spectacular frozen landscape, common throughout Siberia and the Arctic.*

THE NORTHERN LIGHTS AND THE OLD MAN

THERE WAS ONCE an old man who was the oldest person in Lapland. He had lived to be almost 2,000 years old with the help of three rays from the northern lights. These three rays were the souls of dead people which the old man had caught when they had come too close to the earth, and who now wished to remain on earth. They made a bargain with the old man. As long as the old man kept them in his lamp, the three souls could not be retrieved by the northern lights and taken back to the heavens. In return, they would capture the souls of young people to transfer into the body of the old man so that he would continue to live.

One day, a curious young man sees the old man out walking and follows him home. The old man invites him into his house and locks the door. He then releases the three souls from his lamp. Grabbing hold of the young man, the three souls plunge their hands into his body and try to pull out his soul. At that point, the northern lights descend to earth and several rays of light enter the old man's house through a window, seizing the three souls. The young man is saved and the three souls are taken back to the heavens. Without them the old man soon withers and dies.

SIBERIAN YUP'IK CEREMONIAL MASKS

MASKS EXPRESS the unity between humans and animals and bring the mythical world of the past into the present. The Siberian Yup'ik Eskimos of the coasts of southwest Alaska, the Bering Straits, and eastern Siberia carved elaborate masks from driftwood for ceremonial purposes. These masks depicted animal spirits and represented mythical figures. Masks were worn at community feasts, ritual trade festivals, and dances to celebrate the memory of the ancestors. According to Yup'ik myth, a person can be incarnated into the animal or its spirit by using its own form. A person wearing a mask can gain influence over the animal's spirit, and shamans commonly wore masks in rituals to insure success in hunting and fishing.

GUARDIAN SPIRITS OF THE HOME

AMONG REINDEER herders such as the Koryak and Chukchi, each family has a guardian spirit in the form of a sacred wooden fireboard. The fireboard is carved in human form and is used to light the fire in the hearth which is the center of each home. The fireboard represents the deity of the family fire, which protects the family, the home, and hearth from evil spirits. The sacred fireboard is also thought to be an aspect of the master of the herd, and for both Koryak and Chukchi the fireboard is carved in the shape of the Reindeer Being. The fireboard not only protects the family, fire ceremonies also play an important part in the welfare and sacrifice of reindeer. Reindeer have their origins in fire: in Koryak and Chukchi myth the supreme being pulled the first reindeer out of a sacred fire. In Koryak tradition, the return of the reindeer from pasture is celebrated in a fire ceremony. A new fire is started with the fireboard, and burning sticks are then thrown to greet the herd as it approaches the camp. When Chukchi sacrifice a reindeer, its blood is collected in a ladle and fed to the fire. Blood is also smeared over the fireboard and used to paint designs representing the Reindeer Being on people's faces.

▲ *The fireboards in Chukchi and Koryak homes are traditionally carved in the form of the reindeer-being as a mark of respect.*

▼ *The bear is so important to the Arctic peoples that it has its own elaborate ceremony, during which the slaughtered bear is considered an honored guest.*

THE BEAR IN ARCTIC MYTHOLOGY

THE BEAR HOLDS a preeminent place in the mythology of virtually all Arctic peoples. The bear is humanlike, it can stand on its hind legs, and it looks like a human corpse when skinned. The bear is also the most common helping spirit for a shaman. A recurring theme in Inuit myths is that a polar bear has sexual intercourse with a woman, and this symbolizes the close, yet ambivalent nature of both humans and animals. Some people are said to be descended from such unions. The bear is a great hunter and has special power. Bears are also known to track humans as prey, and stories illustrate how the bear hunter is placed in a precarious position because he himself is at once the hunter and the hunted. Although the killing of a bear brings prestige to the hunter, it also brings danger. In Saami tradition, hunters who take part in a bear kill are regarded as unclean and must undergo ritual purification during a period of seclusion. In Siberia, the bear festival is one of the most elaborate forms of animal ceremonialism anywhere in the Arctic. After a bear has been hunted, a feast is held where the dead bear is treated as an honored guest and people ask its forgiveness for slaying it.

HELPING SPIRITS

THE SHAMAN depends on spirit helpers to assist in journeying to the spirit world. Often, the helping spirit is an animal which carries the shaman on its back, flying silently through the air, or swimming effortlessly to the bottom of the sea. Helping spirits can also be humans, but whatever form they take they instruct the shaman in magic and spiritual teaching and may impart some of their powers to the shaman. For the Nenets of Siberia, the shaman's most powerful helping spirit may be a boar which he or she leads by a magic belt, while the Inuit shaman may be helped mainly by a polar bear.

HUMAN HEALTH AND HEALING

WHILE THE RELATIONSHIP between humans and animals depends on humans respecting the spirits and souls of animals, the proper treatment of human souls is of equal importance. While the body, as the material part of the person, is subject to disease and decay, human souls are prone to attack by malevolent spirits. The Netsilik Inuit of the central Canadian Arctic believed that all physical illness was the result of malevolent spirits inhabiting the body and hurting the soul, while Inupiaq Eskimos believed illness to be the result of the temporary departure of the soul from the body. If the soul strayed too far away, then the person would die unless the shaman could retrieve the lost soul. Shamans also had the power to cause harm and bring illness. The Inupiaq Eskimos believed illness to be caused by the intrusion of a foreign object by a malevolent shaman who used his spirit powers for personal advantage and gain. Among the Koyukon Athabaskans of the Alaskan boreal forest, the spirit powers of trees were especially valued for curing illnesses. White spruce, for example, was believed to have a benign spirit, and its needles were boiled to make an infusion prescribed by the shaman and drunk to allay a variety of ailments.

▶ *Early illustration depicting the clothing worn by the peoples of the Arctic.*

WOMEN'S MAGIC AND POWER

THE MYTHS OF ARCTIC peoples tell of the power of women in terms of the magical knowledge some women possess and the influence they have over the elements and animal spirits. In Greenland, a woman who has recently given birth can bring a storm by sucking in air and then blowing it out again. Greenlandic myths also describe how death originated with a woman who spoke to the spirits and told them to let people die gradually, or else there would be no room left in the world for people to live. Through the production of skin clothing, women express the mythical and religious beliefs of their society. By making beautiful garments and caring for the animal skins they use, women are able to please and gain influence over the spirits of the animals essential for the survival of the group. But the opposite can hold true. In southwest Alaska, for example, women had to be careful not to trap their hair in the seams of animal skins they were sewing together. If this happened, it would bring danger to whoever wore the clothes. Inuit stories also tell of actions of women having an effect on the outcome of the hunt. In Greenland a successful whale hunt depended, in part, on women remaining indoors in darkness until the men returned home with the whale.

SIBERIAN CLOTHING AS SACRED ART

FOR SIBERIAN PEOPLES, clothing provides more than warmth and protection from the elements. Whether for everyday use or for ritual and ceremonial use, clothing is an expression of religious and spiritual beliefs and offers protection from malevolent spirits. Animal skins are used to make clothes, but animal spirits retain control over these skins and taboos must be observed when clothes are being made. Sacred imagery depicting animal spirits and mythological characters appears on a person's clothes, and the clothes of a shaman have designs which make symbolic reference to his or her helping spirits. Clothing also pays a vital role in funerary rituals.

India

INTRODUCTION

THE PEOPLES OF ANCIENT India did not think it important to record their history in a chronological way. They lived simply in a climate which quickly eroded anything man-made and they cremated their dead. So they left little in the way of historical records, ruins, or burial grounds, the usual yardsticks by which we measure ancient history. We must therefore speculate about the ancient history of their remarkable civilization and mythology.

Our main sources of clues are the Sanskrit hymns called the *Vedas*, which in their present form might date back to about 1500 B.C.E. These hymns show the influence of the early Indo-Iranians of Iran, the most easterly group of the Indo-European peoples. It is assumed that these people, who called themselves "Aryans," entered India between 3000 and 1500 B.C.E. How much their beliefs contributed to the development of the *Vedas,* and how much the Vedic wisdom was already present in India, is a matter of conjecture.

In north India the Aryans met a culture already well established. The city of Mohenjo Daro, in present-day Pakistan, flourished between about 3500 and 1700 B.C.E. It shows evidence of an advanced civilization in its paved streets and meticulous sanitation. At the same time in South India the Deccan Neolithic culture flourished between about 2500 and 1000 B.C.E. India's religion and mythology are the result of the fusion of these three cultures.

THE VEDIC HYMNS

THE ORAL TRADITION that gave rise to the *Vedas* was called *sruti,* meaning "that which is heard." It was passed down through chains of spiritual teachers, called brahmins, who were the keepers of the wisdom. They taught that the Vedic wisdom had been given to Brahma, the creator, at the beginning of the universe and passed down by word of mouth since then. But at the onset of the present age, called Kali Yuga or the "age of iron," when human memory and intelligence would deteriorate, this wisdom had been written down to preserve it for future generations. Since then it had been expanded, first into the four *Vedas,* then into a vast body of spiritual learning called collectively the Vedic literature. The stories described in this literature relate the actions of a divine race of beings whose lives were intertwined with ordinary mortals, yet who had direct access to a higher realm inhabited by immortal beings headed by Vishnu (or Shiva), the supreme being.

This mythology grew to be more than a collection of stories; it provided a complete alternative reality and belief system which formed the basis of the Hindu religion and contributed to the religions of Jainism and Buddhism.

◀ *Depiction of a Brahmin, dating from C.E. 600.*

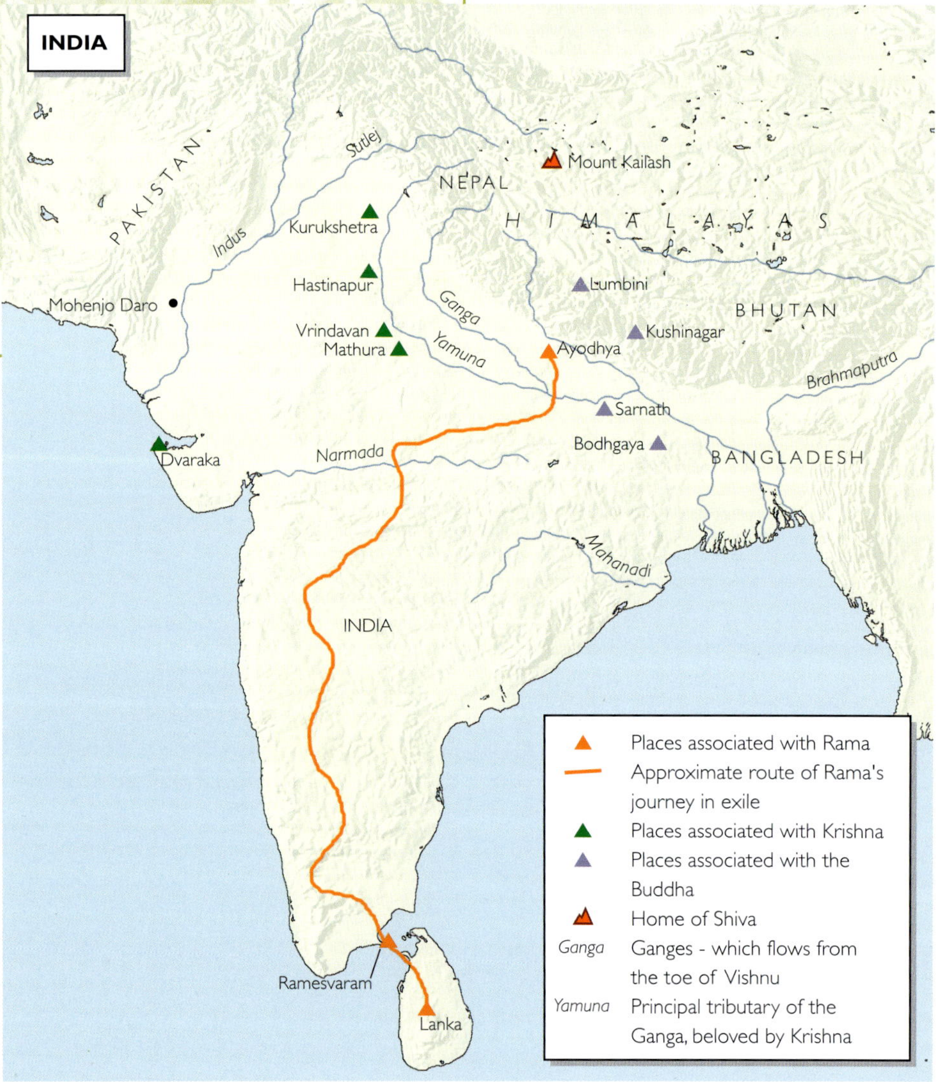

TWO CONTRASTING THEMES

VEDIC MYTHOLOGY has two contrasting themes: the achievement of worldly comfort and prosperity, and the search for a higher reality through asceticism and philosophical inquiry.

The early focus on prosperity emphasized the ritual of the fire ceremony and gave prominence to the gods of nature who could guarantee that prosperity, such as Agni the fire god and Indra the rain god. During the first millennium B.C.E. the emphasis shifted to the search for spiritual knowledge and release from this world. During this period emerged the great gods of later Hinduism: Vishnu, Shiva, and the goddess, Devi.

This shift is demonstrated in the life of King Bharat, recounted in the *Bhagavat Purana*. He retired to the forest to find release from the cycle of rebirth. But at the moment of his death he was distracted by his affection for an orphaned deer and so was reborn in the body of a deer. In time he was reborn as a human and gained enlightenment and release from rebirth. He is so significant a figure that he gives his name to modern India: Bharat.

▶ *Theater and dance, such as this Dance of Krishna, are the media through which Indian myths and beliefs are retold.*

FREEDOM AND SPONTANEITY

THERE ARE TWO broad sources for Indian myths: the Vedic literature, which carries the divine authority of being descended from Brahma and Vishnu through lineages of spiritual teachers and whose influence extends across India; and the local traditions found in hundreds of regional languages and dialects, with their own literature, local gods, and festivals. The *Vedas* contain the epics of the great deities such as Vishnu, Shiva, and the Goddess, with a great deal of philosophical discourse and religious teaching. On the other hand, much of the wisdom of daily life, and the color and vibrancy of Indian culture, is carried in the local stories and traditions that have grown up alongside, or have sometimes prefigured, the Vedic tradition. These local traditions are expressed in dance, drama, song, and folk art. They underscore and add strength to the broader culture of which they form a part. To these could be added the traditions that grew up around Jainism and Buddhism.

SANCTITY OF NATURE

FOR HINDUS, the whole world is sacred: mountains are Vishnu's bones, clouds are the hairs on his head, the air is his breathing, rivers are his veins, trees are the hairs of his body, the sun and moon are his two eyes, and the passage of day and night is the moving of his eyelids.

Everything rests on me as pearls are strung on a thread. I am the original fragrance of the earth. I am the taste in water. I am the heat in fire and the sound in space. I am the light of the sun and moon and the life of all that lives.

EARLY BEGINNINGS: THE *RIG VEDA*

THE EARLIEST MYTHS were gathered in the *Rig Veda*, believed to be the world's oldest surviving text, written at least 3,000 years ago. It is a collection of hymns to accompany the rituals offered to the cosmic deities. Among its stories we find the cosmic initiation ritual which took place at the beginning of this universe, when the primeval male was sacrificed by the deities of space and time. This event symbolized the union of gods and men in acting out the play of life, in which all sacrifice their time and energies in service to the supreme being. The supreme being is himself the substance of the universe, offered in sacrifice to himself. This theme of self-sacrifice recurs throughout Indian mythology as duty and honor. The Sanskrit word approximating "duty" is *dharma*. Roughly translated, it means "the essential purpose of life." It gave rise to a set of principles governing behavior, such as obedience to one's father. These principles at their best embodied a spirit of service which expressed love. This spirit of love was later to flower in the *bhakti*, or spiritual devotion, of the *Bhagavad Gita*.

THE PANTHEON OF GODS

THE UNIVERSE is pervaded by the great spirits, called *devas* in Sanskrit. They each have responsibility for an aspect of nature, which in their personal form they embody, such as Agni, the god of fire. Another example is the goddess Ganga, spirit of the River Ganges. She is the daughter of the Himalayas. She was taken up to heaven as the celestial Milky Way and brought back to earth by the penances of King Bhagiratha to be caught in Shiva's hair. Her devotees believe that she washes away sins. This mystical story coexists with the physical existence of the river in a union of myth and reality which typifies the world of Indian myth, where the line between the visionary and the material substance is subtle and shifting.

The gods have their devotees and their festivals. The high gods, such as Indra, the king of heaven, or Kartikeya, the god of war, are celebrated throughout India. At the local level village gods are worshiped, such as Sitala, the goddess of smallpox, who gives protection from the disease. All the gods and goddesses, however, are intermediaries of the three great deities—Vishnu, Shiva, and Devi—and ultimately of the one supreme spirit.

NARADA AND GANESH: MESSENGERS OF THE GODS

THE GODS have their human or celestial helpers. Narada is the messenger of Vishnu. He warned the evil King Kamsa that Krishna had already been born, thus hastening the unfolding of Krishna's mission on earth. His main purpose is to clear the way for the grace of Vishnu to descend among humans.

Ganesh is the elephant headed son of Shiva. It is said that he removes obstacles from the path of any undertaking. He is jovial and well fed, much loved by Hindu shopkeepers, who make daily offerings to him to avoid obstacles in their business. As the scribe of Vyasa he wrote down the epic *Mahabharata.*

▲ *Vishnu rests between the destruction of the world and the creation of the new universe.*

THE VEDIC CREATION STORY

LONG AGO VEDIC sages described Vishnu as the one whose existence spans the cosmos. When this universe first came into being, it was but one of countless seeds springing from the body of Vishnu, seeds which floated in the Ocean of Creation like clusters of bubbles. Each seed became a golden egg into which Vishnu entered as the Purusha, the cosmic person. Appearing inside its dark hollow, he transformed primeval matter into earth, water, fire, air, and ethereal space. As his universal body developed, corresponding elements of the physical and mental world came into being.

The Vedic hymns recount the sacrifice of Purusha, the cosmic man, at the dawn of the universe. The gods prepared a sacrifice in which the principal offering was the gigantic form of the Purusha himself. From the different parts of his body were produced the elements of the universe. His mouth became speech, presided over by the fire god Agni; his nostrils became breathing and the sense of smell, controlled by the wind god Vayu; his eyes became the sense of sight, controlled by the sun god Surya; movement appeared along with his legs, rivers along with his veins, and mind along with his heart. Brahma and Shiva were his intellect and ego. The four divisions of human society—priests, rulers, merchants, and workers—came from his mouth, his arms, his thighs, and his feet.

Elsewhere there are more specific accounts of the development of the universe undertaken by Brahma, the creator god born from the navel of Vishnu. Brahma made the planets and stars and all the thousands of demigods, each of whom was given charge of a particular part of the cosmic order. Indra was given the rain, Vayu the wind, Surya the sun, Chandra the moon, and Varuna the oceans and rivers. The goddess Bhumi was given the earth.

Brahma and the gods produced the myriad life-forms of the universe, among them human beings. The gods were given the power to grant great blessings to their worshipers. They are the powers behind the elements of the natural world such as wind, rain, and the earth itself. The goddess of the earth, Bhumi, is considered by Hindus as one of the seven mothers. However, powerful though the demigods are, behind them lies Vishnu, and it is really he who creates and controls all. Without him they can do nothing.

▶ *Vishnu rests, with his ever-present attendants, on the serpent, Ananta.*

▼ *The creator god Vishnu seen here riding on Garuda with the godess Lakshmi.*

VISHNU

THE TWO GREAT DEITIES to emerge from the early myths are Vishnu and Shiva, the gods of maintenance and destruction respectively. Both have their ardent devotees, who honor them as the supreme deity, and their separate traditions of learning and worship.

Vishnu is the background to existence, who enters the universe as Narayana, the "one who lies on the waters of life." He sleeps at the base of the universe, attended by the goddess Lakshmi. Whenever there is disturbance in the balance of the universe, he enters the human world to restore the true religious teachings and protect righteousness. He is characterized as full of mercy and patience, and his symbols are the lotus flower and the conch shell by which he blesses the good, and the club and discus with which he subdues the bad.

His role as keeper of the balance is well illustrated in the story of Kurma, the tortoise incarnation, where he sets out to help both the demons and the gods but finally takes the side of the gods. His role as teacher is exemplified by Krishna who taught the *Bhagavad Gita* (see Krishna's Song). In the form of the fish incarnation, Matsya, he re-established the Vedic teachings, which were lost in the great flood, by instructing King Satyavrata.

AVATARS OF VISHNU

THE 10 INCARNATIONS of Vishnu are called avatars, from the word *avatar,* meaning "one who descends." They take progressively more developed forms, from aquatic to mammal to human. Their stories have had a profound influence on Hindu culture. They are: Matsya the fish; Kurma the tortoise; Varaha the boar, who rescued planet earth from the bottom of the universe; Narasimha the man-lion, who protected the boy Prahlad; Vamana the dwarf, who defeated the demon Bali; Parasurama the warrior, who defeated the warlike kings and established peace; Rama the good king; Krishna the cowherd and his brother Balarama; Buddha the teacher, who taught nonviolence and compassion; and Kalki the slayer, who will come at the end of this age riding a white horse to kill the demons and inaugurate a new cycle of the universe.

Thus, from outside, Vishnu reassures the good that he will always insure that evil never triumphs. Meanwhile he is also revered as Antaryami, the "one within," the eternal friend who lives in the heart of each being and gives inner wisdom and guidance.

THE WHEEL OF REBIRTH

VEDIC WISDOM teaches that each living being in this world is an eternal soul inhabiting a temporary body. The individual soul, called *atma,* is a particle of the divine nature. By its presence as the self, it gives energy to the body. Each soul has its own desires to enjoy the world, and to fulfill these desires it enters the cycle of rebirth, called *samsara.* When the soul leaves the body that dies, it is born into another body, like an actor changing clothes. Moving from body to body in search of happiness, it passes through all forms of life, from insect to god.

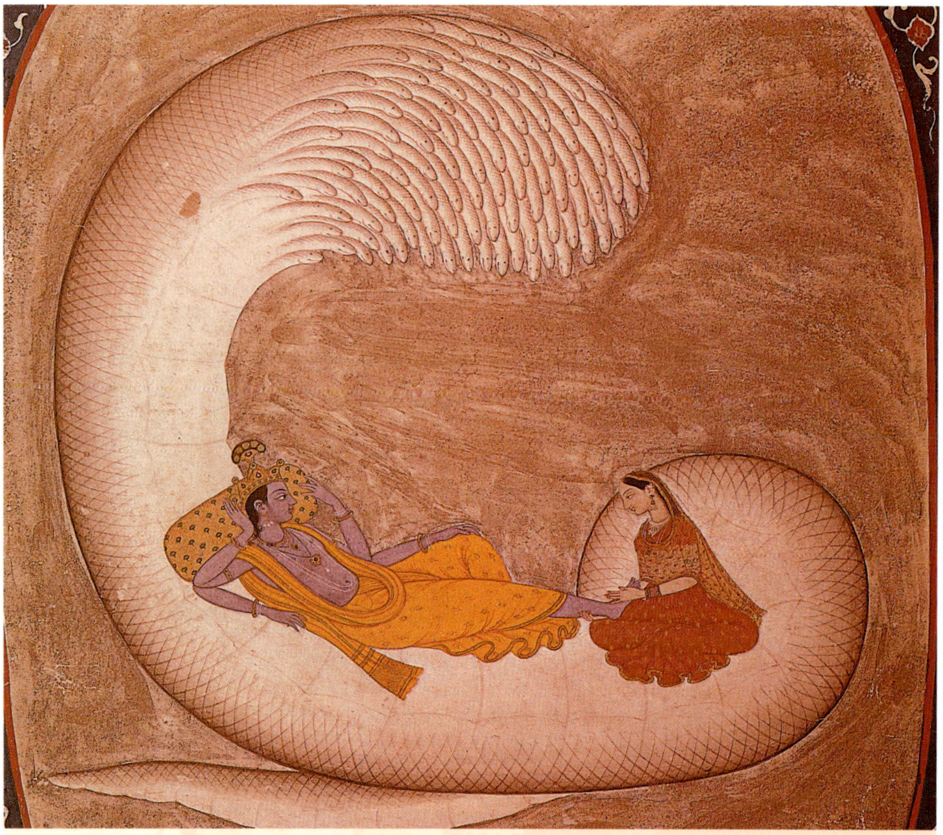

▲ *Vishnu and Lakshmi repose on the Serpent of a Thousand Heads.*

▶ *Traditional art depicting Krishna on a lotus leaf (left).*

MATSYA THE FISH

ONCE A KING named Satyavrata found a tiny fish in the river and took it in a bowl to his palace. Next morning the fish had grown so he transferred it into a pond, but it very quickly outgrew that too, so he put it into a lake. Soon it had grown so large that it had to be put in the ocean.

The king asked the fish why it had taken this form. The fish replied that he was Vishnu, come to save all the creatures of the earth from a devastating flood. The king should gather samples of all species of plants and animals to be saved.

Soon huge clouds appeared and poured water on land and sea, and the ocean overflowed on to the land. Then Satyavrata and all his companions saw a large boat floating toward them across the waves. Satyavrata led them aboard, and Matsya, by now a golden fish of inconceivable size, towed the boat with its precious cargo of all species of life across the waters of devastation. For countless years darkness covered the worlds and they wandered across the stormy wastes. During their journey Matsya instructed King Satyavrata in spiritual knowledge.

It is said that whoever hears this story is delivered from the ocean of sinful life.

▶ *Bronze statue of the deity, Shiva.*

KURMA THE TORTOISE

ONCE, THE GODS and the demons both wanted the nectar of immortality. On the advice of Vishnu they made a pact to co-operate together. Vishnu told them to throw all kinds of vegetables, grass, creepers, and herbs into the ocean of milk and churn it. To churn the ocean they would have to use the golden mountain, Mandara, as a churning rod and Vasuki, the giant serpent, as a rope. Taking the mountain and wrapping the serpent around it, the demons held his head and the gods held his tail.

They tried to churn, but the mountain sank into the ocean floor, so Vishnu appeared as a gigantic tortoise, Kurma, to support the mountain on his back. Using Kurma as the pivot, they began to churn. The first thing the churning produced was a deadly poison, which was drunk by Shiva. They continued to churn, and eventually the ocean produced the nectar of immortality. Both groups wanted it, and a quarrel developed. Vishnu came to the aid of the gods and helped them win the nectar for themselves. The demons, seeing they had lost the nectar, attacked the gods, but after a terrible battle the demons were defeated.

CYCLE OF LIFE

PERHAPS THE GREATEST theme which underlies all Indian myth is the everlasting play between the world of illusion and the world of reality: on the one hand the perpetual cycle of birth and death, of creation and destruction, of the duality of good and bad, on the other hand the divine existence of the immortal soul and the supreme deity. This tension is replayed in the drama of reincarnation, the periodic descent of the avatars of Vishnu from the eternal to the temporary worlds, and the tireless search of ascetics and devotees for *mukti*, liberation from the world of birth and death.

SHIVA

SHIVA MANIFESTS the dark side of the divinity, the power of death and destruction. He is easily moved to anger and can be a frightening figure, surrounded by ghosts and goblins. But Shiva is also easily pleased and merciful to his devotees, showing special favor to the wayward elements in the universe, called the *asuras* ("ungodly"), and those who are at odds with the world. He carries a small drum to accompany his dance of destruction, and his carrier is the bull Nandi. On his head is a crescent moon and a symbol of the descending waters of the Ganges, which he caught in his hair to save the mountains from being crushed by her weight. His mountain home is Mount Kailash and his followers are numerous in the Himalayas, but he is also found in cremation grounds, where he smears his body with ashes and sits in a trance of meditation. Among his followers are the ascetics who wander India smeared in ashes, seminaked, smoking ganja.

Shiva's and Vishnu's followers, the Shaivites and Vaishnavas, are often at odds with each other, and the myth of Daksha's sacrifice (see Shiva's Anger at Daksha) accounts for the origins of this enmity. But they each acknowledge Vishnu and Shiva to be aspects of the same supreme divinity.

COSMIC DESTRUCTION

WHILST BRAHMA is the creator and Vishnu the preserver, Shiva's anger is the destructive force which annihilates the cosmos. Death is the inevitable consequence of life and holds no fear in Indian myth, for in this world of duality neither life nor death has meaning without each other. Death is the precursor of life, which all must come to terms with, as described in the *Bhagavad Gita*: "One who is born must die, and one who dies must be reborn. Do not mourn the inevitable."

At the end of the universe the sun and moon shine no more and all becomes dark. Shiva begins his *pralaya,* dance of destruction, accompanied by his drum called *damaru,* to draw the curtain on the universal act. With his hair scattered he subdues the lords of all planets with his trident. He generates the fire of eternal time, which blazes throughout the universe. This fire blazes for a hundred celestial years, destroying all creatures. From Shiva's scattered hair rains torrential water for a further hundred celestial years, inundating all directions. The universe fills with water and is swept by howling winds. Then follows the long, silent night which precedes the next cycle of creation.

▼ *The teachings of Buddha had a strong influence on Indian mythology.*

SHIVA'S ANGER AT DAKSHA

THE GODS ONCE assembled for a thousand-year sacrifice. When Daksha, leader of the brahmins, arrived, everyone stood to receive him except Shiva, who was deep in meditation. Although Shiva was married to his daughter, Daksha was offended. "Shiva is not worthy to be part of this sacrifice," he cursed. Then he stormed out of the arena.

This led to a confrontation between the followers of Shiva and the followers of Daksha, from which originated the age-old antagonism between the worshipers of Vishnu and the worshipers of Shiva.

Daksha organized another sacrifice and Shiva was not invited. But Shiva's wife, the goddess Sati, went to the ceremony. She found that no oblation had been offered to Shiva, and she was insulted by Daksha, her father, who refused to acknowledge her presence. It was as if she and her husband did not exist.

"Daksha is envious of Shiva," she declared. "I no longer want to be his daughter, or to keep this body which was born of him."

So saying, she sat on the ground and focused her fiery anger between her eyes. Flames burst forth and consumed her body. A great cry went up from the followers of Shiva. When Shiva heard of this terrible event he laughed in demented rage and began his dance of cosmic destruction. Plucking a hair from his head, he dashed it to the ground. From it a great demon sprang up, high as the sky and bright as three suns.

"What would you have me do, O master?," the demon cried.

"Kill Daksha," shrieked Shiva.

Darkness fell over the arena of sacrifice as the great demon appeared. He caught Daksha and in a moment cut off his head, throwing it onto the sacrificial fire. The brahmins fled for protection to Brahma, the father of all beings, but he told them they must beg forgiveness from Shiva himself.

▲ *Shiva and his female aspect, Parvati.*

Mount Kailash is the heavenly home of Shiva, surrounded by forests of flowering trees, filled with the eerie cries of peacocks and the sound of waterfalls. In its midst sat Shiva, grave and peaceful in the company of sages. The brahmins fell before him in contrition. Shiva gladly forgave them and agreed to bring Daksha back to life. Since Daksha's head had been burned to ashes he gave him a goat's head instead.

This story illustrates how Shiva is easily angered and easily satisfied. It is said that one who hears it with faith is released from sin.

THE WORLD AS SYMBOL

INDIAN MYTH has made every aspect of nature into a symbol of divinity, celebrated in dance, poetry, music, sculpture, painting, and architecture. One of the oldest symbols is the ritual fire sacrifice, in which the fire symbolizes Agni, the fire god, or Vishnu the preserver, and becomes the mouth of god to accept the offerings of grains and fruits placed in it. Another daily ritual is meditation on the sun at sunrise, noon, and sunset, in which the brahmin prays: "O Sun, who illuminates the three levels of the universe: upper, middle, and lower, similarly illuminate and inspire my inner consciousness."

▲ *Stones such as this are worshiped as phallic symbols representing the mighty Shiva.*

THE GODDESS

EACH HINDU DEITY has come to be associated with his female half. As all gods are aspects of the One Supreme Divinity, so their female halves are aspects of the Supreme Goddess. This became a fundamental principle of Hindu theology: the combination of the male energetic source, called *purusha,* with its female energy, called *prakriti,* gave rise to the material cosmos. In time prakriti became a goddess in her own right, called Devi, with her own devout followers. She is the female energy who provides the universal womb in which the male energy conceives the abundance of life, as memorably symbolized in the image of the Shiva *lingam* emerging from the womb of Devi, shaped in stone and worshiped in temples all over India. Devi appears as the terrible Kali, to whom goats are sacrificed, or as the merciful Radha, the lover of Krishna. As Durga she rides a lion and protects her devotees from harm. As Bhumi, Mother Earth, she is the giver of abundant life, prayed to in the Vedic hymns:

O mother, with your oceans, rivers, and lakes, you give us land to grow grains, on which our survival depends. Please give us sufficient milk, fruits, water, and cereals.

MAGICAL POWERS

MAGICAL POWERS, called *siddhi,* are so common in Hindu mythology that they have become for many an accepted reality, since the boundary between myth and reality is, in India, an indistinct one. It is generally believed that these powers are achieved by the practice of austerity. There is a higher plane called Siddhaloka where all inhabitants are born with fully developed magical powers. Sometimes an advanced yogi may manifest those same powers on earth, and there are many reported cases of this in modern times in India. These powers include making oneself very small or very large, traveling instantly to another place, being able to bring something instantly from another place, becoming very heavy or very light, and controlling the minds of others.

Typically in the stories of conflict between gods and demons, magic is used. In the story of the Goddess killing the buffalo demon, she acquires her powers by practicing penance in the seclusion of the mountains. Her opponent, the buffalo demon, has the power to change his shape at will and to expand his body to a very large size, both common *siddhis* in Indian stories. Such beings were virtually unassailable, but he was eventually defeated by trapping his soul outside his body.

HANUMAN

SON OF THE WIND GOD, the monkey Hanuman is popular for his selfless devotion to Rama and his good humor. He is worshiped at countless roadside shrines all over India. It is said of Hanuman in the Ramayana that no one is his superior in strength, amiability, sweetness of temper, cleverness, or wisdom and that he is master of all branches of Vedic learning. When Hanuman was young he misused his strength to play mischief, upsetting the forest sages. As a result they cursed him to be unaware of his own strength, making him meek and submissive.

▲ *Mohini with the nectar of immortality.*

DEVI, THE GODDESS, KILLS THE BUFFALO DEMON

MAHISHA WAS BORN with the head of a buffalo and the body of a man, and was said to be destined to be the enemy of the gods. In time he led a great army of demons and captured the throne of heaven, casting out the gods from Paradise. The chief gods became so angry that from their combined anger blazed the form of a woman terrible and beautiful to behold. Her head emanated from Shiva, her arms from Vishnu, her feet from Brahma, her waist from Indra, the king of heaven, her hair from death, her breasts from the moon, her thighs from the ocean, her hips from the earth, and her toes from the sun. This beautiful young maiden was named Devi. She found a secluded mountain where she spent a long time in meditation and lived a life of asceticism. Her penances brought peace and prosperity to the earth.

While she was absorbed in her penances the armies of Mahisha entered the mountains. They came upon the slender figure of Devi, deep in meditation, and reported her astonishing beauty to Mahisha. Full of passion he went to her in disguise and asked her to marry him. She replied contemptuously that he must first prove his manhood. Mahisha tried to capture her, but she escaped from him. In anger he grew in size and as he lashed his tail the oceans were swept into fury, the earth shook beneath the pounding of his feet, the clouds were scattered by his horns, and Devi's armies were hurled before him on the hurricane of his breath. Devi assumed a terrible form and mounted her lion carrier to attack him, but Mahisha kept changing shape. She bound him with ropes but he changed into a lion; she cut off the lion's head but he was transformed into a man; she pierced the man but he became an elephant. She cut off the elephant's trunk but again he became a buffalo. The Goddess, enraged and intoxicated by blood-lust, sprang upon his back, pierced him with her trident and delivered a kick to his neck so powerful that his spirit sprang from his mouth. At that instant she grabbed his sword and cut off his head. His spirit had no way to re-enter his body and he was slain. The gods praised Devi, shouting "Victory!" Since then she has been worshiped as the slayer of the buffalo demon.

RAMA

RAMA IS the seventh avatar of Vishnu. His humanity and the fact that he fell in love have endeared him to Hindus and made him one of the most popular of Hindu deities. His life is often given as the perfect example of one who follows honor and duty. His rule, called Rama-rajya, is even today cited in Indian politics as an ideal to aspire for. His story, retold here, begins with a question to the storyteller:

"Tell me who is the greatest person in the world. Who is accomplished, learned, powerful, beautiful, noble, and cares for all creatures? Who is without anger, yet sends fear into the hearts of enemies? Who can protect the world from evil?"

The storyteller replies:

"The person you seek is hard to find among mortals. There is, however, a famous king by the name Rama. He is strong and beautiful, wise and compassionate, pure in character and loved by all. He has deeply studied the ancient wisdom, is brilliant in archery and courageous in battle. In gravity he is like the ocean, in constancy like the Himalayas, in strength like Vishnu, in beauty like the moon, in generosity like rain and in devotion to truth like religion itself."

▲ *The god Rama and goddess Sita sit enthroned beneath a canopy.*

THE *RAMAYANA* AS ALLEGORY

THE *RAMAYANA*, the "journey of Rama," tells of Rama's banishment from his kingdom and his battle with the forces of evil to rescue the goddess Sita. The divine Rama's human journey provides an allegory for the journey every soul must make, in which each of us has to endure our own banishment, our own loss, face our own demons and hope eventually to find redemption. Thus to hear or to witness Rama's struggles is to relive our own lives, but in a divine context.

The *Ramayana* story is interpreted by some as an allegory for the meeting of the Aryan and Dravidian cultures. The civilizing Aryans, represented by Rama and the kingdom of Ayodhya, encounter the indigenous Dravidians, represented by Ravana and the kingdom of Lanka. This historical interpretation is only a partial one, since the themes of the *Ramayana* go much deeper, to the age-old struggle between good and evil. Nevertheless Ravana, regarded by worshipers of Vishnu as demonic, is in parts of south India still revered as a hero. This ambiguity of good and bad recurs throughout Indian myth, in which the dualities of this world are portrayed as the play, or *lila,* of the divine.

▼ *The god Rama stands surrounded by gods from the* Ramayana.

THE INTERPLAY OF MALE AND FEMALE

THE BALANCE of male and female is at the heart of Indian myths. All deities have their female aspects, such as Vishnu and Lakshmi, Krishna and Radha, Rama and Sita, and Shiva and Parvati. The female aspect of the deity embodies mercy and the spirit of devotion to that deity, while the male aspect represents the outward flow of power and protection. The union of male and female as the creative source of the energy of life is symbolized in the image of the Shiva *lingam* surrounded by the *yoni* of the Goddess. This image is revered in Shiva temples throughout India.

THE COSMIC STRUGGLE BETWEEN GOOD AND EVIL

THE HINDU UNIVERSE is divided into three great levels. The upper levels are the home of the *devas,* godly beings invested with supernatural powers. The middle levels are earthly, the domain of humans, and the lower levels belong to the *asuras,* the demons who possess occult powers. The *devas* and the *asuras* are in a constant state of war. Vishnu protects the *devas,* while compassionate Shiva takes the side of the *asuras.* If one or other side gains too much power, Vishnu incarnates to restore the balance (as in the case of Rama), and there are occasional lulls in the storms of universal war, as when the gods and demons churned the milk ocean.

In the midst of this cosmic struggle, and caught in its throes, is humanity. Human life is thus at the heart of the struggle between good and bad. In human life the soul has the choice of how to behave and must struggle with its own demons, real or imaginary, to find its inner balance. With the help of Vishnu, the indwelling spirit, the soul can rise above good and bad to perceive the divine goodness of all in the cosmic embrace of God.

▲ *Bronze statue of Shiva and Parvati.*
▼ *Traditional Indian scene, showing two lovers.*

RAMAYANA: THE EPIC OF RAMA

THERE ONCE LIVED a wise king called Dasaratha who ruled the prosperous kingdom of Ayodhya in north India. He was old and tired but had no heir. In answer to his prayers a son was born to him: Rama, the seventh incarnation of Vishnu. When Rama reached manhood he married the divine Sita, who was

miraculously born from the earth. He was loved by all except his stepmother Kaikeyi, who forced him into banishment in the forest so that her own son could become king. There he lived with his beloved Sita for 14 years. In the last year of their exile the evil king Ravana stole Sita by sending the wizard Maricha disguised as a golden deer. When Sita saw the beautiful deer she begged Rama to capture it for her. While Rama was in pursuit of the deer, Ravana kidnapped her and carried her through the air in his chariot pulled by donkeys to the golden city of Lanka.

Rama fell into depression, with no hope of finding Sita. But he was encoraged by his brother Lakshmana, and together they met the monkey god Hanuman, possessed of supernatural strength. Hanuman promised to find Sita and after searching the whole subcontinent discovered her imprisoned in a mango grove on the island of Lanka, modern-day Sri Lanka. He set fire to the golden city and hastened back to Rama with the news. Together they led a huge army of monkeys to Lanka across a bridge of floating stones, and a fearful battle ensued, in which Rama finally met Ravana in single combat and killed him. In doing so he fulfilled the original wish of the gods, who had prayed for Vishnu's descent to rid the universe of the tyranny of Ravana.

Rama returned triumphantly to Ayodhya with Sita and became king. But the story does not end here. Tragically, he sent Sita away because she had lived in the house of Ravana and in the eyes of the people had lost her chastity. This cruel twist to the story is typical of so much of Hindu myth, where the line between right and wrong is rarely black and white. In exile, Sita bore Rama twin sons then ended her life by being swallowed back into the embrace of Mother Earth from whence she came. Rama lived on with a broken heart and, after ruling Ayodhya for 11,000 years, vanished with all his followers.

▶ *Krishna dances to the music of young cowherd girls.*

RAVANA, A TRAGIC HERO

IN THE GREAT HINDU MYTHS, evil is often ambigiuous, and the antiheroes can be tragic characters. Ravana, the enemy of Rama, was cursed to fall from Paradise to endure three births as a demon and to be killed each time by Vishnu. In his first birth he was Hiranyakashipu, who was killed by Narasimha, the fourth incarnation of Vishnu; in his second birth he was Ravana; and in his third birth he became Kamsa and was killed by Krishna. His enmity with Vishnu was his way of assisting in his divine play. After being killed by Vishnu for the third time he returned to Paradise.

KRISHNA

KRISHNA IS RECKONED as the eighth avatar of Vishnu. In the person of Krishna, the image of God in Indian myth evolves to encompass the full range of emotion and poetry. For his devotees Krishna occupies a unique position as the fountainhead of all other incarnations.

His story is chiefly told in the *Bhagavat Purana,* thought to have been written around C.E. 500 but believed by the faithful to be far older. He is also woven into the *Mahabharata,* the epic history of India. He was born in the dungeons of King Kamsa and smuggled out to the forest of Vrindavan to live in hiding with the cowherd community. Kamsa wanted to kill the divine child, fearing a challenge to his rule, and in an act reminiscent of the biblical story of Jesus ordered the death of all male children under the age of two years. The demons sent to kill Krishna were killed by him. By killing them, Krishna released them from the cycle of rebirth.

In the forest Krishna, amidst the abundance of nature, herded cows and played with his cowherd friends, delighting his mother with his mischievous ways.

KRISHNA THE COWHERD

INDIANS HAVE PERSONIFIED all aspects of nature and spirituality in the form of their numerous deities. For some these deities are symbolic only, whereas for others they have a life and reality beyond the temporary world. The best-loved deity is Krishna the cowherd, eighth incarnation of Vishnu. He lives as a child in the forest surrounded by his childhood friends and by the cows and peacocks. There he dances with his young lover, the divine Radha, rejoicing in the bounty and simplicity of rural life. Together they share perfect spiritual love. Followers of Krishna offer him their unconditional devotion as the One Supreme God.

KRISHNA'S SONG: THE *BHAGAVAD GITA*

IN LATER LIFE Krishna spoke the immortal words of the *Bhagavad Gita,* or "Song of God," in the form of a dialogue with his friend and disciple, Arjuna, set at the dramatic climax of the *Mahabharata,* as the war is about to begin.

Krishna begins by teaching about *atma,* the self. He describes the self as an immortal soul which is reincarnated from one body to another, the soul's next life being decided by its behavior in this life. This soul, he says, cannot find satisfaction in the temporary pleasures of this world. According to the laws of *karma,* or action, the soul should work without attachment to the results of its actions. Krishna advises Arjuna that he must fight without attachment to victory or defeat, simply for the sake of doing his duty.

Krishna ends the *Gita* with a call for surrender. All living beings are the eternal children of God and will find happiness if they surrender their every action to God as an act of devotion. This surrender will release the self from the cycle of birth and death and allow it to return to the eternal spiritual realm to be reunited with its true eternal friend, Krishna.

RADHA'S LOVE FOR KRISHNA

AT THE HEART of the myth of Krishna is his deep love for Radha. Her story is

touched upon in the *Bhagavat Purana* and developed in countless songs and poems in local dialects across India. She is the goddess of devotion who orchestrates the affairs of love in the enchanted forest of Vrindavan.

Sometimes Radha controls Krishna: he will do anything to please her. This is an important feature of the tradition of *Krishna-bhakti,* or devotion for Krishna: God is bound by the love of his devotees. The old hierarchical order created an image of God, displayed in the creative might of Vishnu and the destructive force of Shiva, based on awe and reverence. This is replaced by a softer, more responsive image of God as the lover of his devotees.

Krishna used to meet Radha at night in the company of her intimate friends, who helped in their love affairs. To dance with them he mystically divided himself into many to be with each one simultaneously. Later, when Krishna grew up, he left Radha and her friends and went to the city to become a king. Some of them died from broken hearts. The longing of Radha to be reunited with Krishna expresses the soul's longing for God.

THE COSMIC CIRCLE DANCE

KRISHNA ENJOYED the company of the cowherd girls in his *rasamandala,* or circle dance, in the forest at night. The dance is depicted in countless paintings and wall hangings. The dancers are arranged alternately in the great circle, with Krishna's multi-forms present between each girl, surrounded by the nighttime forest with its huge array of flowers, trees, and animals, under the star-strewn heavens in which the gods fly so as to witness the magic of the occasion. The *rasamandala* provides the perfect symbol for the dance of life, in which the soul is eternally entwined with its lover, the supreme soul.

◀ *Krishna performing his cosmic circle dance.*

THE *MAHABHARATA:* KRISHNA AND THE GREAT WAR

THE *MAHABHARATA* is the story of the struggle for the throne of India. It centers upon the rivalry between the five sons of King Pandu, called the Pandavas, and the 100 sons of his brother Dhritrashtra, called the Kauravas.

Pandu died young and his brother Dhritrashtra was made regent. Pandu's young orphaned sons were adopted by Bhisma, grandfather of the royal dynasty, who trained them as brilliant warriors and statesmen, fit to rule the kingdom to which they were heirs. But Dhritrashtra wanted his sons to inherit the kingdom, and a feud sprang up between the two groups of princes. The Kauravas plotted to burn the Pandavas alive in a house specially built for the purpose. The Pandavas escaped, and the feud darkened into bitter hatred. In a gambling match the Pandavas were cheated and forced into exile for 12 years. They swore to be avenged.

During this time Krishna was a great friend to the Pandavas, especially Arjuna. He used his influence to try and bring about a peaceful solution to the dispute. But after 12 years in exile, when the Pandavas returned to claim their kingdom, the Kauravas refused to give them any land. All the royal houses of India were drawn into the conflagration, pitting brothers, relatives and friends against each other in mortal combat.

Bhisma sided with the Kauravas, though he loved the Pandavas as his own sons, and Krishna's armies fought for the Kauravas. Krishna himself refused to fight, but as an act of personal friendship he drove Arjuna's chariot. At the moment the battle was about to begin, Arjuna lost his nerve at the prospect of killing all those he loved. He turned to Krishna for help and Krishna delivered his immortal teaching, the *Bhagavad Gita,* in the course of which he revealed his divine identity as God himself.

The battle raged for 18 days. Millions died, including Bhisma and the 100 sons of Dhritarashtra. The Pandava brothers were almost the only ones to survive. Disillusioned, they lived on to rule their kingdom, having lost all their friends. At the end of their lives they left for the Himalayas to prepare for death. In Paradise they were re-united with their cousins, their enmity over, and the whole drama was revealed as the illusory play of the material world, in which nothing is as it seems.

FABLES AND MORALITY TALES

THE COLLECTION of morality tales found in the *Pancatantra* has passed into cultures all over the world. Although the stories are about animal characters, they illustrate the full range of human concerns, including daily ethics, political wisdom, and examples of elevated moral behavior. The stories were originally recorded in Sanskrit over 2,000 years ago by a brahmin named Vishnu Sharma, but their origins lie in a far older oral tradition. Storytelling was central to the Vedic tradition. The ancient Sanskrit literature abounds with stories, most of which are presented as accounts of actual historical events but with a strong didactic element. The stories of the *Pancatantra* are different in that they are pure story and as such form possibly the world's earliest surviving works of fiction. The example given here (The Bird Who Overcame the Ocean) is typical of some *Pancatantra* stories in that it freely incorporates its fictional animal characters into the traditional framework of divine beings, in this case Garuda, the bird-carrier of Vishnu, and Vishnu himself, demonstrating how religious and secular culture are wedded in Indian mythology. It also ends with a moral which reinforces the overall religious framework of Indian culture.

THE BIRD WHO OVERCAME THE OCEAN

A SMALL BIRD and his wife lived by the ocean, and he built a nest on the shore. His wife protested that the ocean waves were too close and would carry away the nest, but he assured her that the ocean was his friend and would never do such a thing.

The very next day the ocean laughed and stretched out his foam tipped hand to snatch their nest with its tiny eggs. The mother bird was in despair and ready to die, but her husband proudly told her not to worry. He would peck the ocean dry and get back their nest. He called upon the other birds to help him. They agreed to help, but the ocean simply laughed, so they went to seek the help of Garuda, king of the birds. When Garuda heard the situation he sent word to his master, Vishnu, that his servant's eggs had been stolen by the ocean. Hearing this, Vishnu himself, in angry mood, threatened the ocean: "If you do not return this little bird's eggs, I shall personally dry you up!" The ocean, full of fear, at once returned the eggs. The moral of this story is that God helps those who help themselves.

▲ *Bronze statue of the god Krishna dancing.*

PEACOCK, ELEPHANT, AND COW

ANIMALS ARE ever present symbols in Indian art. The peacock is a native of the woodlands of north India and a favorite symbol of beauty and grace. The peacock feather is the symbol of Krishna, who always wore one on his head.

The elephant is often kept by temples to lead their religious processions as the bearer of the temple deities. To harm an elephant brings great misfortune, while to feed one brings blessings.

The cow is revered as one of the seven mothers and must never be harmed. All things to do with the cow, including her dung, are pure. Ghee, or clarified butter, made from her milk, is universally used for cooking, illuminating lamps, and fueling the sacred fire.

THE LIVES OF BUDDHA

THE *JATAKA* STORIES recount the many previous births of the Buddha in human and animal lives. In all there are 547 stories, originally told by the Buddha to his disciples. They were written down in the Pali language around 400 B.C.E. and absorbed into the Buddhist canon not long after his death. The stories show the progression of his lives through many incarnations, gradually acquiring the wisdom, selflessness, and thoughtfulness that eventually lead to enlightenment. In each birth he performed some meritorious deed to bring him spiritual progress. In the later stories the being who was to become the Buddha developed such love toward others that he was prepared to sacrifice his own life for their sakes, demonstrating the quality of compassion which lies at the heart of Buddhist teachings and which is the over-riding characteristic of an enlightened being. Some of the stories are adapted from traditional folktales to provide guidance and teaching for ordinary Buddhists. They lend themselves to storytelling, as material for traveling actors, and as an ever fresh source of inspiration for artists, such as in the cave paintings of Ajanta. Their theme is generally the workings of *karma,* the reward and punishment of previous deeds, in the passage from one life to another.

▲ *The elephant was used to lead religious and royal processions. They were often decorated with jewels.*

BUDDHA'S LIFE AS A HARE

BEFORE THE BUDDHA was born as Siddhartha Gautama, he had many animal lives. This story is about his birth as a hare.

A hare once lived in the forest with his animal friends, the jackal, the otter, and the monkey. The animals respected the hare for he was wise and gentle. One day he said they should all fast and give whatever food they gathered to whoever needed it. So the monkey found ripe mangoes, the jackal found a lizard and a pot of milk, and the otter found fresh fish. But the hare could not find any food and vowed that if anyone was hungry, he would offer them his own body. His tremendous vow was heard by the earth herself, who told Sakka, lord of the *devas*. He decided to test the hare.

Sakka entered the forest disguised as a beggar and asked the hare for food.

"Please eat my body," the hare replied without hesitation.

So Sakka built a fire, and the hare willingly ran into the flames. Feeling no pain, he rose up to heaven. In gratitude Sakka drew an image of a hare on the moon for everyone to see and remember the hare's selfless sacrifice.

◀ Wooden panel from a portable altar showing a meditating Buddha.

▶ Indian miniature art showing a goddess holding a lute in a garden. The surrounding peacocks are symbols of beauty and grace.

SACRED TREES

BECAUSE THEY lived in the forest, the early Vedic teachers attached great importance to trees, such as the banyan and peepal, which symbolized patience and tolerance. "These trees are completely dedicated to the welfare of others. How great they are that they bear the storms, rains, snow, and scorching sun and then they protect us!" This tradition was passed on into Indian culture and ultimately led to a relationship between human communities and the forest community of trees, plants, and animals that recognized the rights of the trees, forest dwelling animals, and plants to a life of their own, free from exploitation by humans.

Sri Lanka

INTRODUCTION

SRI LANKA IS A SMALL ISLAND located just north of the equator, off the southernmost tip of India. Its location on the sea routes between Europe, Africa, and Asia has insured contact with many great civilizations, and it had a highly developed culture as early as the fifth century B.C.E.

Apart from a small aboriginal group, the majority of Sri Lankans are descended from Indian migrants. Although there is no firm evidence of a Sinhalese presence before the second century B.C.E., chronicles relate that the first Sinhalese speakers, thought to have originated in north India, arrived in around the sixth century B.C.E. They conquered the earliest inhabitants, the Yakkhas, and the Nagas, and went on to establish themselves in the northern plain. Tamils, probably immigrants from Dravidian India, arrived on the island between the early centuries CE and c. 1200. There are also Moors of Arab origin, and Burghers, descendants of Portuguese or Dutch settlers.

A loose form of Hinduism was introduced to the island by the earliest settlers, and this gradually came to incorporate native deities and spirits. Buddhism was established between 270 and 232 B.C.E. Records relate that it was introduced by the monk Mahinda, who may have been the son of the great Indian ruler Asoka. He is also credited with having brought to Sri Lanka the Pali canon, Buddhist scriptures in the Pali language. Following him, monks from Buddhist monasteries in north India traveled and taught along the eastern coast of India before crossing to establish monastic communities on the island. Buddhism quickly became the dominant religion and remains so today.

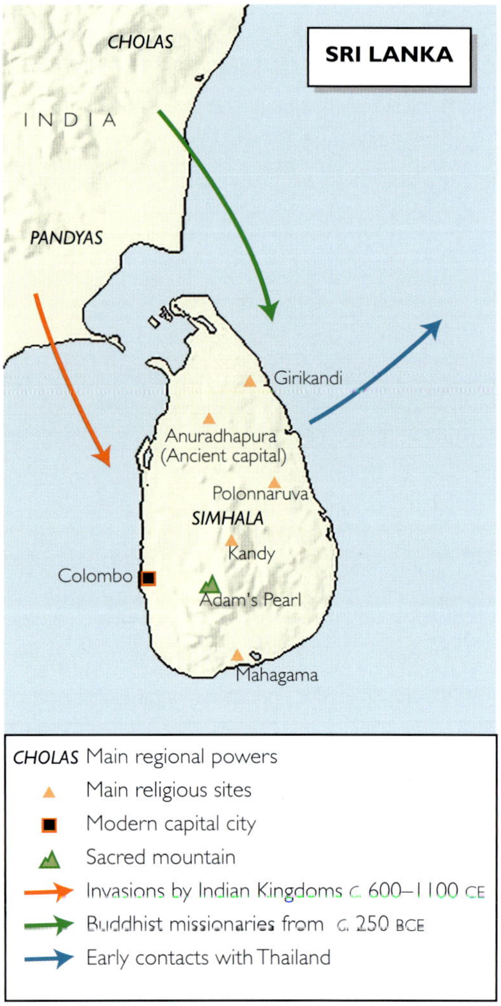

FROM ABOUT THE third century B.C.E. the Tamils were based at Anuradhapura in the northern plain. The Sinhalese defeated the Tamils in 101 B.C.E., and Tamil history after that time is obscure, although the Tamil community remained largely in the north and east of the island, while the Sinhalese lived mainly in the south and west.

Foreign contact with Africa and the Middle East was common in coastal areas. Arab and Indian traders frequented the coastal towns. The Portuguese, Dutch, and British were involved in trade on the island from the sixteenth century. Christianity was introduced at this time into both linguistic groups. In the nineteenth century the British, who had annexed the island in 1815, introduced Tamil workers from south India to work the plantations, emphasizing the division of the population into the majority Buddhist Sinhalese and the smaller Hindu Tamil community.

◀ *A young woman gives offerings in worship of Shiva.*

SRI LANKAN MYTHS

SRI LANKA POSSESSES a rich store of myths which fall into various categories: myths concerning spirits, origin myths, Hindu myths concerning the gods and heroes, and Buddhist myths, including the *jataka* stories.

Various myths reveal how the Nagas and Yakshas, two groups inhabiting the island in ancient times, were defeated by the Sinhalese settlers, who arrived in about the sixth century B.C.E. Nagas are known to have been Hindu and thus were almost certainly of Indian origin. They appear to

▲ *The detail on this casket depicts two spirits in a ritual dance.*

have had a sophisticated method of water control and may have had a *naga* (Sanskrit: serpent) as their totem. Little is known about the Yakshas, but they appear in Hindu epics and in the *Ramayana*. Ravana, the villain of the story, was the ruler of the Yaksha people.

Both local and national deities may act in a protective capacity if treated with reverence. *Devata*, which are nature spirits, and fertility spirits such as the goddess Pattini are also popular. Origin myths associated with the birth of *yaksas,* nature spirits, and other superior beings are recited in ritual when these beings are invoked. This is in order to assure the spirit of the respect in which it is held before persuading it to permit an action on its territory.

ORIGINS OF THE MYTHS

DIFFERENT MYTHS explain the origin of the Sinhalese race and also that of such phenomena as the sea, mountains, gods, and different species of animal. Many of these are undoubtedly derived from the Indian tradition, but they have variations in detail which have been added by Sri Lankans. There is evidence that even before the arrival of the Dravidian and Aryan peoples there had been a preoccupation with nature spirits, fertility deities, and the solar bodies. The gods of the sun, moon, and stars were known and worshiped. Sumana, prince of the *devas,* may have originated as a solar deity. He was believed to dwell on the peak of Sumanakuta, the sacred mountain in the southwest center of the island, which has long been a holy site from which to watch the sun rise. Its ancient role as a holy place is emphasized by the fact that even today this mountain is sacred to Buddhists, Hindus, Christians, and the small community of Muslims. It is the site of what resembles the natural imprint of a huge foot. Buddhists claim that this is the footprint of Gautama Buddha, the fourth Buddha to have visited the mount in the present world cycle. Hindus claim that it is the footprint of Shiva, while Christians and Muslims say that the mark was left by Adam, hence its popular name, Adam's Peak.

◀ *Bronze statue of Shiva.*

INDIAN LINKS

HINDU MYTHS are well known. Vishnu, Shiva, Brahma, and the other major gods and goddesses all feature in innumerable tales. The avatars or incarnations of Vishnu are well known, and the great epics, the *Ramayana* and the *Mahabharata,* are popular, frequently enacted in dance and drama. The *Ramayana* is particularly important as much of its action takes place on the soil of Lanka, home of the wicked Yaksha Ravana. The Yakshas were an ancient people inhabiting Sri Lanka before the arrival of the Sinhalese in the sixth to fifth century B.C.E.

Stories explaining the status of the various castes are also told. The caste system exists in Sri Lanka, although among the Sinhalese it takes a simpler form than in India. The highest, brahmin, caste does not exist among the Sinhalese, and there are no untouchables. Although Buddhism never adopted the caste system, teaching equality for all, there is still a modified system of caste within the Sinhalese Buddhist community.

Buddhist myths are extremely popular, especially those concerning the life of the Buddha. Of these, myths that relate miracles greatly outnumber the others. There are also stories concerning the shrines that contain relics of the Buddha, or sites which were blessed by the Buddha or Buddhist saints, although there is no reliable evidence that the Buddha did in fact visit Sri Lanka. The *jataka* stories, which relate the previous lives of the Buddha, provide Buddhists with moral guidance.

THE BUDDHA

THE BUDDHIST CHRONICLE, the *Mahavamsa,* records the arrival of the first Sinhalese colonists. In the sixth century B.C.E., Prince Vijaya and 700 followers landed on the island and defeated a band of Yakshas, whom they chased into the interior. Vijaya, called a "Sinhala" because he was descended from a lion (*sinha*), later married a Yaksha princess who bore him two children, but he sent them away and they fled to the forest. His wife was later killed by Yakshas. Vijaya then sent to India for another princess, as well as wives for all his followers. His nephew continued the Vijayan line. This probably reflects actual events when the early Dravidian inhabitants were pushed farther inland by the Indo-Aryan settlers.

According to the *Mahavamsa,* the Buddha summoned Sakka, king of the gods, just before he died. He instructed the god to protect Vijaya and his followers, who had just arrived in Lanka, because it was on that island that his religion would be established and come to fruition. This myth reinforces the importance of the legacy of Buddhism, already strengthened by myths relating the Buddha's visits to Lanka.

Central to Sri Lankan culture is the belief that the Buddha stepped across the sea to visit Sri Lanka and left his footprint on the sacred mountain. Carvings of his footprint are popular. They are marked with the 107 symbols of the Buddha's ascendence over all the universe to symbolize the phenomenon.

RAMA AND SITA

IN THE GREAT EPIC the *Ramayana*, the princess Sita was abducted and carried over the sea to Lanka, where she was held against her will by Ravana. Rama and his brother Lakshmana only rescued her with the aid of the monkey general Hanuman and his army of monkeys, who formed a living bridge across the sea to the island. Ravana is referred to as lord of the Yakshas, or demons, and rides in a sky chariot. In the ancient past he was probably identified with the sun. The god Sumana, more often associated with the mountain and also with the sun, may have been a later Buddhist substitute for Ravana.

According to one account the Buddha is believed to have preached to Ravana at the summit of Sumanakutu, suggesting the ascendance of Buddhism over the Yaksha belief in the sky god. Typical of the myths about holy places is that linked up with the stupa at Ruvanvaliseya. The king apparently searched the countryside to find an auspicious site on which to build a stupa and finally selected a place where the telamby tree grew. Unfortunately the tree spirit Swarnamali lived in this tree, and when the king's men arrived to fell it, she wept bitterly. The king managed to persuade Swarnamali to leave the tree, which she did. The tree was felled, and the king went on to build the great stupa. This myth suggests that the site of the stupa was already sacred and that people had long made offerings to the tree spirit before it became a Buddhist site.

THE SACRED TREE

TREES ARE OFTEN SACRED, and it is thought by many that the bodhi tree, under which the Buddha attained Enlightenment, has the power to produce rain, as does the Buddha himself. The bodhi tree at Anuradhapura is believed to have grown from a shoot of the original tree at Bodh Gaya, under which the Buddha meditated, and was brought to Sri Lanka by the first Buddhist missionaries. Many miraculous happenings have been connected with it, and it remained the center of Buddhist ritual until the arrival of the sacred tooth relic, which was enshrined at the stupa in Kandy some 600 years later.

STUPAS

BUDDHIST STUPAS act partly as reliquaries and partly as a visual symbol of Buddha's Enlightenment. The different levels of the structure represent stages on the path toward Enlightenment, and a stupa can also be seen as a meditational aid. The most sacred Buddhist stupas are believed to contain relics of the Buddha's body, brought to Sri Lanka after his death. The Buddha image is popular, usually seated in meditation or protected by the *naga*, and *jataka* stories are often depicted in mural painting and silverwork. There is a tradition of colossal Buddhist sculpture in limestone, which magnificently portrays the vastness of the Buddha's doctrine.

MYTH AND ART

HINDU AND BUDDHIST myths are depicted in painting, sculpture, and architecture. Fine Hindu sculpture, which shows the influence of southern India, reveals the importance of the gods, particularly the Great Goddess and also Shiva. Temples are elaborate and are built in landscaped gardens set with lakes, which mirror the harmony of the universe.

SRI LANKAN GODS

ANCIENT GODS such as Pattini, goddess of fertility, and Sumana, once a solar deity, still hold a place in Sri Lankan consciousness. Emblems of the sun and moon are found everywhere, and nature spirits and household spirits are still widely respected. Vishnu, Shiva, Brahma, Ganesh, and the Goddess are worshiped by the largely Tamil Hindu community, whereas the Buddha is revered by the larger Sinhalese population. Nature spirits are often thought to inhabit trees, rocks, and rivers and may be spiteful if not honored. In addition, Sri Lankan mythology is full of the creatures which populate Indian and Southeast Asian mythology: yaksas, nagas, garudas, the latter part bird, part human being.

▲ *The lotus position and the position of Buddha's hands indicate that he is teaching.*

◄ *Shiva is brought to the floor and attacked by the she-ogre, Kali.*

Tibet

INTRODUCTION

AT WHAT MIGHT be considered a crossroads between India and China, the original religion of Tibet is typically animistic and based on dualism. The religious aspiration of its inhabitants is to live in harmony with the unseen forces operating all around them: benevolent spirits are to be thanked for their kindness with regular offerings and caution must be exercised at all times so as not to offend the malevolent.

Before the dawn of history, Tibet is said to have been held together by a succession of nonhuman rulers. Eventually the first human ruler of Tibet "descended from the sky" on to a mountain in Kong-po and was proclaimed king by a grateful people. At the end of his reign he ascended once more to the heavens from whence he had come by means of a dmu cord, leaving no earthly remains. When the seventh of his royal line finally cut the magical cord connecting his family to the sky, he was buried in the Yar-lung valley and thus began the cult of the royal tombs.

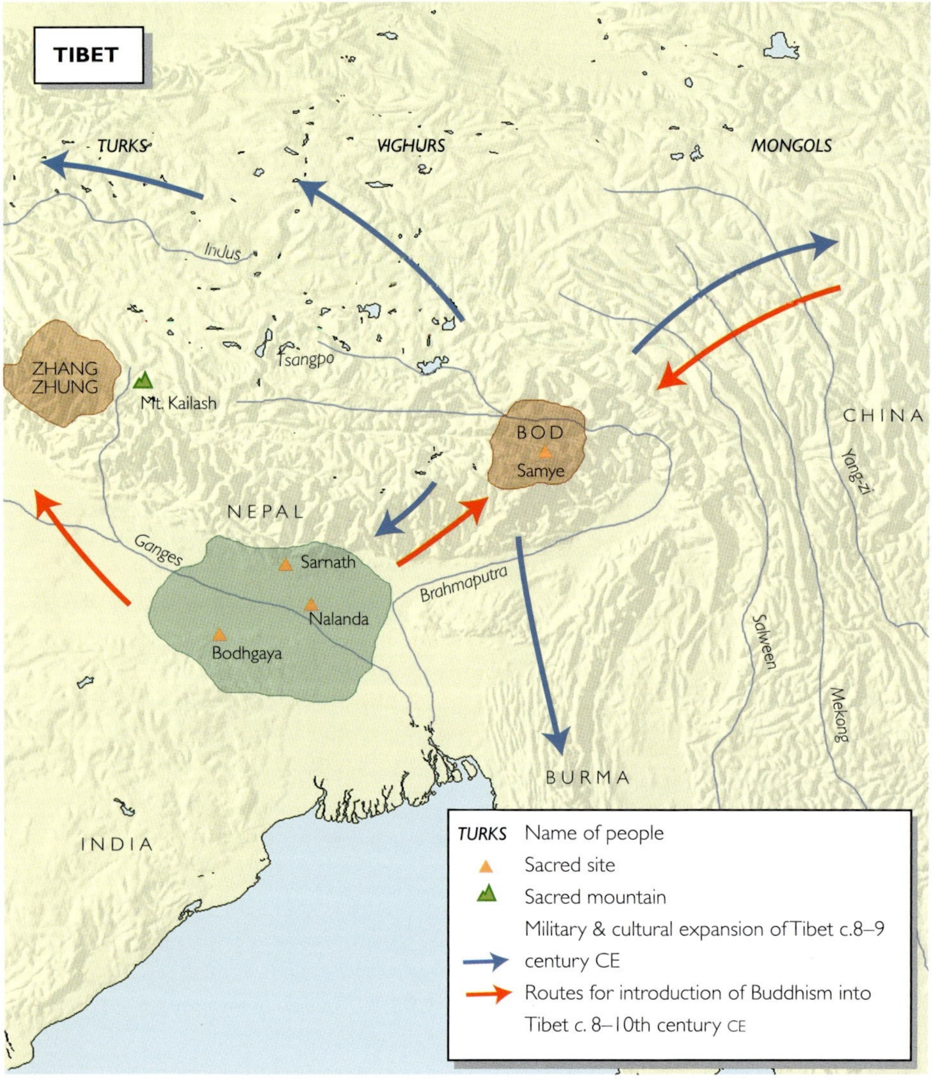

▲ *A Tibetan wooden plaque decorated with a figure of Vairocana.*

THE FIVE AGGREGATES

THE INNUMERABLE transcendent gods of tantric Buddhism imported from their homeland in India cluster around the five families of Buddhas headed by Vairocana, Akshobhya, Ratnasambhava, Amitabha, and Amoghasiddhi. Typically arranged in the circular formation of a *mandala,* with one in the center and the others surrounding him in the four cardinal directions of the compass, each Buddha has his own distinctive color, posture, and attribute. Evoked during the course of profound meditation, these five Buddhas are thought to arise naturally from the basic constituents of the human personality, known as the five aggregates, and they sit in union with their female consorts who embody the five elements of earth, water, fire, air, and space.

THE FIRST HUMAN RULER

AFTER 27 GENERATIONS of kings from the time of Tibet's first human ruler,

Lha-tho tho-ri came to the throne and, in the waterbird year of 433, at the age of 60, he became the first king to learn of Buddhism. Legend has it that the sky one day filled with rainbows and onto the roof of his palace fell Buddhist texts and images. He was unable to comprehend even a single syllable of the sacred writings, but it was predicted to the king that their meaning would be revealed to his family after five generations. Worshiping the miraculous objects as sacred, Lha-tho tho-ri lived to the age of 120, although his body appeared no older than 16.

In fulfillment of the prophecy, after five generations, King Srong-btsan sgam-po (*c.* C.E. 617—650) commissioned the production of an alphabet for the language of Tibet, thus introducing the art of writing. He was the last powerful Tibetan king prior to the country's domination by the great monasteries. Among his five wives there were two Buddhist princesses from the neighboring countries of China and Nepal. It is said that these two queens, as part of their dowries, brought with them precious statues of the Buddha and Buddhist saints. At their insistence, Srong-btsan sgam-po began to tame the wild terrain of Tibet, which was thought to be in the form of a malignant ogress, and prepare the country for the advent of their foreign religion.

ROYAL TOMBS

UP UNTIL the ninth century C.E., sacred tombs of the kings of Tibet were constructed in the Yar-lung valley and kept under constant supervision. The guards and attendants who dwelled within these royal tombs were permitted to see no one from the outside world, and any animal that strayed onto the sacred precincts became forfeit. At the time of the annual feast offered to the ancestor kings, the guards remained hidden until all the royal guests and shamanic priests had departed. Only then could they emerge from the gloom and partake of the lavishly arrayed food and drink.

▲ *Traditional Tibetan art depicts deities and divinities.*

ROOTS OF MYTHOLOGIES

IN A TIME before humans, the first rulers of Tibet were black *gnod-sbyin,* demons who knew the use of bows and arrows but not of ornamentation. Then came the *bdud,* who lived in the forested regions of the "nine valleys" and possessed knowledge of hammers and axes. After them came the *srin* with slings and catapults, and the *lha* with tempered steel. The *dmu-rgyal* arrived next on the scene and were the first to employ black magic and rituals. Following them were the malignant *'dre* who abandoned the wooded valleys and made their homes upon the high mountain slopes. The heroic *ma-sang* brothers were next in command, and it was they who gave the country of Tibet the name of Bod by which it is still known to this day. Protective shields and armor were invented during their dynasty, and they were followed by mysterious beings of great miracle power: the *klu*, the *rgyal-po,* and the *'gong-po*. Thus, by slow evolutionary process, the land became ready for humanity.

FUNDAMENTALS

WHILE VILLAGE shamans have become relegated to a merely marginal sociological role, Buddhist priests in many cases have assumed the role of oracular mouthpiece for converted shamanic deities. Dressed in the attire of a warrior god with heavy metal helmet, lance, and armor, such priests regularly fall into a state of ecstatic shamanic trance and act as mediums for the prophesies of the old deities. The ordained priestly class now adorn their temples with such archaic paraphernalia as the shaman's divination arrow, his magic mirror, and his precious pieces of fine rock crystal, all reinterpreted as symbols of Buddhist doctrine, and from the feathers, horns, bones, and fur on the old shaman's tunic have been derived theatrical costumes for the "Buddhist" dances of the eagle, stag, snow lion and skeleton.

The shaman's eagle, by means of which he once ascended to his nest in the world tree, became identified with the Indian Garuda. The stag is said to be the one who first heard the teachings of the lord Buddha in the deer park at Varanasi, the snow lion became identified as the mount of such Buddhist deities as Vairocana or Manjushri, and the dancing skeletons of the wounded shaman's own traumatic initiation by dismemberment became the guardians of the sacred Vajrayana charnel grounds.

▲ *Padmasambhava sits with a* vajra *in his right hand, a skull and bowl in his left.*

▲ *Early decorative Tibetan scripts.*

THE BIRTH OF PADMASAMBHAVA

THE INDIAN MYSTIC Padmasambhava is popularly believed to have emanated miraculously as an eight-year-old child within the heart of a lotus blossom in the Dhanakosha lake in Oddiyana, the Swat valley in what is now modern-day Pakistan.

Raised by the king of Oddiyana as his own son, Padmasambhava enjoyed all the luxuries of palace life until the time came for his great renunciation. Having murdered a minister of the king, he was banished from the kingdom and condemned to live the life of a penitent ascetic in the fearful charnel grounds beyond the borders of human habitation. There he is said to have conversed with supernatural beings and attained great spiritual power.

He is believed to have been ordained as a Buddhist monk by Ananda, the Buddha's cousin, and to have lived for over a thousand years as a follower of the Buddhist path.

Arriving in Tibet as a result of the king's invitation, Padmasambhava then traveled throughout the land and subdued the hostile forces that arrayed themselves against the new religion, so that he remains worshiped as the founder of Buddhism in Tibet.

THE "LOTUS-BORN GURU"

DURING THE SECOND HALF of the eighth century C.E., King Khri Srong-lde'u-btsan, full of admiration for the sophisticated cultures of his Buddhist neighbors, sent messengers to India in search of the most learned men of his day who, he hoped, would found a new temple and teach his people the ways of righteousness. In particular, the king was advised to invite the *tantrika* (practitioner of occult religion) known as Padmasambhava, the "Lotus-born Guru," and thus a new wave of mythology inherited from the Buddhist magicians of India swept the land.

THE CREATION

THE EARLIEST MYTHS of the shamanic culture that was once prevalent over the whole of Central Asia and the north concern the origins of the world and all that it contains. According to these tales, the world is created and sustained by an enormous number of gods and demons that reside unseen in countless locations of power. Their assistance is called upon before the commencement of any undertaking, and they are to be controlled and exorcized by the shaman priest whenever they cause trouble, stagnation, or sickness.

While the allotted realm of man covers the face of the earth, the gods and demons dwell in the heavens above and in the subterranean labyrinths beneath the surface.

Only a shaman when under trance has the power to travel the three realms and understand the intricate workings of the universe. Only he may divine the causes of illness and misfortune or retrieve lost souls abducted by spirits. It is he who recommends the performance of a particular sacrifice, typically the weaving of a "thread cross" *(mdos)* and the presentation of a ransom to the offended or malicious spirit. It is he who points out the sacred features of the landscape and keeps the myths alive.

STATUES OF THE BUDDHA

DEMONSTRATING her skill in the ancient Chinese art of geomancy, Queen Kong-jo, the Chinese bride of Srong-btsan sgam-po, pointed to those locations in the land where specially designed temples could be built to press down upon the earth demoness's shoulders and hips, elbows and knees, hands and feet, and heart. The large, jewel encrusted golden image of the 12-year-old Buddha that she brought with her from China is nowadays to be found in the Ra-sa 'phrul-snang Temple, built upon a lake in Lhasa formed of the ogress's heart-blood. This statue remains the most revered image in the whole of Tibet.

GURU PADMASAMBHAVA

HAVING INVITED Padmasambhava to assist him in Tibet, the king and the guru were of different opinions concerning who should salute whom. Padmasambhava therefore made a gesture of salutation to the king's staff, causing it to break into 100 pieces, so that the king immediately raised his hands in salutation. Muttering a spell and throwing some mustard seed, Padmasambhava then caused fire to blaze up all around them.

At that time Pe-dkar, the leader of the *rgyal-po* demons, could not bear to see a human with miraculous powers to rival his own and he therefore dispatched his retinue of 1,000 *the'u-rang* demons to destroy the guru. When they arrived there, however, they had no opportunity to kill him owing to the burning fire and they returned to their master in defeat. Even by the time Pe-dkar himself arrived, the fire had not died down, so he began to wonder how it could have been caused. Inquisitive about the spells the guru had recited, he crept forward to listen. Knowing this, the guru pierced him in the hearing ear with his magic *kila* and made his ear deaf. Piercing him in the seeing eye, he made his eye blind. Piercing him in the leg, he crippled his leg. Pe-dkar was thus subjugated and bound under oath to protect the doctrine of Buddhism forever.

▲ *Shamanic mask representing the queen of demons.*

▲ *A* bodhisattva, *one who has renounced* nirvana *to help people on earth.*

FORCES OF NATURE

THE CHAOTIC FORCES of nature, both feared and honored by the original shamanic tradition of Tibet, became systematically categorized and ordered under the influence of Buddhism and made to fit harmoniously into the Indian cosmological model. The wild spirits of the land are all said to have been "converted" and tamed as protectors of the Buddhist faith. Stripped of their former malignancy, such terrific forces of nature would now harm only those whose own wrongdoings could be pointed to as the causes of their misfortune. According to the doctrine of *karma,* the morally upright citizen has nothing to fear from the unseen world of spirits, and the patterns of nature became respected as the unfolding of natural *dharma* or universal law. Indeed, as the special protectors of the doctrine, these forces could be summoned by the Buddhist meditator and set to work at his request. Old shamanic rites of healing, ransom, and exorcism with their characteristic effigies and thread-cross structures wound with colored wool were readily adopted by the Buddhist clergy and heavily overlaid with Buddhist liturgy and symbolizm.

NATURE AND LANDSCAPE

TIBETANS BELIEVE their country to be sacred. Many features of the landscape are especially sacred, being associated either with myths of the gods or with the gods themselves. Even the most mundane areas are believed to contain valuable treasure belonging to the spirits of the land, and this has never been exploited for human profit for fear of offending those spirits upon whose goodwill and co-operation man depends at all times. Dotted here and there throughout the country are "hidden lands," areas of especial virtue for religious practice, and these have been opened up by seers known as "treasure revealers" *(gter-ston).*

BLACK MISERY AND RADIANCE

AT ONE TIME, it was said, when nothing existed, two lights were born. One of these was black and called Black Misery *(myal ba nag po),* the other was white and called Radiant *('od zer ldan*). Then, out of chaos arose multi-colored streams of light which separated in the manner of a rainbow, and from their five colors arose the five qualities of hardness, fluidity, heat, motion, and space. These five elements came together and fused into the form of a huge egg which was under the guardianship of Black Misery and Radiant. Black Misery produced the darkness of nonbeing from that egg, and he filled the darkness with pestilence and disease, misfortune, drought, and pain. Radiance thereupon filled the world with the light of auspicious becoming. He sent forth vitality and well-being, joy, prosperity, longevity and a host of beneficent gods.

As the gods and demons met and mated, many creatures were born and eventually the world became filled with their progeny. The stories of their exploits and creations are often localized in Tibet so that the very earth itself is seen as a manifestation of these divine beings and their children. The mountains, trees, rocks, and lakes that make up the sacred landscape may be recognized as the abodes of gods or as the very gods and demons themselves.

DARKNESS AND LIGHT

THE CONCERNS of Tibetan mythology are categorized as either worldly or transcendental. Mundane myths concern the origin of the world and the history of all that has taken place here since time began. Within this ongoing story are countless episodes of struggles between the forces of darkness and light engaged in by gods, demons, and men from the realms above, below, and upon the surface of the earth. In the realm of the enlightened ones beyond the understanding of ordinary mortals are the countless Buddhas of the five families, whose existence is symbolically expressed in sacred tantric texts and in artistic representations of circular *mandalas.*

THE DEIFIED SPIKE

THE CULT of the deified wrathful spike (Skt: *kila,* Tib: *phur-ba*) was consolidated from Indian sources around the middle of the eighth century C.E. The three scholars Padmasambhava, Vimalamitra, and the Nepali Shilamanju conferred together during a period of religious retreat in a mountain cave in the Kathmandu valley, near modern Pharping. There they composed a detailed commentary on all the wisdom that had thus far been gathered in India concerning the *kila,* and these teachings were then propagated in Tibet. Such a spike, it is said, is the very embodiment of a powerful winged god, as well as being his own special symbol and tool. By merely hammering it into the ground, all malign influences are subdued. If pegged into the corners, or at or across the entrance, of a sacred site, it creates a magical barrier across which evil elements may not pass. Although originating in India and known in all places to which Vajrayana Buddhism has spread, the elaborations of the cult with its extensive worship of the deified spike seem to have been lost there and are today seen as special characteristics of Tibetan Buddhism.

THE FIRST ROYAL TOMB

THE FIRST seven kings of Tibet descended from the sky on ropes. At the end of their lives they returned to the heavens leaving no earthly remains. The son of the last of these was called Gri-gum, and his was the first royal tomb in the land. Made furious by the prophecy of his shamanic soothsayer that he was to die by the sword, Gri-gum challenged his ministers to a duel and was taken on by Lo-ngam, keeper of the king's horses. For superstitious reasons, the king went into battle surrounded by a herd of yaks with bags of soot upon their backs. Wearing a black turban on his head, with a shining mirror affixed on the forehead, the king wore the corpses of a fox and a dog upon his shoulders. As soon as combat began, however, the sharp horns of the yaks burst the bags of soot and the air was filled with a cloud of dust. Wildly waving his sword above his head, Gri-gum severed the magic rope that connected him with heaven, but inflicted no injury whatsoever upon his opponent. Deserted by his protector gods, Gri-gum was slain by Lo-ngam, who carefully aimed an arrow at the only thing visible in all that cloud of gloom—the shining mirror on his king's forehead.

VAJRAPANI

THE THREE *bodhisattvas* Avalokiteshvara of the Lotus family, Manjushri of the Tathagata family, and Vajrapani of the Vajra family, who are the very embodiments of compassion, wisdom, and power, were, at one time, all extremely beautiful in form. One day, however, at the end of a long rite for the production of the elixir of immortality, the Buddhas entrusted Vajrapani with the care of the nectar while everyone else took a break. He failed in his duty, and the nectar was stolen by the planetary demon Rahu who drank down the contents of the golden vessel and replaced it with his own urine before escaping. When the Buddhas realized what had happened, they commanded Vajrapani to drink the demon's poisonous waste. As a result, his eyes bulged out of their sockets, his hair stood on end, and his body turned blue and became contorted with pain, with every muscle and sinew contracting and knotting in his limbs.

With the help of the sun and moon, Rahu was caught and cut in half by the furious Vajrapani but, having drunk the elixir, he could not die. Ever since then, Rahu has pursued those luminaries across the sky, and he regularly catches and devours them, causing periodic eclipses. They are soon released, however, for Rahu's severed trunk cannot keep them contained for long.

◀ *Brass statue of Avalokiteshvara encrusted with copper and turquoise.*

▲ *Red Yama, the Lord of Death, shown here turning the Wheel of Life.*

AVALOKITESHVARA

HAVING MADE A solemn vow to bring all beings to liberation, the *bodhisattva* Avalokiteshvara began teaching the way of wisdom and compassion. Migrating throughout the six realms of existence he brought release from suffering until he had emptied the very hells themselves. As he began his return journey home to Paradise, he happened to glance behind him and saw that, as soon as he left them, creatures everywhere had reverted to their former sinful ways and were living in misery. Unable to bear their suffering, he cried tears of grief and his body burst into a million fragments. The goddess Tara was born from his tears, and the *bodhisattva* arose with 11 heads and 1,000 arms.

THE MONKEY

AT ONE TIME a saintly monkey made his way to the quiet solitude of the Himalayas in order to enjoy there the ecstasy of undisturbed, profound meditation. The beauty of the monkey's personality, however, captivated the heart of a female rock demoness within whose locality he had taken up his abode, and she promptly fell in love with him. All her attempts at seduction, however, were unable to weaken the would-be meditator's vow of chastity and so she suffered greatly from the pangs of unrequited love. Now, a frustrated and angry demoness is a great danger in this world and so, his heart full of sympathy for the ogress's pain and his mind intent on bringing benefit to all beings, the *bodhisattva* monkey finally relented and succumbed to her entreaties for love. In due course, six children were born of their union and from these, it is said, the entire population of Tibet eventually descended. As the six children of the monkey rapidly multiplied, food became scarce and they began to fight among themselves for survival. It is said that the old monkey patriarch then divided the population into four large tribes and two smaller groups and taught them to sow seeds in order to insure a plentiful supply of food for the future.

▲ *The goddess Tara sits enthroned in the center of her universe. This particular paradise is characterized by the Chinese style towers.*
◀ *A form of Avalokiteshvara the Merciful. In one of his many arms he holds a rosary.*

▶ *The modern Tibetan spiritual leader, the Dalai Lama.*

THE MONKEY GOD

AS PIOUS BUDDHISTS, Tibetans believe that their original ancestors were none other than the holy *bodhisattva* sPyan-ras-gzigs (Avalokiteshvara) in the guise of a monkey and the goddess sGrol-ma (Tara) in the form of a rock ogress *(brag-srin-mo)*. These patron deities of Tibet have watched over their descendants ever since—especially Avalokiteshvara, who has repeatedly become manifest for his people in the form of the Dalai Lama. The Tibetans account for the variety of personality types among them by claiming that the first six monkey children included one representative from each of the six realms known to Buddhist cosmology.

THE OVERTHROW OF RUDRA

IN THE PAST the world was ruled by a self-centered tyrant called Rudra, who was the very embodiment of egotism. Having attained great power by misuse of the sacred teachings, he had all the worldly gods and demons under his thrall and there were 24 great cities in his domain. Eight of these cities were controlled by spirits from the realm of the sky, eight were controlled by creatures that crawl upon the surface of the earth, and eight by demons from the subterranean darkness. It was a time of great fear, for malicious demons were to be encountered roaming abroad both day and night. In their hands they carried sharp tridents and other weapons, and upon their bodies they wore human and animal skins for clothing. Adorning themselves with the shining bones of their victims, these demons wore tiaras of skulls upon their heads while around their necks hung garlands of severed heads dripping with blood. Whenever they were thirsty they would satiate themselves on human blood, and at night they would cohabit with one another's wives.

Witnessing this dreadful situation upon the earth and deeply moved by the plight of suffering humanity, the Buddhas assembled on the peak of Mount Meru and elected from among their ranks the *bodhisattva* Vajrapani to subdue the monstrous tyrant. His body having been blessed by Vairocana, his speech by Amitabha, his mind by Akshobhya, his attributes by Ratnasambhava, and his deeds by Amoghasiddhi, the invincible Vajrapani confronted Rudra on the summit of Mount Malaya and overthrew him. Rudra's body was cast down from the mountain with such force that his dismembered parts were scattered into the eight directions, and these sites subsequently became famous as "the eight great charnel grounds."

With the overthrow of their evil lord, the various gods and demons who had been his subjects were converted by the power of Vajrapani to the path of Buddhism and the 24 places under their control became incorporated into the sacred domain of the Wrathful Buddhas. Nowadays, tantric devotees of this cult of Wrathful Buddhas in Tibet carry tridents and wear ornaments of bone. Proclaiming the defeat of Rudra by mimicking his attributes, they visit the sacred sites throughout the Himalayas that are associated with this myth, and they gather together in order to celebrate rites of enlightenment and the triumph of good over evil.

Mongolia

INTRODUCTION

THE SHAMANIC ART of traveling in a trance to unseen worlds in order to resolve the dilemmas of life (once common across the whole of Central Asia and the north) is said to have been introduced to Mongolia in ancient times by a 15-year-old youth called Tarvaa. This lad, having fallen ill and fainted one day, was mistaken for dead. In disgust at the haste in which his relatives removed his body from the house, Tarvaa's soul flew off to the spirit realm where he was accosted by the judge of the dead and asked why he had come so early. Pleased by the boy's courage in travelling to that realm where no living man had traveled before, the lord of the dead offered the boy any gift of his choosing to take back with him to life. Shunning the proffered offerings of wealth, pleasure, fame, longevity, and the rest, Tarvaa chose to return with a knowledge of all the wondrous things that he had encountered in the spirit realm and the gift of eloquence. By the time he returned to his body, crows had already pecked out the eyeballs but, although blind, Tarvaa could foresee the future, and he lived long, and well with his tales of magic and wisdom brought back from the far shore of death.

THE SACRED COW

AMONG THE KHALKHA tribe of Outer Mongolia there is a belief that their origin is due to the love of a shamanic nature spirit and a cow. The first Khalkha having been born from a cow and raised on her creamy milk, the tribe inherited a natural inclination toward cattle rearing and the nomadic life. In order that their coming into being should not be forgotten, married women of this tribe wear their hair parted in the middle and combed outward, stiffened with mutton fat, in the form of a long pair of horns. Their dresses, also, are notable for the high projections on their shoulders, reminiscent of the prominent shoulder blades of cattle.

▼ *Skulls are used in masks such as this as they are believed to hold the personality of a being.*

ROOTS OF MYTHOLOGIES

THE COSMOS OF the Mongolian shaman is essentially vertical in structure, consisting of Blue Eternal heaven above and Mother Earth below. The father of heaven rules 99 realms *(tngri)*, 55 of which are said to be located toward the west and 44 toward the east. The domain of the earth mother is made up of 77 such *tngri,* and all of these realms are interconnected and sustained by a web of life in which every living being, both above and below, has its part to play. The whole is shaped like a cosmic tree with spreading branches on every level and there are holes between the layers through which the shaman can climb.

Shamans know the hunting spirits and the god of heroes. They know the protectors of horses and cows and the star of fate which, although born in the south, now dwells in the zenith. All such knowledge, retrieved at the cost of intense personal crisis from the spirit realms beyond the limits of the ordinarily perceived world, is put by the shaman at the disposal of his fellow men.

THE WASP

AT A TIME when the world was still young, the king of all flying creatures ordered the wasp and the swallow to go and taste the flesh of all living creatures. The two subjects were to report back to him in the evening and declare which meat was sweetest, most fit for the diet of a king. It being a beautiful day, the swallow lost himself in transports of joy—singing and soaring in the blue, blue sky. The wasp, on the other hand, did as he was bidden and spent the day biting whomsoever he met and tasting their hot blood. When the two met up at the end of the day, prior to their reporting back to the king, the swallow asked the wasp for his verdict. "Without doubt," said the wasp, "the sweetest food to eat is humans." Fearing that this could cause great trouble for the future, the swallow pulled out the tongue of the wasp with his beak so that, when the king asked him again that night, all the poor creature could do was buzz incoherently. "We have decided, your majesty," said the swallow, "that the meat most suitable for a king is the flesh of serpents." To this day, then, the eagle and the hawk who are the descendants of that royal line love to dine on snakes.

FUNDAMENTALS

BEGZE SUREN, the fierce protector of Mongolia, is described in the liturgy of his cult as a ferocious warrior attired in the armor and golden helmet of a military leader. Brandishing over his head a flaming copper sword with scorpion handle, Begze carries a bow and arrows and "devours the hearts of his enemies." Accompanied by his sister Okin Tngri, "the spirit of insight," he tramples upon the corpses of men and horses in his dwelling on the peak of a mountain that rises up from a sea of blood. Begze's general is the red Master of Life who rides to battle on the back of a ferocious wolf. Prancing around them in an orgiastic war dance are the eight sword-wielding butchers who devour the flesh, blood, and life breath of their enemies.

It is said that Begze and his horde attempted to prevent the transmission of Buddhism to Mongolia by obstructing the path of the third Dalai Lama in 1577. The Dalai Lama, however, assumed the form of Avalokiteshvara and the hooves of his horse imprinted the spell "Om Mani Padme Hum" upon the ground. Being overpowered, Begze was bound under oath as a protector of Buddhism from then on.

▲ *The Orhon River, Mongolia. However, the unseen lands of the spirits and the dead are just as important to the shamans as the physical environment of the living.*

◄ *Modern Mongolian societies still pay homage to ancient shamanic rituals.*

MYTHOLOGICAL GROUPS

MONGOLIA WAS TWICE converted to the Buddhism of Tibet. In the thirteenth century, Khubilai Khan, grandson of the great Chinggis Khan, together with members of his court, adopted the religion when Khubilai became ruler of an empire stretching from China to the gates of Europe. 300 years later, virtually the entire population of Mongolia became converted when Altan Khan professed his faith in the religion. It was Altan Khan who gave the Mongolian title "Dalai Lama" to his priest, the title by which he subsequently became known throughout the world in all his successive incarnations.

Since the introduction of Buddhism to Mongolia during this period, the ancient shamanic myths have become devalued and lost. The Mongolian Buddhist figure of the "white old man," for example, represents all that remains of the once proud shamanic deity that ruled as father over the 99 regions of heaven. It is said that he was converted during a meeting with the Buddha, and now he acts as an assistant to the clergy and as a supporter of the Buddhist path.

SHAMANS

SHAMANS WHO have followed in the wake of Tarvaa speak of being summoned by the spirits of their ancestors, who force themselves upon the young person and cause his or her personality to crumble. As the neophyte shaman experiences the dismemberment of his physical body on the worldly plane, his spirit takes refuge in a nest upon one of the branches of the world tree. There it stays until it has been nurtured back to health and the spirits that attend it have taught it how to see the world from the high vantage point of the tree.

While resting in their nests in the branches of the world tree, fledgling shamans learn the way of sacrifice to insure harmony and order within the web of life. They return to men with a knowledge of the gods of wind and lightning, the gods of the corners and the horizon, of entrance and borders, of steam and thunder, and countless other gods, and such knowledge gives them great power. Since they are able to summon whomsoever they please with their drums, it is said that the god of death himself, in a fit of rage, reduced the originally double headed shamanic drum to its current single headed style in order to protect his sovereignty, for early shamans could call back the souls even of those long deceased.

THE TIGER

MOST OF THE SACRED dances performed in the Buddhist temples of Mongolia feature the "white old man" as buffoon and symbol of regeneration in the new year. Stiff with age, his horse-headed magic staff now become a walking stick, the old man totters into the arena and begins to beat upon a tiger skin until the tiger is "dead." Absorbing the tiger's vitality, the old man now dances with youthful vigor and enjoys himself, exchanging gifts and jests with the crowd and drinking prodigious quantities of alcohol. When he finally collapses in a drunken stupor, the skeleton dancers of the graveyards cover him with a blanket.

HAYAGRIVA

RENOWNED AS "the five animal people," Mongolians are pastoral nomads with sheep, goats, cattle, camels, and horses under their care; animals as familiars and helpers feature large in their native shamanic cosmology. With the introduction of Buddhism, however, the animal fables of yore have largely given way to such tales as those of the horse necked tantric deity Hayagriva who resides as the fierce aspect in the heart of the *bodhisattva* Avalokiteshvara. Hayagriva's horse dance is thought to pound down upon the heads of demons and conquer the world.

THE KING AND THE SHEEP

AT THE END of every year the breastbone of a sheep is traditionally offered to the fire god who maintains fertility among the herds. Shamans know that the shoulder blade of a sheep is capable of accurate prognostication.

Once, in ancient times, there was a king who kept his beautiful daughter hidden from the world, but Tevne dug a deep pit in the ground into which he enticed one of the princess's maidservants. Over the hole he built a fire and, placing a kettle full of water upon that, he used a length of iron pipe wrapped with cotton to speak to the old woman below. After she had revealed to him the secret identity of the princess, he let her go. When he correctly identified the princess from among a number of similar looking girls, all dressed alike, the furious king was forced to bestow upon Tevne the hand of his daughter. Consulting his magic book of divination, the king learned that the informant was a man with earthen buttocks, a body of fire, lungs of water, and an iron pipe for vocal cords. Being unable to discern the meaning, the king lost faith in his book and burned it. It is because sheep licked up the ashes that they now have the power of divine sight.

THE GESAR KHAN EPIC

LONG AGO, as a man, the marmot is said to have shot down six of the seven suns that dessicated and scorched the earth, causing famine and misery to all beings. In order to escape the final arrow, the seventh sun began to circle the earth, so that we now experience periods of darkness and light as a result of its setting and rising. And all Mongolians know that the marmot's body contains "man flesh," a piece of its meat that is never to be eaten.

In 1577, Altan Khan issued the first antishamanist edict, outlawing such ancient myths, followed in 1586 by the second edict of Abadai Khan. Since then, the predominant mythology of Mongolia has been inspired by the teachings of Buddhism from Tibet.

The epic cycle of Gesar Khan, however, although permeated in its present form with the ideology of Buddhism, nevertheless retains the memories of many older shamanic gods whose myths are included within it. Among them are to be counted the powerful mountain deities as well as numerous lesser spirits of the locations through which the narrative runs.

Said to have been born from a white egg marked with three eye shaped spots that issued forth from the crown of his mother's head, Gesar's birth is reminiscent of shamanic myths of origin. Making his first appearance amid a host of excellent omens, Gesar arrived on earth with three eyes but had one plucked out by his terrified mother at the time of his birth.

▲ *Stones dating from the time of Chinggis Khan, possibly tombs or places of worship.*

▼ *Depiction of Avalokiteshvara.*

GESAR KHAN

GESAR KHAN was a ruthless and powerful warrior king who crushed violent injustice wherever he encountered it. Having descended from heaven to earth commissioned to destroy certain demons whose maledictions threatened to destroy the stability of human existence, Gesar often became forgetful of his quest in the aftermath of individual victories and required the prompting of his guardian angel (now identified as a Buddhist *dakini,* a female spirit of wisdom) to set his feet back on the path. The tales of his exploits are full of the dramatic effects of mortal weaknesses, and the episodes twist and turn in an unpredictable manner as a result of treachery, deceit, cowardice, greed, and envy.

RELIGIOUS SYSTEMS

RELIGIOUS SYSTEMS that are to be found in Mongolia include not only the predominant Buddhism but also Islam and Nestorian Christianity. None of these, however, has managed to completely supersede the ancient cults of shamanism and ancestor worship. Being concerned only with the immediate affairs of this life and having no specific creed of moral retribution and the afterlife, these archaic practices remain buried not too far beneath the surface of the lifestyle of all Mongolians, no matter to which formal religion they may outwardly adhere. Thus, when personal illness strikes, and especially in cases of nervous disorder, fever, or paralysis, the shaman is called in to assist.

Going into a trance while beating hypnotically upon his drum, the shaman invokes the powerful spirits of the natural cosmos (sky, landscape, or the nether regions) and solicits their aid in exorcising the malignancy. For clan affairs, however, such as widespread epidemics, childlessness, drought, or famine, family members themselves pray to the spirits of their ancestors *(avrak)* for help. This ancestral cult is also expressed in the worship of such clan totems as the horse, bull, or deer.

THE *GER*

TRADITIONALLY a nomadic culture, Mongolians have very little permanent architecture but prefer instead to dwell in domed tents called *ger*. These circular constructions of latticed wood and felt are symbolic of the universe, with the roof representing the sky and the smoke hole the sun. The central hearth brings all the elements together in harmony: a metal grate on the foundation of earth contains wood and fire which heats water for cooking. Thus the fireplace is sacred and no stranger will ever take a light from it, nor will any member of the family ever throw in rubbish for disposal.

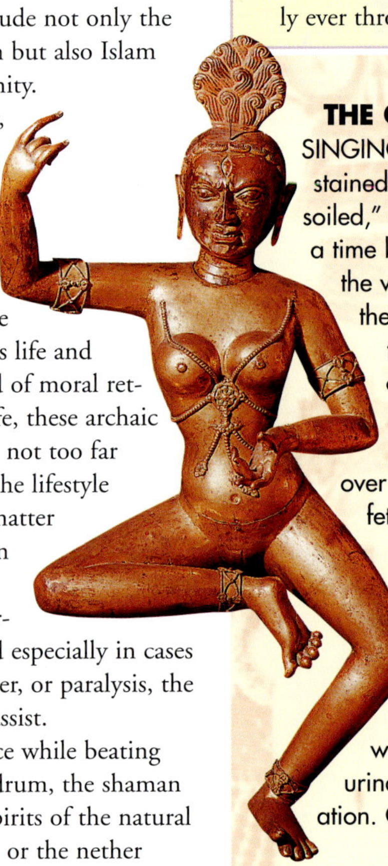

▲ Dakini, *a female spirit of wisdom.*

THE CAT AND THE DEVIL

SINGING "The cat's tongue is stained and the dog's hair is soiled," shamans are reminded of a time long ago when the seas of the world were yet mud and the rising mountains no more than hillocks. Then God created the first man and woman of clay and set a cat and a dog to watch over them while he went to fetch the waters of eternal life from the spring of immortality. While he was away, however, the Devil beguiled the guards by offering them milk and meat and, while they were distracted, urinated on God's new creation. God was then furious to find the fine fur of his handiwork so defiled and he ordered the cat to lick it off—all except for the hair of the head, which alone remained unpolluted. The cat's rough tongue took off all the dirty hair it could reach, leaving sparse stained hairs on the armpits and groin. Whatever the cat licked off, God placed on the dog. He then sprinkled his creations of clay with the sacred waters of the eternal spring but was unable to grant us immortal life owing to the Devil's defilement.

▲ *Rock carving showing the Buddha, from Mongolia.*

CHINGGIS KHAN

HAVING CONQUERED all the tribes of Mongolia, General Tumujin was proclaimed "King of the World" (*chinggis khan*). Gathering all the defeated chieftains under his command, Chinggis Khan inspired his troops with such an intense loyalty that he was able to lead them into victory against the entire known world of his day. The shaman Kokchu announced that Blue Eternal Heaven (*mongke koko tngri*) had elected Chinggis Khan as his representative on earth with divine right to rule over all who dwell there. Those who submitted to his inspired authority were treated well, the others were ruthlessly slain. His royal standard (*tuk*) consisted of a sacred tuft of nine yak tails, and it is said that after his death the soul of Chinggis Khan merged with the *tuk*, which thereafter became known as Borjigin, the guardian spirit and protector of the Mongolian troops.

Although he himself never learned to read, Chinggis Khan is remembered for his *yasa* or system of laws. This document, containing the moral precepts and strict code of honor of his troops, is regarded as a magical talisman of victory and worshiped as part of the cult of the ancestors, for Chinggis Khan was truly the grandfather of the nation.

VIOLINS

THERE WAS ONCE a pretty shepherd girl who was regularly courted at night by a visiting prince from heaven. Each morning at dawn, however, her divine lover would disappear into the depths of the sky on his flying horse. To keep him by her side, she clipped the horse's long feathered wings. As the prince began his ascent to heaven the horse fell down in the desert and died. Lost in the wilderness, the heavenly prince could no longer visit his shepherdess, nor could he return home. Fashioning a violin from the horse's bones, the prince then became a wandering minstrel, and to this day Mongolian violins are carved with the head of a horse.

▲ *Khori Tumed returns his wife's dress of feathers and she once again becomes a beautiful swan and flies away.*

▼ *Gers on the Mongolian plains.*

THE SWAN

LONG AGO, on the little island of Oikhon on Lake Baikal, fed by the river Khudar lined with birch groves, Khori Tumed saw nine swans fly down from the northeast. Removing their feathered dresses, they became nine beautiful girls who bathed naked in the lake. Khori Tumed silently stole one of the dresses so that only eight swans were able to fly off and he married the one who remained. She bore him 11 sons. They were very happy together but Khori Tumed would never show his wife where he had hidden her swan dress. One day she asked once more, "Oh please let me try on my old dress. If I try to walk with it out of the door then you may easily catch me, so there is no danger of my escape."

Being persuaded, he let her try it on and suddenly she flew upward through the skylight of their ger. Khori Tumed was just in time to catch her ankles and he pleaded with her to stay at least long enough to give names to their sons before departing. So the 11 sons became men; Khovduud, Galzuut, Khalbin, and so on. Then Khori Tumed let his swan wife go and she flew around the tent bestowing blessings upon their clans before disappearing back to the northeast.

China

INTRODUCTION

THE ORIGINS OF CHINESE civilization are inextricably linked to its favorable environment. Three zones of eco-geographical systems developed in the land mass of China. The temperate North China belt with its fertile plains benefiting from the rich alluvium from the Yellow River permitted a seed culture of millet, hemp, fruit trees, mulberry, and grasslands conducive to the evolution of wild and domestic plants and animals and to human habitation. But it was prone to harsh winters, drought, and floods. The South China belt forms a second zone, with a stable, mild and humid climate, and with alluvium from the Yangtse River that permitted a vegetative propagation culture of all-year growing seasons. It is characterized as an aquatic agricultural system favorable to rice, beans, lotus, bamboo, fish, and turtles. A third zone is the Deep South China belt with rich coastal fishing grounds and a tropical ecosystem.

The different environments of north and south contributed to the dual origin of human culture, with the emergence of communities of similar economic levels but with varying cultural systems. Their earliest known sites are the Neolithic settlements of the Yangshao culture, at Banpo near Xi'an in the north and Hemudu in Zhejiang Province in the Southeast. The Neolithic people of North China had Mongoloid features and show no significant ethnic diversity. This physical homogeneity indicates that in Neolithic times there is no evidence of migration to North China from neighboring regions. The first Chinese state, the Shang, emerged in the North China bio-geographical belt. Emerging from the Longshan culture of Henan Province, the Shang rose to prominence in an era of unprecedented cultural and technological development.

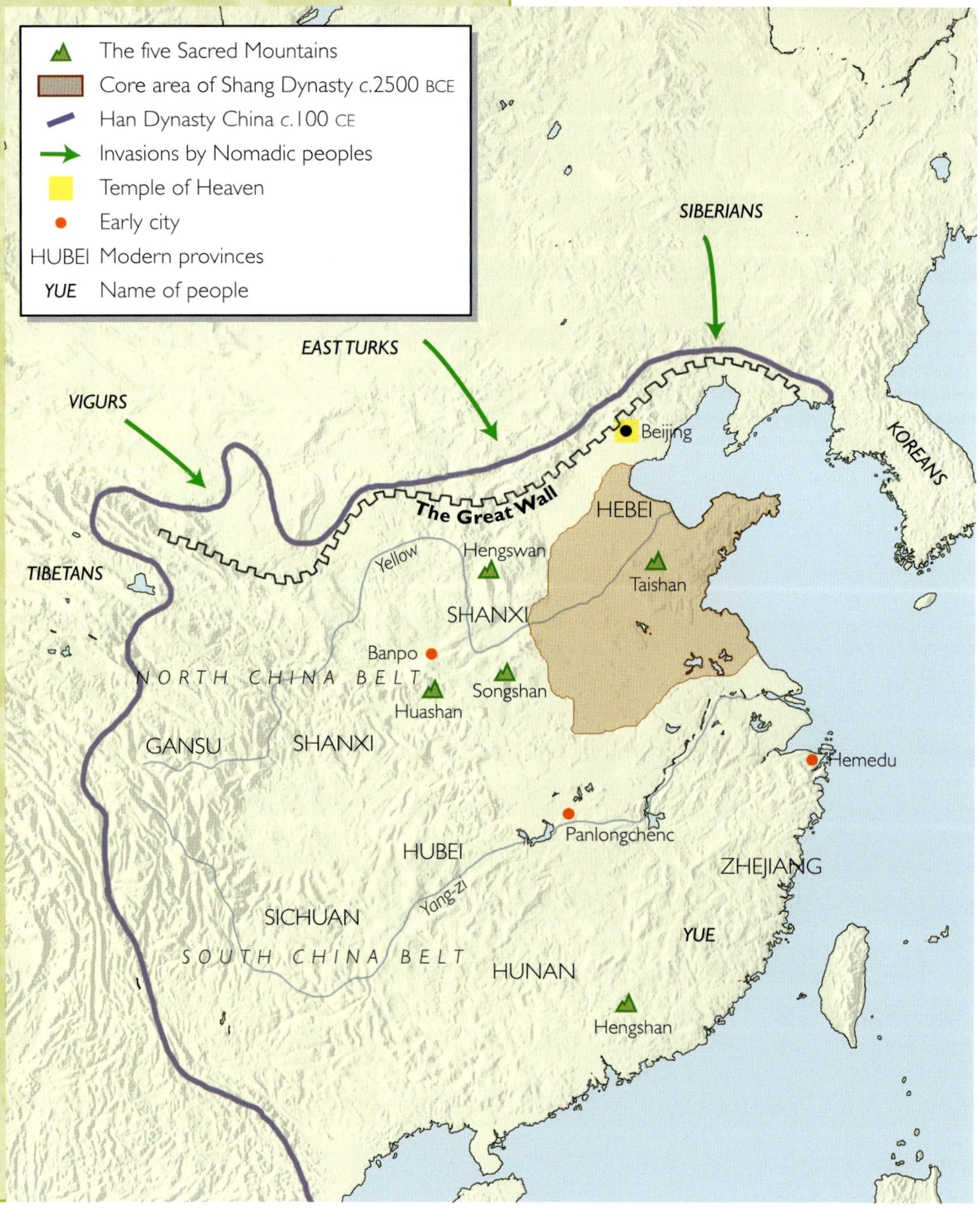

◀ *Chinese Buddhist saint from the Qing Dynasty.*

FUNDAMENTALS: RELIGIOUS CUSTOMS, CULTS, INFLUENCES

CRUCIAL TO THE IDENTITY and central control of the state was the Shang concept of a priestly king. The king's functions were to make divination to the royal ancestors, to conduct rituals in honor of the ancestors, to make a sacred progress through Shang territory, to lead in war, hold audiences, bestow honors, and lead the royal hunt.

There was no fixed capital, except for some ritual, technological and funerary sites. The king ruled through the intercession of the great god, Di. One of the north-west regions visited by Shang kings was the Wei valley, west of the Yellow River, inhabited by the Zhou people. The Zhou absorbed Shang cultural influences, but they were a warrior people, and in time they conquered their Shang overlords, establishing the Zhou dynasty in 1123 B.C.E. The Zhou kings embarked on a military strategy to unite the diverse communities of north and south, extending their power into Manchuria, Inner Mongolia and the regions north and south of the Yangtse River. The Zhou introduced moral rigor to their political and social systems. They abandoned the great god of the Shang, worshiping instead the sky god, Tian, the Zhou king being designated "Son of the sky god" (Tian Zi).

In 771 B.C.E. Zhou power was effectively diminished, but the king had nominal power over a loose federation of kingdoms. These kingdoms gradually merged and became enlarged, and in the Warring States era (fifth–third century B.C.E.) contended for supremacy over a reunited state. The most militaristic of these kingdoms, the Qin, based on what is now Shaanxi, in the north-west, successfully unified the residual Zhou states into the first Chinese empire, followed by the Han empire, which lasted for some 400 years.

It was only with the disintegration of the Zhou dynasty that classical writers were stimulated by the imperative need to record for posterity the remembered heritage of their sacred history. They achieved this, not by writing a seamless, artistic account of their myths, but by incorporating mythic narratives into their books on philosophy, government, law, literature, and social customs. Since their versions of the myths are relatively consistent, it must be assumed that they were drawing on a communal fund of oral traditions that dated from before the first recorded myth of 600 B.C.E. Although the dating and origin of the myths were for ever lost, their stories were preserved in the fragments scattered in classical texts.

THE COMPLEXITY OF THE COLLECTION OF CHINESE MYTHS

THE MYTHS of ancient China emerged from the oral tradition to be preserved in classical texts in the Age of Philosophers and with the advent of early literature. China had no Hesiod, Homer, or Ovid to retell the mythic oral tales. Instead, Chinese writers introduced fragmentary passages of mythic narrative into their works to illustrate their argument and to give authority to their statements.
Chinese myth exists as an amorphous, diffuse collection of anonymous archaic expression preserved in the contexts of philosophical, literary, or historical writings. They are brief, disjointed and enigmatic. Incorporated into miscellaneous classical texts, these mythic fragments vary in their narration. Often authors adapted the myth according to their point of view. The result is that Chinese myth exists in numerous versions, mostly consistent but with significant variation in the details. Whereas the reshaping of archaic oral Greek and Roman myths into artistic narrative literature meant the loss of the authentic oral voice, the Chinese method of recording mythic fragments in a wealth of untidy, variable narrative forms demonstrates a rare aspect of primitive authenticity.

THE ORIGIN OF THE WORLD FROM THE BODY OF PAN GU

CHINA HAS A RICH TRADITION of cosmogonic (or universal) myth. There is the world picture of a primeval earth covered by a sky cupola fastened together by cords, mountains, or pillars. There is the creation of the universe from vapor. A third myth relates that the world was created from matter like a chicken's egg that separated into sky and earth. Another, this time more obscure, myth tells how the goddess Woman Gua created all things through her 70 transformations.

The most colorful creation narrative derives from a minority ethnic group in south-western China, recorded in the third century C.E., and probably transmitted from Central Asia. It relates how the world and humans were formed from the dying body of the first-born, semi-divine human, the giant Pan Gu. His breath became the wind and clouds, his voice thunder, his eyes the sun and moon, and his limbs mountains. His bodily fluids turned into rain and rivers, his flesh into soil. His head hair became stars, his body hair vegetation. Teeth, bones, and marrow became minerals. His body bugs turned into humans. This myth is a series of metamorphoses. It is referred to as the myth of the cosmological human body.

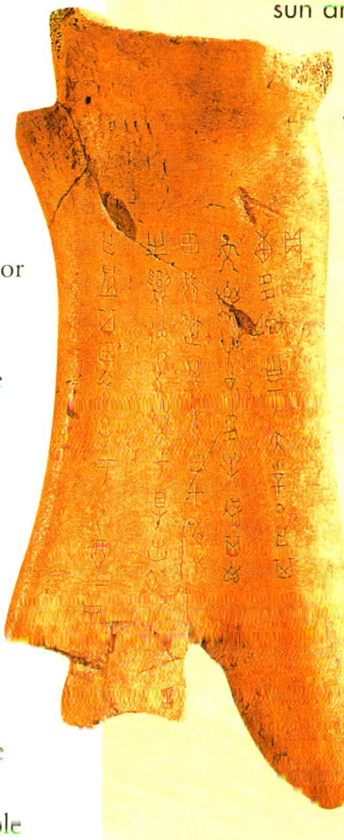

▲ *Ancient inscribed oracle bone, used for divination.*

CALENDRICAL AND CULTURAL DEITIES

CLASSICAL TEXTS relate mythic episodes of numerous famous or shadowy deities. Two play a role in the creation myth (Woman Gua and Pan Gu), and four play a role in the flood myth (Woman Gua, Gong Gong, Gun, and Yu). While the celestial and calendrical deities are female (Xi He, the sun goddess, and Chang Xi, the moon goddess), the cultural deities are male (the Farmer God and Fu Xi). Deities of destruction have different functions. Chi You is the god of war, Gong Gong the marplot, and the Queen Mother of the West the sender of plagues and punishment.

◀ *Spectacular statue of the sky god.*

TEXTS THAT PRESERVED THE MYTHS

THE EARLIEST CLASSICAL text which preserved mythic narrative is a Zhou dynasty anthology of poetry of 600 B.C.E. It contains the rare myths of the divine origin of the Shang and the Zhou, each through an ancestral goddess. The later texts of Confucian philosophy refer only briefly to mythical figures, but the Confucian text by Mencius (350 B.C.E.) records two versions of the myth of world catastrophe by flood. The anonymous *Ancient History*, adopted by the Confucian School, relates myths of the origin of government, the concept of the sage–king and the transfer of political power. The texts of Daoist philosophy, especially *Zhuang Zi* (340 B.C.E.), recounts the myth of chaos, the god Hundun, and the metamorphoses myth. The two major sources of myth are the "Questions of Heaven" chapter of the *Songs of Chu* (400 B.C.E.) and the *Classic of Mountains and Seas* (third century B.C.E.–second century C.E.). The first text records the sacred narrative of the people of Chu in Central China from creation to the era of human history. The second text contains numerous narratives of over 100

▲ *Confucius (in yellow) was one of the first philosophers to record his beliefs and thoughts.*

mythical figures. Both texts preserve major and minor myths in their great diversity. Miscellaneous ancient and medieval writings and later encyclopedias also preserve fragments of myth.

THE CREATION OF HUMANKIND BY WOMAN GUA

THE PAN GU creation myth relates one of three versions of the myth of the creation of humankind. A second relates that out of primeval vapor two gods formed and divided into the cosmic powers Yin and Yang. They produced all living things, and humans were created from primeval vapor. A third myth has a female creator figure. It contains dramatic and colorful detail. The narrative begins after the creation of the world. The creator goddess Woman Gua kneaded yellow clay like a potter and made images of humans which came to life. She wanted to create more but could not. So she made a furrow in the mud with her builder's cord and lifted it out so that the falling mud became humans. The myth goes on to explain the origin of social hierarchy. The yellow clay humans became the class of plutocratic nobility, while the inferior mud produced the mass of the poor underclass. The color motif of yellow resonates through Chinese culture. The Yellow Emperor god was the supreme deity of philosophical and religious Daoism; yellow symbolized the divine earth; and it was the emblematic color of some dynasties. Woman Gua's emblems are her knotted cord and compass.

FIGURES AND ARCHETYPES IN CHINESE MYTHOLOGY

MANY FIGURES depicted in mythical episodes represent cultural archetypes. Woman Gua and Pan Gu in cosmogonic myth, Yi the archer in the world catastrophe of fire and Yu in the flood myth symbolize order out of chaos, and they are archetypal savior figures. The mothers of the suns and the moons, Xi He and Chang Xi, and the culture-bearing deities are archetypal nurturing figures. The female Drought Fury and Responding Dragon denote divine vengeance. Gun is the archetypal failed hero, who also represents the trickster figure. The grain god Hou Ji, Shun and Yu are stereotypical successful heroes. Shun is the archetypal moral leader.

WAYS OF READING CHINESE MYTH

THE MOST REWARDING and practical way of reading the very complex and fragmentary collection of Chinese myth is to apply the various approaches formulated by scholars of mythology worldwide. The naturist approach identifies solar and lunar myths of the goddesses Xi He and Chang Xi. Modern gender theory underscores their myths and those of the creatrix and savior goddess Woman Gua. The anthropological approach uncovers important charter myth in the transfer of power from the sage-kings Yao and Shun. The ethnographic approach reveals the creation myth of Pan Gu from the south-western subculture of ancient China. The etiological approach underscores myths of origin, from the creation myths of Woman Gua and Pan Gu to the discovery myths of the culture-bearing deities, such as the Farmer God and Fu Xi. Etiological myth is evident in the female-gendered foundation myths of the Shang, through a bird's egg, and the Zhou, through a god's footprint, besides the animalian myth of the Yao people through the divine dog Pan Hu. The motif or mythic theme approach helps the reader to discern myths of world catastrophe by fire and flood through the figures of Yi the archer, Woman Gua, Gong Gong and Yu. The stereotypical features of the hero figure identify the child hero and grain god Hou Ji, the failed hero Gun and the successful heroes Shun and Yu.

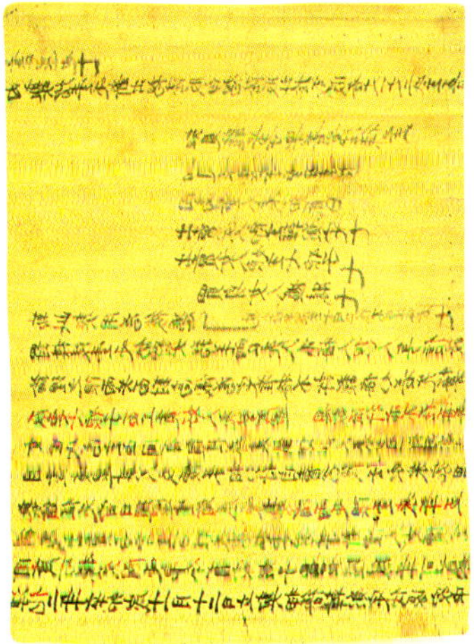

▶ *A page of a sutra, discourse of a Buddha.*

THE WORLD CATASTROPHE OF THE FLOOD

THE FLOOD MYTH is told in four main versions. The myth of the worker god Gong Gong relates how he stirred the world's waters so they crashed against the sky barrier, threatening a return to chaos. The myth of the dual catastrophe of flood and fire is recounted through the figure of the goddess Woman Gua who controlled the disaster. Another account tells how the hero Gun risked all by stealing divine cosmic soil to stem the flood, but he failed and was executed. His son Yu was born from his belly, and then Gun metamorphosed into a bear.

The version of the flood myth which became standard relates how the hero Yu controlled the flood through his superhuman physical prowess, intelligent flood plans and moral virtue. Supernatural creatures, the aquatic dragon and turtle, aided his labors. Yu worked so long and hard that his body became disfigured. After controlling the flood, he divided the world into nine regions and he thus became the founder of the mythical Xia dynasty, the first in the Golden Age.

In Chinese flood myth, the themes of the flood as divine punishment, the drama of human escape, and the recommencement of humankind by divinely favored survivors do not occur.

MAJOR CHINESE THEMES

MAJOR MYTHIC THEMES are narrated in several versions, such as the four cosmogonic myths and the four flood myths. Divine warfare and the marplot themes are significant. The re-establishment of natural order after world catastrophes is followed by the theme of a Golden Age of sage-kings. The theme of the warrior and moral hero is represented in numerous episodes. The rarely expressed theme of love occurs in the myth of stellar lovers. Less emphasized themes include agricultural and pastoral themes, migration and exile, animalian and vegetal themes, gender-based conflict, and the "cultural other."

WORLD PARALLELS AND INDIGENOUS TRAITS

THE MAIN THEMES of Chinese myth reveal significant parallels with world mythologies. Chinese cosmogonic myth differs by the absence of a creator or the concept of divine will, and by the absence of an authorized version (such as that given in *Genesis*). The myths of creation and of catastrophe by flood each have four distinct versions. World catastrophe by fire has only one mythic version whose central concern is with the solar calendar, but there are several drought myths. In myths of cultural benefits the two themes of deities voluntarily bestowing gifts on humankind and of first teaching humans how to use them find close parallels in world mythology. Several divine gifts from Fu Xi, such as divination through the Eight Trigrams (the *Yi jing*), are uniquely Chincsc. The archaic Shang and Zhou foundation myths are vividly detailed. The absence of a foundation myth of a named city derives from the custom of multiple capital cities in ancient China rather than one sacred citadel. The myth of the hero reveals stereotypical parallels, such as the divine birth and trials of the child hero Hou Ji. But Chinese heroic myth differs in its early emphasis on the moral virtue of the warrior hero, such as Yu.

▲*Chinese plate decorated with a green and red dragon motif. Dragons are often central to Chinese mythology.*

THE DISCOVERY OF MEDICINE BY THE FARMER GOD

THE MYTH of the Farmer God relates how he taught humans the discovery and uses of medicine. He took pity on humans who were suffering illnesses from eating toxic plants and drinking contaminated water. In an effort to help these humans, the god tasted all the plants and taught humans the difference between those that were poisonous and those that were edible. His method was to thrash plants with his rust-colored whip and then judge their value by their taste and smell. He organized plants into four categories: bland, toxic, cool, and hot. This taxonomy forms the basis of traditional Chinese medicine. The Farmer God also taught humans how to distinguish between types of soil and terrain. He created a wooden plow and taught humans how to till the soil and sow the five grains. His function as agricultural deity overlaps with that of the grain god Hou Ji. The Farmer God's emblem is a forked plow. He became the divine patron of medicine.

THEMES IN ART

THE EARLIEST artistic expression of myth occurs on funereal stone carvings and murals. Favorite themes are the acts of the deities, flood and fire myths, the tree of life, the paradise of the Queen Mother of the West, and the trials of the hero, such as the filial Shun. The most popular poetic theme is the tragic myth of two stellar lovers. In novels, recurring figures are military heroes of antiquity and intelligent animals such as Monkey. Temple architecture colorfully represents such deified figures as Confucius. The life-giving symbol of the dragon appears on textiles and ceramics.

◄ *This animal shell, covered with special markings, would have been used in medical divinations.*

▼ *Vase with a dragon motif, dating to the early Ming dynasty.*

THE SEPARATION OF SKY AND EARTH

THE MYTH OF THE SEPARATION of sky and earth belongs to the category of creation myth, of which there are five cosmogonic accounts. The earliest version tells of the monstrously deformed sky god Zhuan Xu, who presides over the pivot of the sky and commands his two grandsons, Chong and Li, to eternally prop the sky up and press the earth down to keep the elements separate. If this separation is not maintained, the cosmos will revert to chaos.

A much later version of this myth, which was probably a cultural diffusion from Tibet in the third century C.E., relates that at the beginning of time primeval matter was like a chicken's egg. After 18,000 years this matter separated, and sky and earth opened out, the Yang ethereal matter rising to form the sky, the Yin heavy matter falling to become earth. Between the two unfolding elements the first semi-divine human, Pan Gu, was born and he went through nine metamorphoses, growing as divine and wise as sky and earth. The three attained their maximum development 18,000 years later, and formed the trinity of Heaven, Earth, and Humankind. Later on the Three Sovereigns emerged (primeval rulers whose divine names vary). This myth relates that numbers were then created and cosmic distance was established, providing the etiology of the science of mathematics and the calculation of the distance between the sky and earth of 60,000 miles. This second version became the orthodox myth of creation in traditional mythology.

THE MYTH OF CHAOS

THE NUMEROUS cosmogonic myths describe primeval matter as formless vapor, a chicken's egg, or a dark, shapeless expanse. The myth of chaos is represented in three versions. One is the abstract concept of a primordial shapelessness before creation, called hun dun. Another version of the tale describes chaos as the god Hun Dun who lives on Sky Mountain in the west. He is like a yellow bag and red like a cinnabar flame, with six feet and four wings, but no face or eyes. Hun Dun can sing and dance. The third version is narrated by the Daoist philosopher Zhuang Zi (fourth century B.C.E.). He tells how the god Hun Dun ruled the center of the world, with the gods of the south sea and north sea ruling on each side. They visited his land often, and in return for his generosity they decided that since he had no face they would give him the seven bodily openings so that he could see, hear, eat, and breathe. They chiseled an opening each day, but on the last day Hun Dun died. This Daoist myth illustrates the moral of misguided charity and the danger of interventionist policies.

◀ *Chinese art showing the Goddess of Spring and some of her companions.*

THE MYTH OF THE FIRST MARRIAGE

THE MYTH of the institution of marriage illustrates the way a mythical figure may play different roles in several major myths. This myth features the goddess Woman Gua, who has important functions in other myths as the creatrix of humankind, creatrix of all things in nature, as divine smith and as savior of the world in the catastrophe of fire and flood. Most of these accounts appear in early texts. A much later medieval text relates the myth of the first marriage, in which Woman Gua also figures. But in the period between late antiquity,

when her myths were first recorded, and the medieval era, the position of women was devalued and the goddess was demoted from a primeval divinity to the first female human. The myth tells how she and her brother wanted to enjoy a sexual relationship but were ashamed and decided to ask permission from God. God performed a miracle to show his approval and the first humans made love, hiding their ashamed faces behind a grass fan. This rare account of sibling marriage may contain a rationale for incest in times of dire need, such as floods, famine, war, or epidemics which decimate populations and threaten the survival of the human race.

LADY XIN CHUI

THIS SILK PAINTING found in the tomb of Lady Xin Chui, who died in 168 B.C.E. in the vicinity of Changsha, a city in Hunan Province, depicts her mythological journey into Paradise. The lowest scene shows the watery underworld where her mortal soul will rest in peace and die. Above this is a funeral scene and over this are motifs of the sky in the form of a round jade disk, the aerial messenger birds with human heads, and the chart of the heavens. The central scene shows the immortal soul of the dead woman in her human form, complete with her walking stick, asking the way to Paradise from heavenly guides. The skeletal figure of the owl, symbol of impending death, hovers above. In the center of the painting is the presiding goddess, probably the creator goddess Woman Gua with her serpentine tail. Votive smoke rises from the funeral feast to the goddess and the bell of destiny tolls for the arriving soul, guarded by animal deities. The gates of heaven are opened for her.

◀ *Example of Chinese script used as art. The writing surrounds an image of the Chinese god of longevity.*

THE INVENTION OF WRITING BY FU XI

THE MYTH OF FU XI'S invention of writing, divination, and hunting weapons is told through the device of mimesis, which is the imitation of an observed act and its application to an analogous method. The narrative relates that at the time when the divine Fu Xi ruled the universe, he looked at the sky and earth, observed the marking of birds and beasts, and contemplated their images and patterns. With this knowledge, based on the natural order of things, the god created the Eight Trigrams for humans to make divination. (This was the prototype of the *Book of Change*, or *Yi jing*.) Fu Xi also watched a spider weaving its web and he fashioned knotted cords into nets and taught humans how to use them for hunting and fishing. The god also created music for humans, patterned on the divine harmony of the cosmos. Fu Xi is represented in art with his emblem of a carpenter's square, and in human form with a snake's tail. In the late classical period (first century B.C.E.) he was linked to Woman Gua as a divine married couple with serpentine tails intertwined. In the traditional masculine pantheon Fu Xi often appears as the first and major deity.

▲ *Detail from a silk painting found in the tomb of Lady Xin Chui*

THE MOTHER OF THE TEN SUNS

BY THE MEDIEVAL period, when classical texts were being codified and printed and classified into bibliographies, the history of women was being rewritten, so that major mythical goddesses were given a subordinate role and status and sometimes disappeared from the record. Modern theories of gender have helped to rediscover the identity, function, and role of primeval goddesses who survive only in a shadowy way in the texts. This is particularly true of myths of the sun goddess, which are fragmentary and elusive. These fragments relate that a goddess named Xi He (Breath Blend) gave birth to 10 suns, one for each day of the ancient week. As each sun returned from the worldly sky she washed it and dried it in the world tree in the east. Her nurturing role as mother and restorer is also seen in her concern that humans have life-giving light by day. Breath Blend appears in another version of the sun myth as the charioteer of the sun. Her myth was degraded in writings of the patriarchal Confucian tradition, where the person of the sun goddess and her cosmological function were divided to become two male officials named Xi (Breath) and He (Blend) who were in charge of the regulation of the calendar. This masculine version of her myth became the orthodox version

DROUGHT

A DROUGHT PERSISTED for five (or sometimes seven) years in the reign of a mythical founding Shang king, Tang the conqueror. The people were reduced to starvation. Diviners wanted to offer human sacrifice in expiation, but Tang went to the sacred grove of Mulberry Forest and prayed to God to forgive human error by accepting himself as sacrificial victim and removing the punishment of the drought. He lay on the pyre, and just as the fire was taking hold the skies opened with a great downpour of rain. This myth does not appear among Shang writings, but it reflects the semi-arid environment of the Shang territory in the north.

Another strand of drought myth exists in fragmentary form. It relates how a surrogate female named Woman Chou was exposed on a mountain-top dressed in green, the emblem of water and vegetal regeneration. As the sun beat down mercilessly on her she tried to screen her face with her green sleeve (or sometimes her hand), but she died and her dessicated corpse became divine. In the myth of the war of the gods Chi You and Yellow, drought was one of the weapons of the god Yellow in the form of his daughter, Drought Fury, who defeated the war god Chi You.

THE HUNTER GOD SAVES HUMANKIND FROM THE WORLD FIRE

THE CATASTROPHE MYTH of a world fire is told in two versions. One version relates how the cosmos collapsed, and fire and flood threatened to eliminate humankind. Woman Gua intervened to save the world by using her skills as the divine smith to repair the cosmos. The other version focuses on the catastrophe of the world fire and features the intervention of the hunter god, Yi the archer. This myth is linked to the myth of the 10 suns born to the sun goddess Breath Blend. It is related that one day, instead of one of the 10 suns rising in the sky in its sequence of 10 days, all 10 suns rose at once and threatened to extinguish the world. The hunter god was the first deity to feel pity for humankind, and he interceded with a sky god, Di Jun, who gave him a magic vermilion bow and plain arrows with silk cords to shoot the 10 suns down. In another version of this myth, it is the ideal ruler Yao who orders the hunter god to shoot down the suns and avert the disaster, and at the same time to slaughter six monsters preying on humans.

ARCHETYPAL CHARACTERS

THE ARCHETYPAL FIGURE who creates order out of chaos is seen in the myths of Woman Gua, Pan Gu, and the sky god Zhuan Xu. The culture bearing-deities represent the archetypal figure of the nurturer, teaching humans how to survive and improve their lives. Linked to this is the archetypal savior figure who rescues humans from catastrophes, such as Yi, the hunter god, in the solar fire myth, Woman Gua and Yu in the flood myth, or the Shang king Tang in the drought myth. The mythical figure Gun symbolizes several archetypes: the savior, the hero, the dying god, and the trickster. Yu is the archetypal hero, both warrior and moral exemplar, who became the ruler of the first dynasty, the mythical Xia.

◀ *When a world flood threatened mankind, Woman Gua intervened and repaired the cosmos.*

CULTURAL MYTH: METALLURGY

TWO MAJOR MYTHS present the etiology of metal and the symbolic power of metal. One of these myths features the war god Chi Yu; it relates how, when two mountains burst open pouring forth water and metal, Chi Yu gathered the metal and fashioned weapons and armor from it. This god is represented with a bovine aspect of horns and hooves, and he and his 72 brothers had bronze heads and ate stone pebbles. The god of war achieved supremacy through his invention and challenged the great god Yellow in a war of the gods. But the god Yellow's allies were his daughter Drought Fury and Responding Dragon who defeated Chi Yu and executed him. At his death his fetters and manacles turned into a grove of blood-red maple trees.

The other myth of metallurgy relates how the demigod Yu received nine sacred bronze cauldrons, each of which was engraved with images of the knowledge of the world. These cauldrons were endowed with the power to discern moral worth. They were handed down from dynasty to dynasty. During an era of benevolent government they remained with the ruler and were heavy with moral virtue, but in evil times they became light and flew away. The cauldrons served as a symbol of legitimate dynastic rule and as emblems of wealth, ritual, and state control over the strategic production of metal.

ORIGIN MYTHS

THE MYTH of the divine origin of the Shang tells how the sky god commanded a divine dark bird to descend to earth and give birth to the Shang, whose first founder was the hero Xie. Another version narrates that a lovely girl named Jian Di went bathing with two maids. They saw a dark bird lay an egg, and Jian Di ate it. She became pregnant and gave birth to Xie. Jian Di became the semi-divine ancestress of the Shang, with Xie as its male founder. The myth of the divine origin of the Zhou dynasty similarly features a semi-divine ancestress and a male founder. It relates how the girl Jiang Yuan (Jiang the originator) trod on the big toe of a great god and conceived a child which she named Sovereign Millet (Hou Ji). She thought her child was unlucky and tried three times to abandon it. The child hero survived the three trials and was rescued by animals, woodcutters, and birds. Jiang Yuan then nurtured her baby. He grew up to possess divine knowledge of the seed culture of millet and the vegetal art of propagating beans, and he taught humans his arts. He also taught humans how to cook millet and offer it in sacrifice to him as the grain god and founder of the Zhou. This myth of millet serves as the etiological myth of divine sacrifice.

▲ *An example of the robes worn by the Chinese Emperors, showing the intricate and detailed decoration.*

◀ *Animals feature in some Chinese myths, playing a protective role to those lost or abandoned.*

◀ *A painting on a wooden panel depicting the God of silk, one of the male chinese Gods.*

THE MOON GODDESS

THE LUNAR MYTH is told in two distinct story lines featuring Ever Breath (Chang Xi) and Ever Sublime (Chang E). The earliest narrative tells how Ever Breath gave birth to the 12 moons in the western wilderness near Mount Sunmoon. She nurtured her lunar children by bathing them after their nightly journey through the sky. The second narrative tells how Ever Sublime was the consort of the hunter god, Yi the archer, who saved the world from the solar conflagration. She stole his elixir of immortality, ate some, and was transported to the moon as a goddess. Living on the moon with her were a hare which pounded the drug of immortality and a toad which danced in drugged ecstasy. The motif of regeneration in this myth is expressed through the waxing and waning of the moon and the apparent rebirth of the toad when it sloughs off its skin. The numerological feature of the 10 suns and the 12 moons is reflected in the ancient calendrical system of the 10 Celestial Stems and the 12 Earthly Branches, by which days, months, years, and cycles of time were calculated.

THE PANTHEON

THE ORTHODOX pantheon is limited to about 10 deities or mythical figures. The functions of male deities are to do with agriculture (the Farmer God, Sovereign Millet or the grain god, and Sovereign Earth); war (Chi You); fire (Flame); cosmogony (Pan Gu); cultural benefits, including material culture; and calendrical systems. The functions of female deities are cosmogonic (Woman Gua); cosmological (the solar and lunar goddesses Xi He and Chang Xi); calendrical systems, paradisial bliss (Queen Mother of the West); savior and nurturing aspects; and wreakers of sacred violence in the form of plague and punishments.

STELLAR MYTHS

Stellar myths are few in Chinese mythology. Some relate how a wise man was metamorphosed into a star, or how quarreling brothers became two stars in opposing trajectories. The myth of the stellar lovers Weaver Maid and Draft Ox relates the doomed love of these celestial beings. It appears only as a fragment in the *Book of Poetry*, but by the medieval era it had developed into a romantic story. Weaver Maid was the daughter of a sky god, and she lived by the eastern Sky River (Milky Way) weaving cloudy robes. The sky god took pity on her lonely life and allowed her to marry her stellar lover. But she began to neglect her weaving, so the sky god punished her by separating the lovers each side of the Sky River, only allowing them to meet once a year on the seventh night of the seventh month. The theme of love in this myth is expressed decorously, and in common with other Chinese myths contains no narrative of the rude promiscuity, violent couplings, and lustful passions that are usually related in world mythologies. This sanitized version of love in myths suggests that early accounts may have been more robust but were censored by editors of classical texts in the Han period (206 B.C.E.–C.E. 220).

MYTHS OF ETHNIC MINORITIES

CLASSICAL AUTHORS were acutely aware of the difference between themselves and the numerous peoples living adjacent to the Shang, Zhou and Han borders from 1700 to 100 B.C.E. and often referred to them in a scornful way to emphasize their perceived cultural inferiority. In around 100 B.C.E., during the Han period, Chinese travelers first went to foreign lands and recorded their experiences. While historical records maintain a reasonably unbiased viewpoint, travel writers of an imaginative mind embellished their impressions of foreign peoples, often in a negative manner. They chose abusive graphs to represent foreign names, with such meanings as simian or bestial. They saw foreigners as oddly colored, misshapen people and their mythicized names reflect this attitude, such as the countries of Forkedtongue, Threehead, Hairy Folk, Loppyears, and Nogut.

Despite the increasing cultural homogeneity that ensued from unification policies in the Qin and Han empires, minority peoples treasured the stories of their own origins and retained the heritage of their cultural identity. The Yao people preserved their ancestral myth. It tells how their ancestor was born from the ear of a palace woman. She treasured this worm and it grew into a dog named Pan Hu (Plate Gourd). The dog saved its country from invaders and the king gave it his daughter as a reward. The dog and the princess migrated to a fertile valley. They had six daughters and six sons who mated and produced a new generation, the new race of the Yao people in South China.

CHINA IN WORLD MYTHOLOGY

THE THEMES OF CHINESE myths have significant parallels with those of world mythologies. Where they diverge is in their central concern and cultural distinctiveness. Certain versions of the creation myth are unique for their lack of a divine cause or a creator. The flood myths are also unique for the absence of the motif of divine retribution or intervention in halting the deluge. The myths of cultural benefits fit the pattern of world mythologies in the two aspects of deities being the first to teach humans how to make use of them, and being the divine originators of them. Myths of dynastic foundation are unique for the emphasis given to female ancestors followed by male founding figures, as with the Shang and Zhou myths.

◄ *The moon goddess, Ever Sublime holding her companion, the hare.*

► *All mythologies have their own distinct characters and protagonists, such as this Chinese three-legged toad. However, some traits and themes are shared between the mythologies of cultures that are geographically distant from one another.*

Japan

INTRODUCTION

THE FOUR MAIN ISLANDS that make up the Japanese archipelago have been inhabited for at least 50,000 years. Land bridges linking present-day Japan to mainland Sakhalin in the north and Korea in the south existed until about 12,000 years ago and these overland routes would have enabled early migrants to settle in Japan. Traces of the various waves of people who arrived in Japan can be distinguished archeologically into the Old Stone Age (50,000–12,000 B.C.E.), the Jomon culture (11,000–300 B.C.E.) and the Yayoi culture (300 B.C.E.–C.E. 300). Sites connected with the Jomon culture are located throughout Japan but especially in the northern half of the main island, Honshu. In contrast, the settlements of the later Yayoi people were originally centered on Kyushu, Shikoku and the Kii Peninsula south of Osaka and Nara. The proximity of Korea suggests a close racial connection with these people.

The Yayoi people are thought to be the main cultural and racial ancestors of the present-day Japanese population with the exception of the small group of Ainu, numbering around 20,000, who live on the northern island of Hokkaido. These Ainu may be the remnants of the Jomon people.

ROOTS OF MYTHOLOGY

IT IS UNLIKELY that any of the surviving Japanese myths date back before the arrival of the Jomon people, and what remains of their mythology is unclear. However, there does seem to be a division between the main mythology which links the rulers of Japan with the High Plains of Heaven, centering in Amaterasu, and the colonization of Japan by Susa-no-o and his descendants in the Izumo Cycle. Just as it seems that the incoming Yayoi people subjugated the earlier Jomon civilization, Okuninushi and his clan in Izumo were subjugated by Amaterasu and her gods whose cult is centered on Ise and the Kii Peninsula. It should be noted however that the main shrine to Izanagi and Izanami is located in the Izumo region.

Furthermore, Japanese myths are often related to specific places in the country. There is even a site in Nara Prefecture called Takama-ga-hara, the High Plain of Heaven, near Ise in neighboring Mie Prefecture, as well as a Floating Bridge of Heaven near Kyoto. Elsewhere is the cave in which Amaterasu hid herself, the beach in Izumo where Okuninushi met Sakunabikona and so on. This creates a strong impression that many Japanese myths concern actual people and their clans as they migrated through Japan after their arrival from the mainland.

FUNDAMENTALS

SHINTO, THE NATIVE Japanese religion, is intimately connected with Japanese mythology. Many of its shrines are dedicated to the deities who are mentioned in the myths, since the historical state of Japan and its prosperity was thought to be the product of Amaterasu's divine intervention. Though it does not have an elaborate theology, Shinto deals with the relationship between the natural world and its human inhabitants. Through rituals of purification it attempts to maintain the balance which is vital to the harmony between the human

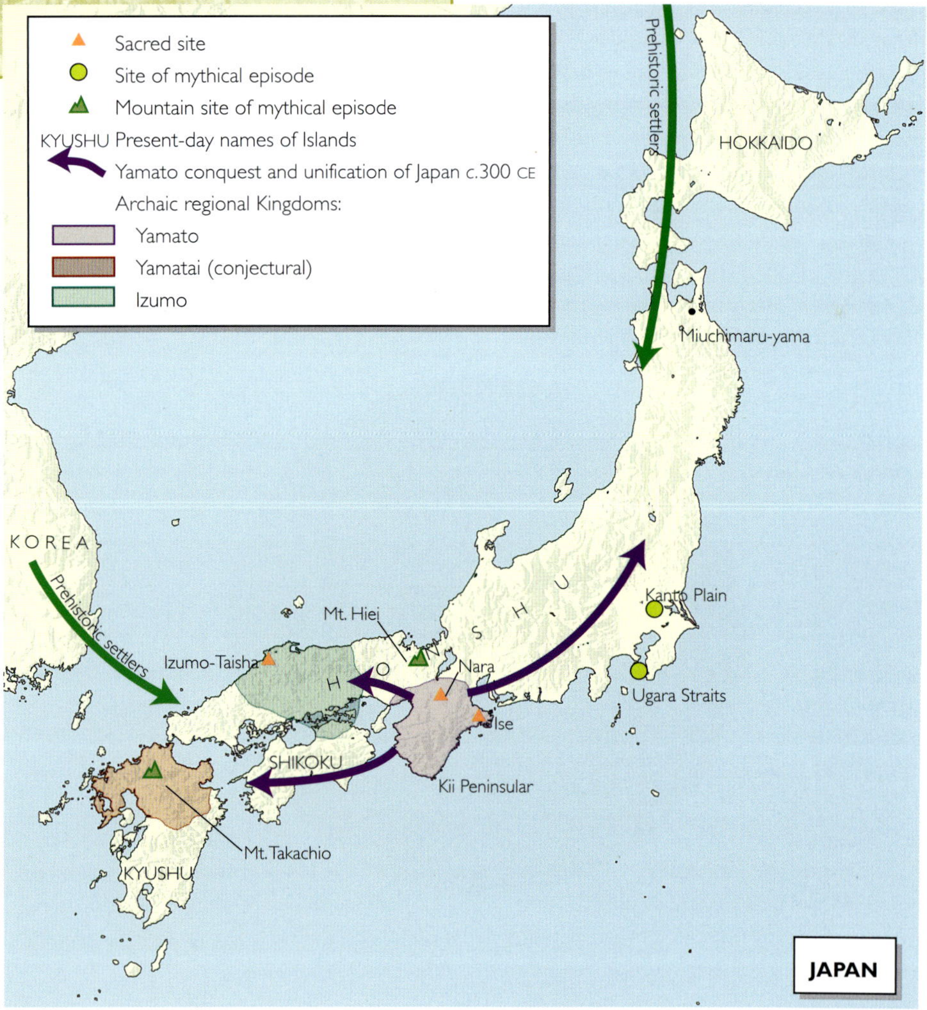

and natural world. The concept of *kegare* (ritual pollution) was very important in early historical times when it more closely resembled the ideas of taboo found in other cultures. Any event—be it birth or death, the construction of a house, the felling of trees, the slaughter of animals—which upset the balance was deemed to be charged with awesome power which needed to be contained and purified. Apart from the regular rituals of purification at shrines, there was a special class of people who were thought to have sufficient spiritual power to deal with these events. Originally respected for their vital role in society, their status was drastically reduced in medieval times and they became classed as *eta* or outcasts. Their descendants are still subject to prejudice in modern Japan.

▶ *Shrines such as this were dedicated to the Japanese deities.*

◀ *A Japanese god encounters the apparition of the fox goddess.*

THE CREATION

THE *NIHON-SHOKI* and the *Kojiki* generally agree in their accounts of creation. Some scholars discern a degree of Chinese influence in these accounts. It is possible that this is not because of later influences dating from the introduction of Chinese culture to Japan from the sixth century C.E. onward but perhaps because these myths were brought to Japan by people who migrated from northern China and Korea. According to these myths, the universe originally existed only as an unformed, oily, jelly-like lump. A single god called Amanominakanushi-no-kami arose from this mass. He was followed by the appearance of another four gods, thus forming a group of five primordial gods. Then, in turn, a further seven generations of gods and goddesses came into being. All these divine beings inhabited the High Plains of Heaven (Takama-gahara) for at that time there was no solid land. The youngest of these gods were Izanagi and Izanami. They took on the task of creating land. Standing on the Floating Bridge of Heaven, together they stirred the murky depths below with a sacred spear. When they lifted the spear out, drops fell down and formed the first land, an island called Onogoro.

IZANAGI AND IZANAMI

IZANAGI AND IZANAMI descended from the heavens to the newly formed land and built a palace for themselves there. As they were the first couple, they invented the ritual of marriage and then procreated. Their first-born, Hiruko (Leech Child), was deformed, so they placed the child in a reed boat and set it adrift in the sea.

Divination showed that this child was deformed because the goddess Izanami had spoken first during the marriage ritual. After correctly performing the marriage ritual again, Izanami gave birth abundantly. Her first group of offspring were the islands that make up the Japanese archipelago. Next, she gave birth to a series of gods and goddesses linked with natural phenomena such as the wind and the mountains. Finally, she gave birth to the god of fire (Kagutsuchi) who burnt her so badly as he was being born that she died. More gods arose from her dead body and also from the tears of Izanagi.

After Izanami's death she entered into Yomi, the dark underworld realm of the dead. Overcome with inconsolable grief, Izanagi decided to visit Izanami to entreat her to return with him, but Izanami told him that she would need to talk to the gods of the underworld about this, warning him not to look at her.

Overcome by a desire to see her once again, Izanagi broke off a tooth from his hair-comb and lit it as a torch. He was horrified to see that Izanami was now a maggot-infested rotting corpse and tried to flee from her.

Angered by his act, Izanami sent a horde of demon hags and warriors to pursue him. When he reached the entrance back into the realm of the living, Izanagi found three peaches which he threw at the frightening horde chasing him and so managed to turn them back. At this point, Izanami herself, transformed into a demon, gave chase.

Before she could reach him, Izanagi barred her way with a great boulder with which he sealed the entrance to the underworld. Here they confronted each other one last time and finally dissolved their marriage vows.

UNIVERSAL THEMES

THOUGH GENERALLY less complex than those found elsewhere, Japanese myths share some features in common with those of other cultures. The emergence of certain deities, land, and food from the living and dead bodies of the gods has echoes in the dismemberment concept of creation found in India and elsewhere.

The first death of Izanami and Izanagi's visit to the underworld are similar to the Greek myth of Orpheus and Eurydice, as well as that of Persephone, and also that of Yama and his sister in Indian mythology. The events surrounding this first death also reflect the early Japanese concern with taboos and pollution. Some scholars believe that the repeated relocation of the capital during the Yamoto and Nara periods following the death of the ruler is linked with this myth, with its decisive separation of the living and the dead.

◀ *Raijin, Japanese god of thunder.*

EARLY RULERS

INITIALLY, THE YAYOI people were organized on the basis of loosely related clans with independent territories. Strong ties with Korea on the mainland were maintained by these people and their descendants even as late as the seventh century C.E. The earliest accounts of Japan survive in Chinese historical annals from the first century C.E., which mention the names of the various clan "kings" or chiefs. However, by the third century C.E., a process of conquest and consolidation of these small separate territories led to the emergence of the large single state of Yamato which included southern Honshu and Shikoku. The lineage of the present-day emperor of Japan can be traced in an unbroken line back to the early legendary rulers of Yamato.

Most surviving Japanese mythology concerns the divine ancestors of these early rulers as recorded in the *Nihon-shoki* and the *Kojiki*, chronicles written during the eighth century C.E. It may be assumed that this mythology was primarily linked to the Yayoi people and may have formed part of their culture even prior to their arrival in Japan.

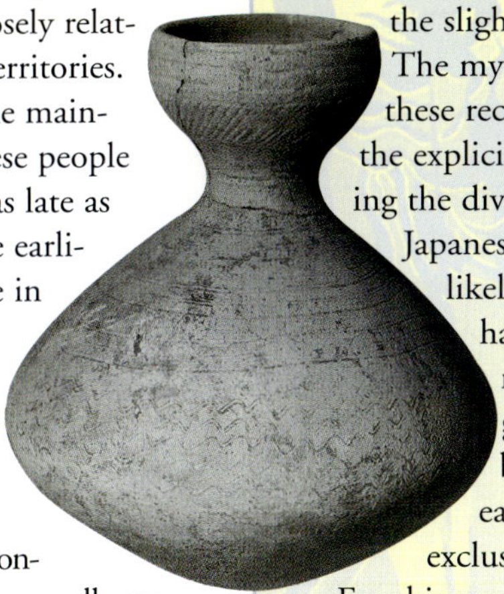

SOURCES OF MYTH

THE SOURCES OF surviving Japanese myths are very limited and derive from virtually two sole sources: the *Kojiki* and the slightly later *Nihon-shoki*. The mythological sections of these records were written with the explicit intention of establishing the divine descent of the Japanese imperial family. It is likely therefore that what we have now were the clan myths of the particular group which eventually became overlords of the early Yamato state to the exclusion of rival claimants.

For this reason there are few recurrent figures or themes in the mythology, with the exception perhaps of the small group of myths connected with Susa-no-o and his sister Amaterasu.

AMATERASU

FOLLOWING IZANAGI's return alone to the land of the living, a number of gods and goddesses emerged from his body and clothing. The most important of these were the sun goddess Amaterasu, the moon god Tsuki-yomi, and the storm god Susa-no-o. Izanagi set Amaterasu up as the ruler of the High Plains of Heaven, Tsuki-yomi as the ruler of the night, and Susa-no-o as the ruler of the seas. However, Susa-no-o was jealous of the status of his sister Amaterasu, rebelled against his father's wishes and hence was banished by Izanagi.

Suspecting that Susa-no-o was plotting to overthrow her, Amaterasu armed herself and confronted her brother. He challenged her to a contest that would prove who was really the mightiest—whoever could give birth to male gods would be the winner. Though Amaterasu won, Susa-no-o refused to accept defeat and embarked on a series of foul outrages against Amaterasu which so terrified her that she sealed herself inside a cave. The entire world and the heavens were cast into darkness and misery.

In vain the gods tried to lure her out. Then the beautiful goddess of the dawn, Ama-no-uzume, a prototype of early Japanese female shamans, stood on an upturned rice barrel and began a sacred erotic dance. The other gods were greatly excited by this. Hearing the excitement of the gods and their praises for Ama-no-uzume, Amaterasu peeped out and asked what was happening. She was told that the gods were rejoicing at the sight of a goddess more beautiful that herself. As she peeped out, one of the gods held up a sacred mirror and Amaterasu saw her own reflection in it. At this moment, one of the other gods seized her by the hand and pulled her out of the cave. Finally, the entrance to the cave was blocked. Amaterasu then resumed her place in the heavens, and Susa-no-o was punished by the other gods and banished to the land of mortals. Amaterasu is viewed both as the chief protector of Japan and as the ancestor of the emperors. She is worshiped to this day at the most important shrine in Japan at Ise.

▲ *Ancient Yayoi terracotta vase.*

◀ *The goddess Amaterasu emerges from the earth.*

Reed Plain, he encountered an old couple with their beautiful daughter Kusanada-hime (Rice-Field Princess). They were being terrorized by an eight-headed and eight-tailed monster which had eaten all their other daughters. Susa-no-o agreed to kill this monster if he could marry the daughter. Leaving tubs of rice wine for the monster to drink, Susa-no-o succeeded. In one of its tails he found the legendary sacred sword, the Kusanagi (Grass-Cutter). He then married Kusanada-hime and took up residence in a palace at Izumo.

◀ *The sacred gateway or* torii *leading to a Shinto shrine.*

▼ *Shinto shrine in Kyoto.*

THE RISE OF THE ICON

THE NUMEROUS *kami* or gods of Japanese mythology and the Shinto religion based on them were not represented in any art form prior to the introduction of Buddhism with its complex range of scriptures, paintings, and sculptures. Instead the gods were thought to be invisible spirits or the spiritual power that inhabited objects, whether living or inanimate. Shinto shrines usually have no statues in them but only symbolic objects. The introduction of Buddhism resulted in the identification of the mythological gods with various Buddhist deities, and this facilitated the depiction of the gods and goddesses in visual form.

SYMBOLS OF THE GODS

THE THREE most important religious symbols associated with the Japanese gods are still enshrined in Shinto shrines. These are a necklace of *magatama*, curious comma-shaped stones, like those given to Amaterasu by Izanagi as a symbol of sovereignty, a metal mirror representing the one used by the gods to lure Amaterasu from her cave, and a sword symbolizing the Kusanagi found by Susa-no-o and later owned by Jimmu, the first Japanese emperor. Shinto shrines are usually marked with avenues of trees or rocks with a sacred gateway, or *torii* through which the gods enter into the shrine itself.

SUSA-NO-O

SUSA-NO-O was a trouble-maker even before he quarrelled with his sister Amaterasu, and he caused a number of earlier conflicts with other gods. According to the *Nihon-shoki*, he made advances toward Ogetsu, the goddess of food. He demanded that she give him some food to eat but flew into a rage when she drew this from her nose, mouth, and rectum. He killed Ogetsu, but after her death the various orifices of her body gave rise to the staple crops eaten by the Japanese: rice, millet, wheat, red azuki beans, and soya beans. After his exile to the Land of

THE IZUMO CYCLE OF MYTHS

THERE IS A SMALL group of myths, known as the Izumo Cycle, concerning the activities of Susa-no-o and of his descendants. Izumo was the place where the god Susa-no-o lived after he was exiled from heaven, corresponding to the northern region of present-day Shimane Prefecture. After he killed the eight-headed monster, Susa-no-o married the princess Kusanada-hime and settled in Izumo. This land seemed too small for him so he broke off pieces of territory from nearby lands, dragged them by rope and added them to Izumo. Susa-no-o also played a role in developing the region for human habitation. One of Susa-no-o's descendants, possibly his grandson, the god Okuninushi, also features in many of these myths as a bringer of civilization and culture.

OKUNINUSHI AND THE WHITE RABBIT

THE GOD WHO LATER became known as Okuninushi lived in Izumo with his 80 brothers of whom he was the youngest. There was a beautiful princess Ya-gami-hime in the neighboring land of Inaba and each of the 80 brothers wanted to marry her. They decided to set out together to woo her, agreeing grudgingly to let Okuninushi go along as their porter. As the brothers crossed into Inaba, they came across a furless rabbit, its skin all red and raw, lying in pain on a beach. Being malicious in nature, the brothers told the rabbit that its fur would grow again if it washed in salt water and then slept at the top of a wind-swept mountain. The rabbit tried this, but it only made matters much worse.

Some time later, Okuninushi came along, weighed down with his brothers' luggage. He saw the miserable rabbit and asked him why he was crying. The rabbit told Okuninushi about the cruelty of the 80 brothers and then explained how he had lost his fur in the first place. He had been born in Inaba, but all the bamboo he lived on had been washed away by a flood. He had clung to a single piece of bamboo and floated out to the island of Oki. Living there for a while, he became lonely and wanted to cross back to Inaba but there was no way of crossing the sea. One day, some crocodiles appeared and the rabbit thought of a plan. He was deliberately rude to them, boasting that there were many more rabbits in the world than crocodiles. To settle the matter, the crocodiles agreed to lie end on end and form a bridge from the island to Inaba. The rabbit told them that he would run across them and count them as he went. But when the rabbit reached the end, he laughed and told the crocodiles that he had tricked them—he only wanted to use them as a bridge! Enraged, the crocodile nearest land grabbed the rabbit and skinned him.

Okuninushi then told the rabbit to wash in the pure fresh water flowing from a river mouth near the beach and then to lie on the soft grass growing there. The rabbit did as Okuninushi told him and he regained his white fur. In gratitude the rabbit, who was actually a god, told Okuninushi that his brothers would fail with the princess Ya-gami-hime but that Okuninushi himself would marry her while his brothers would become his retainers.

▼ *The troublemaker Susa-no-o.*

FESTIVALS

EVERY SHINTO SHRINE in Japan has its *matsuri* or festival. A highlight of these festivals is a parade where portable shrines, *mikoshi*, are carried erratically through the streets, guided by the power of the god. Other festivals are dedicated to fertility and purification—long-standing elements of Shinto dating back to prehistoric times. These festivals are important religious events that bind the inhabitants of towns and villages joyfully together in a sense of shared community. Some shrines also hold displays of ancient ritual dances, *kagura*, often performed with masks. These may have their origins in the kind of shamanic dance that drew Amaterasu from her cave.

OKUNINUSHI AND HIS BROTHERS

THE IZUMO CYCLE may concern the separate mythology of another clan or group of people who inhabited Japan in early times whose rule was ultimately supplanted by people from the Kii Peninsula and Ise area. The myths relate the colonization of the Izumo area by Susa-no-o and his grandson Okuninushi and say that Okuninushi and his descendants eventually became the rulers of much of Japan. After Okuninushi married Ya-gami-hime and presumably incorporated Inaba into his territory, his brothers became jealous and plotted against him. They managed to kill him twice, but each time his mother restored him to life. The first time they heated a rock until it was red-hot and rolled it down a mountain at him. Okuninushi thought it was a red boar his brothers were hunting, so he grabbed hold of it and was burnt to death. The second time they crushed him in the fork of a tree. His mother told him to visit Susa-no-o, now living in the underworld, for advice about ending the rivalry.

▶ *Wooden masks such as this may have been used in ritual dances.*

OKUNINUSHI AND SUSA-NO-O

SEEKING ADVICE from his ancestor Susa-no-o, Okuninushi descended into the underworld of Yomi where Susa-no-o lived. When he arrived there, Okuninushi soon noticed Suseri-hime,

▼ *Painting showing people surrounding the* torii *at the entrance to a temple.*

Susa-no-o's beautiful daughter. They fell in love and were married. However, Susa-no-o was angered by this and he decided to kill Okuninushi. He pretended to be friendly but told Okuninushi to sleep in a room which he had filled with poisonous snakes. However, Suseri-hime had given Okuninushi a magic scarf that drove away the snakes when waved three times. The next night, Susa-no-o told Okuninushi to sleep in a room that was full of bees and centipedes, but again he was saved by the scarf. Then Susa-no-o shot an arrow into a large grassy plain and asked Okuninushi to retrieve it for him. As he did so, Susa-no-o set fire to the grass. Okuninushi could find no way to escape until a mouse told him to stamp hard on the ground as it was hollow. A hole opened up and Okuninushi hid in it until the fire had passed by. The friendly mouse even found the arrow and gave it to Okuninushi.

When Susa-no-o found that Okuninushi was alive and had the lost arrow, he became less hostile to him. Nevertheless, Okuninushi planned to escape from Susa-no-o's realm. One day, he was asked to clean Susa-no-o's hair of the insects living there. No matter how hard he combed, more and more centipedes appeared in it. Suseri-hime gave Okuninushi some red clay and seeds to chew and then to spit out. Susa-no-o noticed the red-spattered ground and was impressed to think that Okuninushi was chewing the centipedes. Susa-no-o then fell asleep. Deciding it was time to make their escape, Suseri-hime brought Okuninushi the bow, sword, and a magical koto belonging to her father. Okuninushi took these things and then tied Susa-no-o's hair to the rafters of his palace. Carrying Suseri-hime on his back, he left Yomi for the Land of the Reed Plain. After they had gone some way, Susa-no-o was woken by the sound of the koto and finally gave chase but, delayed by his entangled hair, was unable to reach them in time.

He halted near the boundary between the underworld and the land of the living and shouted out to Okuninushi. In recognition of his bravery, he told Okuninushi how he could defeat his quarrelsome brothers if he used the bow and sword taken from Susa-no-o. Susa-no-o also foretold that Okuninushi would become master of the entire country.

▼ *Modern rice cultivation in Japan continues, in many ways, as it has done throughout the ages, with farmers working on their own paddies.*

OKUNINUSHI

AS IN OTHER CIVILIZATIONS, Japanese mythology venerates several cultural heroes. These are especially connected with the Izumo Cycle. Despite his negative image in the Amaterasu myths, it was Susa-no-o who began the process of colonization of Japan after his exile from heaven. The exploits of his descendant Okuninushi are very important, as he is credited with the introduction of millet and rice cultivation, medicine, silk-worm breeding, weaving, and so forth. There may be echoes here of the efforts of the early migrants into Japan to colonize the country. The evil spirits met by Okuninushi may be the demonized forms of earlier inhabitants of the land.

OKUNINUSHI'S LATER LIFE

AFTER HIS RETURN from Yomi, the underworld, Okuninushi followed Susa-no-o's advice and hunted down all his older brothers. Eventually, he killed all of them and became sole ruler of Izumo. He then went to live with Suseri-hime in a palace he built at Uga-no-yama in Izumo. Hearing that he had returned safely from the underworld, Ya-gami-hime of Inaba went to see Okuninushi as she had given birth to a child while he was away. But when she reached the palace, she felt ashamed and inferior to Suseri-hime, so she remained outside and just left the child in a tree outside the gate. This child was found by Okuninushi's retainers and taken to him by them. Suseri-hime said she would raise the child as one of her own, which she did, calling the child Kimata-no-kami, the Tree-trunk God.

When Okuninushi settled down in Izumo, most of the country beyond was still wild and unformed at that time. There was nothing but dense forests, swamps, ferocious animals, and evil spirits. Mindful of Susa-no-o's prediction, Okuninushi began to clear the regions near Izumo with the weapon called Yachihoko ("8000 spears"). With it he tirelessly walked around the land and killed many demons, making places safe for people to live in. Because of these exploits he became known as Yachihoko-no-kami.

OKUNINUSHI AND SUKANABIKONA-NO-MIKOTO

ONE DAY WHEN Okuninushi was by the sea at Cape Miho in Izumo, he saw a mysterious tiny god dressed in a robe of glowing firefly skins sitting in a small boat made of sweet potato leaves. Eventually, Okuninushi was told by a lame god called Ku-e-hiko that this was the youngest son of Kamimusubi-no-kami. Okuninushi reported his discovery to Kamimusubi-no-kami, who said that this was Sukunabikona-no-mikoto, who had fallen from heaven while playing. Okuninushi was asked to take this tiny god as his brother, which he did. They became inseparable companions and continued the work of clearing the land of evil and opening it up for habitation. Together they introduced silk worms and weaving, new crops, and many medicinal herbs. The two of them became renowned as guardians of human life and prosperity.

A time came when Sukanabikona-no-mikoto went off alone to the island of Awashima (Millet Island) where millet he had planted had grown prodigiously. He climbed up a stem of millet to get a better view but, after bending under the weight of the tiny god, it then straightened up and catapulted him far away over the sea to Tokoyo (the Land of Eternity) where he stayed and did not return. This loss made Okuninushi very unhappy for a long time, but eventually he resumed his duties by himself.

COMMUNICATION WITH THE DEAD

THERE ARE MANY sacred caves in Japan, often thought to lead into the underworld of the dead. Though the dead were regarded with terror by the living, they were also a source of wisdom and reassurance and hence were visited by the living for advice. From ancient times in Japan down to the present day, special groups of women with the ability to communicate with the dead have functioned as shamanic intermediaries and mediums on the fringes of society. One such group of women were the *miko*, descendants of the mythical union between Ama-no-uzume, the dawn goddess, and Sarutahiko, a local monkey god. *Miko* still exist as attendants at Shinto shrines but no longer act as shamans.

◀ *A demonic Japanese statue.*

AMATERASU'S TAKE-OVER

AFTER SEVERAL HUNDRED years, the rule of Okuninushi and his descendants grew lax and evil gods once again made life unpleasant for the people. Amaterasu wanted to extend her rule to that region and sent a son to subdue the area, but after three years he failed to return. She then sent a god called Ame-no-waka-hiko to find out what had happened. Ame-no-waka-hiko married Okuninushi's daughter and plotted to take over Okuninushi's territory for himself. After eight years Amaterasu sent a divine pheasant to ask Ame-no-waka-hiko why he had been absent for so long. He shot the pheasant with an arrow which passed straight through it and reached the god Takami-musubi. He sent it right back, killing the traitor as he lay in bed. Amaterasu then sent two trusted and brave gods, Futsunushi-no-mikoto and Takemikazuchi-no-mikoto, to tell Okuninushi to surrender the land to her. They sat on the tips of their upturned swords embedded in the crest

▲ *Rice gods were thought to have a very strong influence on whether a harvest was successful or not.*

of a wave in the sea off Inasa in Izumo, and then delivered their ultimatum. Okuninushi was impressed by this and gave in on condition that a place should be reserved for him among the gods worshiped in Izumo. Amaterasu agreed to this, and the shrine built for him at Kizuki in Izumo is still second only to Ise in importance.

◀ *A magnificent example of an ornamental Japanese sword.*

FIRESHINE AND FIRESHADE

AFTER OKUNINUSHI surrendered, his clan was supplanted by Amaterasu's descendants. Amaterasu's grandson Ninigi-no-mikoto came to earth carrying the three symbols of sovereignty: the mirror, the *magatama* beads, and the Kusanagi sword. He had two sons: Ho-teri (Fireshine) and Ho-ori (Fireshade). Fireshine, the eldest, fished using a hook, while Fireshade was a hunter. Fireshade was dissatisfied and suggested changing their occupations. This they did, but Fireshade was unsuccessful and even lost the fishing hook. When asked to return it, he offered several substitutes but Fireshine wanted only the original. Fireshade drifted far out to sea in shame and eventually reached the palace of the sea god, Watatsumi-no-kami. Watatsumi-no-kami retrieved the fish-hook and also gave Fireshade his daughter in marriage. After several years, Fireshade wanted to return home. Watatsumi-no-kami gave him two jewels, one to make the sea rise and one to make it fall. When Fireshade got home, he returned the hook to Fireshine. However, Fireshine continued to complain, so Fireshade threw one jewel in the sea and made it flood. Terrified, Fireshine begged for forgiveness so Fireshade threw the other jewel into the sea and it receded. In gratitude, Fireshine swore that he would serve his younger brother in perpetuity. The grandson of Fireshade was Jimmu, the legendary first emperor of Japan.

INARI AND HACHIMAN

A NUMBER OF GODS venerated in Shinto are not mentioned in the classical sources of Japanese mythology but are nevertheless of considerable importance. One of these is Inari, the rice god, responsible for good rice harvests and general prosperity. He is associated with foxes, seen as his messengers, a pair of whom always flank Inari's image in his shrines. He was also the patron of merchants and swordsmiths. Another important Shinto deity is Hachiman, the god of war, the deified form of the legendary emperor Ojin (*c.* 394 C.E.) famed for his military prowess. Hachiman was very popular in the past in Japan in less peaceful times, particularly venerated by warriors who would dedicate themselves at his shrines.

Korea

INTRODUCTION

THE ORIGINS of the Korean people can be traced to around 1000 B.C.E. when Bronze Age warriors belonging to the Tungusic racial group invaded Manchuria and the Korean peninsula, mixing with its original inhabitants. The Tungus are one of the three major ethnic groups in northern and central Asia, today occupying most of Manchuria and south-eastern Siberia. Thus the Korean people have a racial and cultural origin distinctive from the Chinese people, although they have also absorbed considerable elements of Chinese elite culture and use substantial amounts of Chinese vocabulary in their language. Their mythology, however, is a reflection of a non-Chinese culture. The structure of the tales, the characters, and the motifs which appear in them are on the whole remnants of an earlier period. Korean myths are of two types: foundation myths about the people and state, and creation myths about the origin of the world. Because the foundation myths are so ancient, most of them are known only from ancient Korean or Chinese records and not from narration by contemporary storytellers. The only exception to this statement are the creation myths, which are sung by shamans as part of their ritual repertoire.

Foundation myths recounting the origins of the Korean nation, state, and ruling families have been recorded since at least the first century C.E. and are found in both Chinese and Korean records. The earliest record of a Korean myth is found in the Chinese miscellany the *Lunheng*. The most important extant early record of Korean myths and legends is the *Samguk yusa* "Memorabilia of the Three Kingdoms" which was compiled by the thirteenth-century Buddhist monk Iryon (Ilyon), who was quite possibly the first Korean folklorist. The *Samguk yusa* contains the fullest record of the myths describing the origin of the Korean people, their state, and their clans. Other sources include the *sillok* or "veritable records" of the reigns of the kings of the Choson dynasty (1392–1910). None of these records, however, contain examples of creation myths, which are found only in the *muga* or shaman songs. Creation myths were not recorded until the early part of the twentieth century when the muga were collected by folklorists, most notably Son Chint'ae (*c.* 1900–50).

BECAUSE MOST FOUNDATION myths exist now only as textual records, there are no longer any traditional rituals associated with them. One exception is the myth of the three clan ancestors of Cheju Island, where the ancestors have rituals addressed to them both as clan ancestors and as the ancestors of the island's society. With the growth of twentieth-century Korean nationalism, foundation myths have inspired the creation of new religions and new rituals, most notably Tan'gun-gyo and Taejong-gyo, which worship Tan'gun as the founder of the Korean nation.

For the followers of these religions, *Kaech'on-jol* (Heavenly Foundation Day) held on October 3 is the most important day in the year, as it is believed, variously, that this was the day on which Tan'gun was born or on which he ascended the throne. It is also celebrated as a national holiday without any religious rituals. As creation myths are an integral part of the songs performed by a shaman, they are only heard during performance of a *kut* or shamanistic rite. For example, the rite devoted to the guardian spirit of the home begins with the singing of the story of the creation of heaven and earth before proceeding to a description of earthly history.

The nation or state foundation myths of Korea may be divided into three principal types based upon the formal structure of the mythic narrative: the Tan'gun Type, the Chumong Type, and the Three Clan Ancestors Type. In addition there are clan foundation myths describing the origin of individual clans, particularly the three royal houses of the kingdom of Silla (traditional dates *c.* 35 B.C.E.–C.E. 936).

THE TAN'GUN TYPE

THE MYTH OF TAN'GUN, lord of the sandalwood tree, is the quintessential foundation myth of Korea describing how: the son of the ruler of heaven was selected to go to rule mankind; heaven's son descended to earth and established culture there; a tiger and a bear vied to become men; the transformed Bear Woman pleaded to have a child; and the child Tan'gun established the first Korean kingdom. Assuming the pre-existence of humanity, the tale serves three functions—to describe how civilization was brought to this world, how the first Korean royal house was established, and how the first Korean kingdom was created. A redaction of the myth, not translated here, explains how the change from one dynasty to another took place. Among the motifs used in the myth are the world tree and a cosmic mountain which form the link between earth and heaven. The only other example in North-East Asia of this type of myth is the myth of Jimmu, the tale of the first ruler of "Japan," as recorded in the *Kojiki* (Records of Ancient Matters) and the *Nihon shoki* (Records of Japan).

▲ *Ch'amsong-dan altar, said to have been erected by Tan'gun, mythical founder of the Korean nation*

▲ *Typical image of the mountain god, seated upon a tiger under a tree.*

THE MYTH OF TAN'GUN

IN ANCIENT TIMES, the ruler of heaven had a son by a concubine. he was called Hwanung and wanted to descend from heaven and rule the world of men. The father descended to the world's three great mountains and saw that mankind would benefit from his son's rulership. He gave his son the three heavenly regalia and commanded him to rule over mankind. Taking with him 3,000 spirits Hwanung descended upon the summit of the Great White Mountain by the sacred sandalwood tree. Hwanung called the spot Sacred City, and he was known as the heavenly king. Together with the earl of wind, the master of rain and the master of cloud, he instructed people in agriculture, the preservation of life, the curing of disease, punishments, and the difference between right and wrong—in all some 360 kinds of work. At that time, there was a bear and a tiger living in a cave who constantly pleaded with Hwanung to transform them into men. Hwanung gave them some sacred mugwort and 20 pieces of garlic, telling them to eat the plants and avoid daylight for 100 days. The bear and tiger ate the plants and fasted for three times seven days. The bear received a woman's body, but the tiger, who was not able to fast, did not. As there was no one with whom the Bear Woman could marry, she went every day to the sacred sandalwood tree to pray for a child. Hwanung changed form and married her. She became pregnant and had a son who was called Prince Tan'gun, lord of the sandalwood tree. Tan'gun made P'yongyang his capital and called the nation Choson.

THE MOUNTAIN GOD

PAINTINGS OF THE MOUNTAIN god are found in shrines on mountain passes and in shrines within virtually every Buddhist temple. Called *sanshin-gak*, these shrines are dedicated to the mountain god as the ruler of all the mountains of Korea. In the pictures hung behind the altar, San-shin is often depicted as a grandfatherly figure with a long white beard, seated on a tiger, and resting beneath a pine tree. He is identified with Tan'gun, who upon his death is said to have been transformed into the mountain god.

THE CHUMONG TYPE

THE MYTH OF CHUMONG relates the story of the founder of the kingdom of Koguryo, a militarily powerful state that ruled most of Manchuria and half the Korean peninsula from the fourth to the seventh centuries C.E. The mythic narrative as recorded in the Samguk *yusa* is composed of four scenes which describe how: a king discovered the daughter of a river spirit who had been raped; the river spirit's daughter gave birth to a giant egg out of which the hero emerged; the hero fled because of the jealousy of his half-brothers; and the hero established his kingdom.

The four-fold pattern of the narrative scenes in the myth is the basic pattern of the foundation myths of the Tungusic peoples of North-east Asia, whether the people had state-level societies such as the Manchus or lived in tribal communities. Unlike the Tan'gun myth, this myth is only concerned with the establishment of the state and not with the origin of the people's culture. It also differs from heroic tales told in Europe and the Mediterranean area which use the motif of the flight of a hero from his place of birth. In those myths the hero eventually returns home. In the Chumong myth the hero never returns.

THE MYTH OF CHUMONG

TRAVELING NEAR the Great White Mountain, King Kumwa met Yuhwa, the daughter of the earl of the river, who told him she had been raped by the son of the ruler of heaven near Bear Spirit Mountain on the Yalu River. Angered, her parents had banished her. The king secluded Yuhwa in a room. Sunlight caressed her body, she became pregnant and gave birth to a large egg. The king gave the egg to the dogs, pigs, cows, and horses, but they would not harm it. Not being able to smash the egg, Kumwa gave the egg back to its mother. A heroic baby broke open the egg and came out. When the boy was seven he could make his own bows and arrows and hit the target 100 times in succession. He was called Chumong, "Good Shot." As his half-brothers were jealous of him, his mother told him to flee. Fooling the king, he took some good horses and with three friends fled until they came to a river. Chumong cried out that he was the descendant of the ruler of heaven and the earl of the river. Instantly, terrapin and fish rose up and formed a bridge. Chumong crossed over, built a capital city, called his nation Koguryo, and gave himself the surname Ko.

▶ *Stone Monument giving the history of Won'gak Temple. The stele rests on a granite tortoise*

▶ *San-shin with his messenger tiger*

THE RULER OF HEAVEN

THE RULER OF heaven, Hanullim, is the supreme deity of the Korean pantheon. In the ancient myths, he is called Hwanin, Chesok (a Buddhist term) or Ch'onje. A dialectical variant, Hanulim or Hanunim, is the Korean word for God in the Bible.

San-shin, the mountain god, is ruler of all the mountains and owner of all the creatures and objects on the mountains. He is thought by many to be Tan'gun, the father of the nation. The tiger is his messenger.

The spirits called Earl of the River, Earl of Wind, Master of Cloud, and Master of Rain are master spirits, rulers of aspects of nature. The terms are similar to spirit names from the Zhou dynasty (eleventh to third centuries B.C.E.) in China.

THE THREE CLAN ANCESTORS TYPE

THE MYTH OF THE THREE Clan Ancestors of the island of Cheju is unique among the myths of Korea. It is different from foundation myths told on the Korean peninsula both in terms of its narrative structure and the motifs used in the narrative. The mythic narrative is composed of five scenes which recount how: the primal ancestors of the three clans came up out of the ground together; the ancestors established a hunting/gathering society; the three ancestors discovered a floating box with three princesses in it; the three ancestors married the three princesses; and the male and female ancestors established an agricultural society.

The narrative of this complex myth describes the origin of the three primal clans of Cheju, the origin of the island's culture, and the change from a hunting/gathering society to an agrarian society. There are no parallels to this myth in Korea outside of Cheju Island. The narrative structure, however, is parallel to foundation myths for tribal groups in Melanesia, Micronesia, and Taiwan. In these cases, the myth consists of scenes depicting the emergence of the ancestors from the ground or from a rock, the marriage of the male and female ancestors, and the establishment of society, paralleling some of the scenes from the Cheju myth.

THE MYTH OF THE THREE CLAN ANCESTORS

THREE DIVINE MEN CAME up out of the ground near Mount Halla on Cheju Island. The eldest was Ancestor Yang, the next Ancestor Ko and the youngest Ancestor Pu. These three ancestors lived by hunting—eating animals for meat and wearing their skins for clothes.

One day as they were out hunting they saw a large wooden box wrapped in a purple cloth washed up on the shore. Opening it, they saw that it contained a stone box and a royal envoy. Inside the stone box were three princesses, calves, ponies, and the Five Grains. The envoy told them that his royal master had sent the princesses to them because they had no wives.

The three ancestors married the three princesses according to the order of their age. Now that they had wives, the three ancestors wanted to give up their lives of hunting and settle down. So the three Ancestors, Yang, Ko and Pu, in order of their ages, shot arrows from their bows to determine where their new homes would be. Where the arrows landed, there they settled and began to practice agriculture and farming.

A MUGA CREATION MYTH

THE CREATION MYTHS contained in the *muga* songs recount the origin of the world and aspects of the world as we now know it. In one example of this type of myth, the narrative is composed of five scenes which describe in turn the creation of the world, the origin of fire and water, the origin of human beings, the origin of time, and the origin of the social and physical ills of the world. The protaganist of the tale is a figure called Miruk.

In the first three scenes Miruk creates the world and its inhabitants. Then the antagonist, the trickster Sokka, appears and challenges Miruk to a series of trials. Even though Miruk is always successful, he finally leaves the world to Sokka with the result that not only is time as we know it created, but all the ills and woes of this life begin.

Although Miruk (Maitreya) and Sokka (Shakyamuni) are names for Buddhist figures, they are probably substitutions for the original names, which are now impossible to reconstruct. The creation narrative uses a structural pattern and characters similar to tales told by Paleo-Siberian and North American Indian tribes.

ANCESTORS

THREE ARCHETYPAL characters of Korean myths occur in world mythology—the clan ancestor who descends from heaven, the culture bearer, and the trickster. The most typical motif for a primal ancestor among the myths of Korea and Japan are the ancestors who descend on a mountain top near a sacred tree and who are often the bearers of the people's distinctive culture, those traits that make the people "civilized." Uniquely for Korean myths, the foundation myth of Cheju Island makes the founders of the people male, and the bearers of advanced culture female. The trickster, a figure who uses his wits to gain his ends, appears in the *muga* creation myths as the devious opponent of the creator, who is responsible for the ills of our age.

◀ *Marble figure of a seated Bodhisattva.*

▶ *Painting of religious figures seated in front of a Buddha.*

THE CREATION OF THE UNIVERSE

IN THE BEGINNING, heaven and earth were stuck together. Miruk separated them by putting four copper pillars at the corners of the world. He set the sun, moon, and stars in place. Then hemade clothes and a hat. Eating uncooked rice, Miruk thought he needed fire and water. He asked Grasshopper and Frog if they knew the origin of fire and water. They did not, but Mouse knew. He showed Miruk how to make fire by striking quartz on iron and where to find a spring of water. Deciding to make man, Miruk held a silver tray in one hand and a gold tray in the other. He prayed to heaven and insects came down. The insects on the gold tray became men and the insects on the silver tray became women. They grew up, married, and mankind began. Then Sokka came down to abolish Miruk's Time. He challenged Miruk to see whose chain would break in the sea. Miruk won. He challenged Miruk that he could unfreeze a river which Miruk froze. Miruk won. He challenged Miruk to see on whose knee a peony would flower. Miruk won, but Sokka stole the flower. In disgust, Miruk left this world saying that now that Time was Sokka's, the world would be full of superstition, immorality, and rebellion. This is what happened.

Southeast Asia

INTRODUCTION

SOUTHEAST ASIA is a complex region, both geographically and ethnically, and this complexity is reflected in the rich cultural diversity of its people. Much remains to be discovered about its ancient past and extensive mythology.

Bordering the earth's greatest ocean, the Pacific, Southeast Asia is made up of the mainland and the island arc. The mainland comprises Burma, Thailand, Cambodia, Laos, Vietnam, and Malaya. The Indonesian archipelago, which contains 13,677 islands, lies across one of the earth's most active and dangerous volcanic regions. The Philippine Islands also form part of the region. Between the Indo-Australian plate and the Pacific plate lies the Makassar Strait, which separates the islands of Borneo and Bali from those of Sulawesi and Lombok. To the east of this line the climate becomes drier, and there is a transition from the Asian to the Australasian species of flora and fauna. The peoples of the regions also differ racially, many being more Melanesian or Papuan in appearance.

The majority of the population of Southeast Asia is of Mongoloid extraction. Between 5000 and 1000 B.C.E. there was a continuous drift of peoples from the north, possibly from Southern China, into mainland Southeast Asia and the islands of Indonesia and the Philippines. The path of this migration is not certain, but it is thought that those from the Austro-Asiatic linguistic group settled in the river valleys and hills of the mainland, while the majority of Austronesian-speaking people moved farther south, possibly via Taiwan and the Philippines, into Malaysia, the Indonesian archipelago, and east into the Pacific. Some practiced shifting agriculture in remote upland regions while the majority settled in river valleys and along coastal strips.

Apart from the huge influx of peoples from Southern China, the greatest influence on Southeast Asia was that of India. Indian traders frequented the coastal towns and there was also interaction between the courts of India and Southeast Asia. From about the beginning of the Christian era the Buddhist and Hindu religions and cosmologies were introduced to the larger, more cosmopolitan groups in the region. Buddhism remains the principal faith in Burma, Thailand, Laos, and Cambodia and is also practiced in Vietnam. In the fourteenth century, Islam, brought by Arab traders, began to be adopted in the islands of Sumatra and Java, and in Malaya, where it remains the principal faith. In the more remote upland areas these ideas had little impact, and tribal groups retained their individual beliefs and customs. Vietnam, the northern half of which was controlled by the Chinese courts from 111 B.C.E., retains much of its Chinese culture despite the fierce nationalism of the Vietnamese, who overthrew the Chinese in C.E. 938. Direct Indian influence was restricted to the southern part of Vietnam and the early kingdom of Champa, although Chinese Buddhism, which was introduced into Vietnam from the north, was of course the result of Indian ideas entering China at an early date.

CREATION

AS BOTH THE ANCIENT foundation myths and the modern shamanistic creation myths are tales of creation, the recurrent themes of the tales have to do with the creation of the world, the foundation of the nation, the bringing of the nation's culture, the foundation of the ruling family, the establishment of the state and, in the case of the Cheju Island foundation myth, the change from one form of culture to another.

Southeast Asians have long been skilled navigators and sailors, trading for centuries with China, Arabia, and India. From the early sixteenth century, European powers also competed for trade in Southeast Asia, which was on the sea route between China and India and was itself a vital source of spices. The Spanish, Portuguese, Dutch, French, and British all traded there, becoming increasingly powerful politically. During this period Christianity was introduced, especially into remote regions. The Philippines, which also experienced a strong American influence, are largely Christian today.

During the nineteenth century Chincse and Indian migrants moved to the cities, attracted by economic opportunities. The population of Singapore is today mainly Chinese. Many Chinese Southeast Asians practice Confucianism and Buddhism, as do large numbers of Vietnamese, while Hindu temples serve the smaller Indian communities.

▲ *Ornate head of a Buddha.*

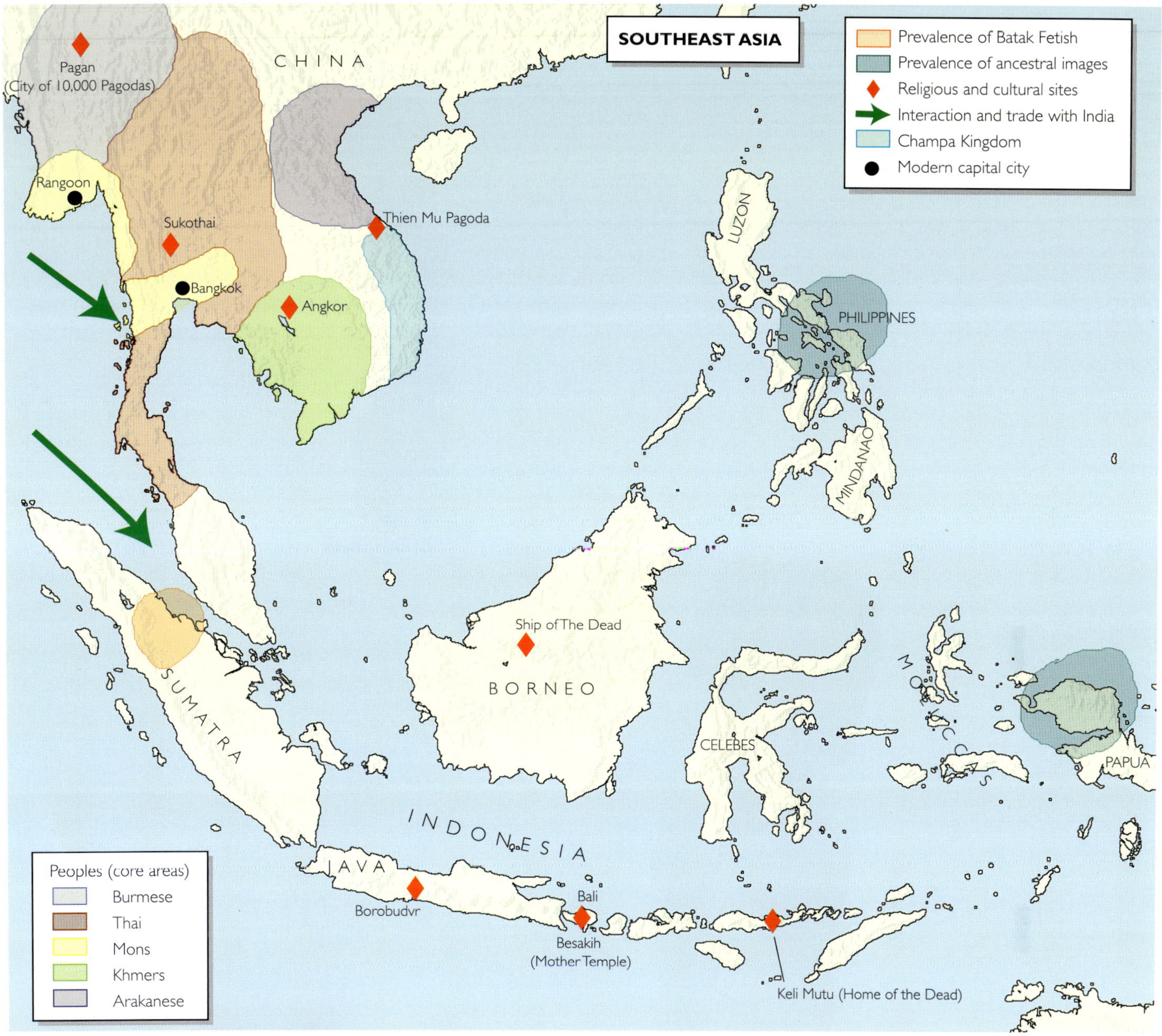

◀ *Cloth worn in Indonesian ritual ceremonies; the two figures are symbols of male achievement.*

RELIGIOUS CUSTOMS, CULTS, AND INFLUENCES

ALTHOUGH LITTLE can be stated with certainty about the origins of early Southeast Asian culture, there are certain underlying factors which suggest common patterns in the ancient past. To reinforce the unity of the group small societies frequently deified their ancestors, tracing descent to a common ancestor. Many groups today trace their origins to remote figures who sailed from the north, or to animals, or semi-divine beings.

The practices of human sacrifice and head-hunting among remote peoples may have predisposed them to accept the complex Christian doctrine of communion—partaking of the blood of Christ—and the crucifixion, or sacrifice of a god.

Direction has a symbolic significance for the people of this region. Depending on the society, a house should be built aligned as nearly as possible to the "right" direction. In Thailand, for instance, people sleep with their head pointing north or east; the room of the household head has to be higher and further north and east than the other rooms, while the less sacred areas such as the kitchen are at the westernmost side of the house. Every important stage of the building of a house is marked by a protective ceremony in order to keep evil spirits at bay.

ANIMAL MYTHS

THE TURTLE IS A POPULAR FIGURE, often appearing in Hindu myth, sometimes supporting the world on its shell, or acting as a wise counceller and guide on the journey of life. In the famous relief *The Churning of the Milky Ocean* at Angkor Wat in Cambodia, the turtle supports Mount Meru, the churning rod with which the seas are churned to produce the elixir of life and other wonders.

Were-wolves and were-tigers are feared in deeply forested areas, and there are also many tales of women who walk alone in the forest becoming possessed by spirits, whom they are forced to marry.

In New Guinea the bird of paradise is thought to have received its feathers from the spirits of heaven, or indeed to have escaped from heaven, for it is so beautiful and rarely touches the earth. In Indonesia the souls of the dead may take the form of birds, which fly above the lands of their descendants.

The Ngaju people of Kalimantan (Borneo) speak of their creation from the Tree of Life by Tambarinang, the hornbill of the Gold Mountain. The water serpent is also created by the hornbill, but the bird later destroys the serpent in its battle with the female hornbill. The canoe, in the shape of a serpent, but with a prow in the shape of a bird, also emerges from the Tree of Life at the dawn of time.

▶ *A male figure rising from a tree—it is the wood that is considered sacred in Indonesia, not the figure.*

WOOD CARVINGS

ORIGIN MYTHS are often depicted in the wood carvings of Indonesian and Philippino islanders. Human and animal ancestral figures such as lizards, hornbills, and praying mantises, also related to sacred head-hunting practices, are carved protectively into clubs, spears, and canoes. Particularly popular are sculptures of the Buddha protected from the rains by *naga* (Skt: serpent) and the Buddha pointing to the ground, "calling the earth to witness." A series of 557 *jataka* stories relate the previous lives and good deeds of the Buddha. Episodes from these stories appear in paintings, lacquerware, woodcarvings, and silverwork.

NATURE SPIRITS

MYTHS FALL into various categories according to belief systems developed over centuries: animism and ancestor veneration, Hinduism, Buddhism, Confucianism, Daoism, Islam, and Christianity are all practised here, and within all these faiths myths have grown and developed, strengthening belief.

The majority of Southeast Asians still live by the land, as can be seen by the many myths connected with nature spirits. The belief in such spirits is very ancient, probably pre-dating the acceptance of Indian religions. They may inhabit unusual trees, rocks, and other natural phenomena, and offerings are often made to them by passers-by. The spirit may be a true nature spirit, or it may be the spirit of someone who died in that place. Many stories recount the unnatural death of the person who haunts such a spot, and these spirits are known to be malevolent if not respected. Branches may fall on unsuspecting passers-by, or other misfortunes—even madness or death—may overtake someone who fails to pay due respect to the rock or tree. Some spirits confine their activities to the immediate site of their death or habitation, whereas some rise in stature to become known throughout the region, or even throughout the country as a whole.

NATURE MYTHS

THE DUAL NATURE of the world is emphasized in many myths. The creation myth of Flores in eastern Indonesia reflects this idea. According to this myth Mother Earth and Father Sky were united in marriage, connected to each other by a vine. The vine was severed by a dog, and earth and sky flew apart, ending up in their present position. The love of the sky for the earth can still be seen today, for as the sky embraces the earth the bamboos are pressed down and bend toward the ground.

There are many stories about the rice goddess and the soul of the rice. The Modang of Kalimantan (Borneo) perform a sacred dance in which masked dancers represent the ancestors. These ancestors enter the village from the forest, bearing rice grains which contain the soul of the rice. Thanks to their intercession the new crop of rice is blessed and fertile.

OFFERINGS AND SACRIFICE

BOTH THE SEA and the mountains are considered sacred, and in many places people feel comfortable only if they know where they are in relation to mountain and sea. The importance of the sea has given rise to many myths about great ocean journeys, princesses on far islands, magical fish, and fearsome monsters. Boats are often decorated with painted eyes which protect the sailors from the sea monsters known to lurk in the deep. These monsters, or *makara*, also adorn temple gateways, where they are thought to ward off evil. In many places offerings are made to the god of the sea before boats set sail and after their safe return.

The ritual of human sacrifice is a common legacy of Southeast Asia and the concept of a god or divine being shedding its blood for the good of mankind is also familiar. Heads were regularly taken in some areas well into the twentieth century. The life force, which is seated in the head, was thought to increase the store of fertility within the head-hunter's community. Heads were placed for added protection and power in the roofs of clan houses, above doorways or at the entrance to the village. On the island of Sumba, trees adorned with human heads guarded the entrance to the village, and the "skull tree" motif still appears on Sumbanese textiles.

ANCESTOR WORSHIP

VENERATION of ancestors is a widespread phenomenon, and ancestors also played a major role in head-hunting communities. The earliest ancestor is important in strengthening group identity. Every community can relate the story about their first ancestor, who may have been semi-divine, human, or animal, and ancestors are often deified. Stories relate the founding of ethnic groups by such mythical figures.

In the south, tales are told of the arrival of the original ancestor by canoe. More immediate ancestors are also important. They are thought to watch over their progeny, guiding and empowering them, especially in battle. Among New Guinea tribes and in many of the islands, warriors traditionally carved their own weapons which they decorated with the images of their dead parents or grandparents.

SERPENTS

THE DRAGON-SNAKE or *naga* (Skt: serpent) is a fabulous creature known throughout the region. It appears in many Indian myths, where it is associated with both Vishnu and Shiva. The Angkor dynasty in Cambodia and the Mons of Burma traced their descent to the union of a brahmin prince and a *naga* princess. According to one Chinese account of the thirteenth century, the king was expected to pass the first watch of the night in a high tower with the princess. If he failed to do this, the empire was doomed to fall. The Vietnamese tell the story of their origin thus: Kinh Duong Vuong, ancestor of the Hung dynasty, married the daughter of the Dragon Lord of the Waters. Their son, Lac Long Quan, is considered to be the father of the Vietnamese people and the originator of agriculture, cooking, and other elements of civilization.

The image of the serpent fighting the bird is frequently seen from Burma to New Guinea. It presumably symbolizes the balance of the elements of sky and earth. In Indian myth the bird is Garuda, the mount of Vishnu, while the serpent is associated with both Vishnu and Shiva.

▼ *Turtles, snakes and other Underworld creatures support this temple's pagoda roof.*

THE GODS OF ASIAN MYTHS

AS A RESULT of its complex history, a whole range of deities and spirits have been worshiped in Southeast Asia. Among nature spirits Sri, the rice goddess, is particularly honored, and the god or spirit of the mountain or volcano is also feared, especially in the islands, as is the god of the sea.

In the Hindu phase many temples were dedicated to Shiva and Vishnu. In Hindu Bali, these gods and many others remain, their characteristics having merged with those of ancient indigenous deities. In the north the Buddha is revered, and Hindu deities such as Indra, Sri Devi and Brahma, who feature in Buddhist mythology, figure in Buddhist stories.

RITUALS OF DEATH

ACCOMPANYING THE CULT of the ancestors in many island groups is a preoccupation with the paraphernalia of death. Some societies perform a dance at which the masked spirit-guide leads the departed soul away from the village to the land of the ancestors. The Toraja of Sulawesi place effigies of the dead in niches carved into cliffs overlooking the village. Legend and myth accompany and support all these important rituals. On the island of Flores the great volcano Keli Mutu has three craters, each containing a lake. The waters of the three lakes are of startlingly different colors, which change over time but which always contrast with each other. At the moment they are colored black, white, and aquamarine respectively. These lakes hold the souls of the dead: the souls of sinners go to the black lake; the souls of young men, virgins and the pure of heart live in the white lake; whilst the souls of those who have died a natural death in old age dwell in the aquamarine lake. This belief is consistent with the widespread belief in the sacred nature of mountains, and volcanoes in particular, which stand closer to the heavens than any other natural feature.

▲ *Mask representing benevolent rice spirits in dances held to promote crop fertility.*

▶ *This cloth painting shows the churning of the ocean by gods and demons at the dawn of Creation.*

the genuine faith in the Buddhist creed, however, Hindu stories concerning gods and heroes are too exciting to be forgotten and the most famous are known to those of every faith. In the Muslim south, Islamic legends of semi-historical kings and warriors are enacted alongside Hindu myths in dance-drama.

RECURRING THEMES

CREATION MYTHS occur throughout the region, and myth also accompanies the ritual of death and passage to the world of the dead. Myths concerning heroic figures are popular and often relate to the glorious past of the community or to a founding ancestor. These tales may tell of great ocean crossings in the dawn of time, or of union between men and gods or semi-divine creatures.

Death is hedged about with myth and ritual. The deceased is sometimes transported to the land of the gods and ancestors in a fantastic coffin or boat, or there may be a second funeral at which the remains are disinterred and cremated.

◄ *Illustration from the* Ramayana *showing a nymph seducing the king of the demons.*

SACRIFICIAL RITUALS

THE RITUALS OF SACRIFICE and blood-letting are thought to restore fertility to the earth and the community. Rituals surrounding fertility and sacrifice are often explained through myth. The ritual of human sacrifice is a common legacy of Southeast Asia. As late as the nineteenth century, live victims were buried beneath gateways and posts of palaces and important buildings. In the past children were offered in sacrifice to the volcano, and heads were regularly taken in some areas well into the twentieth century. The life force, which believed to be seated in the head, was thought to increase the store of fertility within the head-hunter's community.

LINKS WITH HINDU MYTHOLOGY

HINDU MYTHS, particularly stories from the *Ramayana* and the *Mahabharata*, are well known throughout Southeast Asia and appear in the dance-drama and puppet theater of most countries. Although Hinduism has largely disappeared from Southeast Asia, many stories concerning the god Vishnu and his incarnations, Shiva and the Goddess, are remembered. They are depicted in the magnificent reliefs of ancient temples, which are still visited as reminders of the past by today's Muslims and Buddhists. Buddhist stories are very popular in the north. Particularly common are the last 10 *jataka* stories, tales of the previous lives of the Buddha, and miraculous scenes from his last life as a mortal; despite

THE TEMPTATION OF BUDDHA

VERY POPULAR in the north of the region, particularly in Burma, Thailand and Laos, is the story of the temptation of the future Buddha by Mara, the evil one. As he sat in deep meditation beneath a bodhi tree, the sage was seen by Mara, who tried to distract him from his purpose by sending his two scantily clad daughters to parade before him, but the prince remained unmoved. Next Mara sent an army of ugly howling demons to terrify him, but the ascetic seemed oblivious to them. Finally Mara taunted him, demanding to know by what right he should become a Buddha (literally "Enlightenment Being"). The Holy One then pointed to the earth, calling upon it to bear witness to his countless good deeds in this and previous lives, enough to warrant him becoming a Buddha. At this the earth quaked. In response, the heavens opened and there was a great deluge, causing Mara and his devilish followers to flee. The sage then went on to attain full enlightenment and to formulate his doctrine, the essence of Buddhism.

Another well-known story is that of the serpent Mucalinda, who sheltered the Buddha from the rains as he meditated, by stretching its many hoods over the Buddha's head.

▼ *Head of a life-sized wooded crocodile, its back is a seat for the healing goddess, Balam.*

BAS-RELIEFS

MANY HINDU MYTHS survive in the bas-reliefs of Javanese and Cambodian temples. The great twelfth-century relief depicting the "churning of the milky ocean" can be seen at the temple of Angkor Wat in Cambodia. Particularly well illustrated are episodes from the life of the Buddha and from one of his previous lives, depicted in the ninth-century reliefs covering the walls of the stupa of Borobudur in Central Java. Scenes from the *Ramayana* adorn the walls of two of the principal temples of Prambanan. In the north, Buddhist myths appear in wall paintings, illustrated manuscripts and sculpture.

▲ *An example of a Buddhist temple from the Chiang Mai district of northern Thailand.*

KINGS AND LEADERS

THE CONCEPT OF THE KING as intermediary between the celestial and terrestrial worlds was important into the twentieth century. The king, throne, palace, and realm were thought to represent the universe in microcosm, and order within the realm reflected cosmic harmony. An evil or foolish ruler who upset that harmony caused not just political unrest but also floods, earthquakes, droughts, and epidemics. The king was expected to be the foremost upholder of the faith, building temples, mosques or stupas, and supporting the religious leaders. In some cases he was thought to be semi-divine, and any commoner caught looking at the king was put to death.

Twentieth-century political upheavals produced a legacy of stories concerning the struggle for independence. Some nationalist leaders such as Ho Chi Minh have acquired a legendary status. In Indonesia the embellished exploits of these charismatic men and their comrades are enacted in drama and shadow theater, and may well prove to be the basis for myths of the future.

KINGS AND JOKERS

THE KING ONCE PLAYED a vital role in the mythology of Southeast Asia. As a divine being, or as a semi-divine link between man and the gods, he represented the moral order of the known world. Many combined their personal names with that of a god or the Buddha, and several kings who died unnaturally became spirits in their next life.

Throughout the region, but especially in Javanese and Balinese shadow theater, there is found a grotesque clown-like figure, a member of the court. A figure of fun, he nevertheless speaks words of true wisdom and is ranked with the gods. He may have developed out of an ancient deity in the region.

THE HEROIC PRINCE

THE BALANCE BETWEEN the forces of good and evil, light and dark, male and female are played out in dance-dramas typified by Bali's *Barong* dance, in which the lion-like Barong and the witch-like Rangda enact the eternal battle. The heroic prince, courageous, modest, and pure, appears in many dramas. Rama, hero of the *Ramayana*, and an avatar or incarnation of Vishnu, is perhaps the most popular example. The Buddha, himself of royal birth, is known throughout Southeast Asia as a symbol of detachment and enlightenment.

NATS

IN BURMA, the spirits are called *nats*. The brother and sister Nga Tin De and Shwemyethna are probably the best known of the *nats*. Nga Tin De, the strong and handsome blacksmith, was killed in a jealous rage by the king. On hearing the news his sister, who was married to the king and who had been tricked into luring Nga Tin De to his death, threw herself into the flames and burned herself to death rather than continue to live with his murderer. Her husband was left with only her golden face. The brother and sister have become the guardian *nats* of the ancient city of Pagan, and offerings to Nga Tin De also protect houses against fire.

PRINCESS LORO JONGGRANG

IN CENTRAL JAVA the story of Princess Loro Jonggrang is related. This devout princess was courted by a local prince, but she did not wish to marry him and so set him the impossible task of building 1,000 temples in a single night. With the aid of troll-like helpers who could only emerge at night, the prince almost succeeded, but in order to trick him Loro Jonggrang and her maidens began to pound the rice. This task, usually carried out at dawn, caused the roosters to crow and the trolls fled, fearing the sunlight which could turn them to stone. The prince thus failed in his attempt to win her hand. In his rage he cursed her and she turned into the stone statue of the goddess Durga which still stands in the northern temple of Prambanan.

The arrival of Islam in the south is remembered in myth. An Islamic saint appeared before the Hindu raja of West Java and prophesied that he would be the last Hindu ruler, as a new religion would soon sweep the land. His prophecy came to pass, as before long Islam dominated the Javanese lowlands, and the last Hindus fled to Bali.

▼ *A Thai shadow puppet, similar to those found throughout Southeast Asia. Puppet theater shows can last for several days as puppeteers act out the ancient mythologies.*

THE ELEPHANT

THE ELEPHANT is a highly regarded beast, and the rare white elephant is considered sacred. A white elephant entered the right side of Queen Maya, mother of the Buddha, causing his conception; the three-headed elephant Erewan, representing the raincloud, is the mount of Indra, god of rain in Indian mythology. Thai myth, following the Indian story, speaks of white elephants being rainclouds doomed to walk the earth, where they attract heavenly clouds and so ensure rain and prosperity. In former times any white elephant born in captivity or captured from the wild had to be presented to the king; to this day the king of Thailand possesses a sacred white elephant. There are various tales in the Buddhist north of how a sacred Buddhist relic or religious text was carried on the back of a white elephant, which was allowed to wander freely. Wherever it stopped a shrine would be built, and at its final resting place a great pagoda was built.

▶ *Balinese performance of the mythical lion Barong fighting the witch Rangda.*

Oceania

INTRODUCTION

OCEANIA IS USUALLY divided into three regions: the larger islands above Australia or Melanesia long-settled by dark-skinned agricultural people; scattered groups of small islands contiguous to Asia or Micronesia settled by seafaring folk of Asian origin; and the far-flung islands of Polynesia forming a triangle enclosing Hawaii in the north, New Zealand in the south and Easter Island in the east. Unlike the Melanesians and Micronesians, who spoke many hundreds of languages and had as many mythologies, the Polynesians all spoke languages belonging to one language group though their mythologies reflected different influences.

The primal mythologies of Oceania mostly reflected their shamanic origins, the attempts by skilled practitioners and mediums to manipulate and control the spirit world and even visit it. Throughout the region, legends, and folk tales told of celebrated tricksters, shape-changers, and spiritual voyagers. There were, however, great differences. In much of Melanesia and some of the other island groups the more negative facets of the shamanic experience had developed into magic and sorcery. Elsewhere in the region strong religious cults developed or were introduced, some harking back directly to Asia or even the Americas with their own distinctive shamanic underlay.

The Polynesians were great navigators and had settled in Samoa and Tonga by 1000 B.C.E. Over 25 centuries they spread to other groups in the triangle. Although many of the myths of exploration reflected real voyages, they were also understood to represent spirit journeys. In so far as demigods such as Rupe and Maui were originally real people they were more likely to have been famous shamans than explorers. Apart from the folk tales or fables, the older myths in the region usually concerned nature, especially the stars, and the origin of places and obvious things such as fire or animal species. These stories were often told in narrative cycles added to from time to time by the storytellers on ritual occasions.

One of the migrations from South-East Asia into Polynesia, possibly via the island of Futuna, introduced an Indo-European cosmology of numerous heavens and underworlds, a world tree, waters of life, and a mirror-image world called Pulotu. The Pulotu people dominated in western Polynesia and Fiji, while the Papatea people, those who supported a pantheon emanating from the parent gods Papa and Atea, held sway in eastern Polynesia, including New Zealand where Rangi replaced Atea.

ROOTS OF MYTHOLOGIES

ALTHOUGH PREHISTORIANS and linguists have constructed models to account for the spread of settlement and language in Oceania, these models only account for underlays of material culture and overlays of socio-cultural influence. The distribution of mythological motifs and the apparent diffusion of cults suggest more varied patterns of inter-island contact. Thus, despite its eastern Polynesian pantheon, Hawaii has more in common with Indonesia through its mythological motifs, puppetry, and concept of sacred kingship.

In mytho-historical terms Oceania can be divided into regions subject to geographical and cultural influences. In the Melanesian region, vestiges of ritual cannibalizm existed together with snake god cults, concepts of bisexual mythic beings, and pig domestication in a belt which linked Indonesia with northern Australia and some remote islands.

Eastern Polynesia not only shared many plants, most notably the sweet pota-

▼ *Huge monolithic figure sculptures on Easter Island.*

to, with South America but apparently similar fertility rites, human sacrifice, body marking, and probably some gods. In the Micronesian area, classic animist beliefs and the role of the priestess-sister linked the Ryukyu Islands, the Micronesian islands, and parts of western Polynesia. Many of the myths and god names of Polynesia have been so transformed in Micronesia that they are barely recognizable.

CULTS AND CUSTOMS

THE OLDEST GODS were usually fertility gods or "gods of the land" to whom first fruits and other offerings were brought. Important annual or seasonal rituals developed and certain families, usually of chiefly origin, provided priests to maintain the ritual. In the Tongan and Yapese "empires," or spheres of influence, these rituals were extensive and usually involved the assembly of many people from throughout the region. Cults developed around the major gods and were probably linked with trading rings as well as chiefly hegemonies. Some of the Polynesian cults were far reaching. The Ta'aroa (Tangaloa) cult, later replaced by 'Oro, spread from Raiatea throughout the Society, Cook, and Tuamotu archipelagos with its sacred *marae* or altar meeting-place, Taputapuatea. The cult of Rongo spread from Mangaia into different parts of Polynesia and even reached the Gilbert Islands. That of Tane, known throughout eastern Polynesia, was centered on Huahine and possibly spread from there when a large number of Huahineans sailed to Tongatapu (invaded by eastern Polynesians in the reign of Tu'i Tonga Nui Tamatou) before sailing finally to New Zealand. An esoteric cult of Kiho or 'Io, known only to the priestly caste in eastern Polynesia, has caused endless speculation.

▶ *Oceanic spirit man or benevolent devil.*

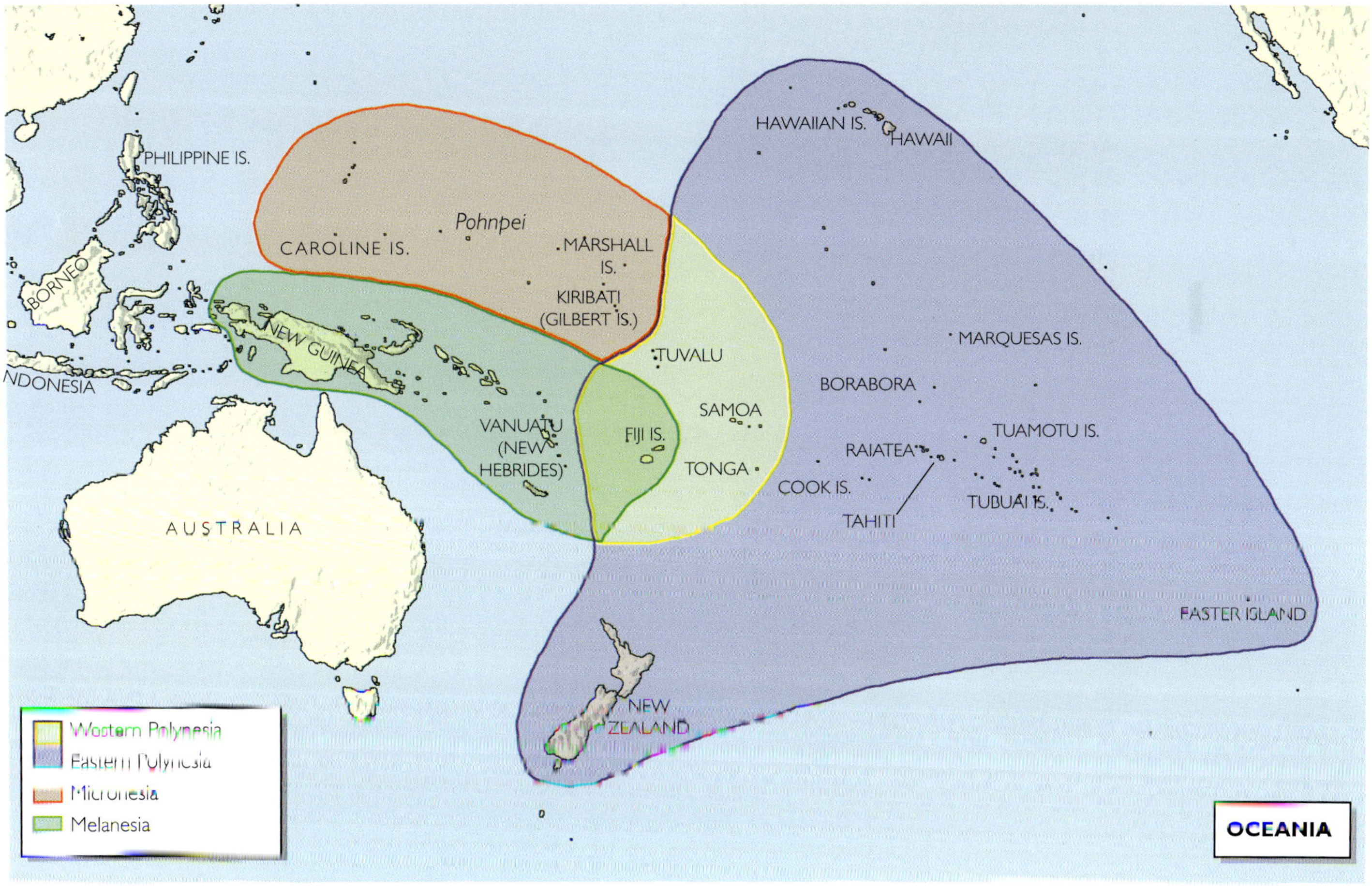

TRANSMISSION OF KNOWLEDGE

MYTHS HELPED the peoples of the islands to relate to their environment and were the basis of their religion. In most societies there were men or women who had the task of transmitting such knowledge, either within a family or as custodians of knowledge for a high chief. In one of the Cook Islands, for instance, the system of ultimogeniture applied to high priestly titles, that is an old priest passed on his mythological and related knowledge to his youngest son, who inherited his title. Craftspeople passed on their specialized knowledge, which was often inseparable from the mythology. In the highly stratified societies, specialized and esoteric knowledge was taught at schools of learning. The Maori schools in New Zealand were taught by priestly "experts" known as *tohunga*, those in Hawaii by their equivalent, the *kahuna*. In the Society Islands, youths were trained by the principal chief and senior members of the 'Arioi Society or players. The myths were often presented to the people in the form of dance or drama with elaborate costumes, Greek-style choruses, falsetto voice parts, and clowning.

▲ *Temple image of the Hawaiian war god, Ku.*

THE *DEMAS* OF WEST IRIAN

ALL THE LAND was once a "garden of Eden" inhabited by animals, plants, and powerful beings called *demas*, half man and half spirit, who could do prodigious things. However the *demas* started to play with fire and very soon they had burnt up everything. Even the mountains caught fire, the earth trembled and shook, and great cracks appeared which became rivers when the great *dema* Darvi sent rain to quench the flames. Darvi was so angry he threw a large piece of earth into the sea which became the land of New Guinea. The animals and plants already on this piece of earth became the ancestors of the people, who were divided into clans according to their original species. The snake people, the sago people, and the kangaroo people all had their own *dema*, who appeared at festivals in an appropriate towering headdress. The fire of the *demas* is said to have caused the legs of herons to turn red and crabs to sizzle. Cassowaries have scorched necks, toasted red flabs, and quills instead of proper feathers, while all bald men are claimed as relations of the first men singed by the fire.

OCEANIC THEMES

MOST MYTHIC THEMES were contained in the major myth cycles to be found in most island groups, namely descent from gods, obligations to the gods associated with birth, procreation and death, spirit journeying, and further rites of passage associated with flood, famine, and war. At a lower level were the numerous fables intended to familiarize the young with the world of nature containing themes of metamorphosis or shape-changing and miraculous origins. Some cycles or parts of cycles had a strong erotic component telling of romance and sexual passion. More philosophical themes explored the antithesis between light and darkness.

VISUAL REPRESENTATION

THE PRESENCE of the major gods was always an ecstatic experience. While mediums might induce possession by eating certain fungi, berries, or large quantities of bananas or by drinking green kava and more potent beverages, the gods also "came down" at the celebration of artistic excellence, especially during dancing and musical performances. In most of Polynesia the principal solo dancers were young women, but the polyandrous Marquesans preferred a handsome youth who danced Krishna-like before them. Masks and other props were used to play the parts of gods, and even in Christian times in Mangaia in the Cook Islands, the winged figure of the ancestor spirit Tangiia takes part in public festivals.

Masks were used to portray events as well as gods. The Mali-Baining people of the Gazelle Peninsula of New Britain hold a Mandas festival, supposed to represent events from primordial mythic time. The story of creation is chanted by a choir of women while 80 masks portray the birth of the sea, the origin of the earth, the forest and various plants, the winds, animals and birds, and finally the first human beings. The mask representing the birth of the sea symbolizes a whirlpool rather than a god.

MYTHIC REPRESENTATION IN ART

WOOD-CARVING was the great mythic art of Oceania, though mythological motifs were also rendered in stone, ivory, and greenstone. Sennit-binding, barkcloth, feather and shell decoration, and dog hair were also used in representing the gods, often portrayed as kites, adzes, and ceremonial artifacts. Mythological symbols were also used in tattooing. Carved objects ranged from large and elaborate god figures to decorative war clubs, pedigree sticks, and bowls for domestic use. Canoe-prow carving was widespread through Oceania, while elaborate house-lintel carving was restricted to New Zealand.

THE OCTOPUS AND THE RAT

THREE LAND ANIMALS once joined a party of birds to travel in a canoe. When a kingfisher picked a hole in the bottom of the canoe it filled and sank. The birds all flew off. The flying fish emulated them but fell into the water and found that it could swim. The hermit crab fell on to the reef below and found that it could come and go on the reef as it pleased. The rat, however, floundered about expecting to drown, until a passing octopus answered his distress cries and agreed to take him to the shore. The rat refused to hang on to the tentacles so climbed on to the head of the octopus where he urinated and defecated on it. Indeed, he was so ratty that he would not jump off but insisted on his obliging carrier taking him to dry sand so that he would not get his feet wet. The rat then rudely asked the octopus to feel his head. On discovering the rat droppings the octopus was incensed and that is why it has tubercles on its head and why it always attacks the imitation rat used as a lure by fishermen.

DUKDUK AND *DEMAS*

IN MANY MELANESIAN societies, the ancestors return at annual New Year festivals or well-marked ritual periods to praise or rebuke the local people, bless the crops and preside at initiations. The secret society of the Dukduk of the Tolai people of New Britain are famous for their distinctive masks or headdresses and are accepted as a visitation of the dead. Mythic masked visitants occur throughout New Guinea, northern Australia, and Vanuatu, and headdresses are often extremely elaborate. The towering structures worn by the *demas* of West Irian, for instance, weigh as much as a hundred pounds and the bearers frequently pass out under the weight of their burdens during the extended festivals. The woven palm tree headdress of the coconut *dema* would be three feet high with red clay-covered leaves, wooden coconuts attached and roots consisting of long straws woven into the hair. The coconut *dema* was chief of the friendly spirits, followed by the sago *dema*, the kangaroo *dema*, and the banana, sweet potato and tobacco *demas*. The master of ceremonies was the Diwa-Zib, the great *dema* of the head-hunt, who alone refrains from drunken excess and who cannot be cursed like the *demas* of floods, droughts, fevers, famine, and war.

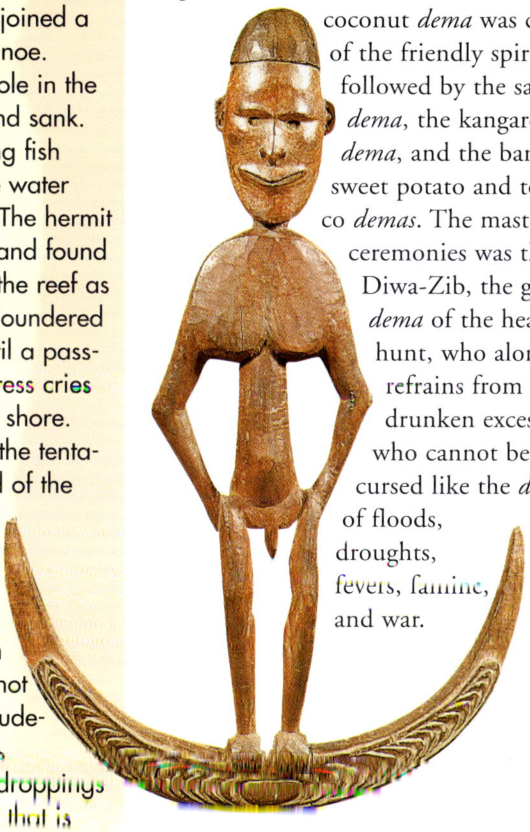

▶ *Spectacular Oceanic wooden masks such as this were used to represent gods and events.*

▲ *Carved figure and hook used for hanging skulls on*

FERTILITY

THE GODS OF FERTILITY and warfare were often linked. In head-hunting societies the head was seen as a source of power, and many Oceanic myths tell of heads and bodies which were buried and gave birth to valuable plants such as the coconut, sugar cane, and kava plant. The male gods of war and fertility were always well endowed, and this also applied to sacred kings who received the first fruits. Myths concerning Rongo, Tane, and Hikule'o were closely linked with the cultivation of food plants. Mother goddesses in Melanesia were also a source of vegetable wealth.

▶ *Carving of a staff god or ancestral figure, possibly Tangaroa.*

GODS NEW AND TRANSFORMED

WHILE THE REVIVAL of old gods in Melanesia is partly to be expected, given the late arrival of Christianity and the absence of chief-based theocracies, revival of the gods in Micronesia and Polynesia would seem unlikely. Yet in both Samoa and Tahiti there have been attempts to replace Jehovah in the *Old Testament* with Tagaloa (Ta'aroa), the assumption being that Jehovah and Tagaloa are the same creator god. Indeed, it is a widely held belief that the Samoans had embraced the religion of the *Old Testament* before the arrival of the missionaries and were simply waiting for the *New Testament.*

On another level, a Polynesian delegation to Tahiti to protest against the atomic testings at Mururoa in 1995 chose to invoke the aid of the gods Tane and Tangaroa. In Hawaii, the Polynesian revival is much more anti-Christian or pagan.

New gods in the Oceanic pantheon are likely to be angels and saints of Christian, Muslim, Bahai, and Mormon provenance or even allegorical characters from *Pilgrim's Progress*. Of the modern shamans and living gods, perhaps the strangest is the female prophet in the Cook Islands who takes on the physical appearance of Jesus Christ when claiming to be possessed.

THE GOD TAGALOA

AN OCEAN GOD from the Sanguir Islands, Tagaloa was probably a late arrival in Western Polynesia, where he became a god of shipbuilders. As a sea god he soon reached the eastern islands and New Zealand. In the Society Islands, as Ta'aroa, he probably usurped the role of the creator god Atea, presiding over a fearsome cult until replaced in turn by 'Oro. His reputation reached Hawaii where, as Kanaloa, he had a minor role. In contrast he returned to Manu'a and the west as a powerful sky god and royal ancestor. He sometimes appeared as a man-devouring shark.

MYTHS OF EXPLANATION

MANY MYTHS throughout the region were simply fables to explain geographical features and natural phenomena such as fire. Invariably particular gods, such as Tagaloa in Samoa and Tonga were attributed with having thrown down rocks which became islands. Kura in the Tuamotus, Motikitik in Yap, and Maui in Tonga and New Zealand were credited with having fished up islands from the sea with magic fish-hooks. All the islands, however, from Guam and New Guinea in the west to remote Easter Island, had entertaining myths that explained the markings on certain creatures or why certain characters became particular birds, animals, or stars. One popular myth in Central Polynesia was that of the rat and the octopus, which explained the markings on the octopus. Myths relating to one flood, one famine or the exploits of one hero usually reflected cumulative experiences scattered over time incorporated by the storytellers into shamanic song cycles. Numerous myths told of battles between birds and fish, fish and ants, or between different species of birds. These myths may have been referring to real battles between totemic groups, or more likely they referred to struggles, not necessarily physical, between rival groups of shamans.

THE ORIGIN OF MAKING FIRE

THE TRICKSTER GOD was always responsible for stealing fire and bringing it to earth. Olifat, the son of a woman of the Carolines and the sky father, accidentally saw his father through a hole in the coconut he was drinking and determined to visit him. He ascended to the heavens on the smoke from a burning pile of coconut shells. After various adventures in which he was killed by his relatives and restored by his father he was given a place in the heavens. He sent a bird back to earth with fire in its beak which was placed in certain trees thus enabling men to obtain fire by rubbing sticks together.

Unlike the Micronesian tricksters, the Maui heroes of Polynesia brought fire from underground. In the Maori

versions, Maui changed to a bird to visit the netherworld, where he fetched fire from the goddess Mahuika whose fingertips and toes glowed with fire. Mahuika gave him the end of a big toe as a firestick which he extinguished in a stream and returned until she had removed all her fingers and toes but one. This she threw after him in anger with a curse that it would consume forests, but he called on the rain gods to save him. Enough seeds of fire were left in certain trees for fire-making.

MYTHIC BEASTS

Although many of the Oceanic gods appeared in animal or reptile form they were mostly anthropomorphic. There were, however, numerous creatures that appeared in the myths which might equate with dragons or monsters. The most famous of these was the *taniwha* of New Zealand. The *taniwha* myths probably derived from a memory in Western Polynesia where saltwater crocodiles occasionally arrive during abnormal weather and cause havoc. Other Maori beasts were the bird-headed *manaia* used in art, the bulldog-headed *kumi*, and the man-eating Dog of Moko. A god in Fijian waters is thought to have been an extinct marine reptile.

SHAMANS OR SPIRIT ANCHORS

THROUGHOUT THE OCEANIC world, ancestral and other gods were believed to communicate through mediums, persons of both sexes and of varying social status, who became possessed, shook violently and spoke in the voice of the spirit or god. These mediums were supposed to travel in the spirit world, heal diseases, change shape, levitate, and fly to distant places in the flick of an eye. In Polynesia the mediums were known as "spirit anchors." A Samoan myth of a pigeon with nine heads refers to a shaman (symbolized by a winged creature) who had access to the nine heavens of Samoan mythology. In another myth Maui had eight heads, suggesting that the most popular trickster was not a full adept. Tafaki, on the other hand, was a master shaman, similar to the Irish Fintann, who had "climbed" to the uppermost heaven in Maori legends. He acquired many characteristics of the Christian God, which suggests that the storytellers were influenced by the ideas of early Spanish or whaling residents. Just as the shamans were shape-changers, the gods also appeared in their favorite animal forms, particularly the shark and the octopus. The Tongan spirit Fehuluni regularly changed sex to entrap both men and women.

◀ *Double-headed wooden figure, possibly used for sorcery.*

▼ *Statue formed around a central "eye of the fire," itself encircled by a snake biting its own tail; the ends are the heads of mythical fish.*

KAMAPUAA AT KAUAI

ON THE ISLAND of Kauai can be seen many rocks and springs which commemorate the visit of a notorious trickster and shape-changer god named Kamapuaa. Swimming to the island as a large black fish, he changed to a hog and rooted in the sand for water. He satisfied his hunger by eating all the sweet potatoes and sugar cane and then fell asleep, having grown so large that it took 20 men to carry him to the village where they prepared an earth oven to cook him. No sooner had they attempted to strangle him than he broke the ropes and changed to a handsome warrior, his bristled boar's back covered with a feather cape.

When the spirit guardians of a spring refused to give him water he became a hog again and rooted for the spring. He then hurled the two spirit men across the valley where they became two large rocks. The spring gave sparkling water which was taken in gourds to other islands. In another spring he lay down as a hog, fouling the water so that it became too bitter for any animal to drink.

On another occasion when he was sleeping hog fashion, the giant Limaloa attempted to kill him by rolling down a giant boulder. Becoming a handsome warrior Kamapuaa hurled a wedge-shaped rock into the slope so that it held the boulder. The two instantly became friends, Limaloa persuading his new friend to help him court the sisters of the lord of Puna. Kamapuaa went to their bathing pool, where the sisters fell in love with his handsome reflection. When he said he would not oblige them unless his spirit friend went with him, they recognized Limaloa as their annoying suitor but relented in order to obtain Kamapuaa as their husband.

In the wars between Puna and the chiefs of Kona, Kamapuaa proved a great warrior, being invisible except for his hand holding his warclub. After the battle he removed the feather capes and helmets of the slain chiefs, returned to his dwelling, became a hog and fouled the mats. While his wives went to wash the mats he hid the trophies under the sleeping mats which eventually rose to a great height. Attempts to find the thief failed, though he was known to have an injured hand. When found out Kamapuaa was given the choice of death or banishment and chose to leave Kauai for ever.

▲ *Tricksters, such as the god Kamapuaa, were able to change shape into animals, such as the wild boar, to suit their purpose.*

▼ *Schools in Hawaii and New Zealand made great efforts to codify and refine ideas in cosmology and mythology.*

OCEANIC COSMOLOGY

THROUGHOUT THE OCEANIC world, the mythmakers adhered to the shaman's three-tiered universe. Most people thought of the heavens in terms of the rainbow: that the arches touched the earth at two points. Those who voyaged for long distances were considered to have passed through several heavens; they were, in Polynesian, terms *papalangi* or heaven-breakers, the name given to Europeans.

In the advanced schools of learning in Hawaii, New Zealand and elsewhere, cosmological debate rivaled that of medieval scholastics. The universe was divided into *Po* and *Ao* (loosely translated, darkness and light), positive and negative, male and female, reproduction and decay, fire and water, and life and death. Various schema for the unwise were worked out, often on the analogy of the coconut or the human head. The number of heavens varied from 10 to 21, the more numerous being in the more distant places such as the Tuamotus and New Zealand, either the result of two systems coming together or an estimate of distance from their homelands. Missionaries, antipathetic to the parallel views of the Pulotu people, turned the waters of life into the "Lake of Death" and the world tree into the "Tree of Death."

THE NEW PACIFIC ARTISTS

The renowned New Guinea artists profess to paint *fasin bilong tumbuna*, "the way we traditionally do something." *A Benevolent Devil* is the title of one such acrylic painting on masonite by the established Port Moresby artist Mattias Kauage (born Chimbu Province), exhibited in 1977. It depicts Yogond, a spirit man, who lived in a cave in Chimbu. Yogond had fins like a fish and at night he went out hunting. According to Kauage, Yogond's drawings can still be seen on cave walls today.

Although most of the "new Pacific" artists tackle urban subjects, Timothy Akis of Tsembaga prefers mythic bush subjects.

HEROES OF THE PEOPLE

AS WELL AS BEING shamanic tricksters, many of the semi-divine figures come across as being popular folk heroes like Robin Hood, especially in the more hierarchical societies of Polynesia. Even today Maui is seen as a champion of liberty in Tonga's pro-democracy movement. Heroes such as Maui, Olifat, Qat, and Kamapuaa may also represent the gods or ancestors of an earlier wave of people who managed to survive and were at length adopted by the dominant cult.

One cycle of the Hawaiian Kamapuaa was so long that it took 16 hours to recite. His exploits were not unlike those of Herakles, particularly as he fought an eight-headed chief, reminiscent of the Hydra, an episode in which native cunning was victorious over esoteric knowledge. His feud and eventual union with the volcano goddess Pele probably reflect a union between two different traditions. In the myth from Kauai his thefts and earthly behavior are in direct contrast with the regulated behavior of the Puna chiefs and make him one with the common people.

Other popular heroes probably derived from various conquered peoples, but the connection was weakened because these groups were usually treated as almost invisible spirit folk.

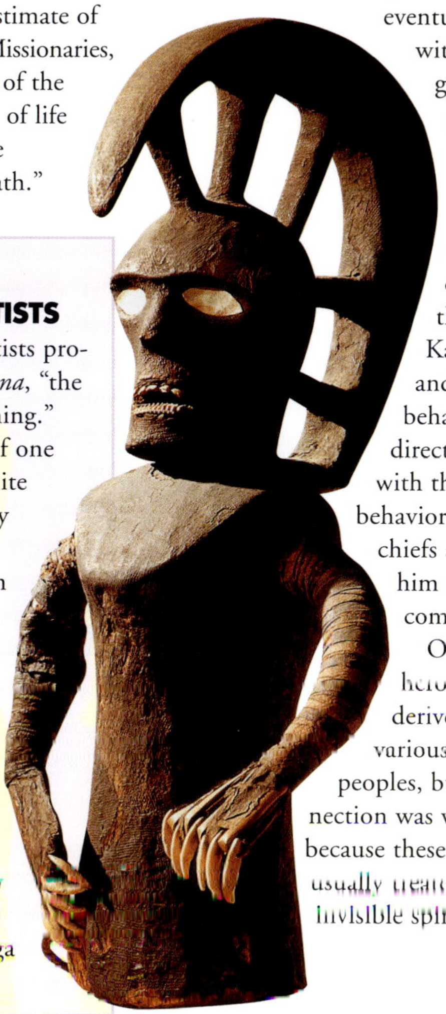

HINA AND TUNA

THE HIGHBORN lady Hina, or Sina, was a protected virgin living in Samoa, probably a female Tu'i Manu'a or high chief of Manu'a. A god in the form of an eel came to Samoa and lived in Hina's bathing pool. When Hina became pregnant everyone wanted to know who was her man. "It is the eel, the Shining One." Her protectors bailed out the pool, lifted out the eel and cut it to pieces. She asked for the head to be buried properly, and after five nights the head had sprouted into a coconut tree which provided oil and shelter for their child.

The Tahitians and Tuamotuans incorporated the story into the Maui cycle. In the Tuamotuan version, Hina was the daughter-wife of Tiki who introduced death into the world when she failed to revive him. She then took Tuna of the eternal waters as her lover. When she tired of him, all her potential lovers were afraid of Tuna until Maui fought and killed him in an epic battle. Maui cut off the head which his mother planted and it became the coconut palm. The Tahitians told that Hina left the head by a stream while she bathed, and it immediately sprouted.

◄ *Hawaiian sculpture of the goddess Pele.*

▲ *A god in the form of an eel made its home in Hina's bathing pool.*

ASTRONOMICAL MYTHS

MANY OF THE EARLIEST myths were universal in type because they drew on the antiquity of star lore. As the Maori scholar Hare Hongi pointed out, many of the Greek and Oriental solar and star myths could only be interpreted properly when compared with their Maori variants which retained essential detail. Maui in particular was the demigod who ordered, arranged, and controlled the solar system. While the classic myth of his snaring the sun survived, his own cult was superseded by the cults of Rongo, Tane, and Tangaroa. All events and seasons were determined by the movements of the heavenly bodies, and the gods associated with certain stars and planets became the tutelary gods of certain crops. The rising of the Pleiades signaled the coming of the wet season and was often an occasion of great excitement. In one Maori myth the Pleiades were seven white pigeons being snared by Tautoru the fowler or Orion.

Hina, the name of numerous goddesses and manifestations, was identified with phases of the moon, appearing in myths as the goddess respectively of death, childbirth, the tides, the west wind, fire, water, and women's crafts, her styles being similar to those of the Virgin Mary.

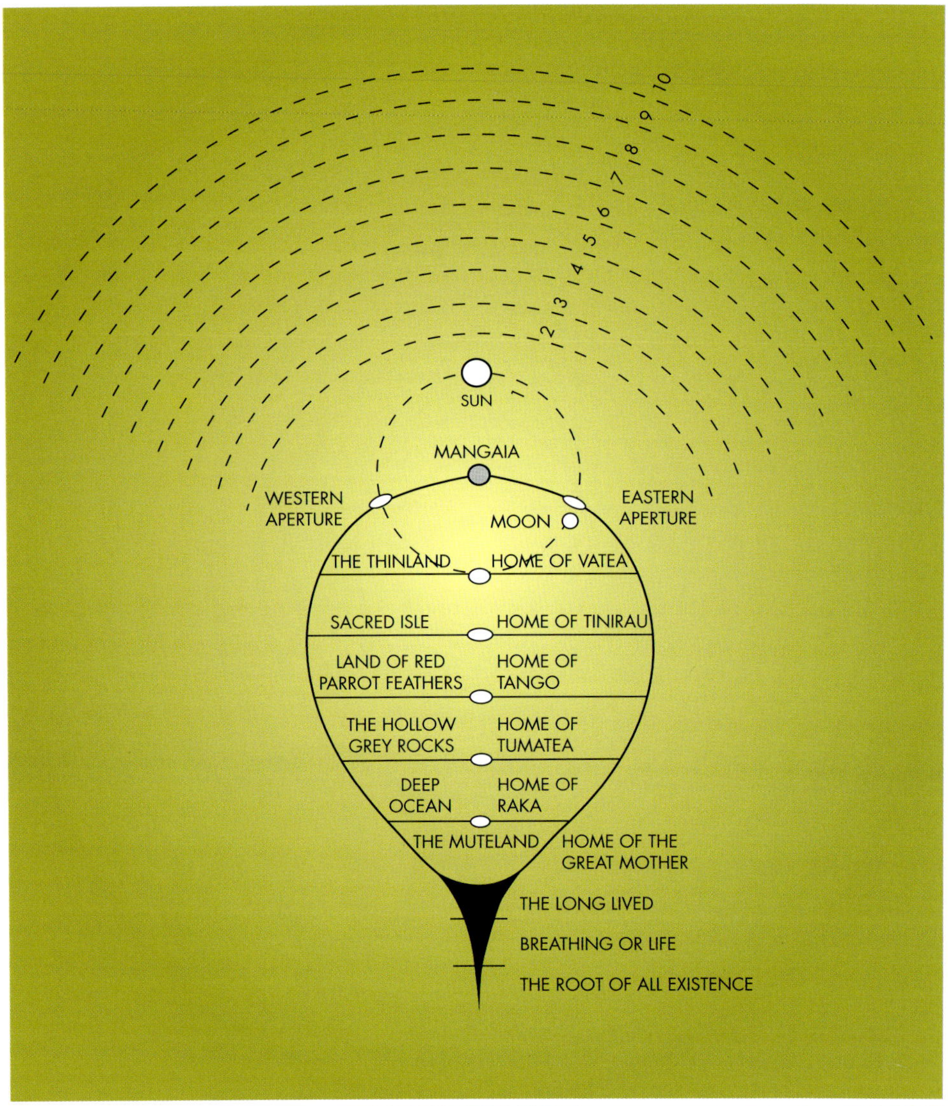

▲ *One representation of the Polynesian universe.*

DEMIGODS

LIVING GODS, such as the most powerful shamans, sacred kings and specified culture heroes, were believed to be half god and half human. The greatest of these, such as Maui and Olifat, were often indistinguishable from gods, their status changing according to local beliefs. Some ancestors and anthropomorphic spirits could also be considered demigods, though they had no cults and seemed to be more spirit than otherwise. Such were Fehuluni of Tonga and many of the *aitu* or spirits of Samoa such as Moso and the family *aitu* of Mata'afa. Living gods such as the Samoan despot Tamafaiga ruled until 1829.

MAUI SNARES THE SUN

WHEN MAUI WAS YOUNG the sun traveled so swiftly across the sky that his mother and other earth people did not have enough time to complete their work in the gardens. Maui determined to slow the sun down so, armed with strong ropes and a club, he traveled to the east to wait for the sun to appear. When the sun put his head into the snare Maui got his brothers to pull on the rope ends until the sun was completely at his mercy. According to the Hawaiians Maui lassoed six of the sun's legs, or rays, and lashed them to a tree. Maui then gave the sun a sound beating with the club, which was said to be the jawbone of his grandmother. The sun was only released when it agreed to travel more slowly and allow the earth people more time to tend their gardens. This myth was retold to suit the conditions of many islands and formed part of the song cycles of Maui in Tonga and Samoa, Hawaii, New Zealand, the Tuamotus, and the Marquesas.

FEMALE DEITIES

MOTHER GODDESSES and moon goddesses proliferated in areas where matrilineal systems prevailed, but female deities tended to be either complementary to male gods or malicious spirits in patrilineal societies. Beneficent serpent goddesses include Kagauaha of San Cristoval and the python goddess Niniganni in New Guinea who reward their followers with wealth. Murdered creator goddesses were usually sources of vegetable products. Uti of Mangaia stalked the earth in search of food and taught the art of night fishing. Predatory and cannibal female spirits were common, particularly in the outer islands of Polynesia. In the Marquesas, the *Vehine Hae* or wild women, were forever trying to steal or rape wandering males. Female spirits in Tonga and the Gilberts were said to strangle mortals they made love with. Maori, Tuamotuan, and Tahitian myths tell of cannibal goddesses. These predatory goddesses may explain why the Samoans and Tahitians often had female war gods. Nafanua, the principal war god of Samoa, was thought to be a man until her breasts were exposed during a battle. To'imata, 'Aitupuai, and Mahufaturau were three battle maidens who accompanied their father 'Oro. Volcano goddesses, such as Pele of Hawaii, shared some of the characteristics of both mother goddesses and malignant spirits.

THE GOD HIKULE'O

HIKULE'O, AN ANCESTRAL deity from Samoa, was the great god of the Tu'i Tonga or sacred king of the Tongan islands to whom first fruits were offered. The god dwelt in the mirror-image world of Pulotu. He had a reptilian tail like the god Dengei in Fiji which encircled the world tree and was tied down by his brothers to prevent him from wrecking the earth. He sometimes appeared as a white shark. When the Tu'i Tonga line passed through two females, Hikule'o took on a female manifestation and is now regarded as a goddess on Tongatapu.

A statue of the Avatea of Rurutu, the original creator god of eastern Polynesia.

THE CURSE OF NAKAA

NAKAA WAS THE *IKAWAI* or eldest of the gods, of one of the dark-skinned earliest inhabitants of the Gilbert Islands. He was the creator god of these dark-skinned people. He created people, both men and women, but let them live separately on their island of Bouru. Both the men and the women had a single tree each in their different sectors. The men's tree was *tarakaimaiu* and the women's tree was *tarakaimate*. Like Nakaa, their god, the men and the women were immortal. Nakaa one day announced to them that he was going on a journey. To remain immortal and live forever, they must remain separated, the men in their part of the land and the women in theirs.

Both the men and the women knew about the existence of the other but did not understand why Nakaa kept them separated and would not allow them to visit one another. The wind, which blows every evening from the direction of the women, would bring the scent of the *tabaa* (flower) of the women's tree to the men, and each time it blew the men would think of the women and desire to visit them. Soon everybody lost count of the "moons" and the "seasons," and they thought Nakaa was not coming back. And the wind, which never ceased to bring the scent of the *tabaa* from the women's tree to the men, kept tempting the men to venture into the women's sector. After several more moons and seasons, Nakaa, to the surprise and dismay of everyone, returned. Everyone pretended nothing had happened.

One day Nakaa called his people together and said, "So you have disobeyed me and have come together, and because of that, your kind is no longer immortal, and soon you will all die." The people denied everything, but Nakaa said to them, "Indeed you have visited one another and have come together, for gray hair is growing on

your heads, your skin is wrinkling, your teeth are rotting, and your health is getting bad day by day.... You can no longer stay with me. You are to leave, but select which tree to take with you." They chose the women's tree—the *tarakaimate*. It was the pandanus.

"You have chosen badly, but your tree will serve you well. You will build your houses from its timber; it will provide you with fruits to eat; its roots will heal you when you are ill, and provide drops of water for you when adrift at sea. Its leaves will shelter you from the sun, wind, and rain, and when you die, to return to me, you will be wrapped in mats made from pandanus leaves...."

SOCIAL MYTHS—CREATION STORIES

THROUGHOUT OCEANIA, MYTHS were used to instil social values such as family obligations, the rights of the first-born, respect for the sacred, condemnation of incest and, in the stratified societies, obedience to chiefs and priests. Although these social myths contained some ancient elements and sometimes obsolete language they were constantly reworked and reinterpreted according to the political agenda of those controlling society. Creation myths, far from being the earliest, were often the most recently composed, as they contained the guidelines for social interaction. As a general rule, one finds that the most stratified societies had the most elaborate creation myths.

While in parts of Melanesia and the subcultures of Micronesia and Polynesia there seemed to be little interest in how the world was formed, curiosity being confined to the first human beings, the creation chants elsewhere reached great poetic and philosophic heights. A hymn to Ta'aroa from the Society Islands resembles a hymn from the *Rig Veda*, while the *Kumulipo*, the Hawaiian hymn of creation, composed as late as the eighteenth century, provides an evolutional account as opposed to spontaneous creation. These hymns provided an introduction to lengthy genealogies connecting the divine with the ruling families.

THE LEGEND OF TIKI: A CREATION STORY

THE GOD TIKI lived in Havaiipo, the mirror-image world of darkness, where he commanded many spirits. He found that he was lonely, so he went to the seashore and created a child in the sand which he then covered over and went away. Three days later he returned and was surprised to find a small hill where he had buried the child. He scraped the loose sand away and found a beautiful woman whom he named Hinatunaone. She became his wife. A son and daughter were born who were able to procreate. Tiki decided to find them a place to live, so he left Havaiipo and found a place in the ocean where he commanded the land of Nukuhiva to appear and placed his grandchildren there. Soon there were too many people and he looked over the water and commanded Uapou to rise. He now left Nukuhiva, where the people made an image of him in stone, but he still created new lands as the population increased: Uahuku in the east, Hivaoa in the south, Tahuata peopled from Uahuku, Mohutani as a resting place, and Fatuhiva peopled from Hivaoa.

◀ *An ancient Oceanic statue believed to have been held sacred. Myths were repeated by the elders to install a respect of the sacred in children.*

▶ *A statue to pay homage to the ancestors.*

DISOBEDIENCE AND ITS REWARD

MISSIONARIES AND SCIENTISTS who held the pre-evolution doctrine of the degeneration of culture often believed they had found evidence of biblical revelation, while evolutionists believed many myths had been contaminated by early Christian influence. What is more likely is that the myths of primal cultures had evolved in much the same way as the myths recorded in *Genesis*. Micronesian myths relating to the ancestor god Nakaa, probably of ultimate Asian Indian origin, formulated in pre-Christian times, have strong biblical resemblances. The curse of Nakaa, retold here by a Gilbertese informant, could be interpreted as the expulsion from Eden except that the island of Bouru (Pulotu) is more likely to be Bhurloka, the home world of the *Vedas*. Other versions make it clear that the men possessed a tree that continually replenished its single coconut and a fish trap that was always full of fish which Nakaa took back with him when he left. He then sat at the entrance to the spirit world weaving a net to catch the souls of the dead. Those who could refrain from consuming fruit from Nakaa's tree, fish from the fishtrap, and water from his well for three days could return to the living.

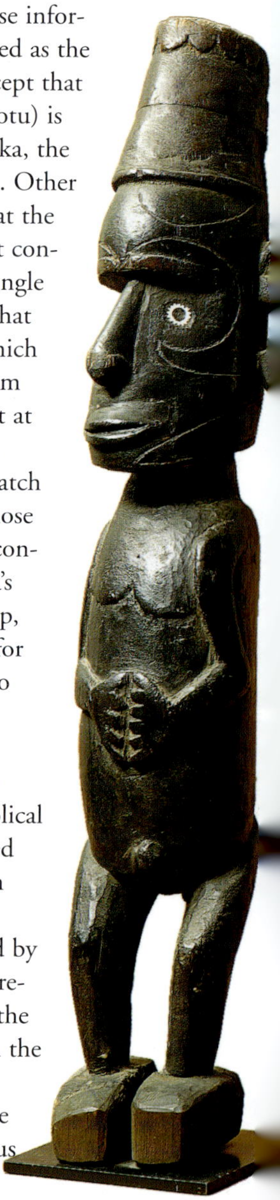

FLOOD MYTHS

THOSE SEEKING "biblical survivals" eagerly collected flood myths. The English beachcomber Thomas Lawson was so convinced by the supposed biblical correspondences in a cycle of the Take people of Hivaoa in the Marquesas which he collected in 1861–62 that he announced to the religious

world that he had found oral confirmation of the Bible narrative. Although Professor Alexander of Hawaii published the flood account, serious scholars shied away, perhaps failing to recognize the universality of the myth and the fact that, in shamanic cycles, every flood is subsumed into one flood just as famines, wars and even heroes are recast in the melting pot of storytelling. Confirmation of the authenticity of Lawson's texts was obtained by a German collector early this century who recorded numerous myths and songs relating to natural catastrophes, most of them in an archaic dialect of the language. Although few of these survive, enough remains to show they correspond with Lawson's text. The Marquesan myth of a lost homeland

▲ *Spectacular coastline surrounds most of Oceania.*

to the north which was entirely destroyed is matched by a modern myth elaborated in the 1930s by the eccentric traveler Colonel James Churchward, who believed that all humankind originated on the sunken Pacific motherland continent of Mu

OCEANIC CHARACTERS

BESIDES TRICKSTERS such as Qat in Melanesia and Maui, most of the early cults revolved around sea gods (Tinirau known from Japan to the Tuamotus, Tefatumoana, and Tangaroa) and land gods (Nafanua). Gods who separated earth from heaven were also archetypal. The cult figures that next emerged were phallic fertility and war gods who were often interchangeable. Thus Rongo presided over agriculture in one group and war in another. Wild women with bulging eyes, bird men and water monsters were recurring characters. Heroes, clowns, living gods and little people filled the mythic landscape.

TAGALOA'S SACRIFICE

WHEN A TERRIBLE PLAGUE ravaged their homeland, Faitaulaga, the chief priest of the sea god Tagaloa, urged 42 strong youths and seven beautiful maidens to offer themselves to the god and flee from the death gods in seven canoes. With the help of the sea god they outraced the death gods and rowed and sailed for seven days and seven nights. Arriving at a northern island they filled their canoes with fruit, only to be shot at with poisoned arrows. As the seventh man on each canoe was pushing from the beach he was shot and became the first sacrifice. A storm next arose in which a house-high wave carried off the rowing man in the front of each canoe to the watery home of Tagaloa, who now craved further sacrifices; they became seven powerful fish which pulled a fisherman from each canoe as a third sacrifice.

The depleted voyagers next arrived at the Nukuor lagoon where they were regaled with pigs and coconut milk and stayed for a year until a dancing feast was held in their honor. Seven of the men got drunk on palm wine and blasphemed the god by shouting *"malosi Tagaloa."* The ancient breadfruit tree under which they sat suddenly split open, spattering their brains and blood over the others. Banished from the island for fear of retribution the voyagers carried the smashed corpses to sea in mats and surrendered them as a fourth sacrifice to the deep. They sailed past the Ralik and Ratak Islands, but for many days they sighted no land and were reduced to starvation. The two men in each canoe drew lots to see who would be killed, but when the losers were bound the men refused to kill them. The women then made love to and strangled their lovers whom the men now butchered. The bones wrapped in mats became the fifth sacrifice. The women now made love to the remaining men, planning to kill them if necessary. A hurricane prevented further slaughter, and Tagaloa spoke from within it commanding no more sacrifices and telling the remaining seven pairs to travel south for 77 nights where they would find fertile islands to be named Samoa.

Arriving at the island of Oahu they were received by King Umi and joined by two Hawaiian chiefs, Leapai and Tualagi, and their families and made the voyage south until they reached Manu'a.

▲ *Spirit figures such as this became cult figures in Oceanic mythology.*

◀ *Mask from New Guinea depicting a "bird man," a typical character in Oceanic mythology.*

SOCIAL MYTHS—NEW INSTITUTIONS

SOCIAL MYTHS were either invented or completely changed following dramatic historical events. After tribal warfare it was not unusual for a peaceful fertility god to become a war god or a defeated war god to preside over a garden. With the collapse of the Samoan-oriented government of Tonga in the sixteenth or early seventeenth century, new myths were invented to justify the use of the psychoactive kava plant as a drug of social control. At the same time the myth of the origin of the Tu'i Tonga was invented or restructured to reinforce the sacredness of the ruling lineage. The first Tu'i Tonga was not only given a divine father but he was also made exceptionally sacred as youngest son of the god reconstructed from shamanic dismemberment.

In the Society Islands, when the cult followers of Tane were defeated sometime early in the eighteenth century, the god of dalliance, 'Oro, replaced his father Ta'aroa as god of the firmament and principal war god. The 'Oro cult created a new priestly caste of players, the 'Arioi Society, who acted out the new stories of the gods and served as a cultural guild to ensure mythological conformity.

THE ORIGIN OF KAVA

THE MAN FEVANGA attended the Tu'i Tonga and invited his master to visit him and his wife Fefafa on Eueiki Island. The visit took place during a famine, and there was nothing to eat except one big kape plant with its edible peppery root. The chief Lo'au rested his canoe so that it sheltered the kape plant. Fevanga then persuaded Lo'au to move and dug up the root which he put into the earth oven together with his leprous daughter Kavaonau. When the food was presented to Lo'au he would not eat the girl but had her head and body buried separately. After five nights a big kava plant grew from the head and sugar cane from the body. Lo'au ordered Fevanga to bring the kava and sugar cane to him and said "Chewing kava, a leper from Faimata, the child of Fevanga and Fefafa! Bring some coconut fiber to strain it, a bowl to contain it, someone as master of ceremonies, some young leaves of the banana as a receiver, and someone for the bowl to be turned to," thus celebrating the occasion when an only child had been cooked for the reception of the ranking chiefs.

DEATH

IN MELANESIAN myths, death was often linked with sorcery. Perhaps the most prevailing myth was that of the return of the spirit to his or her ancestral homeland. In Fiji there was an elaborate route for spirits to travel. In many Polynesian islands there was a jumping-off point at the western end of the major islands where the spirit descended into the sea and later emerged in the mirror-image world. While chiefly persons went to appropriate heavens, commoners had few prospects in the hereafter and in Tonga they were supposed to have no souls, having been created from insects.

◄ Tagaloa revenges himself on disrespectful voyagers— killing them with a falling breadfruit tree.

MYTHS OF THE 'ARIOI

THE MYTHIC TEXTS regarding the institution of the 'Arioi Society provide one of the most specific chapters in Pacific prehistory, having been recorded in Tahitian by the English missionary J. M. Orsmond. Other versions exist but are either derivative, bowdlerized or lack essential detail. Several accounts which outlined initiation and fertility rituals have been lost or destroyed because their content was thought to be offensive. The myth of origin given here appears to contain some historical elements. The union of 'Oro and the highborn lady of Borabora appears to be a union of the people of the land who wear grass skirts and the paperbark- (*tapa*-) making people who had settled in Borabora from their homeland Rotuma. Although some sources state that 'Oro's brothers or sons who were turned into pigs were never to be killed and were worshiped as patrons of the society, the whole purpose of their metamorphosis seems to have been to offer Vairaumati a human sacrifice, an idea which is reinforced by Mahi saying he wished one pig to become a roller to launch his canoe, a function of the human sacrifice. The killing of infants born to members was obligatory, perhaps in memory of 'Oro's sacrifice.

◀ *Grass skirts and other items of traditional costume are still worn by the oceanic peoples when they celebrate their heritage of dance, rituals and stories.*

THE ORIGIN OF THE 'ARIOI SOCIETY

THE GREAT GOD 'Oro cast off his wife, who became a sightless mass of sand. His two sisters took pity on him and, dressed only in the leaves of the ti plant and armed with reed darts, they set off to find him a wife. The people of Tahiti assembled but no wife was found, then the people of Raiatea, but again no wife. The women had wrinkled faces beneath their green chaplets. On Borabora, however, they found the beautiful Vairaumati screened by white and scarlet cloth. When they withdrew the folds of her screen they shrank from her beauty as from lightning. Her face was like the moontide light and her eyes were dark sky-blue.

The sisters returned to the heavens, woke their brother and told him his wife awaited him at Vaiotaha. 'Oro flew in a horizontal line until he was over the place, then descended, and he and his new wife made love for three days and three nights. Ashamed that he had no property to present to her he returned to the heavens where his sisters wept at his plight. He then called for their two younger brothers and turned one into a boar and the other into a sow to take to his wife. That night they made love and at the same time the two pigs engendered, conceived and brought forth five piglets which the priest dedicated to 'Oro, each piglet assigned to one of the privileges of the followers of 'Oro, the master of the pig.

Then 'Oro sought for a place for his hog and sent Mahi to Tahiti, but the people were all at their *marae* praying for their fleet and would not invite him. After returning to Opoa empty-handed three times, Mahi formed an alliance with Hua'atua of Afa'ahiti through his daughter Taurua. Hua'atua presented

◀ *The Fiji Islands.*

Mahi with pigs which were shared with four chiefs and one was kept alive to be a roller over which Mahi would pull his ship *Hotu*. Mahi went to Tahaa to eat certain food, plant paperbark, feed pigs, and roll cloth for his friend at Tahiti. He gave the gifts of a double canoe, cloth, feathers, and pearls to King Tamatoa in exchange for his name and 17 ritual objects which were shared between Taramanini in Raiatea and Hua'atua in Afa'ahiti, and this was the origin of the players who came from 'Oro's house in Raiatea.

ANACHRONISTIC MYTHS

SOME MYTHS are very difficult to date, as new material is often added by the storyteller to help his listeners understand. In the case of shamanic cycles the older portions retain their ancient forms while the new material can be adapted by simply replacing relevant sections. In the case of less formalized myths, such as "fireside tales," the storyteller has more latitude, so that many Oceanic myths recorded since colonial times often have details which are anachronistic, referring to bottles, glass windows, and other introduced artifacts that were unknown to previous storytellers. The myth of Tagaloa's sacrifice, recorded at the turn of the nineteenth century from a chief of Manu'a, may have a traditional base, but there are grounds for doubt. The places mentioned in Micronesia shared German administration with Samoa at that time, kissing the European way is mentioned, and Tagaloa speaks from the skies like Jehovah. A story of migration from the Sunda Islands to Hawaii was current at that time. Similarly a prize essay published in a newspaper told of African migration to Fiji in the Kaunitoni canoe. Based on speculation, the story was accepted by many Fijians and is now told as a cherished relic of Fijian mythology.

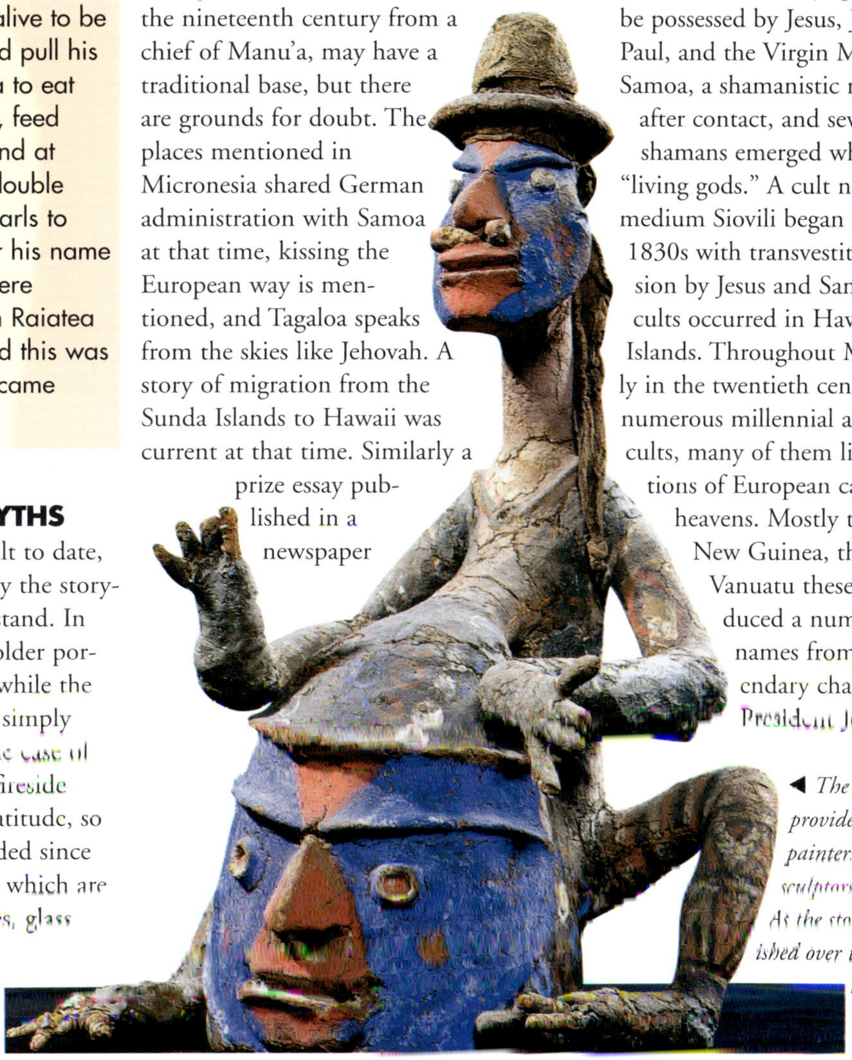

POST-CHRISTIAN MYTHOLOGY

WITH THE INTRODUCTION of Christianity, first to Micronesia in the seventeenth century, then to Polynesia from the late eighteenth century and from the 1830s in Melanesia, there was rapid nominal conversion to the new religion. The contact experience led to the formation of a number of syncretist cults. In the Society Islands, a major cult from 1826, known as Mamaia, was led by "prophets" claiming to be possessed by Jesus, John the Baptist, Paul, and the Virgin Mary. In Tonga and Samoa, a shamanistic revival occurred soon after contact, and several powerful shamans emerged who were regarded as "living gods." A cult named after its chief medium Siovili began in Samoa in the 1830s with transvestite priests and possession by Jesus and Samoan spirits. Feather cults occurred in Hawaii and the Gilbert Islands. Throughout Melanesia, particularly in the twentieth century, there have been numerous millennial and traditional-type cults, many of them linked with expectations of European cargo sent from the heavens. Mostly to be found in Papua New Guinea, the Solomons, and Vanuatu these cults have introduced a number of new god names from indigenous legendary characters to America's President Johnson.

◀ *The ancient stories have provided the inspiration for painters, storytellers, and sculptors over many generations. As the stories have been embellished over the years, so the art has become more and more spectacular.*

OCEANIC GODS

GODS AND SPIRITS were legion throughout the region, particularly in Melanesia and the Marquesas where tribal groupings were separated by mountains and valleys. High gods were more prevalent in Eastern Polynesia and Tonga than in Samoa and Micronesia where spirits predominated. Each Polynesian group developed its own pantheon, often grouped around its three most important gods as in Tonga, Tahiti, and Hawaii. Samoa had two main cults, while the Marquesas and New Zealand had family pantheons that seemed to reflect multi-tribal diversity. Most gods had human or anthropomorphic forms though they could also be worshiped as inanimate objects.

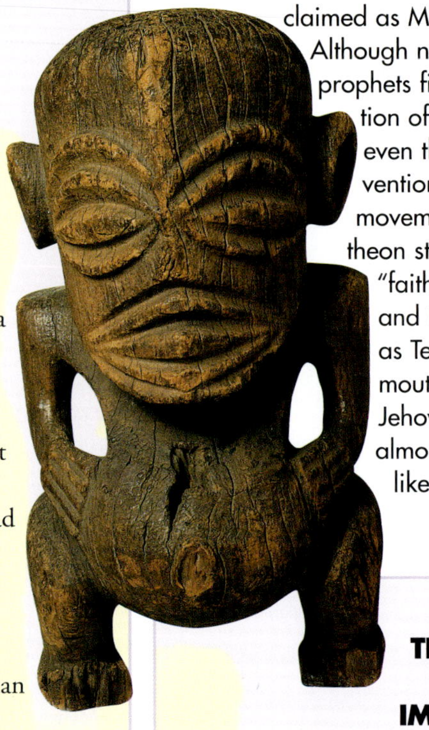

MODERN MAORI MYTHOLOGY

SYNCRETIC CHRISTIAN cults have been prevalent among the New Zealand Maori since the emergence of the Papahurihia movement in 1833. This early religion was in opposition to the Protestant missionaries and invoked the biblical serpent Nakahi, the prophet claiming to be the medium for Te Atua Wera (the Fiery God), the fiery serpent on the rod of Moses. In all these movements the old *tohunga* was replaced by Maori prophets. Of special interest was the Tuhoe prophet Rua Kenana Hepetipa, a Maori messiah, who experienced a vision on Maungapohatu, the sacred mountain of the Tuhoe, in 1905, after being sent there by the archangel Gabriel. On the mountain he encountered the ancestor Whaitiri, a potent goddess of the night world (*po*), who revealed to him a sacred diamond of great power. In 1906, Rua was baptized as Hepetipa (*Hephzibah*), the one who would make the land fruitful, and claimed as Messiah. Although not all the prophets fit into the tradition of living gods, even the fairly conventional Ratana movement gave pantheon status to the "faithful angels," and Ratana himself as Te Mangai (the mouthpiece of Jehovah) had almost god-like status.

THE SEARCH FOR IMMORTALITY

A CARVED LINTEL from a Maori meeting house exhibited in the Wanganui Museum, replicated in many villages, shows Maui attempting to pass through the body of his ancestor Hinenuitepo, the personification of death. Maui, accompanied by a flock of birds, came upon the goddess asleep. Warning the birds to be silent Maui wriggled his way into her body. Hardly had he got his head inside when the birds could not control their mirth, and the fantail's twitter woke the goddess who brought her giant thighs together in a thunderous clap and snapped Maui in two, ending his quest for immortality.

TRANSITION ORIGIN MYTHS FROM THE NEW GUINEA EASTERN HIGHLANDS

IN THE BEGINNING there were three brothers. One became the father of the grasslands people, one became the father of the bush people, and the third brother went away and never came back. When the white people came to New Guinea the old ones said: "These are the children of the third brother. He went away and obtained all kinds of possessions and learned all kinds of magic, and now he has returned. His children have access to clothing and tools, vehicles and tinned food from the outside world. The whiteman does not make anything he has so it must be made by the spirits. The spirits are our spirits too. The whiteman should share these goods with us. Some of us have seen goods arriving by sea in ships. These goods are brought from a great hole in the bottom of the sea. Men take their ships out there and spirits go down on ladders to bring the cargo up from the depths."

The people of the Binumarien valley now have a new myth: "In the beginning God made heaven and earth, and he made a garden in which he put man. God took a knife and scratched Adam's arm and found that the blood wasn't flowing in his veins. So God killed a chicken and gave it to Adam. When Adam ate the chicken, the blood began to run in his arm. God made Adam and Eve both men and, when Eve ate the fruit, as punishment God turned her into a woman."

▲ *Some gods, such as this fisherman's god, were portrayed with some human characteristics, such as clearly defined face and limbs.* ▶ *This sculpture is believed to represent the war god, Ku. He is portrayed here as a shark, a common synonym for a chief. Some of the gods possessed the ability to change their form so are depicted in many different ways.*

CARGO CULTS

THE GODS OF the cargo cults, if they can be so called, were really returning dead or the ancestors, though, as among the Maori, the "prophets" often assumed semi-divine status. Many of these prophets, like the perovera Genakuiya of Buna, were traditional shamans able to visit the invisible spiritual realms, and now claiming to visit the Christian heaven and the gates of the Christian hell. Most cults were millenarian, though often God was not Jehovah or Jesus but a syncretistic deity such as God-Kilibob of the Madang District, New Guinea, in 1942. Other cults were strictly "custom" without Christian content. Even some of the leaders who used the language of the missionaries really meant their local god.

The myths from the eastern highlands of New Guinea are taken from actual accounts given by the people of the Binumarien valley to missionaries and recorded in their diaries between 1954 and 1992. The first helps to explain cargo doctrine as the people had never seen the white man "fashioning an airplane or a motor car, making any of the clothing he wears, putting all that food in tins." The second adapts the biblical myth to the local culture.

▲ *A painted Maori dancer in modern day New Zealand.*

Australia

INTRODUCTION

HUMANS SETTLED AUSTRALIA during a time when the continent was linked by land to the islands of what are now Indonesia and Papua New Guinea. The earliest recorded evidence for human presence in Australia comes from the Upper Swan River region in Western Australia and dates to almost 40,000 years before the present. It has been estimated that at the time of European contact (1788), there were at least 300,000 human beings on the continent of Australia. Although difficult to estimate because of the rapid depopulation and dislocation of Aboriginal people that ensued shortly after European settlement, a conservative estimate is that there were 500 distinct tribes or dialect groups in Australia at the end of the eighteenth century. The Torres Strait Islands, though officially within the national boundaries of Australia, are more appropriately considered culturally to be part of southern Papua, at least traditionally.

In terms of human lifestyle, the continent of Australia at the time of European contact was dominated by the hunting and foraging mode of subsistence The climate and terrain in Australia varies markedly, from the arid desert of the major portion of the inland region to the more fertile and watered valleys and watercourses of the coastal areas. However, even in the coastal areas of, for example, Queensland and South Australia, where abundant fish, vegetable and animal resources afforded the possibility of permanent residence, fixed habitation was rare. Populations moved over considerable distances, not only for the purposes of obtaining food, but also to establish and maintain political, marital and ceremonial alliances between groups.

DESPITE THEIR isolation on an island continent, Aboriginal Australians had regular and important contacts with the people of what is now Papua New Guinea—through the linking Torres Strait Islands—and to the islands of eastern Indonesia. Macassan traders regularly visited the coast of Arnhem Land, and the effects of these visits are recorded in the myth, song and painting of the Yolngu people of north-east Arnhem Land.

Anthropologically, the Aboriginal populations throughout Australia first became renowned for the intricacy of their kinship organisation. In all areas, relatives were divided by categories called sections and subsections, based on the intersecting of male and female descent principles. The sections and subsections stipulated what category a person's spouse should fall into and therefore made marriage subject to specific kinship rules. These sections and subsections also fulfilled important ceremonial functions, such as initiation and the transmission of secret religious knowledge between groups.

The links between the great mythological traditions of Australia and Melanesia are pronounced. However, contrary to what might seem like geographical and historical intuition, the movement of mythical themes evidently went from Australia to New Guinea rather than the other way around. In Australia and in the southern part of New Guinea the cult of the bull roarer was a central focus of male ritual life. In the case of the Aranda, bull-roarers are called by the same name as the sacred boards (*tjuringa*). The cult is essentially a glorification of male phallic power. Myths are re-enacted by performers who, in a disguised form, bear a phallic symbol identical with the ancestor who is represented.

Along with this movement of phallic imagery between Australia and New Guinea there also traveled the serpent motif. The python or serpent is a more complicated symbol than the bull roarer, because it has both female and male characteristics, and these ambivalent properties are seized upon in myths of both regions. The Souw myth of the interior Daribi of New Guinea stresses the linking of sexual knowledge and shaming with human culture. It is cognate with the central myth of the Wagilak cycle in Arnhem Land, where the revelation of women's menstrual capacities cancels and limits the power of male phallic capacity.

◀ *Traditional aboriginal art depicting animals.*

Influences upon Australian Aboriginal cultures came from Asia as well as Melanesia. For at least 200 years, Macassan fishermen from eastern Indonesia made annual voyages to the coast of Arnhem Land in search of the exotic delicacy *trepang* (sea-slug). Among the Yolngu of north-east Arnhem Land, Warramiri clan members of the Yirritja *moiety* (marriage class) once mediated relations between local Aboriginal and Macassans. The Macassan traders used the title Rajah (king) for those Aboriginal elders who acted as their brokers. In turn, these leaders controlled trade with other Aboriginal tribes of the interior.

We should, however, be careful not to see mythology as solely a relic of primordial history, a way of preserving in the present events that occurred before written history. A system of mythology is a theory of the world as it is as much as a portrait of a world that has been, and it explains as much, if not more, about how people should and can act today. Today, it is the mining companies who confront the effects of Aboriginal mythical landscapes most concertedly, in their attempts to win mining and exploration leases on Aboriginal land. Sacred sites, validated by knowledge of mythology, are one obstacle in the way of mining companies seeking permission to operate on Aboriginal land. The way in which Aboriginal communities have used their mythology to resist the encroachment of mining interests is Aboriginal mythology's most signal feature in Australia today.

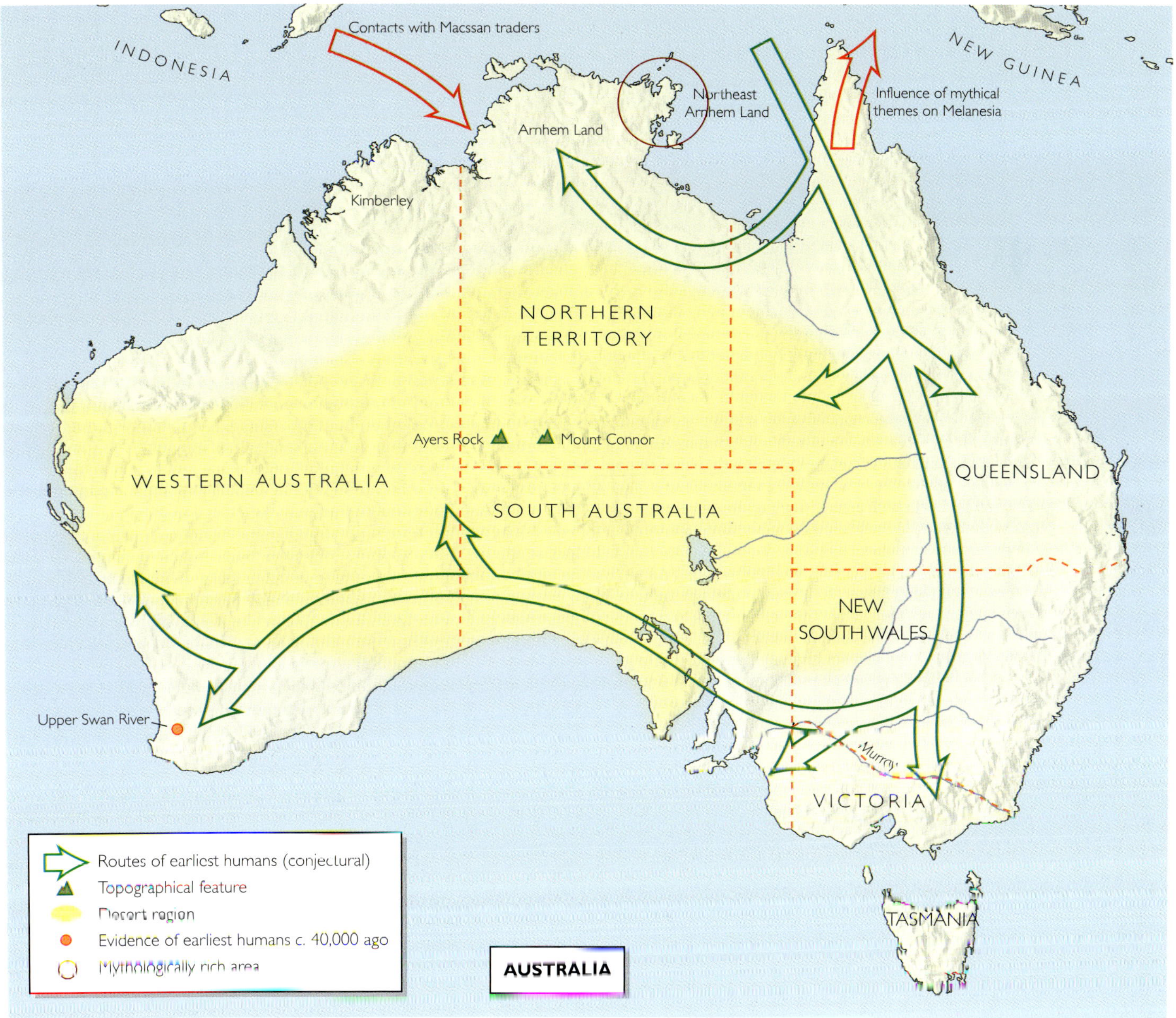

◀ *Figure believed to have been created by clan ancestral beings who formed the landscape during the Dreamtime.*

THE FURNACE OF BIRRINYDJI

THERE ARE INTERESTING twists to the confrontation between Aboriginal and foreign cultures in the myth of Birrinydji that demonstrate the creativity and resiliency of Aboriginal mythology as a mode of knowledge. Macassans may well have made iron on the Arnhem Land coast, and local Aboriginals probably witnessed this and may have participated in its production. The many Aboriginals who traveled to Macassar during the 200 years of the trepang trade would also undoubtedly have come across the industry.

In 1988, 80 years after the end of the Macassan era, the Yolngu man David Burrumarra promoted the view that mining on his land at Dholtji would help restore wealth and status to Aboriginal people—a wealth and status that had been usurped first by these Macassan traders and then later by European settlers. Burrumarra became certain that mining was a part of Aboriginal history and a path to the improvement of Aboriginal life. Since the Dreamtime, Burrumarra maintained, coastal hematite outcrops had been transformed into iron-bladed tools by Yolngu people working under the guidance of the Dreamtime figure Birrinydji. Burrumarra sought a return to this "golden era." This story seems to have much in common with the "cargo cult" mythology that has flourished in Melanesia since the coming of the Europeans.

CREATOR BEINGS

THROUGHOUT AUSTRALIA, the subject of the great majority of myths is the wanderings, journeys, and actions of certain ancestral creator beings. Characteristically, they moved across the landscape creating its notable features and distinguishing landmarks, such as waterholes, mountains and specific rock formations, and also bringing into being the various species, human and non-human, which now populate the earth. For example, in Arnhem Land, the Wagilak sisters are centrally important creator beings. As they traveled north from their origin in central Australia, they plunged their digging sticks into the ground at various spots. From these spots waterholes gushed forth.

While they created the landscape and its plant and animal species, these creator beings also named the places they visited and the species they created that inhabit them. Along with the names, the beings also sang songs in which these acts of naming featured. Thus, myth is commonly recited through the medium of song throughout Aboriginal Australia. For example, in part of the myth of the two Mamandabari heroes among the Walbiri of central Australia, they pass a waterhole named Wurulyuwanda. On the waterhole they see whistling ducks and galah cockatoos eating grass seeds. They name these creatures by "singing" them.

TRACKS AND TOTEMS

THE ROUTES OF THE CREATOR beings are referred to as their tracks. The tracks of important ancestor beings characteristically went across and through the countries of different groups of people. Thus it is common that no local group, clan or language group owns or knows a complete myth. Usually, a local group knows the segment of the myth that narrates the story of the being while it sojourned in their country. This necessitates different groups coming together periodically in order that the ritual recreation of the entire myth can be fully accomplished. For example, in central Australia, the two Mamandabari heroes traveled over an enormous area; no one man knew the myth in its entirety. This necessitates custodians from different areas coming together to perform the Gadjari ritual which is based on this myth cycle.

The concept of totemism is integral to Australian Aboriginal mythology. This is, broadly speaking, the use of a natural species or feature as an emblem of a person or group. Each clan has a variety of different totemic species and items that are specific to it and which differentiate it from other clans in the same area. Since all totems are associated with a particular place, totem designations are always designations about which locality a person is associated with in specific ways.

THE ALL FATHER

IN SOUTH-EASTERN Australia, we can speak of a single male creator being, whom the early anthropologist A. W. Howitt referred to as the "All Father." Among the people of the Lower Murray River area of South Australia, he is referred to as Ngurunderi; further up the Murray River he is called Baiame, Daramulun, and other names. In other parts of Australia the feminine principle is also important, and it is possible to speak of a Great Mother. In north-east Arnhem Land, the two Djanggawul sisters are called "daughters of the sun": they represent the sun and its life-giving properties.

THE WAGILAK MYTH

AT THE BEGINNING of time, the Wagilak sisters set off on foot towards the sea, naming places, animals, and plants as they went. One of them was pregnant and the other had a child. Before their departure they had both had incestuous relations with men of their own *moiety* (marriage class). After the birth of the younger sister's child, they continued their journey and one day stopped near a waterhole where the great python Yurlunggor lived. The older sister polluted the water when her menstrual blood flowed into it. The outraged python came out, caused a deluge of rain and a general flood, and then swallowed the women and their children. When the python raised himself the waters covered the surface of the earth and its vegetation. When he lay down again the flood receded.

◄ *Aboriginal female figure, which represents different sacred beings in different clans.*

► *Sacred disks represent the immortal spirit, the patterns represent a sacred site.*

SERPENTS AND RAINBOWS

SERPENTS OF ALL KINDS recur in Australian Aboriginal mythology, from the Rainbow Serpent, which is found in its archetypal form among the groups of the central desert, to the Carpet Snake whose dreaming tracks stretch along the coast of eastern Australia. Throughout Australia, the Rainbow Serpent is an important figure and motif in myth. The serpent is usually of immense size and lives in deep waterholes. The Rainbow Serpent appears in many guises throughout Australia. In central Australia, the *wanambi* traveled from Aneri Spring, near the South Australia–Northern Territory border, to the Musgrave Ranges. At times, it made long journeys around the circumference of Mount Connor. The tracks he made at this time are often symbolized in painting by large concentric circles. The path that the *wanambi* traveled became marked with rock formations and sandhills, visible today.

The groups near the Proserpine River in North Queensland believed that rain is transformed into quartz crystals at the spot where the rainbow touches the ground. In south-eastern Queensland, the rainbow—*takkan* among Kabi Kabi speakers—would sometimes reveal the presence of such crystals in the bodies of men. These men would be able to become *gundil*, or sorcery-doctors, capable of healing and other feats of magic.

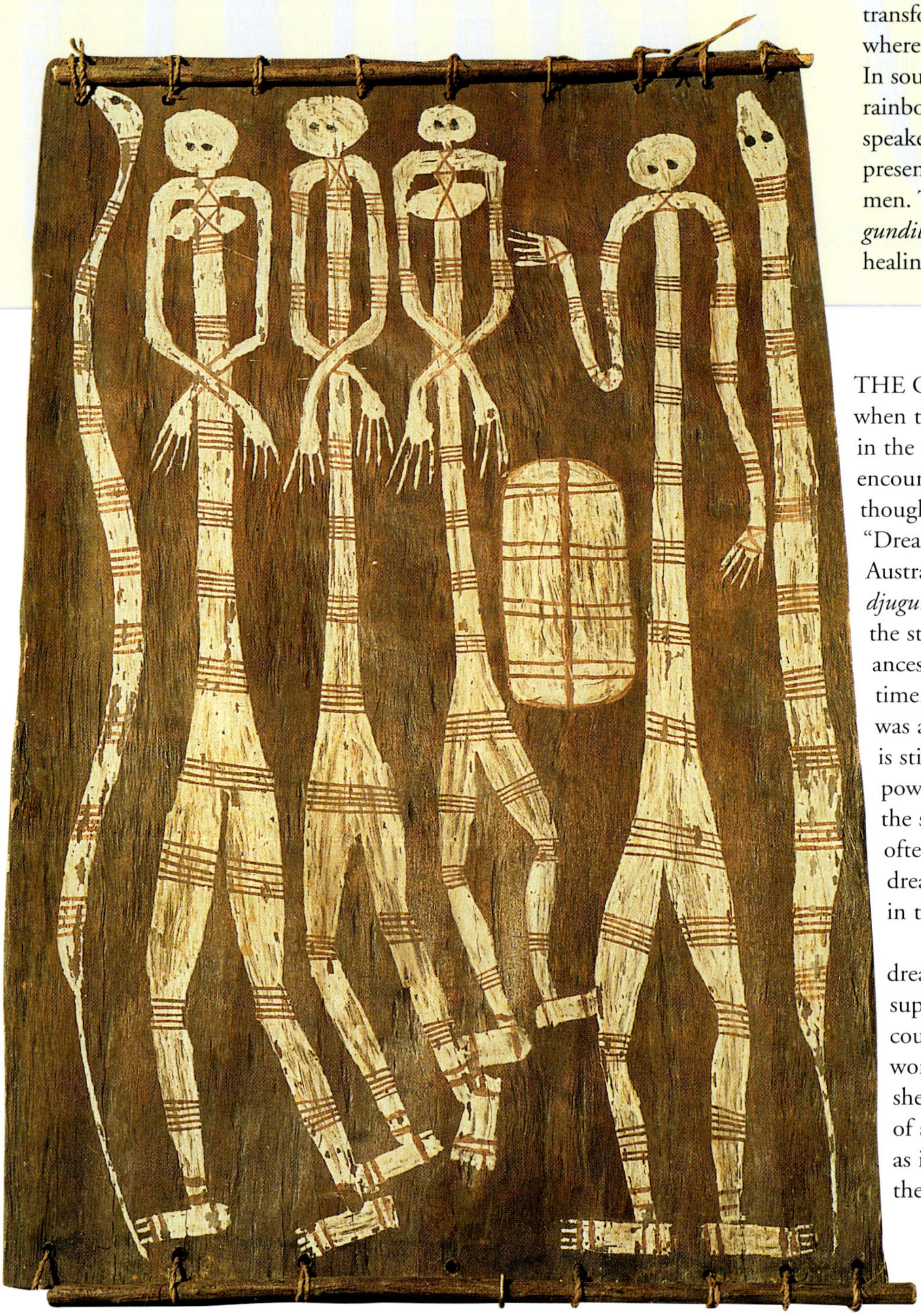

THE DREAMING

THE CONCEPT OF the Creation Time, when the ancestral beings made the world in the form in which present-day people encounter it, is widespread in Aboriginal thought. This is commonly called the "Dreamtime" or "the Dreaming" in Australia. The Walbiri call this period *djugurba*, which strictly speaking refers to the stories and attendant designs about ancestral actions during this creative time. It means an act of creation which was an actual event in ancestral times but is still on-going and still exerting creative power in the human present. Access to the significance of ancestral creation is often gained through the power of dreams, which is why the term is used in this way.

The Walbiri say they themselves dream of the designs their ancestors are supposed to have laid down across the country. In other areas of Australia, a woman may, shortly before learning she is pregnant, dream of a species or of a certain place. This is interpreted as indicating the totemic affiliation of the child and its spiritual progenitor.

◀ *Male and female figures accompanied by snakes.*

THE BULL-ROARER

A BULL-ROARER is an oblong, oval piece of wood, usually inscribed with sacred designs. It is tied to a cord and then swung through the air over the head. The loud noise it makes when this happens is said to be the voice of the male ancestor come to swallow the male initiates. This is done to frighten the boys and expose them to the power of the cult. Later in their entry to the ritual life, older boys will have the secret of the bull-roarer revealed to them.

ANCESTORS

ANOTHER ASPECT of this inscriptive mythic activity is that the bodies of the ancestral creator beings themselves become detached and fixed in the landscape. The ancestor beings, for example among the Aranda of the central desert, left parts of their bodies in the places in which they traveled. A married woman, engaged in the daily search for food, might feel a sudden pain inside her body which she recognizes as an early sign of pregnancy. Later she would show her husband the exact spot at which this sensation occurred. After consulting with the leading old men of his own clan, the man learns which original totemic ancestor either dwelt in this locality or visited it on one of his wanderings. It is then concluded that this totemic ancestor has caused the woman's pregnancy, either by entering into her body himself, or else by hurling a small bull-roarer at her hips and thus causing the acute pains which suddenly came upon her. The child when born will belong to the totem of this ancestor.

The relationship between myth and ritual is central to Australian Aboriginal ceremonial life and to its graphic representation by way of various visual media, primarily painting and carving. To simplify matters, it can be said that the myths provide the charters or templates for human ritual action whereby people attempt to keep ancestral creativity and fertility alive and working on behalf of present-day human groups.

CREATION MYTH OF THE UNAMBAL

IN NORTH-WEST AUSTRALIA, the Unambal say that, in the beginning, only sky and earth existed. Ungud, the creator being, lived under the earth in the form of a great python. Ungud is associated with both the earth and the water. The sky being, Wallanganda, is associated with the Milky Way. Wallanganda is supposed to have made everything, but it was Ungud who made the water deep and caused the rain to fall, and this is how life began on earth. Together, Wallanganda and Ungud created everything.

However, the acts of creation only occurred at night, when the two beings dreamed. Ungud transformed himself into the beings of which he dreamed, while Wallanganda also dreamed the beings he gave birth to. By means of a spiritual force, Wallanganda projected these dreamed beings into red, black, and white designs, the images of which, according to the Unambal, can still be found in caves and rocks.

In Arnhem Land, the Djanggawul and Wagilak creator beings were responsible for creating and naming all the species and places in the landscape. They also placed sacred emblems, *rangga*, in waterholes. The *rangga* are re-created by living human beings as adjuncts of ritual re-enactments of these primordial acts of mythic creation.

WANDJINA

WANDJINA ARE CLAN SPIRIT beings in the Kimberley region of Western Australia. They are named creator beings, each of whom is responsible for forming a portion of the landscape, its animals and plants and significant topographical features. The Wandjina were the first people. Each one entered a cave and laid himself down and died when his creative activity was finished. The cave paintings of the Wandjina that are found today are considered to be the literal incarnation of these ancestral beings. They are still approached by present-day Aboriginal inhabitants to aid in increasing the fertility of plants and animals upon which Aboriginal people depend for food.

◀ *An incised wooden sacred board.*

▲ *Wandjina are ancestral beings from the sea and the sky*

NGURUNDERI

NGURUNDERI TRAVELED down the Murray River in South Australia in search of the great Murray Cod (*pondi*). He speared the fish and it swam away, thrashing its tail and widening the river to its present great size. Ngurunderi sent a signal to his brother-in-law Nepele. Nepele waited for the fish and speared it near Point McLeay (Raukkan). The two men cut the fish up and, throwing bits of fish into Lake Alexandrina, called out the name of every fish species now found there, and each fish was brought into being in this way. With the last piece, they said, "You keep being Murray Cod."

Ngurunderi continued to pursue his two wives, who had run away from him after a quarrel. At the place Larlangangel, he lifted his canoe and placed it into the sky, where it became the Milky Way.

After further pursuing the women, he came upon them at Encounter Bay. He caused a great storm to appear which drowned the women, who turned into the two small islands called The Pages, off Kangaroo Island. Afterward, Ngurunderi himself crossed over to Kangaroo Island. Sitting under a casuarina tree, he dived into the water first to cleanse his spirit, and eventually died and went into the sky.

◀ *Artwork on bark showing a hunter, a kangaroo, and other figures.*

▼ *This aboriginal bark painting depicts a pair of whales. Aboriginal mythologies recount the stories of creation of every living thing.*

MYTH AND RITUAL

THE MYTHS DETAIL important acts of creation and naming. They detail the power of ancestral fertility. In this respect, they demonstrate the importance of gender difference as a general principle of Aboriginal social and cosmological organization. Throughout Australia, much important sacred lore and ceremonial knowledge is in the hands of men. Women were traditionally forbidden to hear or view anything pertaining to men's knowledge, often on pain of death. In western Arnhem Land myth, for example, after Yirawadbad passed on the *ubar* men's ceremony to Nadulmi, Nadulmi asked the bird Djig, "Shall we show it to the women?" and in response was told, "No, this is only for older men, we cannot show it to women and children." More recently, anthropologists have also discovered the previously unreported existence of parallel domains of women's religious knowledge in central and south Australia. This knowledge is described as exclusively the right of women to control, pass on, and manage.

▶ *X-ray style bark illustration of kangaroo.*

THE *GUWAK* CUCKOO

IN THE PAINTING by the Yolngu artists Banapan Maymuru, the subject of the painting is the mythical journey of the *guwak*, or koel cuckoo. The site of this painting is Djarrapki, a brackish lake between sand dunes along the Gulf of Carpentaria, just to the north of Blue Mud Bay in North-East Arnhem Land. Two *guwak*, two possums, two emus and other creator beings (*wangarr*) started out from a place in the Ritharrngu country. Each animal gathered food for itself. The possum would spin its fur into lengths of string. After spinning a certain length, he would be told to stop by the *guwak*. These strings, which varied in length from place to place, were then given to the human clan members of the different places where the creator animals camped and found food. They became sacred objects used in clan rituals.

In some versions, they finished their journey at Djarrapki. There they found a landscape without features. But by their actions they transformed it into the place with the topographical features it has today. The painting shows the possums on the sides, and the cuckoos in the center facing each other. Along the lengths of their bodies are shown the cashew trees where they foraged for nuts each night. The emus are shown in the center, back to back underneath the cashew tree with its spreading vegetation.

COMPONENTS OF MYTHOLOGY

THERE ARE THREE components to Australian mythology and its religious significance. The first is the body of mythology itself, considered as a set of stories. The second is the system of graphic designs which provide a visual form of the actions of myths. The third is the country itself, the creation and distinctive features of which, the myth and visual art provides an origin account. Thus myth is always localized: knowledge of and control of a mythic episode and its attendant ritual-artistic complex is always restricted to the present-day custodians of the sites of which the myth gives an account in religious and cosmological terms.

Songs, the form through which myths are commonly recited, characteristically focus on key words and references which themselves are connected with specific localities within the country. The songs provide a way to help people remember appropriate details concerning the sacred history of the site in question.

THE ALL-MOTHER AND THE ALL-FATHER

FERTILITY IS A CENTRAL concern of Aboriginal religions throughout the continent, and it is common for the sexual capacities of human men and women to be the focus of broader attempts to maintain the regenerative nature of the cosmos. Both males and females figure as key creator beings in different parts of Aboriginal Australia. In the north-west and north-east of Australia, male culture heroes are the most important mythical figures. In the south-east there is a single great hero; Baiami, Bundjil, Ngurunderi and so forth, and he is male as well.

But in the center of the country, in the Central Desert and throughout the Northern Territory into Arnhem Land, it is the female figure which is dominant. The great Gunabibi myth-ritual cycle centers around the "Old Woman," a figure that is also found prominently in the areas of the Roper, Macarthur, and Victoria rivers. She is known variously as Kunapipi, Mumuna, Kliarin-Kliari. She is said to be the source of life in both the human and the natural world. The Old Woman is tied to fertility rites centering around the Rainbow Serpent. The serpent is said to have "made the path" into the female womb so that ancestral spirits can revivify present-day humans when they are born.

MYTH AND ART IN AUSTRALIA

THROUGHOUT AUSTRALIA, but particularly in the Northern Territory, graphic designs are an important adjunct to the public narration of myth for ritual and ceremonial purposes. In central Australia, people such as the Walbiri and Pintupi have become renowned for the iconographic designs they paint on various surfaces—for example, the human body, sand, sacred artifacts such as shields and bull-roarers, and more recently with acrylic paints on canvas—which depict certain mythic episodes. In Arnhem Land, on the north coast of the Northern Territory, local painters inscribe their designs on bark and wood-carvings.

Common motifs in central Australia include the concentric circle, which can stand for a camp, waterhole, person, tree, or ceremonial ground, connected by a series of dotted patterns depicting the movement of an ancestral being from place to place. In Arnhem Land, designs tend to be less abstract but are also concerned with the visual representation of certain mythic episodes of ancestral movement and creation.

In both areas, the knowledge of these designs and the rights to paint them are governed by an elaborate social and political system which distributes access to sacred knowledge unevenly within the community. The strategic revelation of secret/sacred designs in the course of public ritual is a major factor in the social impact of ritual itself.

MOON AND DUGONG

A MAN FROM THE YIRRITJA *moiety* named Moon, lived with his sister named Dugong. Once they were out digging for edible bulbs of the lily and lotus plants. While doing so, the sister was bitten by leeches. To relieve the itching, she ran down to the sea. Before she dived in, she asked her brother what he himself would do now. After speaking with him, she decided to turn herself into a dugong. Her brother Moon agreed to go with her. When they died, Dugong's bones were found but she herself did not come back. Moon however did not die; his bones became seashells and he himself revived after eating lily and lotus roots.

The painting of this myth of the Yirkalla of North-East Arnhem Land shows a crescent moon and a full moon. The area of cross-hatching surrounding the moon disk is said by the Yolngu to be Moon's wet-weather camp. The elongated designs are probably the lily and lotus bulbs and roots. The cross-hatching in the background stands for the swamp where these plants are growing as well as the shimmer of light caused by moonlight on water. It could also represent the light of the evening star shining on the sacred totemic site of Moon and Dugong, as recorded in the song cycle associated with this myth.

GURUWARI

THE BEST DOCUMENTATION of the intimate relationship between myth and visual representation in Aboriginal Australia comes from the Central Desert and Arnhem Land. In the Central Desert, there is among the Walbiri the notion of *guruwari*. This term refers both to the name of conventional iconographic elements of their painted representations, and to the essence of ancestral fertility, which are thought to be both represented and made incarnate through these designs. *Guruwari* thus have both an "inside" and an "outside" manifestation. As the invisible inner essence of a thing, it denotes the hidden, potent power of the landscape, placed there by the ancestors yet still exerting fertile power on today's beings. As the outer manifestation of such potency, it means any visible sign of such potency, such as the designs painted on young men's bodies when they are undergoing initiation and which represent their ancestors.

BULARDEMO: CORONATION HILL

STARTING IN 1985, a dispute arose around the question of whether uranium mining should proceed on a site in the Northern Territory called Coronation Hill, which might become the site of a major uranium excavation project. A Government-appointed body heard evidence from the Jawoyn people, who lived in the area and claimed that unimaginable destruction, as far away as Sydney and Melbourne, would be caused by disturbance of the male hunter-creator Bulardemo, who was embodied in the landscape. Coronation Hill was later incorporated within the boundaries of Kakadu National Park in the early 1990s, as part of the then-Federal Government's decision not to allow mining to proceed.

THE RAIN MAN, ATAIN-TJINA

AMONG THE ARANDA of the Central Desert, the mythical creator being, Atain-tjina, was the most important of the rain men. His totem was the *murunta* or water snake. He made his camp on a far-away seashore along with many other younger rain men.

Atain-tjina would prey upon these younger men, capturing them and hurling them into the sea, where they would be swallowed by a gigantic water snake. After two days, Atain-tjina would order the water snake to disgorge the body of the young man it had swallowed into the smoke of a fire.

While in the body of the water snake, the young men would acquire some of the snake's scales, which were gleaming white in color. After being released, one of the young men traveled to an area of open plain, and there he rubbed the scale on a stone. At this point, the young man turned into a cloud and rose into the sky. In this form, he turned himself upside down, letting his hair hang down in the form of rain. The rain poured onto the earth. The young man threw down more scales that he had taken from the snake's body. These became lightning flashes.

Then the spirit of Atain-tjina left his sleeping body and rose into the sky as a rainbow. The young cloud man grasped the rainbow and fastened it to his head. They traveled together to the west, and the rain stopped. This is why there are long droughts in Central Australia. They continue until Atain-tjina throws another young man into the sea and begins the cycle again.

◀ *Carved aboriginal ancestor boards.*

▼ *People of the Malaiische tribe.*

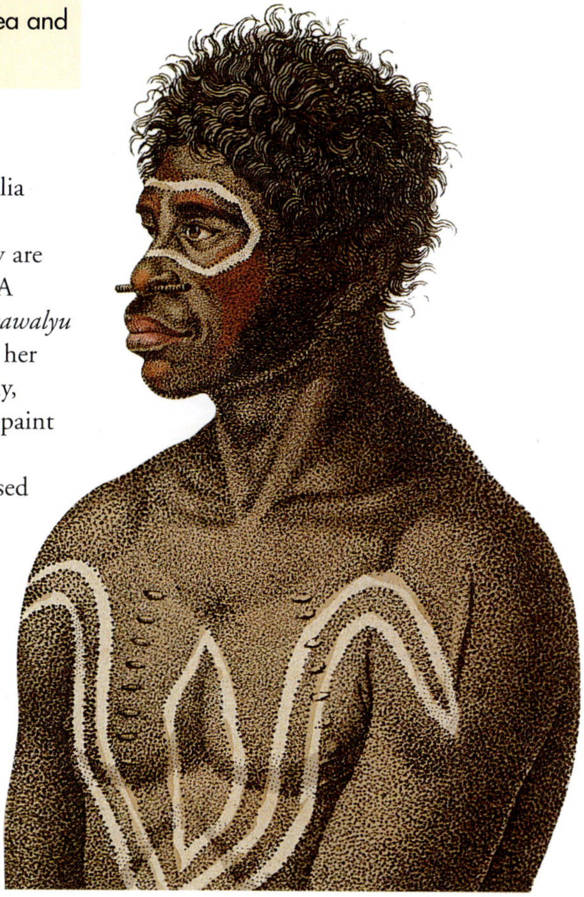

WALBIRI DESIGNS

THE WALBIRI of Central Australia have several categories of designs. *Yawalyu* are women's designs; they are painted only on women's bodies. A woman receives the vision of the *yawalyu* design in a dream but may pass on her own designs to her daughters. Ideally, women related as sisters-in-law will paint each other's bodies with their own designs. The designs are supposed to promote the fertility and sexual attractiveness of women.

A parallel class of designs are called *ilbinji* by the Walbiri and are painted by men. They are supposed to promote men's sexual attractiveness. Common motifs for these designs are the emu and other birds, because of their phallic significance, and fire, because the smoke of fire is used to attract a woman.

More ritually important men's designs are termed *guruwari* proper and can be said to be the primary manifestation of ancestral power. They are painted on the ground, on *tjuringa* boards and stones, and on weapons.

An important dimension of this form of representation is how intimately it is tied to the sense of touch. Walbiri women will accompany a narrative with iconographic designs traced out in the sand on which they are sitting, so that a sign-language version of their spoken narrative is always given alongside the verbal story.

MIMI SPIRITS

THE *MIMI* ARE SMALL, very thin spirits. They are very fragile and can only hunt in calm weather. When humans approach, they escape by blowing on a rock face—a crevice opens up into which they hide. They are considered harmless to living people but are not trustworthy. Their staple food is a type of yam that grows in Arnhem Land. Paintings of *mimi* spirits are very common in cave art throughout western Arnhem Land. The drawings show them as stick-like figures, often with prominent genitalia shown on the male figures and large pendulous breasts on the females.

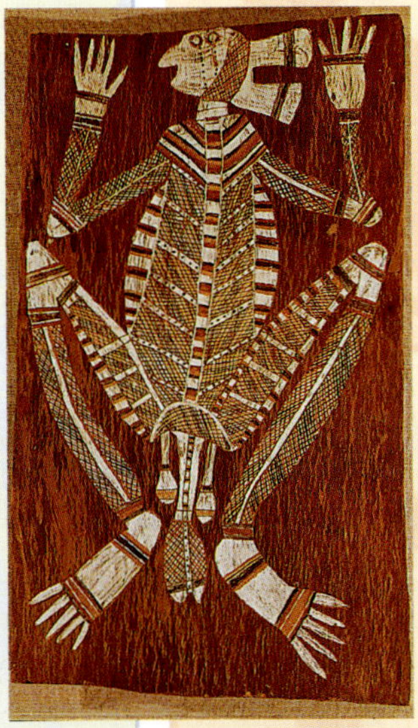

THE STORY OF EMU

IN THIS STORY of the Dalabon (Northern Territory), the emu used to consume all the food that her fellow birds brought back. In vain they appealed to her to share. One day, the jabiru and brolga birds spotted a kangaroo and they returned to camp to inform others of their find.

The cuckoo-shrike had a sore foot and could not come with them. So they dressed its foot and left the camp. They speared the kangaroo and roasted it by a creek.

The jabiru and brolga birds convinced the emu to search far afield for soft grass to soak up the gravy from the roasting kangaroo. While it was away, the jabiru and brolga cut up the kangaroo and flew up into the sky with the pieces, leaving only the tail behind with the grass pigeon. Emu finally returned and found the deserted cooking spot, but there were no fellow birds and no meat. Finally she spotted the grass pigeon, who flew away with the kangaroo tail. All the birds laughed and cried out, "We don't want to stay with that old woman." The emu had had many followers but now because she did not share, she had lost them all. The emu then swallowed a stone, which is why emus lay eggs now.

DESIGN ELEMENTS

THE USE OF FINGERS to trace designs in sand or paint attests to the seamless way in which peoples' hands both generate a mode of livelihood from the earth as well as an artistic and mythical account of that life at one and the same time. The iconographic elements represent a visual counterpart to spoken language. Since ancestral myths and other stories usually take the form of a journey over land, the designs in effect make a map out of a narrative that has at its center a journey or other movement through territory. For example, a straight line can be a spear, a fighting stick, or a digging stick; or it can be the direction of movement of an actor. A series of circles in a row means an actor walking or dancing. A shallow curved line is an actor sleeping or reclining. A parabolic arch is an actor sitting. Circles have a wide range of meanings: they can be a nest, hole, waterhole, tree, fruit, egg, or camp. An oval is a food or water container, a bark carrier for a child, a shield, a spear-thrower, or a hollow scooped out of the sand for sleeping.

◀ *A bark painting showing an aboriginal male spirit of the rocks, or* Mimi.

▼ *Every picture has hidden depths in aboriginal art. Beyond the easily recognizable forms of animals and people lie the stories, told by the curvature of the lines, the symbols and spatial relationships.*

THE DJANGGAWUL

THE THREE DJANGGAWUL beings, a man, his elder sister, and his younger sister, all of the Dua *moiety*, were living on the island of Bralgu off the coast of Arnhem Land. The man had an elongated penis, and his two sisters had elongated clitorises. These dragged along the ground as they walked and left grooves in the ground. The brother's penis and sisters' clitorises were like sacred *rangga* poles. The brother would lift his sisters' clitorises out of the way and have intercourse with them; at this time there were no prohibitions against having sex with people of one's own *moiety*.

Having left dreamings on Bralgu Island, they loaded their canoe and left for the mainland. As they paddled, they named various creatures, such as the *lindaridj* (parakeet), *damurmindjari* (wild duck), *djandja* (goanna), and they left dreamings in the places they visited. The brother made waterholes by inserting his mauwalan rangga pole in the ground, so that water flowed from these places.

They continued to travel. At Nganmaruwi, the elder sister was seen to be pregnant. The brother now placed his finger in her vagina up to the first joint, and a baby boy came out. He was very careful, because if he had opened her up too much, many people would have fallen out because there were many people stored in her uterus.

They continued to travel, leaving sacred objects, and the brother made additional wells with his mauwalan *rangga* pole. They saw various creatures and gave them names. They continued on, dragging their penis and clitorises on the ground, and the women remained pregnant. They named other creatures and left more dreamings but avoided places of the Jiritja moiety. They left sacred *rangga* emblems as they traveled and gave "inside" (secret) and "outside" (public) names to things as they encountered them.

The brother kept inserting his finger into his sister's vagina to make children fall out, each time placing his finger further and further in until he was putting his entire hand and then his whole arm in, and many children were falling out. These people became the ancestors of the various *mada* (language) groups in Arnhem Land.

JULANA AND NJIRANA (WESTERN DESERT)

WHILE THE MAN NJIRANA was wandering, the penis Julana became separated from him. It frightened the Seven Sisters, the Minmara, by swinging a small bull-roarer in an attempt to lure one of them away. Another time, and from another direction, Njirana hears a woman named Minma Mingari passing water. Julana enters the woman, but she stands up and sings for the dogs to bite Njirana's penis. When they do, Njirana retracts his penis. The dogs continue to attack the organ, with Minma Mingari following, as the penis moves and withdraws. They arrive at Anmangu where they all turn into stone boulders.

▲ *Various creatures, including the wild duck, were given their names by the three Djanggawul beings.*

THE ACRYLIC MOVEMENT IN THE CENTRAL DESERT

ABORIGINAL ARTISTS from the Northern Territory are now marketing their art in Europe and North America. Geoffrey Bardon, in the 1970s and 1980s, helped artists from the Western and Central Desert transfer their painting on to canvases for sale to museums and private collectors. Today, Central and Western Desert artists from Yuendumu, in the Walbiri country, as well as other centers such as Papunya and Kintore, paint ancestral designs using acrylic paints. Paintings by such now-renowned artists as Charley Tjungarrayi and Clifford Possum Tjalpatjari are part of the central corpus of Central Australian work in all the major galleries of Australia. In Tjungurrayi's painting *Frog Dreaming*, the subject matter is the creative process that underwrote the last Ice Age, stories that apparently have lasted over 30,000 years in the center of Australia. Many Western Desert stories concern the Tingari dreaming cycle. In this cycle of myths, groups of old men wandered around the country composing song cycles and ritual sequences.

DREAMS IN ART

A 1987 PAINTING by the Pintubi artist Riley Major Tjangala is of the Snake Dreaming at Kakarra, near Kintore, near the border of the Northern Territory and Western Australia. It depicts the snake man of the Tjakamarra subsection and his wife who inhabited this site. The circles represent the sand hills at Kakarra. The legend says that the gap between these sand hills was created by the snake when he traveled through this country during the Dreamtime.

A more modern fusion of Aboriginal and Western cosmologies is shown in a 1986 painting by Brogus Nelson Tjakamarra, a Walbiri man of Yuendumu. The artist was inspired by a depiction of Haley's comet and he utilized this as the central design of this painting. The comet's trajectory is depicted as a loop, with the comet shown in its various positions as it circles the sun. The other planets shown are the Earth, the Moon, the constellation of the Pleiades (commonly called the Seven Sisters throughout Aboriginal Australia), and Venus, the morning star. The Seven Sisters is an important Walbiri dreaming, indeed an important dreaming throughout Australia.

◀ *Geographically distant aboriginal tribes have been found to have stories, beliefs, and artifacts, such as this dreamtime bird carving, in common. As people traveled and groups met individual sub-cultures became enriched.*

▼ *This bark painting shows an x-ray view of two crocodiles. This drawing may be as a result of post-dissection studies, or may be depictions of how shamans might see them, having consumed hallucinogenic plants.*

PAINTING TECHNIQUES

IN WESTERN ARNHEM LAND, the style of painting now known as "X-Ray" is most highly developed. These show the elaborate internal anatomy of beings and animals: in the latter case, it often indicates which parts of the animal are edible.

An interesting variation on the X-Ray motif in western Arnhem Land is by means of the in-fill technique called *rarrk*. This is reserved for representations of ancestral beings. It shows the internal organs of the bodies of these beings, but these are at the same time features of the landscape. Here we are confronted with an artistic reversal. Rather than ancestral beings leaving parts of their bodies on the landscape and marking it in this way, the paintings show the landscape "inside" the ancestor itself, as if the land were part of its bodily composition. This technique is associated particularly with the Mardayin ceremonies, where the relationship between a person and his clan lands is focused on.

Yolngu bark paintings from north-east Arnhem Land make use of both geometric designs, akin to the circle, dot, and line of central Australian visual representation, and figurative designs, similar to the naturalistic depictions of western Arnhem Land art. They have two kinds of meaning. They may refer either to events in myths or to topographical features of the landscape, although they can also refer to both at once. The paintings therefore always have a double function: they refer both to mythic events and to the geographic map of the land.

BARK PAINTINGS

IN 1959, ON ELCHO ISLAND off the coast of north-east Arnhem Land, a collection of highly secret sacred objects and bark paintings was displayed publicly outside the church. It was a syncretically inspired attempt by Aboriginal leaders to show White society that Aboriginal people possessed artifacts and designs of great power, and that they would be willing to share these if European society was itself willing to reciprocate. It was a way for Aboriginal people to demand recognition, aid and assistance in their struggle to survive with their culture in the Euro-Australian nation state.

INTERMARRIAGE

THE MURRAY AND DARLING River system covers much of southern New South Wales, northern Victoria, and eastern South Australia, and was an important focus of traditional Aboriginal regional life as well as a conduit along which myths, artifact,s and trade occurred. Eaglehawk and Crow stories have been recorded from different Aboriginal groups throughout the Murray–Darling region. Usually they are the name of the two *moieties* or halves of the society. They are depicted as antithetical creatures, always in conflict, who, in some cases, agree to make peace—as a result of which the people divide into two groups and begin to intermarry.

▲ *This beautiful bark painting shows a pair of crocodiles with their young and unhatched eggs.*

Africa

INTRODUCTION

THE MYTHOLOGY of Africa is both unique and impressive in its sheer diversity. Although many peoples shared a common language and geographically lived in close proximity to one another, local beliefs varied widely. There are, of course, shared themes, characters, and gods that recur in the mythologies across the continent, but individual cultures generally formed their own pattern of beliefs and customs.

Some believe that, in the history of the cosmos, there were three ages, including a perfect time, a golden time when god, human, and animal existed in perfect harmony. Then, during the second of the three periods, the age of creation, the creator god brought into existence the earth, along with humans and animals. It was a period of differentiation, as God originated life by using himself as material and model, an attempt to re-create the golden age on earth. But something happened during this period to indicate that the perfect age was gone for ever, that it could not be transferred to the earth: death came into the world, and the earth and humankind were flawed. It was a period of chaos and order, of fear and hope, of the diminishing of the past and the promise of a new future. The chaos-order dualism was sometimes seen as the nature of the creator god.

In some religious systems, this creator was a divine trickster, both a benevolent and creative god, and an unpredictable and frequently destructive trickster. He was a god who had within him both life and death. He was a trickster who contained sublime and outrageous characteristics. This same dualistic mixture persists in the creation of humans: they have within them both life and death, sublime and outrageous conduct. That is the result of the flaw experienced during the age of creation, that primal period of transformation, that rite of passage on a cosmological level.

As time went on, the godly, creative part of the divine trickster and the dualistic god repaired to heaven, that is, moved further away from humans and earth, and the destructive part of the divine trickster and dualistic god went to the earth, with the echo of perfection and the potential for good remaining: the divine trickster had become the profane trickster. This third age was the contemporary age, the world of today, a realm in which humans and gods have become remote from each other, in which humans, through their rituals and traditions, seek to duplicate that long-lost perfect age, only a dimly perceived echo now.

In the movement from the perfect age to the contemporary age, humans or animals frequently express their free will, thereby separating themselves from God. This is a part of the differentiation process that is characteristic of the creation period. As humans and animals isolate themselves from God, they retain certain qualities of that original oneness (theirs during the perfect age), but they lose an essential godly quality—everlasting life. For a variety of reasons, as they separate themselves from God, they become mortal. Death comes into the world. Death is often the result of an act of free will on the part of the human or animal; this act is at the center of the age of creation.

THE CREATOR GOD

IN AFRICAN RELIGIONS, the creator god takes various forms. There may be a single god or a pantheon of gods. God may be a wholly positive being, or a dualistic force composed of both good and evil, order and chaos. God may be a divine trickster, both majestic and outrageously debased, a spirit of order and a spirit of disorder, by turns creative and destructive. The divine trickster is a symbol of the period of transformation that characterizes the age of creation: as he moves from the perfect or golden age to the contemporary age, he embodies the changes—the move from the perfection of God (the creative side of the divine trickster) to the flawed human (the destructive side of the divine trickster).

In the contemporary age, the divine part of this trickster is gone, and what remains is the profane trickster, an unpredictable character whose residual creativity is seen in the illusions that he establishes, whose amorality is witnessed in his outrageous conduct, often anti-social. From chaos comes order: the struggle between order and chaos, between creativity and destructiveness. That primal cosmological

▼ *Wooden double figure of ancestors.*

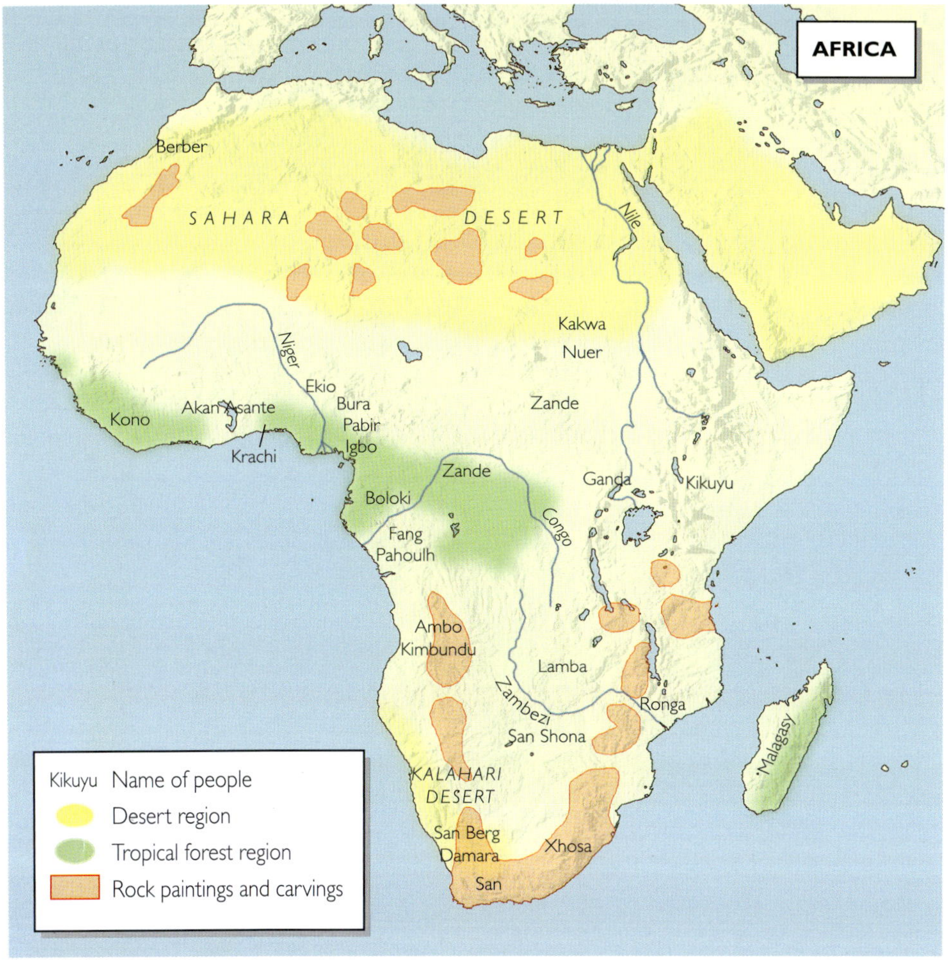

struggle is our struggle writ large. The dualistic god is everyman and everywoman, struggling with the two sides of their nature. The overcoming of chaos and the ordering of the world become our promise and our hope, but the divine trickster and the profane trickster, ever amoral and ever ready to obscure order with chaos, are a part of us as well.

MYTH AND METAPHOR

Myth becomes a constant metaphor for what humans can become, moving from the chaos of their lives to a kind of eternal order. It becomes a ritualizing of their everyday lives, a linkage to their gods. But while they may long for that sense of order, there can be danger in yearning for a oneness with God, for the golden age, if that means a loss of free will. The myths often begin with a familiar domestic scene, something the audience can at once relate to: an outrageous human activity, a bride or groom quest, someone under attack. From out of these often antisocial events comes new life. The outrage is purposeful because it represents chaos; the contrasting creation that emerges represents order. Humans long for that original completeness that they have lost. Within them, a battle rages—between the desire for oneness and the demand for independence. This battle they witness as they move closer to the contemporary age, and they see it especially in the trickster character and in the hero, where the struggle between free-willed humanity and God-related unity goes on. That unity is lost as they move closer to their world, and the profane trickster becomes the specter of what humans could become if they move away from God, toward amorality, from the morality of perfection to the amorality of indifference.

MYTH AND TALE

MYTH CAN BE FOUND at the heart of all stories, including tale and epic. In an Ekoi (Nigeria) story, a sheep generously gives of the food of his farm to his neighbors, but when he sells his farm for a python's shining stone, those neighbors refuse to reciprocate, informing him that it was ridiculous for him to sell his farm for such an object. Dying of starvation and grief about his neighbors' attitudes, the sheep gives the bright stone to Efflon Obassi, as that god moves into the heavens. God places the stone in a box with a lid: when it shines, it is the full moon, a symbol of the sheep's generosity, but once a month the lid is closed and there is no light, suggesting the gods' displeasure with the selfish attitudes of the sheep's neighbors.

▶ *Gods were believed to have two sides to their character.*

COMMON THEMES

THE MYTH-MAKER BUILDS his repertory of stories around an initial sense of oneness that was surrendered, to be followed by an effort to regain the lost accord. Considering the many stories that comprise the African myth systems, a number of common threads can be discerned.

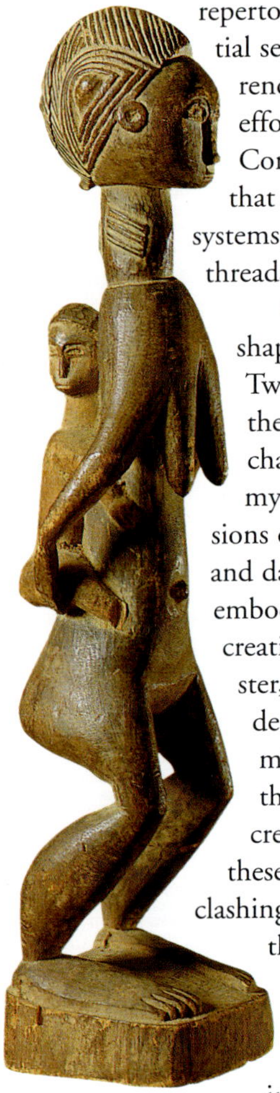

God created the universe, shaped it and then created life. Two forces contended during the age of creation: forces of chaos and order. In some myths, these forces were extensions of the creator god—his son and daughter, for example, embodying his destructive and creative sides, or a divine trickster, at once life-giving and death-dealing. Such divinities mirror the transformation that characterizes the age of creation, a time during which these opposing energies were clashing in the cosmos. So it was that the world and humanity were created, and the struggles writ large in the cosmos became woven into life on the earth and into human nature: in every human being can be found in microcosm the forces that existed in the earliest days when God was in the process of crafting the universe.

THE COSMIC EGG

MEBEGE (Fang, Pahouin/Congo African Republic, Congo, Gabon) is very lonely. He pulls hair from under his right arm, takes substance from his brain, and takes a pebble from the sea. He blows on them, and an egg is formed. He gives the egg to Dibobia, a spider suspended between sky and sea, and when the egg becomes hot, Mebege descends and puts sperm on it. The egg cracks and people emerge, the three children of Mebege. Mebege then takes a strand of raffia, works it into a cross, thereby establishing the four directions. He takes hair from under his arms along with the lining of his brain, rolls these into a ball and blows on them, creating termites and worms. They disperse in all directions, and with their droppings they build up the earth upon which, when it hardens, the three humans step.

GOD'S FOOTPRINTS

WHEN LESA (Lamba/Zambia), the high god and supreme being, visited the earth in the beginning, he did so under the name of Luchyele. He came from the east, arranging the entirety of the countryside—rivers, hills, trees, grass. He came with numbers of people, planting the nations and the communities in their respective places, passing on to the west. On the Itabwa plain can be seen the footprints of Lesa and his people as they passed. The stones were soft like mud, but as soon as Lesa passed, the mud hardened and the marks have been preserved ever since. Then Lesa went back into the heavens, high in the sky, having promised his children that he would return.

◀ *Female statue with infant, reflecting maternity.*
▼ *A rare Fang (Megebe) mask.*

THE DUALISTIC GOD

TO DRAMATIZE AND SYMBOLIZE the forces active during the early creative period, God is sometimes depicted as a complex, ambiguous figure, both creative and destructive, two contending forces within a single being which becomes a means of revealing the transformational processes at work during this time. Gulu (Ganda/Uganda) is such a creator god. He has a daughter, Nambi, who represents his creative side, and a son, Walumbe, who symbolizes his destructive side. Nambi, married to the first man, Kintu, brings life into the world, while her brother, Walumbe, brings death. Kintu and Nambi refuse to share their children with Walumbe, and he therefore begins to take them through death.

HEAVEN AND EARTH—CONNECTION

INITIALLY, THERE WERE connections between God and the mortals he created, between the place where God resided and the earthly home of humans. There was commerce between the heavens and the earth. The daughter of God could visit the earth and there walk among humans. And humans could move to the heavens, and visit and live among the gods. The creator god moved on the face of the earth, bringing new life into being, reshaping and detailing the place he had brought into existence. He met with humans, lived among humans, and the humans were his children. He taught them, he punished and rewarded them, as he made an effort to give order to the place that he had created.

The first connections were present, if not always firm. A goddess arched over the earth, maintaining vigilance and concern. Chains, threads, ropes, strings, webs, and trees connected heaven and earth, and God and man remained relatively close to each other. Wulbari (Krachi/Togo), the creator god, sent men and women down to the earth by means of a chain. Among the Holoholo (Democratic Republic of Congo/Tanzania), a gigantic tree joined heaven and earth. An old woman (Ronga/Mozambique) sees a rope uncoiling from a cloud. She climbs the rope and finds herself in the country above the sky, in a land similar to her own country. When the soul leaves the body (Berg Damara/Namibia), it takes a broad road that leads to the highest deity Gamab's village in the heavens.

A lone tree dominates the African plain.

▼ *A rare statue of a male African figure.*

got many mortars, piling them one on top of the other. In the process, she moved closer and closer to the sky. Now, to get to Nyame, she needed just one more mortar. She asked a child to get one for her, but he could find none. In desperation, she told him to take one of the mortars from the bottom of the pile. He did so and, when the mortar was removed, the entire tower collapsed.

HUMANS ENTREAT GOD

LONG AGO, PEOPLE were plagued by wild beasts. And, they wondered, if Nguleso, the supreme being (Kakwa/Sudan), exists, why then were they eaten by these creatures? Some concluded that it was because they were not acting properly, that Nguleso had sent the animals to punish them. But when they considered the men who had died, they determined that God had treated them unfairly, because these men had not taken others' property, they had not entered the houses of other men, so Nguleso was troubling them for no reason. They therefore called together the spirits, Nguloki, and through them called upon Nguleso in the sky.

SEPARATION

SOMETHING OCCURRED to provoke a separation between heaven and earth, between God and his creations—a disobedience, a struggle, an error, fate. Death came into the world. Humans erred and incurred the wrath of God, a message of eternal life sent by God to the earth was somehow tragically intercepted or misconstrued, God for some reason became disgusted by the activities of humans, human vanity triumphed over modesty and selflessness. There might have been a quarrel, the breaking of a prohibition. Whatever the impetus, the ordered ties with heaven were broken, the gods left the earth, and man was left with a flawed environment. People tried to re-establish contact with the heavens, building towers to the sky, but these crumbled under their own weight and under the weight of their insolence. And so a gap was created between heaven and earth, and the gap would yawn into a chasm. And in the end the break was complete. Humans were on their own.

GOD RETREATS FROM THE EARTH

ABEREWA, THE PRIMORDIAL woman, pounded her mortar with a pestle as she prepared food for her children, and the pestle routinely bumped against the sky. Annoyed, Nyame (Akan, Asante/Ghana) went away. Then Aberewa attempted to re-establish her relationship with him. To do that, she

▲ *A mask of Nimba, the Baga's goddess of fertility.*

▶ *A Nigerian statue of a goddess, made of painted wood and metal.*

THE STRUGGLE BETWEEN GOD AND MAN

ON THE EARTH, there is a continuation of the primal struggle between the forces of good and evil, as humans make efforts to regain and maintain their contacts with the heavens. Fantasy and supernatural beings work their way through the interstices of human life, mirroring the internal clashes as humans struggle to move to the best part of their nature. In their daily lives, in their rites of passage, in their social intercourse, humans are engaged in a struggle with God, as they work to sort out their lives, and the fantasy and supernatural beings become the indices of their daily skirmishes and their resultant transformations.

Heroes are emblematic of the temporal struggle, containing within themselves both the positive, god-like qualities and the negative qualities. In the tales, everyman and everywoman, obeying cultural injunctions and following social rituals, seek to restore the lost harmony: the second connection. Not just heroes are engaged in this gargantuan labor; everyman and everywoman are also contenders, which is why the tale is inevitably built around a mythic core. This is the argument: humans have been separated from God, but they have echoes of God within themselves.

RITUAL STRUGGLES

IN STORIES that make up the African myth traditions, there are beginnings—the origin of the universe—and there are endings: the onset of death. Between these beginnings and endings is the struggle to re-achieve the first and to obviate the second. Initial connections between heaven and earth are severed, a separation between God and man is the result. To recover those connections, a conflict erupts on the earth between contending forces, sometimes given form in mythic heroes, other times in the ritual struggles of everyman.

HUMAN FAILURE

CULTURAL INSTITUTIONS and ceremonies are the immediate manifestations of inner godliness, and it is such institutions and ceremonies that show humans the way to God. If humans faithfully and fully observe such social mores, they can once again, if only for a cosmological moment, touch the face of God.

Death in the end is victorious, although there are some suggestions of a reunion in death with the god of the beginnings. In some myths, humans exulted in the sense of freedom that resulted from their separation from God. It was a nervous exultation, but in severing the relationship with the heavens, humans were on their own, and they had to discover the means of their future survival not from the cosmos but from within their own inner beings. And so the hero who bestrode the earth and the heavens gave way to the earthbound human, and the only echoes of that earlier union with God resonated within rather than without.

DEATH COMES INTO THE WORLD

LONG AGO, there was no such thing as death. All were therefore surprised when a man died. They sent a worm to the sky to ask Hyel, the supreme deity (Bura, Pabir/Nigeria), what they should do. Hyel said they should hang the corpse in a tree and throw mush at it until it came back to life. Then no one else would ever die. On the way back, a lizard named Agadzagadza, having overheard God's words, ran ahead of the worm to deceive the people on the earth. When he reached the earth, he told the people that the sky said they should bury the corpse. The people did this. Later, when the worm arrived and gave them the true message, they were too lazy to take the corpse from the grave. They refused to do what God had told them to do, and people still die.

◀ *Masks may have been used to indicate the dual nature of the gods. This beautiful mask originates from Angola.*

THE DIVINE TRICKSTER

THE CREATOR GOD, when he is cast in the role of divine trickster, suggests the order–chaos duality of the creator, this character mirroring the duality of the universe as the supreme being moves to bring order out of disorder. Kaggen (San/Botswana, Namibia, South Africa), a *mantis*, is a divine trickster. Revealing his trickster nature he steals the sheep of some primal ticks, his dispute with the ticks establishing a necessary disjuncture in the mythical world that will lead to its dismantling and reconstruction in earthly terms. The ticks, who possess shelter, clothing, and domesticated animals, become the victims of the divine trickster as he removes them from their world, that world providing the initial infrastructure of early San civilization.

IN THE BEGINNING...

THERE ARE MANY IDEAS, varied stories about the initial shape of the universe and about the primal activities of creator gods—a cosmic egg, a mat hurled through the void, an earth perilously perched on a bull's horns, two worlds encased in a sphere. There was a flurried maelstrom of shaping, chiseling, organizing, hewing, sculpting industry in these formative periods, and out of the scramble of competing forces emerged from the heavens, from the earth, by means of serpents, spiders, chameleons, heavenly bodies, the rainbow, lightning, an egg, and man himself. Animals also emerged, and trees and plants. People, sometimes suspended between heaven and earth, had connections in both realms.

RITUAL MOVEMENTS

THE SYMBOLISM OF A character that is part animal and part human (Lamba/Zambia) reveals the movement of a human from one identity to another, as he moves from the potentially worse part of himself to the potentially best part of himself. So it is that lion-child and cow-child move from an animal world in which the "might is right" dictum rules. Now the two ambiguous children—part animal, part human—leave the animal world and journey into a human world where they set things right by destroying eight old men who withhold life-sustaining water from people, and so move to the celestial realm. There one of them takes over the role of God himself, a suggestion that, having moved away from the animal in himself, he has touched the God in himself.

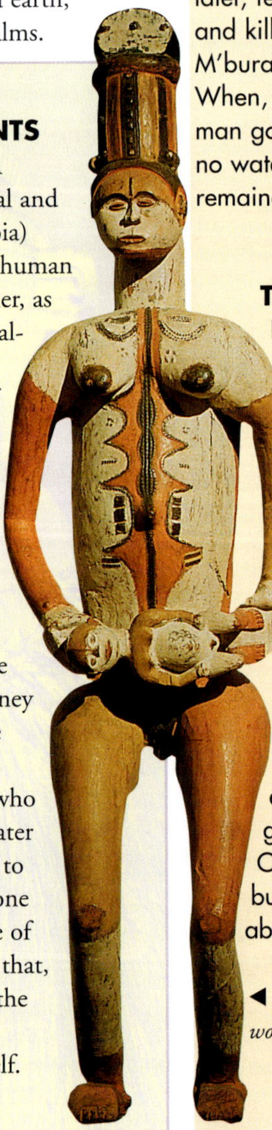

◀ *Statue of an African goddess made of wood with pigment color and metal.*

THE MYTHIC RAINBOW

A BOY (KIKUYU/KENYA) herds cattle on the grazing grounds of Mukunga M'bura, the mythic rainbow, who, in retaliation, swallows the boy's father and all the people, the livestock, and the homes—all except the boy. When the youth grows to manhood, he takes his weapon and goes to fight Mukunga M'buro who, now afraid of the mortal, implores him to make a hole in his finger rather than his heart, so that he may survive. The youth does this, and everything that Mukunga M'bura has swallowed emerges. The young man initially spares Mukunga M'bura but later, fearing his evil, he goes back and kills him. But one leg of Mukunga M'bura throws itself into a pool. When, the following day, the young man goes to destroy the leg, he finds no water, only the livestock that had remained in Mukunga M'bura.

THE CREATION OF EARTH

IN THE BEGINNING, when the earth emerged from chaos, Ale, the earth goddess (Igbo/Nigeria), made a decree that when any man died he should be buried there, in the earth. And so it was that, from her womb, she bore the earth. From that time, when the dead are buried, they return to earth; the people believe that they are then of one body with Ale. But much earlier, while Ale was absent from the earth, the mother of a big bird called Ogbu-ghu, the hornbill, died, and Ogbu-ghu could find no place to bury his dead mother. He flew about, seeking, carrying her body on his back, making a grave for her on his head—this is why the hornbill has a mound on his head to this day. In his quest, Ogbu-ghu flew over the water, restlessly looking for a final resting place for his mother. But he was able to find none. Finally, he saw a woman and a man. They were huge beings and they were swimming in the water, creating something. Land began to appear. It was when this land had become expansive that Ale was heard to say, "When a man dies, let him be buried here." And she stretched her own body over the land. Ogbu-ghu had found a burial place for his mother.

THE CLOUD PEOPLE

MOTU (BOLOKI/CONGO AFRICAN Republic) planted a large garden with bananas and plantains. The fruit ripened, but when he came to his garden one day, he discovered that the ripe bunches of bananas and plantain had been cut off and carried away. This theft continued, and at last he secretly waited for the thief. After a time, Motu saw a group of Cloud people descending from the sky. When they had alighted on the earth, they commenced to cut down his bananas. What they did not eat at once, they tied into bundles and carried away. As they did so, Motu rushed out, and, caught one woman, one of the Cloud people. He took her to his house and, after a short time, he married her. She was very bright and went about her housework and farming like an ordinary woman of the earth. Up until that time, neither Motu nor the people of his village had ever seen a fire. They had always eaten their meat raw and on cold, windy, rainy days had sat shivering in their houses because they did not know anything about fire and warmth. So it was that Motu's wife told some of the Cloud people to bring some fire with them next time they came to visit her. She taught the people how to cook food and how to sit around a fire on cold days.

Motu was very happy with his wife, and the villagers were very glad to have her among them. In time, she persuaded many of the Cloud people to settle in her husband's village. But then things changed. One day, she received a basket that was covered. She placed the basket on a shelf in the house, instructing her husband never to open it. If he did so, she warned, the Cloud people would all leave him. Motu made a promise that he would not open the basket. He was very happy, for he now lived among many people, he had a clever wife, and the villagers treated him as if he were a great man. Even so, he frequently wondered about the basket. Then one day he foolishly decided to open it. When his wife had gone as usual to the farm, he opened the basket, and found nothing in it. Laughing, he shut the basket up and put it back in its place. But when his wife returned, she asked him why he had opened the basket. Then, while Motu was away hunting, she gathered her people and ascended with them to Cloud land, never again to return to earth. And so the earth people received fire and the knowledge of cooking.

▲ *This image covered with nails originates from the Congo. It may have served as an offering to make peace with or to recover a spirit.*

NAMBALISITA

NOW, SEPARATED one from the other, the gap between God and humans grew. Upheavals persisted in heaven and earth. It was often an unhappy time, a time of evil unleashed, of omens, plagues, curses. But it was also a period of exhilaration, a time of new-found freedom. At times, man and God engaged in contests, and at other times humans took on limited roles of God and combatted evil. Nambalisita (Ambo/Angola), the first man, born from an egg, became a heroic warrior during a series of quests while he journeyed about the earth with his mother. Kalunga, who created all men, heard of the prowess of this man, who boasted that he had given birth to himself, and he called Nambalisita to him. Then the two of them competed, each demonstrating his prowess. In the end, Kalunga locked Nambalisita in a doorless room, but Nambalisita called the animals that he commanded and they made a passage for him to escape, at the same time filling the room with pumpkins. At the same time, Kalunga set the room on fire. When the pumpkins became hot, they burst, and Katunga concluded that these sounds indicated that Nambalisita was dying. But Nambalisita then appeared and went on to have other adventures.

◀ *This fearsome-looking mask made in the Congo could have been used for decoration or for dances.*

TURE BRINGS FIRE TO MAN

THE EARTHLY STRUGGLE between order and chaos, between union and separation, was nowhere more graphically revealed than in the divine trickster, symbolic of this period. Ture, a divine trickster (Zande/Democratic Republic of Congo, Sudan), went to visit his uncles who were forging iron. He worked the bellows for them, then deceitfully took fire from them, because at that early time his people did not have fire. He kept blowing on the fire, then returned the next day with a strip of bark-cloth wrapped around his body. He again blew on the fire until the bark-cloth glowed and the ironsmiths put the fire out. This happened again, and again his uncles immediately put the fire out. But they could not extinguish it completely, try as they might. Finally, the trickster fled with the fire, going into the dry grass. And fire spread everywhere behind Ture. It is because of him that humans have fire.

THE HERO

IF CHARACTERS FIND God in themselves, heroes bestride heaven and earth, assuring that the culture that they embody has heavenly sanction.

Heroes, successful or not, sublime or not, provide the promise of union with the heavens. A stone falls from the sky, a hero emerges and later, with a fearful noise, the stone splits—and rain falls. A hero comes out of an egg, and proceeds to struggle with God for ascendancy. Pale and hairy, a hero arises from the water and establishes a model government. A hero's strength is in his shadow and, as long as his secret remains safe, he plays the role of God. Waters part for the hero, miraculously born. The hero, mortal and flawed, has within him the capacity to reach godliness.

IBONIAMASIBONIAMANORO

IBONIAMASIBONIAMANORO (Malagasy/Madagascar) was born miraculously. His mother, Rasoabemanana, had gone to a seer, Ranakombe, to get help for her barrenness. She soared into the heavens where she found a grasshopper, then the grasshopper helped her to secure a child-bearing talisman. All of nature reacted. Ranakombe warned the mother about the child's destiny, and had cannons fired as the grasshopper leapt into the fire, then moved into the mother's womb through her head, remaining in her womb for 10 years.

Now Iboniamasiboniamanoro caused his mother to wander the earth, seeking a place where he might be born. He finally decided that it should be a farm. He asked his mother to swallow a razor, then he cut himself out of her womb. His mother died, and nature again reacted. The child leapt into a fire, was unharmed, but would not be silent until cannons were fired into the four cardinal directions. Ranakombe gave him names and, after rejecting a number of them, he accepted his name, Iboniamasiboniamanoro. He remained in the fire and nature responded.

At a distant place, the villainous Raivato strangely thought about his future enemy. Iboniamasiboniamanoro grew up. As he did so, he proved his abilities by fighting other children, routinely defeating them. Now he wanted to marry. He praised himself, and Ranakombe told him what he must do to get a wife: he must get a bull, move through trees that were imposters, get talismans, stop a whirlwind, roast a bull, dive into water with the talismans, stay under water until daybreak, and he would have a wife.

Iboniamasiboniamanoro did this. He became an irritable trickster, causing people's goods to fall into a ditch. His mother challenged him four times, and each time he rose to her challenge, defeating a crocodile, two ogres, and a swallowing monster. He opened the swallowing monster, and released the people who were inside.

Iboniamasiboniamanoro, although his mother suggested alternative brides, insisted that he would go to seek Iampelamananoro, who had been kidnapped by Raivato. To gain access to Raivato's homestead, Iboniamasiboniamanoro, after learning the old man's habits, killed Ikonitra, Raivato's old retainer, and put on his skin. As Ikonitra, he entered Raivato's homestead and, as he did so, a plate and spoon broke, a mat flew apart, and Raivato's charms rattled.

Iboniamasiboniamanoro as Ikonitra defeated Raivato at chess and wooden crosses, and in the fields with oxen. Finally, he got Raivato's charms, then hammered Raivato into the ground and destroyed him. He took Iampelamananoro as his wife. They were married for three years. Then, three years before his death,

Iboniamasiboniamanoro prepared his testament: let no man tamper with the sacred bonds of marriage. And he died.

▼ *Wild beasts, such as the crocodile, were both feared and respected.*

SUDIKA-MBAMBI

WHEN THE MYTHIC HERO, god-like and heroic, undertakes to move through the stages of a ritual, he establishes a model for all human kind. Sudika-mbambi (Kimbundu/Angola) is a godly being who moves to earth where, after being born miraculously, speaking in his mother's womb, springing forth a fully grown man, he engages in a variety of struggles with villainous creatures on the surface of the earth. He then moves to the underworld, where, in one monumental struggle, he wrests life, in the form of a bride, from the death-dealer of this nether realm, Kalunga-ngombe. He is subsequently swallowed by Kimbiji, a crocodile, from the belly of which he emerges reborn.

THE MESSAGE OF LIFE

QAMATHA, THE CREATOR (Xhosa/South Africa), sent the chameleon to earth to tell the people that they would never die. The chameleon journeyed to the earth, and on the way it got tired and had a rest. A lizard came along; it asked where the chameleon was going, and the chameleon told it. But the lizard hurried ahead and told the people that they would indeed die. An outcry erupted on the earth, the people crying because they were going to die. The chameleon, hearing this wailing, proceeded to the earth to tell people that it would not be like that—they would never die. But the people did not believe the chameleon, accepting instead the word of the lizard. That is why people die.

The first man and woman had one child, a boy, and Yataa, the supreme being (Kono/Sierra Leone), told the three of them that they would never die, that when their bodies grew old he would give them new skins: the old ones would be shed, they would put on new ones and would become young again. God wrapped the new skins in a package and gave it to the dog to carry to the people. The dog carried the package until he met other animals who were eating, and the dog, anxious to share in the feast, put the package down and went to the food. One of the animals asked him what was in the package, and he told the story of the new skins. The snake heard the story and, when the dog was not looking, he stole the package, carried it home, and shared its contents with other snakes. When the dog reached home, the man asked him for the skins, and the dog told him how the snake had stolen them. They told Yataa about it, and God said that he would not take the skins from the snakes, but from then onward the snake would not be allowed to live in the town with other animals but would be driven out to live by himself. So now, when man grows old, he must die. Because the snake stole the skins, man always tries to kill him.

DEATH PREVAILS

IN THE END, the death that was prefigured at the beginning is triumphant and man must die, receiving in many ways the message that he is not eternal. Often this message seems unsubstantial, but that only reinforces the delicate balance that sustains and defines the human condition. A chameleon often brings the message of life but is overtaken by a swifter rival or garbles the message. Sometimes the message of life is cruelly subverted, or it is lost because of a mortal craving for food or rest. Or God changes his mind. Implied in many of the myths is the chance of everlasting life—tantalizing, tempting, teasing—but it remains only a vague promise, now lost. In some stories humans, out of greed, arrogance, curiosity, or desperation, break a commandment, transgress a prohibition, overlook a possibility, misinterpret a message, and eternal life becomes a distant and haunting hope.

▲ *A wooden initiation mask from the Ivory Coast. Birth, reaching adulthood, and death are milestones in the lives of the African people that are celebrated with particular ceremonies, rituals and customs. The reasons behind the cycle of life are recounted in various mythologies.*

▶ *The snake has been condemned in Africa to always be hunted by man in punishment for having stolen the skins that would keep man eternally young.*

COMPETING FORCES

EVERYMAN REACHES for the gods; his positive activities are rewarded and remembered, and sometimes his ritual activities result in permanent good. But there are two sides of everyman, as there are in creation. On the mythic level, these two sides are represented by the divine trickster and by the dualistic god. Humans long for that heavenly counterpart of themselves, that resurrection—the rebirth of their souls as represented by dualistic gods who, like the divine trickster, are both life-giving and death-dealing. The mythic struggle finds its counterpart in the routine lives of humans in the contemporary age.

The Caribbean

INTRODUCTION

THE ISLANDS OF THE CARIBBEAN offered a variety of landscapes to early Amerindian peoples. By 5000 B.C.E. in Trinidad, the first humans had arrived from the tropical rainforests and savannahs of mainland South America. They were hunters and gatherers and quickly adapted to island life, moving north in sea-going canoes to Tobago, Grenada, Martinique, and beyond. These first human settlers must have seen the region as a unique blend of sea, land and sky—quite different from the endless rivers and forests of their homeland.

Around 300 B.C.E., a new wave of settlers arrived from the mouth of the Orinoco River in Venezuela, bringing with them a settled village life, agriculture, and the kind of shamanic religion and mythic world view typical of tropical rainforest societies in lowland Amazonia. These people grew manioc (cassava) and sweet potato, and made the first pottery in the Caribbean. With sharp stone axes they felled trees and cleared areas for fields and villages—changing the Caribbean landscape for ever. By C.E. 300 they had spread throughout the Caribbean, the sea continuing to play an important role in their everyday and religious lives.

Christopher Columbus arrived in the Caribbean in 1492. At this time, the region was occupied by two main Amerindian groups—the Taíno (Arawak) in the Greater Antilles, and the Carib in the Lesser Antilles. Taíno society had evolved out of the previous migrations from South America and was based on manioc cultivation, which supported large villages ruled by chiefs (*caciques*). In Puerto Rico and Hispaniola, they played a rubber ball-game in great stone-lined courts. Taíno religion was based on ancestor worship, with their shamans contacting the spirits by snuffing the hallucinogenic powder *cohoba*.

The Caribs appear to have been late arrivals in the Caribbean, sailing large sea-going canoes from South America around C.E. 1000 and colonizing the Lesser Antilles, especially Dominica, St. Vincent, and Guadeloupe. Carib society and religion were less sophisticated than that of the Taíno, with villages centered on the men's meeting house and their society ruled by war chiefs. One of the most dramatic and misrepresented aspects of Carib culture was cannibalizm. This usually took the form of the ritual consumption of the powdered bones of a relative mixed with liquid in a ceremonial drink. Such practices were misunderstood by Europeans but played an important role in Carib religion and mythology.

▲ *The sea plays a fundamental role in the life of the people of the Caribbean.*

ROOTS OF CARIBBEAN MYTHOLOGIES AND RELIGIONS

CARIBBEAN MYTHOLOGIES have their roots deep in South America, and particularly in the tropical rainforests of the Amazon lowlands. It was the fundamentally shamanic world view of these peoples that was taken to the Caribbean, albeit adapting to local island conditions.

Although the region was populated in a series of migrations, indigenous Caribbean peoples probably were always in contact with their mainland cousins through trading and warfare. Ideas and influences in pottery styles, language, customs and dress, and in the rituals which converted their beliefs into actions, were in constant flux. This, in turn, produced the distinctive mosaic of peoples and beliefs so characteristic of Caribbean prehistory.

The geographical nature of this necklace of islands separated by wide stretches of sea imposed religious, social, and economic constraints on Taíno and Carib life, yet many elements retained their South American character. This is especially true in the shared concept of a spiritually animated world alive with ancestral beings. Illustrating this, both Caribbean and South American societies regarded trees as symbolic and mythical ladders, bridging the divide between heaven and earth, supplying the supernatural as well as physical materials for voyaging canoes and coffins for the dead. In both regions, trees were ancestral beings that walked the land at night.

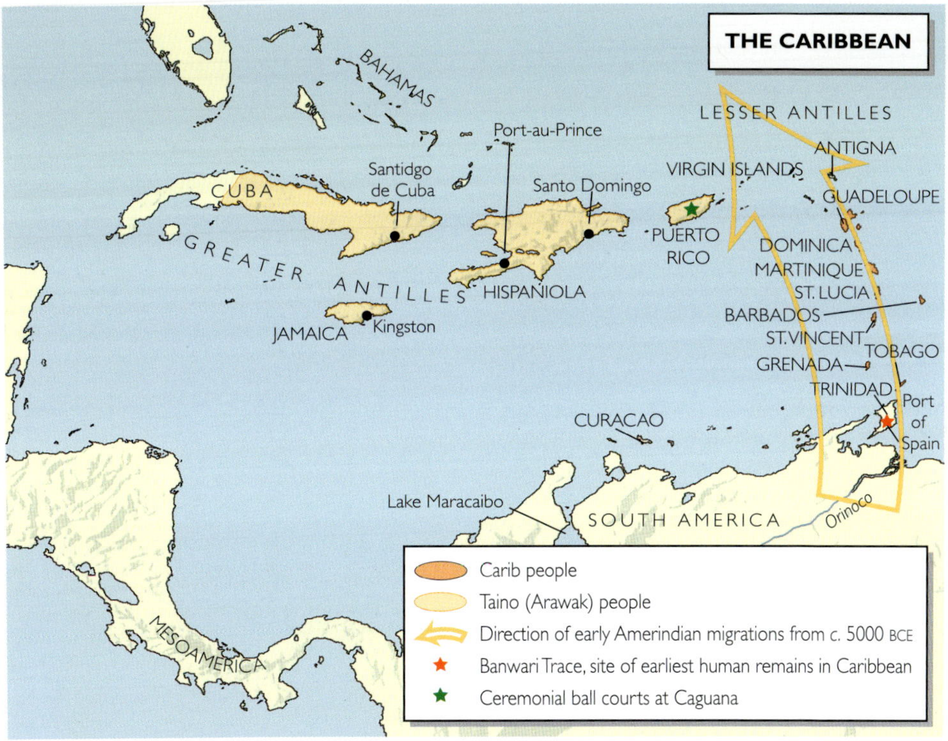

CARIBBEAN MYTHOLOGY

THE MYTHOLOGIES of indigenous Caribbean peoples were similar in many ways to those of their better-known neighbors in Mesoamerica and South America. In particular, they shared ideas of successive creations of the cosmos, and of the spiritual animacy of the physical world. What sets these myths apart is our fragmentary know-ledge of them and the social and physical settings of the Caribbean island landscapes in which they are set. Central to an understanding of Taíno myth is metamorphosis, the ability to change outward appearance from animal to human forms, or vice versa.

Behavior and feelings too could alter, with mythic figures having superhuman animal strength and animals possessing human sensibilities. Some animals could be tribal ancestors, and some trees were the spirits or souls of dead chiefs or *caciques*. The souls of the dead were believed to hide themselves during daylight hours, only to emerge at night to seek out and eat the guava fruit. Taíno myths, like all myths, are philosophical statements of how they regarded and made sense of their uniquely fragmented natural world. The events of Taíno myth take place not in linear, but in mythic time, where movement, nearness and distance have little meaning.

Despite this underlying unity, the Caribbean islands were not as rich in flora or fauna as South America. In response, Amerindians adapted not only their hunting, gathering, and eating habits, but their spiritual ones as well. They replaced such powerful predators as the jaguar and Harpy Eagle with locally available animals in examples of so-called "mythic substitution." In particular, it seems that dogs may have replaced the jaguar in many instances—partly because of the similarity between the fangs of both species and partly also because, even in Amazonia, some dogs are identified with jaguars. Other animals, which inhabited both islands and mainland, retained their mythical importance. Bats, for example, played a significant part in Amazonian myth, as did frogs, and both appear to have been important images portrayed as Caribbean *zemís*.

Caribbean shamans were hardly distinguishable from those in South America and Mesoamerica. Taíno shamans snuffed hallucinogenic *cohoba* powder to enter into a trance, soar in spirit flight with mythical bird helpers to the spirit realm, and cure illness in the time-honored tradition of their mainland cousins. Cosmological links also existed, giving rise to a trade in gold, gold-and-copper alloy, and carved greenstones—all symbolic representations of preciousness and cosmic fertilizing power, and the preserve of the local chiefs who wore them as bodily adornments.

◀ *Columbus is greeted by the* caciques.

ZEMÍS

THE INDIGENOUS PEOPLES of the Caribbean did not build temples or cities adorned with monumental art. They represented their mythic heroes and gods in carvings of wood, stone, and shell. These objects, called *zemís*, possessed supernatural power, both in their finished form and in the raw material itself. Carved wood *zemís* took the form of birds, human figures, and elaborately polished ceremonial benches called *duhos*, on which shamans and chiefs reclined during their narcotic trance journeys to the spirit world. Greenstone frogs, enigmatic faces with staring eyes, spiral decorations, and half-human, half-animal beings represented the powers of nature in visual form.

OPITA

THE TAÍNO PEOPLES of Haiti, who have long been associated with the cult of voodoo, believed that the souls of the dead still walked upon the earth, in particular on the island of Coiabi. These souls were known as *opita*, and were believed to be very powerful; engaging in confrontation with one of these *opita* would lead to certain death. The Haitian Taínos also shared a belief with other Caribbean peoples in the *zemís*, the protecting spirits.

CREATION OF THE TAÍNO WORLD

CARIBBEAN MYTHOLOGY is less well known than the epics from Mesoamerica and South America. Nevertheless important, if fragmentary, evidence has survived of various creation stories. According to the Taíno chiefs (*caciques*) of Hispaniola, the creation of the universe spanned five eras. The first began when the supreme spirit, Yaya, killed his rebellious son, placing the bones in a gourd which he suspended from the rafters of his house. On examining the gourd one day, Yaya and his wife saw that the bones had been transformed into fish, which they ate. In a variation of this story, the quadruplet sons of Itiba Cahubaba, "Bloodied Aged Mother," who had died in childbirth, arrived in Yaya's garden. One of the brothers retrieved the gourd and they all gorged themselves on the fish it contained. Upon hearing Yaya returning they hastily replaced the gourd, but it broke, spilling water full of fish which covered the earth and became the ocean. The brothers fled to their grandfather's land, where, when one of them asked for some cassava bread, the old man became enraged and spat on the boy's back. This spittle was transformed into the narcotic *cohoba* which all Taíno shamans used as a gateway to the spirit world.

▼ *Carribean mythology tells of how the oceans were created by Yaya.*

GUAYAHONA

GUAYAHONA IS ONE of the most significant archetypal figures in Taíno mythology. As a culture hero, he departs from the cave of origin in Hispaniola and journeys westward to the island of Guanín—the name given to the alloy of gold and copper revered by the Taíno. Thus, apart from calling the Taíno out from the bowels of the earth, Guayahona undertakes distinctly shamanic journeys in cosmic time to mythic places full of bright spirit power. In such events, the role and identity of human shaman and mythical being are fused with the symbolizm of cosmic brilliance which re-creates the world through ritual.

MEANINGS OF TAÍNO MYTHS

TAÍNO CREATION MYTHS are often difficult to explain owing to scanty and often confused historical material and an almost complete lack of comparative anthropological evidence after the European conquest. What does seem clear, however, is that the god Yaya is a prime mover deity who personifies cosmic time, and that the four brothers who take his gourd full of fish are lesser but more active supernatural beings. Itiba Cahubaba, their mother, is probably Mother Earth, from whom all life comes. When one of the brothers asks his grandfather for cassava bread, he is in fact discovering the use of fire used to bake the food. Cooking is the essence of civilized life. The Taíno used metaphor and allusion in their myth of the creation of people. Caonao is not in fact a province of Hispaniola, but a magical place full of the brilliance of gold and gems. During the third, civilizing period of cosmic time, Guahayona travels to various islands and is given shiny gifts. This has been seen as a mythical account of a rite of passage during which Guahayona acquires the symbols of tribal leadership and power.

TAÍNO GODS AND SPIRITS

THE TAÍNO PEOPLE worshiped both ancestors and nature, personifying the supernatural forces of both as powerful gods. Sacred *zemí* images of stone and wood represented these powerful supernatural beings. The two major Taíno deities were Yúcahu, the "spirit of cassava"—the staple food of the Taíno, and Atabey, goddess of human fertility. In a world of violently destructive weather, the Taíno also worshiped a female deity, Guabancex, the "Lady of the Winds," mistress of hurricanes. As with Amerindians elsewhere, the gods and spirits of the Caribbean Taíno symbolized their intimate relationship with the natural forces which shaped the world.

CREATION OF THE FIRST PEOPLE

THE SECOND ERA of Taíno cosmogony was the creation of the first people. According to one account, there were two caves in a land called Caonao on the island of Hispaniola. From one of the caves, the Taíno emerged. When one man neglected his guard duties at the mouth of the cave he was turned to stone by the Sun. The others, who had gone fishing, were captured by the Sun and turned into trees. One of these, called Guahayona, washed himself with the digo plant and went out before sunrise. But he was caught by the Sun and changed into a bird which sings at dawn.

From the second cave came other, less numerous people of the Caribbean, those who did not share Taíno customs or identity. The second era ends with Guahayona calling to those remaining in the cave to come forth and populate the fertile islands of the Caribbean.

In the third era, humans became civilized, and women were created as sexual partners for men. During the fourth era, the Taíno spread over the Caribbean, perfected cassava production, lived in well-ordered villages and developed a sweet sounding tongue. Columbus's arrival marked the end of the fourth era. The calamitous fifth era saw the disappearance of Taíno society through European maltreatment, disease, and assimilation.

ORIGINS OF SOCIETY

THE MAIN THEMES of Caribbean, and especially Taíno, mythology concern the origins of the world and the emergence of people from what appears to be a physical place but is actually a golden land located in mythic time. This links the physical and supernatural worlds, providing a mythic charter for the social order of Taíno society. Similarly, the ability to change form, to deceive by physical appearance, is a recurring motif. Taíno myths play on the idea of metamorphosis, integrating everyday and sacred life, acknowledging the presence of death, but infusing spiritual power into the very fabric of their society.

▲ *Sir Walter Raleigh watches the sacrifice of a baby.*

▼ *Opiel Guabiron, the door-keeper to the Underworld.*

THE GIFTS OF BREAD AND HERBS

AS SOON AS THEY came to the door of the house of the old man known as Bayamanaco, the four sons of Itiba Cahubaba saw that he possessed *cazabe* (cassava bread). On seeing him, the brothers called out "Ahiacabo guarocoel!"—which means "We know our grandfather!"—a possible ritual greeting among the Taíno. One of the brothers, known as Deminán Caracaracol, entered through the door to see if he could get some *cazabe*. Caracaracol asked Bayamanaco for some cassava bread—the offering of *cazabe* and *cohoba* snuff being common etiquette for the Taíno. At this request, the old man put his hand to his nose and threw some *guanguayo* (tobacco-juice spittle) onto the boy's back. In this way, the brothers were given *guanguayo* spittle (and its magical connotations) rather than cassava bread. The old man then left, having become very angry at the temerity of the brothers to greet him by asking for *cazabe*.

THE CULTURE OF TOBACCO AND FOOD

THE SYMBOLIC relationship between food, especially *cazabe* (cassava), tobacco and the shaman's hallucinogenic *cohoba* snuff is embodied in the myth which describes Deminán Caracaracol's encounter with the old man Bayamanaco. Here, *guanguayo* is identified as the shaman's spittle which is produced when he chews a wad of tobacco. In this myth, tobacco spittle has been mixed with *cohoba* powder which has a purifying and hallucinogenic effect on the taker. Tobacco in this context is the raw and strong *Nicotiana tabacum*, and its narcotic, vision-inducing effects are released by fermentation in the mouth's saliva. The *guanguayo* which Bayamanaco takes from his nose and throws on to Deminán may in fact be the mucus which streams from the shaman's nose after he has ingested *cohoba* and which, in South America, is also identified symbolically as semen.

The ensuing visions are often part of shamanic curing sessions in which the illness-inducing spirits are interrogated and a cure suggested. Deminán's meeting with Bayamanaco suggests a shamanic curing aspect to the encounter. Bayamanaco is Deminán's grandfather but may also be the supreme deity. Invoking one's grandfather may be more than a social greeting, perhaps associated ritually with divination and communion with the ancestors.

IMAGES OF POWER

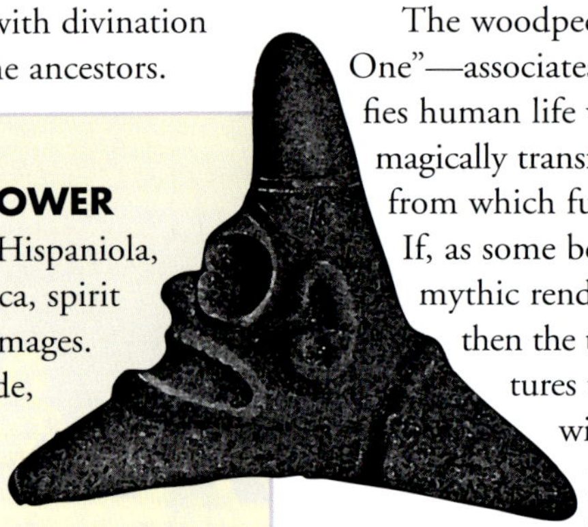

FOR THE TAÍNO of Hispaniola, Puerto Rico, and Jamaica, spirit power resided in *zemí* images. Of the many kinds made, small but elaborately carved stones known as "three pointers" are the most enigmatic. Uniquely Caribbean, they were made from white marble, gray stone or andesite and carry the faces of different Taíno spirits. Each stone possessed its own symbolizm—a cosmic power embodied by its distinctive shape and concentrated by its godly design. *Zemí* stones guarded the soul when buried with the dead and promoted fertility when placed in agricultural fields. Together with the ceremonial ball game, stone *zemís* symbolized ideas of duality in Taíno religious life.

BIRDS, SHAMANS, AND WOMEN

THE SYMBOLIC RELATIONSHIP between birds, women, and trees or logs in Taíno mythology relates to widespread ideas of the remoteness of women from men. Myths of the Taínos of Haiti, for instance, include how a great flood drowned all the women and how all the men were transformed into trees. Part of this is geographical as well as cultural; Carib men raided Taíno islands and took their women as wives. More directly, the myth of the woodpeckers creating women by boring holes into asexual creatures appears related to the social distance of prepubescent girls from sexually mature men. The heavy rain recalls the tropical downpours of the rainy season and links this to rites of female initiation which announce the "social appearance" and public acknowledgment of a woman's sexual maturity. As the myth unfolds, shamanic imagery comes to dominate the proceedings.

The woodpecker—or "Ancient One"—associates birds with logs, identifies human life with ancestral trees and magically transforms a hole into a vagina from which future races will emerge. If, as some believe, this account is a mythic rendering of a puberty rite, then the tying of the asexual creatures to trees is a parallel to widespread Amazonian practices of menstruating women being isolated in the jungle. This myth illustrates the shamanic origins of sexuality and fertility, and the incorporation of both into society in an ordered fashion that links the natural and symbolic worlds.

▲ *A* zemís *stone with its three cardinal points to the sky, the dead, and the land of the living.*

▼ *Woodpeckers are features in Caribbean mythologies, providing the link between human life, ancestral trees, and new life.*

▲ *Afro-Jamaican with local produce. Cooking signifies civilized life for the Taíno.*

MYTH OF THE BIRD-MADE WOMEN

IT IS SAID THAT one day some men went to bathe in the river and while they were washing it began to rain heavily. These men were anxious to possess women, and on many previous occasions they had searched everywhere for evidence of women but had been unable to find any. On this day, however, they looked up to see curious creatures falling from the branches of nearby trees. These were neither men nor women as they did not possess any sexual parts. The men chased them, but every effort to seize them failed. Then the men called out for some men who were under the chief's orders and who were called *caracaracol* because of their rough hands which could get a grip on the slippery creatures. They told their chief that there were four of these creatures and were given four *caracaracol*. After the asexual creatures had been captured, the men conferred as how best to make them into women. They sought out a bird known as Inriri. This bird makes holes in trees (i.e. a woodpecker). The men bound the hands and feet of the creatures, then attached the Inriri bird to them. The woodpecker believed the creatures to be trees and so he began boring a hole in the place where a woman's sexual parts are found. And so in this way, it is believed, women were made for Taíno men.

THEMES

THE THEMES OF these myths focus on cosmic energy as channeled through food, hallucinogenic plants, human sexuality and brilliance. Deminán Caracaracol's encounter with Bayamanaco links physical well-being with spiritual sustenance through the symbolic equivalence of cassava and the shaman's tobacco-juice spittle. Human sexuality, and the interrelatedness of social and natural worlds, is evident in the making of women by the activities of woodpeckers. Such connections also underscore the transformation of motherless children into frogs at Matininó. Finally, there is the association of sexual disease, and the assumption of chiefly power by Guahayona, symbolized by his receiving shiny guanín ornaments—themselves associated with sexual energy.

SEASONS, CYCLES, AND WOMEN

THE MYTH of the "Flight of the *Güeyo* Women" is an account of the symbolic and physical associations between seasonal fertility and that of women. In typically shamanic fashion, Guahayona must attain mastery over these natural rhythms, and to do so he uses the shaman's skills of persuasion, inventiveness, and trickery. *Güeyo* is formed of the ashes of an algae gathered near waterfalls and is a necessary additive to tobacco to make it into *guanguayo*—the narcotic and magical spittle of the shaman. By persuading women to take the *güeyo*, shamanic spittle is neutralized, and by going on a journey women are separated from men. In this way, the separation of *güeyo* from tobacco symbolizes the separation of men from women; in both cases, the two elements belong together if fertilizing power is to be produced. Although Matininó has been identified as the island of Martinique, it is most probably a mythical place, as is Guanín, the region called after the shiny alloy of gold and copper. The episode of the frog marks the appearance of a creature which possessed seasonal and sexual connotations for the Taíno. The rainy season appearance of frogs ties in with moisture, the earth's fertility, and the planting of cassava.

FLIGHT OF THE *GÜEYO* WOMEN

AND GUAHAYONA said to the women, "Leave your husbands and let us travel to distant lands and gather up much *güeyo* (ashes with magical qualities). Abandon your children and take only the herb, we shall return for them later." *Guahayona* thus persuaded the women, and they all left on a journey to search for other lands. They came to a place called Matininó, which means "No Fathers." Here Guahayona left the women behind, their children separated from them by a brook, while he went off to a land known as Guanín. After a while, the children became hungry and began crying for their mothers. The children's fathers could offer no sustenance to the children, who cried out piteously for their mothers' breasts. As they were asking to be nursed, they cried "toa, toa," and were magically transformed into small frog-like creatures called "tona," due to the sound they made. Thus were the children turned into frogs. From this time onward, the call of the frog was said to be the voice of springtime and earthly renewal. In this way also, all men were left without women.

▲ *A view of one of the magnificent bays on the island of Martinique.*

GODS OF NATURE

TAÍNO RELIGIOUS LIFE is characterized by the deification of elements important in everyday existence. Their supreme deity was Yúcahu—"Spirit of Cassava"—invisible lord of fertility on land and sea. In *zemí* representations, Yúcahu is shown with an open mouth, to eat away the soil thereby making room for the sprouting cassava tubers. His feet, likewise, are joined together to scratch away the earth. Yúcahu's female counterpart, and possibly his mother, was Atabey. As "Mother of Waters" she was associated with freshwater streams, ponds, and the rain needed to fertilize the cassava crops.

▲ *The glittering, shiny sea that surrounds the Caribbean islands provides a setting for some of the Caribbean mythologies.*

GUANÍN

FOR THE TAÍNO, as for all Amerindian peoples, sacred power that heals, energizes, promotes fertility and symbolizes status was conceived as bright light and shiny objects. In this myth, Guabonito is rescued by Guahayona from the glittering sea, and in return she cures him of sexual disease, placing him in shamanic isolation—the place called guanara. While the absence of sexual relations between the two may suggest an incest taboo as well as a complex mythical relationship, it is the term *guanín* which carries a heavy significance. As the name of a mythical place, Guanín is the gift of Guabonito to Guahayona and, at the same time, the term describes objects made from the merging of gold and copper. Some believe that in Taíno myth, anín was a rainbow bridge connecting the varied realms of east, west, sky, and underworld. *Guanín* objects retrieved from archaeological sites are often in the form of a crescent or rainbow. The shamanic nature of guanín objects as symbols of chiefly power account for their conferral as gifts from Guabonito to Guahayona. The small pebbles, *cibas*, may refer to the stones inside ceremonial rattles that spark when shaken and which are used in South American tobacco shamanism.

THE SHAMANIC JOURNEY

IN TAÍNO MYTHOLOGY, a recurring theme is the shamanic journey made by a culture hero which ends with his transformation after being cured of a sexual disease. In one instance, Deminán, who arrives on earth on a tidal wave, is struck down by a tortoise-shaped swelling on his back. The story ends when he is cured and a female turtle offers her shell as a sacred refuge for the renewal of life. A second myth involves the adventures of Guahayona, who takes women on a sacred journey and experiences a desire for a woman beneath the sea. He is then cured of his desire and of a sexual disease and is transformed into a chief.

GUAHAYONA BECOMES BRILLIANT

GUAHAYONA FOUND that he had left a woman at the bottom of the sea and so returned to retrieve her. After rescuing her, he took her back to the mountain known as Cauta from which he had originally taken her and was very pleased. Immediately he sought to discover how he might purify himself of the terrible sores which afflicted his body. The woman he had rescued was known as Guabonito, and she put him in a special place known as guanara. While he was there his sores disappeared, and he changed his name to Albeborael Guahayona. Guabonito asked permission of him to be able to continue her journey and this he gave. Guabonito then gave Albeborael Guahayona many *cibas* and *guanines* so that he could wear them attached to his arms and neck. *Cibas* are small, possibly shiny stones, and *guanín* is the term applied to shiny metal such as gold-copper alloy. Albeborael Guahayona decided to stay in that land along with his father, Hiauna, whose name means "He who was made brilliant." His father's son was named Hiaunael Guanín, "Son of Hiauna," and ever since he has been known as Guanín.

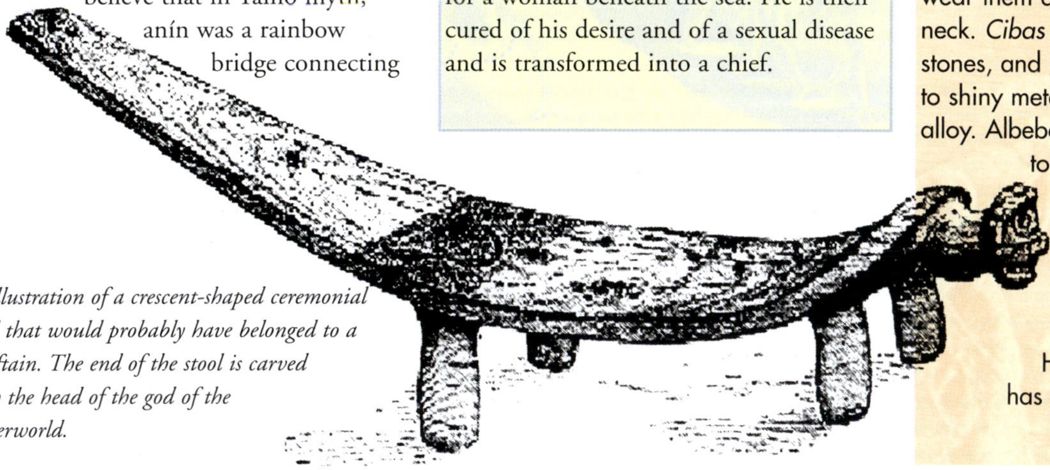

▶ *Illustration of a crescent-shaped ceremonial stool that would probably have belonged to a chieftain. The end of the stool is carved with the head of the god of the underworld.*

North America

INTRODUCTION

THE ORIGINS OF THE NATIVES of North America may be traced down the ages to a time, as distant as 60,000 years ago, when a colorful horde made its way up from the warm plains of Central Asia, northeastward into Siberia. They did not stop at Siberia's boundaries; they crossed from the Chukotka Peninsula into America—for at that time a land or ice bridge connected Chukotka with what is now Alaska.

They were hunters and gatherers, living on the edge of game herds. From Alaska; generations of these people moved down the Columbia River that flowed to the warmer regions in the south, and across the Rockies. They met strangers, fought with some and banded together with others. They followed bison and buffalo south across the plains, eastward to the Atlantic, and all the way south along the Sierra Madre Oriental, over the Mexican Plains, through rain forests and into the jungles of Yucatan. They settled and moved, learning to use the bow and bola, chipping flint, weaving baskets, and making clay pots.

So far did they travel that today ties of language, culture, and physical appearance still loosely connect the Indians of Peru and Bolivia with the Inuit of Siberia and Alaska, the Huron and Iroquois of New York State with the Chukchi and Koryak of northeastern Siberia.

There were as many tribes as there were "stars in the sky" and they spoke at least 300 languages. But they were always under pressure to move on. A turning point came in 1492 when Christopher Columbus landed in the New World. Thinking he had arrived in India, he mistakenly called the peoples "Indios"; the English followed suit and called them "Indians."Later the French added *peaux rouges*, "redskins." Over the next four centuries, from 1492 to 1890, the native Americans found their lands invaded, and during that time much of their culture and civilization was destroyed.

The native American oral tradition does not easily divide into myths and other forms of storytelling. The peoples themselves mostly use the term "stories," distinguishing "true stories" about the present world and "mythic stories" that describe events which happened in an earlier time before human beings appeared.

Because the peoples had no written language, their stories were not set down on paper until white men traveling among the tribes recorded them from the 1830s. Each village had at least one old man who knew the tales and acted them out, imitating the various characters with a growl, squeal, roar, or groan.

In the days before the US Government confined native peoples to reservations, the tribes had extensive inter-tribal contacts, as a result of which tales were exchanged, so the same stories may be found, albeit in different variants, all over the continent.

▲ *"Hole-in-the-Sky" pole, decorated with mythical and historical events.*

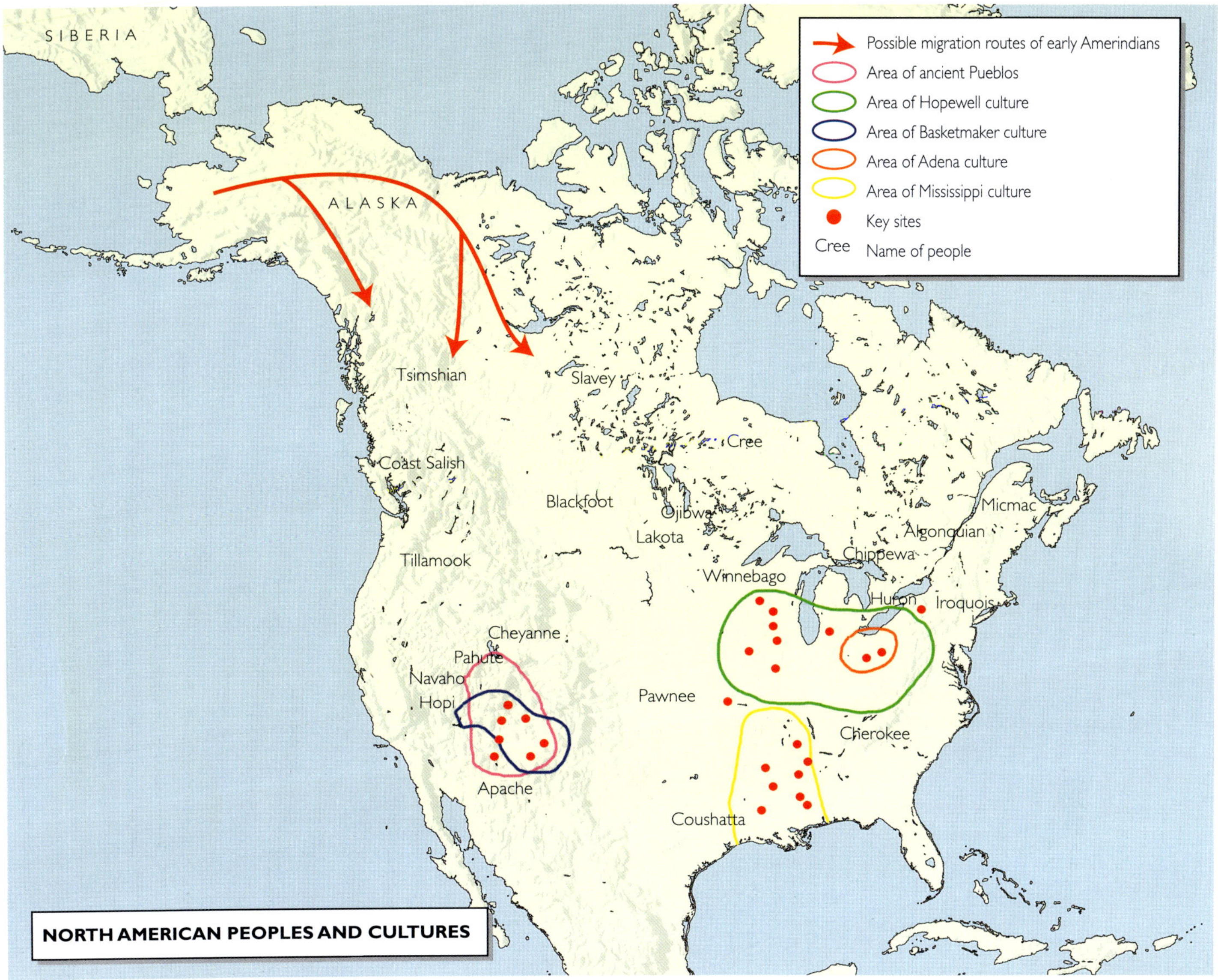

NORTH AMERICAN PEOPLES AND CULTURES

ROOTS OF MYTHOLOGIES

THE MOST SIGNIFICANT MYTHS, spiritually, are those which tell of the activities of the gods, particularly myths of the creation of the universe and of humans, and of the origins of death, animals and plants such as corn and tobacco. The peoples only told such myths at certain times of the year and in particular circumstances. Myths told the whole year round may fall into the category of entertainment or education myths, recounted for moral instruction and diversion, and therefore flexible in their interpretation and elaboration.

◀ *Hide painting of a post-hunt buffalo dance.*

FUNDAMENTALS

ALL THE TRIBES shared the belief that everything that moves is alive. Thus, to these animists, a spirit lurks in every stick and stone, tree and animal, and each object may take another form with gay abandon: the girl hiding from the moon changes into a mound of soil and a lamp, or she can turn into a block of stone, a hammer, a tent flap, a hair, or a grain of soil. Each object can act according to its own will and has its own separate existence.

This form of understanding arose as a direct expression of people's feelings of impotence before the mysterious, powerful, and terrible forces of nature. Being wholly dependent on nature, people did not divorce themselves from it, and their fear of it caused them to attribute supernatural powers to natural phenomena. They may struggle with natural objects and vanquish them; they may sacrifice to them and ask them for protection. They may pick up the smaller ones and use them as charms. These charms or spirits of objects—an owl's or bear's claw, piece of buffalo horn, or walrus tusk—carried about the body would ensure safety against hostile forces.

Life under such primitive circumstances would have been an endless fatalistic round of terrors had there not been some defence against the evil spirits. The various charms, chants, and sacrifices, even the telling of myths, provided hope in countering the forces of destiny.

TRICKSTERS AND MISCHIEF-MAKERS

THE MOST POPULAR personage of North American mythology is the trickster. This being combines human and animal features and is, at once, a figure of fun, a joker, a gullible fool, and the creator of the universe. The trickster god is best shown in the Raven stories of the North Pacific coast and the Coyote cycles of the Great Plains.

The trickster takes many forms. He is the Great Hare for the Winnabago people of Wisconsin, Nanabush or Glooskap in northern and eastern North America (the Woodlands), Rabbit in the south-east, Spider in parts of the Great Plains, and Mink or Blue Jay on the north-east coast. Whatever form he takes, the trickster offers the storyteller great scope for acting and mimicry, which no doubt explains why such stories are so widespread.

In the Raven cycle, the character of Raven is a transformer, part god and part clown. His insatiable appetite has him searching for something to eat, tricking animals out of their food supply. He is also an incurable womanizer, though he is often thwarted in his quest. Like Coyote, however, he is often creative and invaluable to the tribe. Hence the Haida name for Raven is He-Who-Must-Be-Obeyed.

CREATION MYTHS

THE MOST WIDESPREAD creation myth concerns an animal which dives to the bottom of the sea for mud. The duck (or raven, loon, coot, mink, eagle, hawk) brings up the mud in its beak and it grows to form the earth. In a Cheyenne myth, the earth is said to rest on the back of Grandmother Turtle.

The earth-diver story is closely related to stories of the flood, which occurs through non-stop rain, or from the tears of those in the world above who, on looking down, grieve at the wrong-doing on earth.

In most myths, humankind is created out of clay (Hopi) or grass, feathers, sticks, or ears of corn. Humans also emerge from the bones of the dead, the Earthmaker's sweat, or merely by making a wish.

Some tribes have the gods mating—Mother Earth with Father Sky, the Sun with the Moon, Morning Star with Evening Star. According to the Iroquois and Huron in the north-east and the Navaho in the south-west, the first being was a woman.

The Micmac of eastern Canada see creation as in a constant state of flux. Their universe consists of six worlds: the World Beneath the Earth; the World Beneath the Water; Earth World; Ghost World; the World Above the Earth; and the World Above the Sky. But reality is never set for ever; it changes according to people's will.

THE CREATION OF THE WORLD

AWONAWILONA—The-One-Who-Contains-All—was invisible, enshrouded in darkness and engulfed in emptiness. Then out of Awonawilona rolled mists and flowing streams, and he fashioned a fiery ball—the sun—which touched the billowing mists, and they gathered together to form raindrops which became the ocean. Next Awonawilona planted his seed upon the ocean's waters and the seed grew to form a green cover that spread across the waters. This Awonawilona split in two: one half became Mother Earth, the other Father Sky.

Mother Earth spat upon the sea and stirred it with her fingers until a foam arose. She breathed upon this foam and created black and white mists which floated as clouds above the ocean. Father Sky breathed upon the clouds so that they dropped life-giving rain upon the earth.

Father Sky then rose into the heavens. Life grew swiftly inside Mother Earth and it was not long before she gave birth to living beings, first ugly serpents, then fearful monsters and, finally, giant twins who hurled thunderbolts that made deep holes in the earth.

Binding trees, vines, and grasses together, they made a rope ladder so that human beings could escape from the dark bowels of the earth. Those that succeeded in climbing out found the soil neatly furrowed and ready to receive the first corn seeds. The people began to till the soil and reap the harvest.

This is a Pueblo story of the creation, from the desert areas of south-west America—Arizona and New Mexico.

▼ *Portrait of a Navaho chief wearing traditional clothing.*

▶ *A young Apache whose name means "The Son of Many Goats."*

NAVAHO CREATION MYTH

THE NAVAHO and their cousins the Apache, who live today in Arizona, New Mexico, and Utah, are the largest group of surviving North American native peoples, with a population of some 160,000. Their traditions contain the most complete account of the creation myth, which consists of four stages. The first, the Beginning, tells of the ascent of the first people from the underworld to earth. The second, the Animal Hero Age, describes how the earth was set in order and the adventures of the early inhabitants. The third, the God Age (the Yei, led by Talking God), tells of the slaying of monsters. And the fourth age portrays the growth of the Navaho nation in its early wanderings.

SUPREME BEINGS, GODS, AND HEROES

MOST NATIVE AMERICANS have a supreme god or spirit. It is Awonawilona (The-One-Who-Contains-All) for the Pueblo peoples in what is now Arizona and New Mexico; Tirawa (Heavenly Arch) for the Pawnee of Oklahoma; Sagalie Tyee for the Coast Salish in British Columbia; Gitchi Manitou for the Algonquians of north-east Canada; and the twin brothers Tobats and Shinob to the Pahutes of Utah.

Whoever the supreme god is, he normally leaves the everyday affairs of the world to other gods to manage.

Stars are personified heroes who hunt through the sky. The thunder, wind, and storm, for example, live in human form and can also take the shape of an animal. Thus, it is the beating of the Thunderbird's wings that creates the noise of thunder as well as the storm below as it flies through the sky. Anything struck by the Thunderbird's lightning exerts a spiritual power to be either avoided or venerated.

Heroes who overcome seemingly impossible obstacles may be demigods or ordinary mortals who have to go through certain ordeals, like going to the sky world or down to the land of the dead to rescue a maiden who has died. The demigods rid the earth of primeval monsters in mythical times.

◄ *A headdress in the form of the Thunderbird, identified by its hook beak and feathered horns.*

ORIGIN OF DRY LAND

ONE OF THE MOST popular motifs regarding the appearance of dry land involved earth-divers: when various animals attempted to dive to the bottom of a great ocean to gain a small amount of sand or other materials to make the earth appear.

All manner of birds and fish feature in this tale. Among the tribes of southern California, it is the duck (who is successful), eagle, hawk, crow, and hummingbird. Among the Coushatta tribes of Texas it is the crawfish who succeeds after the frog and beaver have failed. However, instead of bringing up soil in his claws, as in versions related by other tribes, the crawfish built a mud chimney that eventually reached the surface of the water.

THE STORYTELLING STONE

THERE WAS ONCE an orphan who grew up strong and wise. One day his aunt gave him a bow and arrows, saying, "It is time for you to learn to hunt. Go to the forest and bring back food." He set off early next morning and shot three birds. At about midday, however, the sinew that held the feathers of his arrow came loose, and he sat down upon a flat-topped stone to mend it.

All of a sudden, he heard a deep voice, "Shall I tell you a story?"

He glanced up, expecting to see a man standing there, but there was no one.

"Shall I tell you a story?", came the voice again.

The boy was beginning to feel afraid. He looked in every direction yet still could see nobody. When the voice called out again, he realized that it was coming from the stone on which he was sitting.

"Shall I tell you a story?"

"What are stories?" asked the boy.

"Stories are what happened in the long-ago time. My stories are like the stars that never fade."

When the stone had finished one story, it began another.

All the while the boy sat, head bowed, listening. Towards sundown, the stone suddenly said:

"We will rest now. Come again tomorrow and bring the people of your camp to listen to my stories. Tell each to bring a gift."

That evening the boy told the whole camp about the storytelling stone. And so it was, next morning, the people followed him into the forest. Each person put meat or bread or tobacco on the stone before sitting down.

When all was quiet the stone spoke:

"Now I shall tell you stories of the long ago. Some of you will remember every word I say, some only part, others none at all. Now listen closely."

The people bent their heads and listened. By the time the stone had finished, the sun was almost down. The stone then said:

"My stories are all told. Keep them and tell them to your children and your children's children, and so on down the ages. And when you ask someone for a story, always give a gift."

And so it was. All the stories we know come from the stone, and from the stone came all the wisdom we have.

This is told by the Seneca, from the area around what is now Toronto in Canada. Stones are the bones of the earth; they are alive and must be treated with respect.

SHAMANS AND MEDICINE MEN

ONLY THE SHAMAN has the power to commune with the gods or spirits, to mediate between them and ordinary mortals, to talk with the souls of the dead on behalf of the living. The shaman is often an extraordinary character both in physical appearance and in acting

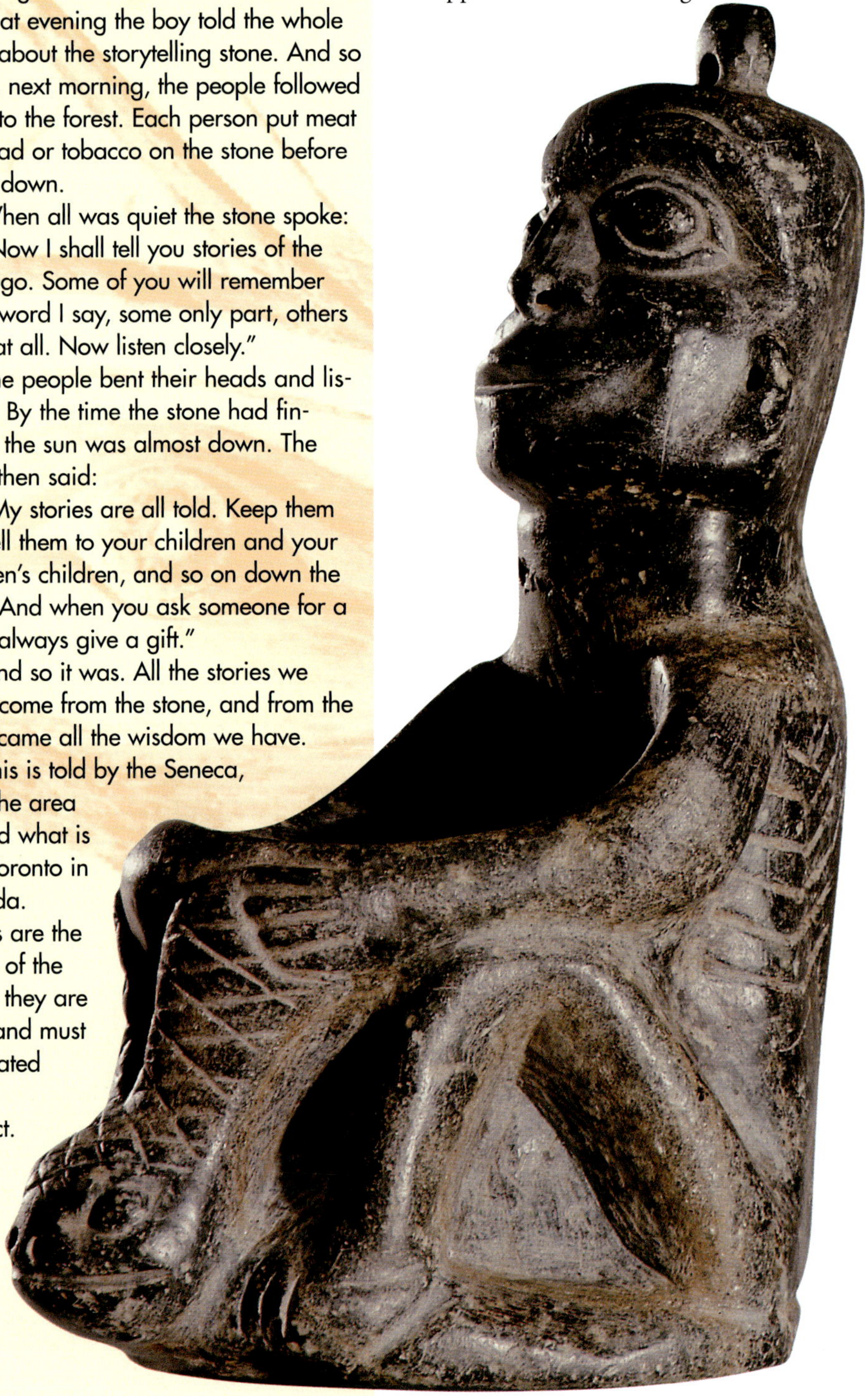

talents. He would be a mystic, poet, sage, healer of the sick, guardian of the tribe, and repository of stories.

To become a shaman, a person had to "receive the call," to suffer a religious experience and be initiated into the mysteries of the art. By symbolic death and resurrection he acquired a new mode of being, his physical and mental frame underwent a thorough change. During this period of initiation the novice would see the spirits of the universe and leave his body like a spirit, soar through the heavens and the underworld. There he would be introduced to the different spirits and taught which one to address in future trances.

Those who do not possess the full range of shamanistic attributes become only "medicine men." Since sickness was thought to be caused by an evil spirit entering the victim's body, the shaman could call it out and cure the patient. He would do so in a special ritual, beating a rhythm on his drum, swaying and chanting, steadily increasing the sound, and interspersing it with long-drawn out sighs, groans, and hysterical laughter.

TOTEM POLES

CARVED ON WOODEN totem poles are representations of mythic beings, often animals (such as eagle ancestors) that had helped the clan and gave it its power. The totem poles were also erected as memorials and mortuaries for the deceased; these were set alongside the grave of a dead chief of the clan. Some memorial poles are put up on a riverside or lakeside, where they can be easily seen by visitors approaching by water. Such memorial poles are usually erected by a chief's son and heir to show his claim to the chief's title. The Haida tribe of Queen Charlotte and Prince of Wales Islands were famous carvers of these monuments.

▶ *Carved figure of a medicine man.*
◀ *Ceremonial dish, probably used to grind tobacco or paints.*

LITTLE STAR

EARLY ONE MORNING as the Sun rose from his bed, his handsome son, Morning Star, told him, "I have fallen in love with a maid of the Blackfoot tribe and want her for my wife."

Despite his father's warnings, Morning Star painted his bronze body, stuck an eagle's feather in his hair, put on his scarlet cloak and shining black moccasins, and appeared before the maid he loved.

She fell in love at once and agreed to be his wife, leaving her home on the plains and flying up to his home in the skies. The Sun warned her she must never look down on her earthly home, and she gave her word.

After a while a son, Little Star, was born. One day, as she sat in the tepee of her mother-in-law, the Moon, she asked why the big iron pot in the center always boiled without a fire.

"It has a source to fuel it," said the Moon. "But heed my words: you must never move the pot. If you do, misfortune will befall you."

At midday, when the Moon was asleep, the maid could not restrain her curiosity. She approached the pot and pulled it aside. To her surprise, she could see right through the hole beneath the pot. And there was her former home, the green prairie, the blossoming wolf willow and dog rose. And she was filled with a longing to see her kinsfolk again.

As soon as Morning Star's father, the Sun, heard of her disobedience, he ordered her to return to earth with her child. "No more will you see your husband," he said. "That will be your punishment for disobedience."

The maid and her son were wrapped tightly in a caribou skin and lowered on a leather thong through the hole beneath the iron pot. But before they reached the earth, the little boy forced his head out of the skin and was cut along the side of his face by the thong. Ever afterward he was known by the tribe as Poia, Scarface.

He grew up ugly and scarred, and one day he decided to journey to his father to have the scar removed. After many moons, he came to a rocky shore and saw a path of light stretching before him across the waters to the sky.

When he reached his father, he did indeed have the scar removed; he returned to earth and married the chief's daughter whom he loved.

This is the story of the Blackfoot tribe, from the plains of Alberta in Canada.

▲ *Native American medicine man from the Blackfoot tribe. His bear costume shows the respect the Blackfoot felt for the bear spirits.*

◀ *Shield cover decorated with a turtle, a thunderbird, stars, and the Milky Way.*

THE OTHER WORLD

THE AFTERWORLD is generally described as a place of peace and happiness, and especially of plentiful game for hunting—hence the name "Happy Hunting Grounds" given to it by the Plains peoples. Because of the absence among many tribes of an underworld or hell, death

appears to present little fear. After death, the person merely travels to the spirit land and remains there, living as he or she did on earth.

The Other World may be reached by the living through various means. Some cross the rainbow or a swirling river or sea. With help from demigods, mortals may tread over a magic chain of arrows or a tree that is stretched into the world above. More simply, some people may just shut their eyes and wish themselves there.

Numerous tales exist of men of the afterworld looking down and falling in love with an earthly maiden, then coming down to earth, having a child and taking his family back home. Almost inevitably the earth wife breaks a taboo and must then depart with her child by descending a rope or leather thong. In a Blackfoot story where the marriage is successful, the tepees of their many children may be seen in the evening sky as the Milky Way.

GREAT SNOW IN THE NORTHLANDS

ONE NIGHT in the long-ago time, the darkness was very black and snow began to fall. It fell all through the long, black night, which seemed endless. The snow became deeper and deeper, covering plants and bushes; the animals had difficulty finding food, and many died.

At last the council decided to send messengers to the Sky World to discover what was causing the long night and snow. A member of each family of animal, bird and fish that lived on the shores of the Great Slave Lake was sent; those that could not fly were carried on the backs of those that could. So all entered through the trapdoor that led to the Sky World.

Beside the trapdoor stood a great lodge made of deer skins. It was the home of Black Bear. Hanging from the cross-bows overhead were some curious bags. On asking what the bags contained, they were told that one contained the winds, one the rain, one the cold; Black Bear refused to tell them what was in the last bag.

When the Bear went out, however, the curious animals pulled down the last bag and threw it through the trapdoor to the earth below. The bag had contained the sun, moon, and stars, and the snow now started to melt from the sun's rays.

Thinking the earth world would now be safe, the animals began their flight down to earth. But some had accidents on the way: beaver split his tail, spilling spots of blood over lynx; moose flattened his nose and buffalo bumped his back.

The peaceful and friendly life on the lake was no more. When the flood waters had gone, the fish found they could no longer live on land because the birds and animals ate them; the birds found they were safer high in the trees. Each animal chose the place that suited it best.

Soon the birds and fish and beasts could not even understand each other's language. Not long afterward, the first humans came to the lake. Since then there has been no peace at all.

This story comes from the Slavey tribe, from the shores of Great Slave Lake in what is now Canada's Northwest Territories.

▲ *The impressive Chief Mountain, a sacred site for the Blackfoot, who would visit the area for meditation and to gain spiritual power.*

Animals can marry humans, and the children of such unions possess a human intellect combined with animal strength.

Animal tales were sometimes told during the hunt when a storm forced the hunters to take shelter; and then the storyteller would speak loudly because it was generally thought that animals listened to the tales as well. Typically, few tales were told of domestic animals such as the dog, goat, horse, or chickens, since whatever did not serve as an object of the hunt had little interest for hunting tribes; some, indeed, had no names for creatures that were not hunted. The most common actors in the tales are the bear, fox, wolf, wolverine, and, of course, the raven.

◀ *The ritual robes and equipment of a shaman: staff, rattle, necklace, and bear claw crown.*

ORIGINS OF ANIMAL CHARACTERISTICS

ANIMALS ARE FREQUENTLY the principal actors of North American tales and sometimes appear as cosmic creative agencies. Animals had chiefs, councils and lived in cabins or tents like those typically built by the tribes. Often the animals are found mingling with people and speaking their language.

Animals often personify certain traits and characteristics. Rabbit is commonly a trickster and mischief-maker; the turtle is regarded as the type of plodding slowness, while the fox, deer, and rabbit represent speed. The race between two types is common to many tribes, with the victory naturally going to the patient striver rather than the self-confident boaster.

ANIMISM

NORTH AMERICAN natives are animists: they believe that everything that moves (clouds, water, leaves, wind) is alive. They therefore live in harmony with nature and give a story to each part of it, trees and flowers, birds and animals, moon and stars. Thus, the water lily which looks up as we paddle past is really a star fallen from heaven. The Milky Way is the snow shaken from the cloak of Wakinu, the bear, as he crosses the Bridge of Dead Souls on his way to the Eternal Hunting Grounds. The Pleiades are seven poor boys who, forever cold and hungry in this world, were changed into stars.

ANIMAL MYTHS

FOR MOST TRIBES, hunting animals was the main occupation and the sole condition for survival. The difference between people and animals was regarded as slight and surmountable. In countless tales, it is related how certain animals were once human beings and vice versa. The Navaho say of the bear that he was once a hunter or a shaman who was changed into a bear, and they tell of a land where people are born as large dogs; even fish are human beings who have been drowned. The Hopi believe that when the beaver was a human being, he was skillful with the bow.

THE HUMAN-ANIMAL RELATIONSHIP

WHEREAS TALES about spirits reflect people's fear of the unknown, in the animal tales people often enjoy a close friendship with the animals; though they are the object of the hunt, they are not

▲ *Burial bowl, punctured at the base to let the spirits out, painted with a male and female figure.*

the tribe's enemy. Even when game is killed it was not thought an offence against the beast, since it had come as a guest of its own accord. The slain beast was highly praised and persuaded not to be offended but to return again to the hunters in another form at another time. For that to happen the hunters had to offer sacrifices: they might cut off small pieces of the animal's nose and throw them on to the ground or back into the river, all the while muttering thanks and pleading for it to come back again.

Some animal tales are told by old women to children who first get their knowledge of animals in this way. And when they ask why an animal is such a size, shape, or color, the myth provides an answer.

▲ *This necklace of bear claws would have been worn as a mark of distinction by men who had carried out acts of bravery resulting from contact with the bear spirit.*

THE BEAR

THE CULT OF THE BEAR holds a special place in North American tales, largely because of the bear's apparent kinship with humans. Above all animals, the bear is believed to possess a soul like that of humans and to understand the language of both people and other beasts. The Micmac actually believe themselves to be descendants of the bear, and the Chippewa call the bear "old man in a fur coat" or sometimes "forest woman" or 'woman of the hills."

The Ojibwa of Canada similarly regard the bear as a female and associate it with a menstruating girl. Approaching the time of a girl's first period, she is known as *wemukowe* - literally "going to be a bear"—and during her seclusion she is known as *mukowe*—"she is a bear."

In many myths bears are described as a race that has human form (often walking on two legs and having skeletons like those of a human) but always wear their coats outside their home. There are many tales about a girl being taken home by a handsome young man only to find that his village was a bear village. She marries the young man, bears twin cubs and returns to her own village, where the twins take off their bear coats to appear as two handsome boys. Naturally, they have good luck in the hunt.

▲ *A robe worn at potlaches by men of high rank. The design represents the brown bear, an animal held in high esteem by native North Americans.*

NANABOZHO

IF YOU LOOK across the blue waters of Lake Superior, you may see a low, rocky promontory that looks rather like a man lying asleep with his hands folded on his chest and his face turned towards the sky. This Sleeping Giant was once Nanabozho, a great creator-magician.

Nanabozho came into being as follows. The Great Spirit, Citche Manitou, sent the Ojibwa a teacher. She was a wise old woman named Nokomis, daughter of the moon. And she had a daughter by the name of Wenonah who was carried off by the West Wind. From that union came two sons; but Wenohah and one of her sons soon departed for the Land of the Spirits. Nokomis found a small white rabbit. She picked him up and called him her Nanabozho, her little rabbit.

WHY THE NORTH STAR STANDS STILL

THE SKY IS FULL of living things. They are as restless as the Pahutes themselves, traveling around the universe and leaving trails all over the sky. Some of the stars are birds who travel to warmer climes; some are animals hunting for better grazing land. The sky is their happy hunting ground.

Yet there is one who does not travel. He is Qui-am-i Wintook, the North Star. Once he was Nagah, the mountain sheep, and one day he found a high mountain with steep sides, ending in a sharp peak reaching up into the clouds. He climbed to the very top. Shinob, the Great Spirit, was walking across the sky when he spotted Nagah stranded on the mountain peak. He decided to turn the sheep into a *see* (a star), shining through the sky for everyone to see. He would be a guide for all living things on earth and in the sky.

And so it was. Nagah became the only star that can always be found in the same place. Travelers can find their way by him since, unlike other stars, he stands quite still. And because he is in the north sky, the people call him Qui-am-i Wintook Poot-see, the North Star.

This is a story from the Pahutes, an ancient people, once large and prosperous, now living mostly in the state of Utah.

THUNDERBIRD

IN AN ENVIRONMENT so dependent on the elements, it is natural that many myths should interpret the weather in a fantastic way. Many tribes imagine thunder to be a mighty bird whose beak and eyes flash lightning, while the beating of its wings is heard as thunderclaps. To the Lakota, Wakinyan, the Thunderbird, is an assistant deity and manifestation of the Supreme Being, with awesome powers of creation and destruction. To the Iroquois, this eagle-like creature takes on human form as Hino, the spirit of thunder and guardian of the heavens. Tribes in the west of North America believe there are four such thunderbirds, one in each corner of the world. All the while, the thunderbird is engaged in constant struggle with evil spirits and monsters; their fighting is said to be the cause of earthquakes, floods, terrble thunderstorms.

The Tsimshian of the north-west make a wooden image of the bird and fix it outside their tents on a long pole. It is thought to protect the soul of the shaman who may encounter many dangers in his flight through the sky. They see proof of its powers in lightning-damaged trees which the Thunderbird has torn to shreds with its "claws of stone."

▼ *Transformation masks, worn for ceremonial dances, were opened at different points in the dance to reveal another aspect of the character. This thunderbird mask opens to reveal a human face to express the dual human/animal nature of the spirits.*

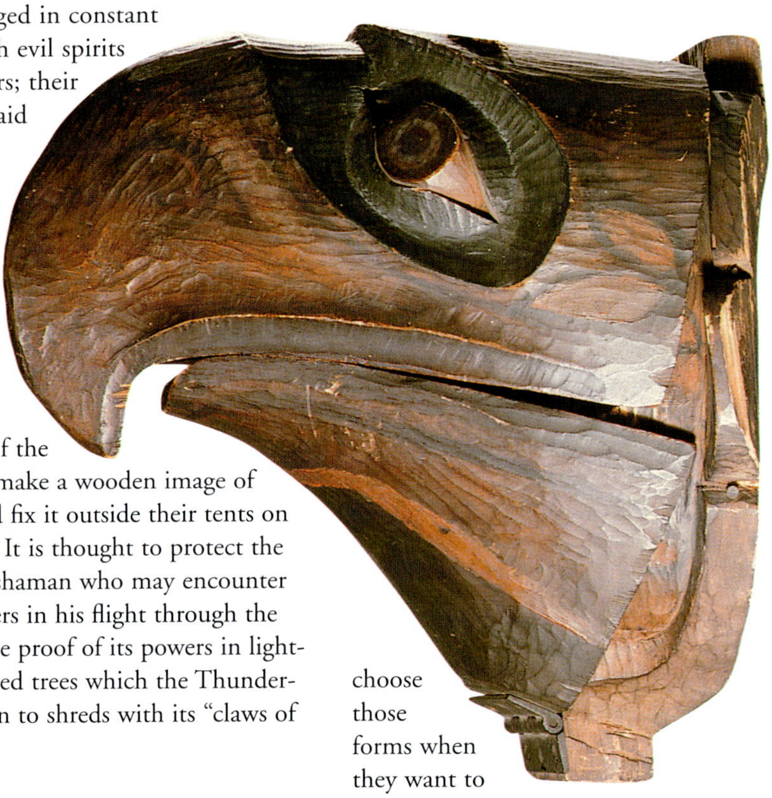

ANIMATE GEOGRAPHY AND WEATHER

IN THE SIX WORLDS of the Micmac of eastern Canada and northern New England, the very geography is animate. Stars are persons who hunt through the sky; thunderclaps are powers of the natural world and, at the same time, people—the Kaqtukwag, and as thunderers they live both in human form and in bird shape. It is the beating of their wings that creates the noise and great winds of storms below them as they fly.

Winds are themselves persons, as are seasons and directions. Mountains are alive, as are lakes and rivers, and the icebergs floating on the sea. Strange features in the landscape are persons thought of with affection or placated with gifts. Cliffs and boulders are sometimes revealed in stories as "shape-changers" who choose those forms when they want to hide or rest. Such rocks can be potent and terrible beings, as Ki'kwa'ju discovers when the rock he has disturbed begins to rumble after him, crushing the forest in its path.

Hail is the stone of thunder, which falls from the sky in round balls or even in the form of roughly chipped arrowheads and spears. Cold winds and blizzards are produced by a giant who lives on the borders of our world and who spends his time shoveling snow and ice from his dwelling.

RAVEN

THE MOST FREQUENTLY recurring creature in animal myths is the raven. He holds a special place in North American mythology, just as he does in that of related peoples of Siberia and the Arctic regions. The raven, and sometimes the

spider, is considered to be a sacred being, the creator of the universe, and representative of age and wisdom. Killing him is taboo among many tribes. The raven is thought to have helped create the earth, all animals, and humans; he brings light and fresh water, and teaches humans the ways of earthly life.

At the same time, he is the common laughing-stock, foolish, and even somewhat lascivious. He plays tricks on others but is also the butt of various tricks played on him by others. Some peoples, such as the Tlingit of southern Alaska, distinguish two ravens, the culture hero and the trickster.

In the desolate landscape of the far North-West and along the Pacific seaboard the cry of the birds, especially the raven, can be the most noticeable sign of other living beings in the vicinity. Raven's black color also singles him out from other birds: this is explained in tales by his quarrel with an owl, seagull, or loon, in which he has black paint or soot thrown over him.

THE AFTERWORLD

REFERENCES TO A DUAL afterworld with reward and punishment are very rare in North American narratives, and most tribes recognize only an upper world. In the tale "Journey to the Sky," told by the Alabama-Coushatta tribes, the soul of the deceased has to encounter several dangerous obstacles. A great body of water and a place filled with snakes are among the traveler's hazardous problems. A huge eagle attacks anyone moving along the prescribed route, and so a big knife is buried with each dead person to be used in fighting this fierce bird. The final obstacle is crossing under the domed sky as it rises and falls at the edge of the earth.

HEROES

THE HERO WHO overcomes seemingly invincible foes is a universal theme in world mythology and one well developed in North America. In certain regions, like the south-west and California, the heroes tend to be demigods and their adventures are concerned with ridding the earth of primeval monsters in mythical times. For most of the continent, however, the myths deal with the exploits of extraordinary mortals in a world roughly conforming to its present form.

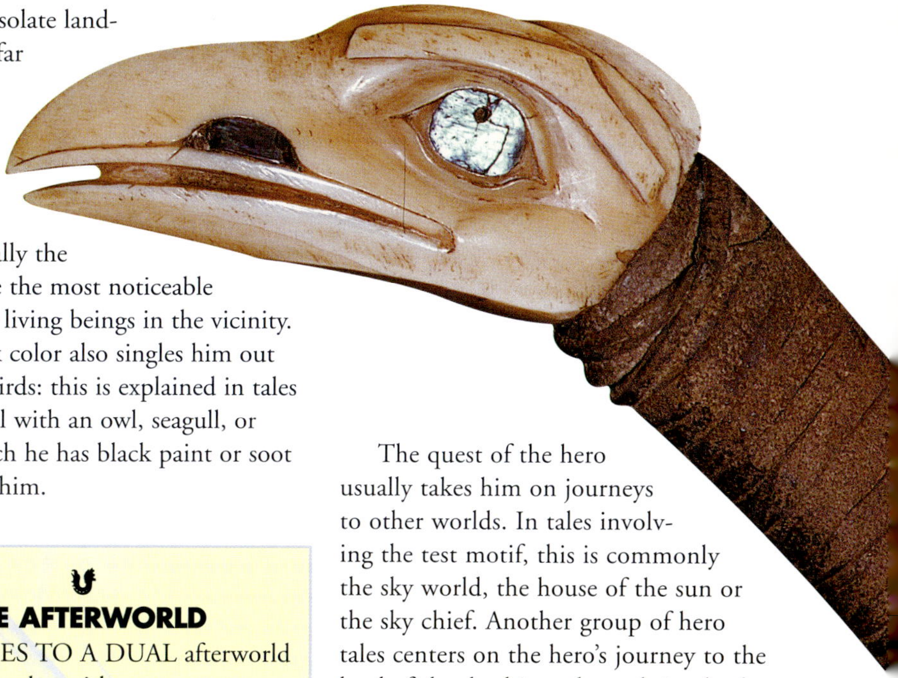

The quest of the hero usually takes him on journeys to other worlds. In tales involving the test motif, this is commonly the sky world, the house of the sun or the sky chief. Another group of hero tales centers on the hero's journey to the land of the dead in order to bring back a loved one. In some versions the return of the dead wife is prevented because of the breaking of a taboo; in others the dead wife is successfully restored to life, as in a Winnebago tale which, in contrast to a Cherokee version, gives the story a happy ending.

◀ *The eyes of this Kachina doll represent the rain clouds, the lashes symbolize the rain.*

▲ *Knife hilt shaped as a raven. Ravens are believed to have brought fire from the sky and were blackened as punishment.*

HEADDRESS AND OTHER CEREMONIAL CLOTHING

ALL THE CEREMONIAL costumes worn by members of the tribe, especially the chiefs and warriors, were dictated by mythic custom or religious vision. Feather bonnets or headdresses were made from the skin and horns of a buffalo, while the feathers were traditionally from eagles. The decorated shirts, the shape of the standards, the patterns of paint on both man and horse—all had mythic significance. Such clothing was worn on ceremonial occasions, on return from successful raids and in battle itself.

Tribes naturally used decorative materials that were at hand. Thus, the Plains Cree were expert at making ornaments of dyed porcupine quills, while the Blackfoot wore crow and owl feathers. In all cases, that animal's special qualities were believed to be transferred to the wearer.

▶ *Traditional headdresses were made from eagles' feathers.*

COYOTE

COYOTE APPEARS in a wide range of roles all over the central plains and in the south-west and west of the country. The part he plays varies from creator to trickster, from lover to magician. Sometimes, especially in tales found among the tribes of the Great Plains, Coyote appears as the personification of unbridled appetite and of all possible vices. Cruel, deceitful, and licentious, he is shown in many tales as seducing even his own daughter or grandmother by his trickery.

Coyote is particularly well known for his gluttony, eating almost every kind of animal or plant. In the tales, a favorite motif is his transformation into a dish so that he may receive the food people place on it.

He is also depicted as a gullible fool, outwitted by the animals he tries to trick. His lack of mercy and his ingratitude to those who help him make him almost monstrous. Yet in other tales he figures as the powerful sorcerer who brings order into the world and bestows great benefits on humankind. True, the benefits are usually less a result of his own altruism than an indirect outcome of his efforts to satisfy his own selfish appetite.

The story told here is a Tsimshian tale from the Canadian Pacific coast.

COYOTE AND THE SALMON

COYOTE CAN CHANGE shape whenever he wants. One day, while crossing a river, he fell into the water. To escape drowning he changed himself into a wooden board and was swept downstream until he ran into a dam.

Soon an old woman noticed the board and decided it would make a good food dish. So she took it home and put salmon in it for her dinner. Imagine her surprise when the salmon disappeared so quickly she hardly got a bite to eat. She grew so angry that she threw the board into the fire.

At once Coyote, finding himself in the fire, changed himself into a baby which cried in pain. Quickly, the woman grabbed him from the fire and brought the baby up as her own.

Time passed and the baby grew up, but it was always naughty and disobedient. One day the woman was going on a journey, but before leaving she told the coyote-child:

"While I'm gone, do not open any of the boxes in my barn."

Coyote promised, but being disobedient he had no intention of keeping the promise. He was curious to know what was inside. First of all, however, he wanted to get rid of the dam that had stopped him being swept out to sea. There were no salmon in coyote's country and he wanted his people upstream to enjoy the tasty salmon. So he had first to destroy the dam so that the salmon could swim upstream.

No sooner had the old woman gone than Coyote smashed the dam with an ax, letting the salmon swim upstream.

To satisfy his curiosity, he began to open the four boxes. To his dismay, out of the first box poured a horde of angry smoke-wasps; out of the second a black cloud of salmon-flies; out of the third a cloud of blow-flies; and out of the fourth, a swarm of meat beetles.

From that day on, Coyote was able to provide his people with as much tasty salmon as they wanted. However, because he was so disobedient, his people are tormented by smoke-wasps, salmon-flies, blow-flies, and meat beetles. Every year they reach their peak in the spring, at the very time the salmon begin their run upstream.

◀ *A shaman's rattle in the form of a salmon.*
▼ *This area was known as "'Hell's Half Acre'" by the Plains Indians that lived there due to its sulfurous springs.*

THE CHANGER OF THE PACIFIC NORTH-WEST

AT FIRST THE EARTH was flat, without mountains or trees; and it was full of cannibal monsters. Then came the Changer. The Qhilleute say this was the clever and crafty mink; the Makah say raven and the Puget Sound people say fox. The Chehalis think it was the moon turned into a human being, and the Tillamook make it a woman. North to Alaska and east to the Rockies, the tribes tell of the Changer in various different forms.

Wherever the Changer camped, creeks and springs sprang up and they have never run dry. He piled up the mountains. He made the rocky cliffs of the Pacific shore by dumping out a sack of wooden combs such as the people use for their hair. He stole the sun from the miser who kept it, and he threw it up into the sky.

CHIPPEWA MYTHS

THE CHIPPEWA are Algonkian-speaking native Americans who lived in the region of the Great Lakes with hunting, fishing, and gathering as their means of subsistence, supplemented by growing corn and squash in summer, harvesting wild rice in fall and tapping maple trees for sugar in the spring. This cycle involved a nomadic or semi-nomadic way of life. Dome-shaped wigwams were constructed which could be built quite quickly. Travel was on foot or by birchbark canoe, or by toboggan in winter.

Chippewa myths may be divided roughly into the following classifications: Wenebojo (a real person) creation myths; tales about Matchikwewis and Oshkikwe, mostly cautionary tales told by women to young girls showing them how to behave; *windigo* tales about people's fights with cannibal giants; animal tales about people's true encounters with animals, and anecdotes involving tricks played by one animal on another; and tales of spells and magical powers about persons who have come under the magical domination of a powerful evil person.

Part of the Wenebojo cycle was told in the course of the Medicine Dance ritual. Other stories were supposed to be told only in winter. Some said that one could not tell stories unless the frog and snake were in the ground because they were bad spirits which should not be allowed to hear the stories.

◀ *A Chippewa warrior wearing ceremonial costume.*

HIAWATHA—THE-COMBER-OUT-OF-SNAKES

THE GREAT SPIRIT, weary of the wars that were slowly destroying his earthly children, called a council to which he invited braves from all the tribes. He scolded them for their strife and told them that he would send a medicine man who would show them the ways of peace.

Years passed, and a young boy grew up in the Mohawk tribe. One night he had a dream of the future given to him by the Great Spirit. The boy's vision was of a world without war.

When the boy grew up he tried to plant the seed of his vision into others; and gradually the Iroquois were converted to the idea of a league of tribes (Ho-de-no-sau-nee). Only the Onondaga remained outside the league, under their evil medicine man Atotarho.

The young man journeyed into Onondaga territory and sat at the council fire in the Onondaga camp. Upon the head of Atotarho, snakes writhed and wrapped their slimy coils in a seething mass, but the young man gained the tribe's consent by proposing Atotarho as the Sachem Chief and the Onondaga as keeper of the sacred fire.

Taking up the sacred deer antlers, he placed them upon Atotarho's head. To everyone's astonishment, the snakes fell to the ground, dead. From that time the young man was known as Hy-ent-wat-ha—the Comber-Out-Of-Snakes.

THE CHIPPEWA MEDICINE DANCE, AND RELIGION

SUMMER WAS the time for Chippewa village life. The Midewiwin, or Medicine Dance, was held in the spring when people assembled in the villages, and again in the fall before the bands split up for the winter hunt.

The Midewiwin was the most important collective religious ritual of the Chippewa and contained many ancient features, notably the origin myth about Wenebojo, the trickster culture hero, part of which was told in the course of the ceremony. Only initiated members could take part in the dance. Application for membership in the Midewiwin could result from sickness or from the death of a close member of the family; or it might come from a dream which was interpreted to mean that the individual should join the Medicine Lodge. A person could "go through" the Medicine Dance several times, attaining different stages of initiation.

Although Midewiwin rituals differed from community to community, the usual performance consisted largely in parading around the Medicine Lodge in a counter-clockwise direction to the accompaniment of drumming and singing. The climax of the ceremony came when the new initiate was magically "shot" by some selected members of the lodge, who aimed their medicine hides at him and supposedly injected small white shells into his body.

MASKS

IN MANY CEREMONIES, especially those to cure the sick, the actors wear masks representing various supernatural beings who possess great healing powers. The Yei masks of the Navaho are made of buckskin from deer that have been ceremonially killed. The spilling of blood must be avoided, so the deer is suffocated by having sacred meal or corn pollen stuffed into its nostrils.

These masks are worn during the Yeibichai winter curing ritual or Night Chant; it can only be held at night, when snakes are asleep. The rite is performed to cure patients of madness or fits. During the last two nights of the ceremony, however, the Yeibichais initiate young boys and girls into the secrets of the masked gods.

◀ *Illustration of the wedding of the Indian chief Hiawatha.*

▲ *Mask with articulated eyes and jaw—these were used to convey different emotions.*

SUPERNATURAL BEINGS

MOST SOUTHERN tribes commonly believed that something supernatural resided in every created thing. So people were surrounded at all times by these supernatural beings, who would make themselves visible to travelers in the dense forests or would indicate their presence by weird sounds.

One of the fundamental, characteristic beliefs was the helplessness of humans against their environment when unaided by the magic power of some favored being. The good and bad spirits possess the power of bestowing all things of social and economic value; and one may bring spirits into a relationship with humans by fasting, mental concentration, self-castigation, and even torture, offerings and sacrifices, prayers and incantations, and charms and fetishes.

Central and South America

INTRODUCTION

THE FIRST HUMANS made their way to the Americas between 30,000 and 20,000 years ago across a land bridge which connected Siberia and Alaska. By 15,000 years ago humans were living in the southernmost part of South America, at the site of Monte Verde in Chile. For some 15 millennia, until Christopher Columbus landed in the Bahamas in 1492, Amerindian peoples developed in cultural and geographical isolation from the rest of the world. This had profound consequences for the course of Pre-Columbian civilization and the shape of its mythologies and religions. Untouched by the political, religious, military, or cultural upheavals in the rest of the world, and Mediterranean Europe in particular, the Americas were insulated also from the ravages of many Old World diseases. The Amerindians' lack of immunity turned even the common cold and smallpox into killers, bringing about a cataclysmic decline in indigenous populations as they came into contact with Europeans. However, this same isolation had produced a unique blend of religion, world view, and mythology—one which, broadly speaking, was shared throughout the Americas by tribe and empire alike.

What Europeans discovered in the Americas from the late fifteenth century onward was a pristine world where the power of myth was a concrete reality, the natural world infused with spirit power, and the spark of divinity visible in every rock, plant, and animal. Mesoamerican and South American peoples lived in a variety of contrasting natural surroundings. In both areas, volcanoes, mountain chains, arid deserts, and humid tropical rainforests made up a landscape of dramatic contrasts. In South America in particular, the twin rivers of the Amazon and Orinoco flowed through the Amazonian lowlands, producing the world's most diverse plant life and supporting a startling variety of animals. The close physical relationships between Amerindians and their surroundings influenced their views of the natural world and the spirits they believed inhabited it. Civilization developed to varying degrees in each of these environmental areas. The great Pre-Columbian societies arose in Mesoamerica and in the central part of the Andes in South America. The gradual move away from hunting and gathering in these areas and the development of agriculture formed the basis for civilized life, increasing populations, and the rise of villages, cities, and eventually imperial states. The mythologies of Mesoamerica and South America were as varied as the people, but they shared a unity of purpose and a coherence in a typically Amerindian world view where physical and spiritual matters were indissolubly linked.

ROOTS OF MYTHOLOGIES

AT THE HEART of Amerindian mythologies were the accumulated formative experiences of hunter-gatherers for untold millennia before the development of agriculture. The intimate understanding of the environment of hunting societies brought familiarity with a vast range and amount of practical information. They knew which plants to eat and which to avoid, which could cure and which poison, they understood the breeding cycles and movements of animals, the whereabouts of fresh water and of raw materials to make tools, pottery, clothing, and weapons. They knew how to move through a landscape by recognizing the smallest detail—animal tracks, smells, birdsong, shifting winds, and the feel of the earth beneath their feet.

This close understanding forged a bond between Amerindians and their surroundings, in such a way that the natural world was understood in terms of their own social world. Landscape was not only a place of physical realities but also of myth and magic. Amerindian landscapes were crisscrossed by invisible lines of power—connecting myth, kinship, and knowledge of the physical and supernatural worlds. Remembering and passing on this information was a cultural act, achieved through observation, instruction, rites of passage and mythic stories which gave a spiritual dimension and sacred explanation to the details of everyday life.

This fundamental and shared world view of Amerindians nevertheless found different cultural expressions in the variety of Pre-Columbian civilizations of Mesoamerica and South America. The proximity of adjacent contrasting physical regions led to a mixing of customs and beliefs, of trade, and of influences on art, religion, and mythology. The symbolizm of Pre-Columbian America's first civilizations—

the Mesoamerican Olmec, and the Chavín culture of the Andes—is full of images and ideas from the tropical rainforests. Both societies possessed sophisticated art, representing in carved stone jungle animals, portrayals of animal-human transformation, the ritual use of hallucinogens, headhunting, cannibalizm, and the building of monumental architecture. These precocious societies made solid the mythic world of the rainforest and bequeathed their technological advances to the long line of civilizations that came in their wake. In Mesoamerica, the Zapotec, Teotihuacanos, Maya and Aztec shared ideas and beliefs which first appeared in material form in Olmec times. Similarly, the influence of Chavín was felt throughout the Andes, affecting the Moche, Wari, Tiwanaku, Chimú, and Inca civilizations. Each society had its own myths of origin, its own ideology and ethnic identity, yet all were keyed into a fundamentally Amerindian world view.

▶ *Page from the* Codex Fejervary-Mayer *showing the fire god at the center of the universe being fed on sacrificial blood.*

▼ *The pyramid of the Magician at Uxmal.*

Mesoamerica

INTRODUCTION

MESOAMERICA IS THE TERM used to describe that part of Central America whose inhabitants shared important cultural features from around 1000 B.C.E. until the Spanish conquest of 1519–21. It encompasses most of modern Mexico, Guatemala, and Belize, as well as parts of Honduras, El Salvador, Nicaragua, and Costa Rica. For almost 3,000 years, a variety of civilizations flourished in the contrasting landscapes—from arid high plateaux to lowland tropical rainforests.

Despite underlying differences in language, politics, and art styles, the peoples of Mesoamerica displayed a surprising unity in their religious beliefs and mythologies, in their use of hieroglyphic writing, a 260-day sacred calendar, and in playing a rubber ball-game. Mesoamerica's distinctive combination of agriculture, village life, and religious ritual had appeared by 2000 B.C.E. Around 1200 B.C.E., the Olmec emerged as the region's first civilization, introducing a pantheon of half-human, half-animal gods, monumental architecture, human sacrifice, and blood-letting. Together with pyramid-building, trading in exotic goods, ancestor worship, and the divine status of dynastic rulers, these were ideas and practices emulated by all subsequent Mesoamerican cultures.

FOREMOST DEITIES

IN MESOAMERICA, Olmec jaguar gods were the earliest deities. Their associations with royalty and fertility influenced many later civilizations. Among the Maya, the supreme creator was Itzamna, lord of all gods and patron of writing. Closely related to him was the jaguar-eared Sun God,

▲ *The animals here represent blocks of time, while the profiles of the gods represent numbers.*

THE NATURE OF MESOAMERICAN MYTH

THROUGHOUT MESOAMERICA, individual myths and groups of related myths served to integrate and make sense of the political, spiritual, and natural worlds of their creators. This they did by placing their society at the center of the universe and by bestowing a sacred legitimacy on the social hierarchy and the activities of the elite. The ideologies of dynastic Maya kings or Aztec emperors were presented in mythical terms as the will of divine rulers who were at one with the supernatural world. In the Mesoamerican world view, the spiritual boundaries between life and death were indistinct, and humans, animals, ancestors, and gods could mingle in spirit form and change their outward appearance. Time itself was cyclical, and events repeated themselves according to patterns established in mythic eras. Births, deaths, marriages, war, and sacrifice were not unique to the physical world, but re-enactments of momentous events enshrined in myth. This explains the widespread Mesoamerican obsession with time and the sacred and secular calendars which measured its passing and predicted the future. At an everyday level, myths illustrated ideas of life and death, the fertility of people, animals and plants, and the fundamental unity of life.

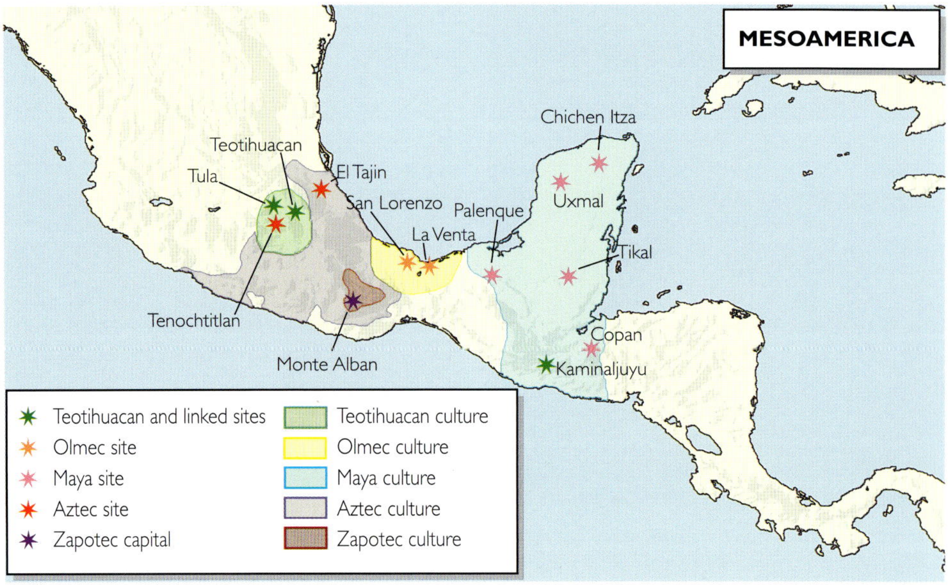

Kinich Ahau, who traveled through the underworld at night from west to east. Among the Aztecs, the foremost deity was Tezcatlipoca, "Lord of the Smoking Mirror," the omnipotent patron of royalty and sorcerers. Uniquely Aztec was Huitzilopochtli, "Hummingbird of the South," the tribal war god to whom human sacrifices were made.

AZTEC CREATIONS OR "SUNS"

THE AZTECS, like many Mesoamerican peoples, believed that the universe was conceived in a struggle between the powers of light and darkness. In the beginning were Ometeotl and Omecihuatl, the male and female lords of duality. Their cosmic offspring were the four Tezcatlipocas: Red Tezcatlipoca or Xipe Totec associated with the east, Blue Tezcatlipoca or Huitzilopochtli with the south, White Tezcatlipoca or Quetzalcoatl with the west, and Black Tezcatlipoca with the north. These were joined by the lords of fertility, Tlaloc the rain god and Chalchiuhtlicue, his consort, goddess of water. It was a series of cosmic struggle between these sibling gods that led to the creation and destruction of successive worlds that is such a feature of Mesomerican creation myths. In Aztec belief, there were five creations or "Suns"—each identified by the cataclysm which engulfed it.

The first creation, presided over by Tezcatlipoca, was called "Four-Jaguar" and was a time when giants walked the earth. After 676 years, Quetzalcoatl knocked Tezcatlipoca into the water and the earth was consumed by jaguars. This initiated the second creation, "Four-Wind," ruled by Quetzalcoatl and brought to an end when Tezcatlipoca took his revenge by casting Quetzalcoatl off his throne, turning people into monkeys and destroying the world with hurricane winds. The third creation was called "Four-Rain" and was dominated by fire. Governed by the rain god Tlaloc, it was destroyed by fiery rain sent by Quetzalcoatl. Then came the fourth creation, known as "Four-Water," which was identified with Chalchiuhtlicue, the water goddess. This world ended when the earth was engulfed by flood and its human inhabitants turned into fish.

With the passing of these imperfect worlds, Tezcatlipoca and Quetzalcoatl were transformed into two great trees and raised the sky above the earth. Quetzalcoatl then descended to the underworld and retrieved the bones of people drowned in the flood. Human flesh was created when the bones were ground into powder and mixed with the penitential blood of the gods. Although the earth was then inhabited by people, it remained in darkness. The gods gathered at Teotihuacan determined to bring about the fifth creation—the Aztec world. The god Nanahuatzin hurled himself into a blazing fire and was magically transformed into the rising sun. When he remained motionless, the other gods sacrificed their blood to give him the energy required for his daily journey across the heavens. This fifth world era is called "Four-Movement."

▲ *The Two Lord Ometecuhtli, was both male and female and the supreme creative deity.*
◀ *Lady Precious Green, Chalchuitlicue, the fertility goddess.*

QUETZALCOATL

THE UNITY OF MESOAMERICAN religions and myths is illustrated by recurring figures who play crucial roles in the epic encounters of the supernatural world. One of the most frequently depicted characters is Quetzalcoatl, whose name means "feathered serpent." Sometimes a god, and other times a king or priest, images of Quetzalcoatl appear most graphically on the Temple of Quetzalcoatl at Teotihuacan. In later epochs, the deity is confused with the historical figure Ce Acatl Topiltzin Quetzalcoatl, ruler of the Toltecs of Tula. During Aztec times, he was the patron of rulership, venerated at the city of Cholula.

HIGHLAND MYTHS

IN HIGHLAND Mesoamerica, myths reflected the physical and cultural realities of life beyond the tropical rainforests. Creation myths in particular were linked to a changing and unstable landscape whose rainfall was unpredictable and where flash floods and volcanic activity presented a constant threat to civilized life. These physical realities played an active part in shaping understanding of the world and appeared also in myths which embodied this knowledge. The third Aztec creation was characterized by fire and destroyed by fiery rain—a reference, some authorities believe, to the devastating effects of volcanic explosions. Similarly, the Aztec glyphic name for the fifth creation—the Aztec era itself—was "Four-Movement," suggesting a link between powerful spirit forces which animated the universe and unpredictable earthquake tremors which shook the Valley of Mexico. In this landscape, heat contended with cold, downpour with drought, and plenty with famine: realities personified as gods of water, sun, and unpredictable fate in creation myths. Highland Mexico during Aztec times was a mosaic of different peoples, dynasties and traditions—most of whom had long preceded the Aztec people. The Aztec myth of the five creations put the Aztecs center stage, describing the past as a series of failures and the present as the gift of Aztec rule, based on regular and bloody human sacrifices to nourish the gods that gave birth to the world.

▼ *Jade plaque showing a Mayan ruler in full regalia standing on a bench supported by two prisoners.*

MAYA CREATIONS IN THE *POPOL VUH*

THE *POPOL VUH*, or "book of counsel," is a unique masterpiece of Mayan literature, preserving ancient myths relating the creation of the world of the Quiché Maya of Guatemala. The *Popol Vuh* tells how, in the beginning, in total silence, the creator gods Gugumatz and Huracan shaped the earth, dividing the mountains from the water, separating sky from earth. After making the trees and bushes, they created a world of animals—jaguars, deer, birds, and serpents. But the creatures were unable to speak and could not praise their makers or call out their illustrious names. So dissatisfied were the two gods that they condemned the animals to offer their flesh to any who would eat it, then set their minds to a second creation.

This time the deities fashioned humans in the hope that they would immortalize their creators' names in prayer. But they were made of mud and crumbled away, dissolving in the swirling waters. Disappointed again, Gugumatz and Huracan tried a third time, calling for help on ancestral diviners, sorcerers, and spirit animals. On this occasion, the humans were carved from wood, and they spoke and looked like real people. Yet, as they populated the earth, the manikins had no memories of their makers and failed to speak their names. The gods wreaked their revenge by turning the world upside down, making the pots, grinding stones, and even dogs rebel against the

people of wood until this third creation too was destroyed.

In the fourth and final attempt at making creatures who would honor their creators, the gods discovered that, to fashion human flesh, they had to use maize. The fox, coyote, parrot, and crow brought ears of white and yellow maize to the deities, who transformed it into the first four men—the mythic founders of the four lineages of the Quiché Maya. The men of maize were handsome and good, they saw and understood everything, and they praised and nourished their creators. Gugumatz and Huracan however were jealous of the perfection of their creations, worried that the men would become as great as the gods themselves. So they subtly changed the nature and powers of the four—limiting their understanding of the world and diluting their uniqueness by creating women and enabling them to procreate. Most of all they clouded their vision, so that now they could see only what was close by. With this creation, the founding of the Quiché nation was assured, and in the east the world's first dawn broke and light spread over the earth.

◄ *Sculpture of the personification of the maize god.*

THE CALENDAR STONE

AZTEC CREATION MYTHS are vividly portrayed in the impressive Calendar Stone. Discovered in 1790 near the Great Aztec Temple in Mexico City, the four-meter-wide disk is less a true calendar than a monumental vision of Aztec creations carved in stone. At the center is the face of the sun god Tonatiuh, flanked by two giant claws and four boxed figures representing the four previous suns—dedicated to the jaguar, wind, fire, and water. Surrounding these are day signs from the sacred calendar and symbolic representations of Tezcatlipoca, Quetzalcoatl and Tlaloc. The calendar stone is a reminder of how entwined art and myth are in ancient Mesoamerica.

► *The Calendar Stone.*

LOWLAND MYTHS

ALTHOUGH LOWLAND peoples shared many features of their mythology with their highland neighbors, they were inspired and constrained also by the tropical rainforests and swampy rivers of their environment. These areas had an excess, not a shortage, of water, possessed lush vegetation, and abounded in plant and animal foods as well as innumerable dangerous animals. They experienced dramatic shifts in climate, from burning sun to hurricane-force winds and electrical storms, tropical downpours and consequent floods.

Maya mythology and art, and their creation stories especially, embodied these natural forces in the successive world eras so typical of Mesoamerican cosmogony. In the Popol Vuh of the Quiché Maya, Hurricane or Huracan was one of the cosmic pair of creator gods who shaped the world, and the power of his storm winds turned the world upside down, ending the third world era. The luxuriance of the tropical rainforest and its animal life is a feature of the first world era, acknowledged in the fashioning of wooden people in the third creation. Unlike the multi-ethnic highlands, the Maya lowlands were inhabited only by Maya-speaking peoples. A deep ethnic unity underlay broader Mesoamerican similarities, bestowing a uniquely Mayan character on their epic myths.

CENTRAL MEXICO, PEOPLES AND MYTHS

MYTHS RELATING the genesis of central Mexican peoples are not as straightforward as they might first appear. During the thirteenth century, central Mexico was a mosaic of different social and ethnic groups, each with their own traditions, gods and languages—though all shared a common Mesoamerican world view. Most myths of ethnic origin are "official" versions, prepared long after the event, and reveal how these peoples manipulated history, weaving it with ancient mythic traditions, spiritual beliefs, and political and military imperatives. There were three major population groups. The first, Chichimec, was a term which confusingly was also applied to all peoples who migrated into the Valley of Mexico. Regarded as semi-civilized, knowing the rudiments of culture but dressed in animal hides and using the bow and arrow, the Chichimec were nomadic tribes who adjusted to the agricultural village life they encountered in the settlements around the Valley of Mexico. The Tepanec came originally from the eastern marches of the Valley of Toluca and were mainly of Matlazinca ethnic stock. A third migrant people were the Acolhua who settled in the eastern Valley of Mexico. Into this melting pot of cultures and overlapping mythic traditions came the last great migrant wave—the Aztecs or *Mexica.*

MEXICA GENESIS

MEXICA (AZTEC) origins are shrouded in mystery and legend and confused by many alternative accounts. Their epic stories are influenced by common Mesoamerican origin themes, such as a primordial emergence from caves, and long and arduous migrations punctuated by dramatic mythical events. Episodes are not always sequential, locations may be geographical or mythic places, and many events were erased, added or suitably elaborated only after the *Mexica* became an imperial power. The god Huitzilopochtli's prophecies of impending greatness for the *Mexica* are probably an example of such later additions. Confusing matters even more is the fact that the language of myth is not that of history—it relies on allusion and metaphor. Many events portrayed as real belonged to the realm of magic and spirits and cannot be interpreted literally. Accounts of *Mexica* genesis are often contradictory, favoring as a point of origin either the island Aztlan or the womb-like caves of Chicomoztoc, or mixing together these and other places, such as Culhuacan. Through the veil of myth we perceive the outline not only of true history but also of political realities—the intrigue, factionalizm, and maneuvering that characterized these formative times and led, for example, to the splitting off of a tribal division mythologized and personified as Malinalxochitl, "sister" of Huitzilopochtli.

MYTHICAL ORIGINS OF THE AZTECS

ACCORDING TO AZTEC tradition, their patron ancestors had emerged from the sacred earth at Chicomoztoc, the legendary mountain of "the seven caves"—a place of cosmic genesis for many Mesoamerican peoples. Yet many accounts state that it was from the mythical island of Aztlan in north-west Mexico that the Aztecs took their name and began their epic migration, south-east to the Valley of Mexico, in the year "1 Flint" (C.E. 1116 or 1168). Aztlan was surrounded by reeds and located in a great lagoon: its name means "the place of whiteness" or "the place of herons."

According to myth, during the journey the Aztecs were guided by a speaking idol of their tribal war god Huitzilopochtli. When they were joined by a group of nomadic hunter-gatherers called the *Mexica*, the god persuaded his people to adopt the latter's name and way of life as well as their weapons, the bow and arrow. They wandered across mountains and deserts for 20 years, never staying long in one place, and always being urged on by the visionary spirit of Huitzilopochtli, who prophesied future greatness for his people. The god spoke to the *Mexica* through his priests, telling them how they would conquer all the peoples of the universe and become the lords and kings of the world. According to the deity, the Mexica would receive tribute of gold, emeralds, coral, quetzal feathers, cacao (chocolate), and cotton.

The mythic journey continued to Culhuacan, the "curved mountain," and, confusingly, to Chicomoztoc, though these may be one and the same. There then followed a series of internal quarrels, one of which led to the abandonment of Huitzilopochtli's sister, Malinalxochitl, who traveled on to found the town of Malinalco. The Mexica continued their wanderings to Coatepetl ("serpent mountain") near Tula. Here, the supernatural Huitzilopochtli was magically conceived by Coatlicue, "She of the Serpent Skirt," the earth mother, from a ball of precious feather down. The embryonic god was forewarned of an attempt by his jealous sister, the moon goddess Coyolxauhqui, and her 400 star brothers, the Huitznahua, to kill his mother and himself. Forestalling the murder, Huitzilopochtli sprang fully grown from his mother's womb as an invincible cosmic warrior, and with a flaming fire-serpent cut off Coyolxauhqui's head and dismembered her body. He then scattered his star brothers to every corner of the sky. The *Mexica* left Coatepetl, making their way to Tula, and from there into the Valley of Mexico.

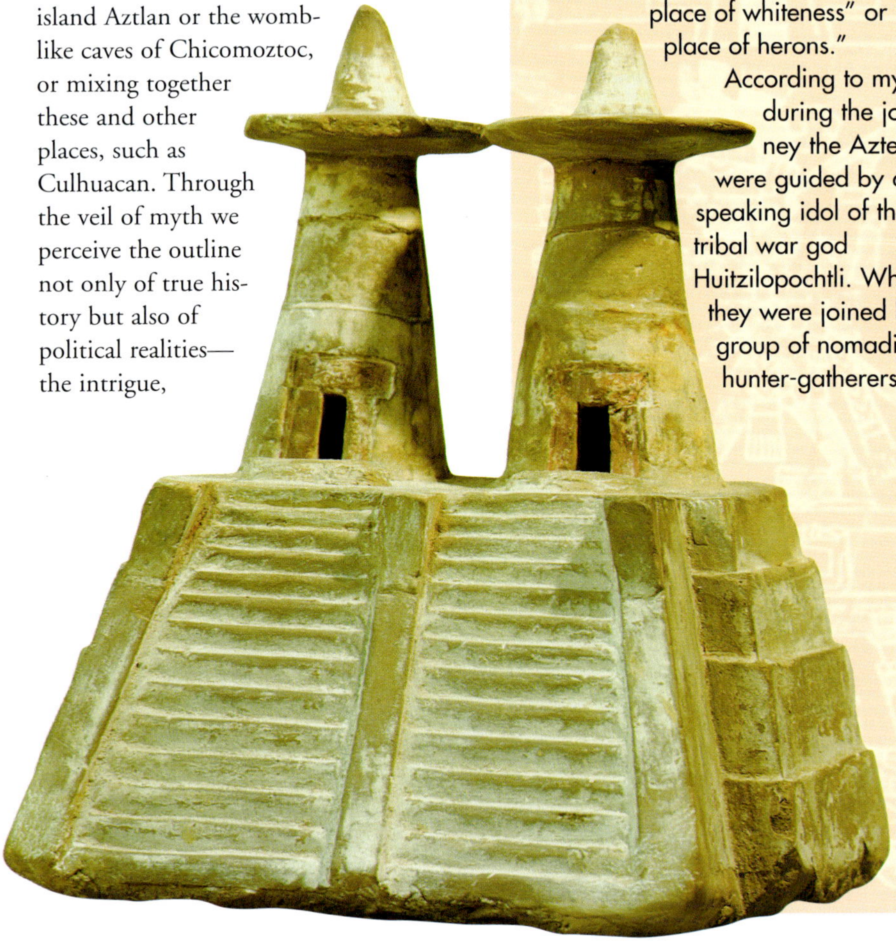

◀ *Model temple used as a household shrine to the god Quetzalcoatl.*

▲ *Stele representing the sun and the moon.*
▶ *Shied Jaguar stands here with a torch whilst his wife, Lady Xoc, draws a rope through her tongue as a blood sacrifice.*

XIPE TOTEC

ONE OF THE MOST DRAMATIC artistic representations of myth is the *Mexica* deity called Xipe Totec, the god of vegetation and springtime renewal. In stone sculpture, and in the painted screenfold books known as *codices*, this god wore the flayed skins of his sacrificial victims. Personifying the idea of fertility, Xipe Totec, "Our Lord the Flayed One," embodied ancient pan-Mesoamerican ideas of maize fertility. The god's priests dressed in human skins which, as they dried and cracked, fell away in imitation, so the *Mexica* believed, of new corn casting off its husk.

COSMIC BATTLES, MYTH, AND HISTORY

THE EPIC BATTLE between Huitzilopochtli and his sister Coyolxauhqui at Coatepetl, near Tula, is a dramatic example of *Mexica* mythic history. It is the climactic event in the preparation of the *Mexica* for their entry into the Valley of Mexico. It is usually interpreted symbolically, to show how Huitzilopochtli as the deified *Mexica* sun defeated the forces of night personified as his sister Coyolxauhqui the moon goddess and the "four hundred" stars. This cosmic battle prepared the universe for the fifth "Sun," the *Mexica* world era. The myth is important for various reasons. Coatepetl is a place of rebirth and renewal for Huitzilopochtli—the place where the world is made anew. What happened here may have served also to re-establish his authority over his people. His mother's name, Coatlicue, means "She of the Serpent Skirt"—a ritual name applied to the sacred earth. The "four hundred" stars who assist Coyolxauhqui actually signify "innumerable" in ancient Mexican thought. The dismemberment of the moon goodess is a mythic charter for human sacrifice in general, and female sacrifice in particular, and the martial nature of Huitzilopochtli is a sacred justification for the Mexica's imperial aspirations and the imposition of tribute on conquered peoples.

THE EAGLE AND THE CACTUS

ACCORDING TO *Mexica* myth, they entered the Valley of Mexico looking for the signs which their patron god Huitzilopochtli had foretold. These were a white juniper tree growing from two great rocks around which two streams, one red, the other blue, were flowing. The reeds, rushes, frogs, and fish living around the streams all were pure white, recalling Aztlan, the "place of whiteness." On seeing these signs, the *Mexica* priests and tribal leaders wept for joy. They announced that Huitzilopochtli had kept his promise and their wanderings were at an end. That night, the god spoke again to the priests in visions, telling them how the sacrificed heart of his nephew had fallen on to a stone, and how a large and beautiful *nopal* cactus had sprouted from it. A great eagle had nested in the cactus,

and all around were scattered the multicolored feathers of birds which he had killed and eaten. This place, said Huitzilopochtli, was called Tenochtitlán. The next day the elders and priests searched the area until they found the eagle perched atop a great *nopal* cactus, clutching in its claws a bird with shimmering feathers. They bowed low to the eagle, which greeted them with similar respect. At this, the assembled leaders wept again and gave thanks to the Lord of Creation and to their own patron Huitzilopochtli.

THE GREAT TEMPLE

THE *MEXICA* expressed their imperial destiny by building the Great Temple of Tenochtitlán, in what is today Mexico City. All Mesoamerican temples were god-houses, *teocalli*, and embodied the cosmic essence of the god's people. The *Mexica*'s Hueteocalli, or Great Temple, was a dual pyramid dedicated to Huitzilopochtli and Tlaloc, and thus materialized myths relating to both deities. Re-built and enlarged by successive emperors, the Great Temple was a symbolic recreation of Coatepetl, and the human sacrifices which took place there repeated Huitzilopochtli's bloody victory over Coyolxauhqui. The presence of the shrine and offerings to Tlaloc suggests the temple was also conceived as a great cosmic mountain symbolizing water and fertility.

PROPHECIES FULFILLED: THE FOUNDING OF TENOCHTITLÁN

THE ARRIVAL of the *Mexica* in the Valley of Mexico, their sojourn among the peoples already settled in cities fringing Lake Texcoco, and the eventual founding of their own capital at Tenochtitlán, was a series of events encapsulated in a blend of myth and history. Although portrayed simply as the will of Huitzilopochtli, in reality the *Mexica* encountered a Valley of Mexico whose best lands were already occupied by a multitude of peoples. At first, they went to the city of Colhuacan, whose ruler Achitometl allowed them to settle nearby in exchange for tribute and fighting as mercenaries on his behalf. During this time they enhanced their status by marrying Colhuacan women, Achitometl himself giving a daughter to one *Mexica* leader, who promptly sacrificed her to Huitzilopochtli. Chased by Achitometl's army, the *Mexica* took refuge in the swampy marshlands on the western side of Lake Texcoco which belonged to Tezozomoc, king of the Tepanec city of Azcapotzalco. Here they stayed as vassals of the Tepanecs until CE 1428 when, under their leader Itzcoatl, the *Mexica* routed the Tepanec forces. The historical victory of the Mexica with all its attendant complexities was finally rewritten as a triumph of Huitzilopochtli—the self-fulfilling prophecy of his divine will.

SACRED EARTH, MIRROR OF HEAVEN

TWO MAJOR THEMES of Mesoamerican myth are the linked ideas of the sacred earth and a concept of cyclical time often described as mythic history. Time and again, in the Maya, Teotihuacan, Zapotec, and *Mexica* cultures, we encounter deifications of the earth, water, and celestial bodies. Uniting the rhythms of nature with human life-cycles and the realities of everyday social, economic, and political life, Mesoamerican peoples conceived a landscape permeated by spiritual essence and the power of their ever-present supernaturals.

Part of this world view arose from wider, pan-Amerindian shamanic ideas of transformation, but part also was uniquely Mesoamerican. Exemplifying this was the supreme *Mexica* deity—Tezcatlipoca, "Lord of the Smoking Mirror." Omnipotent and omnipresent, Tezcatlipoca spied on the world through his magical mirror, made from shiny black obsidian mined from the living volcanic earth itself. Capricious but generous, donor of gifts to humankind yet inhumanly cruel, Tezcatlipoca saw into the very thoughts of his subjects.

Characteristically, the *Mexica* regarded themselves as the slaves of Tezcatlipoca and the *Mexica* emperor as a living manifestation of the god. The complexities of this deity illustrate the distinctive way in which all Mesoamerican peoples saw themselves in relation to each other and to forces of nature and supernature.

◀ *The early American Indian civilizations built magnificent pyramids that rivaled those of the Egyptians.*

THE HERO TWINS OF MAYA MYTH

ALTHOUGH MUCH of the *Popol Vuh* is concerned with various attempts at world creation by the gods, it also describes the adventures of two sets of twins. The story begins when two brothers, Hun Hunahpu and Vucub Hunahpu, are summoned to the underworld of Xibalba by its gruesome rulers. On arrival, the brothers fail one tortuous test after another until finally they are defeated in a ball-game by the gods and suffer decapitation. Their remains are buried in the ball-court, with the exception of Hun Hunahpu's head, which is suspended in a calabash tree. A young underworld goddess named Xquic visits the tree and its strange fruit, whereupon the head spits into her hand and she becomes pregnant with the Hero Twins, Hunahpu and Xbalanque. Xquic is banished in disgrace to the earth's surface where she stays with Hun Hunahpu's mother until she finally gives birth. In Quiché Maya thought, the Hero Twins display great wit and cleverness, becoming skillful ball-players, blow-gunners, and tricksters. They confront and defeat not only the terrible anthropomorphic macaw Vucub Caquix but also two half-brothers whom they turn into monkeys.

Like their fathers, Hunahpu and Xbalanque are commanded to attend the lords of Xibalba. According to the *Popol Vuh*, every night Hunahpu and Xbalanque play the ball-game with the gods of the underworld, after which gods try unsuccessfully to sacrifice the twins but are constantly outwitted. Every night, the Hero Twins are set a new task which they complete against all odds. However, one night Hunahpu has his head sliced off by a vampire bat, and although Xbalanque replaces it with a pumpkin, the gods use the decapitated head as a substitute for the rubber ball in the next ball-game. Xbalanque concocts a ruse whereby a rabbit impersonates the ball and bounds away, leading the gods astray long enough for him to retrieve his brother's head and restore him to life. The twins permit themselves to be killed and reappear in Xibalba disguised as sorcerers. They hoodwink the gods with feats of magic by killing, then restoring to life a dog, a human, then Hunahpu himself. The gods are so impressed they demand to be sacrificed themselves. The Hero Twins oblige but do not revive the hated deities, and then take their place in the night sky as sun and moon.

▲ *This manuscript shows a week made up of 13 days. The central figure is the water goddess, the deity who overlooks the cycle of the weeks.*

◀ *The hours of the day are illustrated in this ancient manuscript. Each hour is represented by a bird, a number, the symbol for the name of the day, and the divinity representing the hours of the night.*

NATURE GODS

MESOAMERICAN RELIGION was dominated by gods of rain, water, and fertility, whose worship often centered around sacrificial offerings of human hearts and blood. Chac was the Maya god of rain and lightning, identified by his catfish whiskers, scales, and curling nose. The *Mexica* deity Tlaloc poured the rains from four great jars, one for each of the sacred world directions. The tears of *Mexica* children sacrificed to him were an augury of the coming rains. Tlaloc's consort, Chalchiutlicue, "She of the Jade Skirt"—a name alluding to a shining body of water—summoned hurricanes and whirlwinds. She was also associated with human fertility via the "breaking of the waters" which precedes childbirth.

SACRED SKIES OF MESOAMERICA

MANY MESOAMERICAN myths incorporated astronomical information by linking earth and sky in a grand cosmic scheme. Mesoamerican astronomy was not science in the Western sense. Detailed knowledge of the movements of the heavenly bodies gathered by priest-astronomers was used to calculate the alignment of temples, the timing of war and sacrifice, and the accession to power of a new ruler. In Mesoamerica, the earth was sacred and the sky the untouchable realm of gods and spirits, whose power reached down to affect the lives of all who inhabited the land. In other words, astronomical knowledge was filtered through astrological interpretations. In this way, the *Mexica* mythologized the Sun and Moon as Huitzilopochtli and Coyolxauhqui at Coatepetl, and the Quiché Maya saw the dawn of life as the planet Venus announcing the first sunrise. Among the Classic Maya, when a divine ruler died, he had to be prepared to outwit the gods in combat and thus be reborn as a celestial body. Many Classic Mayan temple-pyramids were aligned to the rising of celestial bodies. At Palenque, dynastic events were timed to coincide with observations of Jupiter, and periods of the moon and Venus were used in calculating interlocking calendars for sacred and secular puposes.

◀ *This bearded sun god decorated the front of an elaborate incense burner.*

▲ *Tlaloc the rain god in his mountain temple.*

THE FIRST MAYA DAWN

THE QUICHÉ MAYA account of the first dawn describes the appearance of the sun, moon, and stars in terms of astronomy and myth. The first people ever made were the founders of the four Quiché lineages, Jaguar Quitze, Jaguar Night, Not Right Now and Dark Jaguar. They were overjoyed when they spied Venus, the "sun carrier," who rose before the sun. They unwrapped three kinds of precious copal incense which they had brought and burned it towards the east, in the direction of the rising sun. As the smoke curled into the sky they wept with joy and anticipation at the imminent dawn. As the sun rose, all the animals of the world gathered on the mountain peaks and stared eastward. All were happy as the sun rose into the sky. The first to cry out was the parrot, then the eagle, vulture, jaguar, and puma. As the sun's heat grew, he dried the surface of the earth and turned the original animals to stone. It is said that if the first jaguar, puma, and rattlesnake had not been baked hard by the sun, humans would have no relief from the dangerous beasts today. And the sun himself left only his reflection after the first dawn; today's visible sun is but this shiny disk.

MAYA CALENDARS

UNITING THE VARIOUS aspects of Maya life, religion, and ritual was their sophisticated development of the Mesoamerican dual calendar system. Permeating Maya mythology was the ritual significance accorded to the gods, signs and numbers which marked the passage of time. The system comprised two separate but interlocking calendars which expressed a uniquely cyclical view of time, integrating the parallel spheres of everyday and sacred life. The solar calendar, or Haab, comprised 18 months each of 20 days, to which were added five unlucky days to make a total of 365. Running in parallel, and intercalated with the solar year, was the sacred calendar, or *Tzolkin*, made up of 260 days divided into 20 "weeks" of 13 days. Each of these "weeks" was presided over by a particular deity or deities, and every day also had its own god or goddess. For the Maya (and other Mesoamerican peoples), the intermeshing of the two calendars produced a "Calendar Round" of 52 years. Thus time, and the fate of individuals and society were conceived as cyclical.

▲ *The parrot on this tripod vase is believed to be the bird deity Vucub Caquix. The outstretched wings and the necklace it is wearing signify power.*

MESOAMERICAN THEMES

THE MESOAMERICAN myths recounted here are primarily concerned with the ethnic origins of the *Mexica*, and separately, the Quiché Maya—though all cultures had their own variations on this theme. The *Mexica* myths stress their divine origin from astral deities, thereby glossing over what may have been an ethnically mixed background. Mythical migrations and the legendary founding of their capital at Tenochtitlán are also in accord with official *Mexica* ideology—the sense of predestination to imperial greatness. For the Quiché Maya, ethnicity was less of an issue, the myths of the Hero Twins and the First Dawn being more concerned with the primordial establishment of the natural order between the gods, people, and animals.

Andean South America

INTRODUCTION

IN SOUTH AMERICA, the central Andes of modern Peru and Bolivia were home to the great Pre-Columbian civilizations. From before 1000 B.C.E. until the Spanish conquest in C.E. 1532, a diversity of cultures flourished in this region of contrasting landscapes. Geography stimulated cultural development. The proximity of three distinct environments—high mountains, Pacific coast, and Amazonian tropical rainforests—encouraged craft specialization and facilitated trade.

Although there was never the underlying unity in religion and myth that characterized Mesoamerica, many cultural traits were shared by Andean civilizations over 3,000 years. These included the common view of a natural world animated by spirits and ancestors, pilgrimage, human sacrifice, and the artistic representation of religious and mythological ideas in gold, silver, textiles, and pottery. Yet no Andean civilization developed a writing system and so ideas and beliefs were transmitted orally. Chavín (800–200 B.C.E.) was the region's first major civilization, creating a distinctive art style in which ferocious supernatural jaguars and eagles decorated architecture, pottery, and goldwork. Along with sophisticated stone-built temples and elaborate textiles, these features became the hallmarks of all subsequent Andean civilizations, from the coastal cultures of the Mochica and Nazca to the highland empires of the Tiwanaku, Huari, and Inca.

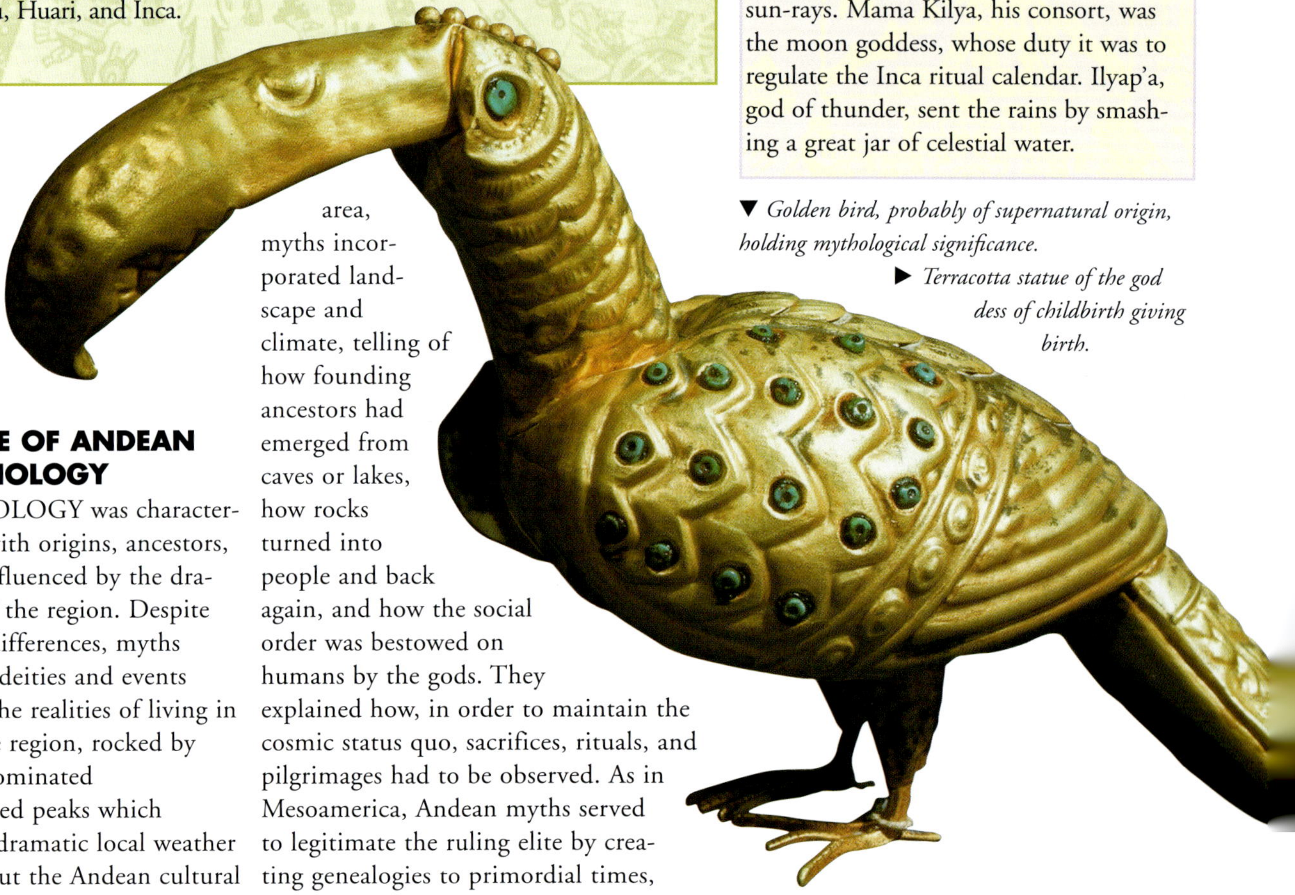

▼ *Golden bird, probably of supernatural origin, holding mythological significance.*

▶ *Terracotta statue of the god dess of childbirth giving birth.*

THE NATURE OF ANDEAN MYTHOLOGY

ANDEAN MYTHOLOGY was characterized by a concern with origins, ancestors, and fertility, and influenced by the dramatic landscapes of the region. Despite local and regional differences, myths tended to focus on deities and events which symbolized the realities of living in a volcanically active region, rocked by earthquakes, and dominated by high, snow-capped peaks which themselves created dramatic local weather patterns. Throughout the Andean cultural area, myths incorporated landscape and climate, telling of how founding ancestors had emerged from caves or lakes, how rocks turned into people and back again, and how the social order was bestowed on humans by the gods. They explained how, in order to maintain the cosmic status quo, sacrifices, rituals, and pilgrimages had to be observed. As in Mesoamerica, Andean myths served to legitimate the ruling elite by creating genealogies to primordial times, establishing the divine status of kings and emperors, and blending the natural and social worlds. Andean mythology provided a framework for living and a sacred charter for ethnic identity. For imperial civilizations, mythology was an integral part of the ideology of military expansion and a method by which the rituals of society and empire were integrated with state religion and social obligations.

GODS OF THE ANDES

THE ANDEAN WORLD, and the Inca pantheon in particular, was ruled by powerful sky gods who presided over the heavens or dwelt atop snow-capped mountain peaks. They sent rain, hail, lightning, and drought to afflict the earth and had to be appeased if disaster was to be averted. Among the Inca, the most powerful deities were Inti, the sun god — divine ancestor of Inca royalty, represented as a golden disk surrounded by sun-rays. Mama Kilya, his consort, was the moon goddess, whose duty it was to regulate the Inca ritual calendar. Ilyap'a, god of thunder, sent the rains by smashing a great jar of celestial water.

ANDEAN AND INCA CREATION MYTHS

THE DOMINANT FEATURE of Andean creation myths was the multiple attempts at shaping not just the natural world but the varied nations who inhabited it. Imperial Inca civilization saw its place of origin not in Cuzco, its capital, but in and around Lake Titicaca to the south. As in Mesoamerica, creations were seen in terms of the relationships between light and dark and successive endeavors by deities to perfect their handiwork. In one Inca version, the god Viracocha first created a world of darkness, inhabited by a race of giants fashioned in stone. When these first people ignored their creator's wishes, Viracocha punished them by sending a great flood to destroy the world. All perished with the exception of one man and one woman, who were transported by magic to the god's abode at Tiwanaku. Viracocha tried a second time, making people out of clay, painting on them the clothes whose varied designs and colors distinguished one nation from another. He endowed each group also with its own customs, language, and way of life.

With his divine breath, Viracocha animated his creations, sending them to earth and commanding them to emerge from natural features of the landscape—caves, lakes, and mountains. At each place of emergence they were to honor their maker by building shrines for his worship. Pleased with his success, Viracocha then created light from the darkness—order from chaos—so that his people could see and live in an orderly world. He caused the sun, moon, and stars to rise up to the heavens from the Island of the Sun in Lake Titicaca.

As the sun ascended in the first dawn, Viracocha cried out to the Inca people and their leader Manco Capac, foretelling that they would be great conquerors and the lords of many nations. As a divine blessing, the god gave Manco Capac a beautiful headdress and a great battle-ax as signs of his royal status among men. Manco led his brothers and sisters into the heart of the earth from where they emerged into the daylight at the place of three caves known as Pacariqtambo.

This account of the magical and transforming activities of Viracocha is but one Inca version of an ancient and pan-Andean cycle of creation myths. At its heart lies the idea of the spiritual unity of people and landscape, of sacred places, journeys, and the appearance of humans at the dawning of first light.

◀ *The god of rain, Viracocha, a creator deity is believed to have created the sun and the moon.*

EXPRESSIONS OF ANDEAN MYTH

FOR ANDEAN peoples, physical and social worlds were inextricably linked by myth in highly distinctive ways. Pilgrimages were made to sacred mountains and snowfields as ancestors who dispensed good fortune and fertility if treated with respect. During Inca times, ancient traditions were re-interpreted. Where once village ancestors had been venerated, local myths and rites were incorporated into the new order and mummies of Inca emperors were worshiped. Women found new roles in the creation of the *Acllas* or "Chosen Women" who attended the royal family and served the cult of the sun god Inti, mythic patron of royalty.

Ancient ideas were manipulated to create the *ceque* system—a series of straight "lines" radiating from the Sun temple of the Coricancha in Cuzco. Each *ceque* line had sacred *huacas* distributed along its length, organizing Inca geographical and symbolic space, and associated with lines of royal kinship, the road system, and the knotted strings, called *quipu*, on which administrative records were kept. Although sacrifices of llamas, guinea pigs and coca were also age-old traditions, the Incas regarded child sacrifices, *capacochas*, as the most valuable gifts to the gods. Brought to Cuzco from every corner of the empire, they engaged in stately ritual before returning home, having symbolically renewed imperial links, and being sacrificed.

CHILDREN OF THE SUN

ACCORDING TO THE INCA chronicler Garcilaso de la Vega, one mythic account of the Andean world was as follows. In ancient times the place was full of mountains, and the people who inhabited the earth lived like wild beasts. They had no religion, no social order, shared each other's wives, and lived neither in houses nor cities. In groups of two or three they inhabited caves and crevices, wore no clothing, and did not know how to make cotton or wool. Instead, those that bothered to cover their nakedness did so with leaves and animal skins. Rather than cultivate the land, they ate human

HUACAS

THROUGHOUT THE ANDES, a feature of religious life is the sacred place—a physical location imbued with mythic significance and supernatural power. Referred to generally as *huacas*, these can be springs, lakes, rivers, rocks, caves and mountains, the tombs of ancestors, or abandoned towns. One of the most common forms are apachetas, piles of small stones strategically placed along mountain paths or at crossroads. Here, travelers may place a stone, offer coca leaves or spill *chicha* (maize beer) as an offering to local deities before continuing their journey. This ancient tradition links people and their myths to the spiritually animated landscape.

▶ *Mythological creatures and figures were used to decorate costumes and jewelry. This silver headdress shows a warrior flanked by two dragons.*

flesh, wild plants, and roots. The Sun looked on these creatures with pity and sent two of his children, a boy and a girl, to instruct them in all the ways necessary for living a civilized life and so that they might also worship him as their god.

He set them down by Lake Titicaca with instructions to thrust a solid golden rod into the soil wherever they stopped to eat or rest. At the place where the rod sank easily into the earth, there they should found the sacred city of the Sun. He then told his two children to nourish, administer, and protect the people whom they civilized and to treat them as their own beloved children in the same way as he had cared for them. "Imitate my example," he said. "I give them my light and brightness ... I warm them ... I grow their pastures and crops ... bring fruit to their trees ... and bring rain and calm weather by turn."

The Sun promised to make his two children the rulers and lords of all whom they instructed and cared for, then departed, leaving his children to journey northward, stopping at many places to test the golden rod. Eventually they came to a small wayside inn known as the Pacárec Tambo or the "Inn of the Dawn." From here they reached the valley of Cuzco which was a wilderness at that time. At a place called Huanacauri, they thrust the rod into the earth and it sank immediately and they saw it no more. Then the princely pair split up and traveled across the land to gather up the varied peoples of the world, impressing them with their demeanor, fine dress and knowledge of civilized living. Their numbers grew, and they venerated the pair as gods and obeyed them as kings. In this way, the great city of Cuzco was populated.

▶ *Ceramic plate depicting a dancing jaguar, crocodile, or supernatural creature.*

GODS OF THE WORLD

AMONG THE INCA, sky gods linked the world of people with the forces of nature and the spirit realm. Apart from Inti, the supreme sun god, the Incas invoked Ilyap'a, the weather god who combined the sound of thunder, the power of thunderbolts and the flash of lightning. Drawing water from the celestial river of the Milky Way, Ilyap'a dispensed fertilizing rains; thunder was the crack of his slingshot and lightning the sparkle of his brilliant clothing as he moved. Mama Kilya, the moon goddess, was Inti's sister and wife, and thus the mythic prototype for brother-sister marriage among Inca royalty. She marked the passage of time and regulated the ritual calendar.

BRILLIANT WORLDS, SHIMMERING MYTHS

IN ANCIENT South America, Andean peoples saw the world as infused with bright spirit matter—the shimmering bodies of supernaturals, the flash of lightning, blinding snow, or the glitter of precious metals and minerals. The various traditions of the Incas used this imagery to illuminate their mythic worlds. If the language of myth employed the metaphors of light and color, so too did artists and craftsmen who worked on behalf of emperors and chiefs. Pottery made from clay, jewelry carved from shells and gemstones, textiles woven from cotton and decorated with feathers, all existed as physical objects whose significance derived from the spiritual qualities of their component parts. In this way gold was widely considered a sacred medium—allied to the brilliance of crystals, silver, and sunlight. Casting gold into lakes was offering one kind of spiritual brilliance to ancestral spirits who dwelt beneath the surface of the waters. These waters themselves once flowed as rivers, originating as rain which fell from sacred skies. This holistic view of a brilliant world partly helps explain the role of the golden rod in Inca creation myths, the Pacific Ocean as "mother of fertility" and the rising of sea level to mountain tops in legendary accounts of floods. It also sets the scene for the recurring importance of Lake Titicaca as a "place of emergence" and as a metaphor for spiritual rebirth.

EL DORADO, GOLD, AND MYTH

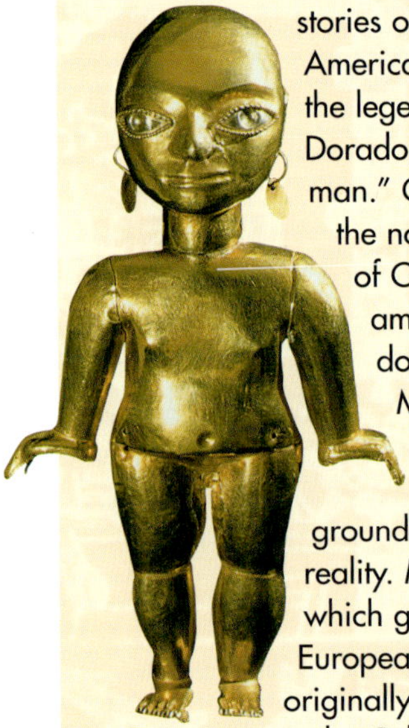

ONE OF THE ENDURING stories of South American mythology is the legend of El Dorado, " the gilded man." Originating in the northern Andes of Colombia, among the chiefdoms of the Muisca people, the El Dorado myth was grounded in historical reality. Muisca rituals, which gave birth to European fantasies, originally took place at the Colombian lake known as Guatavita, in a ceremony celebrating the accession to power of a new chief. After a period of seclusion in a cave, the chief made a pilgrimage to the lake in order to make offerings to the deity. On arrival at the lake's shore, the ruler-to-be was stripped of his clothing and his body smeared with sticky resin on to which was blown a glittering layer of gold dust. Accompanied by four subject chiefs, all adorned with golden jewelry, the golden man set out into the lake on a raft, itself richly adorned and bearing four braziers smoking with sacred incense. As they went, those left behind on the shore blew flutes and trumpets and sang. When the raft reached the center of the lake, silence fell, and the new chief cast his gold into the lake, with his companions doing likewise. On returning to the shore, he was received as the new ruler.

GOLDEN IMAGES

THROUGHOUT THE ANDES, the supernatural power of gold was captured in sacred images. Master craftsmen were often shamans, for Andean goldwork not only displayed technical expertise but was considered a magical transformation of brilliant spirituality into solid matter. Golden death-masks and tumi knives of the Chimú, and the astonishing burial jewelry from Moche tombs, provide a glimpse of the lost splendors of Inca Cuzco. For the Incas, gold was "sweat of the sun," silver the "tears of the moon." In the temple-garden of the sun god Inti, all known life was modeled in gold and silver—symbolic prototypes for the natural and spirit worlds.

◀ *A gold "Venus" statuette.*

▼ *A gold mask of a mummy.*

◄ *The lost city of Machu Picchu, never found by the invading Spanish.*

TITICACA, LAKE OF EMERGENCE

AMONG THE AMERINDIANS who occupied the Titicaca region of the Collao before the Incas there were many creation myths and culture heroes. One of these mythical heroes, called Thunapa or Tonapa, was the bringer of civilization. His imagery later became entangled with that of the Inca creator god Viracocha and probably also was influenced by Christian missionaries and their stories of the Apostles. According to the myth, Thunapa arrived from the north with five followers. He was an impressive man with blue eyes and a beard, and he preached against war, drunkenness, and the taking of more than one wife. Thunapa carried a wooden cross on his back to the city of Carapucu and left his followers there while he visited another town. During his absence, trouble erupted when one of his followers fell in love with the chieftain Makuri's daughter. On his return, Thunapa baptized the girl. Makuri was so angry he killed the disciples and left Thunapa for dead. The hero's body was placed in a totora reed boat and set adrift on Lake Titicaca, whereupon it magically began to move at great speed of its own accord. The boat collided with the shore so hard that it created a river, and on these waters Thunapa's body was borne away to the Pacific Ocean.

MYTHS OF THE FLOOD

ACCORDING TO THE MYTHOLOGY of the Cañari people of Ecuador, two brothers escaped a great flood by perching atop the mountain called Huacayñan, which rose in height every time the floodwaters threatened to engulf it. When the waters receded, the brothers went in search of food, suffering much hardship. One day, after a fruitless search for food, they returned to a hut they had built to find a meal and *chicha* (maize beer) all laid out. This occurred for 10 successive days, until, hiding to see who was bringing the food, the elder brother spotted two macaws arrive and begin to prepare the food. On seeing that the birds had the faces of women, the brother came out of hiding, at which the birds became angry and flew away without leaving any food. The younger brother returned and, on finding no food, decided himself to hide and watch. After three days, the birds returned. When the food was cooked, he slammed the hut door, catching the smaller bird while the larger one escaped. He lived with the bird for many years and had six sons and daughters. From these children, it is said, all Cañari are descended, and they regard the mountain as holy and they worship the macaw.

ANDEAN THEMES

THERE ARE SEVERAL MAJOR, overlapping themes in the myths related here. All in some respects are concerned with creation, the sacred nature of physical locations, the identification of people with named places, and the supernatural transformative power of light. For the Incas, myths tell of their bringing civilization to a savage uncultured world which they are predestined to rule after having tested the earth with a golden rod. The association of mountains and fertility together with the creation of an ethnic group is shown in the flood myth, mixing metaphors of humanity and the animal world to express a universal Andean theme.

Amazonian South America

INTRODUCTION

THE TROPICAL LOWLANDS of the Amazon never reached the heights of civilization attained in the Andes. Although there were no great cities or empires to compare with Chavín, Moche, or Inca, parts of Amazonia were densely populated in prehistoric times. By 2000 B.C.E., pottery making was widespread, and between C.E. 400 and 1300, a sophisticated culture developed on the island of Marajó at the mouth of the Amazon. These people cultivated maize and manioc, built large house-mounds and crafted colorful anthropomorphic burial urns whose female forms suggest the importance of women in everyday life and mythology.

Knowledge of lowland prehistory is limited, however. More abundant and better documented is the seemingly infinite variety of small-scale Amerindian societies occupying this region from the time of European arrival to the present. From the Amazon and Orinoco rivers of northern South America to the Mato Grosso grasslands to the south, groups of Amerindians lived a life of hunting, gathering, and horticulture in a diversity of surroundings. Language, customs, religion, art, and houses differed, but all shared a basic Amerindian view of a world animated by spirits and controlled by ancestors. In these kinds of societies, there was often little room for an elaborate social hierarchy. Chiefs and shamans rather than emperors held sway.

THE MASTER OF ANIMALS

A RECURRING FIGURE in lowland Amazonian mythology is the "Master of Animals." Created in primordial times, these supernatural beings have responsibility for the fertility of the animal kingdom and have to be appeased by the shaman if hunting is to be successful. Every animal has its master, which is often the largest member of its species. It is usually the multicolored jaguar, as the largest lowland predator, which is regarded as the master of all animal species. Jaguars eat all animals but are prey to none, and thus are a natural prototype for an all-powerful guardian of animal spirits.

MYTHIC WORLDS OF THE AMAZON

LOWLAND AMERINDIAN peoples are often described as technologically inferior to the great Pre-Columbian civilizations of the Andes. Yet their societies, rituals, and religious beliefs reveal a spirituality and mythic imagination which recalls the most sophisticated intellectual achievements of the Incas and their predecessors. In many ways, the diversity of Amazonian peoples inhabit a world of myth and magic, where otherwise local myths display an underlying unity. This similarity is produced partly by different groups sharing common concerns and dealing with them with a common logic. It is reinforced by an intimate knowledge of plants and animals, the weather, and an abiding belief in the transformative powers of the shaman. Created in mythic time, the Amerindian universe can be replicated in the design of a house and the shape of the human body. It is ruled by powerful spirits whose capricious actions are tempered only by the shaman confronting them in trance in the shape of a spirit bird or jaguar. The shaman is often a society's most important figure. As keeper of the tribe's mythic traditions, he knows more myths than anybody else and is able to interpret them more meaningfully. In the shaman's hands, myths are powerful tools and weapons, for with them he speaks to the ancestors and accounts for every aspect of life and death.

▶ *Two-pronged silver diadem, originally part of an elaborate headdress worn by chiefs and shaman.*

▲ *Trilogy of masks representing man, the earth, and the sky.*

▶ *Jars decorated with skeletal figures were linked to shamanistic ideas on music, death, and fertility.*

THE ORIGINS OF FIRE

THE MAIN THEMES OF LOWLAND mythology are those concerned with the regulation of human society and its relationship with the natural world. These issues are often entwined, found together in creation myths which relate how light and order was brought into being, how animals—and sometimes women—were the earth's original masters, and how men usurped their position. Defining human culture in opposition to the untamed world of beasts is also a dominant theme. In such myths, the origin of fire is a metaphor for civilized life, yet it was taken from the jaguar who now lives as humans once did. Reversals, transformations, and balance are key features of Amazonian myth.

In Amazonia, fire symbolizes creation and civilized life. In Brazilian Kayapo mythology, the first people possessed no fire and ate their food raw like wild beasts. One day, a young boy, Botoque, was abandoned by his elder brother-in-law while gathering macaw eggs in the jungle. After several days of eating his own excrement, Botoque saw a jaguar carrying a bow and arrow and various kinds of game. The jaguar promised not to eat him, offering instead to adopt him as a son and a hunting companion. Botoque climbed on the jaguar's back and returned to the great cat's house. Here, the boy saw fire and ate cooked meat for the first time. Because of the hostility of the jaguar's wife, the jaguar showed Botoque how to make a bow and arrow. When the jaguar's wife threatened him, he killed her with an arrow, gathered up some cooked meat, his weapons, and a burning ember, and returned to his own village. On seeing these wondrous gifts, the men returned to the jaguar's house, stealing fire, cooked meat, and bows and arrows. Incensed at his adopted son's behavior, the jaguar now eats its food raw, while humans eat theirs cooked.

MEANING OF AMAZONIAN MYTHS

AMAZONIAN MYTHS deal mainly with explaining and ordering human relationships, both within society itself and within the wider natural and supernatural worlds. In a universe where myth and history converge, social life is seen as the result of a careful fusing of antagonistic and spiritually dangerous things, such as men and women, kin and in-laws, or wild beasts and humans. In order for a group to endure, its members must observe social rules and ritual obligations first created by the ancestors and enshrined in myth. If these are transgressed, chaos and disaster quickly follow. Many of these myths, which seek also to explain civilized life in opposition to nature, take the form of creation stories and variations of the origins of fire. Thus many creation myths are concerned with a number of overlapping issues—the origins of hunting, the secret of cooking food, and the relationships between humans and animals and different human groups. Reversal also is a common theme, where animals once were armed but now hunt unaided, or where women once ruled the world until men took over. In the tropical lowlands, processes of creation and decay are magnified by the lush conditions of jungle life, by sudden death and by cannibalizm. Amazonian myths reflect these dramatic conditions, providing a structure for understanding the jungle world.

SPIRITS AND ART

SUPERNATURAL IMAGES and designs are revealed to the shaman in a drug-induced trance. Powerful narcotics, such as *ayahuasca*, create vivid, multi-colored visions in which natural forms can be recombined, made larger or smaller. Many are held to be sacred. Imbued with protective power, these designs are painted on to communal longhouses, applied to the skin for ritual festivities and used as a basis for the making and decoration of baskets, textiles, and pottery. Such designs are symbolic representations of mythological events and culture heroes, and they link the objects and architecture of everyday life with the sacred realm of the ancestors.

AMAZONIAN CREATION

AMONG THE DESANA OF THE Colombian Amazon, creation occurs when an inscrutable and invisible Creator Sun explodes yellow light into the void. The Sun Father, Pagë Abé, sets about creating the natural world in all its details: animals, plants, and forests, each with their own identity, habits, and places. The Sun lays down the principles of existence, spreading brilliance and understanding like solar semen throughout the universe. He then delegates further creativity to a host of supernatural beings—masters of individual realms such as the sky, rivers, and animal kingdom. In Desana cosmogony, dramatic acts of transformative creation are carried out by females such as the Daughter of Aracú Fish. To these culture heroes falls the responsibility of inventing many of the details of existence and cultural life: the shapes and colors of animals, the techniques of human hunting and food production, and the symbolic domains of ritual and art. The Sun now takes two forms. By day he resides in the sky, providing heat, light, and fertility for the life which he and his female protagonists have created. On earth he is the protective supernatural jaguar. The Sun then commands another supernatural, Pamurímahsë, to transport the first people to the earth in a large canoe.

▲ *Amazon Indians from Brazil.*

◀ *Gold statue thought to represent a supernatural being or a shaman.*

"WOMAN SHAMAN" MAKES THE WORLD

IN THE MYTHOLOGY of the Barasana Amerindians of the Colombian Amazon, Romi Kumu was "Woman Shaman," who fashioned the world. She was a virgin who changed her skin with the aid of a magical beeswax gourd—appearing young and beautiful in the morning and old and ugly in the evening. Mother of the sky, grandmother of all people, Woman Shaman's urine is the rain, and she holds fire in her vagina. Thus it was that in the beginning, the world was nothing but bare rock until Romi Kumu gathered up some clay to make a griddle for baking cassava bread.

To support the griddle she made three supports: these were mountains which supported the griddle, which was the sky. Woman Shaman lived above the griddle. When she lit the fire beneath, the supports broke, and the griddle fell on to the earth below, pushing it downward to become the under-world with the griddle now lodged in-between as the earth. A third griddle became the sky. Fashioning the "Water Door" on the eastern edge of the world she then opened it, causing the earth to become flooded.

As the waters rose inside the house, all the items within turned into fierce animals and began to eat the people. The manioc-beer trough and the coca sieve became anacondas, a housepost became a cayman, and pieces of pottery became piranhas. Only those who made a canoe from the kahuu tree survived—every other living thing was drowned. Landing safely on the top of a mountain, the survivors began eating each other as there was no food. Eventually, the rains stopped and the floodwaters receded, and the sun rose high in the sky.

As it became hotter, everything became so dry that the earth caught fire and everything was consumed by the flames. Although Romi Kumu had no husband, she made two daughters and also created all the He People—the ancestral spirit-beings of the world, whom she turned into creatures like women. She was going to give some shamanised food from her beeswax gourd to the He People, but snakes ate from it instead. At midnight she prepared some more food, blew protective spells over it, and offered it to the ancestors but they refused it. Romi Kumu then switched gourds, the original being taken away by the white people who use it to change their skins and become young again. Eventually, the He People were given the gourd they still use today during rituals to celebrate initiations.

BODY PAINTING

IN AMAZONIA, realistic imagery combines with abstract designs said to be experienced by the shaman in hallucinogenic trance. In order to please the spirits, and advertise one's ritual identity and place in society, Amazonian Amerindians lavish time and effort on personal decoration. Body painting is especially important, with red paint made from urucu seeds applied to face, arms, and legs in a multitude of designs. Feather headdresses are made from feathers of mythologically important birds, such as the macaw and Harpy Eagle. Jewelry too expresses culturally defined ideas of aesthetic beauty, items such as mirrors, glass beads, and lip plugs combining to form a sartorial code, making the wearer equally attractive to humans and spirits.

VISIONS OF MYTHICAL LANDSCAPES

THE POWER OF AMAZONIAN mythology belongs to a world moved not by natural forces but by supernatural beings. Where outsiders see endless jungle, Amerindians perceive a rich landscape of symbol and metaphor, of relationships between people, ancestors, animals, plants, mountains, and rivers. In this shape-shifting universe, people transform to animals, wind is the breath of the spirits, and every feature of the forest is invested with spirituality. This may be a philosophical acknowledgement of cycles of rapid growth and decay in a lush tropical environment. One consequence of the shamanic world view is that everyday activities can be shaped by ritual observances. Edible plants and animals may be avoided owing to taboo, and acceptable foods require the blowing of purifying spells over them by the shaman before they are safe to eat. Where not forbidden, the hunting of certain animals needs the shaman to divine the whereabouts of the creatures and to ask the "master of animals" for permission to hunt.

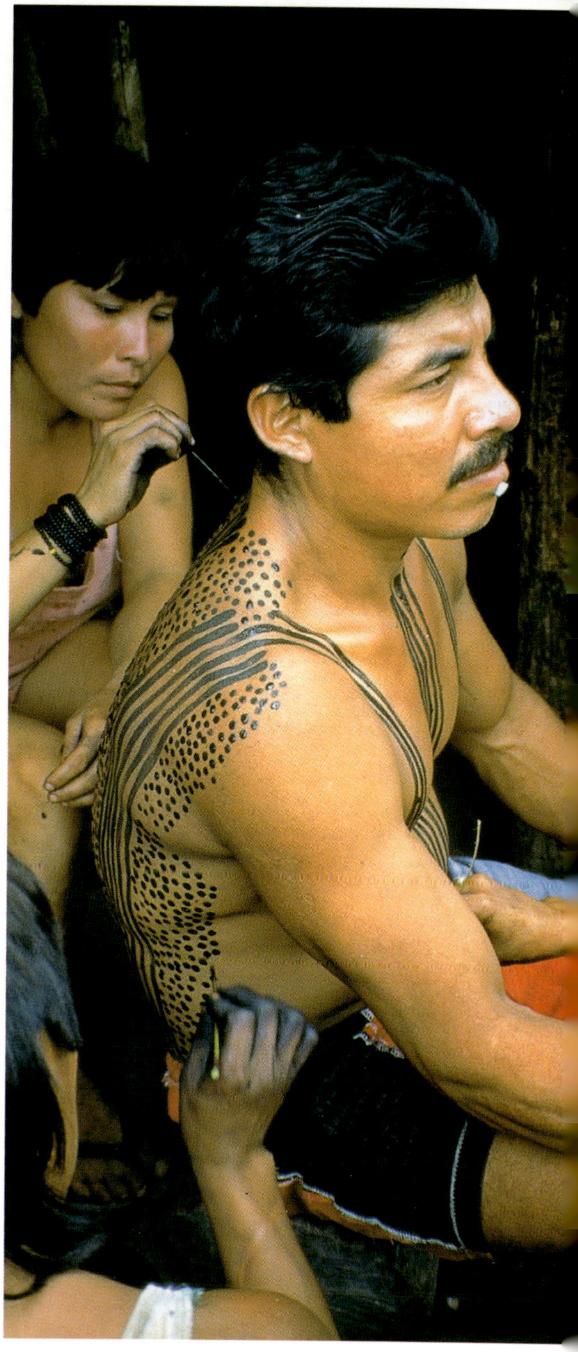

▲ *The art of body painting is still practiced by some communities in North America.*

Felling a tree, gathering tobacco leaves, or collecting clay for pots—all may require spirit permission. Landscapes are places where myth and history collide, where all the senses unite, where sounds have smells and taste has texture. In Amazonia, landscape is living myth, a place of memory.

▲ *A group of Indians, men, women and children, walk through the tropical rainforest.*

MYTH AND THE PHYSICAL WORLD

IN TROPICAL RAINFOREST cultures, different tribes attach their own meanings to the physical world. The Tukano of North-West Amazonia regard lightning as the result of a shaman hurling magical quartz crystals at an enemy: quartz itself is seen as "solid light" and the essence of male virility. The mirror-like surfaces of lakes are shimmering boundaries between the natural and supernatural worlds, rivers are likened to umbilical cords, and rapids seen as the spirit-dwellings of fish. Animals, too, symbolize many different qualities: the jaguar's roar announces the rains, its shiny eyes and brilliant coat represent the sun, and buzzards as carrion-eaters help the shaman to cure illness by devouring the malign agents of disease. For Amazonian peoples, heaven, earth, and sea form an integrated whole, spiritually and materially. The earth is linked to the sea through the exchange of shell-beads, salt is traded widely as the powdered essence of male fertility, and various minerals embody social, gender, and spirit identities. Celestial bodies too are tied to the rhythms of nature through their appearance together with seasonal foods. The Milky Way is a crystalline path of hallucinogenic visions experienced by the shaman in trance, while meteors, comets, and eclipses are heavenly images of earthly matters such as discord, war, and birth.

◀ *A spectacular aerial view of the rainforest, showing the blanket cover provided by the trees interrupted only by the winding path of a great river.*

NIGHT, DAY, AND THE MOON'S BLOOD

FOR THE BARASANA, Sun and Moon were brothers. One day, Moon announced that he was going to be the day and dry up the wombs of women. Sun, the younger brother, thinking of human needs, took issue with this and took the day from his brother and gave him night. While Sun's light was strong and radiant, Moon's was weak, so he turned his body to blood and became like a lump of red paint. Moon then descended to earth and entered a house whose inhabitants had all died. He removed his shiny feather crown which filled the house with light and hung it on a post in the middle of the dwelling. Then Moon transformed into an armadillo and began to scavenge the bones of the dead. A man who had hidden in the rafters picked up Moon's crown and hid it in a pot and the house went dark. Moon eventually retrieved his crown, replaced it on his head and returned to the sky. In this way, Moon descends to earth to eat the bones of men who have made love to menstruating women, for Moon's blood is that of menstruating women. When the Moon becomes red, people cry out: for those about to die, the spirit of a dead relative replies, and for those who will live longer there is no answer.

MEANING AND MEMORY IN AMAZONIAN MYTHOLOGY

AMAZONIAN MYTHOLOGIES account for the world on a supernatural scale yet use ideas from everyday life. In the Barasana myth of Romi Kumu, the universe is seen as a great house, whose constituent parts transform to animals. Even the earth is seen as a great ceramic griddle used to bake the staff of life, cassava bread. Such notions are widespread. Partitions of living space in communal houses reflect mythological divisions, with areas set aside for cassava baking, meat preparation, taking hallucinogens, and for the ritual isolation of menstruating women. Among the Yekuana, roundhouses are regarded as a microcosm of the universe, linked to mountains conceived as houses of the spirits. Symbolic landscapes become symbolic houses and, eventually, are traced through the family group to the formation of life in the womb. Where order and structure are considered of prime importance, the division of night and day represents social and antisocial behavior. The Barasana tale of "Sun and Moon" is a mythic charter against men having sex with menstruating women—women who, for a time, are symbolically and physically distanced from everyday life. In similar fashion, ideas of cannibalizm relate to incest avoidance and the necessity of acquiring strangers as in-laws.

MUSICAL INSTRUMENTS

ANCESTOR SPIRITS haunt the rainforest world of Amazonian peoples. Linking the present with the past, they can appear to a person lost in the forest or be conjured up in rituals which re-enact mythical creations. Ancestors often bestow sacredness on the landscape by wandering through the forest, visiting important places and leaving traces of their passing. Ancestors can inhabit the musical instruments used in rituals. Among the Baniwa and Barasana, flutes are regarded as ancestors, their phallic shape and the magical breath needed to bring them to life recall ancient times, spreading through sound the regenerative power of the spirit world.

THE SPIRIT HELPER

THE IDEA OF the "spirit helper" is widespread throughout lowland South America. It is the effectiveness of the shaman's alliance with his helper which determines his success in dealing with the supernatural world. Spirit helpers can be the ghosts of ancestors, powerful animals—like the jaguar or eagle—or even tobacco smoke, shiny crystals, or lightning. For the Waiwai tribe, spirit helpers called *hyasi* help in childbirth by conveying the newborn's soul to heaven so that it can receive its spirit name. The Mataco shaman obtains his spiritual support from the mythical yulo bird while, for the Canelos Quichua, bees and wasps are spirit-helper souls.

▲ *Gold bead in the form of a snarling jaguar; it signifies a chief's association with spirits.*

GLOSSARY

Aetiology
Today the study of natural phenomena, but primitive people employed naturally occurring events in initiations, religious practices, and rituals.

Afterlife
Believed to be where the spirit goes after bodily death, also known as paradise, the underworld, Hades, Heaven, the Elysian fields, the Netherworld.

Allegory
Storytelling device where one thing is described as another in order to convey a moral or practical lesson.

Ancestor Veneration
Ancestor worship—where people deify their ancestors and trace descent to a common ancestor who watch over their progeny.

Animal myths
Hunter-gatherer tribes often saw close connections between man and animal, believing both capable of transformation; many cultures share a belief in animal myths.

Animism
Those living closely with nature often attached stories to it, believing spirits inhabited anything that moved, such as sticks, trees, stones, and other elements of nature.

Anthropology
Academic pursuit following Darwin's theories to study human evolution, differences in lifestyles, cultures, and societies across the world.

Anthropomorphism
Part of myth or literature where human traits or characteristics are attributed to animals, inanimate objects, or deities.

Aryan
Believed to be the language of ancient peoples living between central Asia and Europe which developed into Indo-European languages.

Asceticism
Where a people may express themselves through art for its own sake, rather than for moral, religious, or educational purposes.

Astral Deities
As explanations for the planets, people, or deities were believed to have transformed into the moon, stars, or sun.

Autochthony
Relating to native or aboriginal people, suggesting ancestry and close connection with the earth, possibly on a spiritual level.

Babylonia
Ancient civilization on the Euphrates River, now Iraq, and site of the Hanging Gardens of Babylon.

Bards
In Celtic and Eastern European cultures, Bards were storytellers passing on myths and legends through generations.

Battle myths
Battle myths and heroics reinforce cultural identity whilst the favors of gods of war can be prayed for or explain losses.

Bronze Age
Period dating from around 3000–2000 B.C.E., when people began using metal-making technology based on copper and its alloys.

Buddhism
Eastern religion based on the teachings of the sixth-century Buddha; these are founded in the destruction of mortal desires, and thus unhappiness, which can be attained by following virtuous paths.

Byzantium
Ancient Greek city, the capital of a Mediterranean empire with a distinctive architecture and orthodox religious art.

Cauldrons
Often magical, cauldrons were seen as life-restoring, brewers of wisdom, holders of visions, and ultimately the Holy Grail.

Christianity
World religion derived from the teachings of Christ, the son of God, who came to earth, suffered persecution for his teachings, and was crucified, before rising from the dead and ascending into Heaven.

Clans
Social grouping based on kinship theoretically descended from a single ancestor, sometimes represented as a spirit being.

Confucianism
Chinese beliefs and practices, based on the teachings of Confucius, relating to nature gods, imperial ancestors, and the balancing of yin and yang.

Cosmogonic myths
Common creation myth where primeval earth is separated from the sky and stars and planets created by gods or humans.

Creation myths
Most cultures have an origin of the world myth, often where the world and order were created out of chaos.

Cycle of life
Cycle of birth, death, and afterlife or reincarnation, depending on specific religions or beliefs.

Degeneration
Where myths are infiltrated by the influence of the different world religions that they resemble, and the original is lost.

Dravidian
Non-Indo-European peoples from southern India and Sri Lanka with around 20 languages and a 2,000-year literary history.

Druidism
Pre-Christian pagan religion of the Celtic people, in which priests were learned, artistic, and important members of the social order.

Dualism
Belief that reality is dual in nature, made up of material objects and how these are perceived by our minds.

Ecogeographical systems
A people's geographical positioning, climate, environment, and resources often determine myths and beliefs.

Enlightenment
Awakening to reality in Buddhist belief is followed by the soul's departure from the cycle of death and reincarnation, known as Enlightenment.

Ethnic identity
Ethnicity is where an ethnic group feels a common sense of identity, based on shared culture, language, customs, and religion.

Evil eye
Some superstitious cultures attributed magical powers to certain individuals, believing they could inflict harm with a glance.

Evolution
Process of change in animal and plant forms as they adapt to environments or learn to manage them as humans have.

Fertility Deities
Most primitive cultures were phallocentric, concerned with reproductive powers and believed certain deities governed fertility.

Fetishes
Belief in the supernatural powers of an inanimate object — the fetish—which has religious or magical importance.

Foundation myths
Common to most cultures and religions are myths concerning the creation of people and their environment or state.

Grail legend
Celtic legends of King Arthur's quest for the supernatural powers held by the cup used by Jesus at the Last Supper, known as the Holy Grail.

Guardian spirit
Widely held belief in protecting spirits or angels, either an animal, the free soul of a sleeping person, or an ancestor.

Heads
For some cultures heads contained the soul, and enemies were beheaded to take possession of their soul.

Hellenistic
Classic period in Greek civilization from 323 B.C.E., when Greek culture and myths spread throughout the Mediterranean.

Heretics
Those accused of religious nonconformity; Christian churches turned pagan myths of vampires, witchcraft, and sorcery against heretics.

Heroes
A hero's ability to overcome seemingly invincible enemies and forces of nature is a universal theme in world mythology.

Hinduism
Dominant religion of India; characterized by a complex system of customs and beliefs, including numerous gods, reincarnation, and a caste system.

Ice Age
Period of widescale glaciation; up to 20 have occurred in the earth's history, the last immediately preceding historic times.

Iconography
Worshiping of symbolic objects, or icons, which have specific significance to certain cultures or religions—such as crucifixes.

Ideology
Set of ideas and beliefs a people hold about themselves, offering a framework for how they should order their lives.

Incantation
In magical or religious rituals certain words or sounds are repeated, often by a group, and sometimes to cast spells.

Initiation
Ceremony or rights of passage whereby young men (generally) are tested or taught the fundamentals of survival and adulthood.

Islam
Founded in the seventh century by the Prophet Muhammad, messenger of Allah, Islam emphasizes God's omnipotence and inscrutability.

Jainism
Ancient ascetic Indian religion emphasizing non-violence and compassion for all forms of life, but not a belief in deities.

Kinship
Human relationships based on blood or marriage, grouped as family, clan or tribe, often with strict rules, customs and taboos.

Masks
Symbols worn in worship rituals to represent supernatural healing beings, gods, ancestors, or to re-enact or retell significant events.

Matriarchal societies
Certain cultures known to have been dominated by worship of female gods and female fertility before phallocentrism.

Medieval
Cultures and beliefs of the Middle Ages, after the Roman Empire's fifth-century decline to the fifteenth-century Renaissance.

Meditation
Individual act of spiritual contemplation, or where a shaman might commune with spirit gods as part of a ritual.

Mesopotamia
Site of powerful ancient civilizations of Sumer and Babylon, now Iraq, with a wealth of art particularly sculpture; dates around 3500 B.C.E.

Mother Goddesses
Some ancient cultures saw goddesses in an overall cosmology with mother goddesses as the earth and the father as the sky.

Muse
In Greek mythology, the nine daughters of the god Zeus each inspire a form of human artistic expression or endeavor; they are known as "muses."

Mythic narrative
Narratives are stories and these were the means to convey myths and keep them alive either orally, in writing, or song.

Nature Spirits
Animist cultures believed that spirits, sometimes ancestors, inhabited trees, rocks, or rivers; this explained their changing appearance.

Neolithic
Final part of the Stone Age period, marked by the development of agriculture and forest clearance around 8000–3000 B.C.E.

Oral traditions
Where a culture has no written tradition myths are passed down through generations by bards, elders, Shamen, and storytellers.

Paganism
From the fourteenth century, worshipers following religions other than Christianity were regarded as pagans, a state associated with superstition and sorcery.

Pastoralism
Belief or ideology in the power and importance of the land, where stories incorporate man and the environment.

Phallic symbol
In patriarchal societies, male fertility was prayed for and worshiped, using symbols in the form of or representing the penis.

Pilgrimages
Journey to worship at a sacred place or shrine particularly, but not only, associated with the major organized religions.

Prehistoric
Period that covers from the beginning of life on earth, 3.5 billion years ago, to approximately 3500 B.C.E., when humans began to keep records.

Primeval
Relates to the earliest period of the world, in mythical terms perhaps the period after creation and before foundation.

Prophecy
Sometimes regarded as a gift where a soothsayer, prophet, or seer can foretell the future, either magically or in visions.

Reincarnation
Depending on cultural variant, part or all of a soul departs after death and inhabits the body of a newborn child.

Religious cults
Many ancient cultures worshiped numerous gods, but those following one of these or an ancestor god were called cults.

Renaissance
Fourteenth to seventeenth century European intellectual and artistic movement, ending the Middle Ages with its emphasis on science and exploration.

Resurrection
Rebirth myths widely held throughout the ancient world, often symbolized by snakes which are able to shed their skins.

Rituals
Religious ceremony with certain set patterns—incantations, dances, singing—to mark particular events such as initiations, births, or deaths.

Sacrifice and offerings
Ancient peoples believed either human or animal sacrifices or votive offerings would appease gods.

Sagas
Traditional Scandinavian prose narratives concerning kings, families, and adventures, part of oral traditions but written down in the eleventh century.

Sages
Profoundly wise men who educated and advised, sometimes foretold the future and were generally honored by their society.

Sanskrit
Sacred classical language of Hinduism, the language of law, medicine, and epic stories; has influenced many Indo-European languages.

Scarab
Often brilliantly colored and industrious, scarab beetles were revered as divine and depicted in their art by Ancient Egyptians.

Semitic
Peoples of ancient cultures in the Middle East, speakers of Semitic languages and founders of Islam, Judaism, and Christianity.

Shamanism
Oldest-known form of organized religion, belief in the power of shamans who transact between the human and spiritual worlds.

Shaman
Ancient priests, believed to be both of the spirit and material world and possess supernatural powers of healing and transformation.

Shinto
Ancient Japanese religion combining oneness with the mysterious forces of nature and devotion to royal descendants of the sun goddess.

Shrine
Religious places of worship marked by statues, rocks, buildings, crosses, or gifts to be offered to or signifying the deity.

Social myths
Used to instill social values, family obligations, taboos against incest, obedience to social hierarchies, and guidelines on behavior.

Solar bodies
Stars and planets, the presence of which were explained as deities as part of many foundation or creation myths.

Sorcery
Magical practices that control the forces of nature by supernatural means, perhaps as part of religious rituals.

Stone Age
Earliest period of human culture, marked by the use of stone implements and covering Paleolithic, Mesolithic, and Neolithic times.

Supreme Being
Where a culture believes in a life-giving being who personifies the life force that animates human and animal worlds.

Symbolic relationships
Where important aspects of a culture's life, such as food, water, and animals are embodied in their myths and worship.

Taboos
Social group and religious prohibitions or restrictions to behavior, such as incest or desecrating sacred objects.

Theriomorphic
Where a god or deity takes the shape of an animal and may be depicted in carvings or paintings.

Totems
Sacred clan or individual totems may be animal, plant, or carved objects and represent the kinship with the totem.

Trances
Shamans in certain cultures experienced drug-induced hallucinogenic trances in order to converse with gods or spirits.

Transformation
Metamorphosis of one animate or inanimate object into another—animals into humans and vice versa, part of animism and shamanism.

Vampires
Evil Slavic and Eastern European mythic creature believed to be dead, yet animated and capable of making others into vampires.

Water nymphs
A life-giving and destructive force; some cultures believed it was alive or contained creatures they wished to please.

AUTHOR BIOGRAPHIES

Arthur Cotterell
GENERAL EDITOR AND INTRODUCTION
Arthur Cotterell is Principal of Kingston College in Surrey. He is a world-renowned authority on the mythologies of the world, and has written, contributed to, and edited many volumes on the subject.

Loren Auerbach
NORTHERN EUROPE
Loren Auerbach gained her Masters degree at King's College (University of London) specializing in Old English and Old Icelandic. She has taught and given lectures at both London University and Oxford University. Her most recent work is *Sagas of the Norsemen* in the Time Life Books series "Myth and Mankind."

Professor Anne M. Birrell
CHINA
Anne M. Birrell is a widely published world authority on Chinese mythology. Her introductory book for Penguin has become a standard work on the subject.

Rev. Dr Martin Boord
TIBET AND MONGOLIA
Prior to attaining his doctoral degree at the School of Oriental & African Studies at the University of London, Martin Boord spent eight years in India training in Buddhist philosophy and practice under some of the most eminent Tibetan lamas of the modern age. Author of *The Cult of the Deity Vajrakila* (Tring 1993), his published translations include *Overview of the Buddhist Tantra* (Dharamsala 1996). He currently resides in Oxford as an independent scholar and translator.

Miranda Bruce-Mitford
SRI LANKA; SOUTHEAST ASIA
Miranda Bruce-Mitford is an art historian and author who has written and contributed to many publications on the art and culture of southern Asia.

Peter A. Clayton
EGYPT
Peter A. Clayton is an Egyptologist and author of many books on ancient Egypt, notably *Chronicle of the Pharaohs* (1994, repr. 1996, 1998) that have been translated into six languages. For the last 25 years, every year, he has been a guest lecturer in Egypt and in many universities and museums in Europe and Australia.

Dr Ray Dunning
THE CELTS
Dr. Ray Dunning was born in 1947 in Brecon, South Wales. He has taught art and art history in schools and colleges for many years and his illustrations appear in books on mythology and the ancient world. He is currently Head of the Department of Design Studies at Kingston College.

Dr. James H. Grayson
KOREA
James Huntley Grayson is Reader in Modern Korean Studies and Director of the Centre for Korean Studies, School of East Asian Studies, University of Sheffield. An anthropologist and former Methodist missionary to Korea (1971–87), he has written widely on Korean religion and folklore. His books include *Korea: A Religious History* and *Myths and Legends from Korea*.

Dr. Niel Gunson
OCEANIA
Niel Gunson is an historian at the Australian National University. His recently published works include contributions to the *Atlas of World Religions* and the *Encyclopedia of the Pacific Islands*.

Stephen Hodge
JAPAN
Stephen Hodge is a linguist in Japanese and an author with a specialist knowledge of Japanese culture.

Dr. Gwendolyn Leick
ANCIENT NEAR EAST
Gwendolyn Leick is a historian of the Ancient Near East. She is widely published in the field and her works include the *Dictionary of Near Eastern Mythology* (Routledge).

Dr. Helen Morales
GREECE; ROME
Dr. Helen Morales is a lecturer in Classics at the University of Reading, having been educated at New Hall and Newnham College, Cambridge. She has published on later Greek literature and Roman art. She is co-editor of the Classical Studies journal *Omnibus*, published for schools and anyone else with a passion for the ancient world.

Mark Nuttall
SIBERIA AND THE ARCTIC
Mark Nuttall is a social anthropologist specializing in the cultures of the Arctic and North Atlantic. He has researched and traveled extensively in Greenland, Alaska, and other northern regions. His most recent book is *Protecting the Arctic: Indigenous Peoples and Cultural Survival* (Harwood Academic Publishers), and he is currently Lecturer in Anthropology and Sociology at the University of Aberdeen.

Richard Prime
INDIA
Richard Prime studied architecture before spending 15 years studying and teaching Krishna Consciousness. He works as a freelance writer and broadcaster, and as adviser on religion and conservation to W.W.F. and to the Alliance on Religions and Conservation. His books include *Hinduism and Ecology* (1992) and *Ramayana, A Journey* (1997).

Professor James Riordan
CENTRAL AND EASTERN EUROPE; NORTH AMERICA
James Riordan was born in Portsmouth, England. He has traveled extensively in central and eastern Europe, lived in Russia for five years, and has published several books on the myths and folklore of the area. He is currently Professor of Russian Studies in the Department of Linguistic and International Studies at the University of Surrey.

Dr. Nicholas J. Saunders
CARIBBEAN; CENTRAL AND SOUTH AMERICA
Nicholas J. Saunders studied archaeology at Sheffield and Southampton Universities, and anthropology at Cambridge University. He has specialized in pre-Columbian America for over 20 years, holding teaching and research positions in Mexico, Trinidad, Jamaica, the USA, and the UK. He is currently a lecturer in archaeology and anthropology at University College, London.

Professor Harold Scheub
AFRICA
Harold Scheub is Professor of African Languages and Literature at the University of Wisconsin. He has recently completed his *Dictionary of African Mythology* for Oxford University Press.

Bruce Wannell
PERSIA
Bruce Wannell was born in Melbourne and educated at Oxford; he taught at Isfahan University and worked with Afghan refugees in Peshawar; he has contributed programs to the Persian and Pushtu service of the B.B.C. World Service, has translated Persian mystical poetry and written on Islamic art and travel.

Professor James Weiner
AUSTRALIA
James Weiner is a senior anthropologist at the Australian National University. His writings include contributions to *World Mythology* (Simon & Schuster).

BIBLIOGRAPHY

Ancient Near East

Black, J., and A. Green, *Gods, Demons and Symbols of Ancient Mesopotamia: An Illustrated Dictionary*, London, 1992

Boyce, Mary, *Zoroastrians, their Beliefs and Practices*, London, 1979

Christensen, Arthur, *L'Iran sous les Sassanides*, Copenhagen, 1944

Clifford, R. J., *Creation Accounts in the Ancient Near East and in the Bible*, Washington, 1994

Dalley, S., *Myths from Mesopotamia, Creation, the Flood, Gilgamesh and Others*, Oxford and New York, 1989

de Moor, J. C., *An Anthology of Religious Texts from Ugarit*, Leiden and New York, 1987

Gershevitch, I., *The Avestan Hymn to Mithra*, Cambridge, 1959

Gibson, J. C. L., *Canaanite Myths and Legends*, Edinburgh, 1978

Kovacs, M. G. *The Epic of Gilgamesh*, Stanford, 1989

Leick, G., *A Dictionary of Ancient Near Eastern Mythology*, London, 1991, 1999

Olmstead, A. T., *History of the Persian Empire*, Chicago, 1948

Pritchard, J. B. (ed.), *Ancient Near Eastern texts relating to the Old Testament*, Princeton, 1969

Vahman, Fereydun, *Arda Viraz Namag*, London and Malmo, 1986

Egypt

A Dictionary of Egyptian Gods and Goddesses, London, 1986

Clayton, Peter A., *Egyptian Mythology*, London, 1998

Hart, George, *Egyptian Myths*, London, 1990

Lurker, Manfred (revised by Peter A. Clayton), *The Gods and Symbols of Ancient Egypt*, London, 1980, repr.

Quirke, Stephen, *Ancient Egyptian Religion*, London, 1992

Greece and Rome

Bremmer, Jan, and Nicholas Horsfall, *Roman Myth and Mythography*, London 1987

Dowden, Ken, *The Uses of Greek Mythology*, London, 1992

Nagy, Gregory, *Greek Mythology and Poetics* New York, 1990

Powell, Barry, *Classical Myth*, New Jersey, 1998

Wiseman, Peter, *A Roman Myth*, Cambridge, 1996

The Celts

Cotterell, Arthur, *Celtic Mythology*, England, 1997

Delaney, Frank, *Legends of the Celts*, England, 1989

James, Simon, *Exploring the World of the Celts*, England, 1993

Mac Cana, Proinsias, *Celtic Mythology*, England, 1996

MacKillop, James, *Dictionary of Celtic Mythology*, England, 1998

Central and Eastern Europe

Afanasiev, Alexander, *The Poetic Interpretations of Nature by the Slavs*, 3 vols, St Petersburg, 1865–9

Afanasiev, Alexander, *Russian Folk Tales*, 8 vols, St Petersburg, 1855–67

Jakobson, Roman, 'Slavic Mythology', in M Leach and J Fried (eds), *Funk and Wagnalls Standard Dictionary of Folklore, Mythology and Legend*, vol 2, New York, 1949–50

Riordan, James, *Tales from Central Russia*, Harmondsworth, 1976

Northern Europe

Davidson, H. R. Ellis, *Gods and Myths of Northern Europe*, London, 1964

Faulkes, Anthony, *Snorri Sturluson: Edda*, London, 1987

Auden, W. H., and P. B. Taylor, *Norse Poems*, London, 1981

Simek, Rudolf, *Dictionary of Northern Mythology*, Cambridge, 1993

Turville-Petre, E. O. G., *Myth and Religion of the North*, London, 1964

Siberia and the Arctic

Bogoras, W. G., *The Chukchee*, New York, 1975 [1904–9]

Dioszegi, V., and M. Hoppal (eds), *Shamanism in Siberia*, Budapest, 1978

Lowenstein, T., *The Things That Were Said of Them: Shaman Stories and Oral Histories of the Tikigaq People*, Berkeley, 1992

Kleivan, I., and B. Sonne, *Eskimos: Greenland and Canada*, Leiden, 1985

Merkur, D., *Powers Which We Do Not Know: the Gods and Spirits of the Inuit Moscow*, Idaho, 1991

India and Sri Lanka

Bhaktivedanta Swami, A. C., *Srimad Bhagavatam*, Los Angeles, 1975

Dowson, J., *Classical Dictionary of Hindu Mythology*, London, 1961

Jones, John Garrett, *Tales and Teachings of the Buddha*, London 1979

O'Flaherty, Wendy, *Hindu Myths*, London 1975

Prime, Ranchor, *Ramayana, A Journey*, London 1997

Rajan, Chandra, *The Pancatantra*, London 1993

Tibet and Mongolia

Altangerel, D., *How Did the Great Bear Originate? Folktales from Mongolia*, Ulaanbaattar, 1988

Berger, Patricia, and Terese Tse Bartholomew, *Mongolia: The Legacy of Chinggis Khan*, London, 1995

Campbell, Joseph, *The Way of the Animal Powers: Historical Atlas of World Mythology*, vol. 1, London, 1983

Eliade, Mircea (translated from the French by Willard R. Trask), *Shamanism: Archaic Techniques of Ecstasy*, Princeton, 1971

Heissig, Walther (translated from the German by Geoffrey Samuel), *The Religions of Mongolia*, Berkeley, 1980

Norbu, Namkhai, *The Necklace of Gzi: A Cultural History of Tibet*, Dharamsala, 1981

Project, Yeshe De, *Ancient Tibet*, Berkeley, 1986

Snellgrove, David, *Indo-Tibetan Buddhism*, London, 1987

Stein, R. A., *Tibetan Civilisation*, London, 1972

Tucci, Giuseppe, *The Religions of Tibet*, London, 1980

China

Watson, W., *China*, London, 1961

Bailey, Adrian, *The Caves of the Sun the Origin of Mythology*, London, 1997
Palmer, Martin and Xiaomin, Zhao et al, *Essential Chinese Mythology*, London 1997
Loewe, Michael, *Divination, Mythology and Monarchy in Han China*, Cambridge, 1994
Birrell, Anne, *Chinese Mythology: an Introduction*, London, 1993
Ke, Yuang, *Dragons and Dynasties: an Introduction to Chinese Mythology*, London, 1993

Japan and Korea

Aston, W. G., *Nihongi: Chronicles of Japan*, London and New York, 1956
Choi, In-hak, *A Type Index of Korean Folktales*, Seoul, 1979
Grayson, James Huntley, *Myths and Legends from Korea*, Sheffield, 1998
Ilyon, *Samguk yusa: Legends and History of the Three Kingdoms of Ancient Korea* translated by Tae-Hung Ha and Grafton K. Mintz, Seoul, 1972
Kidder, J. E., *Japan*, London, 1959
Lee, Peter H., *Sourcebook of Korean Civilization* 2 vols, New York, 1993 (vol. 1, *From Early Times to the Sixteenth Century*)
Walraven, Boudewijn, *Songs of the Shaman: The Ritual Chants of the Korean Mudang*, London, 1994

Southeast Asia

Davis, R. B., *Muang Metaphysics: A Study of Northern Thai Myth and Ritual*, Bangkok, 1984
Mus, Paul, *Barabudur*, New York, 1978
Whittaker, Clio, *An Introduction to Oriental Mythology*, London, 1997
Hallam, Elizabeth, *Gods and Goddesses over 130 deities and tales from world mythology*, London, 1997

Oceania

Best, Elsdan, *Moari Religion and Mythology*, Wellington, 1982
Gillison, Gillian, *Between Culture and Fantasy, a New Guinea Highlands Mythology*, Chicago, 1993
Knappert, Jan, *Pacific Mythology*, London, 1992
Finney, Ben and Among, Marlene et al, *Voyage of Rediscovery a Cultural Odyssey Through Polynesia*, Berkeley, 1994
Beckwith, Martha, *Hawaiian Mythology*, Honolulu, 1982

Australia

Sienkewicz, Thomas J., *World Mythology an Annotated Guide to Collections and Anthologies*, London, 1996
Mudrooroo, *Aboriginal Mythology an A-Z Spanning the History of the Australian Aboriginal People from the Earliest Legends to the Present Day*, London, 1994
Poignant, Roslyn, *Oceanic and Australian Mythology*, Feltham, 1985
Turner, David H., *Australian Aboriginal Culture*, New York, 1987
Rutherford, Anna, *Aboriginal Culture Today*, Sydney, 1991

Africa

Beattie, John, *Bunyoro, An African Kingdom*, New York, 1960
Callaway, Henry, *The Religious System of the Amazulu*, London, 1870
Evans-Pritchard, Evan Edward, *Nuer Religion*, Oxford, 1956
Ezekwuga, Christopher U. M., *Chi: The True God in Igbo Religion*, Alwaye, 1987
Iloanusi, Obiakoizu A., *Myths of the Creation of Man and the Origin of Death in Africa: A Study in Igbo Traditional Culture and Other African Cultures*, Frankfurt, 1984
King, Noel Q., *African Cosmos: An Introduction to Religion in Africa*, Belmont, 1986
Parrinder, Geoffrey, *West African Religion: A Study of the Beliefs and Practices of Akan, Ewe, Yoruba, Ibo, and Kindred Peoples*, London, 1949
Quarcoopome, T. N. O., *West African Traditional Religion*, Ibadan, 1987
Sawyerr, Harry, God, *Ancestor or Creator? Aspects of Traditional Belief in Ghana, Nigeria and Sierra Leone*, Harlow, 1970

The Caribbean

Ann, Martha and Dorothy Myers Imel, *Goddesses in World Mythology*, Santa Barbara, 1993
Spence, Lewis, *Introduction to World Mythology*, London, 1994
Derkx, J., *Caribbean Studies*, Leiden, 1998
Malinowski, Sharon and Shhets, Anna et al, *The Gale Encyclopedia of Native American Tribes*, Detroit, 1998
Ferguson, *Eastern Caribbean a guide to the people, politics and culture*, London, 1997

North America

Burland, C. A., and M. Wood, *North American Indian Mythology*, London, 1985

Feldmann, Susan, *The Storytelling Stone: Traditional Native American Myths and Tales*, New York, 1965
Riordan, James, *The Songs My Paddle Sings. Native American Legends*, London, 1995
Spence, Lewis, *The Myths of the North American Indians*, London, 1914
Wright, Ronald, *Stolen Continents: The Indian Story*, London, 1992

Central and South America

Miller, Mary, and Karl Taube, *The Gods and Symbols of Ancient Mexico and the Maya*, London, 1993
Stevens-Arroyo, A. M., *Cave of the Jaqua: the Mythological World of the Taínos*, Albuquerque, 1988
Sullivan, Lawrence E., *Icanchu's Drum: An orientation to Meaning in South American Religions*, London, 1988
Tedlock, Dennis, *Popul Vuh: The Definitive Edition of the Mayan Book of the Dawn of Life and the Glories of the Gods and Kings*, New York, 1985
Urton, Gary (ed.), *Animal Myths and Metaphors in South America*, Salt Lake City, 1985

PICTURE CREDITS

Academy for Korean Studies: 201, 202, 203(j).

AKG: 35(t), 38, 61(r)67(t), 75, 99, 103, 120(t), 126, 129, 142(t), 143, 152, 158, 159(l),191 (r), 194(t), 203, 216, 243(b), 254, 269(t), 281(b), 298.

Christies Images: 30, 33, 51(t), 52(l), 53, 73(b), 134(b), 153(t), 186, 196(t), 197(t), 199(b), 242(t), 243(t), 249, 250(r), 252(b), 253.

Chief Pedro Guanikeyu Torres: 261(b), 262(t).

Circa Photo Library: 136(b), 189(i),Tjalling Halbertsma: 175(b), 176(r), 177(b), Circa 246(l).

Clayton, Peter A: 44, 45(t), 46(all), 47(all), 49(all), 51 (b), 52(all).

Collection Kharbine-Tapbor: 102, 106(t), 107, 108(t).

Courtesy of Kojiki Nikonshoki (Shinchosha, 1991): 195 .

David Lyons: Event Horizons 88.

e.t. archive: 15(bl,t), 23(l), 27, 29, 35(l), 38(b), 42, 62(b), 63(b), 65(t), 110, 153(b), 159(r), 193(b), 229, 244(t), 298(t), 304(t).

Foundry Arts: 251(t).

Gunson, Niel: 224.

Image Select: 133(t), 139(b), 194(b), 205, 227.

Image Select/Chris Fairclough: 109, 222(b), 230, 231.

Image Select/FPG International: 133(b), 139(t), 171, 222(t), 223(r), 233, 262(b).

Image Select/Giraudon: 13, 16(r), 21(b), 23(r), 24(all), 25(all), 36, 37(all), 39, 71, 79(l), 112(t), 113, 137, 138, 193(t), 196(b), 258(b), 259, 261(t).

Mary Evans Picture Library: 14, 17, 18, 20, 21(t), 31, 66(t), 80(all), 82(all), 83, 84, 86, 87(all), 92(t), 95(b), 97, 98, 101, 106(b), 108(b), 109(t), 111, 112 b), 119(all), 128(all), 256(b), 268, 280, 302(t).

Riordan, J.: 104, 105, 217, 228(t).

Sanders, N. J.: 299.

Scandibild: 123, 125.

Still Pictures: Marek Libersky 140, Tony Rath 141 1(t), Christian Decout 177(t), Walter H. Hodge 197(b), Max Fulcher 244(b), Norbert Wu 265(t), Jamie Drummond/Christian Aid 303, Anore Bartschi 304(b).

Topham: 15(r), 16(l), 19(t), 34(b), 41(b), 134(t), 135, 136(t), 141(b), 142(b), 172, 173(all), 191, 199(t), 245.

Travel Photo International: 258(t), 260, 263, 264.

VAL: National Museum of Copenhagen 90(t), 292(r).

VAL/Bridgeman: 19(b), 22, 24(b), 28, 40, 41(t), 43(all), 45(b), 48, 50, 52(r), 56, 58(t), 68(t), 70(all), 72, 77, 85(b), 92(b), 93, 95(t), 96, Oriental Museum, Durham University, UK: 169(t), Chester Beatty Lib. & Gal. of Oriental Art, Dublin: 178, British Library: 181(b), 188, Christie's Images: 189(r), Bridgeman 204, 221(t), 225, 232(1).

VAL/Artephot: Nimatallah 54, 57(all), Held 58(b), Nimatallah 59, Varga 60, Nimatallah 61(l), 62(t), Faillet 63(t), Nimatallah 65(b), VAL/Artephot 66(b), Varga 67(b), A. Held 68(b), Nimatallah
73, 74(t), VAL/Artephot 100, Scandibild 116(t), 120(b), 121, Silvio Fiore 131(t), Pietri 147(t), 150(t), 156(t), Lavaud 163(b), 166(t), Brumaire 167, Lavaud170(0, Faillet 176(b), Lavaud 179, Ru Sui Chu 180, G. Mandel 181(t), Lauaud 182, 183(r), Percheron 183(l), G. Mandel 184, Percheron 185(t), 187(b), Ogawa 192, Lauaud 198, A. Held 219, 228(b), 234, J. Guillot 247, A. Held 248, Varga 252(t), A. Held 255(t), Varga 255(b), A. Held 256(t), 257(all), R, Percheron 291(all), R. Percheron 293(b), Faillet 295.

VAL/Edimedia: 79(r), 85(t), 144, 145(t), 147(b), 148(t), 149, 1500), 151, 154(t), 155, 156(b), 157, 160, 162, 165, 169(b), 218, 219(r), 220, 221(b), 223(l), 226(l), 226(r), 231(b), 232(r), 250(l), 251(b), 301(t).

Victoria and Albert Museum London: 154(b).

Werner Forman: 78, Dorset Nat. Hist. & Arch. Soc. 76, British Museum London 8 1, National Museum of Wales 89, National Museum Copenhagen 90(b), National Museum of Ireland 91, British Museum 94, Universitetets Oldsaksamling, Oslo 114, Universitetetsbiblioteket, Uppsala, Sweden 115, Statens Historiska Museum 116(b), Viking Ship Museum, Bygdoy 117, Statens Historiska Museum, Stockholm 118, Statens Historiska Museum, Stockholm 122(t), 122, Arhus Kunstmuseum, Denmark 124(t), Statens Historiska Museum, Stockholm 124(b), 127(b), Manx Museum, Isle of Man 127(t), Statens Historiska Museum,

Stockholm 130, Viking Ship Museum, Bygdoy 131 (b), National Gallery, Prague 146, Schatzkarnmer der Residenz, Munich 161, 163(t), Werner Forman 164, Philip Goldman Collection 166(b), Werner Forman 168, Philip Goldman Collection 170(b), Werner Forman 174, 175(t), 176(t), Private Collection 206, 207, P. Goldman Collection, London 208 (all), Werner Forman 209, British Museum, London 210, Denpasar Museum, Bali 211 (all), British Museum, London 212, Werner Forman 213, Private Collection 214, Werner Forman 215, 236, Private Collection, Prague 237(r), Private Collection, New York 237(l), Private Collection 238, Private Collection, New York 239(r), Tara Collection, New York 239(l), Art Gallery of New South Wales 240(all) I Private Collection, Prague 241, 242(bl), 246(r), H W Read Coll. Plains Indian Museum, B. Bill Hist. Center, Cody, Wyoming 266(b), Werner Forman 266(t), Museum of Anthropology, University of British Columbia, Vancouver 269(b), Centennial Museum, Vancouver 270, British Museum, London 271, Smithsonian Institution, Washington 272, Werner Forman 273, National Museum of Man, Ottawa, Maxwell Museum of Anthropology, Albuquerque 275(t), Portland Art Museum, Oregon 275(r), Plains Indian Museum, Buffalo Bill Historical Center, Cody, Wyoming 275(bl), Centennial Museum, Vancouver 276, Schindler Collection, New York 277(l), Formerly James Hooper Collection, Watersfielf, England 277(r), Mr and Mrs John A, Putnam 279(t), Werner Forman 279(b), Provincial Museum, Victoria, Canada 281 (t), Werner Forman 282-3, Liverpool Museum, Liverpool 283(r), British Museum, London 284, National Museum for Anthropology 284(r), 285(l), British Museum, London 285(r), Private Collection, New York 286, British Museum, London 287(t), National Museum of Anthropology, Mexico City 287(r), Museum fur Volkerkunde, Berlin 288, British Museum, London 289(tr), Anthropology Museum, University of Veracruz, Jalapa (tl,br), Werner Forman 290, Private Collection 292(r), Private Collection, New York 293(t), Private Collection 294, Museum fur Volkerkunde, Berlin 296(t), Private Collection, Paris 296(b), Toni Ralph Collection, New York 297, Werner Forman 300, Museum fur Volkerkund, Berlin 301(b), David Bernstein Fine Art, New York 302(b), 305.

INDEX OF NAMES

Abadai Khan 175
Abel 32-3
Aberewa 252
Achaemenids 38
Achilles 58, 59, 72
Achitometl 290
Actaeon 61
Adad 25
Adapa 19
Adonis 61, 66
Aeetes 64
Aegisthus 64
Aegyptus 64
Aeneas 70, 71, 72, 75
Aeschylus 6, 54
Aeshma Daeva 43
Afanasiev, Alexander 104-5, 106, 108
Afi 117
Afrasyab 42
Agadzagadza 253
Agamemnon 7, 58, 64
Agdestis 70
Agni 146, 151
Agrippina, St 112
Ahriman 39, 40, 41, 43
Ahura Mazda 38, 39, 41, 42-3
Ai 117
Ailil 83
Ainnle 86
Aither 57
Aitupuai 225
Ajax 58
Aka Manah 43
Akis, Timothy 223
Akshobhya 164, 171
Alalu 28
Albeborael Guahayona 265
Ale 254
Alexander, of Macedon 38
Alexei Mikhailovich, Tsar 103
Alkmene 58, 59
All Father 237, 241
All Mother 241
Altan Khan 174, 175
Ama-no-uzume 193, 198
Amairgin 92
Amanominakanushi-no-kami 191
Amaterasu 190, 193, 194, 196, 198-9
Ambo 255
Ame-no-waka-hiko 199
Amenophis II 51
Amenophis III 53
Amitabha 164, 171
Amma 117
Amoghasiddhi 164, 171
Amphidromia 61
Amulius 71
Amun-Re 46, 49
An 14, 15, 16, 17, 21
Ananda 167
Anat 34, 35, 36
Anchises 72
Andromeda 65
Aneirin 93
Angra Mainyu *see* Ahriman
Angrboda 125
Angus 87
Antaryami 148
Anu 18, 19, 21, 23, 28
Anubis 49, 50, 53
Anzu 14
Aphrodite 56, 58, 61, 66, 72
Apollo 56, 58, 61, 63, 68, 70, 73
Apsyrtus 64
Aqat 36-7
Arawn 91, 94
Ardan 86
Ardeshir 38
Ares 56, 66
Arinna 26
Arjuna 156, 157
Artemis 56, 61, 63, 64, 74
Arthur 93-4, 95, 96, 97, 99
Ashmedai 43
Ashnan 17
Ashur 9
Ask 116
Asklepios 63
Assur 25
Astar 35
Astart 34, 35, 37
Atabey 261, 265
Atain-tjina 243
Atea 220
Athena 65
Athene 55, 56, 58
Atotarho 280
Atra-hasis 9, 10, 20
Atreus 64
Attis 70
Atum 45, 46
Audhumla 116
Augustus Caesar 73
Austri 116
Avalokiteshvara 169, 170, 171, 175
Awonawilona 268, 269
Az 43
Azadeh 40
Azhi Dahaka 40, 43

Baba 16
Bába Yagá 107, 108, 109
Badb 83
Bahram Gur 40
Baiame 237, 241
Balarama 148
Balder 121, 122, 125, 130, 131
Bali 148
Balor 80, 99
Banapan Maymuru 241
Bardon, Geoffrey 246
Bartilek 99
Bayamanaco 262, 263
Bear Woman 202
Bébinn 85
Begze Suren 173
Bel 77
Beli Mawr 89
Bellerophon 65
Benen 92
Bessmertny, Koshchay 106, 107
Bestla 116
Bhagiratha 146
Bharat 145
Bhisma 156, 157
Bhumi 147, 151
Birrinydji 236
Black Bear 273
Black Tezcatlipoca 285
Blue Tezcatlipoca 285
Boloki 254-5
Bor 116
Borjigin 177
Borvo 78
Botoque 301
Brahma 145, 146, 147, 150, 163, 210
Brân 84, 85, 89, 90
Branwen 81, 89-90
Breath Blend *see* Xi He
Brendan, St. 91
Bres 81
Briccrui 81, 84-5
Brigit 77, 78
Buddha 148, 158-9, 162, 164, 166, 167, 208, 212, 214
Bulardemo 242
Bundjil 241
Bura 253
Burrumarra, David 236

Cain 32-3
Cairbre 81
Calliope 75
Cassandra 64
Cathbad 86, 87, 92
Ce Acatl Topiltzin 286
Cei 97, 98
Celeus 62
Cephisus 74
Cerberus 56, 60, 75
Ceres 68
Cernunnos 78
Chac 292
Chalchiuhtlicue 285, 292
Chandra 147
Chang E 188
Chang Xi 180, 181, 188
Changer 279
Charon 67
Chernava 113
Chesok 203
Chi You 180, 186, 187, 188
Chinggis Khan 174, 176-7
Chiron 63
Chong 183
Ch'onje 203
Chrétien de Troyes 94, 96, 97
Chryseis 58
Chryses 58
Chumong 202-3
Churchward, Colonel James 227
Cian 80
Ciaran, St 92
Citche Manitou 275
Clydno 97
Clytemnestra 64
Coatlicue 288
Collatinus 73
Colomba, St 92, 93
Colum Cuaillemech 80
Columbus, Christopher 258, 261, 282
Conaire Mor 82
Conall Cernach 84, 85
Conchobar 83, 86, 87
Cormac 86
Cormac mac Airt 87
Coyolxauhqui 288, 289, 290, 292
Coyote 268, 278-9
Credne 79
Creon 64, 65
Cú Ro' mac Dairi 84, 85, 99
Cúchulainn 78, 79, 81, 83, 84, 85, 91, 93
Culhwch 85, 88, 94-6, 97
Cupid 71, 72, 75
Cybele 70
Cymedei Cymeinfoll 85
Cynon 97
Cyrus 38, 39

Dagda 79, 82
Dain 120
Daire mac Fiachniu 83
Daksha 149, 150-1
Damkina 18
Danae 58, 65
Danaus 64
Daniel 36
Danu 79
Daphne 73
Darius 38, 40-1
Darvi 218
Dasaratha 154
Deianeira 59
Deirdre 79, 81, 8687, 88, 99
Demaphoon 62
Demeter 56, 62-3, 68, 72
Deminán Caracaracol 262, 263, 265
Demna 86
Dengai 224
Deucalion 57, 70
Devi 146, 151, 152
Dhritrashtra 156, 157
Di 179
Di Jun 186
Diana 68
Diarmaid 81, 87-8, 99
Dibobia 250
Dido 71
Dionysus 54, 56, 66, 67, 70, 74
Djig 240
Don 89
Doso 62
Draught Ox 188
Draupnir 119, 130
Drought Fury 181, 186, 187
Drugh 43
Dubthach Doeltenga 86
Dugong 242
Dumuzi 15, 16, 19
Duneyr 120
Durathror 120
Durga 151, 214
Dvalin 120
Dylan 94

Ea 18, 19, 20, 21, 22, 24, 25, 29
Earth (man) 24
Echidna 56, 66

Echo 74
Edda 114, 117
Efflon Obassi 249
Efnisien 89, 90
Eileithyia 56
El 34, 35, 36, 37
Elimelek 36
Embla 116
Empedocles 54
Enki 8-9, 9-10, 13, 14, 15, 16, 17, 20, 24
Enkidu 16, 17, 23
Enlil 8, 9, 10, 15, 16, 17, 20, 21, 25, 28
Enmesh 14, 16
Enoch 32
Enosichthon 56
Enten 14, 16
Eochaid Airem 81-2, 99
Eogan mac Durthacht 87
Epimetheus 57
Epona 78
Erebos 57, 67
Ereshkigal 15, 22, 24
Erewan 214
Eros 57
Erra 20, 21
Erymanthus 61
Etain 81-2, 88, 99
Etana 24
Etar 81
Euhemerus 7
Euripides 54, 66
Eurydice 75, 192
Eurystheus 59
Ever Breath *see* Chang Xi
Ever Sublime *see* Chang E
Ezhdeha 43

Fadir 117
Fang 250
Farmer God 180, 181, 182-3, 188
Father Sky 208, 268
Faustulus 71
Fefafa 229
Fenrir 125, 126-7
Fereydun 40, 43
Fergus 81
Fergus mac Roich 86
Fevanga 229
Fianna 85, 87, 88, 89, 93, 94
Finn mac Cool 79, 84, 85, 86, 87, 88, 91, 93, 94, 99
Finnbennach 82, 83
Fintan 85-6
Fintann 221
Fireshade 199
Fireshine 199
First Lord of the Westerners *see* Osiris
Flame 188
Freki 130
Freyja 118, 119, 120-1, 123, 124, 127, 128Freyr 115, 118, 123, 124, 130
Frigg 121, 122, 127
Fu Xi 180, 181, 182, 185
Fuamnach 81
Fulla 127
Futsunushi-no-mikoto 199

Gabriel 232
Gaia 57
Galahad 97
Galzuut 177
Ganesh 146, 163
Ganga 146
Garshasp 43
Garuda 157, 166, 209
Gautama Buddha 161
Gawain 78, 79, 84, 97
Gayomard 39
Geb 45
Gefion 127
Gefjun 121
Genakuiya 233
Geoffrey of Monmouth 94, 96
Gerald of Wales 96
Gerd 118, 127, 130
Geri 130
Geryon 60
Gesar Khan 175, 176
Geshtinanna 15, 16
Gildas 93
Gilgamesh 16-17, 22-3
Glauce 64, 65
Gleipnir 119, 126, 127
Gna 127
Goibniu 79
Gong Gong 180, 181, 182
Goreu 95
Gorlois 94
Gosh 39, 41
Grainne 79, 81, 87-8, 99
Grandmother Turtle 268
Grannos 78
Great Mare *see* Epona
Great Mother 70
Gri-gum 169
Grid 118
Grol-ma 171
Guabancex 261
Guabonito 265
Guahayona 261, 263, 264, 265
Guayahona 260
Gugumatz 286
Guinevere 96, 99
Gulu 251
Gun 180, 181, 182, 187
Gungnir 130
Gunnlod 131
Gwalchmai 97, 98
Gwawl 87
Gwenhwyvar 98

Hachiman 199
Hadad 34
Hades 54, 56, 62, 67, 75
Hafgan 91
Hakhamenesh 38
Hammurabi 18
Hannahanna 27
Hannibal 71
Hanullim 203
Hanuman 152, 155, 163
Harc Finneces 85, 86
Hariya 37
Hathor 49
Hayagriva 174-5
He-Who-Must-Be-Obeyed 268
Hebe 56
Hector 58
Hecuba 58
Hedammu 29
Heidrun 122
Heimdall 117, 130
Hel 120, 121, 125
Helen 7, 58
Helios 62, 66
Hephaestus 56, 66
Hephaistus 57
Hera 54, 56, 58, 59, 64, 66, 74
Herakles 58, 59, 60, 72
Hercules 59, 60
Hermes 56, 61
Hermes Psychopompos 67
Hermod 121, 130
Hero 73
Herodotus 42, 44
Hesiod 54
Hestia 56, 61, 75
Hiaunael Guan'n 265
Hiawatha 280
Hikule'o 220, 224-5
Hina 223, 224
Hinatunaone 227
Hinenuitepo 232
Hino 276
Hippolyte 60, 65
Hippolytus 65
Hira 40
Hiranyakashipu 155
Hiruko 192
Hlin 127
Ho Chi Minh 213
Ho-ori 199
Ho-teri 199
Hod 121
Hoel 101
Homer 54
Hongi 224
Horus 45, 47, 49-50
Hou Ji 181, 182, 187
Howitt, A.W. 237
Hrungnir 118
Hua'atua 230, 231
Huginn 130
Huitzilopochtli 285, 288, 289, 290,292
Humbaba 23
Hun Dun 184
Hun Hunahpu 291
Hunahpu 291
Hupashiya 26
Huracan 286, 287
Hwanin 203
Hwanung 202
Hydra 56, 60, 223
Hyel 253
Hymir 123, 129
Hypermnestra 64

Iboniamasiboniamanoro 256
Idunn 124-5
Igbo 254
Igraine 94
Ikonitra 256
Ildanach 80
Illuyanka 26-7
Ilya 112
Ilyap'a 294, 297
Inanna 15, 16, 17, 21, 72
Inari 199
Indra 146, 210, 214
Inpu 53
Inti 294, 297
Iole 59
Iphigeneia 64
Iseult 100-1
Isfandyar 42, 43
Ishtar 15, 21, 23, 24, 25, 28, 29, 72
Isis 45, 47-8, 49, 50-1
Itiba Cahubaba 260, 262
Itys 62
Itzamna 285
Ivan, Prince 106, 107, 111
Ivan the Terrible 103
Ixion 64
Izanagi 191, 192, 193, 194
Izanami 191, 192

Jadu 43
Jamshid 40
Janus 69
Jarl 117
Jarnsaxa 118
Jason 64-5, 66
Jian Di 187
Jiang Yuan 187
Jimmu 194, 199
Jocasta 63
John the Baptist 77, 112
Jormangand 123, 125, 126, 130
Julana 245
Jung, Carl 10
Juno 68
Jupiter 68, 71, 75

Kaech'on-jol 200
Kagauaha 225
Kaggen 253
Kagutsuchi 192
Kaikeyi 154
Kakwa 252
Kali 151
Kalki 148
Kalunga 255
Kalunga-ngombe 256
Kamapuaa 222, 223
Kamimusubi-no-kami 198
Kamrushepa 27
Kamsa 146, 155
Kanaloa 220
Karl 117
Kartikeya 146
Kavaonau 229
Kaveh 40
Keret 37
Kevin, St 92
Khalbin 177
Khepri 51, 52, 53
Khnum 46
Khori Tumed 177
Khovduud 177
Khri-Srong-Ide'u-btsan 167
Khubilai Khan 174
Ki'kaw'ju 276
Kikuyu 254
Kimata-no-kami 198
Kimbiji 256
Kingu 18
Kinh Duong Vuong 209
Kinich Ahau 285
Kintu 251
Kliarin-Kliari 241
Kluchevsky, Vasily 102

Kokchu 176
Kong-jo 167
Kono 257
Kothar-and-Hasis 34, 35, 36
Krachi 251
Krishna 146, 147, 148, 151, 155-7
Kronos 57
Ku-e-hiko 198
Kumarbi 28-9
Kumwa 203
Kunapipi 241
Kupala 112
Kura 220
Kurma 147, 148, 149
Kusa-nada-hime 194, 195
Kusanagi 194
Kusuh 28
Kvasir 131

Lac Long Quan 209
Lady of the Wind *see* Guabancex
Lahar 17
Laius 63
Lakshmana 162
Lakshmi 147
Lamba 250, 254
Lancelot 97, 99
Lanval 88, 96
Lawson, Thomas 227
Layamon 94
Leander 73
Leapai 228
Lel 104
Lesa 250
Leto 56, 63
Lha-tho tho-ri 164-5
Li 183
Lif 126
Lifthrasir 126
Limaloa 222
Little Star 272
Lleu 81
Llyr 89
Lo-ngam 169
Lo'au 229
Lochru 92
Loegaire 84, 92
Lofn 127
Loki 118, 119, 121, 124-5, 126, 130
Lomna 84
Lord of the Smoking Mirror *see* Tezcatlipoca
Loro Jonggrang 214
Lucetmail 92
Luchta 79
Luchyele 250
Lucretia 73
Lugh 77, 78, 79, 80, 81, 85
Lynceus 64

Ma'at 44
Mac Dach. 81
Macha 78, 83
Mahi 230, 231
Mahinda 160
Mahisha 152
Mahmud, Sultan 40
Mahufaturau 225
Mahuika 221
Maia 56
Ma'le Dúin 91
Makosh 109
Makuri 299
Malinalxochitl 288
Malory, Sir Thomas 94
Mama Kilya 294, 297
Manawydan 89
Manco Capac 295
Manjushri 166, 169
Mara 212
Marduk 9, 18, 19, 21, 25
Maricha 155
Marie de France 96
Mark 100, 101
Mars 71
Marsyas 63
Mashyagh 39
Mashyanagh 39
Master of Life 173
Mata'afa 224
Math 89
Matholwch 89, 90
Matsya 147, 148-9
Maui 216, 220, 223, 224, 228, 232
Maya 214, 283, 286-7, 291, 293
Mebege 250
Medb 83, 84
Medea 64-5
Medusa 65, 74
Mencius 180
Menelaus 7, 58
Mercury 61, 71, 78
Merlin 92, 94, 99
Merope 63
Metaneira 62
Metis 55, 56
Midhir 81, 82
Midir 99
Minerva 68, 78
Minma Mingari 245
Miruk 205
Mithra 41, 42
Mjollnir 118, 119, 130
Modir 117
Moon 188-9, 242, 272, 292, 305
Moor, Johannes de 34
Morévna, Márya 106, 107
Morning Star 272
Morrigan 83, 94, 99
Moso 224
Mot 35, 37
Mother Ale 109
Mother Earth 208, 268
Mother of the sky 303
Motu 254-5
Mucalinda 212
Mug Ruith 92
Mukunga M'bura 254
Mumuna 241
Mundhir 40
Muninn 130
Mush 43
Mushhushu 19

Nabu 25
Nadulmi 240
Nafanua 225, 228
Nagah 276, 277
Naim 88, 99
Nakaa 225, 227
Nakahi 232
Nambalista 255
Nambi 251
Nammu 9, 13, 16
Namtar 9, 22
Nanabozho 275
Nanahuatzin 285
Nandi 149
Nannar 15, 16
Nanshe 16
Naoise 86, 87, 99
Narada 146
Narasimha 148, 155
Narayana 147
Narcissus 74
Narfi 125
Nasu 43
Nefertum 46
Neith 46
Nemain 83
Nennius 93
Nepele 240
Nephthys 45, 48
Nergal 20, 22
Nestis 54
Nga Tin De 214
Nguleso 252
Nguloki 252
Ngurunderi 237, 240, 241
Nidhogg 120
Nimue 94
Nineveh 20, 22, 25
Ningishzida 19
Ninhursaga 8, 9, 14, 16
Niniganni 225
Ninigi-no-mikoto 199
Ninisina 16
Ninlil 15, 17
Ninmah 13
Ninshubur 15
Ninurta 14-15, 16, 25
Nisaba 16
Njirana 245
Njord 118, 123, 127, 129, 130
Noah 33
Nokomis 275
Nordri 116
North Star 276-7
Nuada 79, 80
Numitor 71
Nusku 14
Nut 45, 52
Nyame 252

Odin 8, 115, 116, 117, 118, 120, 121, 122, 125, 126, 130, 131
Odysseus 59, 66
Oedipus 6, 55, 58, 70
Oengus 81, 99
Ogbu-ghu 254
Ogetsu 194
Ogma 80
Ohrmazd 39, 41, 42
Oisin 85, 88-9, 91, 94, 99
Ojin 199
Okin Tngri 173
Okuninushi 190, 195, 196, 197, 198, 199
Old Bones the Immortal 106, 107
Olifat 221, 223, 224
Olwen 85, 94-6, 97
Omecihuatl 285
Ometeotle 285
One-Who-Contains-All *see* Awonawilona
Orion 61
Oro 217, 220, 225, 229, 230
Orpheus 75, 192
Orsmond, J.S. 230
Osiris 44, 45, 47-50, 53
Our Lord the Flayed One *see* Xipe Totec
Ovid 73
Owain 97

Pabir 253
Padmasambhava 166-7, 168
Pagë Abé 302
Pahouin 250
Pairika 43
Pamur'mahs' 302
Pan Gu 179, 180, 181, 183, 186, 188
Pan Hu 181, 189
Pandora 57
Pandu 156
Parasurama 148
Paris 58, 59
Patrick, St 88, 89, 92-3
Patroclus 58
Pattini 160, 163
Pe-dkar 167
Pele 223, 225
Peleus 64
Pelias 64
Percival 97
Peredur 89, 97, 98
Persephone 56, 62, 72, 75, 192
Perseus 58, 65
Perun 106, 112
Phaedra 65
Philomela 62
Phineus 66
Phoebus 63
Pisistratus 59
Plato 54
Plow 25
Plutarch 68
Poia 272
Polybus 63
Polydectes 65
Polyphemus 66
Poseidon 55, 56, 62, 65, 66, 67
Prahlad 148
Priam 58
Priapus 74
Procne 62
Productive Manager of the Soil *see* Enki
Prokrustes 47, 59
Prometheus 57
Proserpina 75
Pryderi 78, 89
Psyche 75
Ptah 46, 49
Pugat 36
Purusha 146
Pwll 87, 88, 89, 91, 94
Pyrrha 57, 70
Pytho 63

Qamatha 257
Qat 223, 228
Queen Mother of the West 183
Quetzalcoatl 285, 286, 287
Qui-am-i-Wintook 276-7
Quirinus 68

Radha 151, 155, 156
Radiant 168
Rahu 169
Raivato 256
Rakhsh 42
Rama 7, 148, 152-3, 154-5, 162-3, 214
Rameses VI 52, 53
Ran 121, 129
Ranakombe 256
Rangda 214
Rasoabemanana 256
Ratatosk 120
Ratnasambhava 164, 171
Ravana 153, 155, 162, 163
Raven 137
Raven Man 136
Re 46, 49, 50-1, 52
Re-Harakhte 45-6, 49
Red Tezcatlipoca 285
Remus 68, 70, 71
Responding Dragon 181, 187
Rhea 57
Rhea Silvia 71
Rhiannon 78, 87
Rider of the Cloud 34
Romi Kumu 303, 305
Romulus 68, 70, 71
Rongo 217, 220, 224, 228
Rua Kenana Hepetipa 232
Rudra 171
Rupe 216
Rustam 42

Sadb 94
Sadko 113
Saehrimnir 122
Saga 127
Sakka 159, 162
Sakunabikona 190
Salmon of Knowledge 85-6
San-shin 203
Sarutahiko 198
Sati 150
Satyavrata 147, 148
Scarface 272
Sedna 134-5
Sekhmet 46-7
Semele 56
Sencha mac Ailella 84
Set 45, 47, 49, 50
Sextus Tarquin 73
Shakan 24
Shamash 19, 23, 24, 41
Shapash 35
Shatiqtu 37
Shaushga 28
Shimegi 28
Shinob 276
Shiva 145, 146, 147, 149, 150, 151, 152, 154, 156, 161, 163, 209, 210, 211
Shu 45
Shun 181, 183
Shwemyethna 214
Siddhartha Gautama *see* Buddha
Siduri 23
Sina 223
Sinis 59
Siovili 231
Sita 7, 153, 154, 155, 162-3
Sitala 146
Sjofn 127
Skadi 118, 125, 127, 129, 130
Skidbladnir 130
Sleipnir 121, 130
Snotra 127
Snowmaiden 104
Sohrab 42
Sokka 205
Sophocles 6, 54
Sovereign Earth 188
Sovereign Millet 188
Sphinx 56, 63
Sri 210
Sri Devi 210
Srong-btsan sgam-po 165, 167
Stheneboia 65
Sturluson, Snorri 8, 114
Sudika-mbambi 256
Sudri 116
Sukunabikona-no-mikoto 198
Sulis 78
Sumana 161, 163
Sun 137, 224, 297
Surya 146, 147
Susa-no-o 193, 194, 195, 196, 197, 198
Suseri-hime 197, 198
Suttung 131
Sviagriss 124
Swarnamali 163
Sybil 70
Sychaeus 71
Syn 127

Ta'aroa 217, 220, 226, 229
Tafaki 221
Tagaloa 220, 228, 231
Tahmina 42
Tailtu 77
Takami-musubi 199
Takemikazuchi-no-mikoto 199
Taliesin 89, 92
Talking God 269
Tamafaiga 224
Tamatoa 231
Tambarinang 208
Tammuz 24
Tane 217, 220, 224, 229
Tang 186, 187
Tangaroa 220, 224, 228
Tangiia 218
Tan'gun 200, 201, 202, 203
Tantalus 60, 67
Tara 170, 171
Taramanini 231
Taredd 95
Tarpeia 72
Tartaros 57, 67
Taurua 230
Tautoru 224
Te Atua Wera 232
Tefnut 45
Teiresias 61, 63
Telepinu 27
Tereus 62
Teshub 28
Tevne 175
Tezcatlipoca 285, 287, 290
Tezozomoc 290
Thanapa 299
Themis 57
Theseus 47, 58, 59, 65
Thespios 59
Thjazi 118, 124, 127, 129
Thokk 121
Thor 8, 115, 117, 118-19, 120, 122, 123, 125, 130
Thorolf 115
Thoth 46, 52
Thrall 117
Thrym 118, 119
Thunderbird 269, 276
Thyestes 64
Tiamat 18, 24
Tian 179
Tiki 226-7
Tinirau 228
Titus Tatius 68, 72
Tjakamarra, Brogus Nelson 246
Tjalpatjari, Clifford Possum 246
Tjangala, Riley Major 246
Tjungarrayi, Charley 246
Tlaloc 285, 287, 290, 292
To'imata 225
Tonatiuh 287
Tristan 99, 100-1
Tsuki-yomi 193
Tualagi 228
Ture 255
Turnus 71
Tuthmosis III 51
Twrch Trwyth 95, 96
Typhon 66
Tyr 126-7

Uisnech 86
Ullikummi 29
Umi 228
Ungud 239
Upelluri 29
Uranos 57
Urshanabi 23
Uther 94
Uti 225
Utnapishtim 9, 20-1, 23
Uttu 14,16

Vairocana 164, 166, 171
Vajrapani 169, 171
Vali 125
Vamana 148
Varaha 148
Varuna 147
Vassilisa 108
Vasuki 149
Vayu 146, 147
Ve 116
Vedrfolnir 120
Vega, Garcilaso de la 297
Venus 68, 71, 72, 73, 75
Vesta 75
Vestri 116
Vijaya 162
Vili 116
Vimalamitra 168
Viracocha 295, 299
Vishnu 145, 146, 147, 148, 149, 150, 152, 153, 154, 155, 156, 162, 163, 209, 210, 211, 214
Vivien 94, 99
Vlasia Kupalnitsa, St 112
Volos 112
Vor 127
Vucub Caquix 291
Vucub Hunahpu 291

Wace 94
Wakinu 274
Wallanganda 239
Walumbe 251
Watatsumi-no-kami 199
Weaver Maid 188
Wenonah 275
Wepwawet 53
Whaitiri 232
White Tezcatlipoca 285
Woman Chou 186
Woman Gua 179, 180, 181, 182, 184, 185, 186, 187, 188
Woman Shaman 303
Wrnach 85
Wulbari 251

Xbalanque 291
Xhosa 257
Xi He 180, 181, 185, 186, 188
Xia 187
Xie 187
Xin Chui 185
Xipe Totec 285, 289
Xquic 291

Ya-gami-hime 195, 196, 198
Yachihoko 198
Yakshas 160, 162
Yam 34, 37
Yang 181, 183
Yarilo 112
Yassub 37
Yataa 257
Yatpan 36
Yatu 43
Yaya 260
Yelena the Fair 111
Yellow 181, 186, 187
Yggdrasill 117, 120, 126
Yi 181, 186, 188
Yima Khshaeta 40
Yin 181, 183
Ymir 116
Yogond 223
Ysbaddaden 94, 95, 97
Yu 180, 181, 182, 187
Yúcahu 261, 265
Yuhwa 203
Yurlunggor 237

Zal 42
Zande 255
Zeus 54, 55, 56, 57, 58, 59, 60, 61, 62, 63, 64, 66, 67, 70, 74
Zhuan Xu 183, 186
Zhuang Zi 184
Ziusudra 9, 20
Zoroaster 38, 39, 40, 42, 43
Zuhhak 40, 43

SUBJECT INDEX

Aboriginal Australians 234-5
Abydos 49, 73
Acheron 67
Acllas 296
Acolhua 287
acrylic movement 246
Adam's Peak 161
Adhar Burzin-Mehr 41
Adhar Farn-Bag 41
Adhar Gushn-Asp 41
Aegir 121, 129
Aeneid 71
Aesir 117, 121, 122-3, 125, 127, 129, 131
Africa 248-57
afterlife 120-1
afterworld *see* Otherworld
aggregates, five 164
Ainu 190
aitu 224
Aker 51
Alfheim 117
Amasha Spentas 42-3
Amazon 300-5
Amazons 65
Amerindians 258, 259, 282-3
Amorite tribes 18
amulets 119
ancestors 105, 204-5, 209, 221, 238-9, 304
Ancient Greece 6-8
Ancient History 180
Ancient Near East 8-10, 12-43
Andean South America 294-9
Angkor Wat 212
Animal Hero Age 269
animal skins 143
animals 78, 88, 130, 134, 138, 139, 158, 208, 259, 274, 304
see also individual animals; Master of the Animals
animism 274
Annunanki gods 17, 18
Anthology of Religious Texts from Ugarit 34
apachetas 296
Apophis 51, 52
apostles 299
Apples of Hesperides 60
Apsu 8, 13, 14, 18
Aranda 234, 239
archetypal figures 181, 186-7
Arctic 132-43
Arda Viraz Namag 41
Argo, the 64
Arioi Society 218, 229, 230-1
art 59, 109, 163, 183, 242, 246, 302
see also decoration; designs; folk art; paintings; wood carvings
asceticism 145
Asgard 117, 121, 122, 124, 125, 126, 128, 129, 131
Asia Minor 7
Assyrian mythology 9, 25
astronomy 224
asuras 149

Atar 41
Atash Bahram 41
Athens 55
atma 148, 156
Attica 59
Augean Stables 60
aurora borealis 140, 141
Australia 234-47
avatars 148
Avesta 40
Awashima 198
Ayodhya 154, 155
Azcatpotzalco 290
Aztecs 285-6, 288
Aztlan 288

Baal myths 34-7
Babylonian mythology 9, 18-25
Bacchae, The 67
Baniwa 304
bannik 112
Barasana 303, 304, 305
bark paintings 247
Barong 214
bas-reliefs 212
bats 259
battles 289
bdud 165
bears 60, 142, 202, 273, 274, 275
beasts 221
beavers 274
Beginning 269
Beltaine 77, 78, 92
benu bird 45-6
Beowulf 124, 131
Bhagavad Gita 145, 147, 150, 156, 157
Bhagavat Purana 145, 155, 156
bhakti 145
biblical mythology 30-3
Bifrost 117
bird of paradise 208
bird-made women 263
birds 45-6, 60, 157, 262
Black Misery 168
Blackfoot tribe 272
blizzards 276
Boar of Boann Ghulban 87
boars 78, 88, 124
Bod 165
bodhi tree 163
bodhisattvas 169, 170, 171, 174-5
body painting 303
bogie-man 112
bonfire festivals 78
Book of Am-Duat 51-2
Book of Caverns 51, 52-3
Book of Change 185
Book of the Dead 53
Book of the Dun Cow 82
Book of Durrow 93
Book of Gates 51, 52
Book of Invasions 78, 79
Book of Kells 93
Book of Poetry 188
Booyán 110

Borabora 230
boulders 276
brag-srin-mo 171
brahmin caste 162
Brauron 61
bread 262
Breton Lai 96
Brisings necklace 128
Broceliande, forest of 99
Brown Bull of Ulster 82, 83
Buddhism 160, 194, 206, 211
buffalo demon 152
Bull of Heaven 23
bull-roarers 234, 238
bulls 34, 39, 41, 60, 78, 82, 83
Bundahishn 39
Byblos 48

cactus 289
Caerlayw, witches of 98
Calendae 112
Calendar Round 293
Calendar Stone 287
calendars 293
Cañari 299
Canelos Quichua 305
cannibalizm 258
Caonao 260, 261
Capitoline Hill 72
cargo cults 233, 236
Caribbean 258-65
Caribs 258
cariques 259
Carpet Snake 238
cassowaries 218
caste system 162
cats 176
cattle 88
Cattle of Geryon 60
cattle goddess 17
Cattle Raid of Cooley 82
cauldrons 90, 187
cazabe 262
Celts 76-101
Centaurs 72
Central America 282-305
Central and Eastern Europe 102-13
ceremonial costume 278
ceremonial masks 141
Cerynean Hind 60
chameleons 257
chaos 57, 184, 248, 250, 253
charms 110
Chav'n 283, 294
Chehalis 279
Cheju 204
Chichimec 287
Chicomoztok 288
child sacrifices 296
children 70
Chimú 183
China 178-89
Chippewa 273, 280, 281
Chosen Women 296
Christianity 92, 112, 207, 231
Chukchi 134, 135, 136

Churning of the Milky Ocean 208
cibas 265
circle dance 156
circles 242, 244
City Dionysia 54
Classic of Mountains and Seas 180
Cleopatra's Needles 46
cliffs 276
clothing 143, 278
Cloud people 254-5
Coatepetl 288, 289, 290, 292
coconut dema 219
Cocytus 67
cohoba 259, 260, 262
Coiabi 260
comets 246, 304
Coronation Hill 242
cosmic egg 250
cosmic order 14
cosmogonic myth 182
cosmology 117
cows 158, 172
creation myths 9, 18, 25, 30, 39, 45-6, 57, 116, 136-7, 146-7, 167, 179, 181, 187, 191, 200, 205, 206, 208, 211, 226, 239, 254, 260, 261, 268, 269, 295, 301, 302, 303
creator beings 236, 248-9, 250, 257
Cretan Bull 60
Culhuacan 288, 290
Culhwch and Olwen 89, 93
cultural institutions 253
cuneiform tablets 13, 26
Cutha 20
Cuzco 296, 297, 298
cycle of life 149
cycles 264
Cyclopes 57, 66

dakini 176
Dalai Lama 171, 173, 174
damaru 150
Daoism 181
darkness *see* light and darkness
Daughter of Aracú Fish 302
dawns 293
day 305
death 19, 143, 150, 192, 210, 211, 229, 248, 252, 253, 257
decapitation 84, 101
decoration 67
deified spike 168
Delos 63
Delphi 63
demas 218, 219
demigods 224
Desana 302
designs 243, 244
destiny 120
destruction 46-7, 150
devas 146, 154
devata 160
devils 176, 223
dharma 145, 168
Dilmun 14
direction 207

dismemberment 192
disobedience 30-1, 227
divinity 8
Diwa-Zib 219
Djanggawul sisters 237, 245
Djarrapki 241
djugurba 238
dmu-rgyal 165
Dog of Moko 221
dogs 259
donkeys 74
Donn 82, 83
Draft Ox 188
dragon-snake 209
dragons 108
dre 165
dreaming 238
dreams 246
drink 67
drought 186
Drought Fury 181, 186, 187
dry land 270
duhos 259
Dukduk 219
Dunnu 24-5
dvorovoi 112
dwarfs 119

eagles 166, 289, 305
earth 183, 251, 252, 290, 304
earth-divers 268, 270
Eastern Europe 102-13
eclipses 304
Eden, Garden of 30-1
Edfu 50
Egils saga 121
Egypt 44-53
Eight Trigrams 182, 185
Einherjar 122, 126
El Dorado 298
Eldhrimnir 122
elephants 158, 214
Eleusinian Mysteries 62
elves 119
Elysian Fields 44, 67
emu 244
enlightenment 81, 163
Enuma Elish 18
environment 115
ephedra 41
Erechtheus 57
Eridu 8, 16, 19
Esna 46
ethnic minorities 189
Eurymathian Bear 60
Evenk 134
evil *see* good and evil

fables 157
failure 253
families 89
family life 116-17
farmsteads 112
fate 120
feasting 81
feather cults 231
feather headdresses 278, 303
female *see* male and female; women
Fenian Cycle 85
fertility 66, 74, 196, 220
festivals 77, 196
Fields of Iahru 44
Fir Bolg 79
fire 41, 78, 151, 186, 221, 255, 260, 301
Firebird 111
fireboards 142
fireplaces 176
fireside tales 231
fish 49, 148-9, 240
five aggregates 164
Flight of the Güeyo Women 264
flood myths 20-1, 33, 182, 189, 227, 268, 299
flutes 304
folk art 105
food 262
footprints 162, 250
forests 102
Formorians 80, 81, 91
Four Branches 89
Four-Jaguar 285
Four-Movement 285, 286
Four-Rain 285
Four-Water 285
Four-Wind 285
foxes 199
Frashokereti 39
freedom 145
Frog Dreaming 246
frogs 259

Gadjari ritual 237
Ganda 251
Ganges 146, 149
Garden of Eden 30-1
garudas 163
Gatha 40
Gawain and the Green Knight 94
Genesis 30-3, 182, 227
Ger 176
German mythology 8
Germanic tribes 114
giants 85, 118
Giant's Daughter 95-6
Ginnungagap 116
gnod-sbyin 165
God Age 269
goddesses 17, 127, 151, 225
see also individual goddesses
gods 16, 56, 78, 135, 146, 163, 180, 188, 210, 220, 232, 250, 261, 269
see also demigods; individual gods; jaguar gods; nature gods; sea gods; sky gods
gold 298
gong-po 165
good and evil 43, 154, 214, 253
Gorgons 65
Grail legend 94, 97
grain goddess 17
Great Dionysia 54
Great Temple 290
Greece 6-8, 54-67
Green Knight 78, 79, 84
gter-ston 168
guanara 265
guanguayo 262, 264
Guan'n 260, 264, 265
guanines 265
guardian spirits 39, 138
Guatavita 298
Güeyo 264
Gunabibi ritual 241
Gundestrop Cauldron 90
gundil 238
guruwari 242-3
guwak 241
Guwak cuckoo 241

Haab 293
hail 276
Hallstatt Culture 77
hallucinogens 259, 305
Haoma plant 41
Happy Hunting Grounds 273
hardships 57
hares 159
Harpies 66
harpoon head 138-9
Hatti 26
head-hunting 207, 209, 220
headdress 278, 303
heads 101
healing 63, 143, 262
health 143
hearths 61, 176
heaven 251, 252, 290, 304
Hekatonchires 57
Helgafell 115
Heliopolis 45
Hellespont 73
helping spirits 143
herbs 262
herding god 25
Hermopolis 46
Hero twins 291
heroes 58, 59, 72, 79, 211, 223, 236, 237, 241, 253, 255, 269, 277
heroic quests 97
Hesperides 60
hieroglyphs 46
highland myths 286
Hildisvin 124
Himalayas 153
Hinduism 160, 211
History of the Kings of Britain 94
History of Places 79
Hittite mythology 26-7
Hivaoa 227
Holy Immortals 42
home 61, 75, 105, 142
Homeric Hymn to Demeter 62
Hopi 274
horses 88, 121, 130
Hound of Culann *see* Cúchulainn
household *see* home
huacas 296
Huacay–an 299
Huanacauri 297
Hueteocalli 290
human sacrifice 207, 230
human-animal relationships 274-5
humankind 9, 57, 181, 186
hunter god 186
hunting 88, 282
Hurrian mythology 28-9
Hvergelmir 117

icons 194
ilbinji 243
Iliad 7, 54, 58
illness 143
illumination 93
Imbolc 77
immortality 232
imram 91
Inca 294, 295
India 7, 144-59, 206
intermarriage 246-7
Inuit 132
Iroquois 276
Islam 206, 214
ivory 135
Izumo Cycle 195, 196

jaguar gods 284-5
jaguars 300, 301, 304, 305
Japan 190-9
jataka 158, 162, 163, 208, 211
Jawoyn people 242
jokers 214
Jomon 190
Jotenheim 117
Journey to the Sky 277
journeys 51, 265
Jupiter (planet) 292
justice 19

kagura 196
Kailash, Mount 149, 150
Kali Yuga 144
kami 194
karma 156, 168
Kauai 222
Kauravas 156, 157
Kayapo myths 301
kegare 190
Keli Mutu 210
Khalkha tribe 172
Kherneter 44
Khwarna 41
Kiho 217
kikimora 110
kila 168
kings 213, 214
Kish 24
klu 165
knowledge 218, 282
Koguryo 203

Kojiki 191, 193, 201
Korea 200-5
Krishna-bhakti 156
kumi 221
Kumulipo 226

Lake of Death 223
lakes 103, 276, 304
Land of the Living 16-17
Land of No Return 24
Land of the Reed Plain 194, 197
Land of Shadows 140
landscapes 138, 168, 282, 303, 305
Lares 75
Larlangangel 240
law and order 120
leaders 213
Lenaia 54
Lernaean Hydra 60
leschi 110
Lethe 67
lha 165
light 81
light and darkness 168, 214, 222, 285
lightning 304
lila 153
Lindisfarne Gospels 93
lingam 151
living gods 231
logos 54
love 66, 87
lowland myths 287
Lughnasa 77
Lunheng 200
Lyra 75

ma-sang brothers 165
Mabinogion 84, 89, 95, 97
mada 245
maenads 67
Mag Tuiread 78
magatama 194, 199
magic 99, 143, 238
magical powers 151
Mahabharata 155, 156-7, 162, 211
Mahavamsa 162
male and female 154, 214, 240
Malinalco 288
Mamaia 231
Mamandabari heroes 236, 237
manaia 221
mandalas 164, 168
Mandara 149
Mandas festival 218
manikins 286
Maori 232
Mardayin ceremonies 247
marriage 184-5, 192, 246-7
masks 141, 218, 280-1
Master of Animals 135, 300
Mataco shaman 305
Matchikwewis 280
matriarchal influences 109
matsuri 196
Maungapohatu 232
mdos 167
mead 131
medicine 182-3
Medicine Dance 280, 281
Medicine Lodge 281
medicine men 271
mediums 198, 218, 221
Memorabilia of the Three Kingdoms 200
memory 305
Memphis 46
Mesoamerica 284-93
metallurgy 187
Metamorphoses 73, 74
metamorphosis 62, 259
meteors 304
Mexica 288, 289, 290
Mexico 287
Micmac 275
Midewiwin 281
Midgard 117
Mihr Yasht 41
miko 198
mikoshi 196
Milky Way 274, 297, 304
millennial cults 231, 233
mimi 244
Mimir 117, 126
Minotaur 59
mischief-makers 268
Modang of Kalimantan 208
Mohutani 227
Mongolia 172-7
monkeys 170-1, 183
monsters 66, 209
moon 137
morality 19, 157
Morte d'Arthur, Le 94
mosaics 74
Motikitik 220
mountain god 202
mountains 208, 276
muga 200, 205
Muisca 298
mukowe 275
mukti 149
murderesses 64
Murray Cod 240
murunta 243
musical instruments 304
Muspell 116
myal ba nag po 168
mythology 6-10

nagas 160,163, 209
Naglfar 126
Naqsh Rustam 40-1
narcotics 302
Naskapi 135
national identity 19
Native Americans 266-81
Native Tales 89
nats 214
nature 145, 168
nature gods 265, 292
nature spirits 208
Navaho 269, 274, 280
necklaces 128, 194
Negative Confession 44
Nemean Lion 60
Nenets 134, 135
Nepali Shilamanju 168
Nerik 26
Nesha 27
New Guinea Eastern Highlands 232-3
Nidavellir 117
Niflheim 116, 117, 120, 125
night 305
Night Chant 281
Nihonshoki 191, 193, 194, 201
nine (number) 130
Nippur 17
Noatun 123, 129
nopal cactus 289
Norns 120
North America 266-81
Northern Europe 114-31
northern lights 140, 141
Nukuhiva 227

Oceania 216-33
octopus 219, 220
od zer Idan 168
Oddiyana 166
Odyssey 7, 54
Oedipus at Colonus 6-7
Oedipus the King 63
offerings 208-9
Ojibwa 275
Olmec 283
Olympus, Mount 56
Onogoro 191
Opening of the Mouth 53
opita 260
order 248, 250, 253, 305
see also cosmic order; law and order
Orthodox Church 109
Oseberg 131
Oshkikwe 280
Ossianic Cycle 85
Otherworld 91, 110, 273, 277
oxen 88
oxyrhynchus fish 49

Pacárec Tambo 297
paintings 74
see also bark paintings; body painting; wall paintings
Palekh folk art 103
Pali canon 160
Panathenaia 54
Pancatantra 157
Pandavas 156, 157
pantheon 188
Papahurihia movement 232
Parthenon 55, 61
Pasargadae 39
Pcariqtambo 295
peacocks 158
Penates 75
Persian mythology 38-43
phallic power 234
philosophy 54
Phlegethon 67
phur-ba 168
piety 19
pilgrimages 296
Pintipi 242
Plant of Birth 24
Pleiades 224, 274
Poetic Interpretations of Nature by the Slavs 105
poetry 131
pollution 192
Polynesians 216
Popol Vuh 286, 287, 291
pottery 297
power 143, 262
prakriti 151
pralaya 150
Prambanan 212
propaganda 59
prophecies 290
prosperity 145
Pulotu 216
Puna 222
punishment 32
purification 196
purusha 151
Pythia 63, 70

Qadisiya 39
Qin 179
qivittoq 140
Quiché Maya 286, 287, 292

Ra-sa 'phrul-snang Temple 167
rabbits 195, 274, 275
Ragnarok 115, 124, 125, 126
rain men 243
Rainbow Serpent 238, 241
rainbows 238, 254
rainforest cultures 304
Rama-rajya 153
Ramayana 7, 152, 153, 154-5, 162, 211, 212
rangga 239, 245
rarrk 247
rasamandala 156
rats 219, 220
Raven cycle 268
ravens 277
rebirth 148
Red Book of Hergest 89
reincarnation 139
res publica 73
reversal 301
rgyal-po 165, 167
Rig Veda 145
rites of passage 61
rituals 210-11, 237, 240, 241, 253
rivers 103, 276, 304
rocks 276

Rome 68-75
roundhouses 305
royal tombs 165, 169
rulers 164-5, 193
runes 130-1
runic alphabet 114
rusalka 112

Saami 132
Sabines 68, 72
sacrifices 151, 208-9, 210-11, 228, 230, 296
sages 92
saints 92
salmon 278-9
Samain 77, 78
Samguk Yusa 203
samsara 148
sanshingak 202
satyrs 67
sea 208, 304
sea gods 128-9, 228
sea monsters 209
seasons 264
seers 91, 92, 168
separation 183, 252
serpents 209, 234, 238, 241
Sestos 73
sexual knowledge 234
Shahnama 40
shamans 135, 136, 140, 143, 166, 167, 172, 174, 176, 221, 259, 262, 271, 300
Shang 179, 187
shape-changers 94, 276
sheep 175, 249
Shinto 190
ship burials 131
shrines 194
Siberia 132-43
Siddhaloka 151
siddhi 151
sidhe 91
Sila 136
sillok 200
Simurgh 42
Sirens 66
Sirius 61
sky 183, 292
sky gods 294, 297
Slav mythology 102-13
Slavey tribe 273
snow 273
soapsone 135
social classes 117, 181
social myths 228-9
social origins 261
Sol Invictus 41
solar calendar 293
Songs of Chu 180
soul 110, 139, 140, 156
South America 282-305
Southeast Asia 206-15
Spanishta 41
spike, deified 168-9
spirit anchors 221
spirit helper 305
spirits 39, 105, 143, 208, 261, 302
Spoils of Annwn 94, 97
spontaneity 145
Sri Lanka 7, 160-3
srin 165
sruti 144
stars 188, 224, 269, 274, 276, 304
statues 167
steppe 102-3
stones 262, 270, 287
storms 269
storytelling stone 270
struggles 253, 257
stupas 163
Stymphalion Birds 60
Sumerian mythology 8, 13-17
Sun 261, 272, 292, 302, 305
supernatural beings 253, 281, 297
supreme beings *see* gods
Svartalfheim 117
swans 177
symbols 151, 194
Symposion 67

Tablets of Destiny 14-15, 18
taboos 191, 192
Tahuata 227
Táin 78, 82
Taíno 258, 261
Takama-ga-hara 190, 191
takkan 238
taniwha 221
tantrika 167
tarakaimaiu 225
tarakaimate 225
Tefatumoana 228
temples 60-1, 167, 290
Ten Celestial Stems 189
ten suns 185
Tenochtitlán 289, 290
Teotihuacanos 283
Tepanec 287
theater 54
Theogonies 24-5, 54
Thesmophoria 66
Three Clan Ancestors 204-5
three (number) 99
three pointers 262
Thrymheim 129
thunder 269
thunderclaps 276
thunderers 276
Tibet 164-71
tigers 174, 202
Tigris 28
Tir na nOg 88
Tingari dreaming cycle 246
Titans 57
Titicaca, Lake 295, 297, 299
Tiwanaku 295
tobacco 262
tohunga 218, 232
Tokoya 198
tombs 40-1, 165, 169
Toraja of Sulawesi 210
tortoise 149
totem poles 270-1
totemism 236-7
Tower of Babel 33
tracks 236-7
trances 259, 302
transgression 64
treasure-revealers 168
treasures 130
Tree of Death 223
Tree of Knowledge 31
trees 120, 143, 159, 163, 259
tricksters 248, 253, 268
trinities 99, 183
Trojan War 6, 7, 58-9
Troy 7, 58
Tsgeir Oervel 95
Tsimshian 276
Tuamotus 228
Tuatha Dé Danann 79, 80, 81, 82, 91
Tu'i Tonga 229
Tukano 304
Tula 289
Tuna 223
Tungus 200
turtles 208, 265, 268, 274
Twelve Earthly Branches 189
Twelve Labors of Herakles 60
Twelve Months 110
Twelve Tablets 22
Tzolkin 293

Uahuku 227
Uapou 227
Ugaritic mythology 34-7
Ulster Cycle 82-3
ultimogeniture 218
Unambal 239
underworld 15, 19, 51, 67, 192
Uppsala 115, 130
Uruk 15, 16, 17, 23
Urvazista 41
ushabti 53

Valhalla 120, 122
Valkryries 122
vampires 106
Vanaheim 117
Vanir 117, 123, 128, 131
Vazista 41
Vedas 144-5, 146-7, 227
Vehine Hae 225
Venus (planet) 292, 293
Vestal Virgins 75
Vi-dev-dad 43
Vigrid 126
vila 112
violence 72
violins 177
visual representation 218
vodyanoi 103
Vohufryana 41
voyages 91, 211

Wagilak sisters 236, 237
Waiwai tribe 305
Walbiri 238, 242, 243
wall paintings 74
walrus 138-9
wanambi 238
Wandjina 239
war 66
warriors 43, 65
wasps 173
water 94, 103
Water Door 303
weather 276
Welsh myths 89
wemukowe 275
Wenebojo 280, 281
were-tigers 208
were-wolves 109, 208
White Book of Rhydderch 89
winds 269, 276
wine 66
Winnebago tale 277
wise men 43
witches 98, 108
women 65, 143, 262, 263, 264
see also male and female
wood carvings 208, 219
woodpeckers 262, 263
world tree 120
writing 185

X-Ray painting 247
Xibalba 291

yaksas 161, 163
Yamato 193
Yao 189
yawalyu 243
Yayoi 190, 193
Yei masks 280
Yekuana 305
Yi jing 182, 185
Yolngu bark paintings 247
Yomi 192, 197

Zapotec 283
Zarat-hushtra 38
zemi 259, 261
Zhou 179, 187
Zhuang Zi 180
Zoroastrianism 43